REA

D1155980

AFRICAN HISTORICAL DICTIONARIES
Edited by Jon Woronoff

1. *Cameroon,* by Victor T. LeVine and Roger P. Nye. 1974. *Out of print. See No. 48.*
2. *The Congo,* 2nd ed., by Virginia Thompson and Richard Adloff. 1984. *Out of print. See No. 69.*
3. *Swaziland,* by John J. Grotpeter. 1975.
4. *The Gambia,* 2nd ed., by Harry A. Galley. 1987.
5. *Botswana,* by Richard P. Stevens. 1975. *Out of print. See No. 70.*
6. *Somalia,* by Margaret F. Castagno. 1975.
7. *Benin (Dahomey),* 2nd ed., by Samuel Decalo. 1987. *Out of print. See No. 61.*
8. *Burundi,* by Warren Weinstein. 1976. *Out of print. See No. 73.*
9. *Togo,* 3rd ed., by Samuel Decalo. 1996.
10. *Lesotho,* by Gordon Haliburton. 1977.
11. *Mall,* 3rd ed., by Pascal James Imperato. 1996.
12. *Sierra Leone,* by Cyril Patrick Foray. 1977.
13. *Chad,* 3rd ed., by Samuel Decalo. 1997.
14. *Upper Volta,* by Daniel Miles McFarland. 1978.
15. *Tanzania,* by Laura S. Kurtz. 1978.
16. *Guinea,* 3rd ed., by Thomas O'Toole with Ibrahima Bah-Lalya. 1995.
17. *Sudan,* by John Voll. 1978. *Out of print. See No. 53.*
18. *Rhodesia/Zimbabwe,* by R. Kent Rasmussen. 1979. *Out of print See No. 46.*
19. *Zambia,* 2nd ed., by John J. Grotpeter, Brian V. Siegel, and James R. Fletcher. 1998.
20. *Niger,* 3rd ed., by Samuel Decalo. 1997.
21. *Equatorial Guinea,* 3rd ed., by Max Liniger-Goumaz. 1999.
22. *Guinea-Bissau,* 3rd ed., by Richard Lobban and Peter Mendy. 1996.
23. *Senegal,* by Lucie G. Colvin. 1981. *Out of print. See No. 65.*
24. *Morocco,* by William Spencer. 1980. *Out of print. See No. 71.*
25. *Malawi,* by Cynthia A. Crosby. 1980. *Out of print. See No. 54.*
26. *Angola,* by Phyllis Martin. 1980. *Out of print. See No. 52.*
27. *The Central African Republic,* by Pierre Kalck. 1980. *Out of print. See No. 51.*

Historical Dictionary of Swaziland

Second Edition

Alan R. Booth

African Historical Dictionaries, No. 80

The Scarecrow Press, Inc.
Lanham, Maryland, and London
2000

SCARECROW PRESS, INC.

Published in the United States of America
by Scarecrow Press, Inc.
4720 Boston Way
Lanham, Maryland 20706
http://www.scarecrowpress.com

4 Pleydell Gardens, Folkestone
Kent CT20 2DN, England

British Library Cataloguing in Publication Information Available

Library of Congress Cataloging-in-Publication Data

Booth, Alan R.
  Historical dictionary of Swaziland / Alan R. Booth. — 2nd ed.
      p.   cm. — (African historical dictionaries ; no. 80)
  Rev. ed. of: Historical dictionary of Swaziland / John J. Grotpeter. 1st ed. 1975.
  Includes bibliographical references.
  ISBN 0-8108-3749-8 (alk. paper)
      1. Swaziland—Encyclopedias.   I. Grotpeter, John J. Historical dictionary of
Swaziland.   II. title.   III. Series.

DT2714 .B66   2000
968.87′003—dc21   99-053345

For Margaret, True North,
and for Grace, Evening Star

Contents

Editor's Foreword

Among Africa's often relatively artificial states there are few that could qualify as nations. Swaziland is one of them. It is inhabited by a fairly homogenous people living on the same land as their ancestors. They are bound by countless customs and traditions that unite them and permit them to pull together when necessary. This has been a definite strength when they have been attacked by other African peoples or subverted by Western colonialism, and it permitted an exceptionally smooth transition to independence. But these traditions can also be a weakness when they hamper progress toward more "modern" social, economic, and political practices. At one time this drawback could be largely ignored, or at least tolerated, but Swaziland may be heading for a period when it will find it harder than mere states to cope.

More than most volumes in this series, this *Historical Dictionary of Swaziland* is historical. It reaches back into earlier periods when the Swazi nation was being formed. There are thus numerous entries on the Swazi kings, queens, and others who played a significant role and more that describe basic characteristics and customs. The colonial era is also clearly delineated, with entries on important figures, from colonial secretaries and resident commissioners on down to missionaries and concession-hunters, some impeding and others supporting progress toward independence. The current period, however, is not overlooked, whether for persons, places, events, institutions, or other aspects. The considerable material provided in the dictionary is buttressed on a solid introduction, a chronology, and especially a substantial bibliography.

This entirely new *Historical Dictionary of Swaziland* was written by Professor Alan R. Booth. Professor Booth, a specialist on Southern Africa and particularly the former High Commission Territories, has long been focused on Swaziland. He has lectured extensively on the region, both in his courses in the Department of History at Ohio University (where he was also the founding Director of the African Language and Area Center) and at universities there. Along with numerous articles, he has also written several books, one of which deals with Swaziland, namely *Swaziland: Tradition and Change in a Southern African Kingdom*. He is currently working on a political biography of King Sobhuza II. This experience has given him a deep understanding of, and respect for, the Swazi and their country, which is passed along to the readers of this volume.

Jon Woronoff
Series Editor

Acknowledgments

This second edition of the *Historical Dictionary of Swaziland* owes much to the first edition (1975), the third volume in the Africa series, authored by the late Dr. John J. Grotpeter. Much has happened during the generation since its appearance, in terms of both the passage of important events in the kingdom and the appearance of a wealth of significant new scholarship on Swaziland. The second edition therefore constitutes a substantial revision. I owe much to the fresh interpretations of Swaziland's rich history provided especially by the works of Philip Bonner, Jonathan Crush, Carolyn Hamilton, Huw Jones, Christopher Lowe, Hugh Macmillan, and Hamilton Simelane. Perhaps most of all I am indebted to Huw M. Jones's indispensable *Biographical Register of Swaziland to 1902* (1993), which has informed a great many of my observations on important 19th-century royal and political figures. In compiling the Bibliography I am equally indebted to Balam Nyeko's incomparable *Swaziland* (Clio Press World Bibliographical Series Volume 24, 1994). This second edition has also benefited from the unfailingly courteous assistance provided over the years by the successive directors of the Swaziland National Archives, Julius Dlamini and Nomondi Twala. Finally, I gratefully acknowledge research assistance from the Ohio University Research Committee and from the Committee on International Exchange of Persons (Fulbright Committee).

Reader's Note

SISWATI LANGUAGE AND ORTHOGRAPHY

The siSwati language is a member of the Nguni group of the Bantu language family, closely affined to isiZulu. Indeed, siSwati, as distinct from isiZulu, has been used officially in education and the public sector only since the late 1960s. Like isiZulu, siSwati employs click consonants, although only the ones represented by the letter "C," which signifies a dental + velar click. Unlike isiZulu, however, siSwati does not employ the letters "Q" and "X," both of which in isiZulu denote other, different, and more numerous click consonants. The first siSwati grammar was produced by Ziervogel and Mabuza in 1976, and the most comprehensive and widely used dictionary was published by Rycroft in 1981.[1] Rycroft specifies that nouns are listed alphabetically in accordance with their stems, not their first letters, and that is the method generally used here. The most common noun prefixes encountered in this volume are *um-*, *ba-*, *la-*, *li-*, *ema-*, *si-*, *ti-*, *im/in/i-*, *tim/tin/ti-*, *lu-*, and *ku-*. So, for instance, *iNcwala*, *iNgwenyama*, and *iNdlovukazi* are all entered in this volume under "N," not "I."

In this regard, two things should be noted. First, there exists no single standard, recognized usage of siSwati alphabetization and orthography among scholars; indeed, nearly every authority uses a different system, and some scholars use more than one in successive works. In the case of the term *iNgwenyama*, for example, Hilda Kuper refers to the *Ingwenyama* (under "I") in *An African Aristocracy*, but then to the *Ngwenyama* (under "N") in both *The Swazi* and *Sobhuza II*.[2] Second, in cases of ambiguity (which are legion), common usage prevails here. For example, the word *tinkhundla* (regional councils; sing. *inkhundla*) would, according to Rycroft, be listed under "N," but in this volume the word refers almost exclusively to an electoral system implemented during the late 1970s by *iNgwenyama* Sobhuza Dlamini II, which is known universally as the "Tinkhundla system." It is consequently listed here under "T." In this case, as in many others, the reader will find a cross-reference (in "N") under *iNkhundla*.

A second example of the primacy of common usage in this volume involves the siSwati word for "wilderness," which is properly *lihlane*. The modern common usage for specific geographic areas in Swaziland is either *Ehlane* or *Hlane*, both of which terms are found in this volume, under "E" and "H," respectively. The Glossary, on p. xxix, also reflects common usage.

The word "Swazieland" changed permanently to "Swaziland" during the 1890s. The *liqoqo* changed temporarily to *Liqoqo* during the period 1982–1985. Both changes are reflected in this volume.

NOMENCLATURE

All Swazi royalty are found in entries listed under "Dlamini." All Zulu royalty are listed under "Zulu." All Pedi royalty are listed under "Maroteng." Swazi *tingwenyama* (kings), *tindlovukazi* (queen mothers) and *bantfwan-ankhosi* (princes, princesses) are initially referred to in entries by their given names plus surnames (i.e., Dlamini), and subsequently by their given names only. Geographic terminology is in common usage form (i.e., "Usutu" rather than "Lusutfu" River). Occasionally at the beginning of a geographic entry, the common usage term is followed by the proper term.

REFERENCING

Terms appearing in **bold** indicate specific entries on them.

1. D. Ziervogel and E. J. Mabuza, *Grammar of the Swati Language* (Pretoria: van Schaik, 1976); D. K. Rycroft, *Concise SiSwati Dictionary* (Pretoria: van Schaik, 1981).

2. Hilda Kuper, *An African Aristocracy: Rank Among the Swazi* (New York and London: Oxford University Press, 1947); *Sobhuza II: Ngwenyama and King of Swaziland* (London: Duckworth, 1978); and *The Swazi: A South African Kingdom* (2d ed., New York: Holt, Rinehart and Winston, 1986).

Maps

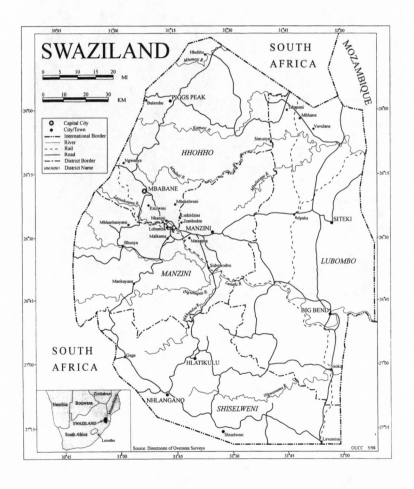

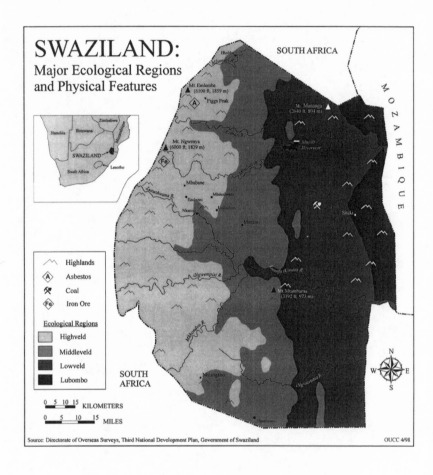

SWAZILAND:
Major Ecological Regions
and Physical Features

SOUTH AFRICA

M O Z A M B I Q U E

Bhabha
Mlumati R.

Mt. Emlembe
(6100 ft, 1859 m)

Piggs Peak

Mt. Mananga
(2640 ft, 804 m)

Komati R.

Mt. Ngwenya
(6000 ft, 1829 m)

Mlilo
Reservoir

Usutu R.

Mbabane

Mbekelweni

Ezulwini

Siteki

Nkanini

Lobamba

Manzini

Lusutfu R.

Ngwempisi R.

Mt Mtambana
(3192 ft, 973 m)

Mhombo R.

N

SOUTH
AFRICA

W   E

Nhlangano

Ngwavuma R.

S

Legend

⌃⌃ Highlands

Ⓐ Asbestos

⚒ Coal

Ⓕⓔ Iron Ore

Ecological Regions

Highveld

Middleveld

Lowveld

Lubombo

0 5 10 15 KILOMETERS

0 5 10 15 MILES

Inset: Namibia, Botswana, Zimbabwe, SWAZILAND, South Africa, Lesotho

Source: Directorate of Overseas Surveys, Third National Development Plan, Government of Swaziland

OUCC 4/98

Chronology

Mid-1700s   Dlamini III settles the Lebombo region north of the Pongola River.

1750   Ngwane III succeeds Dlamini III.

1770   Ngwane III settles southern Swaziland.

1775   Death of Ngwane III; succeeded by Ndvungunye.

1805   Death of Ndvungunye; succeeded by Sobhuza Dlamini I.

1813   Sobhuza I takes Tsandzile Ndwandwe as a wife.

1827–28   Shaka Zulu attacks Sobhuza I in two separate campaigns.

1839   Battle of Lubuya; death of Sobhuza I.

1840   Mswati Dlamini II, successor to Sobhuza I, installed. Tsandzile as *indlovukazi*.

1844   Wesleyan missionaries (Rev. Allison) arrive in Swaziland.

1846   Mswati cedes first Swazi territory to Ohrigstad Afrikaners. Mswati's brother Somcuba defeats Malambule's rebellion at Mahamba.

1852   Mswati moves *lilawu* to Hhohho.

1855   Mswati defeats Somcuba's rebellion; Somcuba slain. Mswati cedes territory to Lydenburg Afrikaners.

1865   Death of Mswati II. Succeeded by Ludvonga Dlamini II. Regency of Tsandzile Dlamini.

1866   Defection of Mblini Ndwandwe.

1869   Swazi expedition against the Pedi. Swazi regiments suffer defeat at Battle of Ewulu.

1874   Death of Ludvonga II.

1875   Installation of Ludvonga II's successor, Mbandzeni Dlamini. Sisile Khumalo becomes *indlovukazi*. Death of Tsandzile. Failure of second military campaign against the Pedi.

1877   Mbandzeni gives permission to Afrikaners to settle a portion of western Swaziland later known as the Little Free State.

1879   Mbandzeni dispatches Swazi army to assist victorious British campaign against the Pedi (Sekhukhune) mountain redoubt. British guarantee Swazi independence in perpetuity.

1880	McLachlan discovers gold near Pigg's Peak. British commission demarcates the Transvaal-Swaziland boundary. Beginning of the era of concessions; Mbandzeni grants large numbers of grazing concessions.
1881	Flight and execution of Sisile. Succeeded as *indlovukazi* by Tibati Nkambule. Pretoria Convention.
1882	Gold discovered in De Kaap valley.
1884	London Convention.
1887	Appointment of Theophilus Shepstone, Jr. as Mbandzeni's resident advisor. Establishment of Swazieland Committee.
1888	Portuguese Boundary Commission delineates Swaziland-Mozambique border to the disadvantage of the Swazi.
1888	Mbandzeni grants royal charter to the Swazieland Committee. Execution of Sandlane Zwane.
1889	Mbandzeni dismisses Shepstone and appoints Allister Miller as royal secretary and advisor. Joint (de Winton) Commission of enquiry. Provisional Government Committee. Death of Mbandzeni. Tibati Nkambule becomes queen regent.
1890	Bhunu Dlamini named successor to Mbandzeni. First Swaziland Convention. Government Committee established at Bremersdrop. Establishment of Chief Court.
1891	Chief Court confirms most of contested concessions.
1893	Second Swaziland Convention.
1894	Organic proclamation rejected by Tibati. Deputation to London led by Mnt. Longcangca Dlamini. Third Swaziland Convention. Shepstone dismissed as secretary to the nation by Tibati.
1895	Bhunu installed as *ingwenyama*. Labotsibeni Mdluli becomes *indlovukazi*. South Africa Republic (SAR) assumes administration of Swaziland.
1896	Hut tax imposed by the SAR and then postponed.
1898	Murder of Mbhabha Nsibandze precipitates constitutional crisis. Bhunu summonsed; flees; tried and fined in SAR landdrost's court. 1898 Protocol to the 1894 third Swaziland Convention.
1899	Birth of Sobhuza Dlamini II. Anglo-Boer War commences. Death of Bhunu. Labotsibeni becomes queen regent.
1902	Burning and sacking of Bremersdrop by Afrikaners. Anglo-Boer War ends. Arrival of first British administration (Special

Commissioner F. Enraght Moony and South African constabulary).

1903   British order-in-council places Swaziland under administration of the Transvaal governor. Native tax reintroduced.

1904   Swaziland Administration Proclamation (3/1904). Appointment of Swaziland Concessions Commission.

1905   Lord Selborne succeeds Milner as high commissioner. Administrative separation of Swaziland from the Transvaal; appointment of Moony as first resident commissioner. Swazi protest deputation to Pretoria, led by Mnt. Malunge Dlamini.

1906   First Swazi National School established at Zombodze.

1907   Appointment of Robert Coryndon as resident commissioner (1907–16). Partition Proclamation. Swazi protest deputation to London, led by Mnt. Malunge.

1908   Delimitation of the territory into settler estates, native areas, and crown lands completed by Partition Commissioner George Grey.

1909   Labotsibeni's first special domestic tax levy to repurchase concessioned lands.

1911   Coryndon and Labotsibeni initiate the Swazi National Fund.

1912   Native Recruiting Corporation established in Swaziland.

1914   Implementation of Partition Proclamation (1907) initiated.

1915   Death of Mnt. Malunge. Replaced as regent by Mnt. Lomvazi Dlamini.

1916   Sobhuza II begins his secondary education at Lovedale Missionary Institution.

1921   Sobhuza II installed as *ingwenyama*. Lomawa Ndwandwe becomes *indlovukazi*. Establishment of the European Advisory Council (EAC).

1922–23   Protest Deputation to London, led by Sobhuza II.

1924   Sobhuza II initiates lawsuit, *Sobhuza II vs. Miller*, in colonial court.

1925   Death of Labotsibeni.

1926   Privy Council rules against Sobhuza II's appeal in the matter of *Sobhuza II vs. Miller*.

1927   First South African Railways and Harbours Road Motor Transport Service buses introduced into Swaziland. Visit to Swaziland of Colonial Secretary L. S. Amery.

1928   T. Ainsworth Dickson becomes resident commissioner (1928–35).

1929 Swaziland Progressive Association formed. Colonial Development Act.

1931 Office of the high commissioner separated from that of the governor-general of the Union of South Africa. Swazi National High School inaugurated by Sobhuza II at Matsapha.

1932 Publication of Pim Report.

1935 Sobhuza II initiates *emabutfo* system at Swazi National High School. Allan G. Marwick becomes resident commissioner (1935–37).

1937 Colonial administration criminalizes chiefs' disobedience to Sobhuza II's decrees; convicts chiefs in colonial courts.

1938 Death of *iNdlovukazi* Lomawa. Succeeded by *iNdlovukazi* Nukwase Ndwandwe. New Amianthus asbestos mine commences production at Havelock.

1940 Colonial Development and Welfare (CD&W) Act.

1941 Sobhuza II petitions parliament for assistance to alleviate acute Swazi land shortage.

1941–42 Sobhuza II oversees recruitment of Swazi *emabutfo* for the World War II African Pioneer Corps.

1942 Swaziland Native Land Settlement Scheme introduced with CD&W funds.

1944 Native Authorities Proclamation gazetted over strong objections of Sobhuza II and *libandla*.

1946 Sobhuza II inaugurates Lifa Fund.

1947 Peak Timbers begins planting first commercial forests near Pigg's Peak. King George VI's royal visit to Swaziland.

1949 EAC becomes Reconstituted European Advisory Council (REAC).

1950 Native Administration, Native Courts and National Treasury Proclamations gazetted. Usutu Forests (CD&W) commences operations near Bhunya. Swaziland Irrigation Scheme (CD&W) established in Swaziland's lowveld.

1955 Sobhuza II establishes the *tinkhundla* administrative system.

1957 Death of *iNdlovukazi* Nukwase. Succeeded by *iNdlovukazi* Zihlathi Ndwandwe. Brian Marwick appointed resident commissioner (1957–63).

1960 Prime Minister Macmillan's "Winds of Change" address. European Advisory Council present memorandum to Resident Commissioner on multiracial Legislative Council. Constitutional Committee established by Marwick. Swaziland Progressive Party formed.

1961   First London constitutional conference.

1962   Report of London constitutional conference released. Construction of Swaziland railway commences.

1963   Second London constitutional conference. (Duncan) Sandys Constitution ("White Paper") announced. Labor strikes lead to administration declaration of state of emergency and British army occupation (until 1966).

1964   Imbokodvo National Movement formed. Elections for the Legislative Council (Legco) held. REAC disbanded.

1967   Pre-independence constitution implemented. Elections for the Swaziland house of assembly. Swaziland becomes a protected kingdom; Britain grants Sobhuza II title of "king" to replace "paramount chief."

1968   Independence constitutional conference in London. Independence constitution vests minerals in Swazi king, not parliament. Swaziland's independence on September 6. Sobhuza II establishes Tibiyo takaNgwane Fund.

1969   First government five-year Development Plan inaugurated.

1971   Land Speculation Control Act passed by Parliament.

1972   Parliamentary elections held. Imbokodvo victory, but Ngwane National Liberatory Congress for the first time wins three opposition seats in Mphumalanga constituency. Government challenges Bhekindlela Thomas Ngwenya's citizenship as means of overturning NNLC's victory. Immigration Amendment Act (IAA) passed.

1973   Court of Appeals rules IAA unconstitutional. Sobhuza II repeals constitution, declares state of emergency, dismisses parliament and rules by decree. Sobhuza establishes the Royal Umbutfo Defense Force. Sobhuza forms Royal Constitutional Commission to study alternatives for a new parliamentary system.

1974   Lilangeni (pl. emalangeni) introduced as Swazi unit of currency.

1975   Death of *iNdlovukazi* Zihlathi. Succeeded by *iNdlovukazi* Seneleleni Ndwandwe.

1976   Retirement of Mnt. Makhosini Dlamini as first prime minister of Swaziland.

1978   Report of Royal Constitutional Commission. Sobhuza II establishes the *tinkhundla* parliamentary electoral system, in which real power remained vested in the *ingwenyama*. First parliamentary elections held under new *tinkhundla* system.

1979	Appointment of Mnt. Mabandla Dlamini as prime minister.
1980	Death of *iNdlovukazi* Seneleleni. Succeeded by *iNdlovukazi* Dzeliwe Shongwe.
1981	Sobhuza II's diamond jubilee.
1982	Sobhuza II signs secret accord with South African government, agreeing to expel the African National Congress from Swaziland in return for the transfer of kaNgwane and iNgwavuma to Swazi sovereignty. Death of Sobhuza II. Nomination of Mnt. Makhosetive Dlamini as his successor, and his mother, Ntombi Twala, as successor to *iNdlovukazi* Dzeliwe. Dzeliwe becomes queen regent. Appointment of Mnt. Sozisa Dlamini as "authorized person." *Liqoqo* initiates constitutional crisis by usurping nontraditional powers.
1983	Traditionalist clique in *Liqoqo* dismisses Prime Minister Mabandla; replaces him with traditionalist Mnt. Bhekimpi Dlamini. *Liqoqo* transfers much of Dzeliwe's functions to authorized person. Queen-regent Dzeliwe confronts *Liqoqo* and is removed. *iNdlovukazi* Ntombi named queen regent by *Liqoqo*. Opponents of *Liqoqo* detained.
1984	Power struggle between *Liqoqo* traditionalists (led by Mnt. Mfanasibili Dlamini) and cabinet (led by Sishayi Nxumalo). Nxumalo detained for "high treason" 1984–85.
1986	Traditionalist faction in *Liqoqo* defeated. Mnt. Mfanasibili removed from *Liqoqo*; detained for "defeating the ends of justice." Dr. Msibi flees abroad. *Liqoqo* stripped of its self-appointed powers and reduced to traditional advisory role. Makhositive crowned as *iNgwenyama* Mswati Dlamini III. Mswati disbands *liqoqo*, reshuffles cabinet, dismisses Mnt. Bhekimpi as prime minister.
1987	Bnt. Mfanasibili, Bhekimpi, and others tried for high treason, convicted.
1988	All treason trial defendants pardoned by Mswati, excepting Mfanasibili, who serves earlier seven-year sentence for defeating the ends of justice.
1989	Plot by jailed Mfanasibili to take power thwarted. NNLC president Dr. Ambrose Zwane arrested for pamphleteering for People's United Democratic Movement (PUDEMO). Zwane goes into exile. Mswati appoints trade unionist Obed Dlamini as prime minister in effort to defuse growing organized opposition.

1990   Arrest, trial of PUDEMO leaders for treason; conviction on lesser charge of "organizing a political meeting." Brutal police repression of student protests at the University of Swaziland (UNISWA).

1991   Mswati responds to rise of popular opposition by launching "Vusela" review of the *tinkhundla* electoral system. Swaziland Youth Congress (SWAYOCO) emerges as second opposition group.

1992   "Vusela II" results in partial reform of *tinkhundla* parliamentary election system, retaining nomination process in grip of the monarchy but allowing for a new second-stage secret ballot. Mswati retains ultimate power over both executive and legislature.

1993   During parliamentary elections, opponents to new system arrested and tried under royal ordinance prohibiting political organization.

1994   SFTU leads militant general strike on behalf of twenty-seven political demands, rocking Swaziland. Local elections met with widespread boycott.

1995   SFTU calls for two-day mass strike, paralyzing the kingdom. Government meets SFTU call for second general strike with show of force. Mass demonstrations in main towns. Firebombing of parliament the first evidence of political violence.

1996   SFTU mass stay-away; its leadership charged under new Industrial Relations Act for instigating the strike. Regional presidents, led by Nelson Mandela of South Africa, pressure Mswati to hasten process of constitutional reform. Mswati forms two bodies, the Constitutional Review Commission and the Swazi National Council Standing Committee, to advise him on constitutional reform.

1997   Unions continue to dominate political opposition. More SFTU mass stay-aways. Month-long strike by Swaziland National Association of Teachers. Government publishes media control bill.

1998   Parliamentary elections (October), held under traditional *tinkhundla* system. Election characterized by voter apathy and trade union boycott (only 30 percent of all those eligible voting). The election, and the king's reappointment of the royalist prime minister, Sibusiso Dlamini, indicates no real political change in the immediate future.

Acronyms and Abbreviations

AME	African Methodist Episcopal Church
ANC	African National Congress
APC	African Pioneer Corps
CDC	Colonial (after 1963, Commonwealth) Development Corporation
CMA	Common Monetary Area
COMESA	Common Market for Eastern and Southern Africa
CRC	Constitutional Review Commission
E	Emalangeni (sing. lilangeni), the principal Swazi monetary unit
EAC	European Advisory Council
EU	European Union
EWA	EurAfrican Welfare Association
INM	Imbokodvo National Movement
Legco	Legislative Council
LFS	Little Free State
Lifa (Fund)	Inheritance (Fund)
MNC	Mbandzeni National Convention
Mnt.	Mntfwanenkhosi (Prince, Princess); pl. Bnt., Bntfwanenkhosi
NIDCS	National Industrial Development Corporation of Swaziland
NNLC	Ngwane National Liberatory Congress
NRC	Native Recruiting Corporation
OAU	Organization of African Unity
ONLC	Overseas Native Labour Contingent
PAC	Pan-Africanist Congress
PM	Prime Minister
PRC	Private Revenue Concession
PTA	Preferential Trade Area
PUDEMO	People's United Democratic Movement
R	Rand, the South African unit of currency
RCS	Resident Commissioner's Secretariat

RDA	Rural Development Area
REAC	Reconstituted European Advisory Council
RMA	Rand Monetary Area
SACU	Southern African Customs Union
SADC	Southern African Development Community
SADCC	Southern African Development Coordination Conference
SAR	South African Republic
SARHRMS	South African Railways and Harbours Road Motor Service
SCOT	Swaziland College of Technology
SDA	Swaziland Democratic Alliance
SDP	Swaziland Democratic Party
SEB	Swaziland Electricity Board
SFA	Swaziland Farmers Association
SFTU	Swaziland Federation of Trade Unions
SIF	Swaziland Independent Front
SIS	Swaziland Irrigation Scheme
SNA	Swaziland National Archives
SNACS	Swaziland National Association of Civil Servants
SNAT	Swaziland National Association of Teachers
SNC	Swazi National Council
SNL	Swazi Nation Land
SNLSS	Swaziland Native Land Settlement Scheme
SNS	Swaziland Sebenta Society/Institute
SPA	Swaziland Progressive Association
SPG	Society for the Propagation of the Gospel
SPP	Swaziland Progressive Party
SWAYOCO	Swaziland Youth Congress
TDL	Title Deed Land
TEBA	The Employment Bureau of Africa
TOS	*The Times of Swaziland*
UBLS	University of Botswana, Lesotho, and Swaziland
UNDP	United Nations Development Program
UNISWA	University of Swaziland
USA	United Swaziland Association
WNLA	Witwatersrand Native Labour Association

Glossary

Entries are alphabetized according to stem, unless common usage prevails. See the "Reader's Note."

liBandla	Council. *See also Libandla*
Bayete	"Hail, Your Majesty." Greeting reserved for the *ingwenyama*
Bemdzabuko	True Swazi
liButfo	Age grade; regiment; pl. *emabutfo*; Regiments; age regiments
umButfo	Royal guard; soldiers at a royal residence
liChiba	Military platoon
umCwasho	Coming of age ceremony for royal princesses and chiefs' daughters
inDvuna	Official; officer; headman
inDvunankhuluyesive	Senior political officer of the kingdom; prime minister
inDvunankhuyemabutfo	Commander-in-chief of the army
Emafika Muva	"Those Who Came Late"
Emakhandza Mbile	"Those Found Ahead"
Embo	Northern Nguni
liFa	Inheritance. *See* Lifa
inHlambelo	Sacred enclosure within the royal cettle-byre
Imitsi	Medicines obtained by ritual murder
kuKhonta	Pay allegiance to (a chief or king)
inKhundla	Regional council; pl. *tinKhundla*; regional councils; system of parliamentary elections (commonly *tinkundhla*)
Koppie	Flat-topped Hill/Mountain (Afrikaans)
Labadzala	Senior advisors
Landdrost	Magistrate (Afrikaans)
Libandla	Swazi National Council
Lifa	Inheritance (as in Lifa Fund; properly, liFa)

liLanga	The sun
liLangeni	Unit of Swazi currency; pl. *emaLangeni*
liLawu	Administrative headquarters
Liqoqo	Inner Council
liLobolo	Transfer of marriage cattle to bride's family
weManti	National priest; water priest, essential to the *iNcwala* ceremony; pl. *beManti*
iMphi	Swazi regiment
iMpi	Zulu regiment
Nabomnftwana	Queen mother-designate
Nagana	Bovine trypanosomiasis
iNdlovukazi	Cow Elephant; traditional title for Swazi queen mother
iNdlu	Hut; dwelling
umNguni	Ethno-linguistic term for Nguni-speakers: Zulu; Khosa; Swazi; Ndebele
liNgwane	A Swazi person
kaNgwane	Place of the Ngwane; in/to/from Swaziland
iNgwenyama	The Lion; traditional title for the Swazi king
iNhlanti	Junior co-wife
iNkhosana	Crown Prince
iNkhosi	Greeting: "Sir," "Madam," "Your Majesty"
iNkhosi Dlamini	Royal line of Dlamini clan
iNsangu	Wild hemp; dagga
iNsila	Ceremonial blood-brother to the *ingwenyama*
umNtfwana	Heir to the throne
umNtfwanenkhosi	Prince; Princess; pl. *baNtfwanenkhosi*
umNumzane	Head of homestead
iNyamatane	Buck; ritual murderer's term for his/her victim
iNyanga	Traditional doctor; ritual practitioner; herbalist
liPhakelo	Royal principality (literally, cattle belonging to a wife)
Sangoma	Ritual practitioner diviner (properly, umNgoma)
luSekwane	Acacia shrub, used in the *iNcwala* ceremony
luSendvo	Family council
Sibaya	Cattle Kraal
Sibongo	Clan name
Sigoldo	Queen's Quarters
Sive Siyingqaba	The Nation is a Fortress; name of a conservative political group

liSolenkhosi	Liaison officer to the king
Somhlohlo	The Wonder; popular name for *iNgwenyama* Sobhuza Dlamini I
emaTala inkhosi	Bearers of kings; term for those clans historically contributing *tindlovukazi* to the royal house
umuTi	Homestead
umuTsi	Medicine
Tjwala	Traditional beer

Introduction

Swaziland is a small kingdom situated in southeastern Africa, lying between South Africa to its west, and Mozambique to its east. It is a small country, about the size of Hawaii or of Wales. In spite of the recency of its origins as a viable kingdom (early 1800s), it is the only one in sub-Saharan Africa that survived the independence period intact as a monarchy, with the possible exception of Zanzibar. It remains so today, an anomaly (along with Morocco) in a continent that is moving—however haltingly—toward democratic governance. Similarly, its diminutive geographic size does not translate into insignificance in other areas. Its strategic position has historically made it a theater of tension and conflict, both diplomatic and military, and its abundance of fertile soil, water, and mineral resources has made it an extraordinarily fecund country, which in turn has made its people comparatively wealthy by sub-Saharan African standards, as measured by per capita GNP.

Wealth, however, has not produced harmony, and modern Swaziland is beset by political and social tensions, caused in no little part by the deep and widening gap between rich and poor. That is mainly the product of two long-standing conditions: the existence of a European community in control of vast portions of the agricultural and manufacturing sector, and an autocratic monarchy that has established mechanisms which ensure that a substantial segment of the remaining wealth flows into its coffers and the pockets of its clients, much of it at the expense of the common citizenry. This gap has led to rising political tensions, manifested—in the absence of representative institutions—by increasingly strident demonstrations in behalf of democratization by organized laborers, teachers, and civil servants. The central issue facing Swaziland at the turn of the century is whether or not the monarchy, which values the benefits of "traditionalism" above all else, will be able to mitigate these tensions to the satisfaction of the populace while at the same time maintaining its grip on the essence of power.

1

LAND AND PEOPLE

The Land

The kingdom of Swaziland is situated in southeast Africa between the twenty-sixth and twenty-seventh parallels south, its borders contiguous with both South Africa and Mozambique. One of the smallest countries in Africa, Swaziland is 6,703 square miles (17,364 square kilometers) in area. It is estimated (based on an annual growth rate of 3.1 percent) that in the year 2000 Swaziland will have a population of 1,064,000. Its two largest cities are Mbabane, the capital (2000 population est. 61,000), and Manzini, the industrial hub (2000 population est. 77,000). Mbabane is 141 miles (226 kilometers) from Maputo, Mozambique, the nearest seaport, and 231 miles (373 kilometers) from Johannesburg, South Africa. Swaziland's climate is subtropical, bordering on temperate in the highveld.

Swaziland's richness in natural resources and strategic position in the subcontinent have historically made it more important than its size alone, comparable to that of the state of Connecticut, might have indicated. Swaziland possesses some of the richest soils and greatest abundance of rivers in all of Africa. That fact, along with its wealth in selected minerals (gold, tin, iron, and coal), made the kingdom historically significant in the region and, beginning in the 1870s, a primary theater for European exploitation and settlement, and, finally, colonization.

Topographically, Swaziland is divided into four regions extending in parallel along north-south axes. They are, from west to east, the highveld, the middleveld, the lowveld, and the Lubombo plateau. The highveld, 6,000 feet (1,830 meters) to 3,500 feet (1,070 meters) in altitude, makes for poor pasturage and subsistence cropping, but its combination of suitable soils and high rainfall make it an ideal region for commercial forestry, making Swaziland one of the world's largest producers of softwood timber and pulp. The middleveld, 3,800 feet (1,160 meters) to 1,500 feet (460 meters) above sea level, is the region with the highest population density and the greatest concentration of subsistence (principally maize) cropping and cattle-herding. Because much of the best land is under irrigation, the middleveld is also the locus of much estate market farming. The lowveld, 1,000 feet (300 meters) to 500 feet (150 meters) in altitude, is prime cattle country, featuring sweetveld (year-round) grazing. Low rainfall levels, however, make it particularly susceptible to drought, meaning that the highly productive soils require irrigation to make them commercially productive. The lowveld consequently is the region most heavily irrigated, and it grows the preponderance of Swaziland's sugar and citrus crops. Human habitation of the lowveld is complicated by the prevalence of malaria and bilharzia. The Lubombo plateau resembles the middleveld in altitude and climate, and like it produces both subsistence crops and cattle.

Swaziland is blessed with an abundance of water from five major rivers that flow through it, generally in a west-to-east direction. They are, from the northernmost, the Mlumati, the Komati, the Mbuluzi, the Usutu, and the iNgwavuma rivers. All of them have been tapped for irrigation projects, and most have the potential for irrigating more acreage. Three of the five rivers rise in South Africa, and all flow back into South Africa or into Mozambique. The use of all river water is consequently subject to bilateral or trilateral agreements. At the end of the 20th century, there were undertakings to dam both the Komati and the Usutu rivers.

Swaziland's agricultural land, either irrigated or rain-fed, is categorized by two types of tenure, the origins of which date from the concessions era. Swazi nation land (SNL) is held in trust for the nation by the *ingwenyama* (king), allocated through chiefs to homestead heads in accordance with traditional principles, in what amounts to communal tenure. SNL, which constitutes some 60 percent of the land total, produces most of Swaziland's rain-fed subsistence crops and cattle. Title deed land (TDL) is held in freehold by both Swazi and Europeans, the deeds dating back to the Partition Proclamation of 1907. TDL accounts for the remaining 40 percent of total area and produces virtually all of Swaziland's estate-owned, irrigated market crops and domestic timber, as well as some cattle. Most estates are owned by foreign capital. The Swazi nation participates in title deed farming principally through the monarchy's investment vehicle, the Tibiyo takaNgwane fund, which has acquired substantial stakes in major enterprises. A few individual Swazi smallholders run cattle and grow sugar and subsistence crops. The system of communal tenure on SNL acts as a substantial brake on Swaziland's agricultural productivity, because such land is not husbanded or improved and is commonly overgrazed. Because the tenure system constitutes a major underpinning of the monarchy's hegemony, however, it stands little chance of being reformed under the prevailing system of government.

The People

The Swazi are a southeastern Bantu people in both language and associated culture (mixed farming). They speak the siSwati tongue, a dialect of the Nguni branch of the Bantu language group, although early admixtures of both Sotho speakers (prominently) and Tsonga speakers (to a lesser degree) have left discernible traces in their language, culture, and nomenclature. The forebears of the Ngwane (the nucleus of what became the Swazi) were part of the Nguni expansion southward from east-central Africa, who settled in southern Mozambique during the 15th century. Although other Nguni-speaking clans, such as the Zulu and the Ndwandwe, eventually moved further south and west, the Ngwane under their ruling Dlamini clan tarried along the Mozambique coast.

HISTORY

Pre-Colonial

It was only during the 18th century that the Ngwane under a Dlamini descendant, Ngwane III, occupied what is now southern Swaziland along the north bank of the Pongola River and gradually assimilated those clans already occupying the region. During the 1820s, the Swazi, led by *iNgwenyama* (king) Sobhuza Dlamini I, moved northward into north-central Swaziland in order to escape the depredations of the Ndwandwe south of the Pongola. There, centered in the fertile and defensible Ezulwini Valley, Sobhuza gradually built up his kingdom of diverse peoples, whom he assimilated either by diplomacy or by force of arms. To be sure, the Swazi state that he had fashioned by the time of his death (1839) was by no means secure, buffeted as it was internally by rivalries and occasional rebellions and externally by the growing threat of the expanding Zulu empire to the south.

It lay to Sobhuza's successor, *iNgwenyama* Mswati Dlamini II (1840–65), to secure his father's gains, to defend the state against the Zulu, and to project Swazi power far to the north and west into what is now South Africa's Transvaal region. Mswati is justly known as Swaziland's greatest fighting king, but he was much more than that. Necessity forced him to become a diplomat, to deal with powers possessing growing influence over his sovereignty and imperial reach. First were the Transvaal Afrikaners ("Boers"), who formed two successive governments with hegemonic designs, the Lydenburg (1845) and the South African (1852) republics. Second was the British administration in Natal (from 1843), which held the key to Mswati's efforts to contain aggressive Zulu expansionism. His diplomatic efforts led him to invite the first foreign missionaries to settle along his borders and to concession away the first Swazi territory to Europeans. Necessity in the form of fraternal threats to his legitimacy forced Mswati to become an innovator of domestic institutions as well. It was he (aided by the powerful *indlovukazi* [queen mother] Tsandzile Ndwandwe) who solidified his grip on power by establishing nationwide *emabutfo* (regiments) loyal to him and by building royal villages strategically located throughout the kingdom, commanded by trusted *bntfwanenkhosi* (princes) and manned by *emabutfo* of unquestioned allegiance. By the time of his death Mswati had built a state that was both cohesive and internally secure, and whose sphere of influence reached along several compass points deep into the Transvaal.

Mswati's death ushered in an extended period of intrigue and darkness that lasted until at least the turn of the century and arguably into the 1920s. It was a period that tested the political institutions and alliances that Mswati and Sobhuza had fashioned. All things considered, they withstood the test of time, but often just barely. Certainly one difficult period was the decade following Mswati's death, which constituted in effect one long, violent interregnum, strewn with the corpses of royal pretenders and their allies. The king to emerge from the fray (1875) was Mbandzeni Dlamini, whose selection by the *indlovukazi* (itself a flawed process) proved to be the single most disastrous royal decision in all of Swaziland's history. Mbandzeni, orphaned in both body and soul, spent the duration of his reign seeking legitimacy and understanding in the face of a cabal of powerful regents, led by Tsandzile, who were unwilling to relinquish their power. Consequently, Mbandzeni turned to the growing community of European concessionaires for his recognition, granting land, grazing, and monopoly concessions so haphazardly and promiscuously over the following dozen years as to shatter any hope Swaziland might have had of maintaining its sovereignty. Many of the concessions ran two or three deep over the same territory; others, monopolies covering the mechanisms of government, eventually were sold off to the South African Republic (SAR) by the original concessionaires. Although Mbandzeni bore the brunt of the blame for the concessions disaster, everyone involved—regents, councillors, European advisors and concessionaires, and most of all the governments of the SAR and Great Britain—were also culpable. The sorry fate of Swaziland was reflected in a famous photograph of its king, taken near the end of his life and located in the files of the Cape archives. It is of a man besotted by drink and gone massively to fat, his expression betraying a broken spirit, his eyes lifeless. Undefended any longer by a strong monarchy, Swaziland lay open to the imperial designs of far larger powers, Britain and the SAR.

The kingdom's fate was sealed during the regency following Mbandzeni's death (1889) and the ensuing reign of the equally ill-fated *iNgwenyama* Bhunu Dlamini (1895–99). During that decade, Britain, once sufficiently concerned with Swaziland's fate to be willing to guarantee its independence, gradually shifted the focus of its strategic interests northward toward Rhodesia, while Pretoria looked increasingly toward the kingdom as its last best opening to the sea. The result was a series of conventions signed by both powers that sacrificed Swaziland's sovereignty on the altar of their combined geopolitical designs. The last, the third Swaziland Convention of 1894, allowed the SAR to administer the kingdom just short of incorporation, and with a British resident in place. That arrangement lasted from 1895 to 1899. The most significant events to occur during that period were the SAR's imposition of a heavy "native" tax designed to force the Swazi to migrate to the gold mines of Johannesburg for labor, and its expropriation—with Britain's accord—of the Swazi monarchy's criminal jurisdiction.

Colonial

When Britain took over Swaziland's colonial administration following the Anglo-Boer War (1899–1902), it reimposed both the SAR's labor tax and the ban on royal criminal jurisdiction. Britain's administration entrenched its program of underdevelopment by legitimizing the preponderance of the concessions granted during the Mbandzeni era and, on that basis, expropriating two-thirds of the Swazis' historic landholdings (Partition Proclamation of 1907). Beginning in 1914, that land was redistributed either to European concessionaires in freehold, or to the government itself as "crown land" for later disposal. Swazi finding themselves occupying the newly confiscated land either made agreements with the new settler-owners to remain in return for farm labor or removed themselves to one of the 32 "native areas" scattered throughout what remained of Swazi Nation Land. Within a generation many of those areas, the vast majority of them on inferior and ill-watered land, were becoming overpopulated, eroded, and unable to support their new inhabitants without the supplementary income derived from migrant labor. Those conditions were only exacerbated by the effects of the world depression of the 1930s, which for the first time pushed significant numbers of Swazi over the line into destitution.

Politically, things were only marginally better for the Swazi monarchy. Following Bhunu's death in 1899, the *indlovukazi*, Labotsibeni Mdluli, became queen regent until such time as Bhunu's son and successor, later to be named Sobhuza Dlamini II, reached majority. That was not to be until

1921. In the meantime, Labotsibeni was forced to rely on her own intelligence and character, along with the advice of a small circle of Swazi and Zulu mission graduates, for her strategies to effect the kingdom's survival. Fortunately, her innate wisdom and moral strength turned out to be formidable, for she needed all the armament she could muster to confront the forces arrayed against her.

Those forces were many and formidable. First was the British administration, determined to undermine every aspect of her authority so that its plan for Swaziland as an agriculturally productive settler economy based on an abundant and compliant African labor force could be accomplished without undue Swazi resistance. Second were both the Swazi chiefs and *banumzana* (homestead heads), who sought to use the circumstance of royal disarray following the disastrous reigns of *tiNgwenyama* Mbandzeni and Bhunu to distance themselves from the monarchy both politically and in terms of fealty obligations, especially labor. Third were Labotsibeni's educated advisors, both African and European, who were all too often prepared to betray the monarchy's and nation's interests if it meant furthering their own. Even the relatively honest ones, such as Johannesburg attorney (and African National Congress founder) Pixley kaI. Seme, proved to constitute a mixed blessing. For all of Seme's considerable abilities as a lawyer and advisor, his fondness for embarking on undertakings and acquisitions through heavy debt financing placed Labotsibeni, and later Sobhuza, under such crippling obligations as to seriously undermine their positions with the colonial administration. Fourth was the settler farmer population, which by 1911 was forming itself into the first of various lobbying organizations and regional and territorial farmers' associations. Their aim was to channel as many government resources as possible (the main source of which was the native tax) into subsidizing their otherwise marginal, and often failing, farms.

Given those obstacles it was remarkable that Labotsibeni was able to preserve the nation's sovereignty and the monarchy's viability. Her ability to do so sufficiently frustrated an early resident commissioner, Robert Coryndon, that he attempted to get rid of her in favor of her pre-adolescent grandson Sobhuza. When that failed, Coryndon resorted to measures that hobbled her financially and prevented her from obtaining competent outside advice. He also—blatantly—infiltrated her court with spies. In many cases, he acted in ways that would have led to his imprisonment in Britain, although in each he had the assent of the high commissioner in Pretoria. Labotsibeni responded with unflagging determination to all those challenges, her tactics varying in accordance with the circumstances from confrontation, to supplication, to guile, and finally to a few mendacities and illegalities of her own. There were also times when, if all else failed, she entered into collaboration with Coryndon and his successors. After 1911, for instance, she used the colonial court system to enforce her civil decrees against chiefs who balked at forfeiting fines. That collaboration earned her the enmity of a good many chiefs, particularly in southern and eastern Swaziland, as well as powerful elements within both the *libandla* (Swazi National Council) and the *liqoqo* (inner council). As a whole, however, Labotsibeni's actions in defense of her people and their institutions proved to be highly effective, and she handed over to Sobhuza in 1921 a monarchy stronger both domestically and diplomatically, and more widely popular with her own people, than the one she had inherited at the time of Bhunu's death in 1899.

iNgwenyama Sobhuza II (ruled 1921–82) clearly had inherited some of Labotsibeni's most distinguished traits—character, resoluteness, and intelligence. He also enjoyed the advantage of having achieved the equivalent of a secondary education, through a combination of formal, western schooling at the Lovedale Missionary Institution in the Cape and private tutoring at Zombodze, Labotsibeni's administrative homestead. Sobhuza also had many serious obstacles to overcome, and it was not inaccurate to say that the fate of the throne he inherited in 1921 would turn on the strength of his character and resolve. Domestically, bitter opposition to Sobhuza's legitimacy centered in one of his half-brothers, Mnt. Makhosikhosi Dlamini, whose mother (laMavimbela) had been regarded at the time of Bhunu's death as holding the inside track to the office of *indlovukazi*. The king-makers, considering the chances of Makhosikhosi's having inherited Bhunu's instabilities to be too dangerous, had chosen Nkhotfotjeni's (Sobhuza's) mother, Lomawa Ndwandwe, instead. Sobhuza was also confronted with the same chiefly opposition to a powerful monarchy, centered in the south, that Labotsibeni had failed to overcome. Diplomatically, Sobhuza was faced early in his reign with an oppressively imperial mind-set both in Pretoria (the British high commissioner) and in Mbabane (the resident commissioner). The administration's main goals for Swaziland were to maintain the trappings of a monarchy in place in order to implement its agenda in preparing the territory for handover to South Africa as a thriving, settler-based agricultural society based on a proletarianized Swazi population.

Sobhuza conducted his early reign as a young African progressive. He had been profoundly influenced by his tutors and his years at Lovedale, both of which had imprinted him with Western values to a degree not fully understood until much later, partly because of his strong indoctrination in tradition under Labotsibeni's watchful eye. Sobhuza's progressivism could be seen not only in his dress and lifestyle, but also in his choice of advisors, notably Benjamin Nxumalo, his mission-educated uncle, and Pixley Seme, his American- and British-trained lawyer. Sobhuza demonstrated his progressivism (and Seme's influence) when he chose to defend Swazi tradition in the colonial court system. The case *Sobhuza II vs. Miller* contested the legality of certain Mbandzeni-era concessions on the grounds that they contravened "Swazi law and custom." Sobhuza, through Seme, fought the case all the way to the Privy Council in London, where his appeal was turned down (1926). It is unlikely that Sobhuza truly believed that the Miller case was winnable (although Seme may have), because it was universally understood that the suit challenged the very legitimacy of British colonial rule. The fact remained that it was widely believed among chiefs and commoners that the Europeans would soon be forced to hand back their lands. Consequently, the political shock of the Privy Council decision (on top of his failed 1922–23 deputation to London) forced Sobhuza into a fundamental rethinking of priorities and strategies. The jolt of Sobhuza's legal reversal on his outlook—and by inference his opinion of where his progressivism had led him—can be seen in a poignantly symbolic act which Crush has noted.[1] In 1926, Sobhuza named his newly constructed administrative capital "*Lozithelezi*," or "A Place Surrounded by Enemies."

The courses of action Sobhuza undertook as the result of his soul-searchings constituted a milestone in his reign, resulting as they did in the dramatic reversal of both his and his kingdom's long-term fortunes. Macmillan documents some elements of the *ingwenyama*'s abandonment of "progressivism" for "traditionalism" (Macmillan calls it "ethnic mobilisation") as his guiding strategy for both domestic rule and relations with the colonials.[2] The beginnings of Sobhuza's volte face can even be dated: his remarkable Socratic confrontation with Resident Commissioner de Symons Honey on 18–19 May 1926, following the Privy Council decision (see DLAMINI *iNGWENYAMA* SOBHUZA II). Central to his strategy was the dusting off and use of several moribund traditions and institutions in the mobilization of popular support for the monarchy. In some instances (the "modernization" of both the *libandla* and the *liqoqo* for instance; see below), the exercise included the invention of institutional roles and procedures that, so far as we know, had never before existed. Sobhuza accorded particular importance to modern (mission-dominated) education, which he considered a double-edged sword: necessary for the next Swazi generation, which would (he hoped) push the kingdom into the modern era, but capable also of subverting the very "traditional" values on which he depended for the monarchy's popular support. Although Sobhuza never felt strong enough to express his feelings other than obliquely, he deeply distrusted the Christian missions as rivals to power, and he went to considerable lengths to sap their authority as much as he dared. Those motives were behind his launching of an independently funded and controlled Swazi National High School at Matsapha in 1931 and his attempts to regiment Swazi students in the kingdom's other, predominantly mission schools by using the 19th-century *emabutfo* (regimental) system as his model.

In that and other invocations of "tradition," Sobhuza called on sympathetically minded European authorities, from colonial officials (notably Allan G. Marwick) to the lions of the South African anthropological establishment, for assistance in legitimizing what he was doing. When, in the mid-1930s, a young anthropology student of Bronislaw Malinowski, Hilda Beemer (Kuper), arrived in the kingdom to pursue her dissertation fieldwork, Sobhuza assigned her a constant escort, accorded her unprecedented access to royal informants, and personally befriended her in what turned out to be a strong lifelong relationship for them both. The largely royalist point of view from which she wrote her several (classic) anthropological studies, along with her biography of him, could not but have pleased the king.[3] Indeed, his campaigns to influence all levels of European society were on the whole quite successful, in part because of a change in policy by the British government in the late 1920s that led to its implementation of the substance of "indirect rule" in Swaziland. It was Allan Marwick, for instance, whose creative reinterpretation of old protocols and proclamations in the late 1930s led to the criminalizing of chiefs' opposition to Sobhuza's civil decisions, effectively bolstering his domestic power and prestige.

It was a testament to his political acumen that Sobhuza quickly began to invest his newly won influence in undertakings promising to redouble his authority. They included his and the *libandla*'s prolonged campaign (beginning in 1939) of adamant public opposition to the British proposal for a "native authorities proclamation" that would have institutionalized indirect rule, but only at the expense of undercutting his power to appoint and depose chiefs. They also included his public petition to Westminster (1941) not only on the native authorities question but also to redress what he termed the "urgent" land shortage in the native areas, which was leading to their "denudation and soil erosion." Eventually both aspects of Sobhuza's petition met with success. Britain made funds available through the Colonial Development and Welfare Act of 1940 as the basis for the establishment of the Swaziland Native Land Settlement Scheme (1943). The resolution of Sobhuza's objections to the native authorities question took much longer; it was only in 1950 that the "*ingwenyama*-in-*libandla*" (king in council) was declared the sole native authority with exclusive powers of appointment and deposition over chiefs, under terms of the Native Administration Proclamation of 1950.

That year marked another milestone in Sobhuza's political history. His conspicuous victory over the British in the matter of the Native Administration Proclamation, won after such a difficult and protracted struggle, gained him enormous domestic prestige. That in turn enabled Sobhuza to act with new decisiveness during the post–World War II era, when an entirely new dimension of foreign capital investment was rendering the old political economy of Swaziland almost unrecognizable. Sobhuza used his newly acquired authority under the 1950 proclamation to grant trading licenses in native areas, which opened the way for selected members of royalty and the loyalist elite to enter the nascent Swazi middle class. He also pushed with new vigor and stridency for the return of exclusive royal rights to the proceeds of Swaziland's mineral wealth on crown lands, which had been lost in 1907.

The 1950 proclamation proved to be a not unalloyed boon to his power, for it also marked the rise in assertiveness and power of two bodies which until then he had effectively prevented from checking his own authority, the *libandla* and the *liqoqo*. The latter of these had gradually shifted in its composition under Sobhuza's leadership toward the influence of mission-educated progressives since the 1930s. The *libandla*'s new authority could be seen in its forging links directly with the colonial administration beginning in 1947, when it fashioned a "Standing Committee" to meet regularly with senior colonial officials in a manner similar to the European Advisory Council (EAC). The *liqoqo*'s growing power, gained in large part by its members' acquisition of wealth through privileged access to trader's licenses and similar investments, was strong enough by 1980 to force the king to quash a government inquiry into corruption which threatened to expose prominent council members.

It was the king, newly powerful but also influenced by his councillors as never before, who beginning in the late 1950s entered the political fray in anticipation of internal self-government and eventual independence. Sobhuza entered the period with the overarching goal of transforming his power as *ingwenyama* into that of the head of a modern, independent state. That required both a sufficient capital base and competent advice in modern party politics, neither of which he possessed. Consequently, Sobhuza made two compensating moves in anticipation. First, he and his *libandla* aligned themselves with the conservative wing of the European settler establishment. Sobhuza, in courting the settlers, hoped to transform the separate de facto ruling elites, the EAC and the *libandla*, into the dominant coalition controlling the first elected Legislative Council (Legco). Second, Sobhuza secretly turned to the white exclusivist South African regime for political counsel and funds.

The king's dream did not take into account the pent-up expectations of the growing class of educated Swazi who wished to mark the end of colonialism with movement toward a new, democratic political dispensation and shared economic opportunity. Its members formed several political parties in opposition to the anticipated EAC-*libandla* alliance. When they did so, their claims to legitimacy were supported by the colonial administration, which wished to end its tenure in Swaziland with a truly representative government in place. Following the failure of all parties to agree on the shape of a constitution, the British government in 1963 imposed an interim document which formed the basis for Legco elections to be held in mid-1964. Against all official advice (excepting, presumably, South African) that he remain above the fray, Sobhuza formed his own political party, the Imbokodvo National Movement (INM), to contest the upcoming elections. The INM, in alliance with the conservative European-based United Swaziland Association (USA), swept the Legco polls, the elected members of which were constitutionally mandated to carry out the drafting of the independence constitution.

Sobhuza quickly capitalized on his overwhelming popular mandate. First, he co-opted many of the most prominent opposition politicians into abandoning their parties and joining the INM. Second, he jettisoned his coalition with the USA, much to its members' shock and chagrin, effectively relegating it to political oblivion. Third, he began a relentless campaign to shape the independence constitution so that the monarchy would once more dominate the political economy of an independent Swaziland, as it had during much of the 19th century. Sobhuza's efforts proved to be highly successful. The design of the new parliament, ostensibly on the Westminster model, was on closer reading a creature of the king. One-fifth of the 30-member assembly were to be his nominees, while the rest were elected from eight 3-member constituencies, gerrymandered to favor the rural areas where the king's strength was centered. He also nominated half of the 12-member senate. Furthermore, the king appointed both the chief justice and the prime minister, who served merely in an advisory capacity to the king. Sobhuza's control over Swazi Nation Land (but not European-held Title Deed Land) was also affirmed.

Not the least important of Sobhuza's victories was in his fight with the colonial authorities over the vesting of Swaziland's mineral wealth, most of which had been in the British administration's hands since the early 1900s. Britain held that those resources should be under the parliament's authority, to ensure that their wealth accrued to the people. In the end, Sobhuza won control over them and proceeded to establish (1968) a closely held royal investment trust whose purpose was to provide, for the first time in the 20th century, a secure capital base for the monarchy and, by extension, the source of personal wealth to the king's clients. That trust, the Tibiyo takaNgwane fund, had by the end of the 20th century extended its grip to shares in virtually every foreign capital investment of any consequence in the kingdom, and in addition had amassed an untold private fortune for its controllers.

Post-Independence

That was the political and economic basis on which Swaziland was granted independence by Britain in 1968. Sobhuza dominated the political process by virtue of his constitutionally mandated authority over parliament, his control over Swazi Nation Land, and his immense personal popularity, especially among the peasantry. The king, however, chafed at those signs remaining that his rule was not absolute. They included the sometimes spirited debates in parliament and especially the continued existence of an organized and vocal—but constitutional—opposition, notably the Ngwane National Liberatory Congress (NNLC), which stood for a constitutional monarchy and the redistribution of wealth. Sobhuza, who complained that such an arrangement was "un-Swazi," was at least comforted that the opposition was extra-parliamentary. That abruptly changed as the result of the 1972 elections, in which the NNLC won three seats in parliament, one of the defeated candidates being a prince who was close to the king and a member of the *liqoqo*. Ominously, the NNLC victory came in a constituency heavily populated with industrial workers and Swazi freeholder farmers, none of whom were dependent on the king for their livelihoods. That was enough for the *ingwenyama*. Citing a procedural technicality—the flimsiest of pretexts—Sobhuza in 1973 declared an emergency, revoked the constitution, and outlawed all political parties. Finally, transforming a lifelong mistrust of police loyalty into action, Sobhuza formed a new national army, the Royal Umbutfo Defense Force, staffed it with loyalists, and allowed the white regime in South Africa to equip it. The *ingwenyama* ruled by decree for the next five years, following which he instituted a new parliamentary process based on *tinkhundla* (regional councils), which featured open voting for candidates selected by the king. The resulting "parliament" was a representative lawmaking body in name only. Understandably, Sobhuza's move to suppress the democratic opposition proved to be immensely popular with Swaziland's European establishment, just as it resonated well with the apartheid government of South Africa.

Indeed, on the diplomatic front Sobhuza's last years were marked by his warming relationship with Pretoria, and specifically by his move toward an accommodation with the South African regime, which addressed the needs of both parties. Sobhuza, who had long dreamed of reincorporating all ethnic Swazi lost during the 19th-century border delineations, reached such an agreement with Pretoria in 1982. Basically, the accord stipulated that in return for his elimination of the activities of the African National Congress (ANC) within Swaziland's borders, South Africa would cede to him two large parcels of territory historically claimed by Swaziland: kaNgwane in the eastern Transvaal, and Ingwavuma in northern Natal. Sobhuza carried out his half of the bargain with considerable dispatch, but Pretoria's promised transfer became embroiled in domestic political controversy in both Swaziland and South Africa, and the arrangement remained mired in limbo when Sobhuza suddenly died in August 1982.

The nature of Sobhuza's unexpected death became a matter of immediate and lasting public speculation. First, aged though he was, the leukemia from which he had long suffered seemed to have gone into remission, and from all appearances he was in reasonable, if not robust, health. Second, there had been much in Swazi royal history to make the suspicion of foul play on the part of those wishing to deny nature its course a not unreasonable one. Indeed, according to Sobhuza's lifelong friend, biographer, and principal eulogizer, Hilda Kuper, the *ingwenyama* did die the victim of a regicide, killed by poison administered by an "African doctor . . . [from] Malawi,"[4] in whom the king had placed his trust to restore his vitality after Western-style medicine had failed to do so. It had not been the first attempt on his life, but this time the king had failed to require that the doctor consume some of the medicine in his presence before he himself did. Who put the alleged assassin up to it was never revealed, for he escaped as the king lay dying.[5] If Kuper's account is the correct one—and there seems to be no reason for her to have left an untruthful account behind in her papers—then tradition, which Sobhuza had invoked so often during his political lifetime, had in a manner of speaking determined the nature of his passing. Although the king was old and ailing, and had recently made provision for the interregnum, his senior aides had found him "well" and "alert" on the day prior to his death,[6] and none of his immediate family had had any sense that the end was near. The suddenness of Sobhuza's death left the government in confusion and exerted a profound effect on the politics of the post-Sobhuza era.

The four-year interregnum that followed—interregnums have always been turbulent periods in Swazi history—was chaotic and dangerous. Sobhuza had signed a decree in June 1982 that had provided that following his death, the functions of the *ingwenyama* were to be performed by the *indlovukazi* as queen regent, a provision for which there was long precedent. The decree then went beyond tradition by establishing her co-regent as the "Authorised Person" and by institutionalizing and elevating the status of the *Liqoqo* (which Sobhuza spelled with a capital "L"), defining it as "the Supreme Council of State whose function is to advise the King on all matters of State." On the membership of the new, more powerful *Liqoqo* the decree was silent, most likely because Sobhuza had planned to make his nominations nearer to the time of his death. His sudden passing ensured that that did not happen, and this lack was instrumental in the chaos that ensued.

Into the void created at the center of power stepped a handful of ambitious men. One of them came forward with a list, with which he claimed to have been entrusted at the last minute by Sobhuza, containing the membership of a new *Liqoqo* supposedly to take office following Sobhuza's passing. Although nothing in Sobhuza's handwriting was ever produced, the nominations were accepted by the queen regent.

Over the next several months, a power struggle pitted the new *Liqoqo* (which awarded itself an unauthorized salary) against those loyalist members of the royal family who were determined to transfer power to Sobhuza's legitimate heir. Ultimately the struggle ended with the premature enthronement of a young son of Sobhuza, Mnt. Makhositive (1986), and with the more sinister of the *Liqoqo* members being sentenced to prison or forced into exile. In an indication of the seriousness of the *Liqoqo*'s challenge to his legitimacy, *iNkhosana* (Crown Prince) Makhositive was installed in April 1986 at the unusually youthful age of 18. Young Makhositive assumed the title of *iNgwenyama* Mswati Dlamini III.

The first years of any Swazi king's reign are more often than not times of great challenge and insecurity. Perhaps the best example was that of the young king's namesake, *iNgwenyama* Mswati II (1840–65). It is not uncommon for a young king to be tested politically and sometimes militarily, the grounds often being questions as to his legitimacy as heir. On occasion he is confronted with diplomatic crises as well. If he proves to be a man of character and has surrounded himself with wise and decisive advisors, his insecurity is likely to be of short duration. Mswati III's period of testing, by contrast, lasted more than a dozen years, for several reasons.

First, his legitimacy was widely questioned, in part because his mother, Ntombi Twala, was of relatively low pedigree. Second, he had from the time of his birth been indulged by his aged father and had undoubtedly been aware of the real possibility of his succeeding the king (Makhositive, the name given him by Sobhuza, is translated as "King of Many Nations"). Those circumstances appeared to have generated in the boy a lack of self-discipline and a taste for the privileged life that scarcely diminished as he grew older. Third, not only had his father reputedly been slain, but Mswati himself was in fear for his life from the day of his nomination as heir, when he had been sent into hiding and subsequently spirited out of the country to be educated under constant guard in England. Those circumstances were hardly calculated to afford the young *ingwenyama* the personal sense of security requisite for wise and decisive rule. Fourth, Mswati was not served well by an inherited circle of advisors who were rigidly conservative, lacking in modern vision, and in some instances corrupt, and from whom he appeared unable to distance himself.

In a manner of speaking, the style of Mswati's early reign could be termed "progressive," the same term used to characterize Sobhuza's early years as king. With reference to the successive rulers, however, there was a world of difference in the meaning of the word. King Sobhuza during his "progressive" phase had indeed enjoyed the 1920s-era material perquisites of modern royalty—stylish European dress, a shortwave radio, a Buick touring car, and a house in Sophiatown, to name a few. Beneath all the stylishness, however, had laid almost from the beginning a serious political agenda—his determination to best the colonial-settler society at its own game. Mswati by contrast often appeared to be following no political agenda at all, aside from his determination to preserve the monarchy unchanged. The young king soon became known for his frequent and luxurious travels abroad, often to occasions more ceremonial than substantive, and for a copious taste in the trappings of conspicuous wealth, most notably the construction of a lavish palace outside Mbabane. At the same time, Mswati developed reputations domestically for his inattention to the substance of governance and within the foreign diplomatic community for his reluctance to focus on serious affairs of state. Those reputations stood in stark contrast to those of his late father.

Certainly the challenges faced by Mswati early in his reign demanded a high level of concentration. Not the least of them was a growing impatience within the Swazi middle class with what it perceived to be a closed and authoritarian political system that rewarded kinship and clientism over merit. During the late 1980s, as events in South Africa moved it toward a system of democracy and a modest redistribution of wealth, public impatience in Swaziland became transformed into action. It manifested itself principally in the formation of increasingly bold opposition movements and labor unions with political as well as workplace agendas.

Public opposition came to focus on the *tinkhundla* system of election to parliament, a procedure so transparently rigged as to be widely regarded as the symbol of all that was wrong with the political system. The most prominent of the several opposition groups and unions to emerge were the People's United Democratic Movement (PUDEMO) and the Swaziland Federation of Trade Unions (SFTU). In response to their gradually escalating activism, Mswati, beginning in the early 1990s, entered into a series of apparent concessions whose actual purpose was widely interpreted to be a stall for time. First came back-to-back "*Vusela*" ("Greeting") commissions to undertake studies of the *tinkhundla* system with the declared intent to reform it. Although the process resulted in a modest move toward voter confidentiality, the fundamental nature of the electoral system as a mechanism to perpetuate royal hegemony remained unaltered, and the first election under the revised *tinkhundla* system in 1993 was widely boycotted. That event was soon followed by the beginnings of sporadic political violence.

By 1996 the pressure on Mswati was such that he agreed to the establishment of a Constitutional Review Commission (CRC), whose mandate was to draft a new constitution that would be acceptable to the public and to submit it to him within two years. Quickly, however, the CRC became enmeshed in a succession of procedural controversies, and several of its prominent members representing opposition bodies eventually resigned in frustration. By the end of the decade, it remained unclear when, or if, the CRC would ever be able to fulfill its declared mandate.

Mswati at the turn of the 21st century appeared to be banking for the survival of his monarchy on the prolonged support of his natural constituency, the peasantry, and on the continued patience of the organized opposition, even the most radical elements of which were seeking only the move toward a constitutional monarchy. In the context of the number of moves toward democracy taking place elsewhere in sub-Saharan Africa, the question was how long the Swazi royal house could continue to argue with any credibility that what was happening beyond the kingdom's borders was not in accordance with Swazi tradition, and therefore not relevant.

THE ECONOMY

Swaziland by any standard is, relative to the rest of sub-Saharan Africa, a wealthy nation. To pick one statistic, in 1993 its per capita income was US$670, the fourth highest in the southern subcontinent, behind mineral-rich Botswana ($2,500), Namibia ($1,240), and South Africa ($2,600) but ahead of Zambia ($580) and Zimbabwe ($540). Swaziland's economy is based in large part on commercial agriculture and agriculture-based industry. Sugar is by far the largest export, constituting 28.1 percent by value of all exports during the period 1988–92. Other principal exports are woodpulp (1988–92: 11.6 percent of exports); citrus and canned fruit, including pineapple (1988–92: 6.0 percent); and timber and wood products (1988–92: 4.0 percent). Swaziland's principal export-oriented industries are woodpulp production, soft-drink (including concentrate) manufacturing, fruit canning, and sugar processing. Non-food light manufacturing, especially textiles (1988–92: 11.0 percent), paper products (1988–92: 2.0 percent), and refrigerators (1988–92: 2.0 percent), accounts for a small percentage of exports. The principal mineral exports are asbestos (1988–92: 1.9 percent), diamonds (1988–92: 1.1 percent), and coal (1988–92: 0.8 percent). Swaziland's largest invisible export is tourism, which in 1996 accounted for revenues of E150 million (US$35 million), nearly all of it from South Africa. Another important source of revenue is in the form of remittances from Swazi migrant workers to South Africa, which in 1996 totalled E324.2 million (US$75.4 million), or 6.8 percent of GDP.

Commercial agricultural and forestry production are centered for the most part on TDL, which constitutes approximately 40 percent of total area. That includes the Usutu forests, the deed for which is owned by the Swazi crown. TDL as a category stems from a 1907 colonial proclamation which placed land previously concessioned to Europeans either under freehold (to individuals) or under the status of crown land (to the British administration). Most of Swaziland's extensive irrigation systems service TDL.

Domestic production is dominated by maize (135,000 tons in 1996), grown largely on SNL, which is held in communal tenure dispensed by the king through the chiefs, and which constitutes some 60 percent of total area.

SNL is preponderantly rain-fed and therefore vulnerable to periodic droughts. Some cotton, grown principally for local textile production, is also grown on SNL. A modest amount of sorghum is cultivated on SNL both as insurance against drought and for beer brewing. Much SNL is given over to cattle grazing (in 1986 amounting to 80 percent of all cattle and 93 percent of all cattle owners), which is the perennial source of much controversy: In Swazi society, cattle are both the repositories and the indicators of wealth, but because grazing on SNL commonage is cost-free to the individual owner, the economic premium rests on cattle numbers rather than condition. The result over recent generations has been not only heavy erosion of large SNL areas but also a deterioration of quality in the national cattleherd to the point where commercially speaking, it is nearly useless for anything beyond milk production, local slaughter, and barter. The Swaziland Meat Corporation slaughterhouse, which had once exported beef to the European Union under quota, closed its doors during the late 1980s.

Swaziland's largest trading partner for both imports (1997: 96.3 percent) and exports (1997: 58.4 percent) is South Africa. The character of the trade relationship is one of dependency, determined by Swaziland's membership in two regional organizations dominated by South Africa: the Southern African Customs Union (SACU) and the Common Monetary Area, which guarantee the duty-free flow of goods and capital across borders and which to a large degree tie Mbabane's fiscal and monetary policies to those of Pretoria. Swaziland's second largest trading partner is the European Union (1997: 16.8 percent of exports), by virtue of its membership in the Lomé Convention, which allows quotas for its sugar and citrus products. Swaziland also exports a small portion of its sugar under quota (General System of Preferences) to the United States, ranging from 3.7 to 8.3 percent of its total sugar exports during the 1990s. Mozambique is the second largest regional importer of Swaziland's products (1997: 3.1 percent of exports).

Foreign investment in Swaziland, which had reached high levels during the late 1980s, flattened out after 1990. That was a direct result of the apartheid-era international campaign of sanctions against South Africa, when Swaziland's membership in SACU and the Lomé Convention made it an attractive conduit for foreign investment funds seeking avoidance of international sanctions. The most notable example was Coca-Cola's establishment of its main concentrate plant at Matsapha in 1986 following its much-publicized exit from South Africa, allowing it to conduct business as usual across the open border. With the advent of democracy in South Africa during the early 1990s, Swaziland's attractiveness to the outside investing world quickly diminished, so that by the end of the decade the only new foreign investment in the kingdom was aimed at the expansion of existing industries.

The main domestic obstruction to the healthy growth of Swaziland's national economy is the continued existence of the royal investment trust, the Tibiyo takaNgwane ("Wealth of the Swazi Nation") Fund. Increasingly since its establishment in 1968, Tibiyo has exercised a parasitical influence on the national economy, siphoning much of its lifeblood into a separate treasury primarily for the benefit of the monarchy and its clients, and pushing the economy as a whole into an artificially anemic state. Because its accounts are secret, there is no telling the degree to which Tibiyo dampens national growth, but it is substantial. Since the mid-1970s, Tibiyo's principal means of accomplishing this has been to obtain substantial shares (usually half) of virtually every important foreign-owned enterprise in the modern sector, often at little or no cost to itself. Because Tibiyo pays no taxes, that has meant that the national economy benefits only from wages earned and corporate taxes paid (or what is left of them after Tibiyo's exemptions) from nearly every significant business from hotels, construction, and transport to financial institutions, mines, agribusiness (notably sugar), and forest products. Although *tingwenyama* have claimed over the years that Tibiyo's resources are held in trust for the benefit of the nation as a whole, the fact is that a very small percentage of its profits are ever seen by the common citizenry except in the form of scholarships (often made available to the children of the elite) and support of cultural institutions, which further the monarchist tradition.

Consequently, Tibiyo, which has become a principal capital base of the modern Swazi monarchy, has operated only at the massive cost of skewing national development priorities and draining the central government budget. For all of Swaziland's copious natural resource base, and whatever the effects of foreign influences, its national economy will never achieve its full potential for the benefit of all its citizenry as long as Tibiyo exercises such overwhelming and exploitative dominance over so much of its modern sector.

SOCIAL DEVELOPMENT

If statistics are kind to Swaziland's population in terms of per capita income, they are less so when it comes to indicators of social well-being.

Swaziland is in many ways comparable to Zimbabwe in natural resources and economic profile, but it suffers by comparison in many indicators associated with the quality of life. In 1993 Swaziland's life expectancy rates (males: 51 years; females: 59 years) were significantly below Zimbabwe's (males: 60 years; females: 64 years). Swaziland's infant mortality rate (101/1,000) dramatically exceeded that of Zimbabwe (61/1,000). Swaziland's adult literacy rate (55 percent) trailed Zimbabwe's (67 percent). Given the similarity of the two countries' economies and experiences of colonial underdevelopment and neglect, the inference is strong that a major reason for the disparity lies in the contrasting education and public policy priorities implemented by the two governments (Swaziland's monarchist, Zimbabwe's more representative) following independence.

Swazi society at the turn of the 21st century is in transition from its rural, agricultural, traditional basis to one more urban, middle-class, and cosmopolitan. Change has come slowly but not always smoothly, its nature affected by many factors tracing back to the early 20th century. Among them are land shortage and deterioration stemming from the colonial era; an attendant decline in agricultural productivity; the advent of the money economy and wage labor for both men and women, leading to both demographic and socioeconomic changes in the traditional homestead; increasing access to education, leading to even further changes in the homestead and beyond; the attendant formation of an ambitious middle class; and the attempts by the traditional elite to maintain political control by emphasizing "tradition" and "harmony" in the face of rising popular expectations.

Complicating that social dynamic is the presence of two other significant population groups. The first is a wealthy and vibrant European settler class tracing its roots back to the late 19th century, whose influence grew dramatically during the post–World War II period of capital development. The second is a small but economically powerful EurAfrican community, born of settler and African parentage, benefiting from the privileges accorded it by the colonial government and settler society, and consequently the object of resentment and occasional discrimination in post-independence Swaziland.

Still, in the face of modernization, the focal point in the lives of most Swazi continues to be the rural homestead. According to de Vletter, the homestead remains the residence of about four out of five Swazi and continues to be a rural base—both physical and psychological—for many urban dwellers.[7] In economic terms, even accounting for modern institutions, the homestead remains the locus for lineage wealth accumulation, whether it be (traditionally) cattle or the invested profits from present-day entrepreneurship. Finally, the homestead remains, for rural and urban dweller alike, the ceremonial focal point for the milestones of life's passages (birth, puberty, marriage, and death) and the ultimate place of sanctuary and security from early childhood to extreme old age.

That is not to say that the homestead has ever been a static institution in Swazi life. The greatest changes came during the first half of the 20th century, primarily as the result of colonialism. Europeans forced on the Swazi the cultural baggage they brought with them, notably the money economy, agricultural innovation, migrant labor, and education. Swazi men in great numbers entered into labor migrancy beginning about 1914, leaving control of agriculture and decision making to women for the first time, and returning with cash. Aside from cattle and grain for food, wages were invested in agricultural technologies and in school fees; children thus empowered with education eventually brought even more wealth and resources to the homestead. Some women also entered the workforce or established themselves in small business, contributing further resources.

The effects of all those changes on the traditional homestead were farreaching and profound. Most often patriarchism declined; decision making was delegated; sex and age roles were dramatically altered, with the empowerment of both women and male youths; and homestead labor power was reduced, with a resultant decline in agricultural productivity, making the family increasingly dependent on wages. Homesteads grew physically and demographically smaller with the decline of polygyny, the previous basis of the agricultural labor power on which homestead prosperity had depended, and as sons with independent access to wealth married and established their own homesteads earlier in life.

Greater socioeconomic differentiation of homesteads became a central dimension of modern Swazi society. The process began following the 1907 Partition Proclamation and accelerated rapidly during the period of heavy post–World War II capital development, as some homesteads adapted to the challenges of the new political economy more readily than others. Rose claims that by the 1960s the process had produced separate classes of "haves" (especially Swazi government officials and those owning TDL farms) and "have nots" (mainly Swazi peasantry remaining on SNL).[8] By the early 1980s, 16 percent of the Swazi population claimed landholdings of more than 5 hectares (12.4 acres), taking up 41 percent of the total land area. Wealthier homesteads possessed not only modern amenities (radios, TVs, furniture, and appliances) but also those implements calculated to enhance their relative wealth even further: ploughs and other farm tools, vehicles and access to tractors, sewing machines, fertilizers, and pesticides. Wealthier homesteads were invariably located close to marketing and employment centers, and they included educated members holding modern-sector jobs. Not coincidentally, it was also among the younger, educated membership of those wealthier homesteads that dissatisfaction with the symbols of the closed, royalist society had become so highly discernible by the turn of the 21st century.

Finally, Swazi social development, both urban and rural, at the turn of the century was seriously and tragically disrupted by the epidemic of HIV/AIDS that gripped the kingdom. In 1999, Swaziland had attained by some estimates one of the highest rates of HIV infection in the world. This was in part caused by the fact that the government during the decade 1985–95 had failed to confront or even to admit the seriousness of the growing problem, in part because it was so heavily dependent on foreign tourism. By 1999, however, there was no denying the statistics: an estimated 33 percent infection rate among young and middle-aged adults. Some accounts reckoned that up to 70 percent of the kingdom's teachers were infected, presenting its educational system with a looming crisis. In the urban areas it was the educated, middle-class citizenry which was the hardest hit, robbing the country of much of its greatest future talent and brainpower. In a 1999 report, the United Nations Children's Fund (UNICEF) estimated that up to 40,000 Swazi citizens would die annually of AIDS between the years 2000 and 2015. In the same year, the Swaziland government acknowledged that the HIV/AIDS epidemic constituted a "national disaster" and established a senior government committee (the Crisis Management and Technical Committee on HIV/AIDS) to begin to deal with the challenge. That challenge, creating awareness among an entire population and persuading it to alter its behavior, was a massive one. At the turn of the century the government, citing its own figures that 50,000 had died of AIDS during 1999 (giving the kingdom the fourth highest infection rate in the world), and acknowledging that if the epidemic goes unchecked Swaziland's population would be reduced by 24 percent, began to take serious measures. They included the heretofore culturally unthinkable program of educating prostitutes in safe sex techniques and supplying them with condoms.

THE TWENTY-FIRST CENTURY

The move toward democratization that is sweeping through sub-Saharan Africa at the turn of the 21st century is seen most dramatically in southern

Africa. In that region most countries have opted for representative governments, either directly from colonialism (or white minority rule), or by stages away from military or socialist authoritarianism. Swaziland has moved in the other direction, achieving independence under a functioning monarchy, then falling under much stronger autocratic rule after 1973. *iNgwenyama* Sobhuza II's seizure of all power in that year, which was carefully couched in the name of "Swazi tradition," was in fact much more on the model of the *coups d'état* then sweeping the continent than it was evocative of what had been legitimate in the nation's political past. What was consistent with former practice was Sobhuza's invocation of murky principles of "tradition" to cover for his authoritarian acts. For instance, the "traditional" *tinkhundla* system of parliamentary elections he instituted in 1978 in order to dominate them dated back only to 1955.

In carrying out his coup, Sobhuza counted on the continued loyalty of his main political constituency, the Swazi peasantry, and his calculation proved to be correct. As the rest of the subcontinent moved, often violently, toward democratic rule, Sobhuza was able to argue successfully that as the outside world became "more and more boisterous with grievances destroying one another,"[9] Swaziland's salvation lay in its adherence to its monarchist tradition. That argument proved to be effective only as long as he lived. During the years following Sobhuza's death in 1982, the Swazi were reminded of another truly valid royal tradition, the often deadly chaos that had so frequently dominated Swazi interregnums. That period (1982–86) blatantly displayed, for all—even the illiterate peasantry—to witness, much of the seamy side of the Swazi autocracy: the naked bids for power by those with no legitimate claim to it and the enormous amount of the nation's wealth flowing unchecked and unaudited into royal coffers. Unfortunately, the example of young *iNgwenyama* Mswati III's first years in power did little to mollify the growing public dissatisfaction with the status quo. Simultaneously, across the border in South Africa, the ANC's dazzling success in its peaceful overthrow of totalitarianism contrasted so emphatically with that Swazi status quo as to make a mockery of official claims that those events held no relevance in the face of Swazi tradition.

It is clear that significant change will come to Swaziland, probably early in the 21st century. Impatience for change is rising both domestically, from Swazi opposition groups and labor unions, and from beyond Swaziland's borders, principally from Southern African Development Community (SADC) governments fearing the spread of unrest and instability. In 1997, nearing his retirement, South Africa's president Nelson Mandela urged that SADC sanctions be imposed on member countries that failed to apply democratic values, a clear reference to Swaziland. At the same time, and hardly coincidentally, there was no mistaking the close relationship between the ANC and the main Swazi opposition organization, PUDEMO.

Historically, the Swazi do not hold the reputation for political volatility that, say, the Zulu or the Basotho do. Instead, the prevailing middle-class attitude during the 1980s and early 1990s was one of apparent resignation, as if to say that if one was a friend of the king, there was no point in exerting oneself, because a bright future was guaranteed; conversely, if one was not a friend of the king, there was no point in exerting oneself, because merit counted for nothing against clientism. One consequence was that too many Swazi professionals (doctors, lawyers, academics) left at the first opportunity for the brighter opportunities for self-fulfillment offered by South Africa. Even though lethargy was not to be confused with indifference, it was not at all clear whether by the late 1990s the king and his advisors had come to recognize that Swazi patience, even that of the peasantry, was finite. The irony was that as the domestic pressure was building, even the strongest opponents of the status quo, such as PUDEMO, were calling for nothing more radical than the creation of a constitutional monarchy. How long that attitude would prevail in the absence of any real progress toward democracy was not easy to ascertain.

Absent such progress, Swaziland appeared relegated to the role it had played since independence, that of a small country possessing unusual natural and human resources that its political circumstances prevent it from utilizing toward the fulfillment of its greatest potential. Swaziland's system of communal land tenure delegated from the king placed a premium on land use practices that constituted an affront to human ecology. Swaziland's effective system of dual government, the national administration in Mbabane and the royal government at both Lozita (*ingwenyama*'s administration, Tibiyo takaNgwane and Tisuka takaNgwane Funds) and Lobamba (Swaziland National Trust Commission), prevented it from carrying out the orderly and rational development of its national resources for the benefit of all of its people.

In 1999, the prevailing mood among Swaziland's educated citizenry was one of resignation tinged with an unprecedented sense of cynicism. The public, which viewed the king's 1996 appointment of the Constitutional Review Commission as a stalling tactic, appeared inclined to boycott in large numbers the parliamentary elections scheduled for October under the revised but still widely unpopular *tinkhundla* system. In response to the low number of voter pre-registrations, the government threatened harsh measures against those advocating a stay-away, which would indicate the public's disaffection with the political system as no other non-violent gesture could. Beyond that prospect, absent a political means of expressing popular political dissent, the only way open for such expression was a return to union mass activism, with all the dangers of violence and government repression that it entailed.

The only individual able to turn the kingdom away from that gloomy scenario and toward meaningful reform was *iNgwenyama* Mswati III, but as the century neared its conclusion, he had become increasingly detached, given more and more to ceremonial activities and bland social pronouncements at the expense of the substance of governing. Not even the warnings of the presidents of Swaziland's neighboring SADC countries seemed able to focus his mind on what needed to be done. Whether that was because he was disinclined or was prevented from doing so was impossible for commoners to tell, but the effect remained the same. The vast power of the monarchy, so skillfully amassed by Mswati's father over the span of more than 60 years, was dissipating. Consequently, Swaziland moved toward the new century under the influence of one political certainty only: that constitutional change would take place. What shape that change would take, how soon, to what degree, and how peaceful it would be were questions that only the future could answer.

NOTES

1. Jonathan Crush, "The Culture of Failure: Racism, Violence and White Farming in Colonial Swaziland," *Journal of Historical Geography*, XXII, 2 (1996), 188.

2. Hugh Macmillan, "Swaziland: Decolonisation and the Triumph of 'Tradition,'" *Journal of Modern African Studies*, XXIII, 4 (1985).

3. Most notably *An African Aristocracy; Sobhuza II;* and *The Swazi.*

4. Hilda Kuper, "The Death and Burial of King Sobhuza II" (typescript edited in Kuper's hand, n.d.), Kuper Papers, University of California, Los Angeles, Box 22, Folder 4.

5. *Ibid.* According to Kuper's account, on the day of the king's death his personal physician, Dr. David Hynd, had personally carried what remained of the "medicine," administered to Sobhuza by the Malawian doctor, to the South African government laboratory in Pretoria for analysis. "He [Hynd] had returned that same night but the results came through to the doctor only later—90% poison."

6. Kuper, *The Swazi* (London: International African Institute, 1952), p. 162.

7. Fion de Vletter, ed., *The Swazi Rural Homestead* (Kwaluseni: University of Swaziland, Social Science Research Unit, 1983.), p. 1.

8. Laurel L. Rose, *The Politics of Harmony: Land Dispute Strategies in Swaziland* (Cambridge: Cambridge University Press, 1992), pp. 31–32.

9. iNgwenyama Sobhuza II, "Jubilee Speech," Lobamba, Swaziland, September 4, 1981.

The Dictionary

-A-

ABANTU BATHO. "The People." The official newspaper of the South African Native National Congress (later **African National Congress, ANC**), launched in 1912 by **Pixley kaI. Seme**, one of the ANC's founders. Seme saw the newspaper as a central element in his (and the ANC's) early strategy of allying traditional chiefs and the emerging bourgeoisie of mission-educated intellectuals, and of joining Africans of all ethnicities together toward the common cause of pan-African nationalism. The Swazi royal house became deeply involved in the early ANC and in the founding of *Abantu Batho*. To Queen Regent **Labotsibeni Mdluli** the newspaper's prominent stance against land expropriation (specifically the **South Africa's Union of** Natives Land Act of 1913) resonated with her own opposition to colonial land confiscation in Swaziland as exemplified by the **Partition Proclamation** of 1907. In 1918 Labotsibeni, influenced by Seme, became a significant underwriter of *Abantu Batho*, probably to the extent of £500. Two of the editors of the newspaper, **Cleopas Kunene** and **Robert Grendon**, also had close ties with the Swazi royal house. When in later years (following **Mnt. Malunge Dlamini's** death in 1915) *Abantu Batho* turned its editorial interests away from rural issues toward urban middle-class causes, Labotsibeni's interest and backing turned elsewhere. The paper ceased publishing in the early 1930s.

AERS, IAN. First Speaker of the House of Assembly (1968–73). He was the founder of the Swaziland Broadcasting Service, of which he was the first director of broadcasting. Aers served as an Indian Army officer during World War II, then Colonial Service (district officer) in Tanganyika prior to appointment as clerk of the Swaziland **Legislative Council** (1964).

AFRICAN METHODIST EPISCOPAL CHURCH (AME). Founded in the United States as an African American institution, this church

27

established a strong presence in southern Africa during the latter part of the 19th century. It began work in Swaziland in 1894, and by 1938 it claimed 35,000 members, a wild exaggeration. A 1962 census (the last accurate enumeration) listed approximately 1,550 AME communicants. While often referred to as a separatist church, the AME Church (which is amalgamated with the AME Church in the United States) is doctrinally similar to other Methodist churches. Its liturgy is, however, rich in local idiom.

AFRICAN NATIONAL CONGRESS (ANC). Founded in 1912 as the South African Native National Congress, by South African nationalists, notably **Pixley kaI. Seme**. The ANC has had a long-standing relationship with Swaziland and its monarchy. **Mnt. Malunge Dlamini** became significantly involved with the ANC's house of chiefs. Queen Regent **Labotsibeni Mdluli** lent it funds to help establish its newspaper, *Abantu Batho* (1912), and collected money (ostensibly) in its behalf. **King Sobhuza Dlamini II** was a member of long standing and was the father-in-law of one of Nelson Mandela's daughters. Some members of the **Swaziland Progressive Party**, notably **Macdonald Maseko**, enjoyed especially close ties with the ANC. During the 1980s and 1990s, the ANC supported and advised the anti-monarchist organization **People's United Democratic Movement (PUDEMO)**.

AFRICAN PIONEER CORPS (APC). Also Swazi Pioneer Corps. Early in World War II the British government recruited laborers and support personnel from all over Africa to support the war effort in Europe, Asia, and the Middle East. The APC was recruited in two levies. The first, which by October 1941 had produced six companies totaling 2,200 men, was accomplished with the cooperation of the chiefs. *iNgwenyama* **Sobhuza Dlamini II** understood the political importance of demonstrating loyalty to **Britain** and at the same time imprinting the whole process with tradition and centralized control. Sobhuza personally oversaw the recruiting and saw the corps off to the north with the same ritualization and doctoring as his forebears had sent armies off on military campaigns. He appointed **Mnt. Dabede Dlamini** to lead the corps, assisted by **Mfundza Sukati**, a close advisor to the king. The second APC levy (1942), in response to Britain's augmented requirement, met with spirited resistance in some areas of Swaziland. Consequently, conscription was by military recruiters, largely bypassing the chiefs; older men were conscripted; and the **Native Recruiting Corporation** was persuaded to suspend operations for several months. The 1942 levy netted an additional four companies of about 1,600 men.

The APC served in the Middle East and in North Africa, performing a wide range of support services. The 1991 Company saw action in the Salerno landings and particularly distinguished itself in the first landing wave at Anzio (January 1944), where it laid smoke screens to protect later waves. In July 1946 Sobhuza staged an elaborate public welcoming-back ceremony for the APC at **Lobamba**, to reemphasize royal hegemony over any military undertaking and the paramountcy of tradition over any foreign influences. A few of the war veterans invested their accumulated savings in beginning businesses, entering the emerging postwar Swazi middle class.

ALLEYNE COMMISSION. *See* TRANSVAAL-SWAZILAND BOUNDARY COMMISSION

ALLIANCE OF SWAZILAND PROGRESSIVE PARTIES. *See* JOINT COUNCIL OF SWAZILAND POLITICAL PARTIES

ALLISON, REV. JAMES (?–1875). The founder and leader of the first mission station in Swaziland, the Wesleyan Church mission near **Mahamba** (1844–46). The mission was established in belated response to *iNgwenyama* **Sobhuza Dlamini I**'s request (c. 1834) to the Wesleyans at Kuruman for missionaries, mostly to act as a buffer against the Zulu to the south. Following Sobhuza's death in 1839 the request was repeated by the regents, and in June 1844 Rev. Allison and Rev. Richard Giddy arrived at young *iNgwenyama* **Mswati Dlamini II**'s residence. The site selected for the mission station was Dlovunga, just south of Mahamba. After building a house and chapel and laying out a garden, the two missionaries left the station in charge of two accompanying Sotho evangelists and returned to their parent mission. Allison returned to Swaziland in 1845 along with his family and four African teachers. There he established a new station at Mahamba mountain, leaving the evangelists to carry on at Dlovunga.

Over the next year Allison's successful evangelical work (Sunday congregations of 1,400, many of them converts) was supplemented by the establishment of several outstations and a school of 600 students, reading from **siSwati** catechism books translated by Allison himself. The mission, however, ultimately fell victim to the civil war marking Mswati's early reign. In July 1846 **Mnt. Malambule Dlamini**, a brother and rival of the king, placed his headquarters near Allison's mission, making the evangelist deeply suspect in Mswati's eyes. An attack against Malambule overran the mission in September, killing dozens, including women and children. Allison, his family, and 1,000 followers decamped Mahamba for Natal, where he eventually (1851) established the Wesleyan mission station at **Edendale** (Natal), near Pietermaritzburg. Official Swazi suspicion was such that not until the 1880s were missionaries allowed back into Swaziland. Allison died at Edendale in April 1875.

***AMABHACA* FINES.** Fines in cattle levied against a member of an age regiment (*libutfo*) who marries without the *ingwenyama*'s permission to the regiment. There were several reasons given for the custom: to keep the *emabutfo* in fighting trim, to control immorality; to abide by precepts regarding the purity of the *iNcwala* **ceremony**, and (on another, unstated level) to ensure the monarchy's control over the rate of homestead formation and hence loyalty. According to Macmillan, the 19th-century *amaBhaca* custom, in which the *libutfo* levied the fines and consumed the seized cattle, fell into disuse during the minority of *iNgwenyama* **Sobhuza II**.[1] When he revived it beginning in the late 1920s, he did so in the context of his campaign to make "traditionalism" (real or conjured) the mantra of the monarchy and the vehicle for its revival, a campaign that also included the establishment of the *emabutfo* system in all schools. Sobhuza's restoration of the *libutfo* thus constituted the basis of his reassertion of cultural nationalism, which he saw as the key to the revitalization of the monarchy. The fact that Sobhuza altered the *amaBhaca* fine so that it was he who imposed the sanction, and he who disposed of the seized cattle, implied secondary motives as well. For one thing the cattle would serve to enrich him at a time when his personal finances were, for a variety of reasons, in shambles. For another, because he could choose those to be fined, he could target those whom he suspected of drifting away from his sphere of control: Christians, for instance, and those who were embarking on unauthorized business ventures. *See also* Swazi National Schools

AMERY, LEOPOLD S. (1873–1955). British colonial secretary (1924–29). Added to his office was the newly established dominions secretaryship (1925–29), under whose responsibility Swaziland fell beginning in 1926. Amery, of all Whitehall officials between the wars, took the most active and positive interest in the political and economic fortunes of Swaziland. His visit to the territory in 1927 as part of a tour of southern Africa convinced him that the key to Swaziland's successful transfer to the **Union of South Africa** was to make the kingdom "effectively British" [in his words] before it goes into the Union. That move, which he believed to be inevitable but which he aimed to delay as long as possible, was not to take place until he had completed his self-assigned task of transforming Swaziland into a British settler "center of progress and development." In line with that aim, Amery believed that the benefits accruing to a viable settler state would trickle down to a Swazi population that until then had been "museum pieces" under a "hand-to-mouth . . . indirect tribal rule" administration.

Consequently Amery's 1927 visit spurred the development of the territory with British financial subsidies, beginning with £128,500 in development loan guarantees, an agricultural loan fund, and parliamentary grants-in-aid. Settlement, public transport, and road improvement schemes also dated from this period. Finally, Amery's initiative sparked a formal, comprehensive inquiry into the financial and economic situation of Swaziland undertaken by **Sir Alan Pim** in 1931. Politically, as it turned out, Amery was as much responsible as anyone for preventing South African prime minister James B. M. Hertzog from pressuring Swaziland into the Union during the late 1920s. Economically, however, various South African economic restrictions, combined with the world depression of the 1930s, blunted some beneficial effects that Amery's initiatives might have had on the Swaziland economy.

ANGLICAN CHURCH. One of the significant Christian denominations in Swaziland, with 5,200 communicants in 1962, the year of the last enumeration. Of these, 3,600 were Africans, 1,300 Europeans, and 300 **EurAfricans**. The church's first presence was along the borders of western Swaziland, when Society for the Propagation of the Gospel missionary **Joel Jackson** preached on an itinerant basis during the early 1870s, based at a farm purchased at Derby (**Transvaal**). In 1880 Jackson established the permanent Usutu mission near Luyengweni (west of **Mbekelweni**) on land concessioned by *iNgwenyama* **Mbandzeni Dlamini**. The king promised to send his children to Jackson's school, but they never appeared.

During the early 20th century the church, under Archdeacon **Rev. Christopher Watts** (1907–22), established schools for Europeans (St. Mark's, **Mbabane**) and EurAfricans (St. Mark's, Mpolonjeni; St. Michael's, **Manzini**), as well as many elementary and secondary schools for Africans, including St. Christopher's High School.

ANGLO-BOER JOINT COMMISSION (1889). A commission established by the colonial office and dispatched by the British acting **high commissioner** (G. Bower) under the direction of **Sir Francis de Winton** in order to investigate conditions in Swaziland, which was understood to be on the verge of open violence. Swaziland's condition of public unrest stemmed from several factors, notably the deteriorating health of *iNgwenyama* **Mbandzeni Dlamini** and the anticipation of a customarily violent transfer of power, along with his promiscuous and controversial concessioning of land, mineral, commercial, and administrative monopolies to Europeans. *See also* Provisional Government Committee (1889–1890)

ANGLO-BOER WAR (1899–1902). Also South African War. The war between **Britain** and the Afrikaner republics in **South Africa** had profound consequences for Swaziland. First and most significant, the **Transvaal** administration (1895–99) retreated from the kingdom, relinquishing its administration to the Swazi royal house and opening the way to British colonization in 1903. **Queen Regent Labotsibeni Mdluli**, upon coming to power upon the death of *iNgwenyama* **Bhunu Dlamini** in December 1899, saw the war as an opportunity and acted accordingly. Ostensibly she kept Swaziland neutral, but she had her followers scout for the British, abscond with the cattle driven by Transvaal Afrikaners into the kingdom for safekeeping, and randomly attack Boer columns, hoping to curry postwar British favor. Domestically she used the period of European inattention to despatch her *emabutfo* to destroy her enemies and stifle opposition. Otherwise little fighting between the combatants took place within Swaziland, with the exception of the activities of a troop of British irregulars (450 whites, 300 Africans) commanded by **Ludwig von Steinaecker**, known popularly as "Steinaecker's Horse," during 1901. Ostensibly campaigning for the British, the troop's activities in Swaziland smacked more of brigandage. Finally, in July an Afrikaner commando from Ermelo routed the Horse from its headquarters at Bremersdorp, sacking and burning the town.

ASBESTOS. *See* HAVELOCK ASBESTOS MINE

-B-

BADEN-POWELL, ROBERT S. S., FIRST BARON BADEN-POWELL (1857–1941). British army officer (lieutenant-general in 1907), best known as a hero of the siege of Mafekeng during the **Anglo-Boer War** and as founder of the Boy Scouts and Girl Guides. In South Africa for a second tour of duty in 1889, Baden-Powell was appointed a member of the **Anglo-Boer Joint Commission**, established by **Britain** and the **South African Republic** to investigate conditions in Swaziland in 1889 and led by **Sir Francis de Winton**. A letter to his brother betrayed the hidden agenda behind the dispatching of the de Winton commission: "to give up Swaziland to the Boers in exchange for certain good conditions."[2] Baden-Powell later produced a manuscript titled "Swaziland: Its Past, Present, and Future," which was never published. It was probably in that connection that Baden-Powell was said to have made during his visit a study of the Swazi *emabutfo*, which he may have used as one of the bases on which the Boy Scout movement was founded in 1908.

BAKA NGWANE. Properly *bakaNgwane*; sometimes *Bantu Baka Ngwane*. "The People of Ngwane," referring collectively to the original **Ngwane** (Swazi) followers of *iNgwenyama* **Ngwane Dlamini** (d. 1780), who is regarded as the founder of the modern nation. Ngwane established his headquarters at **Zombodze** on the northern bank of the Pongola River near present-day Nhlangano. KaNgwane, "The Country of Ngwane," is also named after Ngwane.

*li***BANDLA.** *See LIBANDLA*

BAPEDI. *See PEDI*

BARBERTON. A South African city in the eastern **Transvaal** about 12 miles north-northwest of Havelock, Swaziland. Barberton has always figured heavily in Swaziland's history. *iNgwenyama* **Mswati Dlamini II** located outposts there looking toward **Pedi** territory. The discovery of **gold (de Kaap gold field)** in 1882 led directly to the invasion of northern Swaziland by what became an army of European prospectors and speculators. During the 20th century Barberton was a rail and bus terminus for Swazi migrant laborers and was also the terminus of a cableway carrying raw asbestos across the mountains from the **Havelock Asbestos Mine**.

BARING, SIR EVELYN (1903–1973). British **high commissioner** (1944–51) who oversaw the beginnings of the post–World War II era of capitalist development in Swaziland. He did so less from personal inclination (a family background in banking) than from a stern determination to prevent Swaziland and the other **High Commission Territories** from being transferred to **South Africa**. That being the case, he determined that the Swazi would be impossible to defend unless they were more fully developed. Baring was most keenly interested in the areas of agriculture, public health, and education. It was during the Baring era that the first commercial timber plantations were established; the **Colonial** (later **Commonwealth**) **Development Corporation**'s first irrigation schemes were instituted, and early food processing and light manufacturing industries were started. After leaving office, Baring (as Lord Howick) served as Chairman of the Colonial (1960–63) and then Commonwealth Development Corporation (1963–72). Baring was able to achieve such a level of development in Swaziland in part because of the close and trusting relationship he enjoyed with *iNgwenyama* **Sobhuza Dlamini II**.

BATSAKATSI. *See* WITCHCRAFT

"BAYETHE." "Hail, Your Majesty." A Swazi royal salutation reserved for the *ingwenyama* only and conveying the highest honor and veneration. Its historical significance lay in its use (or lack of use) by the Swazi on state occasions over the years to reassert the sovereignty of the *ingwenyama* in the face of British determination to suppress it. Throughout the colonial era the British imposed the term "paramountcy" in reference to the royal house and forced *iNgwenyama* **Sobhuza Dlamini II** to accept the title "**paramount chief,**" on the grounds that there was only one "king" in the British empire. In response the Swazi reserved the salutation "*Bayethe*" exclusively for the *ingwenyama*. Prince Arthur of Connaught (**high commissioner** 1920–23) took deep offense when the salute was withheld from him during his visit in 1922. In 1947 "*iNkhosi*" was used in place of "*Bayete*" to greet Britain's King George VI on the occasion of his royal visit to Goedgegun (later **Nhlangano**).

BEEMER, HILDA. *See* KUPER, HILDA

BEETHAM, EDWARD B. Resident commissioner from 1946 to 1950. The Beetham period, during which **Sir Evelyn Baring** was **high commissioner**, was the era of the first great post–World War II capital development of Swaziland and of several historic administrative agreements. Beetham oversaw the development of timber, irrigated agriculture, and manufacturing, his success due in no little part to his relationship of cooperation and trust with *iNgwenyama* **Sobhuza Dlamini II**. This was an association quite the opposite from that of his predecessor, **Eric K. Featherstone** (1942–46). The cornerstone of Beetham's relationship was his negotiation of (and persuasion of the high commissioner to accept) a revised **Native Administration Proclamation**, first implemented by Featherstone in 1944. The 1950 proclamation finally and officially vested in the "**Paramount Chief** in *Libandla*" such powers as to make him largely sovereign domestically. Notable were Sobhuza's powers to appoint chiefs, to issue orders enforceable by traditional ("native") courts, and to promulgate other orders which, when sanctioned by the administration, had the force of law. The specific assignment of those powers to Sobhuza set Swaziland apart from any other British colony or territory and provided the basis for Sobhuza's subsequent political and diplomatic triumphs during independence negotiations.

BEMANTI. *See iNCWALA* CEREMONY

BEMDZABUKO. "True Swazi." The senior of three early-19th-century Swazi clan groupings referred to by historians describing the progressive settlement of Swaziland by the **Dlamini** followers of *iNgwenyama* **Sobhuza Dlamini I**. Established around his initial headquarters at **Shiselweni**, they accompanied him north as he beat a retreat from **King Zwide Ndwandwe**'s superior forces beginning about 1820. Along with the Dlamini, the *Bemdzabuko* include many of the prominent modern-day clans, such as Mhlanga, Mavuso, Fakudze, Hlophe, Mabuza, Simelane, Matsebula, Twala, Ngwenya, Nkonyane, and Manana. Individual *Bemdzabuko* clans historically have held privileged positions or performed important ritual functions for the royal house. *See also Emafika Muva*; *Emakhandza Mbili*; *Sibongo*

BHUNU. *See* DLAMINI, *iNgwenyama* BHUNU

siBONGO. *See* SIBONGO

BOTHA, GENERAL LOUIS (1862–1919). South African soldier and statesman, commandant of the Afrikaner forces during the **Anglo-Boer War** (1899–1902), and first **Union of South Africa** prime minister (1910–19). Botha had two connections with Swaziland. During May–November 1896 he was the **South African Republic**'s native commissioner and resident justice of the peace for Swaziland, based in **Mbabane**. Later, while Union prime minister (1910–19), Botha held firmly to the position that the **High Commission Territories** (Basutoland, Bechuanaland Protectorate, and Swaziland) must be incorporated into South Africa. Botha pushed especially hard for the transfer of Swaziland to the Union in 1911, a move successfully resisted by the colonial secretary, Lewis Harcourt.

BREMER, ALBERT. A trader/concessionaire who arrived in Swaziland from the eastern **Transvaal** goldfields in 1886. There he established, along with a partner, the firm of Wallenstein and Bremer, on the Mzimnene River in central Swaziland. The wholesale and retail general dealership, forwarding business (to Lourenço Marques), and canteen thrived to the degree that the village that grew up surrounding it was named Bremersdorp (later [1961] **Manzini**). By 1890 Bremer's store had added hotel accommodations and had become the terminus for the post and telegraph facilities from the **South African Republic**. Eventually Wallenstein and Bremer established trading stores in **Mbabane**, **Ludzidzini**, and Lourenço Marques. Bremer himself went into European politics, being elected to the first and third **Swazieland Committees**. Bremer, upon becoming seriously ill in 1897, sold out his stakes and resettled near London, but that proved not to be the end of his dealings with Swaziland. During 1905–06 Bremer, first in league with **Joseph M. Parsonson** and then acting on his own, lobbied in behalf of the Swazi royal house with the Aborigines Protection Society in London and later with the British **high commissioner**, **Lord Selborne**, in Johannesburg. The British government, however, became disenchanted with him and refused to recognize his status as representative of the Swazi monarchy.

BREMERSDORP. *See* MANZINI

BRITAIN. British interest in Swaziland dates from the 1850s, if one counts the colonial administration in Natal. Beginning in 1852 *iNgwenyama* **Mswati Dlamini II** established relations with the British lieutenant governor of Natal in order to persuade him to intervene to keep the Zulu threat to his southern flank at bay. Mswati's first approach occurred in 1852, following Zulu King **Mpande Zulu**'s crippling invasion across the Pongola River, and his tactic was repeated several times thereafter. Mswati's diplomacy was successful throughout his lifetime, keeping the Zulu at a distance until the rise of King Cetewayo Zulu in 1871.

Britain's active involvement in Swaziland dates from the latter 1870s, with its growing strategic interest in the **Transvaal** (which it annexed 1877–81) extending to encompass Pretoria's own geopolitical interests. In early 1876 the British high commissioner in the Cape warned the **South African Republic** (SAR), which even then had begun to covet a route to the sea and had recently sent a diplomatic expedition to the court of the newly installed *iNgwenyama* **Mbandzeni Dlamini**, not to impinge on Swazi sovereignty. Britain then persuaded Mbandzeni to send a sizable army to support its campaign against the **Pedi** in 1879 in return for a guarantee of Swazi sovereignty in perpetuity. That was the first of several such guarantees, all of which were to be rescinded in 1894 as the British shifted their strategic gaze northward across the Limpopo River. So both the **Pretoria Convention** of 1881, ending Britain's annexation of the Transvaal, and the **London Convention** of 1884, amending it, contained clauses recognizing Swaziland's independence within recognized borders. Still, Britain's interest was benign enough that in 1886, when Mbandzeni, alarmed over new signs of the SAR's proprietary interest and fearing that his concessioning had gone out of control, requested British protection, the **high commissioner** refused, citing the guarantee written into the London convention. Nor, of course, could the SAR move unilaterally. What it could do was to buy up those **concessions** which would allow for its eventual administration. In 1887 it acquired the first of them, the railway monopoly, and others were quickly added. All the while Swaziland, besieged by concessionaires, was becoming less and less governable.

That seeming impasse was breached in 1889 with SAR president Paul Kruger's offer to Britain to exchange any claims he had to the north in return for a free hand in Swaziland and access to the sea through **Kosi Bay**. That set in motion the events of the early 1890s, indicating Britain's acceptance of President Kruger's proposal and leading to the governance of Swaziland by the SAR (1895–99). The **first Swaziland Convention** (1890) guaranteed Swazi independence and established the triumvirate **Swaziland Government Committee** (1890–95), while the **third Swaziland Convention** (1894) cancelled previous guarantees by making Swaziland a "political dependency" of the SAR without the monarchy's consent. The SAR's five-year administration of Swaziland with Britain's connivance ended with the outbreak of the **Anglo-Boer War** in 1899.

Britain, which assumed the role of protector over Swaziland following the war in 1903, administered it in authoritarian fashion until the late 1920s. British **resident commissioners** crippled the Swazi monarchy by withdrawing its criminal jurisdiction and expropriating the greater part of both its financial resources and its control over land. More often than not they did so in a fashion calculated to humble if not humiliate the royal house in the eyes of its people. Britain also imposed a heavy native tax on Swazi males. Its effects were to drive them into the migrant labor stream to the Witwatersrand gold mines, thereby undermining homestead productivity. At the same time the administration utilized the native tax revenue to develop and police the modern economy, largely for the benefit of the European settlers, few of whom paid any tax until the 1920s, and relatively little thereafter. **Sir Alan Pim's** 1932 report on Swaziland found the **native areas** progressively overpopulated, overstocked, and less and less able to support those living on them.[3] When Colonial Secretary **Leopold S. Amery** visited Swaziland in 1927 he was shocked to find that the Swazi had become little more than "museum pieces . . . in an Africa that was being transformed at a breathless pace."

A more enlightened policy was pursued by subsequent administrations beginning in 1928. Understaffed and underfunded, and deeming young *iNgwenyama* **Sobhuza Dlamini II** to be more serious and able than they had been led to believe, resident commissioners moved progressively toward employing him along the lines of "**indirect rule**." Resident commissioners bolstered Sobhuza's domestic power and prestige by establishing regular meetings with him, by criminalizing chiefly resistance to his authority, and in other public ways. During the 1940s, in response to his petitioning, London began allocating parliamentary funds toward the enlargement of **Swazi Nation Land** through the purchase and transfer of **crown lands**. At the same time Britain attempted to formalize indirect rule through enactment of native administration, courts, and treasury proclamations. When a strengthened Sobhuza balked at certain provisions that undercut his domestic sovereignty, it eventually amended the **Native Administration Proclamation**.

Following World War II, as part of its program to transform its colonies into economic assets, Britain commenced a massive program of capital investment in Swaziland through the **Colonial Development Corporation**, principally in the areas of timber products and irrigated cash cropping. In both instances care was taken to provide the monarchy with its own direct stake in the projects. Those undertakings proved to be the catalysts for the large-scale foreign capital development of the kingdom from the 1950s to the 1980s. In a couple of instances (the **Swaziland Native Land Settlement Scheme** and **Vuvulane** Irrigated Farms) Britain attempted to combine its investments with experiments in social engineering by offering the Swazi homesteaders relative security of land tenure. Each such initiative was tenaciously resisted by the *ingwenyama* and *libandla*, who saw (correctly) any threat to their exclusive control over land use as a threat to royal hegemony. In the end each experiment was successfully foiled by the Swazi traditionalists (albeit in the case of Vuvulane only in 1983).

That was not, however, the end of British social reformation. During the early 1960s, as the kingdom moved toward internal self-government leading to independence, London, through its local representative, Resident Commissioner **Brian Marwick**, insisted that democratic principles be implemented in the process of drafting the constitution. While the Swazi traditionalists (*ingwenyama* and *libandla*) and the conservative **European Advisory Council** battled during the drafting process to have power devolve jointly to them, Marwick (and the Commonwealth Relations Office) insisted that any legislature be based at least in part on a popular mandate voiced through officially sanctioned opposition parties. That was the basis on which the first multiracial **Legislative Council** was established in 1964 and on which independence was granted to king and parliament in 1968.

Britain has provided bilateral assistance to Swaziland each year since independence ($5.3 million in 1995). Britain has, however, refused Swaziland's requests for parliamentary grants for the purpose of repurchasing partitioned lands. Swaziland's balance of trade with Britain is consistently in Swaziland's favor by a factor of five or six. In 1995 Swaziland imported E30.9 million worth of goods from Britain while exporting goods worth E187.9 million in return. During the 1990s Swaziland's trade with Britain fell to third place in volume, behind that with South Africa and then with the European Union.

BRUCE, VICTOR A. (NINTH EARL OF ELGIN, 1849–1917). Britain's secretary of state for the colonies, 1906 to 1908. Elgin played a key role in preventing Swaziland from being incorporated into the **Transvaal** during the years immediately prior to Union (1910). This was most notable in 1907, when he rebuffed Transvaal prime minister **Louis Botha**'s appeal to annex the kingdom, proposing instead that he assist **Britain** in developing the territory. Lord Elgin became far better remembered for his overly candid remarks to the visiting Swazi **deputation** to protest the **Partition Proclamation** of 1907. In his meeting with them Lord Elgin let slip to the Swazi delegation the promise that future transfers of **crown lands** to the Swazi would ensure that half, not the proclaimed one-third, of the partitioned land would eventually fall to them. That blunder was quite in character with his reputation as a cautious and sometimes subservient administrator. In any event, as Elgin's assertion ran counter to the intent of local administrators in Pretoria and **Mbabane** to use crown lands to subsidize future European settlement in Swaziland, the latter spent the next two and a half decades disavowing his statement. Only in 1942 did Britain begin to allow return of crown lands to the Swazi.

BRUTON, CHARLES L. Resident commissioner in Swaziland from 1937 to 1942. Bruton, together with his successor, **Eric K. Featherstone** (1942–46), attempted to force *iNgwenyama* **Sobhuza Dlamini II** to accept the imposition of a **Native Authority** (later **Administration**) **Proclamation** similar to the ones being implemented in Basutoland, Bechuanaland, and elsewhere in Africa. Bruton pushed its implementation as a necessary step toward realization of true "**indirect rule**," but the Swazi bitterly opposed it as a direct threat to the traditional authority of the *ingwenyama* and the chiefs. Sobhuza also had reason to believe that Bruton, along with **High Commissioner** Sir William Clark, were less than steadfast when it came to the question of opposition to the once-anticipated transfer of Swaziland to the **Union of South Africa**. On his part, Bruton became exasperated at the stalling tactics employed by Sobhuza to resist imposition of the Native Authority Proclamation. Consequently relations between Sobhuza and Bruton ranged from uneasy to hostile during the latter's tenure, the one bright spot being Sobhuza's cooperation in sending forward Swazi recruits for the **African Pioneer Corps**. **Sir Brian Marwick**, who served under Bruton as an assistant commissioner and who later served as resident commissioner himself, referred to Bruton in private correspondence following his own retirement as "ineffective" and "clearly out of his depth."

BRYANT, REV. ALFRED T. (1865–1953). A 19th-century missionary and amateur historian whose scholarship on the early history of the **Nguni** people constitutes a valuable, although hardly infallible, source. His writings centered on the Zulu, but in the process he touched on other histories, such as the beginnings of the **Ndwandwe** and the Swazi nations.

liBUTFO. See LIBUTFO

-C-

CATCHPOLE REPORT (1960). F. C. Catchpole, *Report on Labour Legislation in Swaziland* (1960, mimeo). A report commissioned by the colonial administration with a view toward modifying the labor market to reflect the demands of the post–World War II industrialization of Swaziland. The report found that, although legislation allowing for the formation of unions had been on the books since 1942, there was as yet "no machinery whatever for negotiating wages in any industry." Instead, "the fixing of wage rates [remained] the sole prerogative of employers." Instead of unions an existing, government-approved grievance procedure based on *libandla*-appointed labor representatives (*tindvuna*), which had been in use since the mid-1940s, was implemented as each new industry was established. The report concluded that such a system stood the chance of breaking down in the event of serious labor disputes because labor *tindvuna* were often appointed on the basis of politics rather than industrial experience and because, paid as they were by the companies to which they were accredited, they were likely to be regarded by the workers as company loyalists rather than as fair arbitrators. The Catchpole Report stopped short of recommending any drastic reform of the existing system, and none was implemented before a wave of labor disputes of just the type Catchpole had envisioned broke out throughout Swaziland beginning in early 1963. As the report had predicted, the labor *indvuna* system quickly broke down, contributing to the rapid development of a political crisis serious enough to spark the government's declaration of an emergency in June 1963.

CATTLE. Cattle, as both stores and indicators of wealth, are a central consideration in the daily lives of most Swazi. Cattle constitute a central element in the wealth of both the homestead and the nation. First, there is almost nothing related to cattle that is not useful. Hides, milk, meat, horns, blood and bones, manure—all can be either consumed, worn, or used as fertilizer. Furthermore cattle, under appropriate conditions of weather and health, reproduce exponentially; and on communal land they are cheap to maintain, making a cattle herd in normal times an extremely prudent investment. Cattle are also readily exchangeable for cash and acceptable as loan collateral. They constitute the coin of the central *lilobolo* custom, for instance, legitimizing a marriage and its children through their transfer from the husband's to the wife's family. Finally, the use of cattle is a requirement for many important Swazi rituals and customs, notably the *iNcwala* **ceremony**. Within the homestead, cattle are essential to the various rites propitiating ancestral spirits.

Cattle have played a central role in the accumulation of wealth by the **iNkhosi Dlamini** over the generations since the 18th century. Most offensive wars waged by Swazi kings against the Zulu, **Pedi**, or **Shangane** had cattle booty as one of their objects, most of the cattle accruing to the royal house. The *ingwenyama* collected more cattle from "eating up" the estates of traitors and wizards, and from administrative and court fines. In addition, Philip Bonner and **Hilda Kuper** have shown that the royal preference for endogamous marriage, combined with preferential *lilobolo* valuations for princesses, resulted in high levels of wealth accumulation and recirculation in the form of cattle among the ruling elite.[4] The *ingwenyama's* most sacrosanct cattle are the *mfukwane* (sacred royal) herd, numbering perhaps 200 head, which are used only for ritual purposes. Their rendered fat is considered such a powerful medicine that it is used only by the *ingwenyama*, his mother, and his senior (Matsebula) wife. Dung from this herd is used to doctor an *indlovukazi* initiate.

Among Swazi commoners thoughts of cattle resonate deeply within the individual psyche, to a level not accountable by their representative wealth alone. Each beast within a herd is known by name, color, physical characteristics, and temperament. There is a rich vocabulary in the **siSwati** language to describe all the various characteristics and conditions of cattle. Small children make model oxen and use them in games of cattle herding and raiding. Traditionally the cattle byre (*sibaya*) was the central feature within the homestead, enclosed with heavy logs for defensive purposes and restricted as to access, especially by women. Even today a rural man who does not own cattle is an object of compassion.

CHIEF COURT (1890). A court recommended by the **Anglo-Boer Joint Commission** and established by the **first Swaziland Convention** (1890). That convention also established the **Provisional Government Committee** at the same time. Both bodies were designed to administer the affairs of the growing European concessionaire and merchant population in Swaziland. The Chief Court was to have full jurisdiction over all Europeans in Swaziland. It was also to undertake a judicial inquiry into the validity of all disputed **concessions**. The court, sitting in its latter capacity between October 1890 and January 1891, confirmed 352 out of a total of 354 disputed concessions, including the notorious **unallotted lands concession**.

CHRISTIANITY. Since their introduction into Swaziland in 1845, Christian missions have played an important role in Swaziland's political as well as religious history. This was exemplified by the initial Swazi invitation to the Wesleyans to establish a mission in the south, not only to proselytize to the people but also to establish a missionary buffer against the Zulu. *iNgwenyama* **Sobhuza Dlamini I** made the first request to the Wesleyans in the 1830s, and **Rev. James Allison** established the first Wesleyan mission at **Mahamba** in 1844, during the reign of *iNgwenyama* **Mswati Dlamini II**. Allison and his followers fled for safety two years later after incurring Mswati's wrath for having apparently sided with his rival to power, **Mnt. Malambule Dlamini**. Allison subsequently led in the establishment of a new mission station and school at **Edendale**, Natal, whence came the group of African evangelists who re-established the Wesleyan station at Mahamba in 1882.

That group, headed by Rev. Daniel **Msimang**, and later including its descendants and offshoots, was to play an important role in providing advisors to the monarchy, especially during the era of **Queen Regent**

Labotsibeni Mdluli. John Gama, Stephen Mini, and Lazarus Xaba from the Edendale (Natal) mission via Mahamba allied themselves with *iNgwenyama* **Mbandzeni Dlamini,** largely through his advisor and agent, **Theophilus Shepstone, Jr.** Daniel Msimang's son Jeremiah broke away around the turn of the century with a large Methodist following and formed the Independent Methodist Church, from whose congregation came **Josiah Vilakazi,** Labotsibeni's secretary and advisor. Other Wesleyan-educated royal advisors and tutors were **Alpheus Nkosi,** of the Mahamba mission, and **Benjamin Nxumalo** and **Robert Grendon,** both of the **African Methodist Episcopal Church.**

Meanwhile other missions were establishing themselves in Swaziland, following the Wesleyans' lead. The Anglicans (Society for the Propagation of the Gospel, **Rev. Joel Jackson**) established a mission at Ndlotane in 1871, and at Mbandzeni's invitation they built a school at Luyengo in 1881. The Anglicans under the direction of **Rev. Christopher Watts** opened the first school for European children (St. Mark's) in **Mbabane** in 1909, and later the first **EurAfrican** school (St. Mark's Coloured School) at Mpholonjeni. In 1887 the Berlin (Lutheran) Mission Society built a station at Nduma in the shadow of **Ngwenya** mountain. In 1890 the South African General Mission founded its station at Bethany, west of modern **Manzini** near the banks of the **Lusushwana River.** Rev. William Dawson of the Scandinavian Alliance Mission (Evangelical Alliance Mission) established its initial station at Bulungu in central Swaziland in 1892. One of its missionaries, Ms. **Malla Moe,** started a second mission at Bethel near Hluti in southern Swaziland in 1898. It became an occasional haven for British forces during the **Anglo-Boer War.** In 1912 the Roman Catholic mission was established at Mbabane.

In 1925 the Church of the Nazarene (**Dr. David Hynd**) established a mission at Bremersdorp (**Manzini**). Hynd, a physician and surgeon, began construction of the Raleigh Fitkin Memorial Hospital on government-furnished land nearby, opening it in 1927. Hynd also established Swaziland's first teacher training college and its first nursing college. By the time of his retirement in the 1960s Hynd had become a powerful political figure whose influence furthered the cause of his mission. Hynd became essentially the personal physician to *iNgwenyama* **Sobhuza Dlamini II** and his wives. He served on the Advisory Board for Native Education and on the governing board of the **Swazi National High School.** In 1963 Hynd attended the second **constitutional conference** in London as an independent representative at the request of the colonial government.

Sobhuza's attitude toward the Christian missions was highly ambiguous. On one hand he understood and valued the education they offered, stemming from his own experience at **Lovedale** and his association with the graduates of the Edendale (Natal) and Mahamba mission schools. His own personal identification with Western-style progressivism had been particularly strong until 1926, and thereafter his deep understanding of Western values as put forward by the missions constituted one of his profound strengths. According to the later accounts of two of his children, Sobhuza was strongly influenced by elements of the Christian faith. On the other hand, Sobhuza after 1926 was deeply wary of mission challenges to his tradition-based political authority in the name of modernism. The acculturation that accompanied mission education frustrated him insofar as it undercut his own legitimacy. He was angered during the 1930s when the missions opposed his regimental (*emabutfo*) system in the schools on grounds that it threatened the foundations of Christian teaching. Throughout the king's lifetime missions' claims to ownership of church land, their building of schools without his permission, and their denigration of customary practices such as arranged marriages and polygyny all affronted him.

Sobhuza's lifelong minuet with the Christian missions never amounted to more than that. He had no intention, however he might have hinted at it on occasion, of dying a Christian, as had several other important members of the royal family before him: his uncle and secretary Benjamin Nxumalo, **Mnt.** and **Prince Regent Malunge Dlamini** (although never officially), and *tiNdlovukazi* **Lomawa** and **Nukwase Ndwandwe** (although the latter had been baptized prior to her installation). Sobhuza, honoring Nukwase's request, built the Christian nondenominational **Swazi National Church** at **Lobamba**, completing it following her death. The king hardly set foot in it thereafter. Sobhuza also danced a similar minuet with Dr. Hynd, the greatest missionary of them all, whom he normally consulted on both medical and political matters, but whom he was quick to supplant with trusted *tinyanga* (sing. *inyanga*) and *tangoma* (sing. *sangoma*) in times of greatest crisis—medical or political.

There is no way of knowing what percentage of the Swazi population is Christian, since official enumeration by religion was halted after the 1956 census. A working estimate, including both Christian and separatist churches, would be about 60 percent.

CITIZENSHIP ACT (1974). Prior to the passage of the Citizenship Act (No. 50/1968) there existed no official concept of citizenship in Swaziland. Act No. 50 recognized all persons who had previously been members of the protected state to be citizens of newly independent Swaziland. In 1972 the electoral victory of **Ngwane National Liberatory Congress** parliamentary candidate **Bhekindlela Thomas Ngwenya** over the **Imbokodvo National Movement** candidate in the Mphumalanga constituency, and his subsequent expulsion on the grounds of non-Swazi citizenship, led to the official determination of the need for redefinition of the term "citizenship." The result was the passage of the Citizenship Act (Citizenship Order No. 22) of 1974, which limited Swazi citizenship to those persons whose fathers had been citizens. Exceptions were granted only by application to the deputy prime minister, who oversaw immigration and citizenship. The deputy prime minister in 1974 was **Zonke Khumalo**, who in 1972 had arbitrarily expelled Ngwenya. Since 1974 the Citizenship Act has been used by successive Swazi governments primarily to deny citizenship to **EurAfricans**. EurAfricans, who had been made a privileged class during the colonial era and who consequently became the objects of much jealousy and discriminatory treatment following independence, have consequently found themselves in political limbo. For instance, unable to obtain Swaziland passports, EurAfricans have been able to travel abroad only to those countries willing to accept the "stateless persons certificates" which they were issued by the government in lieu of passports. Successive governments have admitted the discriminatory nature of the 1974 act but have not been willing to change its fundamental nature.

CLAN. *See SIBONGO*

COLONIAL DEVELOPMENT AND WELFARE ACTS. Beginning in 1929 the British parliament passed a succession of separate colonial development acts aimed at providing for the expenditure of funds for capital development projects in the colonies and **High Commission Territories**. Motivation behind these acts differed markedly according to the circumstances of the times. The Colonial Development Act of 1929 followed the tour of the colonies and High Commission Territories by the colonial secretary, **Leopold S. Amery**, which convinced him that a certain amount of capital investment was essential to their viability. The act provided for expenditure of up to £1 million per year for approved development schemes. The Colonial Development and Welfare Act of 1940 was passed with an eye toward enhancing the loyalty of the colonies and territories in the time of grave threat to Britain brought on by World War II. The act broadened the range of approved expenditures and authorized increased appropriations of up to £5 million per year ending in 1951. The

Colonial Development and Welfare Act of 1945 raised expenditure levels to £120 million per year until 1956. A 1950 amendment to the act raised that annual total to £140 million per annum.

In broad terms, colonial development funds were invested over the years in water development, medical services, tsetse eradication, education, and geological and mineral surveys. In Swaziland colonial development funds were used for a variety of capital improvements. Bremersdorp (**Manzini**) received an improved urban water infrastructure and a creamery (butter factory). The 1940 act allocated funds for the transfer of **crown lands** and purchase of **title deed lands** toward implementation of the **Swaziland Native Land Settlement Scheme**; other funds were utilized to convert previous Swaziland development loans into grants-in-aid. Both the 1940 and the 1945 acts provided for the development of social services, especially education (establishment of the Swaziland Teacher Training College and expansion of the **Swazi National High School**), and health (expansion of two government hospitals). Finally, the 1945 act established the **Colonial** (later **Commonwealth**) **Development Corporation**, which was to exert an enormous impact on postwar capital development in the kingdom.

COLONIAL DEVELOPMENT CORPORATION. *See* COMMONWEALTH DEVELOPMENT CORPORATION

COLOURED. *See* EURAFRICAN

COLOURED WELFARE ASSOCIATION. *See* EURAFRICAN WELFARE ASSOCIATION

COMMITTEE OF TWELVE, THE. A rump European political grouping (its core being former members of the moderate **Swaziland Independence Front**) formed in 1965. As the result of *iNgwenyama* Sobhuza Dlamini II's impressive victory in the 1964 election through the triumph of his **Imbokodvo National Movement**, political parties realigned themselves in anticipation of the writing of the pre-independence **constitution** (1967). The main European party, the **United Swaziland Association** (USA), pushed for a bloc of reserved seats in the new parliament for Europeans disproportionate to their small numbers. The Committee of Twelve (most notably **Leopold Lovell**, Frank Corbett, and Peter Braun) rejected racially reserved seats and instead advocated the *ingwenyama*'s appointment of non-Swazi to the new legislature on the basis of merit. The short-lived Committee of Twelve never became a formal party, but its political nonracialism came to be adopted as the *ingwenyama*'s policy following independence. One of Sobhuza's appointments to the House of Assembly in 1967 was Lovell, who later became finance minister. The committee was known derisively by its opponents in the USA as the "twelve apostles."

COMMON MARKET FOR EASTERN AND SOUTHERN AFRICA (COMESA). Formerly the Preferential Trade Area (PTA), established among 12 members in 1981. COMESA was a regional trade organization succeeding the PTA in 1994, covering 23 member states: Angola, Burundi, Comoros, Djibouti, Eritrea, Ethiopia, Kenya, Lesotho, Madagascar, Malawi, Mauritius, Mozambique, Namibia, Rwanda, Seychelles, Somalia, Sudan, Swaziland, Tanzania, Uganda, Zaire (now Congo), Zambia, and Zimbabwe. COMESA's purpose was to liberalize trade and foster cooperation in industry, agriculture, transportation, and communications, all with the aim of establishing a common market by the turn of the century. The ultimate goal was to eliminate all barriers to the free flow of goods, services, and capital, and eventually to establish a monetary union. The goals and timetable of COMESA were universally regarded as ambitious. Member states' economies, being extremely diverse in some cases, did not lend themselves to integration easily or quickly. Furthermore many members of COMESA were also members of the **Southern African Customs Union** (SACU), and it was not clear how the relationship could be accommodated. Furthermore civil unrest in several member states (i.e., Angola, Burundi, Rwanda, Somalia, and Sudan) threw up barriers to regional integration.

COMMON MONETARY AREA (CMA). The CMA, which superseded the Rand Monetary Area (RMA) in 1986, includes Lesotho, Namibia, **South Africa**, and Swaziland as member states. Botswana resigned from the RMA in 1976, and Namibia is expected to leave the CMA eventually. Membership in the CMA holds both advantages and drawbacks for Swaziland. On one hand, it affords liquidity to its economy and provides for the easy flow of capital, credit, and investment across the borders of member states. The drawbacks are also substantial. The Swazi *lilangeni* (like Lesotho's *loti*) is pegged at par with the South African rand, meaning that Swaziland's fiscal and monetary fortunes are dependent to a high degree on South Africa's policies and on the value of the rand on international markets. Swaziland's interest rates, bank credit policies, and rate of inflation are likewise highly dependent on what happens to South Africa's economy, credit, and currency. The precipitous drop in the value of the rand beginning in the early 1990s had profound effects on

Swaziland's economy without the latter's ability to do much about it (Swaziland was not represented on the South African Reserve Bank).

COMMONWEALTH DEVELOPMENT CORPORATION (CDC). Until 1963 the Colonial Development Corporation. Created in 1948 by the British government to implement the **Colonial Development and Welfare Act** of 1945. Swaziland's original share of the act's provisions (totalling £120 million) was set at £830,000, of which an initial portion was expended during 1946–48 on technical studies, economic surveys, and previously approved but unfunded projects. Anchoring the undertakings was the "Socio-Economic Survey of Swaziland," headed by V. Liversage (*see* **Liversage Report**). Its publication in 1948 became the basis for the first Swaziland Development Plan, covering the years 1948–56 and focusing on rural development and conservation projects, at a cost of £163,500. The report also pointed out that the most likely areas of profitable investment were in agribusiness.

This led to the beginnings of heavy CDC capital investment in mining, transportation, agriculture, and forestry, which were to have an enormous and lasting impact on Swaziland's economy. Most notable were an afforestation project and pulp mill along the upper **Usutu River** (Usutu Forests; *see* **Usutu Pulp**); the **Swaziland Irrigation Scheme** (including **Mhlume** Sugar and **Vuvulane** Irrigated Farms), developing irrigated sugar, rice, citrus, and other agricultural projects along the lower **Komati**, Mbuluzi, Usutu, and iNgwavuma rivers; the **Malkerns** Irrigation Scheme along the middle Usutu; and the Big Bend Irrigation Scheme (mainly sugar). Other projects included a fruit cannery at Malkerns and the **Swaziland Iron Ore Development Company** and associated **Swaziland Railway**. By the end of the 1970s the original CDC plan for capital expenditure for Swaziland had grown from less than £1 million to actual spending in excess of £10 million.

CONCESSIONS. Referring to the events of the period from the early 1870s to the turn of the century when most of the land or its usufruct, minerals, and economic infrastructure of Swaziland were bargained or formally concessioned away to European entrepreneurs. The first were Afrikaner cattlemen from the **Transvaal** seeking rich winter pasturage for their cattle and sheep (beginning in the 1860s). Then, commencing in the early 1880s, came the British and South African mineral prospectors and speculators. The great frenzy of concessioneering came during the reign of the profligate *iNgwenyama* **Mbandzeni Dlamini** (1875–89). Mbandzeni and his advisors, driven both by greed and by the need for political legitimacy, concessioned away land, resources, and business monopolies, sometimes several times over. Those concessions in turn became the basis for the establishment of a European settler regime (1890), later (1895) a **South African Republic** administration, and still later (1903) a British colonial government that awarded two-thirds of the lands and all the minerals to the settlers or to itself (**Partition Proclamation** of 1907).

CONSTITUTION (1964). Imposed on Swaziland in 1963 and implemented in 1964 by the British government (Commonwealth Secretary **Duncan Sandys**) following the inability of the second constitutional conference in London to agree on provisions of a local government constitution. The idea of independence for Swaziland, first implied by **Lord William Hailey**'s call for a legislative council in 1953, gained momentum following British Prime Minister Harold Macmillan's "Winds of Change" address before the South African parliament in February 1960. In November Resident Commissioner **Brian Marwick** convened the first constitutional committee, chaired by him and composed mainly of the leading members of the *libandla*; the leading opposition party of the day, the **Swaziland Progressive Party** (SPP); the **Reconstituted European Advisory Council (REAC)**; and government officials.

Commissioned by order of the colonial secretary, the committee's mandate was to determine the character of a local, multiracial representative government and to draft a constitution accordingly. Its report, carried to London in December 1961 (the first London constitutional conference), advocated a "50–50 constitution," a **legislative council** composed of an equal number of Europeans (elected) and Swazi (some nominated by the *ingwenyama* and some elected). When the report was published by the British government in March 1962, such was the storm of opposition from every quarter (including Marwick but excepting the settlers) that a second London **constitutional conference** was convened in early 1963. Conferees at that gathering represented the administration, the *libandla*, the REAC, political parties formed in anticipation of independence, and the **EurAfrican** community.

Discussions, frequently acrimonious, took place over five weeks during early 1963, with no agreement emerging over a number of issues surrounding the principal ideological tension between royalist and democratic forms of government. Finally Sandys disbanded the conference with the announcement that the British government would impose a constitution. The "Sandys Constitution," promulgated in March 1963 and implemented in early 1964, fell far short of what *iNgwenyama* **Sobhuza**

Dlamini II and the traditionalists had had in mind. It replaced the **resident commissioner** with **Her Majesty's Commissioner for Swaziland**, who enjoyed executive powers similar to those of a colonial governor, including direct communication with the commonwealth secretary. The Queen's Commissioner would wield the veto over the Legislative Council (Legco) and would be vested with the kingdom's minerals (the latter provision an especially bitter disappointment to Sobhuza). The Legislative Council would comprise 24 elected members: 8 Swazi (elected by traditional means), 8 Europeans, and 8 of any race elected on a national roll. The Legco would also comprise four official members and a speaker. The *ingwenyama* would enjoy certain royal prerogatives and immunities, and would be vested with all **Swazi Nation Land**.

It was on the basis of the 1964 constitution that the first elections were held in that year, and it was to contest those elections that Sobhuza formed the royalist **Imbokodvo National Movement**, a political maneuver that proved to be spectacularly successful in gaining constitutional power for the throne.

CONSTITUTION (1967). In 1965, with the Queen's Commissioner (*see* **Her Majesty's Commissioner**), **Legislative Council**, and *ingwenyama* all functioning in accordance with the **constitution (1964)**, the commonwealth secretary, in response to an **Imbokodvo National Movement (INM)** request, authorized the establishment of a second constitutional committee. Its charge was to make recommendations for a new constitution providing for internal self-government in immediate anticipation of independence.

The committee's report, issued in March 1966, constituted a political triumph for *iNgwenyama* **Sobhuza Dlamini II**. The new constitution recognized him as king of Swaziland and head of state, and it affirmed the legitimacy of the *libandla* in traditional affairs. The document established a two-house **parliament**. The House of Assembly would have 24 elected members plus 6 members nominated by the king. The Senate would comprise 12 members, 6 elected by the House of Assembly and 6 appointed by the king, plus a speaker (also appointed by the king). Furthermore, the king would appoint the prime minister and name the cabinet.

The king's sovereignty was not complete, however, for although the constitution vested the mineral wealth of the country in him, he was to be advised by a committee appointed by parliament, whose members were mainly elected by universal franchise. Sobhuza continued to oppose that stipulation, although he accepted the rest of the constitutional provisions. The new constitution was implemented in March 1967, making Swaziland officially a protected state with its own king, and elections to the new parliament were held in April. By that time the INM's divorce from the settler party, the **United Swaziland Association (USA)**, was complete, and the USA itself had become factionalized. Unlike the 1964 election, no European candidates were included on the INM roster. The Swazi opposition had also become factionalized. The result was another smashing INM victory, polling nearly 80 percent of the vote and winning every eligible seat in parliament. Sobhuza's political triumph was nearly complete. In his inaugural speech to the new parliament Sobhuza proposed that independence be granted to Swaziland in September 1968.

CONSTITUTION (INDEPENDENCE, 1968). The independence constitution of 1968 was virtually identical to the 1967 **constitution** with the exception of the provision for the vesting of Swaziland's minerals. The constitutional committee, comprising members of the cabinet, proposed that the provision be altered to specify that the minerals committee be selected and controlled by the king, rather than by **parliament**. That proposed amendment was carried by a cabinet delegation to the independence conference held in London during February 1968, where it was accepted (reluctantly) by the commonwealth secretary. That action constituted the genesis of what became the king's separate state within a state, the **Tibiyo takaNgwane Fund**. *iNgwenyama* **Sobhuza Dlamini II's** pre-independence political triumph could also be seen in the makeup of the conference delegation: one European and three Swazi cabinet members (including Prime Minister **Mnt. Makhosini Dlamini**), with no separate representation from either the settler community or the Swazi opposition parties, as had been the case in previous London conferences. The delegation also raised the issue of British compensation for having alienated two-thirds of the land early in the century. The idea was for the British to capitalize the Swazi repurchase of what alienated land remained, as the British had done earlier in the case of the "white highlands" in Kenya. The commonwealth secretary rejected the Swazi claim. Finally, the conference set the date for independence as September 6, 1968.

CONSTITUTIONAL ALLIANCE OF SWAZILAND POLITICAL ORGANIZATIONS. An ad hoc, short-lived political alliance among the antimonarchist ("modern") political parties in anticipation of the second London **constitutional conference** in January–February 1963. It was formed by **Simon Nxumalo** of the **Swaziland Democratic Party (SDP)**, and **Dr. Ambrose Zwane** of the **Swaziland Progressive Party (SPP)** as a result of Nxumalo's appeal for unity of the party leaders against the Swazi traditionalist and European settler forces. It specifically aimed at forming a united front to oppose the traditionalists' "50–50" (European-African) power-sharing proposals and to lobby for a one-man, one-vote constitution and a constitutional monarchy. The alliance immediately came to grief when **John J. Nquku**, Nxumalo's rival for the leadership of the SPP, refused to join and sat in the SPP's lone seat at the conference table. Other alliance members included **Dr. George Msibi** of the **Mbandzeni National Convention**, **Affleck Sellstroom** of the **EurAfrican Welfare Association**, and **Dr. Allen Nxumalo** (later president of the SDP), who defected to the alliance from the traditionalists at the London conference. The alliance was most notable for persuading the British that there was an unbreakable deadlock among the Swazi, leading to the collapse of the conference and Britain's eventual imposition of its own constitutional plan. What remained of the collapsed alliance (once the conference had ended) eventually became the basis of the **Joint Council of Swaziland Political Parties** (1964).

CONSTITUTIONAL CONFERENCE (1963). Held in London from January 28 to February 12, 1963, under the auspices of the Ministry of Commonwealth Affairs, this conference attempted to attain final agreement on the first modern constitution for Swaziland. Constitutional discussions had been taking place in Swaziland since 1960 and had generated a proliferation of political parties and movements in anticipation of independence. The British invited six representatives from the *libandla* (Swazi National Council); four from the **Reconstituted European Advisory Council (REAC)**; one each from the **Swaziland Democratic Party**, the **Mbandzeni National Convention**, the **EurAfrican Welfare Association**, and the **Swaziland Progressive Party**; and an independent delegate, missionary doctor and educator **Dr. David Hynd**.

Each of the political groupings represented a compelling economic interest: the *libandla* stood for traditionalist hegemony, the Swazi political parties represented the emerging and ambitious African middle class, and the REAC sought to further the interests of settler and foreign capital. Consequently the conference quickly reached loggerheads over a number of interrelated political and economic issues, the most notable of which were the extent of white representation in the proposed **Legislative Council**, the nature and extent of the franchise, and the control of mineral and land rights. In spite of all efforts at negotiation and compromise, including the formation of the **Constitutional Alliance of Swaziland Political Organizations**, it quickly became evident that the conference was so torn by disagreement that it would not be able to produce a draft constitution. Ultimately the secretary of state, **Duncan Sandys**, dissolved the conference with the announcement that the British government intended to impose its own constitution. That was done in 1964. *See also* Constitution (1964)

CONSTITUTIONAL REVIEW COMMISSION (CRC, 1996). Formed by *iNgwenyama* **Mswati Dlamini III** in mid-1996 in response to growing popular pressure to democratize the government of Swaziland. That pressure, in the absence of lawful opposition parties, had come primarily from **trade unions** such as the **Swaziland Federation of Trade Unions (SFTU)** and the **Swaziland National Association of Teachers (SNAT)**, and from opposition movements such as the **People's United Democratic Movement (PUDEMO)**. Mswati had previously attempted to mollify popular sentiment for democratization by revising the tightly controlled *tinkhundla* electoral system to allow for a two-stage legislative election which provided for a secret ballot at the second stage. That reform, which stopped short of allowing for the reintroduction of opposition parties, failed in its purpose.

By 1996, as escalating labor activism became transparently political in its intent, the king moved once more to head off a crisis by forming the CRC. The 30-member CRC was commissioned to draft a new constitution by mid-1998, more responsive to the popular will than the previous one repealed by *iNgwenyama* **Sobhuza Dlamini II** in 1973. The CRC quickly became the battleground for power between the traditionalists (monarchists) and the progressives (trade unionists and political activists). Because it became evident just as quickly that the real power in the CRC, chaired by a conservative brother of the king, Mnt. Mangaliso Dlamini, rested firmly with the traditionalists, several of its members resigned, including the vice-chair and the secretary. One of them charged that the CRC constituted nothing more than "an attempt by the authorities to fool donor nations and delay the democratisation process indefinitely while giving the appearance of doing something." Within two years the public had become disillusioned about the real purposes of the CRC, as it became evident that it was consulting only certain constituencies, and as it appeared to be spending more time on securing handsome salaries and other perquisites for its members than on pursuing its announced mandate. That led to the widely repeated charge that the CRC was little more than a "fattening ranch" for its commissioners, which in turn led to the banning of the press from its public hearings. Nevertheless, in mid-1998 the king, perhaps perceiving the CRC's role in determining the kingdom's constitutional future to be more vital than seemed clear to others, extended the body's reporting deadline to the end of 1999. As that time approached, the CRC announced that it would require another two-year extension and that it could not guarantee a revised constitution in place prior to the 2003 general election. At that point the European Union withdrew its financial backing from the commission, on grounds that its procedures lacked openness, financial accountability, and adherence to democratic principles.

CORYNDON, ROBERT THORNE (1870–1925; knighted 1919). Swaziland **resident commissioner** 1907–16. South African born and British educated, Coryndon had a long and eventful career in the colonial service, serving successively in Northern Rhodesia, Swaziland, Basutoland, Uganda (governor), and Kenya (governor). Coryndon's early reputation as a decisive administrator made him **High Commissioner Lord Selborne's** choice to succeed Swaziland **Resident Commissioner Francis Enraght Moony**, who had made too many important settler enemies and was considered too inept by his superiors to be able to deal effectively with anticipated events there.

Those events centered around the **Partition Proclamation**, which was to be announced during November 1907, immediately following Coryndon's arrival, and the anticipated hostile reaction to it by Queen Regent **Labotsibeni Mdluli** and the *libandla*. Coryndon proved to be Moony's opposite in every significant way, forceful to the point of imperiousness with Labotsibeni and her advisors (both European and mission-educated African) and the lion of settler opinion. In Labotsibeni, it turned out, Coryndon met his match, but he ultimately succeeded in floating the Partition Proclamation peacefully, undercutting her protest **deputation of 1907** to London and keeping her advisors largely in check.

At the same time there was never a resident commissioner in Swaziland's colonial history who acted with greater subservience toward every settler interest of any significance. Indeed Coryndon's own biographer allows that his obsequiousness toward European interests was so pronounced as to taint his career as a colonial official.[5] Coryndon's final major task as resident commissioner was to oversee the peaceful removal of the Swazi to the "**native areas**" or to tenancy status on European farms beginning in mid-1914, under the terms of the 1907 Partition

Proclamation. From the settler point of view Coryndon's efforts were highly satisfactory.

COTTON. Cotton has been grown in Swaziland's **middleveld** and **lowveld** since the first experimental crops were planted around Mawelawela in 1904 and Bremersdorp (later **Manzini**) in 1906. Cotton has been grown commercially, however, only since the end of World War I, when the Empire Cotton Growing Association subsidized its introduction as a measure to enhance the viability of European settlement. As a drought-resistant crop (similar to sorghum), cotton proved more suitable as a crop where maize failed for lack of moisture. At first little official attention was paid to African cotton culture; indeed, Africans were excluded from early marketing cooperatives. What developed instead during the 1920s was a handful of Swazi cultivators in the Hlatikulu region who sold their cotton to European farmers at low, set prices, a settler method of offsetting high transportation costs to market in South Africa. European cotton estates employed large numbers of Swazi women and children during growing and harvesting season.

African smallholder cotton culture was therefore a post–World War II phenomenon, with cotton emerging by the 1950s as a major export crop, partly because it was encouraged as part of the **Swaziland Native Land Settlement Scheme** beginning in 1943. By the early 1980s 55 percent of Swaziland's cotton crop was being grown by 7,000 small farmers, marketed either in the **Transvaal** (under the South African Cotton Marketing Agreement) or to the local ginnery at **Matsapha**, where there was also a textile mill producing ticking for the South African market. During the 1980s Swaziland produced 25,000 tons of cotton annually during good years and 9,000 tons during drought years. During the 1990s, droughts and cheap cotton imports reduced cotton production both on irrigated estates and among the 80 percent of all small farmers cropping on **Swazi Nation Land**, leaving the crop's long-term viability in doubt.

COWEN, DENIS V. Professor of Comparative Law at the University of Cape Town, experienced in constitutional development in Basutoland, who was engaged in 1961 by the **Swaziland Progressive Party (SPP)** to prepare a proposal for constitutional reform. The SPP feared that the official constitutional committee (1960–61), laden as it was with Swazi traditionalists, was stacked against it and was incapable of producing anything like a multiracial, democratic document. The Cowen Report (1961), although never coming close to being adopted at the time, became the basis of several political party platforms, and greatly influenced the course of constitutional development in Swaziland, most notably in the provisions of the 1967 independence **constitution**.

CRAIB, IAN (?–1966). South African forestry expert who, following his retirement in 1947 as chief research officer for the South African Department of Forestry, became the principal expert behind the founding of the forestry industry in Swaziland. He oversaw the development of **Peak Timbers, Ltd.** (**Pigg's Peak**) and contributed to the establishment of **Usutu Forests** (**Mhlambanyatsi**) and the Usutu plantations at Gege and Goedgegun (modern **Nhlangano**). With an undergraduate degree from Cape Town and a Ph.D. from Yale University, Craib became a pioneer in the theory of wattle and coniferous forestry development, in the latter instance by virtue of his theories on the relative value of light and soil moisture in the rapid maturing of exotic conifers. Craib served as an executive director of Peak Timbers from 1947 to 1961. He was also a director of Forest Industries and Veneers, Ltd. in South Africa.

CROWN LAND. Also crown lands. The **Partition Proclamation** of 1907 divided the kingdom of Swaziland into three categories of lands: crown lands (approximately 22 percent of total land area), European ("**title deed**") concession lands (45 percent), and 32 native areas (later **Swazi Nation Land**, 33 percent). The delineation of boundaries was carried out by Partition Commissioner **George Grey** during 1908. The creation of crown land was intended to further the administration's political and financial purposes. Crown land was added to each native area where necessary to bring it to a state of viability in terms of carrying capacity and proximity to former areas of habitation, a measure calculated to reduce the chances of Swazi civil disturbances against the partition. Crown land was also intended to be sold off in future years to benefit the administration's fiscal balance sheet, to establish ranching companies, and to attract British settlers, especially following World War I.

The sale of crown land exclusively to Europeans represented a reversal of the promises made at the time of partition to the Swazi by several British colonial officials, including **Lord Selborne** and **Lord Elgin**, that crown lands would be sold to them in the future in order to increase their landholdings. This reversal touched off a sense of betrayal and resentment among Swazi rulers which rose to such a pitch that the British government in 1940 reversed itself and made crown land available for Swazi settlement. That reallocation in turn became the basis for the several **Swaziland Native Land Settlement Schemes** that followed.

umCWASHO. See UMCWASHO

-D-

DAGGA. *See INSANGU*

DE KAAP GOLD FIELD. *See* BARBERTON

DELAGOA BAY. An important Indian Ocean port at which grew the city of Lourenço Marques (now Maputo) in Mozambique. The bay was awarded to Portugal in arbitration (1875) after **Britain** had disputed its claim. Geographically Delagoa Bay is the natural port of Swaziland, whose border is less than 50 miles (81 kilometers) distant. Throughout the 19th century most bulk traffic arrived in Swaziland overland from the bay; only after South African rail service reached Piet Retief did that change. All the proposed railways through Swaziland from the **Transvaal** during the 19th and 20th centuries had Delagoa Bay as their terminus, and when the **Swaziland Railway** was completed in 1964 it terminated there.

DEPUTATION OF 1894. A delegation of Swazi sent to London by the Queen Regent **Tibati Nkambule** to protest the imposition of a **South African Republican** administration on her country and to seek instead British protection. Both the protest and the request proved futile. The deputation was headed by the recently appointed secretary to the Swazi nation, George H. Hulett, a Natal lawyer, and comprised Swazi officials allegedly not of the highest rank. It was officiously treated by the colonial secretary Lord Ripon, who refused to recognize Hulett's authority. The highest-ranking Swazi member of the deputation was Mnt. Longcanga Dlamini, half-brother and confidant of the late *iNgwenyama* **Mbandzeni Dlamini**.

DEPUTATION OF 1905. The first protest delegation dispatched beyond Swaziland's borders by Queen Regent **Labotsibeni Mdluli**. Its destination was the offices of the new **high commissioner, Lord Selborne**, in Pretoria. Its purpose was to protest the imposition of the **Swaziland Administration Proclamation No. 3/1904**. That law defined Swaziland administratively as a district of the **Transvaal** and established a court system similar in powers and jurisdiction to that of the Transvaal. That meant that the criminal jurisdiction of the *ingwenyama* and chiefs, which had first been curtailed by the **protocol of 1898**, was now abrogated. It also meant that while civil litigation remained in the realm of "native law and custom," the **resident commissioner** enjoyed appellate jurisdiction over decisions of the *ingwenyama's* court. That was the crippling blow

to Swazi royal sovereignty that the deputation, led by Labotsibeni's closest son, **Mnt. Malunge Dlamini**, protested, to no avail.

DEPUTATION OF 1907. A delegation sent by Queen Regent **Labotsibeni
Mdluli** to London to protest the British actions taken with respect to the
Partition Proclamation of 1907. Unlike the **deputation of 1894**, this
delegation consisted of the political heavyweights of the realm, among
them **Mnt. Malunge Dlamini**, closest and most influential son of the
queen regent; **Mnt. Logcogco Dlamini**, son of *iNgwenyama* **Mswati
Dlamini II** and a former regent; and **Josiah Vilakazi**, the queen regent's
secretary and close advisor. **Allan G. Marwick**, an up-and-coming assistant commissioner, accompanied the deputation as advisor and interpreter. The deputation's public protest centered on two main issues. The
first was land: the insufficiency of territory allotted to the Swazi under
the partition and the granting of lands in freehold to the concessionaires.
The second issue was politics: lack of consultation with Swazi authorities before legislation affecting them was enacted, and the withdrawal
of criminal jurisdiction from the *ingwenyama*'s court and the transfer
of final appellate jurisdiction in civil cases to the **resident commissioner**.
Also linked to the deputation's visit were two less public agendas, one
Swazi and the other British. For her part Labotsibeni wished to protest
Lord Selborne's expropriation of all but £1,000 of the annual £12,000
revenue accruing to the royal house from the **private revenue concession** which, if not reversed, would seriously undermine the queen regent's
sovereignty.

As for Selborne, both he and Resident Commissioner **Robert
Coryndon** had reversed themselves in allowing the deputation to proceed to London. By doing so they had hoped to so humiliate the queen
regent by London's flat, public rejection of all her protests as to undercut her politically, forcing her to resign in favor of her young (and vulnerable) grandson, the *inkhosana* (crown prince) **Nkhotfotjeni (Sobhuza
Dlamini II)**. In the end all the protests, public and private, failed, while
Lord Selborne's agenda backfired. Labotsibeni gained in domestic stature (for having prevailed in dispatching the deputation) far more than she
lost through any humiliation stemming from its failure, and she continued in office until 1921. Labotsibeni's gain was in part based on the circumstance that in turning her protests down, Colonial Secretary **Lord
Elgin** let slip the statement that his government intended to provide for
sufficient **crown land** to be transferred to the Swazi as to make them the
eventual owners of "half the land." That statement, quickly disavowed
and denied repeatedly by others over the following half-century, influ-

enced certain later events in important ways. They began with the collapse of Selborne's agenda for Labotsibeni's overthrow in 1908 and ended with the reversal of **Britain**'s longstanding refusal to sell crown land to the Swazi in 1940.

DE VRIES, VAN WYK. One of a small group of South African jurists and businessmen, some of them (like De Vries) conservative Afrikaners, to whom *iNgwenyama* **Sobhuza Dlamini II** turned for advice and support during the political and constitutional debates of the early and mid-1960s. De Vries, a lawyer and judge, as well as a member of both the National Party and the Broederbond, was prominent among those who advised Sobhuza in his maneuverings with the Commonwealth Office over the formulation of what would become the independence government of Swaziland. De Vries laid out a scenario for Sobhuza wherein the latter held out for unequivocal recognition as king and as the sole repository of all non-deeded land and all mineral rights. Failing that, his advice was that Sobhuza accept the new constitution imposed by Britain under protest, and then form—and lead—a political party whose platform was effectively that of the *ingwenyama*-in-*libandla*. In broad outline that strategy turned out to be spectacularly successful in fashioning Sobhuza into the dominating political figure he had become by the time of independence in 1968.

DE WINTON, COL. (later MAJ.-GEN.) SIR FRANCIS W. (1835–1901; knighted 1884). Chairman of the **Anglo-Boer Joint Commission** to Swaziland (1889). A veteran of the Crimean War, de Winton arrived in South Africa (1889) carrying an impressive record of civil appointments, including administrator of the Congo (1885) and secretary of the Emin Pasha relief expedition (1887). In 1889 de Winton was appointed by the acting British **high commissioner** (G. Bower, in behalf of the colonial office) to be special commissioner to report on the situation in Swaziland, which was understood to be on the verge of serious unrest. Huw Jones argues that the colonial office's confidential understanding of the de Winton mission was that he was to find a pretense to give the Swazi over to **South African Republican (SAR)** administration in return for SAR political and railway concessions in Bechuanaland, Swaziland, and the **Transvaal** itself.[6] The British high commission dispatched **Lord Robert Baden-Powell** to Swaziland with de Winton as his secretary to ensure that he carried out this hidden agenda. Both conferred with SAR president Paul Kruger in Pretoria about the proposed accommodation before departing for Swaziland.

The joint commission was composed of de Winton, **Lt.-Col. Richard Martin**, Baden-Powell, and the attorney W. P. Schreiner. The SAP representatives were Gens. P. J. Joubert and N. J. Smit. De Winton was elected chairman of the commission by the others while in Swaziland at **Mbekelweni**. The de Winton commission arrived at **Nkanini**, Queen Regent **Tibati Nkambule**'s homestead, in November 1889, where they were informed officially of *iNgwenyama* **Mbandzeni Dlamini**'s recent death. De Winton conducted his inquiries at Mbekelweni, Mbandzeni's administrative homestead and the site of **Theophilus Shepstone, Jr.**'s office as advisor to the Swazi nation. There he conferred with senior princes and *tindvuna*, including **Mnt. Logcogco Dlamini** and **Tikhuba Magongo**, along with Shepstone and a number of European concessionaires, notably **David Forbes**.

Because de Winton was operating in accordance with a secret agenda, his findings were not long in coming. The commission recommended the establishment of a **Provisional Government Committee** to administer European affairs (actually established in December 1889 and superseded by the **Swaziland Government Commitee** in September 1890), and a **Chief Court**. The latter was to have jurisdiction over all Europeans and also was commissioned to determine the validity of the **concessions**, which were being disputed mainly by the Swazi. Those recommendations were meant to constitute the first step toward the accommodation between the SAR and the colonial office, and indeed they became the foundation of the **first Swaziland Convention**, signed in July 1890. Its clauses included the Swaziland Government Committee (but with no jurisdiction over exclusively Swazi affairs), the Chief Court, and a right of way to the SAR to build a railroad through Swaziland to **Kosi Bay**. The latter clause was balanced by article 14, which provided for the renunciation by the SAR of any claims to extend its territories to the north and northwest.

By the time de Winton sent the commission's report to London (February 1890) the colonial office, under pressure from humanitarian and business interests in Britain, had backed away from the latter two understandings. They would be revived in somewhat different form, however, in 1894 as the **third Swaziland Convention**. De Winton's last official act in Swaziland was to pressure Tibati and the *libandla* into signing an instrument in early December 1889 assenting to all the above provisions. With the document in hand, de Winton and party departed Swaziland before the end of December 1889. He later became administrator of the territories under the responsibility of the Imperial British East Africa Company.

DICKSON, THOMAS AINSWORTH (1881–1935). Resident commissioner 1928–35. Dickson brought to Swaziland from his long experience in the Kenya colonial service a strong belief in the efficacy of **indirect rule.** What he found in Swaziland, following the residencies of **Robert Coryndon** (1907–16) and **de Symons Honey** (1917–28), was an absence altogether of an administration "native policy," but rather in its stead an administrative atmosphere of oppressive authoritarianism. Immediately he set out to delegate more authority to the Swazi ruling class including chiefs, and to foster "progressivism," by which he largely meant (as a devout Christian) furthering the aims of Christianity as well as of African Westernization. That translated into various specific acts. Dickson gave active support to the work of Christian **missions** and their schools and hospitals. He instituted monthly meetings between assistant commissioners and chiefs as a means of drawing the latter into the administration, and he proposed to make the *liqoqo* and *libandla* recognized elements of his administration. Dickson supported *iNgwenyama* **Sobhuza Dlamini II**'s establishment of the Western-style **Swazi National High School** at **Matsapha** (1931). He fostered the establishment of the **Swaziland Progressive Association** for educated Africans in 1929, the Coloured (later **EurAfrican**) **Welfare Association** for **EurAfricans** during the same year, and separate committees for educated Africans and EurAfricans in each of the districts to facilitate communications with the assistant commissioners.

During the early 1930s many of Dickson's progressive and administrative initiatives clashed with the growing design of King Sobhuza to emphasize traditional Swazi institutions and values as a means to revive the domestic power of the monarchy, and Dickson consequently retreated from or modified many of his early initiatives. In this he was influenced by **Allan G. Marwick**, assistant commissioner in Hlatikulu, whom he later moved to **Mbabane** as his deputy. Marwick's close ties with Sobhuza translated into his active sympathy toward reasserting the *ingwenyama*'s domestic sovereignty even at the expense of colonial prerogative. Dickson died in office and was succeeded as resident commissioner by Marwick in 1935.

DINGANE. *See* ZULU, DINGANE kaSENZANGAKHONA

DLAMINI. *See* iNKHOSI DLAMINI

DLAMINI III, *iNGWENYAMA* **(?–c. 1750).** A great deal of historical confusion exists concerning the genealogy of Swazi kings going back to the 15th century and even earlier. Various sources list as few as 8 and as many as 25 kings. Dlamini I, leader of the **eMbo** ("northern") **Nguni** and founder of the royal dynasty of the Swazi, is generally listed as the first of those kings. According to tradition he was succeeded by his son Mswati Dlamini I, and he in turn by his son Ngwane (*see* **Dlamini, *iNgwenyama* Ngwane**) and grandson Dlamini II, and so on. The first Swazi king about whom there is general agreement was *iNgwenyama* Dlamini III, who, along with his people around the mid-1700s, took control of the lands just beyond modern Swaziland's southeastern border around the Pongola River where it cuts through the **Lebombo** massif. They did so in company with the **Ndwandwe**; both were distancing themselves from the Tembe, who were consolidating their hold over the eastern reaches of the Lebombo range. Dlamini III was succeeded by his son Ngwane (Ngwane III) after 1750.

DLAMINI IV. *See* DLAMINI, *iNGWENYAMA* MBANDZENI

DLAMINI, *MNTFWANENKHOSI* BHEKIMPI A. (c. 1924–1999). Major political figure during the constitutional crisis following the death of *iNgwenyama* **Sobhuza Dlamini II** in 1982. The son of Chief Mnisi Dlamini of Nkhaba, he received some education before joining the **African Pioneer Corps** during World War II, attaining the rank of sergeant at the age of 20. Beginning in 1960 he served on various constitutional committees and delegations, and in 1964 he was elected to the **Legislative Council** (Legco) as an **Imbokodvo National Movement** candidate. As a Legco and later parliamentary member he served on various committees and in two ministries, but he was never selected by Sobhuza for national office.

In 1983 Dlamini was a deputy minister in the office of the deputy prime minister when he was selected by the traditionalists on the *Liqoqo* to be prime minister following their sacking of the modernist prime minister **Mnt. Mabandla Dlamini**. Later in 1983 Mnt. Bhekimpi, as a creature of the **Mnt. Mfanasibili Dlamini** faction in the *Liqoqo*, was involved in the dismissal of *iNdlovukazi* and Queen Regent **Dzeliwe Shongwe**. Still later that year Dlamini participated in the naming of **Ntombi Twala** as Dzeliwe's successor as *indlovukazi* and in Ntombi's subsequent ratification of the document designating the *Liqoqo* as the "Supreme Council of State." Although Mnt. Bhekimpi ostensibly survived the ensuing disintegration of the *Liqoqo* over the following months, he was dismissed by *iNgwenyama* **Mswati Dlamini III** and succeeded by Sotja Dlamini, the first prime minister to be selected from outside the royal family. In June 1987 Mnt. Bhekimpi was arrested and, along with 10 others (including Mnt. Mfanasibili), convicted of high treason for his part in the dismissal of Dzeliwe in 1983. In mid-1988 Bhekimpi, along with most of the other defendants, was pardoned by the king.

DLAMINI, *iNGWENYAMA* BHUNU (1887–1899). Bhunu ("The Boer") was the eldest son of *iNgwenyama* **Mbandzeni Dlamini** and **Labotsibeni Mdluli**. The legacy of his disastrous reign (1895–99) would burden his successors throughout most of the 20th century. Although he was his father's choice to succeed him, his candidacy to be *inkhosana* (crown prince) was widely unpopular on the grounds that he had two brothers and that no *ingwenyama* had ever been born of a Mdluli woman. His candidacy was therefore disputed by several rivals. In the end his mother's strong character and credentials as a possible *indlovukazi* overcame the obstacle of her background, and it was largely because of her that Bhunu was selected in mid-1890. That became the occasion for his mother's establishment of a new residence at **Zombodze** in the shadow of the **Mdzimba hills** (not to be confused with "old Zombodze" to the south, near **Shiselweni**). Zombodze was to become the seat of power for the duration of her regency.

Although the real power of government during Bhunu's minority lay with the queen regent, **Tibati Nkambule**, Labotsibeni quickly came to contest her authority over a number of issues. Bhunu was brought up at Zombodze and appeared at **Nkanini**, Tibati's homestead, only on occasions of state. To be sure, many of those occasions were significant, involving the machinations of **Theophilus Shepstone, Jr.**, advisor to the nation, and the concessionaires' **Government Committee** throughout 1890. Then there followed the maneuverings of the British and **South African Republican** (SAR) governments during 1893–94, which resulted in the handing over of the Swazi without their consent to the SAR's administration (1895–99), under the terms of the **third Swaziland Convention**.

Those crises required a steady hand at the throne, but as the years moved toward Bhunu's crowning (1895) his temperament proved to be anything but steady. Drunken and hedonistic on one hand, and headstrong and often violently cruel on the other, Bhunu developed a reputation for extreme unpredictability. Not the least of those who became alarmed by his behavior was his mother Labotsibeni, with whom his relations became increasingly strained following his crowning and, shortly thereafter, Tibati's death. Partly as a consequence he distanced himself physically from the *indlovukazi* by building his *lilawu* at Zabeni and establishing a personal homestead off in the Mdzimba range at Mampondvweni. In April 1898 the personal conflict turned into a state crisis when the *indlovukazi*'s chief *indvuna* at Zombodze, **Mbhabha Nsibandze**, was murdered, and Bhunu was quickly implicated.

The SAR administration, eager to clip Bhunu's wings and alarmed at the reports of Swazi regiments being mobilized, summoned the *ingwenyama* to appear at its headquarters at **Bremersdorp** to answer to the circumstances of the murder. Bhunu at first refused, and when he did appear he did so on horseback, rifle in hand, and accompanied by several **regiments** numbering more than 2,000 men. He denied complicity in the murder and then retired with several hundred armed followers to Mampondvweni, where he waited. The administration, seizing the opportunity, brought in troops and artillery from the SAR, then served Bhunu with a summons to stand trial in Bremersdorp for Nsibandze's murder. The *ingwenyama* thereupon fled to Natal, where he turned himself in to the British authorities. They succeeded in persuading him to return and undergo an "enquiry" (which they had negotiated with the SAR) into the affair at Bremersdorp. That proceeding, held in September, resulted in Bhunu's payment of £1,646 in fines and costs for "permitting public violence."

Of much more—indeed historic—consequence, however, Bhunu's disastrous behavior led to the effective termination of the monarchy's sovereignty by handing the SAR what it had long sought, an excuse to terminate the *ingwenyama*'s criminal jurisdiction. In 1898, with **Britain**'s assent, a protocol was added to the **third Swaziland Convention (1894)** that relegated major criminal jurisdiction solely to the European courts, leaving to the **paramount**'s and chiefs' courts jurisdiction only over civil and petty criminal cases.

Those terms were subsequently reimposed by Britain's postwar **Swaziland Administration Proclamation No. 3 of 1904**. Swazi criminal jurisdiction was to be partially restored only in 1950 and fully restored only upon independence in 1968. The **protocol of 1898** marked the beginning of Bhunu's rapid political decline. In 1899 the king gave himself over to his SAR oppressors, traveling to visit President Paul Kruger in April and later contracting with concessionaire **Matthias J. Grobelaar** to supply Swazi labor for the Johannesburg mines at £10 per head. Then in October, unfortunately for him, the **Anglo-Boer War** led to the exit of the SAR and most Europeans from the kingdom. Within a month Bhunu had become seriously ill, and in the midst of the *iNcwala* celebrations (December 10) he suddenly collapsed and died at Zombodze. His son selected as heir was **Nkhotfotjeni**, who would be installed in 1921 as *iNgwenyama* **Sobhuza Dlamini II**. Until then Labotsibeni ruled as queen regent, with her second son, **Mnt. Malunge Dlamini**, as her senior advisor.

DLAMINI, *MNTFWANENKHOSI* DABEDE. Son of **Mnt. Logcogco Dlamini** and grandson of *iNgwenyama* **Mswati Dlamini II**. Dlamini was appointed by *iNgwenyama* **Sobhuza Dlamini II** as his personal representative to and leader of the Swazi companies joining the **African Pioneer Corps** during 1941–45. Sobhuza viewed Swazi participation in **Britain**'s war effort as of prime importance politically and symbolically, and he bent every effort to meet Swaziland's quota for the corps. Diplomatically Sobhuza wanted to demonstrate imperial loyalty at a time when he was at loggerheads with the British over a series of sensitive issues. Specifically he sought to equate his dispatching of Swazi troops during World War II with his grandfather *iNgwenyama* **Mbandzeni Dlamini**'s support of the combined Swazi-British attack on the **Pedi** in 1879, thereby reminding the British of their broken promise to guarantee Swazi sovereignty in perpetuity. Mnt. Dabede, a nephew of Mbandzeni, therefore suited Sobhuza's purposes admirably.

By all accounts Dabede acquitted himself well, both as a leader of the troops and as the keeper of tradition—ensuring that Sobhuza remained demonstrably the military and spiritual commander-in-chief of the Swazi troops abroad. This included the ritualization of the powerfully medicinal war baton's handover to Dabede by Sobhuza in 1941 and its return to the *ingwenyama* by Dabede in 1946, each with elaborate public ceremony. Following the war Mnt. Dabede was one of several returned soldiers who, with back pay as capital to purchase trucks and taxis, and with the *ingwenyama*'s political support in fighting the **South African Railways and Harbours Road Motor Service**'s monopoly, entered the public transport and other businesses.

DLAMINI, *MNTFWANENKHOSI* DUMISA CLEMENT (c. 1938–). Often referred to as Clement Dumisa Dlamini. Nephew of *iNgwenyama* **Sobhuza Dlamini II** and son of *iNdlovukazi* **Nukwase Ndwandwe**, who fashioned an erratic career as an opposition politician during the early 1960s. Mnt. Dumisa articulated his own personal magnetism and driving ambition into the beginnings of a Western-style, charismatic political career. He studied briefly at Pius XII College in Basutoland (Lesotho), where he became involved in, and taken up in, the ideology and workings of the left-wing Basutoland Congress Party.

In 1960 Mnt. Dumisa, now a convert to activist politics, returned to Swaziland. The territory was just entering into its pre-independence period of political turbulence, and he determined to make political capital out of the situation. An evocative radical address in **Mbabane** in December vaulted him to the presidency of the Youth League of the **Swaziland Progressive Party (SPP)**, while the same month he distanced himself from the royal inner circle and traditionalists by his conspicuous absence from the annual *iNcwala* **ceremonies**. His travels to pan-Africanist conferences throughout the continent as SPP representative further radicalized him. Mnt. Dumisa became a protégé of **Dr. Ambrose Zwane**, and when Zwane broke with **John J. Nquku**'s faction of the SPP and formed the **Ngwane National Liberatory Congress** (NNLC, 1963), Mnt. Dumisa followed him and became secretary-general of the new party. Consequently when labor disturbances broke out throughout the territory in 1963, Mnt. Dumisa found the charged atmosphere ready-made for his brand of incendiary oratory. Along with Zwane and **Macdonald Maseko**, he jumped into the fray. Dubbing himself "prince of the oppressed," Dlamini led **sugar** workers' **strikes** around Big Bend in March and a protest march of market women in Mbabane in April, urged the strikers on at **Havelock** in May, and led a general strikers' march on the Mbabane office of the **resident commissioner** in June. For the last offense he was arrested along with several others for public violence and jailed for six months.

That spelled Mnt. Dumisa's end as a national political figure. From then until late 1966 he was either in jail or in exile. After serving his final sentence (for assault against several women) he tired of his life out in the political cold, made his accommodation with the *ingwenyama*, renounced the NNLC, and urged his followers to join the royalist **Imbokodvo National Movement (INM)**. His abrupt volte-face so enraged his followers that he was sent safely out of the country for an extended period of time "in order to further his studies." In 1985, still in enforced exile during the period of political turbulence following Sobhuza's death, Dumisa in London formed the short-lived Swaziland Liberation Movement, aimed at bringing down the *Liqoqo*-dominated government. He returned to Swaziland for a period during the late 1980s to enter business, but subsequently he exiled himself once again to London. There, in the late 1990s, he once more involved himself in politics, becoming once again the secretary-general of the revived NNLC in 1997.

DLAMINI, *MNTFWANENKHOSI* FOKOTSI (d. 1845). First-born son of *iNgwenyama* **Sobhuza Dlamini I** who violently opposed the choice of **Mnt. Mswati Dlamini II** as Sobhuza's successor. Along with two brothers and one or two allies, Fokotsi raised an army in southwest Swaziland and mounted a rebellion. In 1845, in Mswati's first decisive defense of his throne, Fokotsi was met at **Mahamba** hill by forces led by two of Mswati's brothers, **Bnt. Malunge** and **Somcuba Dlamini**. There Fokotsi (many of whose allies deserted him) was decisively defeated and killed, and his body was left to the elements.

DLAMINI, *MNTFWANENKHOSI* GABHENI (1942–). Son of *iNgwenyama* **Sobhuza Dlamini II** by Lomadlozi Nkambule. Gabheni was educated at the National School at **Lobamba** and the **Swazi National High School** at **Matsapha**. Until the early 1980s Mnt. Gabheni was appointed to a number of fairly minor posts: clerk to the Swazi National Court (1968), Land Control Appeals Board (1972), and Constitutional Advisory Committee (1975). His national political life began in 1968 when, as an **Imbokodvo National Movement** candidate, he was elected to **parliament**. He was reelected in 1972, and when the *ingwenyama's tinkhundla* parliament was elected in 1978 he was named minister of home affairs. As Sobhuza's health declined Mnt. Gabheni became his chief personal representative and spokesperson.

It was following his father's death in 1982, however, that Mnt. Gabheni found himself directly at the vortex of royal politics when he was made a member of the *Liqoqo*, allegedly by virtue of his nomination on Sobhuza's (unpublished) roster. Gabheni had once been considered a successor to Sobhuza, but in the end he was passed over in favor of Makhosetive on the grounds that he was not an only son. Still, all those credentials made Gabheni a most forceful chief spokesman among the modernists within the *Liqoqo* and among the royals during the turbulent interregnum period (1982–86). He led the opposition to the *Liqoqo's* dismissals of the prime minister, **Mnt. Mabandla Dlamini**, and that of the *indlovukazi* and queen regent, **Dzeliwe Shongwe**, in 1983. He also opposed the South African-proposed **Ingwavuma** land deal. His principled stances made him the target of the traditionalists on the *Liqoqo*, notably **Mnt. Mfanasibili Dlamini**. Finally in late 1983 Gabheni was ousted from the cabinet as home affairs minister and then (1984) from the *Liqoqo*. After that time his largely behind-the-scenes efforts to modernize the monarchy earned him wide respect.

DLAMINI, *MNTFWANENKHOSI* LOGCOGCO (c. 1860–1922). The son of *iNgwenyama* **Mswati Dlamini II** and **Tibati Nkambule**. Tibati became *indlovukazi* in 1881 following the execution of *iNdlovukazi* **Sisile**

Khumalo. That was principally because it had been she who had brought up her late sister Nandzi Nkambule's child **Mnt. Mbandzeni Dlamini**, who had become *ingwenyama* in 1874. When Mbandzeni died in 1889, Mnt. Logcogco became the senior prince and acting regent along with his mother. He was consequently deeply involved with affairs of state during much of *iNkhosana* **Bhunu Dlamini**'s minority, although as tensions between his mother and Bhunu's mother, **Labotsibeni Mdluli**, intensified, his influence diminished. After Tibati's death in 1895 Mnt. Logcogco's political shadow receded further. Still, he did act as an important stabilizing influence during the political crisis following the murder of **Mbhabha Nsibandze** in 1898. Again for a period following Bhunu's death Logcogco acted as co-regent with Labotsibeni, until such time as the rise of **Mnt. Malunge Dlamini**'s political star eclipsed his own, although Mnt. Logcogco continued to preside over the *liqoqo*. Following his death in 1922, he was succeeded as head of the royal residence at Gunundwini by his son, **Mnt. Sozisa Dlamini**.

DLAMINI, *MNTFWANENKHOSI* LOMVAZI (c. 1885–1922). Son of *iNgwenyama* **Mbandzeni Dlamini** and **Labotsibeni Mdluli**, and full brother to both *iNgwenyama* **Bhunu Dlamini** and **Mnt. Malunge Dlamini**. Mnt. Lomvazi, the youngest and least distinguished of Labotsibeni's sons, was well educated, having spent a brief period at the **Edendale** (Natal) mission school, then having been tutored by **Robert Grendon,** and finally having attended the Methodist mission school at **Mahamba**. Not surprisingly Mnt. Lomvazi was one of those who was influential in urging the dispatch of *iNkhosana* (Crown Prince) **Sobhuza Dlamini II** abroad to be educated at the **Lovedale Missionary Institution** at the Cape. Upon Malunge's death in 1915, Lomvazi was named to replace him in assisting Labotsibeni as regent, but such was the contrast between his undistinguished character and Malunge's charismatic personality that his office in effect withered away.

DLAMINI, *iNGWENYAMA* LUDVONGA II (c. 1855–1874). Son of *iNgwenyama* **Mswati Dlamini II** and **Sisile Khumalo**. Upon his father's death in 1865 the *indlovukazi*, **Tsandzile Ndwandwe**, became queen regent. Among several contenders for succession Ludvonga II was chosen, partly because his mother possessed the correct qualifications (including an only son) and partly because his young age would ensure a long regency for Tsandzile and the other regents. Their plans went awry in March 1874 when Ludvonga suddenly became ill and died. His uncle and guardian, **Mnt. Ndwandwa Dlamini**, who was immediately suspected of the murder on grounds of political ambition, was quickly executed. Ludvonga was the first *ingwenyama* to be buried at **Dlangeni** in the **Mdzimba** range. He was succeeded by his half-brother, *iNgwenyama* **Mbandzeni Dlamini**.

DLAMINI, *MNTFWANENKHOSI* MABANDLA. Swaziland's first and (to date) only reformist prime minister (1979–1983). Although he was the son of a prominent chief (Mnt. Mancibane Dlamini) and was well educated, Mabandla brought no previous political experience to the post. Instead, he had been an agricultural administrator prior to his appointment to the prime ministership by *iNgwenyama* **Sobhuza Dlamini II**. Once in office, finding the government and ancillary institutions rife with corruption, Mabandla established a commission of inquiry to look comprehensively into fraudulent activity. In short order those close to Sobhuza, seeing that the investigation was closing in on individuals of the greatest prominence, persuaded the king to close it down. In the process Mabandla incurred the wrath of those who stood to be exposed by his anticorruption drive, many of whom were either allied to or members of the *liqoqo*.

Consequently Sobhuza's death in 1982 rendered Mabandla vulnerable to the now-empowered *Liqoqo*'s efforts to oust him. He hardly enhanced his security in office by opposing the South African government's offer to transfer **kaNgwane** and **Ingwavuma** to the kingdom in return for its suppression of the **African National Congress**'s activities within its borders, a deal enthusiastically supported by the *Liqoqo*. In 1983 Mabandla was one of those who fell victim to the *Liqoqo*'s moves to shunt the monarchy aside in favor of itself as the "Supreme Council of State." Mabandla, in fear of his life, fled with his family into exile in Boputhatswana for a time, but he subsequently returned to Swaziland, in the eyes of many a revered figure for having sought to bring true reform to the government. By the late 1990s Mnt. Mabandla had become a prominent businessman and farmer.

DLAMINI, *MNTFWANENKHOSI* MABHEDLA. Son of *iNgwenyama* **Mswati Dlamini II** who in 1874 launched a conspiracy to head off the crowning of his half-brother **Mnt. Mbandzeni Dlamini**. Consequently when Mbandzeni became *ingwenyama* in 1875 Mabhedla fled north to raise a rebellion in the Hhohho region. When that failed to gain popular support he decamped to the **Pedi** domains of **Sekhukhune Maroteng**. From that base he became a constant threat to Swazi influence in the eastern **Transvaal** until a Swazi troop helped defeat Sekhukhune and capture him in the 1879 campaign. Thereafter, Mnt. Mabhedla's fealty to his British captors kept him from being murdered by Mbandzeni's forces, and he lived out his days exiled in the Transvaal.

DLAMINI, *MNTFWANENKHOSI* MAGWEGWE (?–1820). Son of *iNgwenyama* **Ndvungunye Dlamini**. Mnt. Magwegwe attempted to take power from his brother, *iNgwenyama* **Sobhuza Dlamini I**, while the latter was campaigning in the Dhlomodhlomo hills in the upper **Komati River** valley. Sobhuza had already subdued another brother and would-be usurper, **Mnt. Ngwekazi Dlamini**, in **Shiselweni** in 1819. Now in 1820 the king moved back into the **Ezulwini Valley**, put down Magwegwe's rebellion, and killed him.

DLAMINI, *MNTFWANENKHOSI* MAKHOSINI (1914–1976). Great-grandson of *iNgwenyama* **Sobhuza Dlamini I** and son of Mnt. Majozi Dlamini, Mnt. Makhosini was the first prime minister of independent Swaziland (1967, prior to independence, until 1976). Mnt. Makhosini was a product of missionary education and a graduate of the **Swazi National High School**, then was trained as a teacher at the Umphulo Training Institute in Natal. While a teacher in Swaziland he served as secretary-general of the Swaziland Teachers' Association, predecessor to the **Swaziland National Association of Teachers**. He served briefly (1946–47) as headmaster of the Swazi National High School before turning to farming, the civil service, and politics. Mnt. Makhosini became a member of the *libandla* or Swazi National Council (SNC) in 1949, and later (1965) a member of its **Standing Committee**. From 1949 to 1962 he served as a rural development officer and a member of the Central Rural Development Board.

By the early 1960s Mnt. Makhosini, with his educational background and civil service experience, had become a member of *iNgwenyama* **Sobhuza Dlamini II**'s inner circle of advisors and was a participant in almost every notable conference, constitutional committee, and delegation to London. In 1964, with the foundation of the **Imbokodvo National Movement (INM)** and with its victory at the polls, Sobhuza appointed Mnt. Makhosini as its head and as spokesman of the SNC in the new **Legislative Council** (Legco). In that capacity Mnt. Makhosini led the INM successfully through the elections of 1964 and 1967, and in that year the *ingwenyama* appointed him prime minister of the pre-independence internal government. He served in that post until ill health forced his retirement in early 1976. He died shortly thereafter. He was succeeded as prime minister by Maphevu Dlamini.

DLAMINI, *MNTFWANENKHOSI* MALAMBULE. Son of *iNgwenyama*
Sobhuza Dlamini I and **laVumisa Ndwandwe**, *inhlanti* of **Tsandzile
Ndwandwe.** Although Tsandzile's son **Mnt. Mswati Dlamini II** was at
first Sobhuza's chosen heir, laVumisa persuaded the seriously ailing
Sobhuza to alter the succession in favor of the older Mnt. Malambule
on the grounds that the kingdom could not withstand a protracted minority. Then Sobhuza recovered and reversed his decision, leading to
mounting hostility between the two princes, complicated by the fact that
such were Malambule's credentials that he became the principal regent
during Mswati's minority.

In 1846, several years following Mswati's installation, things came to
a head. The situation was fraught with danger for Mswati because
Malambule had allied himself with King **Mpande Zulu**, which made his
backing by the powerful Zulu army highly possible. To make matters
worse, Malambule established his rebel camp near **Mahamba** next to the
new station of the Wesleyan missionary **James Allison**, an attack in
whose vicinity could raise all kinds of complications. Yet this was no time
to demonstrate weakness, for there were other conspirators, real and
potential, awaiting the outcome. Mswati launched a skirmish against
Malambule at Mahamba in June, but it was indecisive and the rebel retired for reinforcements. In September a second attack carried into the
mission itself and caused so many casualties that Allison fled with his
entire party. Malambule, now defeated, fled to the fold of his ally
Mpande, but Malambule arrived accompanied by so many stories of his
treachery and murderous behavior that Mpande had him executed.

DLAMINI, *MNTFWANENKHOSI* MALOYI (d. 1890s). The son of
iNgwenyama **Sobhuza Dlamini I** and Lomawandla Ndwandwe, *inhlanti*
of **Tsandzile Ndwandwe.** By the time of *iNgwenyama* **Mswati Dlamini
II**'s death in 1865 Mnt. Maloyi had become a prominent councillor, and
he played an important role as regent during *iNgwenyama* **Ludvonga
Dlamini II**'s minority. Following Ludvonga's death Mnt. Maloyi was one
of a handful of regents who determined that the boy's guardian, **Mnt.
Ndwandwa Dlamini**, was to be executed. Again, Mnt. Maloyi was a
senior councillor determining affairs of state during the reign of *iNgwenyama* **Mbandzeni Dlamini**, and subsequently during the minority of
iNgwenyama **Bhunu Dlamini**. Mnt. Maloyi firmly supported the formal
recognition of the white presence in the kingdom. He signed the White
Charter (*see* **Swazieland Committee**) in 1888 and was a supporter of
Theophilus Shepstone, Jr., as Mbandzeni's resident advisor. Maloyi
also signed the Organic Proclamation of 1890, which established the

Swaziland Government Committee and the Chief Court to administer and adjudicate the affairs of the white population in Swaziland. Mnt. Maloyi died probably during the 1890s and was buried in the **Mdzimba** range.

DLAMINI, *MNTFWANENKHOSI* MALUNGE (d. c. 1874). Malunge was a son of *iNgwenyama* **Ndvungunye Dlamini** who played an important role in affairs of state during the reigns of *tiNgwenyama* **Mswati Dlamini II** and **Ludvonga Dlamini II** and the attendant interregna. In defense of Mswati's throne Malunge, along with **Mnt. Somcuba Dlamini**, defeated the forces of the rebel **Mnt. Fokotsi Dlamini** at **Mahamba** in 1845. When Ludvonga died suddenly in 1874 Mnt. Malunge was one of the regents to whom Queen Regent **Tsandzile Ndwandwe** turned to advise her on the fate of the boy's guardian, **Mnt. Ndwandwa Dlamini**. Mnt. Malunge died a venerated political figure about 1874 and was buried at **Dlangeni** in the **Mdzimba** range. He was succeeded by his son Mnt. Jokovu Dlamini.

DLAMINI, *MNTFWANENKHOSI* MALUNGE (c. 1881–1915). Son of *iNgwenyama* **Mbandzeni Dlamini** and **Labotsibeni Mdluli**, and full brother of *iNgwenyama* **Bhunu Dlamini** and **Mnt. Lomvazi Dlamini**. He was by all accounts an extraordinary person and political figure: tall, handsome, able, articulate, and charismatic. He was clearly his mother's favorite son, and there were strong indications that she conspired to replace Bhunu with the brighter and less volatile Malunge as *ingwenyama*, even to the point of proposing to doctor him for the throne. Later there were signs that she sought to shunt aside the *inkhosana* (crown prince), **Nkhotfotjeni (Sobhuza Dlamini II)**, in favor of Mnt. Malunge. In each case it was said that Malunge refused to go along. What was certain was that after Labotsibeni became queen regent in 1899, Malunge quickly outstripped the designated co-regent, **Mnt. Logcogco Dlamini**, in political influence both with his mother and in the wider polity. That was in part because of his character and in part because of his modern education, first at the Wesleyan mission at **Edendale** (Natal), and later at the hands of a Western-educated tutor, **Robert Grendon**, at **Zombodze**. Mnt. Malunge was a highly placed signatory on the important state documents and petitions of the early years of British administration. He led a protest delegation to the **high commissioner** in Pretoria in 1905 and was a prominent member of the **deputation of 1907** to London. As the ineffectiveness of that type of protest became clearer, and after the South Africa Act of 1909 made it evident that Swaziland would some day be incorporated into the **Union of South Africa**, Malunge's progressive education led him to take an active interest in more confrontational nationalist politics as practiced in the Union. He later influenced his mother to do the same. Mnt. Malunge befriended two of the founders of the **African National Congress (ANC)**, **Pixley Seme** and **Richard Msimang**, and in 1914 he attended an ANC protest conference against the Union's Natives Land Act (in his mind not dissimilar to Swaziland's 1907 **Partition Proclamation**) in Kimberley.

With Seme's legal advice Mnt. Malunge and Labotsibeni put together a land repurchase program based on a Swazi head tax, and later, when that failed to generate sufficient revenue, on loaned capital. During the 1913–14 land levy campaign which he headed, Mnt. Malunge's popularity and reputation suffered markedly as he made heavy demands on the chiefs and as rumors spread that he and others were embezzling some of the collections. Partly (undoubtedly) because of this, Malunge's health began to suffer, and in early 1915 he died of heart failure. Labotsibeni, who believed that Malunge had been poisoned by a chief hostile to the royal family, never fully recovered from the shock of his death, suffering periodic bouts of depression until her own death in 1925. Upon Bhunu's death in 1899 Malunge had taken one of his wives, **Nukwase Ndwandwe**, under his protection, and by the levirate she bore him two sons. Nukwase later became *indlovukazi* (1938–57). Malunge's heir was Mnt. Magongo Dlamini. Malunge was buried at **Makhosini** in the **Dlangeni** hills.

DLAMINI, *MNTFWANENKHOSI* MASITSELA (1930–). Mnt. Masitsela, the son of *iNgwenyama* **Sobhuza Dlamini II**, operated simultaneously at the center of national politics and at the vortex of royal family affairs continuously beginning in the early 1960s. He received his education at the **Zombodze** elementary school and at the **Swazi National High School**, following which he held several lower civil service positions. In 1963 Mnt. Masitsela was thrust into the public limelight in the midst of the national labor crisis when his father appointed him as his chief labor representative to Swaziland's agribusinesses, industries, and mines. Because the Swazi labor force deeply mistrusted *iNgwenyama* Sobhuza's substitution of *tindvuna* for labor unions, and considering that Mnt. Masitsela had no experience in labor relations, his position immediately became untenable, and then irrelevant, in the wave of **strikes** that followed. In announcing his appointment Sobhuza ordered striking workers to return to work and to communicate with him through Masitsela. The workers proceeded to ignore both Sobhuza and Masitsela and, succumbing to the rhetoric of radical politicians such as **Mnt. Dumisa Dlamini**, walked out in increasing numbers and rising militancy until the June 1963 government declaration of an emergency.

Mnt. Masitsela's political fortunes rose with his appointment in 1964 as one of the members of the monarchist **Imbokodvo National Movement (INM)** to serve in the **Legislative Council**. Thereafter Masitsela served on **Sir Francis Loyd**'s Constitutional Review Commission in 1965. In 1967, again an INM candidate, Masitsela was elected to **parliament** and then was made assistant deputy prime minister for labor. Following the 1972 election (by which he was once more returned to parliament) he became Minister for Local Administration in Sobhuza's cabinet. After Sobhuza's repeal of the constitution in 1973, Masitsela became an advisor to his father and pursued his politics within the royal circle. Following Sobhuza's death Masitsela remained largely behind the scenes during the ensuing constitutional crises. By the mid-1990s he had emerged as one of *iNgwenyama* **Mswati Dlamini III**'s closest advisors and a leading opponent of any significant constitutional change that would diminish royal authority.

DLAMINI, *MNTFWANENKHOSI* MASUMPHE (c. 1870–?). Son of *iNgwenyama* **Mbandzeni Dlamini** and Ncenekile Simelane, and the senior uncle of *iNgwenyama* **Sobhuza Dlamini II**. Mnt. Masumphe was a contender to be his father's successor but was passed over in favor of **Mnt. Bhunu Dlamini** because of his mother's volatile temper. During World War I Masumphe volunteered to command the 57-man Overseas Native Labour Contingent which saw action in France. Because Queen Regent **Labotsibeni Mdluli** had been so deliberately and conspicuously deficient in supplying the 480 men to the Contingent requested by the British, Masumphe's response to the call was seen by young Mnt. Sobhuza as helping to salve the wound she had inflicted on the monarchy's reputation, and the crown prince expressed his deep appreciation in writing to Masumphe. During World War II Sobhuza took that lesson and acted entirely differently toward a similar British request for a Swazi complement to the **African Pioneer Corps**. Mnt. Masumphe was also one of those who spoke in forceful rejoinder when the Privy Council's judgment on the *Sobhuza II vs. Miller* case was announced in **Mbabane** in May 1926.

DLAMINI, *iNGWENYAMA* MBANDZENI (c. 1857–1889). Son of *iNgwenyama* **Mswati Dlamini II** and Nandzi Nkambule. Ill-fated king whose profligate concessioning of Swaziland's land and resources to foreigners wrought baneful consequences on the kingdom ever after. The sudden death of Mswati's youthful successor *iNgwenyama* **Ludvonga Dlamini II** in 1874, along with the existence of the 20-odd sons of Mswati who could be candidates for the succession, opened up the probability of yet another long and turbulent interregnum similar to the one following Mswati's own death. To avoid that circumstance the queen regent, **Tsandzile Ndwandwe**, conferred the responsibility for selection on Ludvonga's mother, **Sisile Khumalo**, because she had lost her only child.

Sisile chose Mnt. Mbandzeni, who had already lost his mother, thereby securing her own position as *indlovukazi*. He was installed in mid-1875. The timid and isolated boy, still only 17 years old, was from the beginning overshadowed by his adoptive mother in the affairs of state. It could not have been otherwise, because he had been chosen to suit Sisile's convenience and she in turn stood in the shadow of a venerable group of regents, led by Tsandzile and **Sandlane Zwane**, with its own power agenda. When Tsandzile died in 1874, power polarized between Sisile and Sandlane. Two circumstances changed that alignment. First was Mbandzeni's determination to carve out an area of authority for himself alone, uncontested by the *indlovukazi* and the regents. The area they ceded to him was foreign affairs, and that led directly to the concessioneering era. Second was his liaison, against all advice, with **Somdlalose Hlubi**, daughter of King Langalibalele Hlubi. Somdlalose had previously been betrothed to the late *iNgwenyama* Ludvonga, so that when a son was born of that union, Mbandzeni laid himself open to the whispered charge of raising Ludvonga's seed to produce the real Swazi *ingwenyama*.

That forced him to act with uncharacteristic decisiveness, for he discovered that Sisile, responding to the growing tension between them, had doctored the infant to occupy his "rightful" throne. In early 1881 Mbandzeni had the child murdered and both Sisile and Somdlalose executed, following which the homesteads of their allies were laid waste. Only then did he achieve anything approaching full domestic power. In foreign affairs Mbandzeni was taken up with both the resurgence of Zulu pressure from the south and the revival of enmity with the **Pedi** to the north. The Zulu threat he handled largely diplomatically, while he mounted two separate military operations against the Pedi. The first, in 1876, ended in disaster, while in the second, in 1879, Swazi **regiments** in consort with British and **Transvaal** Afrikaner troops defeated and captured **King Sekhukhune Maroteng**. In return for participation in the 1879 campaign Mbandzeni was guaranteed Swazi independence in perpetuity by the British, a promise that certainly must have colored his later judgments on concessioning, but one that the British broke ignominiously in 1894. Mbandzeni was also caught up diplomatically in the labyrinth of maneuverings between the British and the **South African Republic** (SAR) in its several dimensions: SAR expansionism into the Transvaal interior and British annexation and retrocession (1877–81). In his dealings with the Europeans Mbandzeni frequently acted with considerable skill and acumen, which is not to say that he was often successful in preserving Swazi interests.

Those qualities were conspicuously absent in his domestic dealings with European concessionaires. In fairness to Mbandzeni, his **concessions** were far from the first granted by the Swazi royal house. Concessions (in the form of permissions for European settlement of western and southwestern Swaziland) had been granted during the regency prior to his installation, probably to create white buffers against Zulu and other incursions. That was after all what his father, Mswati II, had done. During the 1880s Mbandzeni, more self-confident after his diplomatic and military victories of the late 1870s, opened the floodgates. First grazing leases were granted to Transvaal Afrikaner farmers for payment in kind, 67 of them between 1881 and 1885, almost half of them orally and without documentation. Then **gold** prospecting concessions were granted beginning in 1883, the year following the **Barberton** strike, and becoming substantial by 1886. By that time he had once again lost his confidence in himself and his *tindvuna*, and he had grown very fat (he died weighing well over 300 pounds).

Mbandzeni also had decided to seek out "an honest white man" to look after his interests. The man he retained, **Theophilus Shepstone, Jr.**, met, despite his background and pedigree, only half of those criteria. Shepstone's appointment turned out to be Mbandzeni's most disastrous miscalculation of all time. During the remainder of 1887, following Shepstone's arrival, both land and mineral concessions proliferated, some of them to Shepstone's friends, and the first of the monopoly concessions were granted. Shepstone also seized the political initiative, creating in 1887 a **Swazieland Committee**, in part to control white affairs but in part also to subvert Mbandzeni's sovereignty and to draw attention away from himself and his doings. From that point onward Mbandzeni, sensing that he was losing control of events, repeatedly made it clear that all concessions were meant to be leases and not sales of ground, and that he was determined to maintain his kingdom's independence. He also initiated at long last a system of written concessions registration. Still concession hunters hounded him, sometimes into the inner recesses of the royal residences. The king began drinking heavily, often at white-owned canteens, notably **John Thorburn**'s Embekelweni Hotel. In 1888 Mbandzeni broke with Shepstone, accusing him of theft of concessions monies and terminating his appointment as advisor. Shortly afterward, however, Mbandzeni signed a White Charter that devolved jurisdiction involving Europeans to the whites themselves. By late 1888 Mbandzeni had begun acting increasingly erratically, moving (consequently) the country toward anarchy. He reappointed Shepstone, placing him on a fixed stipend, and isolated himself from his *tindvuna* and other advisors. He signed away the **Little Free State** and allowed the SAR to begin to acquire monopoly concessions that would lead to its control of Swaziland's administration. In December 1888, frightened by his own deteriorating health, he accused several influential men (including Sandlane Zwane) of witchcraft and had them executed and their homesteads destroyed.

In early 1889 Mbandzeni once again dismissed Shepstone and in his place appointed **Allister Miller**, a member of the Swazieland Committee, as his secretary. That was a choice that proved to be fatefully ill-advised, for it would be under Miller's influence that some of the most egregious concessions were granted. By mid-1889 the parlous state of Mbandzeni's health and other indications of approaching anarchy led first the SAR and then the British to establish the **Joint (de Winton) Commission** of inquiry into the state of affairs in the kingdom. That would eventually lead to an administrative takeover by the SAR. In October 1889, before the commission could ever convene in Swaziland, Mbandzeni died at the age of 32. He was buried near *iNgwenyama* Ludvonga II's gravesite at **Dlangeni** in the **Mdzimba** range. When Mbandzeni had been near death in 1889 and aware of the tragedy he had wrought, he had despaired that the "Swazi kingship ends with me." His own dark self-assessment was entirely justified, but in the end the brilliance of his widow **Labotsibeni Mdluli** and grandson **Sobhuza II** in reviving the fortunes of the monarchy proved him wrong.

DLAMINI, *MNTFWANENKHOSI* MBILINI (c. 1843–1879). Eldest son of *iNgwenyama* **Mswati Dlamini II** and leMakhasiso Dvuba, who considered himself the leading candidate to succeed his father. In fact Mswati was said to have named him as he lay dying in his brother **Mnt. Maloyi Dlamini**'s arms, but that was not how successors were chosen constitutionally. Mbilini was considered by the nominating council under the influence of Queen Regent **Tsandzile Ndwandwe** to be so tempestuous as to be unable to rule wisely. Consequently his brother **Mnt. Ludvonga**

Dlamini II was chosen in 1865, and Mbilini proceeded to validate the judgment of the kingmakers for the rest of his days.

Basing his rebellion in Hhohho to the north, Mblini appealed to his father's strongest **regiment**, the *iNyatsi* (Buffalo), for backing, without apparent success. He thereupon defected to the emigrant Afrikaner community at Lydenburg in the eastern **Transvaal**, offering them 500 head of royal cattle for their support. They accepted, and when Ludvonga sent a force against Mnt. Mbilini it was beaten back by the Lydenburgers. Eventually the Afrikaners tired of the danger that Mnt. Mblini represented. In 1867, rather than accept that ambivalent position, Mnt. Mblini removed to northern Zululand, where he found a certain protection under the shadow of King Cetshwayo Zulu. There, for more than a decade, his brigandage against both Swazi and Afrikaner made him the scourge of the countryside and a major embarrassment to Cetshwayo himself. Then, during the British operations in northern Zululand following the Battle of Isandhlwana (January 1879), Mnt. Mbilini allied himself with Zulu forces, and in April 1879 he was gunned down by British soldiers while returning to his homestead with stolen horses. Mnt. Mbilini's protracted rebellion failed largely because it never succeeded in eliciting Swazi popular support and because he was unable to ally himself to any consequence with either Afrikaner or Zulu.

DLAMINI, *MNTFWANENKHOSI* MDZABUKO (1879–1881). The son of *iNgwenyama* **Mbandzeni Dlamini** and **Somdlalose Hlubi**, the Hlubi princess betrothed but not married to the late *iNgwenyama* **Ludvonga Dlamini II**. Mbandzeni's liaison with Somdlalose was carried on against the strong warnings of *iNdlovukazi* **Sisile Khumalo** that a son born of that union would be considered as Ludvonga's legitimate heir and would thus undercut Mbandzeni's legitimacy. Indeed, when Mdzabuko was born, Sisile did hold him hostage to her own political ambitions by doctoring him to assume the throne. Responding quickly, Mbandzeni had the infant murdered with poisoned milk, touching off a chain of events leading to Sisile's execution and the installation of **Tibati Nkambule** in her place as *indlovukazi*.

DLAMINI, *MNTFWANENKHOSI* MFANASIBILI (1939–). Son of Mnt. Makhosikhosi Dlamini and grandson of *iNgwenyama* **Bhunu Dlamini**. The fact that **Nkhotfotjeni (Sobhuza Dlamini II)** had been chosen in 1899 as Bhunu's successor over Makhosikhosi, Bhunu's posthumous son (for fear that the infant might have inherited Bhunu's cruel disposition), created a permanent split in the royal family. That circumstance explained much about Mnt. Mfanasibili's checkered political career beginning in the early 1960s. Bnt. Makhosikhosi and Mfanasibili, father and son, lived always by the conviction that they, not Sobhuza and his successor *iNgwenyama* **Mswati Dlamini III**, were the rightful heirs of Bhunu. Sobhuza courted the loyalties of both men while he was alive. For Mnt. Mfanasibili that meant a series of political appointments: the *libandla* in 1963, **Legislative Council** in 1964, Constitutional Review Commission in 1965, the board of **Tibiyo takaNgwane** in 1968, and chairman of the Civil Service Board in 1982. In 1967, after election to parliament (as an **Imbokodvo National Movement** candidate), he was appointed Minister of Local Administration.

In 1972 it was Mnt. Mfanasibili who was defeated in his Mphumalanga constituency by **Bhekindlela Thomas Ngwenya** of the **Ngwane National Liberatory Congress (NNLC)**, and it was he who then helped to challenge Ngwenya's citizenship as a means of attempting to overturn his own defeat. Unsuccessful, Mfanasibili was subsequently appointed senator and Minister for Commerce and Cooperatives by Sobhuza.

It was the *ingwenyama*'s death in 1982 that loosed Mnt. Mfanasibili's darkest political instincts. Supposedly named to the *Liqoqo* in Sobhuza's political testament, Mnt. Mfanasibili attempted to leverage that position into the means of righting the wrong, as he saw it, done to his father in 1899. Quickly emerging as the de facto leader of an unconstitutionally activist *Liqoqo* (terming itself the "Supreme Council of State"), he used it to force the resignations of Sobhuza's last prime minister, **Mnt. Mabandla Dlamini**, and Sobhuza's designated *indlovukazi* and regent, **Dzeliwe Shongwe** in 1983. Subsequently Dzeliwe's successor, *iNkhosana* (Crown Prince) Makhosetive's unlettered mother **Ntombi Twala**, was persuaded to sign away her sovereign powers in favor of the *Liqoqo*. The impending success of Mnt. Mfanasibili's coup was trumped only by his rivals' ability to return Makhosetive hastily from his British school, then ritually prepare and crown him prematurely. Thus foiled, Mnt. Mfanasibili and his allies were dismissed, and two of them were arrested. Mfanasibili was convicted of attempting to "defeat the ends of justice" and sentenced to a long prison term. In 1988 Mnt. Mfanasibili and nine others (including **Mnt. Bhekimpi Dlamini**) were convicted of high treason for having dismissed Dzeliwe in 1983. Later that year the *ingwenyama* pardoned them all, except Mfanasibili. After his release from prison in 1993 Mnt. Mfanasibili maintained a low profile, remaining a close advisor only to the *indlovukazi*.

DLAMINI, *iNGWENYAMA* MSWATI II (c. 1825–1865). The son of *iNgwenyama* **Sobhuza Dlamini I** and his chief wife **Tsandzile Ndwandwe**. Mswati II became, along with his father, the greatest consolidator and empire builder of the 19th-century Swazi kings. Mswati's rash and sometimes violent temperament, which later contributed to his reputation as the greatest of the Swazi fighting kings, nearly kept him from the succession, because his father did not view him as a worthy heir. Indeed, late in life when Sobhuza was seriously ill, he had been persuaded by **laVumisa Ndwandwe**, one of Tsandzile's *tinhlanti*, to name her son **Mnt. Malambule Dlamini** as his heir. Once recovered, Sobhuza backed away from his promise, giving the disappointed pretender several hundred cattle as compensation. Thus were the seeds of a later princely rebellion sown. Upon Sobhuza's death in 1839 Tsandzile was able to put forward Mswati's candidacy successfully with the regents in spite of his relative youth (15 years) because of his impeccable political credentials.

Mswati's selection was a circumstance that begged for trouble, considering the handful of elder brothers who viewed their own legitimacy in a different light, and the trouble was not long in coming. The first challenges came at a time when Mswati was still too young to defend himself. First around 1840 an elder brother, **Mnt. Fokotsi Dlamini**, launched a rebellion from his headquarters near **Mahamba**. The revolt never got very far, for lack of hoped-for popular support, before being shattered on the slopes of Mahamba hill at the hands of **Bnt. Malunge** and **Somcuba Dlamini**.

Then came the rebellion of Mnt. Malambule in 1845, centered near modern-day Lavumisa in the southwest, all the more serious because he managed to attract the alliances of two outsiders. The first was Wesleyan missionary **Rev. James Allison**, whose alleged "alliance" with Malambule was more a matter of proximity to the prince's field headquarters than anything else. The second was King **Mpande Zulu**, who saw in Malambule's predicament the pretext to extend his influence into southern Swaziland. In response to that latter threat Mswati also resorted to diplomacy, concluding a treaty in 1846 with **Transvaal** Afrikaners headquartered at **Ohrigstad** by which he ceded land bounded by the Crocodile and Olifants rivers in return for military support and 100 head of cattle. That treaty, which in effect initiated the **concessions** era for which Mswati's son *iNgwenyama* **Mbandzeni Dlamini** was to become infamous, provided the basis for Mswati's calling on Ohrigstad Afrikaner assistance against Malambule. In September 1846 Mnt. Somcuba, aided by the guns of a handful of Afrikaners, overran Malambule's forces at

Rev. Allison's mission station. Malambule fled to Mpande's territory, where he was subsequently executed.

Those very successes of Mnt. Somcuba, who had himself negotiated the Afrikaner treaty and had defeated the princely renegades, now emboldened him to assert his own dynastic claims as one of Sobhuza's senior sons. The issue was his refusal of Mswati's orders to deliver up some royal cattle. Mswati attacked his cave redoubt along the **Komati River**, and Somcuba thereupon fled for protection (c. 1850) to the newly established Afrikaner settlement at Lydenburg. There he remained for five years, establishing his own sovereignty by incorporating neighboring clans and celebrating his own *iNcwala* **ceremony** (a blatantly treasonous act), periodically fending off Swazi attacks and in general poisoning Mswati's relations with the Afrikaners. Only in 1855 was Mswati able to catch Somcuba in a surprise attack and finish him off, ending the last serious threat to his sovereignty—although jealous brethren plagued him until his dying day.

Those domestic challenges, combined with the threats of Zulu expansionism from the south (particularly the 1847 Zulu invasion) and **Pedi** rivalry to the north, sparked as defense mechanisms a succession of royal administrative reforms and ritual initiatives undertaken by Mswati and the influential *indlovukazi* Tsandzile. That many of them mirrored what had been done in other **Nguni**-speaking (especially **Ndwandwe**) societies did not detract from the fact that *in toto* they centralized and immeasurably strengthened the hand of the royal house at a time when it was most embattled at home and abroad. Mswati established royal villages in the countryside and manned them with loyal princes, wives, and functionaries. He formed nationwide *emabutfo* and kept them mobilized around royal capitals and residences for long periods of time. He reinvigorated the *iNcwala* ceremony and added his own innovations, as well as appropriating rainmaking powers and eliminating rival claimants to those and other ritual powers. Finally, Mswati waged a protracted campaign throughout his reign to incorporate, sometimes by diplomacy (such as dynastic marriages) but if necessary by force, those clans (*Emakhandza Mbile*—"Those Found Ahead") which had remained independent of **Dlamini** rule until then. That meant that they then became liable to common forms of royal surplus extraction, differential *lilobolo* demands between royalty and commoners, and tribute labor in royal fields at certain times of the agricultural cycle.

Thus did Mswati's royal house consolidate its domestic control and its ability to project power abroad, and in the process enrich itself. That was best reflected in a new decisiveness in the king's conduct of foreign relations during the latter half of his reign, when he pushed with boldness where he felt strongest and moved with diplomatic cleverness where he did not. Moving his military capital north to Hhohho in the early 1850s, Mswati proceeded to dispatch his regiments north into country claimed by the **Pedi**, and northeast to challenge the Portuguese in Mozambique. During the early 1860s Mswati even dabbled in the politics of succession in the Shangane empire, only to get his knuckles rapped by backing the losing candidate. To the west, he ceded (1855) a 7-mile (12-kilometer) wide strip of territory from the **Komati** to the Pongola rivers (to the **Lydenburg** Afrikaners)—apparently with no intention of making good, for he then proceeded to settle it with his own followers. To the south, where Mpande's incursions in 1847 and 1852 set him back, Mswati appealed to British authorities in Natal to rein the Zulu king in, going so far as to offer a sister in marriage to **Theophilus Shepstone**, secretary for native affairs.

In sum, Mswati's successes in consolidating the Swazi state and in expanding its borders to unprecedented distances were impressive. Perhaps his (and Tsandzile's) greatest accomplishment was to build a set of state institutions so strong that they withstood intact the buffetings of not only the disastrous reigns of the 19th-century kings who followed him but all the various assaults posed against them during the colonial era as well. Many of those institutions constitute the basis of the Swazi polity to this day.

DLAMINI, *iNGWENYAMA* **MSWATI III (1968–).** Son of *iNgwenyama* **Sobhuza Dlamini II** and **Ntombi Twala**. Ntombi was a young queen from a clan not known for producing kings, and whose father was not a chief. In the matter of the succession, in Mswati's favor (as against this relatively low pedigree) were the facts that he was his mother's only son and that he appeared to be very bright and a favorite of his father. It was Sobhuza who had given the infant prince his name, "Makhosetive" ("King of Many Nations"). Makhosetive's selection was therefore one of the most controversial aspects of an interregnum clouded with intrigue. Sobhuza had signed, shortly before his death, a decree that provided for the *ingwenyama*'s functions to be carried out by the *indlovukazi* acting as queen regent, and that in the event of her incapacity they be performed by a senior prince termed the "authorized person." It also provided for the formation of a new *Liqoqo* (with the "L" capitalized), redefined as the "Supreme Council of State." The decree named **Dzeliwe Shongwe** as *indlovukazi* and regent, and following the king's death she in turn accepted the purported nominations by Sobhuza of 15 members of the new *Liqoqo*. Finally, she endorsed the senior princes' choice of Mnt. Sozisa Dlamini, son of the late **Mnt. Logcogco Dlamini**, as authorized person. Because none of those provisions had any constitutional precedent and some were shrouded in suspicion (notably the *Liqoqo* roster, which was never produced), and because the exact nature of Sobhuza's own death was highly suspect, Dzeliwe's position from the outset appeared untenable. Fortunately, although unlettered, she proved to be a woman of extraordinary character and determination.

She needed those qualities, for it quickly became evident that the *Liqoqo*, led by **Mnt. Mfanasibili Dlamini**, meant to set itself up as the new government, leaving only the trappings of the traditional monarchy in place. At first only Dzeliwe, *Liqoqo* member **Mnt. Gabheni Dlamini**, prime minister **Mnt. Mabandla Dlamini** (representing the government), and a few loyalist allies stood in their way. Such was the nature of the struggle that *iNkhosana* (Crown Prince) Makhosetive was first secluded in various royal villages for his safety, then whisked abroad under guard to the Sherborne school in Britain. By November 1983, when parliamentary elections were held, the Mfanasibili faction appeared to have prevailed. First Mabandla was dismissed and hastily fled the country for his own safety, replaced as prime minister by *Liqoqo* loyalist **Mnt. Bhekimpi Dlamini**. Then Dzeliwe herself was deposed (under Mnt. Sozisa's signature) and replaced by the more malleable Ntombi as *indlovukazi*, while Mnt. Gabheni came within a whisker of being arrested. In the end, however, Gabheni mustered enough powerful allies in both the *Liqoqo* and the government to prevail, rallying them in mid-1985 to effect the removal of Mfanasibili and a conspirator, **Dr. George Msibi**, from the *Liqoqo*. It was at that point that the *Liqoqo* reverted to its original advisory function. In early 1986 Mfanasibili was arrested, convicted of "defeating the ends of justice," and sentenced to seven years in prison, effectively ending the *Liqoqo* coup. As part of the modernists' counter-coup, Makhosetive was returned prematurely from **Britain** and crowned as *iNgwenyama* Mswati Dlamini II in April 1986.

Much of Mswati's initial decade in power was devoted to shoring up the institution of the monarchy, which had been so badly undermined during the interregnum. Several circumstances made his efforts less than successful. First, the young king, like his father before him, took the reins of a troubled monarchy before completing his formal education and immediately demonstrated as much interest in enjoying its perquisites as he did in attending to the affairs of state. Whereas Sobhuza arguably had done so with a politician's eye toward demonstrating his "progressivism," there appeared to be little political motivation behind Mswati's lavish spending on luxuries, foreign travel, and an extravagant palace. Second, Mswati's early measures to deal with the *Liqoqo* plotters, reshuffling the cabinet and trying the conspirators for treason, were undercut by the transparent venality of the men he chose as his closest advisors, whose character was perceived as little different from the ones he had had prosecuted. Third, in increasing numbers the Swazi middle class, frustrated politically since 1973 by Sobhuza's return to autocracy and seeing little in Mswati's actions that gave hope for a return to democracy, joined dissatisfied workers in their labor activism and public protests or formed new, extra-legal opposition movements aimed at bringing about a constitutional monarchy. Finally, the dramatic events leading to a parliamentary democracy in **South Africa** after 1990 fueled a general sense of political disquiet among the educated Swazi population and elements of the press, which was not appeased by Mswati's arguments that those events held no relevance to Swaziland's circumstances.

Consequently Mswati's early reign was characterized by moves reactive to domestic crises rather than pursuant to a reasoned and positive agenda. In response to the 1989 formation of the main opposition group, the **People's United Democratic Movement (PUDEMO)**, which took the lead in industrial action, Mswati first appointed a former trade unionist, **Obed Dlamini**, as his new prime minister, but then increasingly resorted to police repression to curb dissent. In 1990 the PUDEMO leadership was arrested and put on trial for treason and sedition, but with none being found guilty. That same year student demonstrations at the **University of Swaziland** and by the nationwide **Swaziland Youth Congress** were brutally repressed. When those measures proved to have served only to heighten social tensions, Mswati moved to defuse them by forming study commissions addressing the root causes of popular dissent. In 1990 he launched a review of the *tinkhundla* electoral system first put in place by his late father, Sobhuza, in 1978. That review, which dragged on for nearly three years, produced a slightly revised system (including a secret ballot at the final stage), but one still firmly under control of the *ingwenyama*. New elections under the revised *tinkhundla* system were characterized by government repression of political parties including arrests of opposition candidates and low voter participation.

Consequently political tensions continued to be expressed in alternative venues. The activist **Swaziland Federation of Trade Unions** led a series of sometimes violent strikes from 1994 onwards. Both the **Swaz-**

iland **National Association of Teachers** and the Swaziland National Association of Civil Servants took on more radical, anti-government stances. In 1995 the parliament building was petrol-bombed. In the face of those circumstances and apparently eager to be seen as newly responsive to popular concerns, the *ingwenyama* in mid-1996 formed a **Constitutional Review Commission (CRC)** to write a draft constitution and submit it to him within two years. In mid-1998 the king extended the CRC's deadline for another two years, but clearly certain radical elements within the opposition took that action as an indication of yet further delay, which was unacceptable. In late 1998 bombs were detonated on a bridge along the main **Manzini-Mbabane** highway, and at the deputy prime minister's office in the capital. The bombing campaign continued, with a massive blast (November 1999) leveling the headquarters of the Royal Mahlanya Inkhundla, just two miles (three kilometers) distant from the Royal Administrative Capital at **Ludzidzini**. That escalation cast new doubt at the very least on the practicality of the CRC's timetable, and ultimately on its efficacy as the chosen mechanism to initiate the solution of the kingdom's constitutional problems.

DLAMINI, *iNGWENYAMA* NDVUNGUNYE (c. 1755–c. 1805). Son and heir of *iNgwenyama* **Ngwane Dlamini** by his chief wife, Lomvulo Mndzebele. Ndvungunye succeeded his father in about 1775. His reign was noted for its violence, partly because of his reputed ill-tempered and cruel personality, partly because he introduced an early version of the *emabutfo* (regimental) system, and partly because of the legendary early-19th-century **Madlathule famine**, which severely strained ecological resources and ensured that whatever food remained would be fiercely contested. Ndvungunye used his regiments to secure his father's conquests and to incorporate new ones, notably a branch of the Simelane clan. It was **Somnjalose Simelane**, *inhlanti* to her older sister **Lojiba Simelane**, who bore Ndvungunye's son and heir, *iNgwenyama* **Sobhuza Dlamini I**. Such was Ndvungunye's terrible bile that when he was struck down by lightning in about 1805, his death was widely assumed to have been the work of ancestral anger. Ndvungunye was buried apart from his father in the koppie at **Mlokotfwa**.

DLAMINI, *MNTFWANENKHOSI* NDWANDWA (c. 1820–1874). Son of *iNgwenyama* **Sobhuza Dlamini I** and File Ndwandwe, sister and *inhlanti* of **Tsandzile Ndwandwe**. When *iNgwenyama* **Mswati Dlamini II** died in 1865 Mnt. Ndwandwa became a regent (with Tsandzile as queen regent) during the minority of *iNgwenyama* **Ludvonga Dlamini**

II. Ndwandwa was, however, reputed to be a treacherous man, and he came to be suspected of harboring evil intentions toward Ludvonga in order to further his own interests. When Ludvonga died suddenly in 1874 Ndwandwa immediately became suspect as his murderer. Consequently, on the orders of Tsandzile and senior princes, he was executed and his homesteads were leveled.

DLAMINI, *iNGWENYAMA* NGWANE (c. 1735–c. 1775). Also Ngwane Dlamini III. Son and successor of *iNgwenyama* **Dlamini III**, who by about 1770 was leading his followers (*baka Ngwane*, "People of Ngwane") west from the **Lebombo Mountains** and north across the Pongola River into southern Swaziland, establishing the first Dlamini presence there. In doing so Ngwane's followers split off from the **Ndwandwe** (who remained south of the Pongola); both were distancing themselves from the Tembe consolidation of the eastern reaches of the Lebombo Mountains. Ngwane placed his royal capital at **Zombodze** in the southern Mhlosheni hills near the Mthambe tributary to the iNgwavuma River. It was at Zombodze that the Dlamini first danced the *iNcwala* ceremony. Ngwane later built his *lilawu* (administrative capital) at Hhohho, 9 miles (15 kilometers) to the northwest, near the confluence of the Ngwedze with the iNgwavuma River. Once established, he conquered and incorporated the Sihlongonyane, Nkonyane, and Manana **clans**. Ngwane died and was succeeded by his son, *iNgwenyama* **Ndvungunye Dlamini**, about 1775. Ngwane was the first of the Swazi kings to be buried at a rocky koppie known as **Mlokotfwa**, near Mhlosheni.

DLAMINI, *MNTFWANENKHOSI* NGWEKAZI. Son of *iNgwenyama* **Ndvungunye Dlamini**, who rebelled and attempted to usurp leadership of the Dlamini following *iNgwenyama* **Sobhuza Dlamini I**'s departure from **Shiselweni** on his expeditions into central and northern Swaziland during the late 1810s. For a brief period Ngwekazi took control of the Shiselweni region, but he was thwarted by **Maloyi Mamba**, who refused to countenance the coup, called Sobhuza to return, and then helped him to place himself back in power.

DLAMINI, *MNTFWANENKHOSI* NKHOPOLO (c. 1845–?). Second son of *iNgwenyama* **Mswati Dlamini II** by his senior ritual wife, Lozinyanga Matsebula. Forbidden by custom to succeed his father because of his maternal parentage, Nkhopolo became an officer in *iNgwenyama* **Mbandzeni**'s crack *iNdhlavela* **regiment**. But Nkhopolo grew disenchanted with Mbandzeni's dissolute concessioning, eventually becoming the leading traditionalist at **Mbekelweni** in opposition to the king's opportunist *tindvuna* led by **Tikhuba Magongo**. In December 1888 Mnt. Nkhopolo was attacked by Mbandzeni's regiments for having been part of a conspiracy to kill the *ingwenyama*. The conspirators, led by **Sandlane Zwane**, had intended to make Nkhopolo Mbandzeni's successor. Zwane and several others were put to death, but Nkhopolo escaped to Forbes Reef, where he was secreted in a mine shaft until things had cooled off, following which he was spirited off to the safety of **David Forbes**'s farm Athole in **New Scotland**. There he later died and was buried.

DLAMINI, OBED M. Swazi trade unionist who was appointed by *iNgwenyama* **Mswati Dlamini III** to be Swaziland's prime minister in mid-1990. Dlamini had been a founder and general secretary of the **Swaziland Federation of Trade Unions**. It was widely assumed that the king appointed him to reduce the danger of **trade union** activism to the future of the monarchy. What the king apparently did not understand was that Dlamini's recent position as a personnel manager in a large food processing company had made his labor credentials suspect with his former constituency. In any event Dlamini's term of office was punctuated by both violent labor protests and highly dramatic demonstrations of political opposition, and the methods his government used to put some of them down triggered public disfavor. Consequently Dlamini remained prime minister only until October 1993, when he lost his seat in the *tinkhundla* parliamentary elections. Dlamini was, however, appointed a senator by the new House of Assembly. He and his cabinet, most of them widely perceived as liberals, were replaced by Mswati with conservative royalists, led by Mnt. Mblini Dlamini as prime minister. Obed Dlamini emerged in the late 1990s as a leader of **Dr. Ambrose Zwane**'s revived left-wing **Ngwane National Liberatory Congress**.

DLAMINI, POLYCARP MAFELETIVENI (1918–1986). A central figure in Swaziland politics from the early 1950s until his death. Dlamini was a graduate of the **Swazi National High School**, then studied for a social science degree at the University College of Natal from 1947–51 while working as a social welfare and probation officer. In 1952 he returned at *iNgwenyama* **Sobhuza Dlamini II**'s request to serve as secretary to the *libandla*, a post he held until 1964. He continued his studies by correspondence, completing his B.A. in social science from the University of South Africa in 1957. Dlamini thenceforth became, along with **Msindazwe Sukati**, one of the two Swazi politicians most in the public's (and the *ingwenyama*'s) eye.

Beginning in 1960 Dlamini became Sobhuza's main representative on constitutional matters when he was appointed to the first Constitutional Committee. In 1961 he attended the first London Constitutional Conference as the *ingwenyama*'s personal representative. In 1963 he participated in the second London **Constitutional Conference** as a member of the *libandla* delegation. In 1964 Dlamini was made one of eight *libandla* representatives to the **Legislative Council** (Legco), and he was subsequently appointed by the Queen's Commissioner, **Sir Francis Loyd**, to the first Legco cabinet as member for education and health. One year later Loyd appointed him to his pre-independence Constitutional Committee. Following the 1967 election *ingwenyama* Sobhuza named him to his first cabinet as Minister of Works, Power, and Communication, a post he held until 1972, when he was made Minister of Justice.

Once Sobhuza repealed the constitution in 1972 he named Dlamini chairman of the Royal Constitutional Commission (1973–75). The commission's 1975 report was never made public; instead, the *ingwenyama* appointed a new commission, which in 1978 opted for a new constitution reconstituting the sovereign monarchy and a parliamentary election system based on *tinkhundla* under control of the *ingwenyama*. Following Sobhuza's death in 1982, Dlamini distanced himself from parliamentary government and threw in his lot with the *Liqoqo* forces, masterminding their strategy but never formally joining them. In 1984 he was rewarded with the directorship of the **Tibiyo takaNgwane Fund**, which he held until his death.

DLAMINI, *MNTFWANENKHOSI* SENCABAPHI (1901–?). Daughter of *iNgwenyama* **Bhunu Dlamini** and laMndzebele, and half-sister of *iNgwenyama* **Sobhuza Dlamini II**. Sencabaphi was 1 of 12 youths sent with Sobhuza for secondary schooling at the **Lovedale Missionary Institution** in 1916. When **Mnt. Tongotongo Dlamini**, who had been sent abroad in 1916 to be the main wife of Chief Dinane **Ndwandwe**, died in 1918, Sencabaphi was sent in her place. She went at Sobhuza's personal request. Sencabaphi produced two daughters for Dinane but no son, a personal tragedy compounded by the fact that Tongotongo's original *lilobolo* had amounted to 100 cattle. The pressure of leaving Dinane without a proper male heir led her to retreat for long periods to **Lobamba**, and she remained there permanently following his death.

DLAMINI, *iNGWENYAMA* SOBHUZA I (c. 1780–1839). Commonly referred to as Somhlohlo, "The Wonder." Along with *iNgwenyama* **Mswati Dlamini II**, the towering figure among 19th-century Swazi kings. Son of *iNgwenyama* **Ndvungunye Dlamini** and **Somnjalose Simelane**, Sobhuza succeeded his father shortly after the latter was killed by lightning in about 1805. Somnjalose, while Sobhuza's mother, was not the *indlovukazi* at first; rather, she was *inhlanti* to Ndvungunye's queen, **Lojiba Simelane**, who later became Sobhuza's first *indlovukazi*. Somnjalose always wielded great influence on her son, and when she later became *indlovukazi* following Lojiba's death, she used her new powers to restrain the *ingwenyama* as none had before her.

Ndvungunye's unpropitious death around 1805 meant that Sobhuza undoubtedly succeeded him precipitously and then hastened to consolidate his power. Huw Jones observes that Sobhuza established no new royal homesteads, simply continuing use of the ones established by his father and grandfather, principally **Zombodze** and **Lobamba**.[7] Ndvungunye had made the **iNkhosi Dlamini** the dominant **clan** among numerous contesting clans in southern Swaziland; it was Sobhuza's immediate accomplishment to transform that dominance into kingship. The region he came to command was known as **Shiselweni** ("Place of Burning"), stretching from modern Hluti (east) to **Mahamba** (west), and from the Pongolo River (south) to the iNgwavuma watershed (north). Its alluvial soils were rich and well watered. Those southern clans, the *Bemdzabuko* ("True Swazi"), formed the core of Sobhuza's following and remain the ethnic heart of the Swazi nation to this day.

Sobhuza's greatest foreign threat lay to the south across the Pongolo River, where **Zwide Ndwandwe** commanded the **Ndwandwe** confederation that dominated northern Natal. The Ndwandwe were longer established than the Swazi, and Zwide was further advanced in consolidating his rule, most probably along age group lines across clans. Zwide was also using those regiments to consolidate his southern marches against first the Mthethwa, and then the Zulu, and also his northern flank along the Pongolo River against the Swazi. That meant periodic raids across the river into Sobhuza's tenuous defenses along its northern bank, especially during the years of drought and occasional famine (i.e., the **Madlathule famine**) during the early 1800s. In desperation Sobhuza, resorting to diplomacy in time of weakness, sought a wife from among Zwide's daughters. Zwide's choice, **Tsandzile Ndwandwe**, was a fateful one. She arrived in about 1813 accompanied by four *tinhlanti* and proceeded to profoundly alter the course of 19th-century Swazi history.

Diplomatically in the short run the marriage did Sobhuza no good at all. In 1816, in the midst of a prolonged drought, Zwide launched a campaign to secure the rich croplands of the Pongolo-iNgwavuma River watershed, and although the Ndwandwe **regiments** ultimately retreated, Sobhuza had escaped by a whisker. Shaken, he determined to move out of Zwide's reach and into a more defensible region. Taking with him those few *Bemdzabuko* followers willing to cast their lots with him, he headed north, skirting the **highveld** in the west of Swaziland. Sobhuza tarried for a while at Nqabaneni (northeast of modern **Mankayane**) and reached as far as the Dhlomodhlomo hills in the upper **Komati River** valley before doubling back and halting again near Nqabaneni. Ultimately he and his followers settled in the **Ezulwini Valley** in the west-central **middleveld** of Swaziland. There they found rich and well-watered soils comparable to Shiselweni, protected by a ring of rugged hills on three sides, and with defensible caves in the **Mdzimba** range to the east offering an emergency retreat. Those caves were to stand him in good stead.

The clans that occupied west-central Swaziland were both Sotho- and **Nguni**-speaking (the *Emakhandza Mbili,* "Those Found Ahead"), and Sobhuza set about incorporating them by various means into his core of followers. Some he enticed into the fold by means of diplomacy, in which case they paid him tribute in return for retaining the trappings of independence. Others he conquered. Still others he destroyed, incorporating the survivors. It was in the Ezulwini Valley that he built his new headquarters, Langeni, and the royal homestead for *iNdlovukazi* Lojiba Simelane, **Lobamba**, where the *iNcwala* ceremony was celebrated.

In the interim two events had transpired to Sobhuza's south which affected his position. First, a brother, **Mnt. Magwegwe Dlamini**, who had attempted to take power while Sobhuza was campaigning to the north in the Dhlomodhlomo hills, was foiled by the refusal of **Maloyi Mamba** to join him. Instead Maloyi sent for Sobhuza, and it was for that reason that the *ingwenyama* returned to central Swaziland in 1820. Those actions secured Sobhuza's southern flank, but at the price of a high degree of perpetual autonomy that Sobhuza was obliged to grant to Maloyi and his Mamba successors in return for his loyalty. The second event was the smashing defeat of Zwide's armies at the hands of **Shaka Zulu** in 1819, which substituted the Zulu state for the Ndwandwe as Sobhuza's (and his successors') principal southern threat. In response Sobhuza again tried diplomacy, sending two of his daughters to Shaka in marriage. Shaka eventually executed them, and in 1827 he sent an army after Sobhuza, who was forced to beat a retreat to the Mdzimba caves with his followers and their cattle. The Zulu finally withdrew but returned the following year and again forced the Swazi to the caves. Shaka's real quarry that year was the Ndwandwe under Soshangane to the north, and again Sobhuza escaped destruction. Consequently the news of Shaka's assassination later in 1828 must have swept through the Ezulwini Valley like a welcome breeze.

It was then that, enjoying for the first time some breathing space, Sobhuza set about aggrandizing himself with captured cattle, trade goods, and human captives. He launched attacks northward against Sotho clans in the central and eastern **Transvaal**, and to the south across the Pongolo River into Zulu territory. He repeated those latter raids several times between 1829 and 1836, finally provoking a Zulu retaliatory attack that year to punish him. The Zulu made off with 6,000 head of Swazi cattle while Sobhuza again sought the refuge of the caves, once more saving himself to fight another day. That occasion came in 1839 when, in quest of stolen cattle and retribution for renewed Swazi raids, **Dingane Zulu** once more launched an attack across the Pongolo aimed at Sobhuza's military village of Lubuya commanding the iNgwavuma watershed. This time Sobhuza was waiting for him, and his troops defeated the Zulu with heavy casualties during the ensuing **Battle of Lubuya**.

Lubuya was, however, Sobhuza's final victory, for he died shortly afterward. Sobhuza's hallowed place in Swazi history is fully justified. He was a brilliant military tactician and strategist who picked able field commanders but who also knew the value of retreat when circumstances dictated. He was a skilled diplomat and politician who understood when to negotiate and when to be ruthless. Using all his skills Sobhuza fashioned a working state out of scattered and disparate clans, and he constructed a regimental system that both forged the Swazi polity and defended it against formidable enemies. Finally, Sobhuza was also known as a visionary who acted on his perceptions. Shortly before he died he was said to have had a vision involving white-skinned people who arrived carrying books and coinage.[8] He advised his councilors to accept the book (Bible) but to eschew the money, and under no circumstances to harm the whites under pain of their own destruction. Parts of the story are undoubtedly mythical, but it points up Sobhuza's worldly wisdom. The fact was that as early as 1834 the king had sent emissaries to the Wesleyan **mission** at Kuruman requesting that missionaries be sent to his kingdom. It took another 10 years for the first of them, **Rev. James Allison**, to arrive, long after Sobhuza's own death. Allison's placement by the regents around Mahamba in the south, obviously as a buffer against the Zulu, unquestionably reflected Sobhuza's strategic thinking.

Sobhuza was succeeded by his son, Mnt. Mswati II, by his chief wife, Tsandzile Ndwandwe.

DLAMINI, *iNGWENYAMA* SOBHUZA II (1899–1982). Birth name **Mnt. Nkhotfotjeni** ("Lizard"). The greatest figure in the 20th-century political history of Swaziland, and along with the 19th-century *tiNgwenyama* **Sobhuza Dlamini I** and **Mswati Dlamini II**, one of the three greatest kings in the Swazi pantheon. Son of *iNgwenyama* **Bhunu Dlamini** and **Lomawa Ndwandwe**, his nomination as successor shortly after Bhunu's death came as the result of *iNdlovukazi* **Labotsibeni Mdluli**'s intervention to end a contentious dispute among the supporters of four contenders. Soon thereafter Labotsibeni had second thoughts about her decision on grounds that a prolonged regency following the previous quarter century of political turbulence constituted a grave threat to the monarchy. She sought to have **Mnt. Malunge Dlamini** enthroned in Nkhotfotjeni's place, but that was rejected by senior members of the *libandla* as an unacceptable break with tradition. Lomawa was named *indlovukazi* while Labotsibeni, who retained the office of queen regent, exercised the dominant influence over Sobhuza's upbringing and preparation to reign.

Labotsibeni, understanding his emphatic need for a Western education in the new colonial era and yet leery of **mission** influence, established an elementary school under her watchful eye at **Zombodze** for Sobhuza and other princes, with South African mission-educated tutors as instructors. In 1916 Sobhuza was sent to the **Lovedale Missionary Institution** school in the Cape for his secondary education. Political opposition to her from various quarters, notably among influential chiefs, rose to such an alarming extent that she recalled Sobhuza to Zombodze before completion of his curriculum. There he began (early 1919) to undergo public ritualization and private preparation for rule as *ingwenyama*. Sobhuza was installed on the Swazi throne in late December 1921.

At the outset of his reign Sobhuza faced three broad, interrelated challenges to his legitimacy and effectiveness as *ingwenyama*. The first was the need to prevent at all costs the proposed transfer of Swaziland to the **Union of South Africa**, which would have been disastrous to both the monarchy and its people. The second was the imperative to continue the domestic effort begun by Labotsibeni to bring rebellious chiefs to heel and to restore the popular reputation (and hence the legitimacy) of the monarchy. The third was the requirement to wrest back from the colonial administration those levers of royal authority previously relinquished to it during the regimes of Labotsibeni, Bhunu, and *iNgwenyama* **Mbandzeni Dlamini**. Most notable among them were the **private revenue concession** monies payable to the royal house, control by the monarchy over the lost concessions, and the crown's monopoly over criminal jurisdiction. In 1921 that seemed to be an impossible set of tasks, but Sobhuza's spectacular successes in achieving most of them held the key to his political triumphs by the time that independence was achieved in 1968.

Sobhuza's initial tactics (1921–26) were influenced by the progressive education (and acculturation) he had received from his tutors and at Lovedale, and by his associations with the progressives influential at the Zombodze court, most notably **Pixley kaI. Seme**. During this period he dressed fashionably and acquired the impedimenta of the African progressive: furniture and a shortwave radio, an expensive automobile—and a substantial bank overdraft. More important, he undertook a modern legal assault on the legitimacy of the Mbandzeni-era concessions by having his American-educated lawyer, Pixley Seme, sue the concessionaire **Allister Miller** in colonial court for trespass and for unlawful ejectment of his subjects. Sobhuza lost both the original case and the final appeal to the Privy Council (1926), a reversal that raised popular questions as to his judgment and left him deeply in debt. In response Sobhuza changed his tactics and at the same time altered his persona, refashioning himself into an arch-traditionalist. Thenceforth "traditionalism," authentic or manufactured, became both the essence and the basis of his political legitimacy. Many years later Sobhuza confirmed the crucial importance of his close friend **Allan G. Marwick**'s advice in his decision to make himself over.

Sobhuza's transformation coincided with the growing British realization that effective colonial administration in the future would depend on a change from past paternalism and repression to the true substance of "**indirect rule**." That change of policy was most notable during the term of **T. Ainsworth Dickson** as **resident commissioner** (1928–35), as advised by his deputy and long-standing Swazi administrator, Allan G. Marwick. Dickson found ways to restore to Sobhuza much of the domestic authority previously undermined by his predecessors, and the *ingwenyama* in turn used some of that power to assist Dickson in local governance—and in the process to discipline rebellious chiefs. That symbiosis was continued throughout the residency of Dickson's successor, Allan Marwick (1935–37), and until such time as later resident commissioners initiated the official campaign to impose restrictions on Sobhuza's domestic sovereignty, in the form of the proposed **Native** Authority (later **Administration**) **Proclamation**, beginning in 1939.

As early as the beginning of the 1930s Sobhuza was investing some of his newly recouped prestige to revive "traditionalism" as the foundation of his domestic authority and to demonstrate to his subjects that he was standing up to the British. There was no better example of that than his establishment of the **Swazi National High School** in 1931 at **Matsapha** as an institution specifically free from all mission influence and from most government funding. Sobhuza, fearing the consequences of Western (even non-mission) education on his traditional authority over Swazi youth, insisted that the 19th-century *emabutfo* system be revived and practiced by the boys in the school. When the European missions opposed his plan, he successfully enlisted (through Marwick) the support of the South African functionalist anthropology establishment to his cause. Likewise he instituted a regimenting *umcwasho* (coming of age) ceremony for all girls.

By 1940 Sobhuza had succeeded in gaining considerable leverage over his own people and with the British. In part this was because the latter needed his assistance in recruiting troops for the **African Pioneer Corps (APC)**. His recruiting efforts provided him with another opportunity to assist the war effort while simultaneously using the APC as a means to reinforce, for both domestic and colonial consumption, his traditional authority over all military affairs. British need to consolidate the empire in support of its war mobilization was behind its passage of the **Colonial Development and Welfare Act** of 1940 (CDW), but in truth it was Sobhuza's forceful petition to Westminster in 1941 that led to the allocation by war's end of £200,000 in CDW funds toward the purchase of several hundred thousand acres for the first **Swaziland Native Land Settlement Scheme** (1943).

Nothing, however, demonstrated the resurgence of Sobhuza's authority as did his protracted and successful resistance to the government's proposed Native Administration Proclamation, first put forward in 1939 as the prospect of Swaziland's anticipated transfer to the Union flickered. Sobhuza and the *libandla* objected principally to the provision that the powers to appoint and depose chiefs, including the "**paramount chief**," be vested in the resident commissioner. The fact that similar proclamations had been successfully promulgated previously in other British African colonies, notably Basutoland (1938), made Sobhuza and the *libandla* no less tenacious in their joint campaign against it. The proclamation was finally gazetted in 1944 but never fully implemented because of Sobhuza's strong objections. Consequently an amended Native Administration Proclamation (1950) stripped out the objectionable clauses, leaving the powers in question solely to the "Paramount Chief in Libandla." That same year the gazetting of the **Native Courts** and **Na-**

tional Treasury Proclamations restored to Sobhuza a substantial degree of autonomy in both civil and criminal jurisdiction lost to the British in 1904, and in the expenditure of Swazi tax funds, untypical of British colonies elsewhere. Those victories, which were unique in sub-Saharan Africa, were the first discernible steps in Sobhuza's triumphal emergence as head of state by the time of independence in 1968.

That was so because the *ingwenyama* was able to enter into the campaigns leading to independence with unprecedented vigor born of his enhanced powers and new prestige. Beginning in 1962 **Britain** took initial steps to form a **Legislative Council** of Europeans and Africans and to write a constitution preparatory to independence. Two **Constitutional Conferences**, held in London during 1962 and 1963, drew representatives from the monarchy, the colonial government, and opposition political parties recently formed by both Europeans and Swazi in anticipation of handover. Issues concerning the constitutional powers of the *ingwenyama*, the vesting of mineral rights, and the method of electing legislative council members remained unresolved, leading to a London-imposed **constitution (1964)** that satisfied no one but formed the basis for the legislative elections held later that year. In what proved to be a political master stroke Sobhuza formed a modern political party, the **Imbokodvo National Movement**, which smashed all opposition parties, Swazi and European, garnering 85 percent of the vote. Over the following three years Sobhuza managed to parlay that mandate into a new independence **constitution (1967)**, which granted executive powers to and vested the kingdom's mineral wealth in him, not in **parliament**. That document in turn helped determine the largely nondemocratic character of postindependence political and economic development of the kingdom.

Sobhuza, following independence, chafed at even the pseudo-parliamentary structure of government left in place by Britain, believing that it threatened to institutionalize opposition to the monarchy in a way that would be inimical to orderly development. Following the 1972 election, in which the opposition **Ngwane National Liberatory Congress** won seats in parliament for the first time, Sobhuza acted. In April 1973, after failing to nullify certain aspects of that election, the *ingwenyama* repealed the constitution, dismissed parliament, banned all political parties, and announced that he would henceforward rule by decree pending implementation of a new constitution reflective of tradition. That constitution, promulgated in 1978 and this time unwritten, placed the parliamentary electoral process unequivocally back under the royal thumb.

Based on regional councils (***tinkhundla***) that he had established in the mid-1950s as a means of extending centralized administration and simultaneously outflanking local chiefs' powers, the system ensured that voting for new parliamentarians would henceforward be indirect, public, and overseen by the *ingwenyama*'s representatives. Emergency regulations including a South African–type preventive detention act, along with the formation of a new army, the **Royal Umbutfo Defense Force** (1973), equipped by Pretoria, ensured Sobhuza that any popular opposition to these measures could be contained successfully.

Opposition there was indeed; but now, without benefit of the democratic process, underlying social and class tensions were forced to find various extra-parliamentary means of expression. Labor **strikes**, often marked by violence, broke out among railroad workers, sugarcane cutters, and teachers (accompanied by student demonstrations) throughout the 1970s. More often than not harsh police measures were employed to counter them. Public criticism of the *ingwenyama* among the working and urban middle classes became unprecedented in its scope and bitterness. In 1978 the first illegal opposition movement, the Swaziland Liberation Movement, made its appearance. That was as far as it went, and among the rural peasantry, Sobhuza's natural constituency, loyalty to the monarchy remained essentially undiminished, and so did Sobhuza's personal popularity.

One of the consequences of Sobhuza's repeal of the constitution in 1973 was undoubtedly one he had not foreseen. That was the rise in the power and the assertiveness of the *liqoqo* by the late 1970s. In a way the king should not have been surprised, because the *libandla*, following the 1950 British declaration of the "*ingwenyama*-in-*libandla*" as the sole native authority (*see* **Native Administration Proclamations**), had asserted itself in a similar fashion. The *liqoqo*, which only began to be recognized with any formality during Sobhuza's early reign, commenced jockeying for more influence once Sobhuza's coup drew the power from parliament and the opposition parties back into the center. As Macmillan has observed, there was no better example of that than the *liqoqo*'s forcing of Sobhuza to close down Prime Minister **Mabandla Dlamini**'s government corruption inquiry in 1980 when it approached too closely the interests of its members and their allies.[9] Following the king's death the *Liqoqo*, shorn of practically all royal restraint, transformed itself unconstitutionally into a "Supreme Council of State" for several months before it was faced down and order was restored in 1985.

Partly because of the *liqoqo*'s challenge, Sobhuza during his final years turned, as some of his predecessors had done, to shoring up his own domestic power by looking to his relations with South Africa. He negotiated with Pretoria for the return of **kaNgwane**, a South African homeland for ethnic Swazi adjoining his western border, in compensation for which he was prepared to assist Pretoria in its regional battle against the **African National Congress**. In February 1982 Sobhuza signed a secret agreement to that effect with Pretoria which, when its existence was made public in 1984, did considerable damage to the late king's stature abroad. Sobhuza died in August 1982, ruling with a firm hand almost until the end. He was buried in a cave near many of his forebears at **Makhosini** in southern Swaziland. Sobhuza was succeeded by Mnt. Makhosetive Dlamini (*iNgwenyama* **Mswati Dlamini III**).

DLAMINI, *MNTFWANENKHOSI* SOLOMON MADEVU (c. 1891–1963). Mnt. Solomon (commonly referred to as "Madevu") was the son of Mnt. Mfokati Dlamini and grandson of *iNgwenyama* **Mbandzeni Dlamini**. Madevu occupied a principality (*liphakelo*) in the hills southwest of Hhohho. He was educated at the Nazarene **mission** at **Pigg's Peak** but later became a Wesleyan church member until he was expelled for polygyny. He then joined the United Swazi Christian Church in Zion and became a power in the Christian community, which pressed *iNgwenyama* **Sobhuza Dlamini II** during the 1930s and 1940s to establish a **Swazi National Church**. In 1936 Madevu was described in the colonial administration's "Confidential Report on Chiefs" as having about 1,200 followers (in whose welfare he was "not interested") and as being a member of the *liqoqo*. Madevu during the 1930s was a close advisor to Sobhuza and wrote (along with **Benjamin Nxumalo**) many of the king's speeches. During 1937–38 Madevu acted as chairman of Sobhuza's special committee to resolve chiefs' boundary disputes in the Hlatikulu region, an extremely delicate and politically important task. However, as one of Sobhuza's "office *tindvuna*" assigned to assistant commissioners' offices during the early 1940s, Madevu was dismissed from the Hlatikulu office for insubordination. Then, sometime during the 1950s, Madevu had a serious falling out with Sobhuza over a dispute involving the borders of his *liphakelo*, during which he accused the king's representatives of corruption. The bitter dispute, which estranged Madevu from Sobhuza's court, lasted until Madevu's death in 1963.

DLAMINI, *MNTFWANENKHOSI* SOMCUBA (c. 1800–1855). Eldest son of *iNgwenyama* **Sobhuza Dlamini I** and laMndzebele, and a principal in the dynastic struggles of his younger brother, *iNgwenyama* **Mswati Dlamini II**. Somcuba became especially powerful during Mswati's minority and early reign, when the young king was beset by serious rivals to the throne. At first loyal to Mswati, Somcuba led regiments successfully against his renegade brother **Mnt. Fokotsi Dlamini** near **Mahamba** in 1844, and again in the same region against another rebellious brother, **Mnt. Malambule Dlamini**, in 1846. Very quickly his relations with Mswati soured, perhaps because of the latter's experience with overly ambitious brothers, and certainly because Somcuba made off illegally with a large number of royal cattle. In 1850 Mswati sent an army north after Somcuba, which Somcuba managed to check on the banks of the **Komati River** long enough to flee to the protection of the Afrikaner community at **Lydenburg**. There he remained for five years, a constant and often provocative challenge to Mswati's claim to suzerainty in the eastern **Transvaal**, repeatedly strengthening himself by successive incorporations of Sotho elements. Somcuba was more or less tolerated by Mswati until such time as word arrived that he was performing his own *iNcwala* ceremony, a blatantly treasonous act. Mswati dispatched a regiment to attack him in his cave redoubt. Achieving total surprise by crossing a supposedly impassable river in flood, the king's regiment attacked and killed Somcuba and many of his followers.

DLAMINI, *MNTFWANENKHOSI* **TONGOTONGO (c. 1879–1918).** Daughter of *iNgwenyama* **Mbandzeni Dlamini** and **Labotsibeni Mdluli** (later *indlovukazi*); full sister of *iNgwenyama* **Bhunu Dlamini** as well as **Bnt. Malunge Dlamini** and **Lomvazi Dlamini**. Tongotongo, extremely close to her mother, was deeply involved with her in the choice of *iNgwenyama* **Sobhuza Dlamini II** as Bhunu's heir. In 1916 Tongotongo was sent abroad to become the main wife of Chief Dinane of the **Ndwandwe**, for whom 100 head of *lilobolo* cattle were exchanged. She died in 1918 while visiting **Zombodze**, leaving no heir. Subsequently **Mnt. Sencabaphi Dlamini** was sent to Dinane as a substitute. The death of Tongotongo, coming so soon after her favorite son **Malunge's** passing (1915), left Labotsibeni in a depression from which she never fully recovered.

DLANGENI. A royal burial ground in the **Mdzimba hills**, approximately four miles (six kilometers) north-northwest of **Zombodze**. Dlangeni is the burial site of *tiNgwenyama* **Ludvonga Dlamini II**, **Mbandzeni Dlamini**, and **Bhunu Dlamini**, as well as several important chiefs, notably **Mnt. Malunge waNdvungunye Dlamini**. The Dlangeni graves are guarded by a branch of the Gama **clan**. The other principal royal burial grounds are at **Makhosini** (originally Mbilaneni) and at **Mlokotfwa**, in southern Swaziland.

DOMINIONS OFFICE. In 1907 the responsibility for administration of the **High Commission Territories** was placed in the Dominions Department of the Colonial Office. That department was recast as the Dominions Office in 1925. It was further recast into the Commonwealth Relations Office in 1947.

DUPONT, CHARLES EDGAR (c. 1860–c. 1940). Eldest son of **Edward DuPont**, who lived at Mnyamatsini, near Stegi (modern **Siteki**). DuPont's only legitimate profession appears to have been as a guide to European visitors to Swaziland. Otherwise he lived by thieving and cattle rustling, often involving murder. His only lasting legacy is a substantial clan of **EurAfricans** bearing his surname, the offspring of a handful of African women who bore his children.

DUPONT, EDWARD CHARLES (c. 1833–?). Paterfamilias of the line of DuPonts inhabiting Swaziland since 1872. DuPont began his career in Swaziland while inhabiting his wife's farm in the **Little Free State**. From the beginning he made a life out of skirting the law, becoming a renowned cattle rustler. In the early 1880s DuPont moved to Stegi (**Siteki**) to work his farming and grazing **concession**. By 1890 he had sold out and invested in mining concessions, most of them invalid. DuPont was the father of **Charles DuPont**.

NOTES

1. Hugh Macmillan, "Administrators, Anthropologists and 'Traditionalists' in Colonial Swaziland: The Case of the 'Amabhaca' Fines," *Africa*, LXV, 4 (1995), 546–548.

2. Huw Jones, *A Biographical Register of Swaziland to 1902* (Pietermaritzburg: University of Natal Press, 1993), p. 19.

3. Sir Alan Pim, *Financial and Economic Situation of Swaziland: Report of the Commission Appointed by the Secretary of State for Dominion Affairs* (London: HMSO, 1932), pp. 20–23.

4. Philip Bonner, *Kings, Commoners and Concessionaires: The Evolution and Dissolution of the Nineteenth-Century Swazi State* (Cambridge: Cambridge University Press, 1983), pp. 34–37; Hilda Kuper, *An African Aristocracy: Rank Among the Swazi* (London and New York: Oxford University Press, for the International African Institute, 1947), p. 151.

5. Christopher Youé, *Robert Thorne Coryndon: Proconsular Imperialism in Southern and Eastern Africa, 1897–1925* (Waterloo, Ontario: Wilfred Laurier Press, 1986), pp. 47–78, 201.

6. Jones, *Biographical Register*, pp. 90–91.

7. Jones, *Biographical Register*, p. 178.

8. James S. M. Matsebula, *A History of Swaziland* (3d ed., Cape Town: Longman Southern Africa, 1986), p. 27. As Carolyn Hamilton has observed, prophesies and predictions have always had their political uses, not the least of which is the suggestion that an important event is inevitable or ordained. Hamilton, *Terrific Majesty: The Powers of Shaka Zulu and the Limits of Historical Invention* (Cambridge, Mass.: Harvard University Press, 1998), pp. 77, 81, 83–84, 153.

9. Hugh Macmillan, "Swaziland: Decolonisation and the Triumph of 'Tradition,'" *Journal of Modern African Studies*, XXIII, 4 (1985), 665–666.

-E-

ECKSTEIN, HERMANN (1849–1893). A South African mining magnate of German background (born and died in Stuttgart). Eckstein's investment in Swaziland **concessions** during the late 1880s (as the representative and sometime partner of Jules Porge & Company) helped bring about the collapse of the kingdom's independence. In 1889 Eckstein and Porge laid out £30,000 toward the purchase of the **private revenue concession** from its original owner, **John R. Harington**, with the intention of turning it over to the government of the **South African Republic** (SAR) upon its annexation of Swaziland. What Eckstein was seeking in compensation were various lucrative monopoly concessions situated along South Africa's Witwatersrand, along with a license to join with Cecil Rhodes in exploiting lands north of the Limpopo River. Control of the revenue and other concessions essential to governing Swaziland later became the basis for the SAR's assumption of the kingdom's administration in 1895. Subsequently the firm of H. Eckstein & Co. became a major shareholder in both Swaziland Coal Mines Ltd. and in Swaziland Tin Ltd.

EDENDALE. The Wesleyan Methodist mission station founded at Edendale, Natal, on the south bank of the upper Mgeni River, in 1851. It was founded by the Wesleyan missionary **Rev. James Allison**, who had fled with his followers from the **Mahamba** mission in southern Swaziland in 1846 to escape the dynastic wars of the early *iNgwenyama* **Mswati Dlamini II** era. Allison and his party of 400, a good number of them

Swazi converts or "believers," settled on a 6,123 acre (2,478 hectare) farm named Edendale. From the outset the African community was characterized by its adherence to capitalist principles and middle-class values. The purchasers of the farm, along with Allison, were an association of 99 African shareholders who held their plots in freehold, while the remainder of the Edendale community became renters. According to Meintjes, Edendale's innovation in African land ownership "shaped the community's into the colonial polity and economy" and became the model for other African initiatives in Natal. It also served to distance the landowner-converts (who numbered nearly 1,000 by the end of the century) even further from their pre-Christian roots. By the 1860s the market farmers of Edendale had become major suppliers of fruits, vegetables, poultry, and cattle to the nearby town of Pietermaritzburg.[1] Men also served as laborers and transport drivers. Several of the Edendale communicants would later become founding members of the **African National Congress (ANC)**, which in its early years was distinctly middle class in its makeup and values.

Edendale's strong connection with Swaziland stemmed from the fact that many of the mission's families, seeking larger landholdings and brighter opportunities elsewhere, moved away and created new settlements in the region, communities which were shaped along the same middle-class lines as the parent mission. One of them was at Mahamba, where Rev. Daniel **Msimang** and his son Joel reestablished the Methodist mission in 1882. Joel Msimang then established an outstation at **Makhosini** in 1890. Other Edendale converts who made a significant impact on Swaziland, either as landowners or as teachers and/or advisors to Queen Regent **Labotsibeni Mdluli**, were **John Gama, Josiah Vilakazi, Cleopas Kunene, Alpheus Nkosi**, and **Stephen** and **Edgar Mini. Robert Grendon**, sometime headmaster at Edendale, later became tutor to **Bnt. Malunge** and **Lomvazi Dlamini**, and subsequently to *iNkhosana* (later *iNgwenyama*) **Sobhuza Dlamini II**. Among Swazi royalty educated at Edendale were (briefly, at Labotsibeni's behest) Bnt. Malunge and Lomvazi, and **Benjamin Nxumalo**, maternal uncle and advisor to Sobhuza, as well as head of the Swaziland branch of the ANC.

EHLANE. "In the Wilderness." A large (25,000 acre, or 10,500 hectare) tract of land in the Swaziland **lowveld** along the Msulutane River, originally owned by **David Forbes, Jr.** Upon Forbes's death in 1941 Ehlane was purchased by *iNgwenyama* **Sobhuza Dlamini II** as his own estate, using **Lifa funds**. Forbes's large farmhouse became Sobhuza's first Western-style residence in Swaziland. There the king retired periodically to rest and hunt wild game (often with local and foreign dignitaries), and there for a time he installed his favorite wife, laMasuku (**Pauline Fikelephi Masuku**). In 1967 he proclaimed Ehlane a game reserve and placed it under the direction of **Terence E. Reilly**. *See also* Hlane ("Wilderness") Royal National Park

1820 SETTLERS ASSOCIATION. *See* MUSHROOM LAND SETTLEMENT SCHEME

ELGIN, NINTH EARL OF. *See* BRUCE, VICTOR A.

ELYAN, SIR VICTOR. The first chief justice of independent Swaziland, serving from 1968 to 1970. Prior to his appointment Elyan had served in the colonial legal service in the Gold Coast, then for the three **High Commission Territories** (Basutoland, Bechuanaland, and Swaziland) as a justice (finally chief justice) of the Court of Appeal.

EMABUTFO. *See LIBUTFO*

EMAFIKA MUVA. "Those Who Came Late." Terminology for a third wave of **clans** which were incorporated into the Swazi polity following the establishment of the *Bemdzabuko* ("True Swazi") and the *Emakhandza Mbili* ("Those Found Ahead"). Some of these latter groups were fleeing the effects of Zulu expansion; others were refugees from Gaza dynastic wars; still others were conquered clans. Most were incorporated during the reign of *iNgwenyama* **Mswati Dlamini II**. They included such prominent *tibongo* as Dladla, Hlatshwako, Manyatsi, Masuku, Mtsetfwa, Nhlengetfwa, Nkambule, Nxumalo, and Vilakazi.

EMAKHANDZA MBILI. "Those Found Ahead." Terminology for the large number of loosely organized **clans** occupying west-central Swaziland which *iNgwenyama* **Sobhuza Dlamini I** incorporated when he moved with the *Bemdzabuko* ("True Swazi") north from his original settlement at **Shiselweni**. As he moved Sobhuza demanded allegiance from these new clans, some of **Nguni**-speaking background and others Sotho. Those who submitted paid tribute but were otherwise allowed to retain their outward independence, often including their hereditary chiefs. Those who resisted were crushed and incorporated. The numerous *Emakhandza Mbili* included such prominent *tibongo* as Bhembe, Gama, Gamedze, Gwebu, Mabuza, Magagula, Makhubu, Maseko, Masilela, Mavimbela, Maziya, Mngometfulu, Mncina, Mnisi, Motsa, Ngwenya, Shabalala, Shabangu, Shongwe, Sifundza, Tsabedze, and Zwane. During the reign of *iNgwenyama* **Mswati Dlamini II** many of the *Emakhandza Mbili* clans demonstrating disloyalty to the throne during the early period of turbulence were in effect reincorporated with their autonomy restricted. *See also Emafika Muva*

EMALANGENI. *See* LILANGENI

EMBO. In Swazi tradition, the legendary place of origin of the **Nguni**-speaking peoples from whom the Swazi are descended. Oral tradition describes eMbo as lying to the north, in the vicinity of the great lakes of East Africa (lakes Victoria, Tanganyika, and Nyasa). They migrated southward during the late 15th century, settling for generations in the kaTembe region of southern Mozambique east of the Lubombo hills. Then, probably during the 17th century, they began their migration inland under the leadership of the **iNkhosi Dlamini**, eventually settling in what is now southern Swaziland.

EMPLOYMENT BUREAU OF AFRICA (TEBA), THE. *See* NATIVE RECRUITING CORPORATION

ENGLAND. *See* BRITAIN

ENRAGHT-MOONY, FRANCIS. *See* MOONY, FRANCIS ENRAGHT

EPHONDVO. Residence of *iNgwenyama* Sobhuza Dlamini II, in the middleveld, two miles (three kilometers) east of **Malkerns**. Ephondvo is an estate stocked with wildlife, originally owned by Baron Klaus von Oertzen, a German citizen who had once chaired the Volkswagen motor corporation before resettling in Africa. Ephondvo was sold to Sobhuza in the 1970s, and a health clinic was built on the grounds as his health failed. Sobhuza died at Ephondvo in 1982.

ESSELEN, DANIEL J. (1851–1919). Transvaal landdrost who served as the **South African Republic**'s (SAR) representative on the Government Committee (established in 1889 as the **Provisional Government Committee**) to administer white interests in Swaziland. During his tenure Esselen strongly represented the SAR's position in Swaziland. Esselen left Swaziland in 1894, but that did not end his association. As an advocate he assisted in the drafting of the **third Swaziland Convention** (1894) by which the SAR assumed administrative authority over Swaziland. In 1898, appointed a justice of the peace in Swaziland, he represented the SAR at the 1898 inquiry into *iNgwenyama* **Bhunu Dlamini**'s involvement in the assassination of **Mbhabha Nsibandze**.

EURAFRICAN. A term used to indicate persons of combined European and African descent, or less commonly, Asian-African descent. The commonplace but less acceptable term is "Coloured." Swaziland's EurAfrican population originated with the arrival of male European settlers and officials beginning in the 1880s. During the colonial era the EurAfrican population, largely by virtue of its preferential treatment by officials (in education, jobs and trading licenses, and social amenities) came to be regarded on a socioeconomic status as intermediate between Europeans and Africans. Separate schools for EurAfricans were founded in **Mbabane** (St. Mark's, 1909) and Bremersdorp (**Manzini**; St. Michael's, 1937). EurAfricans joined the **Swaziland Progressive Association** in 1929 and also later that year formed their own interest group, the **EurAfrican Welfare Association**. In that year EurAfricans residing in Swaziland numbered around 500. Swazi resentment at what they perceived as EurAfrican wealth and exclusiveness surfaced during the years following independence, manifested most notably by governmental refusal to grant them Swazi citizenship. While in 1976 the EurAfrican population had numbered 4,067, by 1991 it had dropped to around 3,200. *See also* Citizenship Act (1974)

EURAFRICAN WELFARE ASSOCIATION (EWA). Originally the Swaziland Coloured Welfare Society. The interest group and political lobbying arm of Swaziland's **EurAfrican** community. The EWA was formed in 1929, the year of the formation of the **Swaziland Progressive Association**, its counterpart Swazi interest group. Its original goals were to better the condition of the EurAfricans as distinct from the Swazi. For instance, the EWA sought special government employment opportunities and pay equal to that of Europeans, and special provision for purchase of **crown lands**, especially in urban areas. By the early 1960s, with the EurAfrican population at about 4,000, the EWA's goals had become directly linked to EurAfricans' status as Swaziland approached independence. Professor **Denis V. Cowen**, advisor to the **Swaziland Progressive Party**, also advised the EWA. The longtime president of the EurAfrican Welfare Association, **Affleck Sellstroom**, represented EurAfrican interests at the 1963 **constitutional conference** in London. There Sellstroom threw his lot in with those who favored a constitutional monarchy and opposed special privileges for Europeans. With the failure of those proposals the EurAfrican Welfare Association rapidly lost its political influence, and following independence it passed out of existence.

EUROPEAN ADVISORY COUNCIL (EAC). Swaziland's main European interest and political lobbying organization, established in 1921, the same year (not coincidentally) as the government imposition of the European poll tax. The EAC may be seen as the lobbying successor to the farmers' associations (**Swaziland Farmers Association**; Hlatikulu Farmers Association; Stegi [**Siteki**] Farmers Association) that had dominated early 20th-century European politics following the *The Times of Swaziland*'s cessation of publication in 1907. The EAC's formation was one result of the fragmentation of the farmers' associations along geographical lines, with the resultant diminution of their lobbying effectiveness. So too was the EAC forever conscious of the tensions raised by the differences, geographical and ethnic, in its membership, stretching north and south of the **Usutu River**.

Prior to World War II the EAC membership leaned geographically toward southern farmers and concerned itself primarily with such agricultural issues as labor, South African market restrictions, government veterinary services, and subsidized bulk transport by road and rail. It also lobbied continually for government-assisted British immigration and against Swaziland's incorporation into the **Union of South Africa**. Following the war, as Swaziland became the theater of forestry, agribusiness, and manufacturing capital investment, the EAC's political center shifted to the central and northern regions of the kingdom where those ventures were located. During the early postwar period its attempts to turn itself into a legislative body failed, when in 1949 its successor body, the **Reconstituted European Advisory Council (REAC),** was denied lawmaking status. The REAC was superseded by the **Legislative Council** in 1964.

EWING, ANDREW ("CAPTAIN") (?-1898). A former Castle Line merchant captain who arrived in Swaziland in 1887 after a short career as a **Barberton gold** mining entrepreneur. Ewing became an ally of **Allister Miller** and a trusted advisor to *iNgwenyama* **Mbandzeni Dlamini**. Ewing led the group that persuaded Mbandzeni to grant the establishment of the **Swazieland Committee** in 1887. Consequently Ewing's influence on Swaziland's loss of independence was strong. An early and substantial **concession** holder (minerals, grazing, and monopolies), Ewing became chairman of the Swazieland Committee in 1888. His was one of the monopoly concessions sold to the **South African Republic** that became the economic basis for its administration of the kingdom beginning in 1895. Ewing sided with the opponents of **Theophilus Shepstone, Jr.,** as advisor to Mbandzeni, leading to the latter's dismissal in 1889 in favor of Allister Miller. Miller then oversaw that period of concessioning, by far the most damaging to Swaziland's integrity.

EZULWINI VALLEY. The "Valley of Heaven." A picturesque valley running from **Mbabane** and the Malegwane hill south between the **Mdzimba** mountain range on the east and the Mantenga hills on the west for more than a dozen miles (18 kilometers). Ezulwini has with only occasional exceptions constituted the geographic and demographic heartland of the Swazi royal house throughout the 19th and 20th centuries. Originally this was because of the valley's fertile soils and abundant water, along with its close proximity to defensible caves in the Mdzimba range to the east. Consequently it is in the Ezulwini Valley that the royal villages of a succession of Swazi *tingwenyama* and *tindlovukazi* dot the landscape. It was, for instance, to *iNgwenyama* **Mbandzeni Dlamini**'s *lilawu* (administrative homestead) at **Mbekelweni** in the valley to which a generation of Europeans pilgrimaged, **gold** coins in hand, to bargain for **concessions**. Later, during the early 20th century, the Mantenga hills adjoining the valley became the scene of a massive mining effort to extract cassiterite **tin** utilizing high-pressure water hoses, indelibly disfiguring that portion of the once-scenic countryside. Still later, beginning in the early 1960s, the Ezulwini Valley became the mecca of a new generation of gold-bearing pilgrims—mainly foreign investors in the canneries, hotels and spas, bottle stores and casinos, souvenir shops, dance halls, racetracks, and more that proliferated along the main **Manzini**-Mbabane road. To traditionalists those enterprises made the Ezulwini Valley appear anything but heavenly.

-F-

FAIRLIE, MICHAEL J. (1920–). A colonial civil servant in Swaziland from 1953 (Mankiana [now **Mankayane**] district officer) to 1968 (secretary for external affairs and labor; member of both the **Queen's Commissioner**'s Executive Council and the **Legislative Council**). Fairlie was instrumental in implementing governmental policies supportive of **trade unions** and outlawing racial discrimination. He was an early advocate of both the Africanization of the government bureaucracy and the social integration of the races. As director of the **Mbabane** choir, he established and oversaw one of the earliest mixed-race organizations in colonial Swaziland. Fairlie's reminiscences were published as *No Time Like the Past* (1992).

FAKUDZE, MBOVANE (?–c. 1887). One of Swaziland's leading councillors and most venerable military commanders. Fakudze was noted especially for his expert generalship as *iNgwenyama* **Mbandzeni Dlamini**'s commander-in-chief in the joint Swazi-British campaign against the **Pedi** King **Sekhukhune Maroteng** in 1879. Later (1881) as *indvuna* of the **Nkanini** royal homestead under *iNdlovukazi* **Sisile Khumalo**, Fakudze tried to persuade her not to carry out her intention to flee from Mbandzeni's kingdom with her **regiments**, a treasonous act. When he discovered her gone, however, he reported her absence to the king, who then dispatched a regiment to capture and kill her. Henceforward until his death Fakudze became one of Mbandzeni's most trusted senior councillors.

FAKUDZE, MNGAYI. A senior *indvuna*, both military and civil, of *iNgwenyama* **Sobhuza Dlamini I**. Fakudze was most noted as the *indvuna* of the *baLondolozi* **regiment** which rolled back the Zulu invasion of 1839. In July, under his command, a Swazi *imphi* fought the invaders to a standstill at the Lubuya stream near modern Hlatikulu. Following the **Battle of Lubuya** the Zulu began a protracted retreat during which they incurred heavy losses of both men and cattle. Fakudze subsequently became *indvuna* of the royal homestead at **Lobamba**, a senior and prestigious position.

FARMERS ASSOCIATIONS. *See* SWAZILAND FARMERS ASSOCIATION

FEATHERSTONE, ERIC K. (1896–?). Commonly referred to as E. P. Featherstone. Colonial civil servant in Nigeria seconded as **resident commissioner** in Swaziland from 1942 to 1946. Featherstone possessed a reputation for obstinacy (hence his Swazi nickname, *Magandeyane*, "The Pounder"). Featherstone's main task was to obtain *iNgwenyama* **Sobhuza Dlamini II**'s acquiescence to the proposed **Native Administration Proclamation**. First put forward in 1939, the proclamation provoked Sobhuza's (and the *libandla*'s) strong and protracted opposition because it undercut his sovereignty by according the resident commissioner the power to appoint and dismiss chiefs. Featherstone's pressing for Swazi assent to the proclamation was so assiduous and Sobhuza's opposition so adamant that relations between them became permanently strained. Finally in 1944 the proclamation (with the offending provision) was imposed on the Swazi by the British **high commissioner**. Featherstone, however, had no such luck in implementing the proposed companion **Native Courts Proclamation**, which gave the resident commissioner appellate jurisdiction unacceptable to Sobhuza. Sobhuza and his *libandla* immediately refused to recognize the Native Administration

Proclamation and continued their noncooperation long after Featherstone returned to the Nigerian colonial service in 1946. The result was that amended Native Administration and Native Courts Proclamations, both without the objectionable provisions, were implemented in 1950, along with the **National Treasury Proclamation**.

FERREIRA, JOACHIM J. (1835–1917). An early concessionaire whose purchase of land from *iNgwenyama* **Mbandzeni Dlamini** in 1877 became the basis for the polity which became known (1886) as the "**Little Free State**" (LFS). That land, east of Derby in the **Transvaal**, was subsequently taken from the Swazi and declared to be part of the **South African Republic (SAR)** (1893). Ferreira, two brothers, and F. Ignatius Maritz, his brother-in-law, obtained the land from Mbandzeni in return for a dozen horses and related items. Allegedly Mbandzeni's motive for the sale was to settle some "reliable" Europeans as a buffer against the incursions of the renegade **Mnt. Mbilini Dlamini**.

For the *ingwenyama* Ferreira proved to be anything but reliable. He and several other Afrikaners established farms on the ceded land, finally reaching about 90 in number by 1886. Subsequently Ferreira obtained a second, substantial grazing **concession** in the same region. Following the retrocession of the Transvaal by the British in 1881, Ferreira became a **South African Republican** official based at Piet Retief, first a native commissioner and later a border commissioner. That was when he began to distance himself from Mbandzeni's original intentions. In 1886, at his instigation, the LFS farmers formed a self-government committee, and in 1888 Ferreira persuaded Mbandzeni to renounce his sovereignty over the region. The LFS was incorporated into the SAR under articles of the **first Swaziland Convention** in 1890. Ferreira also obtained a substantial mineral concession south of the **Usutu River**. He was most likely involved in the sale of one or more of the concessions to the SAR, forming the basis for its governance of the territory. When the SAR assumed administrative control in 1895 Ferreira was made a justice of the peace situated north of modern **Nhlangano**.

FIRST SWAZILAND CONVENTION (1890). This convention, signed by representatives of the British and **South African Republic (SAR)** governments, marked the placing of Swaziland in play as a pawn in the wider game of regional big-power diplomacy. The clash between the ambitions of **Britain** and the SAR in central and southern Africa led to the signing of the convention's accommodation to SAR president Paul

Kruger's ambitions to the east through Swaziland and (he thought) to the sea, and to British ambitions north of the Limpopo River.

For the Swazi, however, the convention proved to be the thin edge of the wedge. There were several reasons for that. First, although the convention again guaranteed Swazi independence, it made that guarantee dependent on joint British-SAR acquiescence and joint administration of the kingdom. That arrangement took the form of a governing council, the **Swaziland Government Committee**, which was to administer European and **concessions** affairs, but which was not to exert any sovereignty over Swazi (including judicial) affairs. Second, the convention provided for the establishment of a **Chief Court** to adjudicate European affairs and to investigate the validity of the concessions. Consequently in Swazi eyes the court was a body that, because the concessions were disputed mainly by them, constituted a danger principally to their interests. Third, Article 24 of the convention provided for the transfer to the **Transvaal** of the "**Little Free State**," a 50-square-mile (131-square-kilometer) tract of land along the Swazi border north of Piet Retief which had been loaned by *iNgwenyama* **Mbandzeni Dlamini** in 1875 to two Transvaal Afrikaners. Finally, Queen Regent **Tibati Nkambule** and the *libandla* were pressured to acquiesce to those humiliating provisions by placing their signatures on the organic proclamation of December 1889. Later (1893), when Tibati was similarly pressured as queen regent to sign an **organic proclamation** abrogating Swazi internal sovereignty (the proposed **second Swaziland Convention** of 1893), she refused. Instead she dispatched the **deputation of 1894** to protest Swaziland's effective incorporation into the SAR, all to no effect. *See also* Anglo-Boer Joint Commission; Third Swaziland Convention

FITZPATRICK, H. DANIEL (1909–). Colonial civil servant and, from 1967 to 1972, senator. Born in Swaziland and educated at St. Mark's School, he joined the Swaziland colonial service in 1928. During the 1940s he served as a district officer and as a rural development officer. He retired officially in 1956 as secretary for African affairs and became a shopkeeper. Following Fitzpatrick's retirement, such was his reputation that he was appointed to successive constitutional committees and ran unopposed as an independent candidate for the **Legislative Council** in 1964. He was then appointed to its executive as member for public works and communications. In 1968, following independence, he was appointed by *iNgwenyama* **Sobhuza Dlamini II** to the Senate, serving until Sobhuza repealed the constitution in 1973.

FORBES, DAVID (1829–1905). Born in Scotland, Forbes emigrated to **South Africa** in 1850, becoming a successful hunter and trader in Natal. In 1857 Forbes settled on a farm near the mouth of the Thukela River and raised cattle. From there he hunted elephants in northern Natal and Swaziland, whose **highveld** topography, strongly reminiscent of the Scotland of his youth, proved an irresistible attraction to him. It was Forbes who persuaded a fellow Scot, **Alexander McCorkindale**, to whom he was related by marriage, to establish the farming community **New Scotland** in the eastern **Transvaal** highveld bordering on Swaziland in 1866. McCorkindale purchased the land from President Martinus Pretorius of the **South African Republic**, but because the title to some of the territory was in dispute, token compensation was paid to the Swazi as well. Forbes purchased four farm plots in New Scotland and consolidated them into an estate, which he named Athole, situated on the western extremity of modern Amsterdam.

Forbes's early years at Athole were prosperous ones, but with McCorkindale's death in 1871 came an end to the viability of New Scotland, and Forbes turned to mineral prospecting. He focused first on diamonds in the Orange Free State, but then **gold** was discovered in Swaziland, and Forbes's brother **James Forbes** obtained a **concession** from *iNgwenyama* **Mbandzeni Dlamini** in 1882 allowing him to prospect south of the **Komati River**. There in November 1883 David Forbes's son Alexander (1860–1885) struck gold at what became known as Forbes Reef near the Malolotja River, 10 miles (16 kilometers) north-northwest of modern **Mbabane**. This was the first major gold strike in the kingdom, and it became the basis of the Forbes Reef Gold Mining Company, capitalized in London (1885) at £100,000 (later £400,000). The Forbeses paid King Mbandzeni an annual rental of £300 on the concession after an initial payment of £3,000.

David Forbes left concessions politics to James and to his son **David Forbes, Jr.**, to concentrate on the family mining interests as managing director of the Forbes Reef company. By 1889 the company was employing 60 Cornish miners and 150 African laborers to work the original and several adjacent reefs. Forbes also became a director of subsequent companies exploiting segments of the main reef, notably the Henderson and Forbes Gold Mining Company and the Southern Forbes Reef Gold Mining Company. During the **Anglo-Boer War** (1899–1902) Athole was rendered destitute by successive occupations of British troops and Afrikaner commandoes. Forbes, who rebuilt the estate following the war, died and was buried at Athole in 1905.

FORBES, DAVID, JR. (1863–1941). Son of **David Forbes**, born and raised on his father's farm Athole in **New Scotland**. Forbes joined his uncle, **James Forbes**, in negotiating the mineral **concession** south of the **Komati River** in 1882 that became the basis of the Forbes Reef Gold Mining Company's fortune. In 1887 Forbes obtained a mining concession over an area south of modern **Mbabane** for the Star Prospecting and Gold Mining Syndicate which he represented. Later deeming it worthless, he sold it to Sydney T. Ryan for £2,000, and then saw Ryan mine it for a fortune in **tin**. Forbes's foray into European politics began in 1888 when he was elected to the third **Swazieland Committee** and became an ally of **Allister Miller** in the campaign to dismiss **Theophilus Shepstone, Jr.**, as advisor to the Swazi nation. Once Miller had replaced Shepstone as *iNgwenyama* **Mbandzeni Dlamini**'s secretary, and as the king edged toward death, Forbes joined the rest of the Miller clique in the gang violation by concession of the kingdom. Forbes's acquisitions were in timber and land, and on the basis of those and previous concessions he embarked on several commercial ventures, principally cattle ranching at **Ehlane** and coal mining along the **Lebombo mountain** range. During the **Anglo-Boer War** (1899–1902) Forbes embarked on a variety of activities on behalf of the British, notably as an intelligence officer on commando-type raids against Boer forces and installations. In 1902 a scouting operation against a Boer troop in southern Swaziland earned him the D.S.O. Following the war Forbes again took up ranching at Ehlane and farming at the family estate, Athole. He was buried there. In 1938 Forbes published an episodic memoir entitled *My Life in South Africa*.

FORBES, JAMES (1835–1896). Born in Scotland, Forbes, the youngest of the three Forbes brothers, emigrated to **South Africa** in 1859. He established himself in Swaziland in 1874 as a cattle trader and transport driver, then quickly cultivated close relations with the Swazi royal house. That relationship led to Forbes's first mineral **concession** granted in 1880 following his discovery of coal in the central **lowveld** near modern **Mpaka**. It was Forbes's second mineral concession, granted in 1882 for prospecting south of the **Komati River**, that led to the creation of the Forbes family fortune. In 1883 Forbes's nephew Alexander discovered the main **gold** seam of what became the Forbes Reef Gold Mining Company's field. By that time Forbes had become a close confidant of both *iNgwenyama* **Mbandzeni Dlamini** and his senior political officer, **Sandlane Zwane**, using his near-perfect **siSwati** to interpret for them on important state matters involving foreigners and writing official letters for the king. Forbes was one of a handful of Europeans to whom the *ingwenyama* awarded a farming and grazing concession free of rent and in perpetuity. Forbes was a member of the first **Swazieland Committee**, serving briefly as its chairman in 1887. Thereafter he concentrated on his business interests, mainly gold, coal, and farming. *See also* Forbes, David; Forbes, David, Jr.

FORSYTH-THOMPSON, PATRICK R. A longtime civil servant serving in staff capacities both during the latter years of British colonial administration and following independence. He served as the first government labor officer (1957–60) and as secretary for local administration until the mid-1960s. In 1967 he was named permanent secretary in the deputy prime minister's office. Following his retirement he served as chief electoral officer in the 1972 election, and for many years thereafter he managed a tourist caravan park in the **Ezulwini Valley**.

FRIEDMAN, DR. FRANCES (FANNIE) (c. 1920–). Minister for health (1987–93), the first female cabinet minister in Swaziland's history. Dr. Friedman, a **EurAfrican** born and trained in **South Africa**, joined the Swaziland government health services as a doctor in the late 1940s. In 1968 Dr. Friedman became Swaziland's first female permanent secretary, serving in the Ministry of Health. She retired as director of medical services in 1979 and was appointed to the House of Assembly in 1983.

-G-

GAMA, JOHN (c. 1842–1905). One of the earliest educated Swazi Christians (the Gama clan was one of those classified as *Emakhandza Mbili*), who began his **mission** association as a follower of **Rev. James Allison** at the Wesleyan station at **Mahamba**. With Allison he fled Mahamba in 1846 after it came under attack during the civil war following the accession of *iNgwenyama* **Mswati Dlamini II** to the throne. Gama prospered as one of the original African landholders at the **Edendale** (Natal) mission, which Allison founded in 1851, and as a trader. He returned to Swaziland as a permanent settler in 1882 during the reign of *iNgwenyama* **Mbandzeni Dlamini** and became a holder (along with 14 other Edendale graduates) of a 4,500-acre (1,823-hectare) land **concession** running from Mahamba to Makhosini.

Gama, along with a few fellow Edendalers, became involved in Swazi politics with the arrival in the kingdom of **Theophilus Shepstone, Jr.**, with whom they became early allies. He worked closely with Shepstone during the latter's advisory tenures from 1887 to 1889 and from 1889 to 1894. Gama and **Stephen Mini** (another Edendale graduate) also became secretaries and advisors to Mbandzeni, which led to their deep and apparently profitable involvement in mineral concessioneering. By the time of his death Gama owned a land concession in the shadow of the **Lebombo mountain** range on which he had built a home and on which he ran 150 head of cattle. Gama became an informant on early Swazi history and culture to both **James Stuart** (in 1898) and **Allister Miller**, with whom he became closely allied during his later years. Upon Gama's death Miller became one of the executors of his estate.

GAZA. *See* SHANGANE

GOEDGEGUN. *See* NHLANGANO

GOLD. The mineral whose allure was most responsible for the early attraction of Europeans to Swaziland during the **concessions** period (beginning 1882). Gold turned out to be more important historically for that reason than for any lasting significant wealth that it produced for Swaziland during the 19th century. The first gold concession was granted by *iNgwenyama* **Mbandzeni Dlamini** in 1882; eight gold concessions were granted from that date until the end of the gold rush in 1899. The first major lode was discovered by Alexander Forbes at what became known as Forbes Reef, northwest of **Mbabane** in 1883. Other mines were established on the **Komati River** and at **Pigg's Peak**, Kobolondo, Wyldesdale, and Horo. For all its early promise, gold mining in Swaziland never became a paying proposition during the 19th century, and by 1897 the industry had become nonviable. High prospecting and operating costs, labor difficulties, and transport inadequacies in rugged **highveld** terrain were all contributing factors. The Forbes Reef mine, the closest to Mbabane, was the only one to be consistently profitable, but it too closed down by the outset of the **Anglo-Boer War** in 1899. What revived the mines was the takeover of the local syndicates by Johannesburg mining houses and British companies, which then proceeded to develop only those mines showing the most potential. The heyday for gold mining came between 1910 and 1915, when 11 mines were on line. During the years up to 1920 gold and **tin** constituted more than 70 percent of Swaziland's exports by value. After 1920, however, gold suffered an irretrievable decline beginning with the plummet in its price brought on by the post–World War I world depression. *See also* Forbes, David; Forbes, David, Jr.

GOVERNMENT COMMITTEE. *See* PROVISIONAL GOVERNMENT COMMITTEE; SWAZILAND GOVERNMENT COMMITTEE

GREAT BRITAIN. *See* BRITAIN

GREAT USUTU RIVER. *See* USUTU RIVER

GRENDON, ROBERT (?–1949). EurAfrican educator and journalist, born of an Irish father and Herero mother in South West Africa (now Namibia). Educated at an Anglican mission school in the Cape, Grendon became headmaster of the **Edendale** mission school in Natal at the turn of the century. In 1904 Queen Regent **Labotsibeni Mdluli**, probably on the advice of the Edendale graduates counseling her, invited Grendon to become the tutor of her two surviving sons, **Bnt. Malunge** and **Lomvazi Dlamini**, at **Zombodze**. Consequently Grendon became the first tutor for **Mnt. Nkhotfotjeni Dlamini**, who later became *iNgwenyama* **Sobhuza Dlamini II**. Grendon, who believed that education included political analysis as well as book learning, became a favorite of Sobhuza but also as a consequence became someone to be viewed with suspicion by court rivals. The fact that Grendon had become an editor of the **African National Congress** newspaper *Abantu Batho* and had made powerful enemies in that role did not make his position any easier. Consequently when Labotsibeni (at Sobhuza's request) sought to have Grendon once again tutor the young crown prince upon his return from the **Lovedale Missionary Institution** in 1919, the **resident commissioner, de Symons Honey**, upon receipt of letters questioning Grendon's integrity and motives, rejected his candidacy. Grendon ended his days teaching at an African Methodist Episcopal school in Swaziland.

GREY, GEORGE. Partition Commissioner appointed by **High Commissioner Lord Selborne** (1908) to delineate boundaries and delimit "**native area**" reserves in accordance with the **Partition Proclamation** of 1907. That proclamation had awarded two-thirds of Swaziland's territory to European concessionaires and the crown. Grey, who had been a close friend of **Resident Commissioner Robert Coryndon** since their Rhodesian campaigning days against the Ndebele, carved out 32 native areas from 181 **concessions**. Working alone but in constant communication with both Selborne and Coryndon, Grey carried out his partitioning in accordance with several criteria. First, boundary lines between European and African lands were to be explicit and indisputable (such as rivers and streams). Second, more than one-third of all "fertile land" would lie in native area. That, however, was inconsistent with the third criterion, which stipulated that any land under settler occupation and cultivation in 1908 (obviously likely to be the most fertile) was precluded from incorporation into native area. In fact nearly 80 percent of native area land was later classified as "poor" to "untillable." Fourth, aggregated blocks of land were to be, as far as possible, desirable for both races: for Europeans, to provide for unrestricted capitalist production and sustenance of market value; and for Swazi, to ensure minimal disturbance of existing homesteads and at least short-term agricultural mobility. The latter consideration had mostly to do with Selborne's fear of a Swazi reprise of the bloody Zulu risings of 1906–8 in Natal. Fifth, enough Swazi were to remain on settler lands as to provide the Europeans with adequate farm labor. Last, the Swazi royal house and chiefs were to be appeased by leaving their large homesteads and holdings substantially intact, so as to minimize official protest against the partition. That final precaution had its desired effect. To further ensure peaceable compliance with the partition, the Swazi were given until 1914 to make labor agreements on settler estates or remove themselves to the native areas. Grey later met his death in Kenya, mauled by a lion.

GROBELAAR, MATTHIAS J. Commonly known as Thuys Grobler. A concessionaire with substantial landholdings, whose ties with both **South African Republic (SAR)** president Paul Kruger and the Swazi royal house (notably *iNgwenyama* **Bhunu Dlamini** and Queen Regent **Labotsibeni Mdluli**) made him something of a local political heavyweight at the turn of the century. Grobelaar acted as Kruger's personal representative and **concessions** revenue courier with the Swazi, and he was Bhunu's interpreter during the latter's visit to Pretoria in 1899. Consequently it was with Grobelaar that Bhunu signed an agreement making him exclusive labor recruiting agent in the kingdom in 1899 as the era of Swazi labor migrancy to the gold mines on the Witwatersrand was commencing. Unfortunately for Grobelaar that agreement was never ratified by the SAR and consequently lapsed with the death of Bhunu, never, in spite of Grobelaar's vigorous efforts, to be renewed. Grobelaar did, however, operate in Swaziland as a labor recruiter, and he maintained a close relationship with Labotsibeni.

GWAMILE. "Firm and Unshakable"; "Indomitable." *See* MDLULI, *INDLOVUKAZI* LABOTSIBENI

GWAMILE VOCATIONAL AND COMMERCIAL TRAINING INSTITUTE MATSAPHA (GWAMILE-VOCTIM). A technical and commercial training institute for secondary school leavers established in

1987, comparable to the **Swaziland College of Technology** in **Mbabane**. Craft-level courses of instruction are in building and construction; business administration; automotive, electrical, and mechanical engineering; and secretarial studies. Final examinations are administered by the London Chamber of Commerce. In 1996 Gwamile-Voctim enrolled 300 students.

-H-

HAILEY, LORD WILLIAM M. (1872–1969). British colonial official who, following 40 years of distinguished service in India (capped by his governorship of the United Provinces), directed the compilation of the *African Survey* (1938). Although Hailey was regarded as the most distinguished Indian Civil Service officer of his time, his African contributions were more renowned and longer lasting. Hailey's *African Survey* set the tone of the British debate over Africa for the generation following its publication and helped determine the agenda for Britain's wartime colonial reforms and post–World War II decolonization. The book set out the revised terms of the system of "**indirect rule**" first implemented by Lord Lugard in Northern Nigeria. Although Hailey agreed that indirect rule was preferable to the imposition of Western parliamentary government at the local level, he viewed it as a preliminary stage toward the eventual goal of African independent governments based along modified Western lines.

An extensively revised *African Survey* was published in 1957, less influential than the first edition because of the continent-wide independence movements well under way by then, which rendered much of its agenda obsolete. In addition, Hailey authored two subsequent works which dealt more specifically and substantially with Swaziland: *Native Administration in the British African Territories. Part V. The High Commission Territories: Basutoland, the Bechuanaland Protectorate, and Swaziland* (1953) and *The Republic of South Africa and the High Commission Territories* (1963). Through all those books Hailey established himself as an exceptionally important influence in shaping British policy toward Swaziland between the early 1940s and independence.

Hailey's tour of Africa in 1935 preparatory to the writing of the *African Survey* included a visit to Swaziland and an extended interview with *iNgwenyama* **Sobhuza Dlamini II** that helped to shape the thinking of both men about the nature of future indirect rule. Hailey proposed to

Sobhuza a form of government whereby a "native authority" would exercise administrative powers only while ultimate political sovereignty and legal jurisdiction would rest with the colonial administration. Hailey pointed to Tanganyika as the example of that concept of "parallelism," which would eventually become the basis for the initial draft proposals (1939) of the Swaziland **Native Administration** and **Native Courts Proclamations**. Sobhuza vigorously opposed Hailey's concept of parallelism, arguing that it was inconsistent with the Order-in-Council of 1903, which preserved "native law and custom," and that its implementation would inevitably usurp his and the chiefs' powers and hence destroy their effectiveness. That position would become the basis for Sobhuza's protracted opposition to the draft proclamations, over which his stance would ultimately prevail in 1950.

Hailey came away from his encounter with the king impressed enough to argue with the **high commissioner** that criminal jurisdictional powers should be restored to Sobhuza by the British administration and that he should be granted a degree of financial sovereignty. The return of those powers proved to be slow in coming; they were eventually restored to Sobhuza only in 1950, by proclamation. None of Hailey's sentiments expressed as the result of his encounter with Sobhuza appeared in *An African Survey*, either the 1938 or the revised 1957 edition. However, in *Native Administration in the British African Territories* (1953), Hailey asserted that Swaziland was ready for a degree of self-government in the form of a joint European-Swazi advisory council.

HARINGTON, JOHN R. (1866–?). The principal agent in the **South African Republican (SAR)** government's acquisition of the significant **concessions** in 1889 and 1890 that later formed the basis of its administration of Swaziland (1895–99). Harington arrived in Swaziland from **Barberton** in 1888. His first transaction involved the postal services concession, which he acquired and then sold to an agent of the SAR in 1889 for £7,000. Later that year he acquired and sold the licenses and mint monopolies to SAR agents for £50,000. The most significant of all, however, was Harington's acquisition in 1889 of the concession allowing him the exclusive right to collect the private revenue of *iNgwenyama* **Mbandzeni Dlamini** and his successors, in return for which he was to pay the *ingwenyama* £12,000 annually in monthly installments. Mbandzeni appears to have signed away the concession, an otherwise unaccountable act, because he suspected that some of his revenues were being embezzled by his agent and advisor **Theophilus Shepstone, Jr.** Harington sold the "**private revenue concession**" to an agent of the SAR for an unspecified amount in 1889, and it was then transferred to the government itself in 1890. In 1894 **Britain** recognized the SAR's legitimacy to administer Swaziland, based in part on those monopolies, principally the private revenue concession.

HAVELOCK ASBESTOS MINE. A crysotile asbestos mine located in the rugged Makonjwa mountain range in northwest Swaziland. The nearest town is Havelock, named after Sir Arthur Havelock, governor of Natal during the 1880s. Havelock has a current population of about 4,800. In 1939 the New Amianthus Mines, Ltd., a subsidiary of the British corporation Turner and Newall, began mining operations on the slopes of Emlembe mountain, near the town. Given the terrain, the mine product was shipped 12 miles (20 kilometers) via aerial cableway to **Barberton** in the eastern **Transvaal**. During the 1950s and 1960s New Amianthus was one of the five largest producers of crysotile asbestos in the world, with production amounting to E5 million to E6 million (£2.5 million to £3 million) in value per year. In 1973 40 percent ownership was transferred to the Swazi nation's **Tibiyo takaNgwane Fund**, and in 1986 another 40 percent was transferred to Credo International Asbestos, a subsidiary of the Consolidated Mining Corporation of South Africa.

The Havelock mine has been the theater for two significant confrontations between labor and management. The first strike, in 1944, was mounted over the issue of the mine's imposition of a liquor monopoly over its workforce. The second strike, in 1963 (*see* **Havelock Mine Strike**), was touched off over the issue of wages, but it quickly assumed political overtones. The drop in worldwide asbestos demand, principally because of concern over its effects on human health, has seriously affected prices. Furthermore, the mines are playing out, forcing operators to go to deeper levels to extract fibers that are of lower quality. In spite of all this, asbestos remains Swaziland's major mineral export. Current mine employment is about 1,800. In 1998 Swaziland exported 27,693 metric tons of asbestos. In late 1999 Credo International Asbestos announced plans for the permanent closure of the mine, citing the precipitous drop in world prices for asbestos and the exhaustion of high-grade fiber seams.

HAVELOCK MINE STRIKE (1963). The key event in a series of labor strikes taking place during May and June 1963 leading to the colonial government's declaration of an emergency and the deployment of British troops in the kingdom. The strikes started in mid-March with brief work stoppages at **Peak Timbers**, **Ubombo Ranches**, and the sugarcane complex at Big Bend over a variety of grievances. In early April a public demonstration erupted in **Mbabane** over the government closure of some food stalls at the public market for health reasons. On May 20, 1,800 African laborers went on strike at the **Havelock Asbestos Mine** over wages (demanding E2.80 [£1] per day, double what the company offered) and the alleged ineffectiveness and corruption of *iNgwenyama* **Sobhuza Dlamini II**'s labor *tindvuna* at the mine. Sobhuza's lifelong opposition to **trade unions** that operated beyond his control had led him to place *tindvuna* at every work site to communicate workers' grievances to management and encourage negotiations in place of strikes. Workers had come to both mistrust and resent the *tindvuna*, whom they perceived as the co-opted and in some cases corrupted tools of management.

By mid-1963 unions had been formed in every major industry, and they in turn came under the gaze of politically ambitious men with an eye toward the approach of independence. At Havelock the fiery rhetoric of **Mnt. Dumisa Dlamini** (a nephew of the king) and **Macdonald Maseko** of the **Ngwane National Liberatory Congress** persuaded the workers to ignore the *ingwenyama*'s order that they return to work. They also threatened to foment the spread of sympathy strikes elsewhere in Swaziland. In mid-June, with Sobhuza's authority being ignored by the strikers and the government's security forces already overextended, the **resident commissioner**, **Sir Brian Marwick**, declared an emergency and called in British troops from Kenya. The occupying army battalion remained for five years, during which further union activity was effectively suppressed.

HER MAJESTY'S COMMISSIONER FOR SWAZILAND. A post established in 1963 by the secretary of state for colonial affairs **Duncan Sandys** to replace the position of **resident commissioner**. The pre-independence constitution for Swaziland was imposed by Sandys (in the form of a 1963 White Paper) following the inability of the **constitutional conference** to agree on the provisions of such a document. Under the Sandys constitution the Queen's Commissioner reported directly to the secretary of state, bypassing the **high commissioner**, many of whose powers now fell to the newly created post. The new position was strongly opposed by *iNgwenyama* **Sobhuza Dlamini II**, who saw its executive powers as a threat to his own sovereignty. The Queen's Commissioner was to have a veto power over all acts of the new **Legislative Council**, for instance, and would hold sovereignty over all minerals. The first and only Queen's Commissioner was **Sir Francis Loyd** (1964–68). The post lapsed upon independence in 1968.

HHOHHO ADMINISTRATIVE REGION. The northernmost of four administrative regions of modern Swaziland. At 1,364 square miles (3,583 square kilometers), Hhohho is the smallest of the four in area. Hhohho District was formed in the 1963 administrative reform from the combination of the former Mbabane and (Pigg's) Peak Districts. In 1986 its population stood at 185,986. Its capital and largest city is **Mbabane**. The region's main commercial assets include the forestry plantations surrounding **Pigg's Peak** and the asbestos mine at **Havelock**. The village of Hhohho, the northernmost town in Swaziland, became the locus of the *lilawu* (administrative capital) established by *iNgwenyama* **Mswati Dlamini II** in the late 1840s as he projected royal power northward from Ekufiyeni in central Swaziland.

HIGH COMMISSION TERRITORIES. The common term used to designate the three territories of Basutoland (modern Lesotho), the Bechuanaland Protectorate (modern Botswana), and Swaziland. The term was derived from the title of their chief colonial administrator, the British **high commissioner**. It was made necessary because of the ambiguous status of the protected territories, which were kept out of the **Union of South Africa** in 1910 but were intended to be incorporated at a later date. The term lapsed with the abolition of the proposed incorporation in anticipation of the gaining of independence by Lesotho and Botswana (1966) and Swaziland (1968).

HIGH COMMISSIONER OF THE UNITED KINGDOM FOR BASUTOLAND, THE BECHUANALAND PROTECTORATE, AND SWAZILAND. The title of the chief British administrative officer responsible to the secretary of state for the colonies for the affairs of the three **High Commission Territories**. Those territories were Basutoland (modern Lesotho), the Bechuanaland Protectorate (modern Botswana), and Swaziland. The post was instituted in 1910 upon formation of the **Union of South Africa** as a joint position with that of the governor-general. The two posts were separated administratively in 1931. The position of high commissioner lapsed in 1964 concomitant with the establishment of the post of **Her Majesty's Commissioner for Swaziland**.

HIGH COURT OF SWAZILAND. The superior court of record in Swaziland, presided over by the head of the judiciary, the chief justice. The High Court has unlimited original jurisdiction in civil and criminal matters in Swaziland, and appellate jurisdiction as prescribed by any law currently in force in the kingdom. Inferior to the High Court are the subordinate courts and the Swazi (traditional) courts, while superior to it is the Court of Appeal. Except where altered by statute, Roman-Dutch law is the common law of the country.

HIGHVELD. One of four topographical regions in Swaziland, a mountainous area along its western side, 1,900 square miles (4,900 square kilometers) in area. Its altitude varies from 3,500 feet (1,070 meters) to 6,100 feet (1,860 meters) above sea level, the highest peaks being the summits of Mt. Emlembe (6,109 feet; 1,863 meters) and Mt. Ngwenya (6,002 feet; 1,830 meters). The area is cut through by numerous river valleys and gorges, with waterfalls not uncommon. The highveld is really an extension of the Drakensberg chain of mountains that courses through South Africa and Lesotho (known there as the Maluti mountains). The hillsides and ridges are mostly grassland ("sourveld"), except for areas commercially planted with forests (conifers and eucalypti). Only about 3 percent of the highveld is suitable for intensive agriculture, with another 7 percent marginally suitable. The highveld is the locus of much of Swaziland's mineral wealth (most recently **asbestos** and historically **gold, tin,** and **iron**). The highveld receives between 40 and 90 inches of rain per year and has a temperate but humid climate. The average annual rainfall is about 53 inches (1,325 millimeters); the temperature range falls between 73°F (23°C) and 51°F (11°C).

HLANE ("WILDERNESS") ROYAL NATIONAL PARK. One of four major game and nature reserves in Swaziland. Hlane is about 70,000 acres (30,000 hectares) in area, of which 25,000 acres (10,500 hectares) forms the nucleus and 45,000 acres (19,500 hectares) serves as seasonal dispersal. It is located in the lowveld 3 miles (5 kilometers) west of Simunye, 40 miles (67 kilometers) by road east from **Manzini.** The Hlane nucleus is the former ranch of **David Forbes,** which, upon his death in 1941, was sold to *iNgwenyama* **Sobhuza Dlamini II.** Sobhuza used it primarily for hunting parties, but its game had become so depleted by the mid-1960s that he declared it a protected area in 1967. It remains held in trust for the Swazi Nation by the *ingwenyama.* It is at Hlane that the *Butimba,* the ritual royal hunting party, is held. *See also* Ehlane

HLOPHE, ABEDNIGO K. (1922–). An important member of both the *libandla* and the *liqoqo,* and occasional cabinet minister. Hlophe was a lifelong, trusted advisor to *iNgwenyama* **Sobhuza Dlamini II.** He was educated abroad at St. Chad's College in Natal and then at the University of Sussex. Both his political and educational qualifications led him to occupy a number of important political offices and administrative posts throughout his lifetime. He became clerk to the **Standing Committee**

of the *libandla*, and from 1951 to 1962 he was private secretary to Sobhuza. He served on the constitutional committee from 1961 to 1963 and was a delegate to London **constitutional conferences** in 1961 and 1963, and to the London independence constitutional conference in 1968. As a member of the **Imbokodvo National Movement**, Hlophe stood successfully from the Mbuluzi constituency in the elections of 1964 (**Legislative Council**), 1967, and 1972 (**parliament**). From 1964 to 1967 he served on the Executive Committee of the Legislative Council as minister of local government and social services, and he was a member of the Constitutional Review Commission during 1965–66. In 1967 he was selected by Sobhuza to be minister of agriculture in his first cabinet. In that capacity it was he who introduced the controversial **Land Speculation Control Act** (passed in December 1971, effective 1972) into parliament. Following Sobhuza's repeal of the constitution in 1973, Hlophe chaired the Constitutional Advisory Commission (1975–78, the second of two such commissions) to recommend the shape of the new document. Such was Hlophe's stature with the *ingwenyama* that he was chosen to coordinate the eulogies at Sobhuza's funeral in 1982.

HLUBI, SOMDLALOSE (?–c. 1881). Daughter of Hlubi King Langalibalele, who was betrothed but not married to *iNgwenyama* **Ludvonga Dlamini II** at his death in 1874. Subsequently Somdlalose entered into a liaison with *iNgwenyama* **Mbandzeni Dlamini**, the issue of which was a son, **Mnt. Mdzabuko Dlamini**. The royal infant was perceived by Mbandzeni's enemies to be the legitimate heir of Ludvonga by leviratic union, and consequently he became the principal issue in a deadly power struggle between Mbandzeni and the ambitious *iNdlovukazi*, **Sisile Khumalo**. Somdlalose allied herself with Sisile in that dynastic controversy. Mbandzeni resolved the dispute by having Mdzabuko poisoned and Sisile executed, and it is most likely that Somdlalose died with her.

HOMESTEAD. (siSwati: *Umuti.*) In rural Swaziland the homestead, not the village, is the major social and productive unit. Depending on its size (a function of wealth and status), it consists of the homestead head (*umnumzane*), his mother (if still living), his wife or wives, and her/their descendants—married sons and their wives, and unmarried sons and daughters. Large homesteads can also incorporate an *umnumzane*'s brothers and their wives and families. The *umuti* of a wealthy, elderly *umnumzane* might incorporate his, his sons', and their children's generations in a single location, offering the appearance of a small village. In a polygynous *umuti* (increasingly rare in modern times) the first wife was generally the senior wife, although she might on occasion be a favored junior wife or one from an especially prominent clan. The senior wife was the key personage in determining succession and inheritance; it was normally her eldest son who was the heir and to whom the estate, notably the cattle, was passed. Upon the death of the *umnumzane* the other surviving sons moved off with their respective mothers and families to found new *imiti*.

Traditionally the *umnumzane* was the lord and master of the homestead. It was he who controlled and allocated resources and he who made the crucial decisions affecting production (timing and extent of ploughing, types of cropping). He mobilized and directed the human labor and animal draft power, and he determined the nature of agricultural investments (seeds, implements, tractor hire). Each wife had her own house (*indlu*) and fields to cultivate. The *indlu* was the basic cooking, sleeping, and cultivating sub-unit for each wife and her descendants. To the extent that she had her own possessions, the *indlu* was also the sub-unit for inheritance. Each wife kept a portion of the harvest from her fields and contributed the remainder for communal use.

Aside from *tindlu* each standard *umuti* contained three other elements. First was the *sibaya* (cattle byre), the center of homestead life, where the cattle were enclosed, where grain was stored in pits, and where important meetings were held. Second was the *indlunkulu* (great hut), opposite the *sibaya*, in which resided—and over which presided—the mother of the *umnumzane* (if she were alive; if not, a classificatory mother or the *umnumzane*'s first wife). The *indlunkulu* was also the hallowed sanctuary for the spirits of the *umnumzane*'s male ancestors. Third was the *lilawu* (barracks), guarding the entrance to the homestead, in which resided the unmarried young men of the homestead.

Homestead labor was allocated in accordance with gender and age. Traditionally women were responsible for child rearing, domestic labor and upkeep, and cultivation. Men were responsible for constructing and ploughing fields, homestead construction, and all aspects of cattle husbandry. The *umnumzane* was also responsible for mediating the homestead's interests with the wider economic and political world. In recent times, with the advent of urbanization and migrant labor, the rigid delineation of homestead labor has given way to more flexible arrangements.

The modernization of Swazi society has also led to the progressive integration of the *umuti*'s economic base into the capitalist economy. By the 1980s more than half of the total income of the average homestead was derived from cash wages, while less than 10 percent of homesteads were supporting themselves by agricultural sales alone. Likewise, about half of the total homestead income was being expended on modern necessities: clothing, school fees, household goods, fuel, and transportation. Still, near the end of the 20th century (1986 census) more than 75 percent of the total population remained classified as "rural," and more than 35 percent of the total population remained illiterate.

HONEY, DE SYMONS (b. 1872; knighted 1932). Resident commissioner, 1917–28. Honey was a former British South Africa Company policeman and **Transvaal** civil servant. His first posting in Swaziland was as government secretary to the first resident commissioner, **Francis Enraght Moony**. During 1914–16 Honey was acting resident commissioner during the extended absence of Resident Commissioner **Robert Coryndon** in Rhodesia. Honey was an authoritarian administrator (in the mold of his predecessor Coryndon) who defined "**indirect rule**" as a coercive rather than a cooperative mechanism of governance. Honey treated both Queen Regent **Labotsibeni Mdluli** and *iNgwenyama* **Sobhuza Dlamini II** as junior civil servants, opening their mail, infiltrating their courts with informers, and occasionally humiliating them in public. Honey's successor as resident commissioner, **T. Ainsworth Dickson**, remarked soon after his arrival from Kenya on the total absence of any productive native policy in Swaziland and proceeded over the span of his tenure to bring Sobhuza into participation in what came much closer to effective joint rule. Honey was also an amateur historian who wrote in manuscript a useful political and social history of the Swazi that is located in the National Archives at **Lobamba** (RCS 115/14). Honey became governor of the Seychelles in 1928 and retired in 1933.

HOULTON, SIR JOHN W. (?–1973). Resident of Swaziland beginning in 1950 who first served as legal secretary to the colonial administration. In 1965 Houlton was appointed speaker of the **Legislative Council**. In 1967 he was appointed speaker of the Senate, then president of the Senate, a position he held until *iNgwenyama* **Sobhuza Dlamini II**'s repeal of the constitution in 1973. For many years Houlton contributed editorials to *The Times of Swaziland*.

HOUSE OF ASSEMBLY. *See* PARLIAMENT

HOWICK, LORD. *See* BARING, SIR EVELYN

HYND, DR. DAVID (1895–1991). A Church of the **Nazarene** medical missionary and educator of uncommon stature and political influence from soon after his arrival in Swaziland in 1925 until his death in 1991.

Dr. Hynd was born in Australia but was raised and educated in Scotland. In 1927 he founded and built the Raleigh Fitkin Memorial Hospital on 35 acres of government-allocated land on the outskirts of Bremersdorp (**Manzini**). At the same time that he was medical superintendent of the hospital and head of the Nazarene mission at Bremersdorp, he also served as government medical officer for the Bremersdorp and Lubombo districts. Dr. Hynd established the first nurses' training institute, the first rural health clinic, and the first leprosarium in the kingdom. In 1932 he became director of the Swaziland branch of the British Red Cross Society. He was also, from 1925 onward, the royal physician for the dowager queen, **Labotsibeni Mdluli**, along with *iNgwenyama* **Sobhuza Dlamini II** and his wives and children.

Dr. Hynd's close relationship with Sobhuza led to his involvement in national educational policy and politics, most often as a supporter of the royalist political perspective. From 1929 to 1961 Dr. Hynd served on the Board of Advice on National Education. He was a member of the first Constitutional Committee in 1960, and in 1963 he was a delegate to the second **constitutional conference** in London. For a number of years Dr. Hynd was president of the Swaziland Council of Churches. He retired officially from his missionary and medical offices in 1961. Dr. Hynd's son, Dr. Samuel Hynd, was minister of health from 1978 to 1982.

-I-

IMBOKODVO NATIONAL MOVEMENT (INM). The victorious royalist party in the three parliamentary elections held in Swaziland in 1964, 1967, and 1972, and thus the ruling political party of Swaziland until *iNgwenyama* **Sobhuza Dlamini II**'s repeal of Swaziland's constitution in 1973. It was formed by Sobhuza and the *libandla* in response to the pre-independence constitutional developments of 1963–64. In 1963 British colonial secretary **Duncan Sandys**, reacting to the inability of the London **constitutional conference** to agree on key provisions of a new draft document, imposed a constitution on Swaziland that Sobhuza regarded to be threatening to his legitimacy. That was so primarily because the Sandys constitution vested unprecedented executive powers with the newly established office of **Queen's Commissioner**, including his control over the disposition of Swaziland's mineral wealth.

At about the same time, Sobhuza was perceiving the mounting danger to his position of two emerging domestic power blocs, the European settlers and the educated Swazi middle class. Neither bloc was under his control, and indeed both were forming themselves into opposition political parties in order to contest the 1964 election. Were either (or both) of them to score respectable showings they might begin, constitutionally, to whittle away at his sovereignty. At the very least what was at stake in the 1964 election was the membership of the new **Legislative Council** (Legco), because it would be the Legco that would profoundly influence the shaping of the projected independence constitution. Consequently the *ingwenyama* and *libandla* formed a proprietary, monarchist party (the INM) to contest the election. *Imbokodvo* can be translated roughly as "Grinding Stone," a metaphor for national unity analogous to the American image of the "melting pot." The *ingwenyama* chose **Mnt. Makhosini Dlamini** to head the party and contest the election, aided by **Dr. George Msibi** as secretary general.

Sobhuza, to neutralize the parties representing the Swazi bourgeoisie (which to varying degrees advocated limiting the powers of the monarchy), placed the INM in an election coalition with the strongest and most conservative settler party, the **United Swaziland Association (USA)**. Mnt. Makhosini also drew on the advice of political strategists from **South Africa**. In organizing the support of its political base among the Swazi peasantry, the INM relied on *libandla* members and chiefs to act as informal electioneering officers. INM candidates were selected through the mechanism of the *tinkhundla*, regional councils that had been established by Sobhuza in the mid-1950s. Despite its Westernized pretensions, therefore, the INM remained firmly rooted in "tradition," the tool of the *ingwenyama*, the *libandla*, and the chiefs. Sobhuza's formulae clearly resonated with the electorate, for the INM-USA alliance won a smashing victory, with the USA winning all the European-roll seats in the new Legco and the INM sweeping every seat on the National roll.

Once victory was won, Sobhuza executed a political volte-face. By early 1966 he had abandoned the INM's alliance with the USA, which thereafter withered away. At about the same time he quietly severed the INM's close ties with the South African political establishment, while he invited the leadership of the more moderate Swazi opposition parties (the most accommodating ones, at least) to join Imbokodvo. Many of the more prominent politicians did, some at that time and others somewhat later. The ultimate effect—and this was the sign of Sobhuza's political genius—was to co-opt in piecemeal fashion the bulk of the Swazi middle class and the European settler population into the traditionalist political fold.

In the 1967 election the INM, now with strong settler backing, won 75 percent of the vote in seven out of eight constituencies, winning every seat in the new pre-independence parliament. The 1972 election was a different story, for in the Mphumalanga (Big Bend area) constituency the democratically inclined middle-class peasant voters combined with militant workers to throw out the three INM members of **parliament** in favor of a radical opposition (**Ngwane National Liberatory Congress**) slate. That proved to be the opening scene in a political drama that ended with the *ingwenyama*'s repeal of the constitution and banning of all political parties in 1973. That act in turn spelled the end of the political usefulness of the INM and consequently marked its demise. *See also* Constitution (1964); Constitution (1967)

IMMIGRATION AMENDMENT ACT of 1972. *See* NGWENYA, BHEKINDLELA THOMAS

INDEPENDENCE CONFERENCE. *See* CONSTITUTION (INDEPENDENCE, 1968)

INDIRECT RULE. A pattern of British colonial administration in Africa expostulated by the administrator of Northern Nigeria, Frederick Lugard, in a series of early 20th-century political memoranda. "Indirect rule" advocated reliance on traditional rulers and institutions as the basis of rule (where not contradictory to British moral standards), in effect making a virtue out of the perpetual understaffing and scanty funding of the British colonial service. Colonial officers were to utilize "native" taxes to support minimal social services and encourage the growth of Western political institutions. In Swaziland the beginnings of true indirect rule were not achieved until the residency of **T. Ainsworth Dickson** (1928–35). Previous **resident commissioners** had placed much emphasis on flaunting their own authority and on reducing the traditional officials to such conspicuous (and often humiliating) dependency as to render them almost wholly ineffective as agents of indirect rule. Under Dickson and his successor, **Allan G. Marwick** (1935–37), enough domestic authority and prestige was restored to *iNgwenyama* **Sobhuza Dlamini II** as to allow him to participate significantly in indirect rule.

Sobhuza then played that new domestic leverage into effective political support for his protracted campaign against the **Native Administration Proclamation**, first proposed by the British on the model of Basutoland's proclamation, in 1939. Its purpose was to formalize indirect rule by placing the *ingwenyama* officially under the authority of the resident commissioner. The king also campaigned against the proposed **Native**

Courts Proclamation, which likewise placed the resident commissioner officially at the pinnacle of the appellate process. Sobhuza ultimately prevailed in his campaign against both proclamations, laying the groundwork for his establishment of his complete sovereignty at the time of independence in 1968.

INDLOVUKAZI. See iNDLOVUKAZI

INGWAVUMA. Properly, iNgwavuma. A horizontal strip of territory about 12 miles (19 kilometers) deep stretching east from Swaziland's southeastern border to the Indian Ocean, contiguous to the Natal-Mozambique border. It is populated (c. 150,000) by **Nguni**-speakers, some of whom have historically *khonta*-ed (paid allegiance to) Swazi kings, while others consider themselves Zulu, Tsonga, or **Shangane**. In 1895 **Britain** designated the region to be part of Zululand over the vigorous protests of the Swazi. In 1976 **South Africa** proclaimed Ingwavuma to be part of the kwaZulu homeland.

All those considerations took on a new urgency in early 1982 when the South African government offered Ingwavuma to *iNgwenyama* **Sobhuza Dlamini II** as part of the **kaNgwane** land deal. Sobhuza, who was not the first Swazi king to dream of sovereignty over Ingwavuma, giving him access to the sea through **Kosi Bay**, was enthusiastically disposed to accept Pretoria's offer. News of the proposed deal touched off storms of protest from the Zulu and from the Organization of African Unity, which opposed the *quid pro quo* demanded of Sobhuza, that he expel the **African National Congress** from his kingdom. Sobhuza died before the deal could be consummated, and Ingwavuma remains part of South Africa.

The village of Ingwavuma, located along the South African side of the border 14 miles (22 kilometers) north-northeast of Lavumisa, was the British colonial magistracy to which *iNgwenyama* **Bhunu Dlamini** fled in 1898 following the political murder of *indvuna* **Mbhabha Nsibandze**.

INGWENYAMA. See iNGWENYAMA

INKHOSI DLAMINI. *See* iNKHOSI DLAMINI

INSANGU. (Properly *inSangu*; also *dagga*.) Marijuana. A hallucinogenic drug, usually smoked, used by the Swazi since the 18th century in doctoring armies for battle and in ceremonial praisings of the *ingwenyama*. Beginning around World War I, with the growing concentration of labor forces in **South Africa**, *insangu* cultivation increasingly became a staple of Swaziland's underground economy. Grown in the rich, manured soil of old cattle kraals primarily in the mountainous regions of western and southwestern Swaziland, powerful Swazi *insangu* became a prized commodity when smuggled into the mining compounds of the Rand. So profitable was its trade that by the late 1920s chiefs controlling certain of those regions took on the character of warlords, powerful enough to repel occasional police incursions with their followers. The *insangu* culture along with its attendant political economy permeates those regions of Swaziland to this day.

INSILA. (Properly *inSila*; pl. *tinsila*.) Literally, "body dirt" or "sweat." Individuals drawn from specific non-royal clans who are ceremonially made "blood brothers" to the ***ingwenyama*** in order to protect him from royal rivals. No others, even royalty, are as close to the *ingwenyama* ceremonially and often personally. The first two, senior *tinsila*, are the most important in his life. They are selected from his age cohort soon after his designation as *inkhosana* (crown prince), so that they may participate with him in all the various ceremonies signifying his advancement in age and status. Blood and other medications are exchanged between the *tinsila* and the *ingwenyama*, applied to incisions in the body. After this ceremony they are referred to as the *ingwenyama*'s "twins." Citizens with personal difficulties or crises, even royalty, appeal to the *tinsila* to request the *ingwenyama*'s intercession. Any attack by an enemy of the *ingwenyama* is said to be deflected or absorbed by the *tinsila* acting as shields to protect him. Other, junior, *tinsila* are appointed later throughout the king's lifetime to assist in various rituals connected with his person. *iNgwenyama* **Sobhuza Dlamini II**'s two senior *tinsila* were Shwapha Mdluli (*insila* of the right hand) and **Ngolotjeni Motsa** (*insila* of the left hand). The death of the *ingwenyama* removes all *tinsila* from office.

INYANGA. (Properly *inYanga*; pl. *tinyanga*.) One of two ritual specialists whom Swazi consult for relief from common body or mental ailments or other misfortunes (such as crop or business failure, or unrequited love). The other specialist is the ***sangoma*** (pl. *tangoma*, ritual practitioners). The *inyanga* specializes in concocting medicines as cures, most commonly herbs or the roots, bark, or leaves of trees. Hence *tinyanga* are often referred to as "herbalists" or "medicine men." *tInyanga* claim experience and past successes in diagnosing and treating specific illnesses and conditions with specialized medicines. They do not often claim, as *tangoma* normally do, special communications with ancestors, "callings," or powerful medical pedigrees. *tInyanga* can offer medicines to cure disease, potions to elicit love, or medicines to defend the homestead or to protect against lightning. There are numerous specialties within the ritual profession. For example the *inyanga vokupengula*, the medical diagnostician, rare among the *tinyanga*, throws bones and observes their patterns for signs. All *tinyanga* are known by their particular arrays of charms, medicine pouches, and other specialized paraphernalia. It was those medicines that constituted the most tangible means of identifying *tinyanga* as distinct from *tangoma*, diviners of occult causations of illness and misfortune.

During the colonial era the British administration took a dim view of the roles of both *tinyanga* and *tangoma* in traditional society. It was responding in part to pressure from the missionary establishment, which viewed them as spiritual competitors, but it was also responding as the political authority, seeing them as alternative loci of power, exerting as they did a strong metaphysical hold on virtually the entire citizenry. In a "**witchcraft**" proclamation in 1930 the government outlawed those *tinyanga* who practiced diagnosis and the prescription of medicines, as well as all divining activities of *tangoma*. The proclamation had little effect on either practice.

IRON ORE. *See* SWAZILAND IRON ORE DEVELOPMENT COMPANY

IRRIGATION. Swaziland's extraordinary fertility is in part the result of post–World War II investment in irrigation schemes that diverted the water from the kingdom's major rivers into **lowveld** and **middleveld** regions of fertile soils but scanty rainfall. The first major undertaking was the British **Colonial** (later **Commonwealth**) **Development Corporation**'s **Swaziland Irrigation Scheme** on the lower **Komati** and Mbuluzi rivers, begun in 1950. Subsequent projects diverted water from the Mlumati, **Lusushwana**, Mbuluzane, Mlumati, **Usutu**, and Mhlatuzane rivers. Major crops produced under irrigation are sugarcane and citrus. Until the 1970s rice was grown, but it proved unsuccessful because of water salinity. Vegetables, pineapples, maize, and **cotton** are also cultivated under irrigation in certain areas. In 1998 a major new hydroelectric and irrigation project, the Maguga Dam, was being constructed on the upper Komati River.

-J-

JACKSON, REVEREND JOEL (1837–1903). Anglican (Society for the Propagation of the Gospel, SPG) missionary to Zululand (1865) who traveled north to establish the first SPG mission in Swaziland in 1871. The station was in **New Scotland**, near the settlement of Derby in the **Transvaal**. Later, when the border delineation by the **Transvaal-Swaziland Boundary Commission** (1880) placed that station in the Transvaal, Jackson moved inland and established the Usutu mission at Luyengweni, near *iNgwenyama* **Mbandzeni Dlamini**'s capital at **Mbekelweni**, in 1881. Jackson proceeded to establish himself in a position of trust with Mbandzeni, occasionally translating for him and obtaining a **concession** for the land on which his mission was situated. It was at that time that Jackson, who had always held a low opinion of the Swazi as potential congregants, began to succumb to the allure of the entrepreneurial world. In 1887 he obtained a share in a mineral concession from Mbandzeni, placing it in his wife's name and selling it in 1889 for a profit that made him for a time a wealthy man. Subsequently Rev. Jackson became deeply involved in European politics, elected a member of the **third Swazieland Committee** and becoming an ally of **Allister Miller** in his efforts to oust **Theophilus Shepstone, Jr.**, as Mbandzeni's advisor. It was possibly because of his political enmities that rumors about Jackson's moral character reached the Anglican bishop of Natal. The charges were, however, never proven. Jackson left Swaziland in 1892 and died, destitute, in Durban. He left the Anglican mission much better established in land and buildings than in communicants.

JOINT COMMISSION. *See* ANGLO-BOER JOINT COMMISSION

JOINT COUNCIL OF SWAZILAND POLITICAL PARTIES. Also Swaziland African National Union (SANU). A short-lived, *ad hoc* alliance of the three main Swazi opposition parties in June 1964 in anticipation of the 1964 **Legislative Council** election. Those parties were the already fragmented **Swaziland Progressive Party (SPP)**, the **Swaziland Democratic Party (SDP)**, and the **Ngwane National Liberatory Congress (NNLC)**. The incentive for the political amalgamation was the overwhelming success of *iNgwenyama* **Sobhuza Dlamini II**'s January 1964 **"Reindeer Referendum"** opposing the British-imposed (1963) internal government constitution. That referendum was known as the "Reindeer Referendum" because the people chose between two symbols: the lion (anti-constitution) and the reindeer, an animal unknown in Swaziland (pro-constitution). The lopsidedness of the vote, 122,000 against and 154 for the constitution, alerted the opposition to the near-impossibility of beating Sobhuza's **Imbokodvo National Movement (INM)** in the legislative elections scheduled for late June. The alliance that they formed as a result was doomed from the start, for it was never able to coordinate the campaign in any of the electoral constituencies, and each party ended up putting forward its own candidates. The result was a total sweep of the election by the INM and its European coalition partner, the **United Swaziland Association (USA)**.

Following the 1964 election the grouping renamed itself the Alliance of Swaziland Progressive Parties, under the leadership of the SDP's **Dr. Allen Nxumalo**. It proved to be as unable as its predecessor alliances to overcome the determinations of its party leaders to go their own ways. One by one its constituent members (including Dr. Nxumalo) resigned. In 1966 it renamed itself the Swaziland United Front under the leadership of **Obed Mabuza** (ex-SPP faction head). When the alliance failed to win any seats in the 1967 parliamentary elections, it folded.

JOUBERT, PETRUS J. (PIET) (1831–1900). Transvaal Afrikaner farmer and politician whose activities peripherally affected Swaziland's fortunes for a generation. As acting president of the **South African Republic (SAR)** during 1875–76, Joubert mounted a diplomatic and military show of force to counter King Cetshwayo Zulu's threat against the Swazi, forcing him to back down. Cetshwayo had approached the SAR in 1875 for permission to attack the Swazi. Joubert feared that the purpose of the proposed assault was to place the renegade **Mnt. Mblini Dlamini**, to whom he had granted asylum, on the Swazi throne. Subsequently Joubert acted as a member of the 1886 **Transvaal-Swaziland Boundary Commission**, as the SAR's chief representative on the 1889 **Anglo-Boer Joint (de Winton) Commission**, and on the SAR delegation that imposed itself on the installation ceremony of *iNgwenyama* **Bhunu Dlamini** in 1895.

-K-

KANGWANE. *See* kaNGWANE

*ku***KHONTA.** To pay allegiance to; serve; worship.[2] A pledge of allegiance offered by commoners to chiefs, and by chiefs to the *ingwenyama*. Supposedly voluntary, *khonta*-ing is in fact obligatory because it is entrenched in the Swazi system of land allocation controlled by the king and delegated through the chiefs. Commonly, in return for an allocation of land the homestead head *khonta*s a chief and owes him and the king tribute labor and/or cash, plus other forms of allegiance, on a continuing basis. It is claimed that the system is mutually beneficial and offers security of land tenure to the homestead, but in fact the arrangement can be, and on occasion is, terminated by the party in authority. For instance, not infrequently in the past a homestead head's improvement of his allocated land through fencing, irrigating, or other visible means has been viewed by his chief as his assumption of permanence of tenure and has led to his expulsion. It is arguable therefore that the *kukhonta* system, combined with the custom of communal cattle grazing, is responsible for much (though by no means all) of the decline of agricultural productivity on **Swazi Nation Land (SNL)** since the 1920s.

According to Macmillan,[3] *iNgwenyama* **Sobhuza Dlamini II** and the *libandla*, in an effort to further entrench the power of the "traditionalists" following his 1973 repeal of the constitution, made the *kukhonta* procedure a mandatory element of Swazi citizenship (Order in Council of 1974).

KHOZA, ARTHUR R. Swazi politician and civil servant whose career commenced in the radical opposition and who ended as an establishment official. Khoza obtained his degree from the University of South Africa and later studied at the Ideological Institute in Winneba, Ghana, where he became deeply influenced by the Pan-Africanist ideology of Kwame Nkrumah. Consequently he became a member of the **Ngwane National Liberatory Congress (NNLC)** in 1962 and embraced the African socialist platform of the NNLC's radical faction led by **Dr. Ambrose Zwane**. In 1965, following the arrest of **Mnt. Dumisa Dlamini** for assault, Khoza became acting secretary-general of the NNLC. In September 1966, with the splintering of the NNLC over ideological and personality issues, Khoza was one of many in the leadership to resign.

In time Khoza joined the royalist **Imbokodvo National Movement (INM)** and became the prime minister's private secretary. During the late 1960s and early 1970s he served as permanent secretary for the Ministry of Works, Power and Communication, and then in the same capacity for the Ministry of Justice. Following *iNgwenyama* **Sobhuza Dlamini II**'s repeal of the constitution in 1973, Khoza was appointed secretary to the Royal Constitutional Commission. At the time of Sobhuza's death in 1982, Khoza was serving as principal secretary for the Ministry of Agriculture. During the struggle for power between the *Liqoqo* and the royal house, Khoza cast his lot with Queen Regent **Dzeliwe Shongwe** and was imprisoned at the time of her dismissal in 1983. Following his pardoning and release in 1984, he became director for agriculture in the Southern African Development Coordination Conference (later **Southern African Development Community**), headquartered in Zambia. In

1988 he was elected to **parliament**, and he served as vice-president of the Senate.

KHUMALO, *iNDLOVUKAZI* SISILE (?–1881). A wife of *iNgwenyama* **Mswati Dlamini II** and mother of *iNgwenyama* **Ludvonga Dlamini II**, her only child. Once Sisile became *indlovukazi* she established herself at the royal village at **Nkanini**. She was described by contemporary observers as a strong personality, intelligent, crafty, and ambitious. Sisile consequently holds a place as one of a handful of females who have strongly influenced Swaziland's history in a society dominated hegemonically by males.

The choice of Mswati's successor was contested by many eligible sons, including **Mnt. Mblini Dlamini**, and Ludvonga's selection while still a minor was mired in controversy. Subsequently Ludvonga left no heir when he died suddenly in 1874 at age 19, entailing yet another contested succession. In this one Sisile figured prominently. The venerated and powerful dowager queen **Tsandzile Ndwandwe** decreed that the choice of Ludvonga's heir should fall to Sisile, who had lost her only son. Sisile thereupon selected the orphaned **Mnt. Mbandzeni Dlamini**, which consequently left her in position as *indlovukazi*. Sisile immediately demonstrated her determination to wield her renewed influence. She inserted herself in border negotiations with the **South African Republic**, heretofore the *ingwenyama*'s realm, and accorded women a prominent place in her previously all-male council. Sisile was said to have regarded the shy, lonely Mbandzeni to be more of a regent than a king. When Mbandzeni fathered a child by a young woman previously betrothed to Ludvonga, **Somdlalose Hlubi**, Sisile quickly recognized the infant as Ludvonga's rightful heir. At that point Mbandzeni acted with uncharacteristic decisiveness, ordering the child poisoned and removing all persons from Nkanini excepting Sisile and Somdlalose. When the two women fled with troops from the Nkanini royal regiment, Mbandzeni's *imphi* chased, caught, and defeated the rebellious troops, then executed Sisile (and presumably Somdlalose).

KHUMALO, ZONKE A. (1927–). Swazi businessman and politician, and personal advisor to both *tiNgwenyama* **Sobhuza Dlamini II** and **Mswati Dlamini III**, both of whom occasionally placed him in government ministries. Khumalo was proprietor of the Mhlanya Trading Store, and during the late 1950s and early 1960s he was secretary of the **Swazi Commercial Amadoda**, a position of considerable power in the emerging Swazi middle class. Khumalo, a member of the **Imbokodvo National**

Movement (INM), was elected to **parliament** representing the Usutu constituency in 1964, 1967, and 1972. He served as deputy prime minister of Swaziland from 1971 to 1980 and as minister of justice during the early 1990s.

Historically the Khumalos held close ties to the monarchy. Khumalo's father, Mashambo, had been an attendant to Queen Regent **Labotsibeni Mdluli**, and following her death he had guarded her grave. Zonke Khumalo had been close to Sobhuza since childhood and had married one of his daughters. He became one of a small circle of advisors to King Mswati after the latter's installation in 1986. In 1990 Mswati named Khumalo minister of justice although he had no legal training. That move, given Khumalo's reputation as a hard-line conservative, was widely interpreted as aimed against popular opposition to the government.

KIRSH, NATHAN (NATIE) (1930–). South African industrialist whose Swaziland Milling Company obtained a monopoly over all maize milling and distribution in Swaziland beginning in 1959. Raised in Potchefstroom, where his family owned a milling and sorghum brewing malt business, Kirsh arrived in Swaziland in 1958 armed with £1,000 and an idea of how to solve the severe problems of maize distribution bottlenecks that were hindering the kingdom's agricultural and industrial development by periodically interrupting laborers' food supplies. Kirsh persuaded the **resident commissioner**, **Brian Marwick**, and *iNgwenyama* **Sobhuza Dlamini II** to allow him to purchase all locally grown maize at a set price, mill some of it, and distribute the maize and maize meal at fixed prices without competition, stipulating only that his prices would be fair and his operations efficient. The Swaziland Milling Co. Ltd. began operations in May 1959, marketing maize, maize meal, and sorghum brewing malt. Although it soon smoothed out the problems of distribution to the employers of large labor forces, the fact of its monopoly inevitably led to some resentment and occasional charges of price gouging, especially on the maize that Swaziland Milling imported from **South Africa**.

Kirsh's success in maize processing and marketing quickly led to his investment in other sectors of the modern Swazi economy. Tracar Ltd. first sold tractors to farmers and then automobiles and trucks to the general populace. Swaziland Warehouse marketed farm implements and general hardware, while Farm Chemicals Ltd. sold fertilizers and pesticides. Sugar Sales Ltd. and Mtimane Forests Ltd. marketed their products in South Africa. Polyplas Ltd. and Prepack Ltd. distributed plastics and packaging materials and services. Fincor Ltd. and Industrial Agencies

Ltd. involved banking and real estate. During the 1980s these corporations were merged into the Swaki Group Ltd. In 1986 Kirsh became a major investor in the National Textile Corporation of Swaziland Ltd. (Natex), which produced cotton ticking and cotton/polyester yarns. In 1988 he established a second bank, UnionBank.

Kirsh in the meantime had become a major industrialist in South Africa (the Kirsh Group) and had also made significant investments in Israel, **Britain**, and the United States. Throughout his Swaziland career Kirsh was active in service to industrial associations, the monarchy, and the government. This service included the chairmanship of the Swazi Electricity Board and the presidencies of the Swaziland Chamber of Industries and the Swaziland Federation of Employers. Kirsh also acted as unofficial advisor to the *ingwenyama*, the *liqoqo*, and the cabinet.

KOMATI RIVER. Sometimes iNkomati River. One of the four major rivers traversing Swaziland, rising in the **Transvaal** and exiting ultimately into the Indian Ocean. The Komati rises near the **South African** town of Carolina and follows an erratic path before it enters Swaziland about 6 miles (10 kilometers) south of Bulembu (**Havelock**). It flows due east to Bhalekane, where it turns north and northeast, exiting near Bordergate. Back in the Transvaal it is joined by the Lomati River, enters Mozambique through Komatipoort, and becomes the iNcomati River, which loops through the country, exiting into the Indian Ocean just north of Maputo.

During the **concessions** period the Komati figured as a boundary of sorts, forming the northern limitation of the infamous **unallotted lands concession** (1889), which granted Frank Watkins and **John Thorburn** the rights to all vacant farm and grazing lands south of the river for an annual fee of £50. Since 1950 the Komati has been a major source of **irrigation** water for the large **lowveld** complex in the Tshaneni-Mhlume area. In 1998 the construction of the massive Maguga Dam project on the upper Komati promised to add new irrigation and hydroelectric power capacity to northern Swaziland. Finally, the Komati figures significantly in the ritual life of the nation, being one of four rivers from which national priests (*bemanti*) draw water during the preparations for the *iNcwala* **ceremony** to strengthen the *ingwenyama*.

KOSI BAY. An Indian Ocean inlet in extreme northern Natal, approximately 50 miles (80 kilometers) east of Big Bend. From the 1880s to the present Kosi Bay has figured significantly in the strategic intentions and dreams of both the **South African Republic (SAR)** and Swaziland. Beginning in the early 1880s the SAR under President Paul Kruger looked on Delagoa, Kosi, and St. Lucia bays as possible termini for his dreamed-of railway and opening to the sea. That ambition appeared to be within Kruger's grasp during the late 1880s when the SAR came into possession through local intermediaries of several of *iNgwenyama* **Mbandzeni Dlamini**'s **concessions** (customs, postal, survey, licenses, railways, and telegraphs), allowing it to administer the kingdom. His dream appeared achieved when the **third Swaziland Convention** (1894) granted him virtually a free hand in Swaziland in return for his acquiescence toward British adventures north of the Limpopo River. At that point Kosi Bay loomed large in Kruger's sights, because it was the last outlet to the sea remaining unannexed by Great **Britain** or not under Portuguese sovereignty. Within months, however, the British attitude toward Kruger's government hardened, and in 1895 Britain demolished the SAR's plans for a railway through Swaziland to Kosi Bay by annexing Tsongaland.

Perhaps in part because Swazi origins lay along the Tsonga coast, Swazi kings have always held Kosi Bay and its environs in their acquisitive gaze. *iNgwenyama* **Sobhuza Dlamini II** demonstrated his interest in direct ocean commerce during the 1970s by establishing two successive maritime shipping companies, the Royal Swazi Maritime Corporation (Swazimar) and the Royal Swazi National Shipping Corporation (Swaziship). In 1982, during the months immediately prior to his death, Sobhuza entered into a controversial agreement with the **South African** government by which the **kaNgwane** homeland would be transferred to his sovereignty in return for his suppression of **African National Congress (ANC)** activities within Swaziland's borders. Part of the allure to the old king was South Africa's offer to transfer sovereignty over a strip of land (**Ingwavuma**) stretching from Swaziland's southeast border to and including Kosi Bay, his long-coveted outlet to the sea. Sobhuza died before the deal could be ratified, and vigorous opposition to the accord from every quarter—the Zulu, the **Organization of African Unity**, and after 1990 the new ANC government in Pretoria—has kept it from being revived. During the 1990s, however, *iNgwenyama* **Mswati Dlamini III** stated his intention of raising the issue once again.

KROGH, JOHANNES C. (1846–1921). Longtime member of the **South African Republic (SAR)** civil service, notably as landdrost of the Wakkerstroom and Utrecht districts. In 1884 Krogh obtained a land **concession** from *iNgwenyama* **Mbandzeni Dlamini**, and there were suggestions that he subsequently used his SAR government position to leverage a large grazing concession from Mbandzeni. In 1894 Krogh became the SAR's representative on the **Government Committee** in Swaziland, and a year later (following the SAR's administrative takeover) he became special commissioner for Swaziland.

Krogh faced three significant administrative difficulties during his tenure. The first was establishing the jurisdiction of his **Transvaal** *vrederechters* (justices of the peace) in the face of Swazi official opposition to the relinquishment of its criminal jurisdiction. The second was participating in the SAR-Portuguese boundary commission's 1897 resetting of the beacons separating Swazi from Mozambican territory, an action embroiled in controversy. The third was his gradual and skillful undertaking to impose SAR government authority over *iNgwenyama* **Bhunu Dlamini** in 1898 following the murder of **Mbhabha Nsibandze**. Responding to Bhunu's hostile resistance to his summonses with diplomacy backed by military force, Krogh ultimately helped maneuver the headstrong king into submitting to a public trial and a fine. That in turn led to the joint SAR-British **protocol** (1898) to the **third Swaziland Convention** (1894), which withdrew Bhunu's criminal jurisdiction and drastically curtailed other royal legal powers. Finally, at the outbreak of the **Anglo-Boer War** (October 1899), Krogh terminated the SAR administration of Swaziland and ordered all European inhabitants to join him in withdrawing. Krogh's final official involvement in Swaziland was his service on the **Swaziland Concessions Commission** (1905), which created the **native areas** later delineated following the **Partition Proclamation** of 1907.

KUKHONTA. See kuKHONTA

KUNENE, CLEOPAS (?–1917). Of Swazi parentage, one of the graduates of the Wesleyan mission school at **Edendale**, Natal, who played a role as advisors to the Swazi monarchy and during the 1890s, and then as occasional functionaries of the British colonial administration after 1903. Of them all Kunene, one of those most deeply imprinted by the seamier aspects of his acquired bourgeois values, played one of the most ambiguous roles. Kunene arrived in Swaziland from Natal in 1894 and immediately became interpreter to the Swazi **deputation of 1894** dispatched by Queen Regent **Tibati Nkambule** to London to protest the **South African Republic's** (SAR's) administrative takeover. Kunene subsequently became Queen Regent **Labotsibeni Mdluli's** interpreter and advisor in certain affairs of state. For instance he was involved in the 1896 settlement of the long-standing dispute between Labotsibeni and **Theophilus Shepstone, Jr.**, over monies owed him as official advisor.

In all those capacities Kunene demonstrated an unseemly acquisitiveness, spending so promiscuously in London for instance that he later asked for reimbursement of several hundred pounds from the British administration. He was also accused (along with **Alpheus Nkosi**, another of Labotsibeni's mission-educated advisors) of persuading her to settle with Shepstone to her great disadvantage in return for a bribe from the SAR.

Beginning in 1912 Kunene, along with Labotsibeni, **Mnt. Malunge Dlamini**, **Robert Grendon**, and other advisors, became involved in the launching of the **African National Congress's** (ANC's) newspaper, *Abantu Batho*. Kunene and Grendon were its first editors, and Labotsibeni became a substantial founding backer. In 1916 Kunene, then a resident of Sophiatown, threw a lavish reception for *iNkhosana* (**Crown Prince**) **Sobhuza Dlamini II**, then on his way to take up his secondary education at the **Lovedale Missionary Institution** in the Cape. Once again Kunene submitted an exorbitant bill to the administration in Mbabane, which the **resident commissioner**—as he had done on the previous occasion—ignored.

KUNENE, MBABANE (?–1914). Swazi chief and *indvuna* of the **Mdzimba** royal cattle station, on whose lands near modern **Mbabane Allister Miller** built his home, Dalriach, at the turn of the century. Miller claimed the area by right of a **concession** and proceeded to encroach gradually but often provocatively on Kunene's lands and authority. It was on Chief Kunene's account that *iNgwenyama* **Sobhuza Dlamini II** petitioned the Special Court in 1924 (*Sobhuza II vs. Miller*) to overturn the legitimacy of the **unallotted lands concession**, held originally by Miller's father-in-law, **John Thorburn**, a portion of which Thorburn had transferred to Miller. It was by virtue of that concession that Miller claimed ownership of Dalriach. By the time Sobhuza filed his suit Chief Mbabane Kunene had died and had been succeeded by his son Maloyi. It is believed by many that Chief Mbabane gave his name to the stream, and hence to the early European settlement that has since become the capital of Swaziland.

KUPER, HILDA (1911–1992). A leading scholar on Swazi anthropology and history whose books *An African Aristocracy: Rank Among the Swazi* and *The Uniform of Colour: A Study of White-Black Relationships in Swaziland* (both 1947) remain widely respected and consulted classics. The most important of her numerous articles and books on the Swazi are noted in the bibliography (during the 1930s she published under her maiden name, Beemer).

Born in Rhodesia (modern Zimbabwe), Kuper received her doctorate in anthropology at the London School of Economics under the direction of Bronislaw Malinowski. Her fieldwork in Swaziland, published in her two 1947 volumes, was conducted during 1934–37, an era when research by women working alone in the field was highly unusual. Although Kuper later studied the Indian community in Natal, the Swazi remained her principal life's work. Beginning in 1934 Kuper developed a close friendship with *iNgwenyama* **Sobhuza Dlamini II** that lasted until his death in 1982. She also developed lifelong relationships with several of his wives and daughters. In 1978 she published Sobhuza's authorized biography, *Sobhuza II: Ngwenyama and King of Swaziland*, and in 1982 she was one of the principal eulogists at his state funeral. In later years Dr. Kuper's attachment to the royal house attracted some question from scholars as to how it may have affected her objectivity, especially considering Sobhuza's known penchant for courting the South African anthropological establishment in support of his political interests. In 1970 Dr. Kuper became a citizen of Swaziland. In 1988 she received an honorary doctorate from the University of Swaziland. Her principal academic appointments were at the Universities of the Witwatersrand and Natal, and (beginning 1964) as professor of anthropology at the University of California, Los Angeles.

-L-

LABOR, MIGRANT. Migrant labor has been one of the pinions of Swaziland's economy and a leading cause of the underdevelopment of its peasantry since the establishment of the Witwatersrand ("rand," Johannesburg) gold mines in the 1890s. The deliberate underdevelopment took different forms. Heavy levels of taxation imposed first by the **South African Republic** in 1898 and then by the British beginning in 1903 were exacted not primarily for revenue but to force the Swazi off their **homesteads** and into the migrant labor stream; "to induce," in the words of one British official, "the Swazis to take to agricultural or mine labour."[4] It was incontrovertible also that one of the primary reasons for British implementation of the **Partition Proclamation** of 1907, which forced the Swazi either to become squatter tenants on European farms or to move to deliberately undersized and agriculturally marginal "**native areas**," was to generate reserves of labor for the benefit of local and foreign capital.

The British policy of underdevelopment and neglect achieved its desired effect. Within a generation of the removals (1914) the native areas were becoming seriously overpopulated, overstocked, and subject to erosion. By the mid-1920s upwards of 40 percent of the male working-age population was absent from homesteads, traveling as migrant labor either to the **Transvaal** or to local farms, estates, and ranches. That inevitably led to the decline of homestead productivity and the transformation of a once surplus-producing agricultural economy into a chronic importer of grains and foodstuffs. By 1941 conditions in the native areas had become so serious that a petition by *iNgwenyama* **Sobhuza Dlamini II** to the British parliament led to the implementation of several land repurchase and settlement schemes aimed at reversing the effects of colonial underdevelopment. Those measures did not begin to offset the effects of two generations of British underdevelopment, however, and migrant labor continued apace.

Following World War II the nature and direction of Swazi migrant labor flows were gradually altered because of the new, indigenous demands of the foreign-owned forestry, agribusiness, mining, and manufacturing enterprises that made their appearance in the kingdom beginning in the late 1940s. Migrant labor became more localized, and relatively fewer men absented themselves to the rand mines. Those conditions altered the economics of the Swazi homestead still further. For one thing, although men may have been absent for shorter periods, pay from local enterprises was substantially less than what could be earned in Johannesburg. One consequence was that female and child agricultural labor became a significant element in the employment market for the first time, further sapping homestead productivity, especially because women and children earned wages at levels far less than men's rates.

The Swazi monarchy has always been involved in the recruiting of Swazi labor in behalf of foreign capital. *iNgwenyama* **Bhunu Dlamini**, **Mnt. Malunge Dlamini**, and Queen Regent **Labotsibeni Mdluli** all made contracts with European recruiters to supply Swazi laborers to the South African gold mines in return for capitation fees. So too did *iNgwenyama* **Sobhuza Dlamini II** on occasion urge Swazi peasants to leave their homesteads for wage labor, first on behalf of the **Native Recruiting Corporation** (1948) and later in concert with foreign forestry and agribusiness capital within Swaziland.

Migrant labor has long been understood to carry socially destructive consequences irrespective of the benefits of the wages it generates. In addition to creation of agricultural dependency in the homestead, these consequences include sexual promiscuity and high rates of illegitimacy and disease, broken marriages, and increasing incidences of depression, alcoholism, and suicide. Subsequent generations are also affected: some children of absent fathers evince significantly diminished academic cognitive development.[5]

LABOTSIBENI. *See* MDLULI, *iNDLOVUKAZI* LABOTSIBENI

LAGDEN, SIR GODFREY Y. (1851–1934; knighted 1897). Lifelong British colonial servant with administrative experience in the **Transvaal**, Swaziland, and (most extensively) Basutoland. Lagden served in Swaziland during 1892–93 as acting British representative (in the absence of **Colonel Richard Martin** on the **Swaziland Government Committee**). Lagden, known as an ardent imperialist, spent his time countering the initiatives of **Theophilus Shepstone, Jr.,** the Swazi monarchy's representative on the committee. Lagden suspected Shepstone of being the stalking horse for the **South African Republic**'s imperial designs on the kingdom, while Shepstone and others on the committee accused Lagden of intriguing to establish a British protectorate. Following the British colonial takeover of Swaziland in 1903, Lagden was placed in charge of Swazi affairs as imperial secretary in Pretoria until 1907. He administered the territory as if, as was anticipated at the time, the kingdom was to be incorporated administratively into the Transvaal. So, for instance, the laws of the Transvaal were made, *mutatis mutandis*, the laws of Swaziland.

LAND SETTLEMENT SCHEME. *See* SWAZILAND NATIVE LAND SETTLEMENT SCHEME

LAND SPECULATION CONTROL ACT (1972). An act of the Swaziland **parliament** (December 1971) aimed at restraining the rapidly escalating price of freehold land in the interests of the emerging Swazi middle class by the mechanism of restricting the market. The law, which took effect at the end of 1972, established a land control board and decreed that any sale of land (or immovable property or company equity) to any non-Swazi required board approval. The law also provided for an appeals board. Finally, the act provided for the expropriation of profits derived from the sale of land attributable to speculation. The act touched off a storm of protest among the European population, but their worst fears were never realized. Many sales of land to non-Swazi were approved by the board, and the speculation clause was invoked only rarely. The act's main beneficiaries have been the Swazi elite and the monarchy, principally through its capital investment mechanism, the **Tibiyo takaNgwane Fund**.

liLANGENI. *See* LILANGENI

liLAUW. *See* LILAWU.

LaVUMISA. *See* NDWANDWE, LaVUMISA

LaZIDZE. *See* NDWANDWE, TSANDZILE

LEBOMBO MOUNTAINS. One of four topographical regions in Swaziland, a range of rocky scarps lying on a north-south axis east of the **lowveld**. The region ranges from 6 to 11 miles (10 to 18 kilometers) in breadth, and from 1,000 feet (305 meters) to 2,000 feet (610 meters) above sea level. The range is broken by narrow breaches cut by the Mbuluzi, **Usutu**, and iNgwavuma rivers flowing into Mozambique. The highest point in the Lebombo is Siteki Hill, which is 2,500 feet (760 meters) in altitude. Drought-resistant crops, **cotton**, sorghum, and occasionally groundnuts grow successfully in the Lebombo region in good rainfall years, with 30 inches (76 centimeters) to 40 inches (102 centimeters) of rainfall annually.

LEGISLATIVE COUNCIL (LEGCO). A multiracial internal law-making body established under the **constitution (1964)**. Such a council had first been proposed by **Lord William Hailey** in the 1950s. The first Constitutional Committee (1960) proposed its establishment to take the places of both the **Reconstituted European Advisory Council** and the *libandla*, but *iNgwenyama* **Sobhuza Dlamini II** would not hear of supplanting the latter body. The council was seen by the committee as an initial step toward a fully responsible and ultimately independent government. The committee's recommendation (1961) that the proposed council comprise an equal number of Europeans and Swazi ("50–50") was met with such hostility among Swazi opposition parties that the British government came to view it as nonviable.

The British-imposed 1964 constitution laid out the details of a legislature that was to be composed of **Her Majesty's Commissioner for Swaziland** (HMC) plus a Legislative Council (Legco). The Legco was to be composed of four officials (*ex officio*) and three members (nominated by HMC), plus 24 elected members. Of the latter, eight were to be Swazi elected under the eye of the *ingwenyama*, eight were to be elected by Europeans, and eight were to be of "any race" elected on a multiracial national roll. Elections for the Legco were held in June 1964, and in spite of the cumbersome nature of its composition it worked relatively smoothly during its tenure. It remained in power until it was replaced by a **parliament** under the terms of the **1967 constitution**.

LIBANDLA. The Swazi National Council. The formal name is *Libandla lakaNgwane*, Council of the Ngwane Nation. The *libandla* is a deliberative body that represents the nation in advising the king. In theory, membership in the *libandla* is open to all adult males (but not females), and when it addresses issues of great import attendance by commoners can be substantial. As a practical matter the *libandla*'s membership consists of *bantfwanenkosi* (princes) of lesser rank, chiefs and their councillors, headmen, and others by virtue of their clan status, education, wisdom, or other special attributes. The *libandla* meets at the royal *sibaya* (cattle kraal), where a representative of the *liqoqo* announces the subjects to be discussed. The *ingwenyama* is often, but not always, in attendance. He frequently does not attend *libandla* debates but is present when consensus has been reached. On occasions of state the *indlovukazi* may also be present. Otherwise there is no formal agenda or structure, while at the same time there is near total freedom of speech. Individuals who appear to abuse that freedom can be shouted down. Once the semblance of consensus has been reached, the *ingwenyama* makes his own observations, and the result is announced to the nation. Normally decisions by the *libandla* are required on all matters brought to it by the *liqoqo*. Following independence the *libandla* has met regularly, often during the winter for as much as a month.

During the pre–World War II period, as *iNgwenyama* **Sobhuza Dlamini II** was attempting both to consolidate domestic power and to strengthen his position with the colonial administration, his relations with the *libandla* became strained. This was because both Sobhuza and the *libandla* were jockeying for advantage in their mutual campaign to restore the power that had been relinquished to the chiefs (a major *libandla* constituency) during the era of Queen Regent **Labotsibeni Mdluli**. Sobhuza complained bitterly, for instance, when the administration initiated scheduled meetings between the assistant commissioners and the chiefs (many of whom were prominent *libandla* members). Conversely the colonial administration admonished the king throughout the 1930s to convene the *libandla* more often and treat it with more respect. Eventually Sobhuza began to prevail over the chiefs, first by persuading the administration to criminalize chiefly disobedience to his orders (1936) and then by conspicuously and successfully championing the chiefs' cause against the **Native Administration Proclamation** during the

1940s. Consequently during that decade the *libandla* worked in relative harmony under Sobhuza's leadership. That relationship took on new tensions following the gazetting of the Native Administration and **Native Courts Proclamations** of 1950, which delegated considerable power back to the "**Paramount Chief** in *Libandla*." That official recognition of the council's status as a powerful consultative body gave it the temerity to challenge Sobhuza's paramountcy on many issues from then until the king's death.

Because the *libandla* membership constitutes the establishment of the nation—royalty, chiefs, and their councillors—it is by tradition conservative in its outlook. During the late colonial era (beginning 1952) a mechanism was established by **Resident Commissioner David Morgan** and Sobhuza whereby a **Standing Committee of the *libandla*** met regularly with the government secretary and other officials to discuss matters of mutual concern. The Standing Committee quickly became an effective means of representing the traditionalist point of view to the government. The initiative came from Morgan and Sobhuza, the latter seeing it as a way to present his and the *libandla*'s case to the administration as effectively as other groups had done over the years. Those groups of concern to the king were the **Swaziland Farmers Association** (since the 1910s), the **Reconstituted European Advisory Council** (since 1921), and the Swazi chiefs, who had been meeting in groups with district and other officials since the late 1920s and whose views were sometimes at variance with those of the *ingwenyama* and *libandla*.

During the 1980s, following the death of Sobhuza and the ensuing period of political turbulence, the *libandla* dropped practically out of existence for about a decade. Beginning in the late 1990s the *ingwenyama*, the *indlovukazi*, and their close advisors (*labadzala*) were occasionally referred to as the Swazi National Council, a historical inaccuracy. In 1996 *iNgwenyama* **Mswati Dlamini III** established the Swaziland National Council Standing Committee to advise him on constitutional reform.

LIBUTFO. (Properly *liButfo*; pl. *emabutfo*.) Regiment, or (in the modern context), age regiment. The *emabutfo* are nationwide regiments, as distinct from *emachiba* (sing. *lichiba*, platoon), which are based on locality. The 19th-century *emabutfo* were organized primarily for war campaigning, cattle raiding, and communal labor for the *ingwenyama*'s fields. Nowadays their role is more ceremonial: dancing and singing on state occasions and providing tribute labor for the *ingwenyama*. Each age regiment shares a central meeting place or ceremonial barracks at royal villages throughout the countryside. The *libutfo* cuts across clan and geographic lines, and its age-mates can develop bonds stronger than kinship ties. *Emabutfo* are therefore important infusers and indicators of nationalism. They are exclusively male institutions, although women's age-groupings also exist.

In the past, a new *libutfo* was formed when a senior regiment was granted permission to marry (at 25 to 35 years of age). Normally this occurred at a rate of one every five to seven years. The new *libutfo* consisted of all young men around the age of puberty. Normally the *ingwenyama* determined the rate of *libutfo* formation and dispersal for marriage, which gave him enormous power over the rate of **homestead** formation and hence over both social reproduction and the loyalty of his male subjects. As a practical matter, because relatively few men could be accommodated at the regimental barracks in royal villages, the degree of participation in the *emabutfo* varied widely, with those living in the barracks being more active and enjoying higher status than those residing in the homestead.

The prominence of the *libutfo* as a national institution has waxed and waned over the years. During the early reign of *iNgwenyama* **Mswati Dlamini II**, the *libutfo*, based previously on locality as well as age, was made a nationwide institution. Because at the same time the number of royal villages was increased, the *emabutfo* were effectively transformed into powerful instruments of intelligence gathering and social control, constituting a major foundation of Mswati's heightened domestic power. The regency of **Labotsibeni Mdluli** witnessed a significant devolution of central power during the early 20th century, when regional chiefs' successful demands for control of tribute labor led to the near dissolution of the *emabutfo*.

It was *iNgwenyama* **Sobhuza Dlamini II** who saw in the *emabutfo* a means to revive the control of the monarchy over the male citizenry as the country gradually underwent modernization. During the 1920s Sobhuza invoked "tradition" in his imposition of the *emabutfo* system in the Swazi national schools in **Zombodze** and **Matsapha**, and his attempts to establish it in mission schools were a counter to the Pathfinder Scouts movement advocated by the Christian missionary establishment in Swaziland. In addition, Sobhuza chose major national events as occasions to establish new *emabutfo*. During World War II the *ingwenyama* dispatched the **African Pioneer Corps** to the war in the Mediterranean theater in a ceremony reminiscent of past kings' dispatching of the *emabutfo* on campaigns. Then in 1946 the king received the corps back from the war in a similar ceremonial fashion.

A listing of the most prominent *emabutfo* would include the following:

iNGWENYAMA	REGIMENT
Sobhuza I	*baLondolozi* (**)
	emaHubulu
	emaHlakabezi
	Mbulalazwe
	Latshane
	Punga
	tiChele
Mswati II	*tiChele* (**)
	tiNdlovu
	emaHubhulu
	iNyatsi
	Malalane
	imiGadlela
	uGiba
	baLondolozi
Mbandzeni	*iNdhlavela* (**)
	iNyatsi
	uGiba
	imiGadlela
Bhunu	*iNgulube* (**)
	Halaza
	liSaka
	Lomkhele
Sobhuza II	*baLondolozi* (**)
	emaGavu
	emaSotja (*)
	liNdimpi
	Sikonyane (*)
	Malindane
	Gcina
Mswati III	*liNdimpi* (**)
	baLondolozi
	emaSotja

(*)Under *iNgwenyama* Sobhuza II the emaSotja and Sikonyane regiments formed the basis of Swaziland's African Pioneer Corps contingent which he dispatched to fight during World War II. The contingent fought under the name "1991 Company" and distinguished itself particularly during the battles at Salerno and Anzio in Italy (1944). It was the emaSotja regiment's shield, spears, and staff that were chosen to be depicted on both the Swaziland flag and the national coat of arms at independence.

(**)Denotes *ingwenyama*'s regiment.

LIFA FUND. "Lifa" means "inheritance." A Swazi treasury fund established in 1946 by *iNgwenyama* **Sobhuza Dlamini II** and the *libandla* for the dual purpose of dealing with Swazi overstocking and land shortage. By royal decree every owner of more than 10 head of cattle would periodically contribute one head, which would be auctioned, with the proceeds deposited in the fund. The fund would then use its resources to purchase European-owned freehold land that came on the market. The fund quickly ran into difficulties connected with the requisitioning of cattle over the objections of individual owners and chiefs. The scheme may have helped to control overgrazing in some areas, although there was no evidence to prove it. Eventually, however, popular opposition combined with accusations of mishandling and disappearance of funds led to the closing of the Lifa Fund in the early 1960s. In the end 268,093 acres (about 108,500 hectares) were purchased as **Swazi Nation Land** through the fund. One of the estates purchased with Lifa funds was the *ingwenyama*'s **lowveld** hunting and game reserve, **Ehlane**, once owned by **David Forbes**.

LILANGENI. (Properly liLangenia; pl. emalangeni.) The unit of currency of Swaziland, equal in value to the South African rand, introduced 1974. The term is also used for a member of the Swazi royal family. The currency's symbol is "E" (e.g., E12 million). Swazi currency is decimalized, so that each lilangeni is divisible into one hundred cents. Since its introduction the lilangeni has been pegged to the value of the rand, often to the detriment of Swaziland's economic health.

LILAWU. (Properly liLauw.) The bachelors' quarters, or barracks: one of the three basic structures in the traditional Swazi **homestead**. The *lilawu* houses unmarried men and male visitors, as well as guarding the homestead entrance. When used in the royal context, *lilawu* refers to the site of the young *ingwenyama*'s new village, built away from the royal capital of his late father (which is now under the charge of his mother, the *indlovukazi*). The *lilawu* serves as the *ingwenyama*'s administrative headquarters.

LILOBOLO. See liLOBOLO

LIQOQO. Inner Council. The most senior and influential confidential advisory council to the *ingwenyama*. The *liqoqo* developed from the *lusendvo* (family council) and hence is predominantly aristocratic. It is headed by a senior prince (the great counsellor). *Liqoqo* membership normally consists of the *ingwenyama*'s principal uncle, the *tindvuna* of the chief and other royal villages, senior princes and chiefs, and able commoners chosen for their wisdom, stature, and attainments. There is no fixed number of members; *iNgwenyama* **Sobhuza Dlamini II** limited his *liqoqo* during the 1920s to less than 30. The *ex officio* members are the *ingwenyama*, the *indlovukazi* (the only woman in the *liqoqo*), and the great counsellor. The *ingwenyama* continues consulting with the *liqoqo* of his father, adding members as he sees fit. Membership is not announced, and there are no set meetings. Instead the *ingwenyama* consults with members individually as the need arises, and only when an important matter requiring a decision comes before him is he expected to convene the full council. In that event the *ingwenyama* normally abides by its decision. In addition the *liqoqo* is expected to relay to the *ingwenyama* the views of the citizenry and to inform him on matters requiring his attention and those that should be brought to the *libandla* for discussion.

Christopher Lowe has observed that beginning in the early 1930s Sobhuza altered the composition of the *liqoqo* markedly, increasing its membership in numbers (to 44 at one point) and incorporating a significant number of mission-educated "progressives," some of them South African-born.[6] This was probably done for several reasons. First, Sobhuza, an educated man himself, undoubtedly found the old and notoriously conservative *liqoqo* membership out of touch with the times. Second, Sobhuza wished to incorporate a number of educated Africans whom he trusted into his governance structure, thereby undercutting the independence of the **Swaziland Progressive Association (SPA)**, which had been in separate communication with the **resident commissioner** and with which he had refused to deal directly. That reform was undoubtedly responsible for maintaining the *liqoqo* in its constitutionally strong position advisory to the *ingwenyama* at a time when the *libandla* was losing influence.

Throughout Swaziland's history the *liqoqo* has frequently played a pivotal role during interregnums. Often it has contributed to their instability and occasional violence. Following Sobhuza's death in 1982 the *Liqoqo* became embroiled in the princely jockeying for power that dominated national politics for the following four years until the installation of his successor, *iNgwenyama* **Mswati Dlamini III**. Various princes and their factions attempted to gain executive power through either the *Liqoqo* or the cabinet. That was made easier because of several actions actually or allegedly taken by Sobhuza just prior to his death. The first was his decree signed in June 1982 ordering the modernization of the *liqoqo* by making it a state body (the "Supreme Council of State") and by capitalizing its title (*"Liqoqo"*), establishing it as a major consultative body. In the same decree he named *iNdlovukazi* **Dzeliwe Shongwe** as queen regent pending installation of the next *ingwenyama*, and he established a new position, the "authorized person," to be filled by a senior prince who would take over her duties if for any reason she was unable to perform them. Finally, Sobhuza was alleged by some senior princes to have left a list naming the 15 members of the new *Liqoqo*, although nothing in his handwriting was ever produced by his officials.

Three days following his death Dzeliwe endorsed the new *Liqoqo* membership (its title now capitalized) and named **Mnt. Sozisa Dlamini** as the authorized person. Quickly the *Liqoqo* fell under the influence of two of its members, **Mnt. Mfanasibili Dlamini** and **Dr. George Msibi**, the latter an outsider and a man of such transparent venality that the appearance of his name on the *Liqoqo* membership list raised serious doubts about its authenticity. Mnt. Sozisa fell in with their faction, leaving only **Mnt. Gabheni Dlamini** and a handful of allies to oppose them. Shortly thereafter the *Liqoqo* placed its own membership on government salary. Next (1983) it dismissed the modernist and popular prime minister, **Mnt. Mabandla Dlamini**, replacing him with a staunch traditionalist, **Mnt. Bhekimpi Dlamini**. When Dzeliwe balked at those moves the *Liqoqo* replaced her as queen regent with *iNkhosana* (Crown Prince) Makhosetive's mother, **Ntombi Twala**. Ntombi's signing of a statement recognizing the supremacy of the *Liqoqo* over the queen regent made the council's victory seemingly complete.

In the end, however, the Mfanasibili/Msibi faction proved to have overreached itself, with large segments of the population and the cabinet rallying to Gabheni's side in opposition to them. In 1985 a government decree was issued restoring the *Liqoqo* to its original advisory function. By 1986 Mfanasibili was in prison and Msibi had fled into exile, while Gabheni and Dzeliwe had, because of their actions, achieved the status of popular heroes. In April 1986 Makhosetive was installed as *iNgwenyama* **Mswati Dlamini III.**

LITTLE FREE STATE. A European (largely Afrikaner) community located on Swazi-owned land along the kingdom's southwestern border with the **Transvaal**, which was granted in 1877 by *iNgwenyama* **Mbandzeni Dlamini** to two hunters, **J. J. Ferreira** and F. I. Maritz. Mbandzeni's purpose appears to have been to use them and their followers as buffers against further attacks by the renegade **Mnt. Mblini Dlamini** into the region. The land consisted of 36,000 acres (14,580 hectares) northeast of the present town of Piet Retief. What Mbandzeni thought he had granted was in the nature of a permanent grazing **concession**, but Ferreira and Maritz opened up the territory to Afrikaner settlement and subdivision into small farms. Soon Mbandzeni gave them permission to form their own *libandla* (council), which led to their establishment of a local government consisting of a president and council, with its own constitution and laws.

In 1886 the settlers declared their independence as the Little Free State and were able to rebuff Mbandzeni's halfhearted attempts to evict them on the grounds that they had exceeded his mandate. In 1888 Ferreira and Maritz requested that the **South African Republic (SAR)** incorporate them into the Transvaal, claiming that Mbandzeni had renounced his authority over them. At that point Mbandzeni reasserted his sovereignty over the territory and demanded an annual rental payment of £21, but by then it was too late. By the terms of the **first Swaziland Convention** (1890) the Little Free State was incorporated into the SAR, with the accord of the British, as part of the Piet Retief district.

LIVERSAGE REPORT (1948). The report of the Socio-Economic Survey of Swaziland, directed by V. Liversage, an agricultural economist, initiated by the colonial secretary. The occasion for the study was the drastic cutback of parliamentary funds allocated to Swaziland under the second **Colonial Development and Welfare Act** (1945) from the proposed £2.5 million to £830,000, occasioned by the postwar financial crisis in **Britain**. Those circumstances led to the cancellation of Swaziland's Ten-Year Development Plan (1946–56) and the recasting of all existing development projects, requiring in turn the commissioning of a new socioeconomic survey to redetermine needs and reset priorities. Liversage conducted his survey during 1947, assisted by R. W. Thornton, agricultural advisor to the **high commissioner**, and a committee of local officials.

The Liversage report, the first post–World War II survey of Swaziland's existing resources and development needs, was vitally important in setting directions for resource allocation that shaped national economic development over the succeeding two generations. Its main findings were that

1. Swaziland possessed the greatest potential resources of the three **High Commission Territories** yet was at that time the most backward of them.
2. Swaziland suffered from a severe lack of transport facilities.

Its main recommendations were that

1. The **Swaziland Native Land Settlement Scheme** was over-administered and underproductive, and needed to be pared in half.
2. A hydrographic survey be made to determine the territory's **irrigation** potential.
3. Stemming from (2), the catchment areas of Swaziland's three main rivers, the **Komati**, **Usutu**, and iNgwavuma, be protected through improvements in native methods of agriculture, husbandry, and general economy.
4. Stemming from (3), a Rural Development Scheme be implemented to impart practical educational programs to the Swazi in agriculture, husbandry, and general economy.
5. Communications be improved by building a railway from **South Africa** to Swaziland and by building and improving domestic roads.
6. Regarding future development, special attention be paid to minerals (especially coal), irrigated agriculture (especially **sugar**), and afforestation.

The Liversage report foreshadowed the **Rural Development Area (RDA) Program** beginning in 1970. The report's immediate result was the implementation of a new Eight Year Plan (1948–56), to replace the old Ten Year Plan, that placed a new emphasis on capital development rather than on past "native welfare" programs such as the Swaziland Native Land Settlement Scheme. More immediately the plan led directly to the government implementation, with the cooperation for the most part of *iNgwenyama* **Sobhuza Dlamini II** and the *libandla*, of the various capital development schemes that dominated the economy of Swaziland over the following generation, principally afforestation, irrigation for sugar and citrus, and mining enterprises.

LOBAMBA. During the era of *iNgwenyama* **Sobhuza Dlamini II** Lobamba was the residence of the *indlovukazi* and the ritual capital of the Swazi nation. The village reflected the blueprint of traditional homesteads, only on a much larger scale. The *sibaya* (cattle enclosure), for instance, was mammoth in its size, because it also doubled as the venue for national ceremonial occasions, including the *iNcwala* **ceremony**. Following independence Lobamba became the locus of several other, modern national institutions. The buildings of **parliament** were established there, as were the Swaziland National Archives next to them. Construction of the **Swazi National Church** was begun there in the 1960s. The **Somhlolo** ("The Wonder"—*iNgwenyama* **Sobhuza Dlamini I**) National Stadium is also located in Lobamba, along with the offices of the Swazi National Trust, which is the repository of some of Sobhuza's private archives that are kept separate from the national archives (and are not open to unauthorized scholars). Finally, a large memorial building and grounds dedicated to Sobhuza II were located at Lobamba across from the national church in 1989.

The original Lobamba was the royal village that *iNgwenyama* **Ndvungunye Dlamini** built for his mother, Lomvulo Mndzebele, which was located in what is now southwestern Swaziland. It is now referred to as Old Lobamba. Ndvungunye died there and was buried at a rocky koppie called **Mlokotfwa** near Lobamba. Later, *iNgwenyama* Sobhuza I chose Lobamba as the name for the royal village he built about 1820 in the **Ezulwini Valley** in the shadow of the **Mdzimba mountains** as the homestead of *iNdlovukazi* **Lojiba Simelane**.

*li***LOBOLO**. Commonly *Lobolo*. Compensation, usually in cattle, transferred to the bride's family by the groom to effect a traditional Swazi marriage contract. The compensation is regarded to be for the family's loss of the bride's reproductive powers and her labor in the **homestead**. *liLobolo* also legitimizes the children of the marriage and guarantees to them the benefits of their father's lineage. Finally, *lilobolo* is seen as a form of security guarantee, because in the event of the bride's return to her family because of mistreatment by the husband the *lilobolo* cattle must be returned. The number of *lilobolo* cattle transferred at the time of the marriage depends on the desirability of the bride in terms of wealth, status, and appearance. For instance, *lilobolo* for a daughter of an *ingwenyama* might run to 15 to 20 times the number of cattle demanded for a commoner.

In modern Swaziland the institution of *lilobolo* has come under criticism from educated women as being gender-discriminatory and reinforcing the underlying patriarchal system. Modernists argue that although *lilobolo* may not amount, as the traditionalists argue, to the buying and selling of women, it does have the effect of commoditizing them. That is particularly the case, they say, in more and more instances in metropolitan Swaziland where marriages are secured with *lilobolo* cash rather than cattle. Such a practice can lead, as even Hilda Kuper, a defender of the system, admits, to "unscrupulous parents who marry their daughter to the highest bidder."[7] Because by tradition women are barred from access to cattle, *lilobolo* is seen by modernists as yet another means of divorcing homestead women from the fruits of their labors.

Certain *lilobolo*-related practices resulting in wealth accumulation by the elite over the years have also lent themselves to the female commoditization argument. Differential *lilobolo* transactions (an *ingwenyama*'s, prince's, or chief's receipt of larger *lilobolo* for daughters than he exchanged for wives) resulted in a substantial net transfer of cattle to the aristocracy throughout the 19th and 20th centuries. Poor families mortgaged infant daughters to wealthy men for *lilobolo* cattle; the family then kept the cattle and their accrued increase until the time the marriage took place. Wealthier patrons would loan *lilobolo* cattle to poor men in return for patrilineal rights over the first daughter of the marriage. Those types of transactions make it difficult to argue that Swazi tradition does not equate women with cattle in commodity value.

Many educated women are choosing not to participate in the *lilobolo* transaction upon marriage, just as they are declining to enter polygynous marriages. That is one reason for the gradual decline of both institutions as the society adapts to modern values.

LOMAHASHA. A border village and customs post high in the **Lebombo** plateau in northeastern Swaziland. Across the border is Namaacha, Mozambique. The town is named after Chief Lomahasha Mahlalela (c. 1825–c. 1896), an important and independent chief in the region. The Portuguese Boundary Commission (1888) deprived the Swazi of the eastern slopes of the Lebombo range as their territory drew the line around the Portuguese military post at Namaacha, which led to the development of Lomahasha.

LOMÉ CONVENTION. A trade and aid agreement signed in Lomé, Togo, between the then European Economic Community, presently the European Union (EU), and 70 African, Caribbean, and Pacific (ACP) countries. The convention guarantees preferential access to the EU for selected commodities produced by the ACP nations. The convention includes all sub-Saharan African countries excepting South Africa. There have been four Lomé conventions: 1975, 1979, 1984, and 1989 (to last for 10 years). Swaziland exports **sugar**, canned citrus, and processed pineapple to the EU under its quotas. Swaziland's most important export to the EU is sugar, with approximately one-third of the crop falling annually under the EU quota. The convention's Stabilisation of Export Earnings (Stabex) Scheme helps to stabilize commodity prices against unfavorable changes in market conditions. The EU's European Development Fund provides multilateral aid to member countries. The convention's European Investment Bank makes commercial loans to member nations.

LONDON CONSTITUTIONAL CONFERENCE (1963). *See* CONSTITUTIONAL CONFERENCE (1963)

LONDON CONSTITUTIONAL CONFERENCE (1968). *See* CONSTITUTION (INDEPENDENCE, 1968)

LONDON CONVENTION (1884). Signed in London by the British and **South African Republic (SAR)** governments, the London Convention amended some provisions of the previous **Pretoria Convention (1881)** objected to by SAR president Paul Kruger. The London convention made no reference to British suzerainty and restored the name "South African Republic." Of greater interest to the Swazi, the London Convention reaffirmed the British guarantee of the kingdom's sovereignty first laid out in the Pretoria Convention, it enjoined the SAR from expanding beyond its eastern or western boundaries, and it provided for the policing of, and placed a border resident at, the **Transvaal**-Swaziland border to ensure that no SAR encroachment took place.

LOVEDALE MISSIONARY INSTITUTION. The Lovedale mission was established in 1824 by the United Free Church of Scotland (Glasgow Society), near Alice, Cape Province, South Africa. Lovedale was widely renowned for the academic quality of its coeducational secondary school, especially in the areas of agriculture and industrial skills. It was to Lovedale that *iNkhosana* **(Crown Prince) Sobhuza Dlamini II** was sent by his grandmother, Queen Regent **Labotsibeni Mdluli**. She did so over the vehement opposition of a number of councillors and influential chiefs on grounds of the *inkosana*'s personal safety. Sobhuza, accompanied by 12 other royal and elite youths (nine boys, three girls), attended Lovedale from 1916 to 1918. It was Sobhuza's first sojourn abroad, and although he was not a distinguished student his educational experience at Lovedale exerted a profound influence on him. His reaction to his formal studies was a positive one—he was disappointed when they were interrupted in 1918—and he traveled as widely as possible during his school holidays. He was also given an opulent reception in Sophiatown by **Cleopas Kunene** on his way to Lovedale, and he learned to appreciate Western dress and culture while he was at the school.

The degree to which Sobhuza's Lovedale experiences imprinted him became evident only after he had become *ingwenyama* in late 1921.

From then until mid-1926 Sobhuza became an African "progressive" in style and substance. He dressed expensively in the Western style, drove a Buick automobile, kept up with world events on his British-made short-wave radio, and purchased a house in Sophiatown, an African township near Johannesburg.

Sobhuza also challenged the legitimacy of the **concessions** by launching a lawsuit against **Allister Miller** in the British court system, engaging an American-educated lawyer (**Pixley kaI. Seme**), and carrying his appeal all the way to the Privy Council. He lost the Miller case (**Sobhuza II vs. Miller**) and in the process came to realize that this and other elements of his progressivism had encumbered him with a massive personal debt, which in turn weakened him in his stance against the colonial administration. It was at this point that Sobhuza reversed course and began to embrace "traditionalism" as his guiding ideology in reviving the fortunes of his office. That tactical change hardly marked the end of his insatiable intellectual curiosity or his determination to beat the Europeans at their own political game. Throughout his lifetime Sobhuza was by all accounts a voracious reader of the daily press (especially the *Rand Daily Mail*) and listener to the news broadcasts of the BBC. The seeds of those vital aspects of Sobhuza's personality had been planted at Lovedale during the years 1916 to 1918.

LOVELL, LEOPOLD. Minister of Finance from 1967 to 1972. A citizen of **South Africa**, Lovell had served in its parliament from 1949 to 1958 as a member of the Labour Party. In 1961 Lovell left South Africa and settled in Swaziland, where he practiced law in **Mbabane**. Lovell was one of four Europeans appointed by *iNgwenyama* **Sobhuza Dlamini II** to the House of Assembly in 1967. Sobhuza then appointed him to his first cabinet as minister of finance (initially finance, commerce, and industry). In 1971 Lovell fell out with the prime minister, **Mnt. Makhosini Dlamini**, over the **Land Speculation Control Act**, which Lovell publicly opposed. Lovell was not reappointed to the cabinet by Sobhuza following the 1972 election.

LOWVELD. One of four major topographic regions in Swaziland, lying east of the **middleveld** and west of the **Lebombo Mountains**. The lowveld encompasses 2,400 square miles (6,200 square kilometers) and is characterized by undulating savannah plain broken by occasional ridges, lying mainly between 1,000 feet (305 meters) and 500 feet (150 meters) above sea level. The climate is dry and near-tropical, the temperature averaging between 85°F (29°C) and 60°F (16°C). The vast majority of the lowveld receives less than 20 inches (51 centimeters) of rain annually, although the western portion (about 25 percent of the lowveld area) can average as much as 30 inches (76 centimeters) annually. The vegetation is broad-leafed savannah and tropical bush, with occasional sweetveld (year-around) grasses. Consequently the lowveld outside the irrigated areas is primarily given to cattle grazing.

Since 1950 portions of the lowveld have been subjected to intensive **irrigation**, transforming them into highly productive agricultural regions. In the north, projects in the Tshaneni, Ngomane, Mhlume, **Vuvulane**, and Simunye areas fed by water from the **Komati**, Mbuluzi, and Mbuluzane rivers produce **sugar**, citrus, and vegetables. In mid-country, the Big Bend region watered by the **Usutu River** produces sugar and citrus. To the south, the Nsoko region fed by the iNgwavuma River produces sugar. Extensive deposits of low-sulphur, high-energy-content coal are found in the **Mpaka** area, and lesser-quality coal underlies much of the eastern lowveld from north to south. Malaria, once thought to be nearly eradicated in the lowveld, has returned, and bilharzia is endemic in the entire lowveld region. The lowveld is sometimes referred to as the bushveld.

LOYD, SIR FRANCIS A. (1916– ; knighted 1965). Her Majesty's Commissioner in Swaziland from 1964 until independence in 1968. Until 1964 Loyd had spent his career in Kenya, serving as permanent secretary from 1962 to 1964. Loyd's appointment as Queen's Commissioner signified a British accommodation to *iNgwenyama* **Sobhuza Dlamini II**, who had just suffered the humiliation of having a pre-independence constitution imposed on Swaziland that challenged his sovereignty by, among other provisions, legitimizing opposition parties. That had been the design of Loyd's predecessor and the last of the **resident commissioners, Sir Brian Marwick**, whose strained relations with Sobhuza had become painfully evident by the time of his departure in 1964.

Loyd's reputation for correctness and diplomacy suited him well for the delicate tasks that fell to him as Queen's Commissioner: to repair relations with Sobhuza, to oversee the 1964 **Legislative Council** elections, and to move Swaziland toward independence at a deliberate pace. Loyd proved to be the man for the job. He and Sobhuza quickly developed what came to be a lasting relationship based on mutual candor and respect. That was an accommodation made easier because Loyd's title of Queen's Commissioner implied a new, higher status for Sobhuza and allowed Loyd to communicate directly with London rather than through the **high commissioner** in Pretoria. Throughout his tenure Loyd found reasons to accommodate Sobhuza's wishes rather than to block them, as

residents had so often done in the past. For instance the London constitutional conference of February 1968 excluded all representatives from
opposition parties, which was quite different from what had occurred
during the London **constitutional conference** (1963). In the final analysis
it was Loyd most of all who was personally responsible for the smooth-
ness of the transition from the Legislative Council period in 1964 to independence in 1968. Significantly, Loyd was chosen to deliver the eu-
logy at Sobhuza's memorial service at St. Paul's Cathedral, London, on
November 18, 1982.

LOZITHEHLEZI. "Sitting Surrounded by Enemies" (colloq. Lozita,
Zitheni). The principal administrative and diplomatic residence of *iNgwenyama* **Sobhuza Dlamini II**. It is situated on the Lancabane ridge of
the **Mdzimba** foothills, about five miles (eight kilometers) southeast of
the ritual capital, **Lobamba**. Sobhuza built Lozithehlezi following his
installation in 1921 and moved from Lobamba in 1926. The irony of his
choice of the name for his new royal residence, in what Jonathan Crush
called "a powerfully symbolic piece of landscape naming," reflected his
extreme bitterness and frustration over the obvious injustice of the Privy
Council's denial of his appeal in the *Sobhuza II vs. Miller* case in 1926.[8]
Sobhuza lived at Lozithehlezi regularly until 1953, when he purchased
a modern house, **Masundvwini**, east of **Manzini**, that henceforward
became his favorite residence.

LUBOMBO ADMINISTRATIVE REGION. One of the four administrative regions of Swaziland, it comprises 2,036 square miles (5,273 square
kilometers) along the eastern side of the country. It stretches from slightly
north of Tshaneni southward to within 10 miles (16 kilometers) of the
southern border at Gollel. At some points it reaches close to the center
of the country. Among its major towns are Tshaneni, Mhlume, **Siteki**,
and Big Bend. The Lubombo region was called the Stegi district prior
to the 1963 administrative reforms. Siteki is the regional administrative
headquarters. The total population of Lubombo region in 1986 was
153,958.

LUBUYA, BATTLE OF. In 1839 Zulu **King Dingane**, on the defensive
because of the defection of his brother **Mpande Zulu** and the open hostility of the Natal trekboers, launched a campaign northward against
iNgwenyama **Sobhuza Dlamini I** to recoup his military and political
fortunes. The Zulu *impi*'s orders were to establish a military camp along
the Lubuya stream, one of the sources of the iNgwavuma River near
modern Hlatikulu. Although Sobhuza was by then infirm (and indeed

near death), the Swazi nation rose up to a man to fight the invaders. The main Swazi *imphi* arrayed against the Zulu was commanded by **Mngayi Fakudze** and included two of Sobhuza's principal **regiments**, which attacked from the hills. The two armies fought hand to hand in the Lubuya Valley for an entire day before breaking off the battle. The following day the Zulu fought a series of skirmishes as they retreated and sought to protect their cattle. Upon hearing of his defeat Dingane reattacked with strong reinforcements but again was repulsed by the Swazi with heavy losses in both men and cattle.

The battle of Lubuya was fought during July–September 1839; Sobhuza died during August. The battle is revered in Swazi military history for the spirit of nationalism that rallied the Swazi against the invader and for the bravery of the regiments facing heavy casualties in fierce combat. Finally, Lubuya marked a sharp reversal for Dingane, both militarily and politically, because he owed his power to the Zulu army. Dingane was deposed the following year and killed while in flight in southern Swaziland.

LUDZIDZINI. The *indlovukazi*'s residence and ritual capital of the Swazi nation during the reign of *iNgwenyama* **Mswati Dlamini II**. Mswati built Ludzidzini for his mother, **Tsandzile Ndwandwe**, about 1840. Mswati initially lived at Ludzidzini, but he later moved his *lilawu* (administrative capital) to Hhohho in the north. Ludzidzini was located halfway between **Zombodze** and the National High School at **Matsapha**. It was there that the *iNcwala* **ceremony** was performed. The senior *indvuna* at Ludzidzini was **Sandlane Zwane**.

In 1984 a new ritual capital was built for *iNkhosana* (Crown Prince) Makhosetive (*iNgwenyama* **Mswati Dlamini III**) and named Ludzidzini. Ludzidzini became the **homestead** of his mother, *iNdlovukazi* **Ntombi Twala**. It was the capital where Mswati was crowned and where the *iNcwala* ceremony was regularly performed.

LUKHELE, DOUGLAS (1932–). Swazi lawyer and legislator, Swaziland's first trained indigenous lawyer. Lukhele received a B.A. from Fort Hare University College and studied law in Pretoria. He then joined the Johannesburg law firm of Mandela and Tambo, practicing there from 1955 to 1964. Several years following the death of *iNgwenyama* **Sobhuza Dlamini II**'s attorney **Pixley Seme** in 1951, Sobhuza began retaining Lukhele for a number of causes in behalf of the monarchy and the state. In 1960 Lukhele participated in some of the early constitutional talks with British officials. He was also one of the government lawyers arguing the case for the denial of Swazi citizenship to **Bhekindlela Thomas Ngwenya** in 1972. Lukhele was appointed senator by Sobhuza following the 1967 parliamentary elections, then reappointed in 1972. In 1973, following Sobhuza's repeal of the constitution, Lukhele was appointed successively as deputy attorney-general, attorney-general, and judge. In the late 1970s Lukhele returned to his law practice in Johannesburg.

Following Sobhuza's death in 1982 Lukhele became a central figure in the constitutional struggles between the *Liqoqo* and Queen Regent **Dzeliwe Shongwe**. Lukhele, by then a well-known and widely respected lawyer, argued Dzeliwe's case before the **High Court** following her dismissal by the *Liqoqo* in mid-1983. When the court refused to rescind the dismissal order, Lukhele and a second defender of Dzeliwe were arrested under the infamous 60-day detention law and jailed for six months before being released.

LUSUSHWANA RIVER. Also Little Usutu River. The Lusushwana River rises in the **Transvaal** about 20 miles (32 kilometers) west of Swaziland near Lothair. The river passes south of **Mbabane** and through **Matsapha** before joining the **Usutu River** near Sidvokodvo. Its precipitous drop north and west of the **Ezulwini Valley** has made the Lusushwana an ideal source of hydroelectric power. Two major projects tapping the river have been completed, one during the mid-1960s and the other (the Lupholo project) during the mid-1980s.

LUSUTFU RIVER. *See* USUTU RIVER

LYDENBURG REPUBLIC. An Afrikaner republic founded in 1845 at Ohrigstad (properly Andries Ohrigstad) in the eastern **Transvaal** by trekboer emigrants from the Republic of Natalia following its defeat by the British in 1842. In 1848 the community, finding Ohrigstad feverous and unhealthy, moved their capital southward to higher ground, where they established the Lydenburg Republic (*lyden* means "suffering"). The Afrikaners' commandant-general was A. H. Potgieter, succeeded following his departure by W. F. Joubert. Early in their history the Lydenburghers were swept up in the African politics of the region, at various times maintaining direct or indirect relations with the **Pedi**, the Swazi (including the renegades **Bnt. Somcuba** and **Malambule Dlamini**), and the Zulu. In 1846 the Ohrigstad volksraad concluded an agreement with *iNgwenyama* **Mswati Dlamini II** by which the latter ceded to them the lands between the Crocodile and **Olifants** rivers (which included both

Ohrigstad and Lydenburg). What Mswati received in return was 110 head of cattle and the assistance of four armed Afrikaners in beating back the incursion of Mnt. Malambule, backed by **King Mpande Zulu**, near **Mahamba**. The Afrikaners did in fact assist in the defeat of Malambule in September 1846.

Following his defeat of Somcuba in 1855, Mswati again negotiated with the Lydenburghers (principally Joubert) over land. That year, in a second agreement, Mswati ceded **highveld** land between the **Komati** and iNgwavuma rivers, as well as a strip along the Pongola River to be occupied by Afrikaners as a buffer against the Zulu, all in return for 70 head of cattle. That seeming giveaway was largely explained by the fact that Mswati had no intention of the land's actually changing hands, any more than the Lydenburghers intended to occupy the Pongola strip. Instead Mswati immediately settled Komati region heavily with loyal chiefs and members of the royal family. The Lydenburg Republic became part of the **South African Republic** in 1860, placing those agreements under Pretoria's authority.

Over the long term the Ohrigstad/Lydenburg agreements proved to be of great damage to Swaziland's strategic interests in the region. Even though Mswati engineered both the 1846 and 1855 agreements to gain an ally against the Zulu threat, the fact remained that they were both made when the Swazi were relatively strong and the Afrikaners comparatively weak. Beginning in the early 1880s that balance of power would be reversed, and it would be then that the Afrikaners would begin to hold the Swazi to the terms of those agreements, on both of which hung the Transvaal's right to much of its land. Finally, during the 20th century much of the land ceded by Mswati would form the basis of the **kaNgwane** homeland, which would figure heavily in Swaziland's diplomatic relations with the **South African government**, the Zulu, and the **Organization of African Unity** during *iNgwenyama* **Sobhuza Dlamini II**'s final years. Thus did Mswati's relations with Lydenburg resonate to Swaziland's detriment well into modern times.

NOTES

1. Sheila Meintjes, "Family and Gender in the Christian Community at Edendale, Natal, in Colonial Times," in Cherryl Walker (ed.), *Women and Gender in Southern Africa to 1845* (Cape Town: David Phillip; London: James Currey, 1990), pp. 127–129.

2. David R. Rycroft, *Concise SiSwati Dictionary* (Pretoria: J. L. van Schaik, 1981), p. 49.

3. Hugh Macmillan, "Swaziland: Decolonisation and the Triumph of Tradition," *Journal of Modern African Studies*, XXlll, 4 (1985), p. 665.

4. Jonathan Crush, *The Struggle for Swazi Labour, 1890–1920* (Kingston and Montreal: McGill-Queens University Press, 1987), p. 44.

5. Margaret Zoller Booth, "Children of Migrant Fathers: The Effects of Father Absence on Swazi Children's Preparedness for School," *Comparative Education Review*, XXXIX, 2 (1995), 209–210.

6. Christopher Lowe, "Elite Reactions to Colonialism in Swaziland: The Case of Prince Mavela Dlamini," paper presented at the African Studies Association Conference, Seattle, WA, November 1992, p. 63.

7. Hilda Kuper, *The Swazi: A South African Kingdom* (2d ed., New York: Holt, Rinehart and Winston, 1986), p. 26.

8. Jonathan Crush, "The Culture of Failure: Racism, Violence and White Farming in Colonial Swaziland," *Journal of Historical Geography*, XXII, 2 (1996), 188.

-M-

McCORKINDALE, ALEXANDER (1816–1871). Scottish-born entrepreneur who migrated to Natal in 1856 with the intent of establishing a Scottish industrial settlement at Sinkwazi, north of Durban. The area proved to be too hot and humid for his fellow Scots. Following its failure he was persuaded by **David Forbes**, his nephew by marriage, to reconnoiter the eastern **Transvaal** as more climatically suitable for a Scottish settlement. In 1864 McCorkindale obtained a grant from the **South African Republic (SAR)** volksraad of farmland 2,700 square miles (7,000 square kilometers) in area in the eastern Transvaal bordering Swaziland. By 1867 the territory, known as **New Scotland**, had been surveyed into 200 farms of 8,650 acres (3,500 hectares) each, to be sold at £40 per farm. The modest price was indicative of SAR President M. W. Pretorius's anxiety to place a buffer between his republic and the Swazi and Zulu.

The grant was divided into three blocks: Industria to the north, Roburnia (after Robert Burns) in the center, and Londina bordering southwestern and southern Swaziland. McCorkindale determined that the eastern portion of the grant constituted the best farmland, and in 1868 he established his principal settlement (Derby) along the Swazi border just south of the iNgwenpisi River. McCorkindale's and Forbes's activities along the border, and their reputed intention of purchasing land in

Swaziland for a railway right-of-way to the coast in behalf of Pretorius, all elicited a nervous response from the Swazi regents. They need not have worried. The New Scotland settlement failed to become agriculturally or economically viable, and many of the settlers pulled up stakes and left. The most viable farm was Forbes's Athole, while McCorkindale died a bitter and frustrated man, of malaria, while visiting **Delagoa Bay**.

It is said that it was McCorkindale, along with Forbes, who popularized the name "Swaziland" for *iNgwenyama* **Mswati Dlamini II**'s kingdom.

McCREEDY, GEORGE B. European concessionaire who obtained a mineral **concession** to prospect for **gold** located in the hills forming the western border of the **Ezulwini Valley** near the confluence of the Mbabane and **Lusushwana** rivers. McCreedy prospected for gold without success, but for a number of years after 1910, McCreedy Tins Ltd. was the second largest **tin** producer in Swaziland. In all of the Ezulwini Valley and environs a total of £400,000 ($2 million) worth of cassiterite tin was mined between 1894 and 1948. Perhaps 20 percent of that amount, or £80,000 ($400,000), came from McCreedy Tins. In 1956 the company was sold to New Union Goldfields of South Africa.

McLACHLAN, THOMAS (c. 1830–1900). Concessionaire and **gold** prospector who arrived in Swaziland from a career in gold exploration around **Lydenburg** in 1878. In that year McLachlan obtained a mineral concession from *iNgwenyama* **Mbandzeni Dlamini** to prospect for all minerals north of the **Komati River,** and he built his camp 4 miles (6 kilometers) northwest of modern **Pigg's Peak**. McLachlan, who became close friends with Mbandzeni, was the first prospector to discover gold in Swaziland. The reason, it is said, was that he was the first to discover that alluvial gold was to be found in reef quartz. It was also McLachlan who invited **William Pigg** to prospect with him, and in 1881 Pigg bought out McLachlan's major claim, although McLachlan retained control of his overall concession. Thereafter McLachlan made his money by forging partnerships with other prospectors and then selling his stake when they struck gold. McLachlan appears to have been a poor husbander of his resources, for he died in poverty.

McSEVENEY, CHARLES. Farmer and businessman. Son of Tom McSeveney, a concessionaire and farmer at Spitzkop in southern Swaziland near Goedgegun (**Nhlangano**). Spitzkop was renowned as one of the premier settler farms in the territory. Tom McSeveney was a member of the **European Advisory Council** for a number of years following its establishment. Charles McSeveney, following a university education in

South Africa, took over his father's farm and became an operative for the **Native Recruiting Corporation** beginning in the 1930s. During the 1950s McSeveney established Skonkwane Stores, general grocers, retailers, and suppliers of farm hardware and implements, in Nhlangano. By the mid-1990s Skonkwane was operating 10 outlets throughout Swaziland. During the 1970s and 1980s McSeveney served as a member of **parliament**.

MABUZA, OBED M. Official of the **Swaziland Progressive Party (SPP)** and various opposition coalitions during the 1960s. Until 1960 Mabuza had been a prominent member of the *libandla* and head of the **Manzini** branch of the **Swazi Commercial Amadoda**. By about then Mabuza had burned his bridges with *iNgwenyama* **Sobhuza Dlamini II** when he had illegally sold a large number of royal cattle and then had audaciously cross-examined the king who had brought suit against him for the return of the cattle in civil court. Mabuza represented the SPP (along with **John J. Nquku** and **Dr. Ambrose Zwane**, during the first constitutional conference in London (1961). Such was the virulence of their disagreement with the traditionalists over the degree of political modernization to be written into the new constitution that Nquku was dismissed from the constitutional committee and Mabuza and Zwane later resigned. In 1962, following Zwane's split from the SPP, Mabuza became its secretary general and later its president. In 1964 Mabuza was the moving force behind the organization of the **Joint Council of Swaziland Political Parties**, becoming chairman of its executive council in 1965. A year later he became president of the successor organization, the Swaziland United Front.

All those coalitions failed in their purpose, to mount a powerful and credible opposition to the traditionalists, especially the *ingwenyama*'s **Imbokodvo National Movement**. For example, in the 1964 **Legislative Council** elections Mabuza lost his deposit, and United Front candidates in the 1967 elections received only 1 out of every 300 votes. In the 1972 elections the United Front ran only six candidates, all of them losing badly.

MADLATHULE FAMINE. Madlathule means "Let One Eat What He Can and Say Naught." This historic famine descended on southeast Africa during the first decade of the 19th century and is remembered for its widespread (Natal, Mozambique, and Swaziland) and catastrophic effects. Stories of cannibalism are associated with it, as are recollections of people concentrating in villages to protect their remaining grain stores from marauders. Such famines bring great political stress in their tow, and historians associate them with mounting conflicts over productive land, both agricultural and especially grazing, and the centralization of political authority. Philip Bonner associates the Madlathule famine with the development of the tributary state in early 19th-century Swaziland and with the rise in violence and coincident beginnings of a crude *emabutfo* system (sing. *libutfo*) during the reign of *iNgwenyama* **Ndvungunye Dlamini**.[1]

MAGAGULA, MNJOLI. Leader of one branch of the Magagula clan (of Sotho origin) during the era of *iNgwenyama* **Sobhuza Dlamini I**. The Magagula headquarters was in the shadow of the **Mdzimba** mountain range in central Swaziland, just north of modern **Lozithehlezi**. The leader of the other Magagula branch was **Moyeni Magagula**. Sobhuza's colonization of central Swaziland from his southern base at **Shiselweni** during the 1820s necessitated his defeat and incorporation of a number of Sotho-speaking clans that had occupied the region for several generations, prominent among them being the Magagula. Mnjoli was the most formidable of the Magagulas by virtue of his command of the strategic and fertile **Ezulwini Valley** and his possession of the renowned Magagula **rainmaking** medicines, the most powerful (rivaled only by the Mnisi medicines) in Swaziland. Sobhuza knew that if he were able to obtain the medicines from Mnjoli, his strength would be significantly enhanced and his job of controlling central Swaziland would be made easier. Sobhuza, unsure of his strength and numbers, first tried diplomacy, but when the king's messengers requested that Mnjoli turn over the rainmaking medicines, they were severely beaten and summarily returned to the *ingwenyama*'s camp.

Sobhuza, the story goes, resorted to a stratagem reminiscent of the Trojan Horse. At dusk his men camouflaged themselves with cattle hides and hid among the Magagula herd. Once the cattle were led into Mnjoli's stronghold for the night Sobhuza's "cattle" attacked the Magagula men from the inside, defeated them, and slew Mnjoli. Mnjoli, however, had managed to spirit the rainmaking medicines away with his sons before his death, and Sobhuza (who even had Mnjoli's stomach opened in his determined search for them) was unable to locate them. His defeat of Mnjoli was, however, successful in opening up central Swaziland to his control.

MAGAGULA, MOYENI (MOYA). The rival (and probably brother) to **Mnjoli Magagula**. Moyeni's headquarters was located in the hills east of modern **Manzini**. It was there that Moyeni fled with his father, Mhlangala Magagula, from *iNgwenyama* **Sobhuza Dlamini I**'s attack in 1815 after refusing to *khonta* (pay homage to) him. Sobhuza, once he had defeated Mnjoli, turned his attention to Moyeni, but this time his campaign was not so decisive. In the conflict Moyeni first attacked Sobhuza's stronghold at **Lobamba**, apparently when the *ingwenyama*'s army was off to the north, and Sobhuza barely escaped. Sobhuza then attacked Moyeni and drove him off but did not kill him.

Sometime following Sobhuza's death Moyeni returned to Swaziland, settled, and prospered conspicuously in both wealth and followers. Eventually Moyeni's prosperity attained a level that sparked the suspicion and jealousy of Sobhuza's successor, *iNgwenyama* **Mswati Dlamini II**. Consequently Mswati, whose degree of tolerance was even less than his father's, planned an attack against Moyeni. He was dissuaded by the influential chief Madzanga Ndwandwe, exiled son of the Ndwandwe king Zwide and half-brother of *iNdlovukazi* **Tsandzile Ndwandwe**. Madzanga was able to entice Mswati into calling off his assault by suggesting that the king instead grant him control over the Magagula chiefdom and place Moyeni under his authority, a humiliation at once equally as politically effective as, and far less costly than, a military defeat.

MAGONGO, TIKHUBA. Senior official during the reign of *iNgwenyama* **Mbandzeni Dlamini** and *indvuna* of his administrative homestead at **Mbekelweni** after its establishment in about 1876. As one of Mbandzeni's chief councillors Tikhuba was involved in practically every major concession granted by the *ingwenyama*, and he was said to have profited handsomely from his position. Magongo was also involved in the appointment of **Theophilus Shepstone, Jr.**, as resident advisor and agent of the *ingwenyama* in 1886, but he later sided with **Allister Miller** and **John Thorburn** in their campaign to torpedo Shepstone and replace him (1889). He was also a senior signatory to the "**White Charter**" in 1888.

Tikhuba's chief rival for influence at Mbandzeni's court was **Sandlane Zwane**, Mbandzeni's prime minister who was also the leader of those councillors opposed to the army of concessionaires besieging Mbekelweni. Tikhuba was finally able to dispose of Zwane as his opponent late in 1888 by taking advantage of the latter's exposure as chief conspirator in a plot to kill Mbandzeni and his likely successor and place a brother, **Mnt. Nkhopolo Dlamini**, on the throne.

It was Tikhuba who was most influential in having Zwane (and those of his senior associates arrayed against his concessionaire allies) executed for treason. Following the executions Tikhuba's own influence at court became unrivaled. Tikhuba was at Mbandzeni's side when he died (1889), and he then spoke at the public introduction of *iNgwenyama* **Bhunu Dlamini** in 1890. As Swaziland edged toward the prospect of governance by the **South African Republic** and the domestic political mood turned ugly, Tikhuba became one of those councillors who were dishonored by their previous association with the establishment (1889) of the **Provisional Government Committee** and the **Chief Court**. Tikhuba consequently retired in disgrace to the Hhohho region, well away from court intrigue and under the protection of his relatives.

MAHAMBA. "The Runaways." A border post village in southwestern Swaziland, connecting the towns of **Nhlangano** (Swaziland) and Piet Retief (**Transvaal**). It was near Mahamba that the first European (Wesleyan) mission was established in 1844 by **Rev. James Allison**. The village's name was derived from the incident in 1846 in which *iNgwenyama* Mswati **Dlamini II**'s troops defeated the renegade forces of **Mnt. Malambule Dlamini** at the mission, forcing Rev. Allison and his staff to abandon the station and flee to Natal. In 1882 the Wesleyans, this time under the direction of Rev. Daniel **Msimang** from the **Edendale** mission in Natal, reestablished themselves on the old site.

Beginning in the 1920s the Mahamba border post and environs became a major transit point for the Swazi-cultivated *insangu* being smuggled into the Johannesburg industrial region.

MAHLALELA, LOMAHASHA. *See* LOMAHASHA

MAKHOSINI. "The Place of the Kings." Originally known as Mbilaneni. The site of Nzama royal graves on a wooded hillside in southern Swaziland, about five miles (eight kilometers) south of modern **Nhlangano**. The first of the Swazi kings to be buried at Makhosini was *iNgwenyama* **Sobhuza Dlamini I**, and the last, *iNgwenyama* **Sobhuza Dlamini II**. *iNgwenyama* **Mswati Dlamini II** was also laid to rest at Makhosini. Makhosini is guarded by a branch of the Mdluli clan. The other major royal burial site is at **Dlangeni** in the **Mdzimba hills**. There is a third site at Mlokotfwa, near Mhlosheni, where *iNgwenyama* **Ndvungunye Dlamini** is buried.

MALALOTJA NATURE RESERVE. One of four protected areas in Swaziland for the preservation of plants and animals. Malalotja is administered by the Swaziland National Trust Commission and was opened in 1983. It is approximately 18,000 hectares (180 square kilometers) in area, its entrance lying 18 miles (29 kilometers) by road north of

Mbabane. Many of its 10 species of large animals were introduced either from the **Hlane Royal National Park** in Swaziland's **lowveld** or from **South Africa**. Malalotja also has recorded 150 species of birds, including the crowned eagle and the bald ibis. The Malalotja River falls are the highest (300 feet, 92 meters) in Swaziland, and hiking trails provide spectacular views of the **Komati River** valley. The Ngwenya mine (Lion's Cavern) is the site of one of the world's earliest Neolithic-era mining operations (c. 41,000 B.C.), producing pigments for ritual and cosmetic purposes.

MALKERNS. An agricultural and food processing center, 23 miles (37 kilometers) south-southwest of **Mbabane** and 5 miles (8 kilometers) west of Mahlanya. The Malkerns valley between the **Usutu** and **Lusushwana rivers** is one of the richest irrigated agricultural areas in Swaziland. Its products are citrus, **sugarcane**, vegetables, pineapples, avocados, maize, and **cotton**. Specialized crops such as miniature vegetables for the French market and flowers sold in Johannesburg are also grown in the valley. Malkerns's 1986 population was 4,994.

The making of the Malkerns valley was an **irrigation** canal drawing water from the Usutu River 20 miles (32 kilometers) distant, built privately in 1952 by a group of farmers led by H. H. Green and Joseph Vickery. *iNgwenyama* **Sobhuza Dlamini II**, who oversaw some **Swazi Nation Land** acreage in the valley, was also a member of the group. The canal (4 feet deep and 16 feet across at the top and 8 at the bottom) was cut through hills and run across valleys with bridges and aqueducts. An exit canal led from the valley to the Lusushwana River. It was built in a year, the tap being turned on in April 1953. Several crops were tried and abandoned before citrus succeeded. Rice thrived until the crop was attacked by a parasite at about the time that the world price plummeted. Wheat was consumed by birds.

Success of the canal quickly resulted in a concentration of wage employment, particularly for females, on the estates. A canning factory, a government agricultural research station, and the agricultural campus of the **University of Swaziland** at Luyengo were later established, providing more employment opportunities. The original cost of the scheme was £100,000, secured by a bank mortgage, about 1/20th of its estimated replacement cost at the end of the century.

MAMBA, BOKWENI (c. 1876–1940). Son of Matja I and chief of the Mamba clan dominating southeast Swaziland throughout much of the colonial era, beginning in about 1888. At the beginning of Bokweni's tenure the Mambas constituted a quasi-independent kingdom, treating the **iNkhosi Dlaminis** more or less as equals, a status won from a grateful *iNgwenyama* **Sobhuza Dlamini I**, whom Bokweni's ancestor, **Chief Maloyi Mamba**, had saved from being overthrown. The British colonial administration altered that relationship by withdrawing capital jurisdiction from the *ingwenyama* and all chiefs, and in particular outlawing the "smelling-out" and execution of witches. Those powers had constituted the foundations of Bokweni's claim to regional sovereignty. Therefore, the Mambas claimed, it was the British, not the Dlaminis, who had abolished their kingship and crushed their hegemony, won from Sobhuza with such *élan* by Bokweni's predecessor Maloyi Mamba, and it was the British who had subordinated them once more to Sobhuza's heirs.

Bokweni ostensibly accepted his new subordinate position with grace, maintaining cordial relations with *iNgwenyama* **Sobhuza Dlamini II** and working cooperatively with the British. Clandestinely, however, he continued to exercise his capital jurisdiction, including the smelling-out and execution of witches, as the basis of his unrivaled domestic and regional authority. His strategy seemed to work: he was treated as an equal by Sobhuza, and a 1936 colonial officer's report on Swazi chiefs referred to him as in all respects "exemplary" and concluded that "he is a chief of outstanding merit and worthy of extended powers." At his death in 1940 Bokweni had 46 wives and 5,100 followers.

MAMBA, MALOYI. Son of Mamba, 18th-century founder of the Mamba clan. According to Mamba tradition the royal clan ruling the Tsonga people in the **Delagoa Bay** region of 18th-century southern Mozambique was headed by Langa. Langa produced two sons: Dlamini (the elder) and Hlubi (the younger). Because Dlamini possessed a cruel personality, Langa broke tradition and decreed Hlubi to be his successor. Followers of the two sons moved off as separate clans during the 1720s to the southwest but were blocked from heading further south by the **Ndwandwe**. The followers of Dlamini headed west along the iNgwavuma River, while the followers of Hlubi followed the Pongola River, settling north of its banks. Maloyi Mamba led the followers of Hlubi beginning in the late 18th century in southeastern Swaziland. Maloyi consequently exhibited a "brotherly" affinity to *iNgwenyama* **Sobhuza Dlamini I**, descended as they both were from Langa.

It followed that when Sobhuza had left his **Shiselweni** headquarters on his northern campaign in the late 1810s, and his brother **Mnt. Ngwekazi Dlamini** attempted to usurp his throne in his absence, Maloyi stepped in to thwart the coup. He did so by refusing to countenance

Ngwekazi's actions, beckoning Sobhuza back from his Dlomodlomo hills (upper **Komati River** valley) expedition and helping him to suppress Ngwekazi's rebellion. Sobhuza, deeply obliged to Maloyi and as yet none too powerful on his own, rewarded him by recognizing his autonomy, allowing him privileges normally considered treasonous if practiced by others. Those included Maloyi's ability to raise his own **regiments**, harbor refugees from Sobhuza, and celebrate his own *iNcwala* **ceremony**. Maloyi was succeeded by his son Matja Mamba. The line of Mamba succession that followed was **Bokweni**, Mabatjane II, and Matja II.

MAMISA (*sibongo* not known). An important *indvuna* of two royal **homesteads** throughout his career and an *indvuna* of the iNdhlavela **regiment**, which, on the orders of *iNgwenyama* **Mbandzeni**, executed the *indlovukazi*, **Sisile Khumalo**, and her fleeing companions in northern Swaziland in 1880. Mamisa was also the *indvuna* commissioned to execute Mbandzeni's allegedly treasonous prime minister, **Sandlane Zwane**, in 1888. Mamisa was the model for **Allister Miller**'s highly romanticized novel *Mamisa, the Swazi Warrior* (1933), for which the author claimed, in obvious exaggeration, historical accuracy. Jonathan Crush exposes Miller's dual political motivations in publishing the book as first, to remind colonial administrators that their first duty was to the settlers, not the "natives"; and second, to remind his readers of the barbaric nature of Swazi society before the "Whiteman" brought law and order. Miller dedicated *Mamisa* to **Robert Coryndon** (**resident commissioner** 1907–16), who was by far the most obsequious of any colonial official to settler interests.[2]

MANKAYANE (formerly Mankaiana). "Little Steps." A village of 913 inhabitants (1986 census) 23 miles (38 kilometers) west-southwest of **Manzini**. Mankayane is primarily a marketing center, but before the 1963 administrative changes it was the district headquarters of the Mankaiana administrative district. The Mankaiana district was one of six, lying in west-central Swaziland between the **Usutu** and iNgwempisi rivers. Modern Mankayane lies within the Manzini administrative region.

MANZINI. The largest city in Swaziland (1986 greater Manzini population 46,058), located in the central **middleveld** in the kingdom. Also the name of the most populous administrative region. Manzini began its existence as Bremersdorp, a hamlet which grew up around the hotel, canteen, and general dealership of **Albert Bremer**, partner in Wallenstein and Bremer. Bremersdorp became successively the headquarters of the European provisional government established in 1890 and the capital of the **South African Republic**'s administration (1895–99). It was partly destroyed during the **Anglo-Boer War**, first by the brigandage of the troop commanded by **Ludwig von Steinaecker**, then by an Afrikaner commando which routed Steinaecker's men out of the village in July 1901. In 1903 Bremersdorp lost its primacy when the new British colonial administration moved the administrative capital up into the hills to **Mbabane**, largely for considerations of health.

Following World War II Bremersdorp's central location made it increasingly the hub of commercial and industrial development and population growth. The name Bremersdorp was changed to Manzini in 1961, probably after a local chief, Manzini Motsa, in whose domain it lay, but possibly also in consideration of Bremer's African name, Manzini ("Water"). Today the greater Manzini area (including the **Matsapha** industrial estate and the international airport) constitutes the country's largest agricultural, commercial, retail, industrial, transportation, and communications center. Manzini is also the capital of the Manzini Administrative Region (the region's 1986 population was 187,030), one of four such regions, which extends from the country's western border with South Africa well into its center. Along with Manzini, it includes such important towns and villages as Bhunya, **Mankayane**, **Malkerns**, Luve, Croyden, Mliba, Mafutseni, **Mhlambanyatsi**, and Sidvokodvo.

MAROTENG, SEKHUKHUNE I (c. 1810–1882). **Pedi** king who, along with King Cetewayo Zulu, deeply influenced the character of 19th-century Swazi military history, especially during the early reign of *iNgwenyama* **Mbandzeni Dlamini**. Sekhukhune did so by perpetuating the historic Pedi-Swazi rivalry for domination of the eastern **Transvaal** between their territories. Sekhukhune's succession to his father Sekwati Maroteng's throne in 1861 was bitterly disputed by his half-brother, Mampuru Maroteng. Consequently Sekhukhune's consolidation of power, bloody as it was, did not settle things for long. Mampuru fled to Swaziland to seek allies against his brother, and in 1869, during the regency following the death of *iNgwenyama* **Mswati Dlamini II**, an expedition was launched to place him on the Pedi throne. The Swazi force was entrapped and slaughtered by Pedi riflemen at Ewulu (Lulu mountains, Transvaal), where Swazi princes "fell like the leaves in autumn."[3] Partly out of revenge for Ewulu, Mbandzeni dispatched a troop of 2,000 men to aid in the **South African Republic**'s campaign to subdue Sekhukhune in 1875. Again, tricked this time by the Afrikaners into bearing the brunt of the attack and taking heavy casualties, the Swazi broke off in disgust and returned home.

Following the British annexation of the Transvaal in 1877, Sekhukhune escalated his battles with the Transvaal Europeans by launching a series of raids on the British. In retaliation, the British under Gen. Sir Garnet Wolesley launched a joint expedition against Sekhukhune's mountain redoubt in 1879 that involved nearly 8,500 Swazi troops under their ablest general, **Mbovane Fakudze**. While the British launched a frontal attack the Swazi stormed up the rear of the mountain and took Sekhukhune from behind. The glory Fakudze's men achieved in that battle, in spite of their heavy casualties, more than wiped away the humiliation of all the previous defeats of the Swazi at Sekhukhune's hands. Sekhukhune was captured and exiled for a while in Pretoria. He was murdered by Mampuru in 1882, an act that marked the end of the Pedi as a cohesive nation.

MARTIN, COL. SIR RICHARD E. R. (1847–1907; knighted 1895). An officer in the British army's 6th Inskilling Dragoons, 77th Regiment, who arrived in **South Africa** in 1882 and saw service against the Zulu in 1887–88. In 1889 the **high commissioner**, Sir Hercules Robinson, dispatched Martin to Swaziland accompanying two representatives of the **South African Republic (SAR)** to investigate reports of possible disturbances there. Martin and the others arrived just as *iNgwenyama* **Mbandzeni Dlamini** was suffering his final illness, and they immediately determined that the kingdom was unsettled enough to warrant the appointment of a joint (British-Afrikaner) commission to determine if Swaziland's independence was in jeopardy. The **Anglo-Boer Joint Commission** was dispatched to Swaziland in late 1889, with Martin serving as its deputy British representative. The commission determined to replace the former **Swazieland Committee** with a **Provisional Government Committee**, representing British, Swazi, and SAR interests. Martin was selected as the British member. The other two members were **Daniel J. Esselen** (SAR) and **Theophilus Shepstone, Jr.** (Swazi).

Martin served on the **Swaziland Government Committee** for five years (1890–95), an eventful era that witnessed all members of the triumvirate government jockeying for position over the future governance of Swaziland. By 1893 the SAR had acquired the **concessions** necessary for it to govern. Meanwhile the British had signaled a shift of their interest elsewhere by signing the **second Swaziland Convention**, which allowed the SAR to administer the kingdom short of incorporation. In 1894 Britain effectively ripped up its previous guarantees of Swazi sovereignty by signing the **third Swaziland Convention**, which obviated the previous requirement that an "**organic proclamation**" be signed by the Swazi before the SAR could assume administrative sovereignty. The

SAR commenced its administration of Swaziland in early 1895. Martin as the British representative was in the thick of all those events, especially during 1894–95 as it became evident to Queen Regent **Labotsibeni Mdluli** that previous British guarantees were not worth the paper they were written on, prompting her angry protests to the British through Martin.

As those events unfolded Martin managed to maintain a reputation of evenhandedness and integrity among all parties involved, until early 1895. It was then that Martin officially attended the queen regent's ceremony "showing" (formally introducing) **Mnt. Bhunu Dlamini** to the nation and foreign representatives as the successor to Mbandzeni as *ingwenyama*. The SAR vigorously protested Martin's attendance as "British resident" which appeared to contradict the sovereignty provisions of the third Swaziland Convention. Martin was removed from Swaziland quickly, and in 1896 he became resident commissioner and commandant of the armed forces of Rhodesia.

MARWICK, ALLAN G. (1877–1966). One of four extraordinarily influential public officials in Swaziland during the colonial era. He had a profound influence on the monarchy's prevailing over its adversaries by the time of independence (1968). Marwick, raised in Natal, the son of a colonial official and labor recruiter, arrived in Swaziland in 1903 with the first wave of British colonial administrators. He gradually moved up the ladder of administrative posts, mainly in the Hlatikulu region in the south, developing a reputation for being an effective official dealing with the Swazi, who considered him extraordinarily trustworthy (in part because of his fluency in the Zulu tongue). He was consequently chosen by **Resident Commissioner Robert Coryndon** to carry out a number of important and sensitive tasks that were destined to profoundly affect the course of his career.

First, Coryndon chose Marwick to accompany the **deputation of 1907** commissioned by Queen Regent **Labotsibeni Mdluli** to protest the expropriation of Swazi lands under the **Partition Proclamation** to the Colonial Office. According to Coryndon's confidential instructions Marwick's duties included passing along intelligence on the deputation's plans to the Colonial Office and arranging the agenda so that the planned rebuff of the delegation by the colonial secretary, **Lord Elgin**, would prove to be humiliating enough to seriously damage Labotsibeni politically. Coryndon's plan backfired when Labotsibeni's domestic reputation was instead enhanced by her show of defiance and when Marwick returned from London an ardent supporter of the Swazi claim that Elgin had promised them that much of their land would be returned to them. Marwick's allegation, which directly contradicted the **high commissioner**'s position, so displeased colonial officialdom that his career was nearly derailed. Marwick, however, never backed away from his claim regarding Elgin's broken promise, going so far as to write an account following his retirement of Swazi political history from his own point of view, "The Attitude of the Swazi Towards Government and Its Causes" (Mbabane, 1955; mss., SNA, RCS 591/30).

Marwick's second assignment stemmed from his advocacy of *iNkhosana* (Crown Prince) **Sobhuza Dlamini II**'s education at the **Lovedale Missionary Institution** in the western Cape. In 1915 Marwick inspected the school in company with four prominent Swazi, and he returned to prepare Sobhuza for his experience. That became the beginning of a close, lifelong friendship between the two, a relationship characterized by unparalleled trust and influence on the parts of each toward the other. This was best exemplified during the residency of **T. Ainsworth Dickson** (1928–35). At the time of Dickson's appointment Marwick, then assistant commissioner in Hlatikulu, was so disappointed at not being named **resident commissioner** himself that he refused to travel to **Mbabane** to greet Dickson. Their relations quickly warmed, however, and Dickson came to trust Marwick's judgment to such a degree that he took him to Mbabane as his deputy. Marwick convinced Dickson of the counterproductivity of the long-standing British policy of undermining Swazi royalty politically and economically, and thus influenced him to set a new course of bolstering Sobhuza's domestic power, thereby forging an effective regime of **indirect rule**. So accomplished was Marwick in that regard that he was named to succeed Dickson as resident commissioner (1935–37).

At the same time Marwick was using his influence with Sobhuza to consolidate the latter's position both domestically and with the British. Here the key event was Sobhuza's decision in 1926 to abandon his dominant persona as an African progressive, which had succeeded only in gaining him a humiliating defeat in the British courts in his lawsuit against **Allister Miller** and in leaving him deeply in debt and hence politically vulnerable. Sobhuza instead began to emphasize Swazi tradition as the basis of his political presence and power. This was manifested in many ways, notably his revival and elaboration of the *iNcwala* **ceremony**, his initiation of an *umcwasho* (coming of age) ceremony for adolescent girls, and his institution of the *emabutfo* (regimental; *see* **libutfo**) system in the **Swazi National High School** at **Matsapha** and (it was planned) in Swazi schools elsewhere. By such means Sobhuza sought to control, as Christopher Lowe has pointed out, the acculturation of young men and women in an era of dizzying social change.[4]

To Marwick's hand could be attributed many of those initiatives. He wrote letters to *The Star* (Johannesburg) defending the more controversial elements of the *iNcwala* ritual. More to the point, Marwick persuaded Sobhuza of the vital importance of enlisting the support of the community of functionalist anthropologists in **South Africa** in support of his traditionalist initiatives. This was especially true of Sobhuza's school *emabutfo* system, which was being strongly opposed by the European missionary establishment. Marwick corresponded with the leading academics in Sobhuza's behalf and invited them to visit Swaziland and discuss Sobhuza's initiatives with the ***ingwenyama*** personally. In the end the king obtained the strong support of the South African anthropological community's luminaries, including Winifred Hoernlé (University of the Witwatersrand) and Isaac Schapera (University of Cape Town). Sobhuza never forgot Marwick's lesson on the importance of cultivating influential European anthropologists and other intellectuals. His efforts to influence the thinking of **Lord William Hailey** during his 1935 visit and to influence the writings of **Hilda Kuper** over a lifetime were only the most prominent examples of that.

Finally, as resident commissioner Marwick intervened directly to bolster Sobhuza's flagging domestic power and prestige, most markedly among the chiefs of southern Swaziland, where the monarchy's influence historically had been the weakest. Marwick did this by reinterpreting the 1898 law that had deprived the *ingwenyama* of criminal jurisdiction, in such a way as to criminalize chiefs' disobedience to him. Sobhuza for his part suddenly became active in deciding a series of perennially difficult boundary disputes between chiefs in the south that had remained unaddressed for years. He then turned over those chiefs who refused to comply with his decisions to the colonial courts for prosecution. Those concerted actions added significantly to Sobhuza's domestic stature and, ironically, contributed to his ability to present his subjects' case more effectively before the colonial authorities in Mbabane, Pretoria, and London. That in no little way contributed to his political triumphs during the run-up to independence during the 1960s.

Marwick retired from the colonial service in 1937. On that occasion Sobhuza wrote to him: "you have won our confidence, love and respect and have left an indelible impression in our hearts." The Marwicks lived out their retirement in Mbabane.

MARWICK, SIR BRIAN A. (1908–1992; knighted 1963). Resident commissioner, 1957–63; **Her Majesty's Commissioner for Swaziland,** 1963–64. Marwick, a nephew of **Allan G. Marwick**, was born into a sugar-planting family in Natal and was educated at the University of Cape Town. He joined the British colonial service in Swaziland in 1925 and, with intervals in Basutoland and Nigeria, served there until his retirement in 1964. During his early years in Swaziland Marwick, who was fluent in **siSwati**, became personally close to the *ingwenyama*, **Sobhuza Dlamini II**, as had been his uncle, Allan Marwick. Those years as a district officer were full of promise. Marwick combined excellence as a colonial administrator with a keen intellectual curiosity about the anthropology of the Swazi. His academic thesis on that subject, the product of fieldwork performed along with his administrative duties, earned him an M.A. degree from Cape Town in 1939. (The costs of Marwick's graduate work and the publication of his book were borne in their entirety by the Swaziland administration.) It was in part Sobhuza's reading of Marwick's thesis that set him on a lifelong interest in the subject and in anthropologists. Marwick published his thesis as *The Swazi* in 1940, and it immediately became the standard work on the subject. *The Swazi* was succeeded but not superseded by **Hilda Kuper**'s two major works published in 1947 (based primarily on mid-1930s field research), *An African Aristocracy* and *The Uniform of Colour*.

The promise of those years added poignancy to the turbulence that beset Marwick's later career as resident commissioner beginning in 1957. Two factors were mainly responsible: the post–World War II penetration of foreign capital investment, which quickly and drastically altered the political economy of the kingdom; and official and popular awareness of the approach of independence, which made its appearance about the time Marwick assumed the resident commissionership. On the first point, by the time of Marwick's appointment there existed in Swaziland a cohort of European entrepreneurs who had shaped the pattern of postwar capitalist development of the kingdom and were then dominating their powerful lobbying arm, the **Reconstituted European Advisory Council (REAC)**. That group had found a friend in the **high commissioner**'s office during the heyday of Swaziland's new development, occupied by **Sir Evelyn Baring** (1944–55), who had personally created a business climate so strongly entrepreneurial that even Sobhuza had been caught up in it (*see* **Stephens, Robert P.**).

It was in the vortex of that go-getting spirit in Swaziland business and politics that Marwick set his priorities as resident commissioner, not without a great deal of controversy and opposition, especially from the Swazi. For example Marwick's decision to grant the maize milling and distribution monopoly to **Natie Kirsh**'s Swaziland Milling Co. was opposed by many European businesses and only grudgingly assented to by Sobhuza. Similarly, Marwick's endorsement of the contracting of all the iron deposits from the **Swaziland Iron Ore Development Co.**'s **Ngwenya** development to Japanese steel producers (1961), with no provision for financial benefit to the Swazi nation, was bitterly but unsuccessfully opposed by Sobhuza. Those and other decisions by Marwick debited his goodwill capital with Sobhuza, making his subsequent political dealings with the *ingwenyama* over independence issues all the more difficult.

The myriad issues that arose as independence approached from the late 1950s onward could be distilled into one fundamental disagreement between Marwick and Sobhuza: whether the Swazi government on which the independence constitution would be conferred was to be democratic (as advocated by Marwick) or autocratic (as insisted upon by Sobhuza). Until 1964, when Marwick departed, that issue remained very much in doubt. Marwick brought his considerable intellect and energies to bear on his efforts. He also had the interests of the emerging Swazi middle class on his side, although that sword proved to be double-edged. Events were to prove, however, that Sobhuza's own intellect and energies were equal to the task of defending his interests. Furthermore the *ingwenyama* was aided—far more effectively than Marwick was, it turned out—by his alliance with the preponderance of the powerful settler interests, along with his unquestioned support by the Swazi traditionalists and peasantry.

The constitutional issues over which this basic tension played out commenced with Marwick's convening of the first Constitutional Committee, composed mainly of delegates from the *libandla*, the REAC, and the **Swaziland Progressive Party (SPP)**, in late 1960. So great was the disagreement between the Swazi modernists and traditionalists, and between them and the Europeans, that even Marwick's skillful maneuverings proved insufficient to push his constitutional ideal through either the committee or two successive **constitutional conferences** held in London in 1961 and 1963. Marwick's ideal was a representative, nonracial, and gender-inclusive form of government, incorporating both checks and balances and a bill of rights. Consequently his principal behind-the-scenes role during the entire period of negotiations (1960–63) was to influence the Colonial Office into vetoing all the committees' recommendations in favor of a constitution loosely modeled on the Westminster style, which London indeed imposed, finally, in March 1963.

Marwick, whose title was changed to Her Majesty's Commissioner at that time, spent his final year (to March 1964) confronting two complicated and highly consequential challenges. The first was to establish the guidelines and set the ground rules for the first **Legislative Council** (Legco) elections to be held under the British-imposed constitution, scheduled for June 1964. The second was to take command of the government's reaction to a series of volatile **labor strikes** in key industries. If not handled properly, these held the potential for derailing the kingdom's movement toward self-government and independence. Marwick's moves were necessarily reactive, given the dizzying speed with which the labor stoppages swept through workplace after workplace. Ultimately the strikes could not be contained because political leaders of the radical opposition movements were quick to seize on them to further their own aims and because Sobhuza, when requested, refused to call out his *emabutfo* in support of Marwick's inadequate numbers of police. In June 1963 Marwick declared an emergency and called in the British army from Kenya to maintain order, effectively putting an end to the strikes. Those events did nothing to create an atmosphere of calm in which to accomplish his political goals.

Those goals centered on Marwick's plan to turn Sobhuza into a constitutional monarch above the fray during the run-up to the 1964 Legco elections and thereafter. To Marwick's consternation, Sobhuza instead succeeded in establishing his own royalist political party, the **Imbokodvo National Movement (INM)**, through which—utilizing the political machinery of the *libandla*—the *ingwenyama* ran his slate of candidates (all of whom were *libandla* members) in the elections. In June 1964 the INM succeeded in winning a smashing victory, although by then Marwick had retired, replaced by **Sir Francis Loyd** as Queen's Commissioner.

Marwick did not go quietly. At a reception on the eve of his departure, given by Sobhuza in his honor, Marwick criticized the REAC for its political opportunism, chastised the *libandla* for meddling inappropriately in the modern political process, and delivered a harsh judgment on Sobhuza's refusal to distance himself from the election, warning that his failure to do so would eventually bring about the end of democratic institutions in Swaziland.

Following his retirement Marwick was employed by the government of the Bahamas (1965–71) as a permanent secretary, following which he lived out his life on the Isle of Man.

MASEKO, MACDONALD M. Member of the **Ngwane National Liberatory Congress (NNLC)** executive and labor activist whose agitation as a **strike** leader during March–June 1963 helped launch a political crisis leading to the government's declaration of an emergency. Maseko was a refugee from **South Africa**, having been an **African National Congress (ANC)** official, who after being placed under house arrest had escaped and fled across the border to Swaziland in 1962. Maseko first joined the **Swaziland Progressive Party (SPP)** but soon broke with its leader, **John J. Nquku**, as being domineering and insufficiently radical. Maseko, along with a second dissident, **Mnt. Dumisa Dlamini**, followed **Dr. Ambrose Zwane** out of the SPP to form the more radical NNLC (April 1963). Maseko was later elected NNLC vice president.

Even before that realignment the three activists, led by Maseko with his ANC background, recognized the political potential of the mass dissatisfaction of the new generation of agribusiness laborers with their pay, working conditions, and inability to unionize. (As early as mid-1962 Dlamini had been involved in the rump unionization of asbestos and sugar workers.) In March 1963 the three led strikes among sugar laborers at Big Bend and **Ubombo ranches**, which in turn touched off stoppages at **Peak Timbers** and the **Mbabane** central market (April), and at the **Havelock Asbestos Mine** (May). In early June 1963 Dlamini and Maseko ratcheted up the tension by agitating for a countrywide sympathy strike, leading a protest march in Mbabane and then sparking a second walkout among sugar workers in the **lowveld**. It was at that point that **Her Majesty's Commissioner Sir Brian Marwick** declared an emergency and called in British troops from Kenya, actions that quickly put an end to all strikes and civil disorders.

Maseko, along with a dozen or so other strike leaders, was quickly arrested and jailed. He was convicted in February 1964 for disturbing public order and inciting to violence, and sentenced to six months in prison. Dlamini, also convicted, was given a lighter sentence, and Zwane was acquitted. Of greater consequence was the fact that the NNLC leadership was so preoccupied with defending themselves in court that the party was never able to mount an effective campaign for the 1964 **Legislative Council** elections, failed to win any seats, and never amounted to anything at the ballot box thereafter. Maseko lost his deposit in the 1964 elections and later that year became vice president (representing what was left of the NNLC) of the newly formed **Joint Council of Swaziland Political Parties** (JCSPP). At that point Maseko wandered off into the political wilderness, first being expelled from Zwane's NNLC and then going down with the sinking JCSPP ship. At that point he formed the Anti-Apartheid Committee devoted to assisting refugees from South Africa.

MASUKU, PAULINE FIKELEPHI (1928–). Commonly known by her *sibongo*, laMasuku. By all accounts the most beloved by *iNgwenyama* **Sobhuza Dlamini II** of all his wives, laMasuku was a **Swazi National High School** classmate of Sobhuza's daughter Pholile Dlamini, whom he spotted on a visit to her school. Sobhuza summoned her, the tradition being that the *ingwenyama*'s proffer of betrothal is not to be declined by any woman. laMasuku, however, was the daughter of devout Christians, educated, and possessed of strong career ambitions. Furthermore, her father let it be known that she would marry no "heathen," and certainly not in polygyny, even a king. She was sent off to Durban for safe keeping, then to Johannesburg. Sobhuza was not to be denied, and he sent emissaries to fetch her back. The marriage took place in 1949. It was said that after a long and difficult period of adjustment to her new circumstances, laMasuku fashioned out an extremely happy and fulfilling relationship with Sobhuza. He first placed her at **Ehlane**, in part to remove her from the jealousies afoot in the *sigodlo* (queens' quarters). Then, in 1953, he installed her at his new, Western residence at **Masundvwini**.

MASUNDVWINI. "The Place of Palms." *iNgwenyama* **Sobhuza Dlamini II**'s Western-style residence in the hilly savannah just east of **Manzini**, built in 1953. Its large, sumptuous house quickly became Sobhuza's most favored residence. He installed several of his wives there. From that time his pattern of living generally was Masundvwini, residence; **Lobamba**, rituals; **Ehlane**, hunting; and **Lozithehlezi** (Lozitha), administration. In Sobhuza's final years he often favored a second residential retreat, **Ephondvo**, 2 miles (3 kilometers) east of **Malkerns**. It was at Ephondvo that Sobhuza died in 1982.

MATSAPHA. Swaziland's major industrial area, situated on the **Lusushwana River**, 5 miles (8 kilometers) west of **Manzini**. At the Matsapha industrial estate, established in 1965, are situated a large and growing number of manufacturing and processing enterprises, including a truck and bus assembly plant, petroleum storage depots, and a brewery. The estate is serviced by a major highway (to South Africa) and a railroad (to Maputo and Richards Bay). Among major governmental facilities located in the Matsapha area are the **Swaziland National High School**, the Swaziland Police College, and the national prison. Accordingly, Matsapha has become a major population center in the kingdom.

MATSEBULA, JAMES S. MKHULUNYELWA (1918–1994). Swaziland's leading Swazi historian and private secretary to *iNgwenyama* **Sobhuza Dlamini II.** Matsebula was best known for his authorship of the pioneering *A History of Swaziland* (1972; 3d ed., 1988). Matsebula's *History* was the first comprehensive history of Swaziland ever published and one of the first accounts (the earliest being the historical writing of **Hilda Kuper**) written from an Afrocentric point of view. The successive editions of Matsebula's *History*, though they have often understandably reflected the royalist perspective, have been used as important sources by subsequent historians of Swaziland. Matsebula authored 11 other volumes over his lifetime, in English, **siSwati**, and Zulu, the last being his autobiographical *The King's Eye* (1983).

Matsebula was an extremely close confidant of Sobhuza during his entire lifetime, by virtue of two qualities. The first was his social status. He was born into a *Bemdzabuko* ("True Swazi") clan with powerful ritual ties to the **Nkhosi Dlamini**, the one that traditionally offered the *ingwenyama* his first wife, who became his senior queen (although not the mother of his heir). The Matsebula also traditionally furnished the *ingwenyama*'s junior right-hand *insila*, and they provided officials for special court rituals. The second reason for Matsebula's influence with Sobhuza was the *ingwenyama*'s estimation of his intelligence, education, and judgment. There is no indication that Matsebula ever disappointed Sobhuza in those regards.

Matsebula was educated at the Mpolonjeni mission school, then the **Swazi National High School** at **Matsapha**. He subsequently trained as a teacher at St. Chad Teacher Training College in Natal and received his B.A. degree by correspondence from the University of South Africa. From 1941 to 1959 Matsebula held a number of posts as teacher and then headmaster in Swaziland and South Africa. In 1959 Sobhuza appointed him his junior *Lisolenkhosi* ("King's Eye"), liaison officer between the *ingwenyama* and the colonial administration. In that capacity he served on the first Constitutional Committee and attended the first constitutional conference in London in 1960–61. From 1962 to 1967 Matsebula was senior inspector of schools, and from 1967 to 1974 he served as private secretary to the *ingwenyama*. Finally, from 1974 until his death he served as chief executive officer of the Swaziland National Trust Commission, overseeing the *ingwenyama*'s secretariat and archives. In that capacity Matsebula chaired the committee of government officials and scholars that oversaw Hilda Kuper's authorship of Sobhuza's official biography, *Sobhuza II* (1978). Prior to his death Matsebula placed his papers in the library of the University of Swaziland. During the final years of his life Dr. Matsebula opted to be referred to as Dr. J. S. Mkhulunyelwa Matsebula.

MAUDLING, REGINALD. British Secretary of State for Colonies during the 1960s who presided over the earliest of Swaziland's constitutional discussions. It was Maudling who in 1959 and 1960 received notes from *iNgwenyama* **Sobhuza Dlamini II** and from the **Reconstituted European Advisory Council** that established their respective positions on issues anticipatory to independence and that led to his authorization of the establishment of the first Constitutional Committee in 1960. Maudling also chaired the first constitutional conference in London (1961), which proved to be inconclusive. Maudling's views on the shape of Swaziland's independence constitution closely reflected those of the **resident commissioner, Sir Brian Marwick**, making the latter's job of pressing for a representative government somewhat easier (although not in the long run successful). Maudling favored a legislature with powers over the monarchy, a common voting roll, and measures to ensure that modern opposition parties had a voice in any independence government.

MBABANE. The administrative and judicial capital of Swaziland and the administrative center of the **Hhohho administrative region**. Mbabane's 1986 population was 38,290. The town is located on the Mbabane River (which flows into the Mbuluzi) in the **highveld** region, 12 miles (19 kilometers) southeast of the main South African border post at Oshoek. Mbabane was originally the site of one of *iNgwenyama* **Mbandzeni Dlamini**'s principal cattle kraals. Until 1902 the administrative and judicial capital of Swaziland was Bremersdorp (**Manzini**), near the geographic center of the kingdom, but with the arrival of the British colonial administration the need for a more amenable, highveld climate was made the paramount consideration. The two sites considered were Mbabane and **Mhlambanyatsi**, but the latter was more remote from the royal capitals and from the mining areas. It is believed that Mbabane took its name from the Mbabane River, which in turn was named after the most important local chief, **Mbabane Kunene**. Until 1963 Mbabane was the capital of the Mbabane district (one of six districts), but in that year the Mbabane and **Pigg's Peak** districts became the Hhohho administrative region. Mbabane is also (like Manzini) a commercial center of the kingdom, with all the businesses and services associated with a seat of government. The main government hospital is located in Mbabane, as are the government radio and television broadcasting facilities.

MBANDZENI NATIONAL CONVENTION (MNC). A short-lived political party created in 1962 by merging two splinter parties in anticipation of pre-independence elections: the Mbandzeni Party, led by **Clifford Nkosi**, and the National Convention Party, led by **Dr. George Msibi**. Nkosi, the MNC's secretary general, had been a clerk in a Johannesburg law firm, while Msibi, its president, had returned from his medical training in India to enter the political fray. The MNC, being more than anything else a creature of its two leaders, never produced a clearly discernible platform. It called for support of the *ingwenyama* and for the principle of one man, one vote. It also called for the formation of a kingdom-wide labor organization under the control of the *libandla*. The MNC was represented by Dr. Msibi at the **constitutional conference** (1963) in London, following which, without any discernible constituency, it vanished. Nkosi withdrew from politics, and Msibi joined the **Imbokodvo National Movement** following its formation in 1964, for a while serving as its secretary general.

MBEKELWENI. Archaically, Embekelweni. The *lilawu* (administrative capital) established by *iNgwenyama* **Mbandzeni Dlamini**, located about 6 miles (10 kilometers) northwest of modern **Manzini**. The ritual capital and *indlovukazi*'s **homestead** during the Mbandzeni era was **Nkanini**, 4 miles (7 kilometers) southwest of Mbekelweni. During the **concessions** era (1880s) Mbekelweni became the mecca of the transactions, the locus around which gathered all the European would-be concessionaires and the *ingwenyama*'s councillors on the take, where gold coinage and spirits were exchanged for a word with Mbandzeni and his "X" on a document. Many of the transactions with the king's councillors—and increasingly with the *ingwenyama* himself—took place at **John Thorburn**'s canteen, the Embekelweni Hotel, a stone's throw from the Mbekelweni royal kraal, where the spirits flowed freely while the deals were struck. By the late 1880s both a postal service and a telegraph line stretched from Mbekelweni across the border to the **Transvaal**.

MBILANENI. *See* MAKHOSINI

eMbo. *See* EMBO

MDLULI, *iNDLOVUKAZI* (also QUEEN REGENT) LABOTSIBENI (c. 1858–1925). Less commonly referred to by her proper name, Gwamile ("Indomitable," "Firm and Unshakable"). The daughter of Chief

Matsanjana Mdluli and widow of *iNgwenyama* **Mbandzeni Dlamini**. Although the Mdluli are an important *Bemdzabuko* ("True Swazi") clan, guarding the royal graves at **Makhosini** and supplying the *ingwenyama*'s junior right-hand *insila*, Labotsibeni's father was a minor chief from an unimportant lineage. Labotsibeni consequently would not have been expected to emerge to the front rank of Mbandzeni's wives on the strength of her pedigree. That did not account for her exceptional character, which was what captured Mbandzeni's respect. Consequently the first child resulting from her marriage to him was destined to become the future *ingwenyama*, **Bhunu Dlamini**. She later gave birth to a daughter, **Mnt. Tongotongo**, and two sons, **Bnt. Malunge** and **Lomvazi Dlamini**.

Upon Mbandzeni's death in 1889, Labotsibeni was selected as *indlovukazi* and her son became the designated successor. It has occasionally been the case, and this was one of them, when the choice of the heir to the throne is based more on the mother's character than on that of the son. Consequently this highly unusual selection was made in spite of the normally disqualifying existence of Bhunu's two brothers. The former *indlovukazi*, **Tibati Nkambule**, became queen regent at the **Nkanini** royal **homestead**, and Labotsibeni established a new homestead at **Zombodze** in the eastern shadow of the **Mdzimba** mountain range. From that location Labotsibeni, first as *indlovukazi* and then (after Bhunu's death in 1899) as queen regent, dominated Swaziland's politics for the following three decades. She relinquished power only upon the installation of *iNgwenyama* **Sobhuza Dlamini II** in 1921, and even then she kept hold of certain ritual medicines out of fear of her enemies until her own death in 1925. It is to Labotsibeni as much as anyone that Swaziland owes the existence of its current form of government, for she tenaciously preserved the royal institutions in the face of the shame that her husband and son had visited on them and despite the assaults on them waged by successive British **resident commissioners**. She accomplished this in a number of ways.

First, she vigorously opposed the imposition of the **South African Republican (SAR)** administration on Swaziland in 1895 and the withdrawal of her government's political and fiscal sovereignty by the British beginning in 1903. When her own remonstrations and her deputations to the **high commissioner** in Pretoria and the Colonial Office in London failed of their purposes, she turned to mission-educated Africans (mostly from the Wesleyan mission at **Edendale**, Natal) and what she thought were politically connected Europeans for advice in furthering her cause. Those Edendale Africans on whom she principally relied were **Josiah Vilakazi**, her secretary, his brother Nehemiah, **Edgar Mini**, Joel **Msimang**, **Cleopas Kunene**, and **Robert Grendon**, a **EurAfrican** who tutored Bnt. Malunge and Lomvazi at Zombodze. Through Msimang Labotsibeni established ties with **Pixley Seme**, a Natal-born lawyer and founder of the **African National Congress (ANC)**. Through Seme she came to appreciate the importance of the ANC's campaigns against land expropriation in South Africa, and as one consequence she contributed funds to help establish and publish the ANC's newspaper *Abantu Batho*. None of the Europeans she chose to advise her, notably **Joseph M. Parsonson**, a Natal speculator, and **Albert Bremer**, a hotelier and concessionaire, turned out to be wise choices. Consequently she received little sound advice during that period of profound change. In the end none of these people nor any of her initiatives succeeded in protecting her sovereignty, although many of them did assist her in standing up to her colonial adversaries, with occasional success.

Labotsibeni also played a deft game of collaboration with colonial authorities when there was leverage to be gained. During the **Anglo-Boer War** she deployed her forces against the Afrikaners, the late administrators of her kingdom, confiscating their cattle, making off with their weapons, and supplying the British with intelligence on enemy movements and on occasion tactical support. Her hope was that the British would restore her sovereignty once the war was over. When instead they recolonized the Swazi themselves, making them an administrative appendage of the **Transvaal** and taking away her criminal jurisdiction (**Swaziland Administration Proclamation 3/1904**), Labotsibeni responded over the next two decades with an amalgam of protest and collaboration calculated to remind the British of the consequences of their policies. During World War I, for example, she refused to recruit Swazi for the **Overseas Native Labour Contingent** on the grounds that she no longer possessed the coercive means to do so; then, once the point was made, she turned around and leveraged £3,000 from her people to contribute to the British war effort. In the end by all these means she preserved enough of the sinews of traditional institutions for Sobhuza to build on in his successful struggles to revive the monarchy prior to independence in 1968.

Second, Labotsibeni came to realize by the turn of the century the value of Western education as a weapon to confront colonial encroachments. Consequently she reversed her previous opposition to Bhunu's education by establishing a national elementary school for her other sons and their peers at **Zombodze** (1906); when it came time for their further education she had them tutored. In 1916 she sent Sobhuza off to the renowned **Lovedale Missionary Institution** at the Cape for his secondary schooling. Although Sobhuza did not finish his course at Lovedale the education he received there stood him in superbly good stead, as she had firmly intended in the face of spirited opposition, in his later political struggles with the colonials.

Third, Labotsibeni solidified her own power within the royal house as she saw the weaknesses of others eroding its defenses against the colonial administration, then used that new power to shore up those defenses as best she could. During Tibati's progressive illness she took over many of her powers. When *iNgwenyama* Bhunu's weaknesses became evident she attempted to shunt him aside in favor of Mnt. Malunge, and failing that she went on to succeed him as queen regent following his sudden death. Whether or not Labotsibeni had a hand in the deaths of Tibati and Bhunu, as was widely believed, remains a mystery. Labotsibeni also sought to bolster her power over the chiefs. When she, a renowned rainmaker, was beseeched by chiefs to make rain during times of drought she always extracted political conditions before acceding. For instance, in 1903, in the midst of a prolonged drought she defied demands that she relinquish her **rainmaking** medicines to *iNkhosana* Sobhuza's mother, **Lomawa Ndwandwe**, by refusing to make rain. Then, when the officials relented, she propitiated the heavens and rains followed.

In that regard it should be understood that many of Labotsibeni's most ambitious initiatives were undertaken not so much to defend her people in the face of colonial depredations as to strengthen the position of the monarchy over her people and their chiefs. Much of the business of her **deputations of 1905** (Pretoria) and **1907** (London), both paid for by levies on the chiefs and their followers, concerned her complaints about the British sequestering of her annual £12,000 personal stipend from the **private revenue concession**. Once again, after exhausting her appeals over the **Partition Proclamation** (1907), Labotsibeni determined to purchase back the concessioned lands just lost to the settlers. Beginning in 1907 she imposed a national levy of £5 per chief and £1 per adult male toward land repurchase and encouraged men to go off to the Johannesburg gold mines to earn the required cash. Eventually the levy reached £10 per chief and £5 per man, yet resistance to it was so determined—partly because of widespread charges of royal embezzlement of funds and favoritism to royalist chiefs in the lands repurchased—that the scheme was finally abandoned in favor of a general tax for the "development and education" of the people, to be administered by the British.

During her term as queen regent Labotsibeni ruled from the center to a degree unprecedented since the latter years of *iNgwenyama* **Mswati Dlamini II**'s reign. That was possible partly because of the absence of a strong *indlovukazi* in office to balance her off. It was also true that both the *libandla* and *liqoqo* fell into near disuse as the years of her rule progressed. Indeed, both bodies came to distrust her and her relationship with the **resident commissioner** that bypassed them, which became the subject of their open and bitter resentment by the end of World War I (RCS 304/19, SNA). The fact was that by the end of her regency Labotsibeni had become so unpopular with certain chiefs for her alleged misdeeds that she feared for her life as she turned over power to her grandson Sobhuza in 1921. She consequently retained some rain medicines in her possession, unconstitutionally, until her dying day. History judges her one of the great figures in the Swazi past, a person who fought tenaciously for Swazi sovereignty as she defined it. It further regards her as the queen who passed on to her grandson in 1921 a monarchy notably strengthened, especially in the esteem of the colonials, over the one she had inherited as queen regent in 1899.

MDLULI, MATSAFENI. The *indvuna* of *iNgwenyama* **Mswati Dlamini II**'s administrative headquarters at Hhohho, established about 1852. In that capacity Matsafeni commanded a large area in what is now the eastern **Transvaal** north of Swaziland to the Crocodile River. Matsafeni enjoyed a reputation as a formidable warrior, earned as the result of several exploits. He led an attack by Mswati's crack iNyatsi ("Buffalo") **regiment** against the Kopa in 1864, capturing their leader in a daring raid up the face of a steep hill. His military reputation was sullied in 1869 when he advocated and led, against the strong advice of Queen Regent **Tsandzile Ndwandwe**, an invasion of the **Pedi** with the object of overthrowing **King Sekhukhune Maroteng**. That attack was stopped in its tracks at Ewulu in the Transvaal, with heavy losses inflicted on the elite Swazi troops. Matsafeni himself was feared lost, but he returned to Hhohho six months later. This setback did not end his military career (he again invaded the Transvaal in 1875), but he did lose his stature during the reign of *iNgwenyama* **Mbandzeni Dlamini**, especially as he descended into an unheard-of running dispute with Mbandzeni over the hand of a young woman whom they both fancied. Finally, in 1891 he was forced to flee from the *ingwenyama*'s wrath, and he was murdered in the Transvaal.

MDZIMBA HILLS. Often Mdzimba mountains. A range of hills stretching south from Mbabane, the ridge-top averaging 3,600 feet (1,100 meters) in height, the peak being 4,200 feet (1,280 meters) in elevation. The Mdzimba range forms the eastern ridge overlooking the **Ezulwini Valley** for a distance of about 7 miles (11 kilometers) along a northwest-southeast axis. The rugged hills at times played an important role in Swaziland's early history. *iNgwenyama* **Sobhuza Dlamini I** chose the fertile and well-watered Ezulwini Valley as his new headquarters in central Swaziland (following his abandonment of **Shiselweni**) during the 1820s in part because the Mdzimba hills offered the most extensive cave fortresses in the region and a quick retreat from the royal capitals in the valley, as well as being well-nigh impregnable. They demonstrated their worth on several occasions, proving unassailable to **Ndwandwe** and Zulu assaults. When the Zulu king **Shaka** attacked Sobhuza with a superior army in 1827, Sobhuza took to the safety of the Mdzimba caves and was saved to fight Shaka again another day, later inflicting defeats on the Zulu king twice before he died. Subsequent royal villages were also built in the shadow of the Mdzimba. There is also a royal gravesite at **Dlangeni**, high on the Mdzimba ridge, where *iNgwenyama* **Bhunu Dlamini** and several senior princes lie.

MEYER, WILLIE. A Sidvokodvo cotton farmer and cattle rancher who entered pre-independence politics beginning in 1960, largely out of determination to preserve European rights and privileges, as the dialogue over the shape of the pre-independence constitution got under way. Meyer, who retained his **South African** citizenship throughout, was possessed of the apartheid-era persuasion that to allow majority rule was to further the aims of international communism. He was made a member of the first Constitutional Committee in 1960 by the **resident commissioner, Brian Marwick**. Meyer was elected chairman of the **United Swaziland Association (USA)** in 1964 during the run-up to the **Legislative Council** elections in June, and he won a reserved European seat on the council. He was then made a member of the second Constitutional Commission in 1965 by the **Queen's Commissioner, Sir Francis Loyd**. Throughout, Meyer remained one of the most vocal advocates of the special place for Europeans in any future constitutional arrangements. Meyer's apprehension over a communist takeover proved groundless, but he was correct in his fear that the USA-**Imbokodvo National Movement (INM)** alliance (formed to contest the 1964 elections) would fall apart once the defeated Swazi opposition parties joined the INM by default, making European support superfluous. Meyer's hard-line position on the demand for a fixed number of reserved seats for Europeans made it easier for the INM to distance itself from them and in fact caused a split among his USA constituency. Once the **1967 constitution**, without a separate roll and equal representation for Europeans, was implemented, Meyer retired from politics and returned to farming.

MHLAMBANYATSI. "Buffalo Crossing." A forestry village with a predominantly European population of 2,146 (1986 census), situated in the forested **highveld** approximately 12 miles (19 kilometers) south-southwest of **Mbabane**. In Mhlambanyatsi is located the administrative headquarters of the **Usutu Pulp Company** and its affiliate, Usutu Forests.

MHLUME. "Good Growth." A **sugar** company town, population 6,509 (1986 census), situated in the irrigated **lowveld** region in northeastern Swaziland, approximately 31 miles (50 kilometers) north-northwest of **Siteki**. Mhlume was established in 1950 by the **Colonial** (later **Commonwealth**) **Development Corporation (CDC)** and is the site of its Mhlume Sugar Company estate. Irrigated citrus orchards are also found in the Mhlume area. The Mhlume Sugar Company was the first **Swaziland Irrigation Scheme (SIS)** sugar enterprise to begin production (1960). The Mhlume-Simunye milling complex is one of the two main sugar production areas in Swaziland, the other being the Ubombo milling complex, which draws from the Big Bend–Nsoko areas. Mhlume was established jointly by the CDC and the Sir J. L. Hulett & Sons firm of South Africa. In 1966 the CDC became the sole owner. Mhlume's main source of **irrigation** is a SIS canal from the **Komati River**, 42 miles (67 kilometers) in length. Processed Mhlume sugar and molasses are shipped by rail from Mlawula to Maputo, Mozambique, and thence overseas.

MIDDLEVELD. Swaziland's main region of population, commerce, and industry. It encompasses an area of 1,700 square miles (4,400 square kilometers), lying on a north-south axis east of the **highveld**. Topographically it is a rolling grassland plateau, varying in altitude from 3,800 feet (1,160 meters) to 1,500 feet (460 meters). Its climate is subtropical, drier than that of the highveld but wetter by far than the **lowveld**. **Manzini** (Swaziland's second major city) in the middleveld normally receives 35 inches (876 millimeters) of rain annually. The middleveld's temperature averages from 79°F (26°C) to 56°F (13°C). Its natural vegetation consists of tall grasses and mixed bush, excellent for cattle grazing, although since the 1930s overgrazing in the middleveld has become an increasingly serious problem.

The middleveld is the principal rain-grown cropping region in Swaziland. Maize is by far the main crop, grown on more than half the ploughed area (much of it **Swazi Nation Land**). Other crops that normally do well in the middleveld are vegetables, sorghum, nuts, fruit, wattle, **cotton**, and tobacco. Much of the best soil is under **irrigation**, and those areas (most of them European-owned **title deed land**) are the most productive of all. The largest irrigation scheme is at **Malkerns (Usutu River)**, where **sugar**, vegetables, pineapples, and citrus are grown, and in the Mhlumati River valley, 16 miles (26 kilometers) northeast of **Pigg's Peak**, where citrus and bananas are grown. The major Swazi nation capitals and *tindlovukazi*'s homesteads traditionally have been placed in the **Ezulwini Valley** (middleveld), most notably Ekufinyeni, Elangeni, Ezabeni, **Lobamba, Ludzidzini, Mbekelweni, Nkanini**, and **Zombodze**.

MILLER, ALLISTER M. (1865–1951). Actual name Alexander Mitchell Miller. Journalist (*Cape Argus*; *Goldfields Times* [Barberton]) who arrived in Swaziland in 1888 to seek his fortune, which he never did (he died in very modest circumstances). His various undertakings and development schemes over the following 60 years profoundly affected Swaziland's history, although they rarely turned out to be successful and the effects were not always for the better. Miller first went to Swaziland as secretary to the **Swazieland Committee** and justice of the peace, appointments strongly objected to by *iNgwenyama* **Mbandzeni Dlamini**'s agent and advisor, **Theophilus Shepstone, Jr.** Thus was started a lifelong enmity between the two men. Miller soon discovered that there were two European factions among the concessionaires at Mbandzeni's capital, **Mbekelweni**: Shepstone's clique and the followers of **John Thorburn**, a concessionaire and owner of the local canteen, the Embekelweni Hotel. Miller quickly sided with Thorburn, partly because he saw that Shepstone was by then falling out of Mbandzeni's favor. Miller was later (1891) to become Thorburn's son-in-law.

In the politics of the *ingwenyama*'s court at Mbekelweni the traditionalists, led by **Mnt. Nkhopolo Dlamini**, opposed the profligate concessioning of Mbandzeni, who was being egged on by a conspiracy of *tindvuna* led by **Tikhuba Magongo**. Thorburn and Miller threw in their lot with Tikhuba, and their position was strengthened when Nkhopolo, caught up in **Sandlane Zwane**'s conspiracy to kill Mbandzeni, fled for his life in December 1888 and left the field open to Tikhuba. Because Shepstone's star had been dimmed by then, Miller's influence with Mbandzeni became greatly enhanced, to the point that he often acted by default as the *ingwenyama*'s personal secretary. By February 1889 Mbandzeni had dismissed Shepstone, and Miller had officially become his secretary and agent. Mbandzeni also appointed Miller as one of his five representatives on the Swazieland Committee. Miller was now in a position to sell the *ingwenyama* out, which he proceeded to do; for instance none of Miller's **concessions** contained the language typical of previous or subsequent royal concessions protecting Swazi sovereignty or rights. Furthermore, as early as January 1889 Miller and Thorburn traveled to Pretoria to peddle monopolies to the **South African Republic (SAR)**. By 1894 the SAR would hold enough monopoly concessions (sold by Miller, Thorburn, and others) to be able to claim practical sovereignty over Swaziland.

The claim that Miller was the arch-villain of the concessions era has been much disputed. What seems fair to say is that a good many of the arguably fraudulent concessions that did the most serious damage to Swazi economic and political viability were directly attributable to Miller's influence and conniving, and that consequently he stands fairly accused of betraying Mbandzeni's trust in a most shameful manner. It was during Miller's tenure as the *ingwenyama*'s advisor for instance that the notorious **unallotted lands** and the **private revenue concessions** were sold to John Thorburn and **John Harington**, respectively, both of them over Miller's signature as witness. The unallotted lands concession granted Thorburn (and Frank Watkins) a grazing and farming monopoly over all lands south of the **Komati River** not previously concessioned, for an absurdly low rental of £50 annually. The private revenue concession (which Harington transferred to the SAR the following year) allowed him the sole right to collect all royal concessions rents and fees, turning over to Mbandzeni £1,000 monthly and pocketing the balance.

Miller resigned as Mbandzeni's advisor in July 1889, replaced once again by Shepstone in October. Shepstone removed Miller from the Swazieland Committee in November 1889. Thereafter Miller concentrated his efforts in developing Thorburn's and his own business interests. In 1891 Thorburn's concessions were consolidated and incorporated in London as the Umbandine Swazieland Concessions Syndicate Ltd., Thorburn and Miller being major shareholders. Miller as local manager toured the Swaziland countryside extensively, prospecting for land and minerals to add to the syndicate's monopolies portfolio. From his geographical and geological reconnaissance Miller produced the first comprehensive map of Swaziland, published in 1896, a copy of which is mounted in the Swaziland National Archives at **Lobamba**. In 1898 the syndicate became the **Swazieland Corporation Ltd.**, with offices in Bremersdorp (**Manzini**). Miller moved his family into a home and experimental farm, Loch Moy, on Thorburn property in the hills east of Bremersdorp. In 1897 he took advantage of Thorburn's publishing monopoly to found a newspaper, *The Times of Swazieland* (later Swaziland; *TOS*), which immediately became the leading mouthpiece of settler interests. He also founded and became the first chairman of the Swaziland Mining, Industrial and Commercial Chamber in 1899. From that point onward, utilizing those platforms, Miller made himself the leading spokesman for the development of Swaziland as a British settler colony based on the "detribalization" (as he termed it) and proletarianization of the Swazi.

During the **Anglo-Boer War** (1899–1902) Miller served as a lieutenant in the British army's field intelligence department along with **David Forbes**, with whom Miller subsequently formed a celebrated enmity. They were based on the Lubombo ridge in order to observe and harass Afrikaner commando movements in the region. At war's end Miller became once again a leading and aggressive proponent of settler interests. That was exemplified by his moving his family to the farm Dalriach on the outskirts of **Mbabane** immediately upon the British establishment of their colonial capital there. Miller served on the **Swaziland Concessions Commission** from 1905 to 1907, as a member of which he pushed for the transferral of up to 90 percent of Swazi territory to the settlers. Following the issuance of the **Partition Proclamation** (1907), Miller ceased publication of *The Times* on the announced grounds that "our work has been done" (*TOS*, 30 Jan. 1909).

Miller proceeded to concentrate his efforts toward other goals. In 1909 he became a member of the Swaziland Water Commission, which ensured that riparian rights from the major rivers accrued first and foremost to the European holders of **title deed lands**. Also in 1909 Miller founded and became first president of another education and interest group, the **Swaziland Farmers Association**. In 1910 Miller became one of the backers of the privately financed **Mushroom Land Settlement Scheme**, the aim of which was to attract British settlers to Swaziland by selling them land at modest prices. The Mushroom scheme purchased **crown land** from the colonial government and sold it off to ranching companies and individuals (many of them war veterans after 1919), helping to attract a steady flow of settlers. In 1912 Miller became the director of the Swaziland Ranching & Development Company, which eventually purchased 271,000 acres (109,755 hectares) in the **lowveld** primarily for running cattle. Those ventures both failed as financial undertakings during the 1920s and 1930s, but the Swaziland Ranches acreage eventually became the basis for the spectacularly successful **Swaziland Irrigation Scheme** beginning in 1950. Miller's personal investment in Swaziland Ranches was his Bar R Ranch, 172,000 acres (69,600 hectares) in extent; that too had failed by the early 1930s. In 1921 Miller became a founding member of the **European Advisory Council**, and he remained an influential member of that body until 1935.

By the 1920s Miller's name had become so notorious among educated Swazi for his rampant settler aggressiveness that *iNgwenyama* **Sobhuza Dlamini II** chose him as the target of his 1924 lawsuit challenging the legitimacy of Mbandzeni's concessions. The monopoly chosen was the notorious **unallotted lands concession** that Mbandzeni had signed while in the depth of his final illness, when Miller had been his advisor. Sobhuza's lawsuit, *Sobhuza II vs. Miller*, stemmed in part from Swazi anger over Miller's previous betrayals and in part over Miller's imperious behavior in expelling Swazi families from that small portion of the original concession that had become his farming property at Dalriach. Sobhuza lost the case by virtue of the Privy Council's decision in 1926, but his action nevertheless proved to be popular with many of his subjects. The colonial administration paid Miller's legal costs; Sobhuza's costs put him personally deeply into debt and thus in a vulnerable position vis-à-vis the administration.

Miller, alarmed by what he perceived to be the dangerous sympathies of the new generation of colonial administrators for Swazi culture and point of view, resumed publication of *The Times of Swaziland* in 1931, this time with financial backing from others. Again his primary goal for *The Times* lay in its value as a lobbying enterprise in behalf of his development goals for a European Swaziland based on an African labor force. The most notable of his editorial positions were in favor of lowering South African agricultural and cattle tariffs, the construction of a railway to Johannesburg, and maintaining Swaziland free from the **Union of South Africa**. As previously, Miller wrote many of the articles and most of the editorials himself. Once more the paper became a failure as a profit-making venture but was successful as a mouthpiece for settler interests. Miller sold *The Times* to a South African firm, the High Commission Territories Printing and Publishing Company, in 1950.

Aside from his newspaper venture, Miller was a prolific writer on Swazi history, geography, and folklore. Those works are listed in the bibliography, the most notable being "A Short History of Swazieland," published in *TOS*, June 5 to August 7, 1897, which Philip Bonner has described as "an extraordinarily garbled version of events";[5] *Swaziland* (1900); *Swaziland: The California of South Africa* (1907); *Mamisa: The Swazi Warrior* (1933); and *Swaziland: The Land of Green Pastures and Running Streams* (1936). Miller is buried in Mbabane, where the main commercial street is named after him. A son, Allister Mackintosh Miller, was an RAF pilot during World War I and was a founder and co-owner of Union Airways, the predecessor of South African Airways. A second son, Douglas Mackintosh Miller, ran the Bar R Ranch until its demise and later managed the Swaziland Printing and Publishing Company until its sale in 1950.

MILNER, LORD ALFRED (1852–1925). In his capacity as British **high commissioner** from 1897 to 1905, Lord Milner had a profound effect on Swaziland's colonial history. Milner's ancillary role as governor of the **Transvaal** (1902–5) accorded him even greater interest in Swaziland's affairs. Milner first affected Swaziland in 1898 when the **South African Republic**'s (SAR's) special commissioner for Swaziland, **Johannes Krogh**, attempted to turn the political crisis of *iNgwenyama* **Bhunu Dlamini** into a pretext for stripping him of his powers. The occasion was Bhunu's direct implication in the murder of the royal *indvuna* at **Zombodze, Mbhabha Nsibandze**. Krogh proposed to prosecute Bhunu and in the process abolish the office of *ingwenyama*. Milner, whose consent was required by the terms of the **third Swaziland Convention** (1894), refused to go along. Instead he assented to the staging of a humiliating public trial of the king and the imposition of a fine on him for "permitting public violence." Milner also agreed to a **protocol** (**1898**) to the 1894 convention that deprived Bhunu of his criminal jurisdiction and consequently in effect reduced the *ingwenyama*'s title from "king" to "**paramount chief**." The Swazi monarchy would spend the following 70 years restoring the powers Krogh and Milner had removed.

Following the **Anglo-Boer War** (1899–1902) Milner established a colonial administration in Swaziland, headed by a **resident commissioner** who reported to him. Milner administered Swaziland as if (as he believed) it were shortly to become another district of the Transvaal. Transvaal laws were therefore made applicable, *mutatis mutandis*, to Swaziland (legitimized by the **Swaziland Administration Proclamation 4/1907**). A tax policy was implemented that was designed to drive Swazi males off the agriculturally based homestead and into the labor stream headed to the goldfields of the Witwatersrand. Milner's **Swaziland Administration Proclamation (3/1904)** confirmed the withdrawal of criminal jurisdiction from the Swazi monarchy and deprived it of some of its civil authority as well. Milner also canceled the monarchy's annual £12,000 stipend from the **private revenue concession** and replaced it with a £1,000 yearly payment, making the Swazi royal house dependent on his office.

To Lord Milner, then, and to his successor **Lord Selborne**, goes the dubious credit for implementing the colonial policy of authoritarianism and official humiliation vis-à-vis the Swazi monarchy that passed for "**indirect rule**" until the era of Resident Commissioner **T. Ainsworth Dickson** beginning in 1928. From 1918 to 1921 Milner served as British colonial secretary.

MINI, EDGAR. Alternative *sibongo*: Mzolo. Son of **Stephen Mini**. Raised and educated at the Wesleyan mission at **Edendale**, Natal, Mini became one of the Edendale/**Mahamba** group of advisors influential at the court of Queen Regent **Labotsibeni Mdluli**. Mini was responsible for her engagement of **Joseph M. Parsonson** as advisor to the Swazi nation in 1905. Labotsibeni appointed Mini as the teacher of the first **Swazi national** (elementary) **school** at **Zombodze**, and it was therefore he who first taught *iNgwenyama* **Sobhuza Dlamini II** formally. Mini retired from Zombodze in 1906 and was replaced by **Rev. Joseph Xaba**. Mini also arranged for **Bnt. Malunge** and **Lomvazi Dlamini** to study at Edendale during several months in 1904.

MINI, STEPHEN (1855–?). Mini was born and raised at the Wesleyan mission at **Edendale** (Natal), the son of its *induna*. He became a protégé of **Theophilus Shepstone, Jr.**, and accompanied him (along with **John Gama**) to **Mbekelweni** in 1886 when he negotiated for his position as advisor and agent to *iNgwenyama* **Mbandzeni Dlamini**. Mini parlayed his relationship with Shepstone into a position as secretary and advisor to the royal house and, in turn, into ownership of both land and mineral **concessions** around **Mahamba**. He may have farmed his land for an interval, but he returned to Edendale as *induna* succeeding his father in 1893. By then he had become a wealthy man, and he behaved like one for the remainder of his life. He fought on the side of the British during both the **Anglo-Boer War** (1899–1902) and the Zulu rebellion of 1906. He was a founder of the Natal Native Congress and active in the college of chiefs in the South African Native National Congress (later **African National Congress**). A son, **Edgar Mini** (Mzoli), was the teacher at the queen regent's school at **Zombodze** where *iNgwenyama* **Sobhuza Dlamini II** began his formal education.

MISSIONS. *See* CHRISTIANITY

MKHAYA NATURE RESERVE. One of four game and nature reserves in Swaziland, 15,320 acres (6,200 hectares) in area. It is located in the **lowveld** near Phuzumoya along the Manzini–Big Bend road, 30 miles (48 kilometers) from **Manzini**. A dozen large animal species (including white and black rhinoceroses) are stocked there, and it is the habitat for 100 species of birds, including the rare Bateleur eagle. Mkhaya is privately owned and operated, principally by **Terence Reilly**.

MLILWANE GAME SANCTUARY. "Little Fire." The original and one of four major game reserves in Swaziland, its main camp located along the western border of the **Ezulwini Valley**, 14 miles (23 kilometers) by road south of **Mbabane**. Mlilwane, 11,490 acres (4,650 hectares) in area, was started in 1960 by **Terence Reilly**, a local conservationist. The basis for the original reserve was the Reilly farm, owned by his father **James W.** ("Mickey") **Reilly**. The elder Reilly had mined **tin** at Mlilwane beginning in 1906 by blasting the soil overbearing with high-pressure water hoses in order to get at the ore seams. The dimensions of the resulting ecological disruption were such that Reilly was fined for pollution of the **Lusushwana River** in 1946; the operation's scars still disfigure large sections of the reserve. In view of that, Terence Reilly's lifetime devotion to conservation at Mlilwane and elsewhere in Swaziland seems especially admirable. In 1959 Reilly appealed to the colonial administration for assistance in establishing the reserve but was turned down. Thereafter the venture became by necessity a private one.

By 1964 the original 1,137-acre (460-hectare) farm had been enlarged by 3,150 acres (1,276 hectares) through the assistance of the South African Nature Foundation, the South African Wildlife Federation, and the Anglo-American Corporation. By 1971 another 5,400 acres (2,187 hectares) had been added with aid from the same sources. With stock donated largely by the National Parks Board of South Africa, Mlilwane opened for visitors in 1964. In 1977 Mlilwane was proclaimed a Nature Reserve under provisions of the National Trust Commission Act of 1972. Forty-eight species of larger animals have been established there, and 238 bird species have been recorded.

MLOKOTFWA. *See* MAKHOSINI

MNGOMETFULU, MBIKIZA (c. 1857–1918). The Mngometfulu clan historically occupied the lower iNgwavuma River valley where it cut through the Lubombo range. Under Mbikiza's father, Lubelo Mngometfulu, the clan attempted to play off the Swazi against the **Ndwandwe** and the Zulu in a complicated game of engineering their independence from all three. Because of his fierce fighting reputation and the availability of strong defensive positions in the Lubombo, Lubelo remained immune from the attacks that *iNgwenyama* **Mswati Dlamini II** was launching northward during his heyday, but only for so long. His downfall came in 1860 when he provoked the other powerful clan in the Lubombo, the **Nyawo** under **Chief Sambane**, and was defeated and sent fleeing into the **lowveld** far from the safety of his redoubts. There he and a large number of his followers were attacked by Mswati and killed.

Among those captured by Mswati's regiments during the attack was Lubelo's young son Mbikiza. He was taken for safekeeping to the **homestead** of Ngolotjeni Nxumalo, the *indvuna* of the royal graves at **Mlokotfwa** and the maternal grandfather of *iNgwenyama* **Sobhuza Dlamini II**. Mbikiza was returned to his people by Mswati, who anointed him to succeed his father with the understanding that he acknowledge **iNkhosi Dlamini** suzerainty. That, however, never happened. For a number of years Mbikiza allied himself with various Zulu factions, until 1884, when once again Sambane Nyawo forced him to flee to the lowveld north of the iNgwavuma River, where he sought protection from *iNgwenyama* **Mbandzeni Dlamini**. Rebuffed by the king, he thereafter attempted to replicate his father's old game of playing three powers off against each other—this time the Swazi, Zulu, and **Transvaal** Afrikaners. From his headquarters in Natal just north of **Ingwavuma** he governed his followers in the Swazi lowveld through an *indvuna*. He also regularly paid court at **Mbekelweni** during Mbandzeni's reign. On the other hand when newly crowned *iNgwenyama* **Bhunu Dlamini** sent messengers to Mbikizi requesting a demonstration of fealty he had them beaten. There remains a substantial population of Mngometfulu in the southeastern Swazi lowveld, divided from their royal headquarters by the Swaziland-Natal border.

MOE, MALLA. Norwegian missionary of the Scandinavian (Evangelical) Alliance Mission who arrived in Swaziland with Rev. William Dawson and his wife. She started her own mission near Hluti in 1898, a rare undertaking by a single woman in that day. During the **Anglo-Boer War** (1899–1902) Moe remained at the mission, isolated from other stations as British columns and Afrikaner commandoes skirted her environs.

MONA. "Jealousy." A childhood name for *iNgwenyama* **Sobhuza Dlamini II**. *See also* Nkhotfotjeni

MOONY, FRANCIS ENRAGHT. Also Francis Enraght-Moony. The British special commissioner for Swaziland who arrived with the first administrative contingent in September 1902 and remained until 1907. **Swaziland Administrative Proclamation 4/1907** changed his title to **resident commissioner**. To Moony fell a number of extremely delicate and potentially dangerous tasks associated with establishing a colonial administration. He had to delineate administrative districts and staff them, and to put in place the South African constabulary he had brought with him. He had to disarm the Swazi and place a tax on them, largely with the intent of driving the men into the migrant labor stream to the farms of the eastern **Transvaal** and the Johannesburg gold mines. At the same time he had been ordered to put a stop to the Swazi monarchy's campaign of "killing-off" its domestic enemies instituted by Queen Regent **Labotsibeni Mdluli** during the **Anglo-Boer War**. That undertaking implied that the previous withdrawal of the monarchy's criminal jurisdiction stipulated by the Anglo-Boer Protocol of 1898, but allowed to lapse during the war, was thereby reimposed—a measure confirmed by Proclamation 1/1904. Finally, Moony had to orchestrate an official scenario whereby the European settler demands to validate their land and mineral **concessions** gained from *iNgwenyama* **Mbandzeni Dlamini** were carried out in such a way that the Swazi accepted the expropriation of their lands peacefully, and not violently like their Zulu neighbors to the south. Moony was forced to carry out all those tasks in an atmosphere of pained hostility on the part of Labotsibeni and the *libandla*, stemming from their realization of the fallaciousness of their previous beliefs that their aid to the British during the late war would earn them their freedom from alien rule.

Given all those obstacles Enraght Moony's administrative record in Swaziland has to be termed a success, although his superiors in Pretoria and London thought differently. That was undoubtedly because settler interests, as voiced directly to the **high commissioner** and colonial secretary by such swashbucklers as **Allister Miller**, were able to convince them that Enraght Moony's attitude vis-à-vis the Swazi was insufficiently authoritarian. In 1907 Moony, judged by the high commissioner not to be up to managing the anticipated Swazi reaction to the pending **Partition Proclamation**, was replaced as resident commissioner by a colonial administrator from Barotseland possessing a far sterner reputation, **Robert T. Coryndon**.

MORGAN, DAVID L. (1904–?). Resident commissioner from 1951 to 1956. Morgan came to Swaziland with 20 years' experience in the Kenya colonial service. He served during a period of rapid capital development of the kingdom, most notably the implementation of the **Colonial De-**

velopment Corporation's **Swaziland Irrigation Scheme** and the Usutu Forests (**Usutu Pulp Company**) project.

MOTSA, NGOLOTJENI (?–1946). The left-hand *insila* of *iNgwenyama* **Sobhuza Dlamini II.** The Motsa clan, one of the *Emakhandza Mbili*, enjoys high prestige, providing the *ingwenyama* with one of two *tinsila* and one of two senior ritual wives, also of the left hand. Motsa accompanied Sobhuza throughout his life, including his first **Zombodze** schooling and his years at the **Lovedale Missionary Institution**, and was a closer confidant to him than most princes—almost an alter ego. A 1925 picture of the two (taken during Sobhuza's "progressive" phase) at a ceremonial greeting for the Prince of Wales shows them identically dressed in elegant Western suits. Motsa (like Sobhuza's uncle, **Benjamin Nxumalo**) made an early and sustained foray into the nascent Swazi middle class, investing in diverse ventures. Undoubtedly his favored position allowed him rare access to coveted native trader's and general dealer's licenses. At various times Motsa was a hotel cook, farmer, cattle dealer, and shopkeeper. Although Hilda Kuper describes him as "individualistic, industrious, [and] intelligent,"[6] Motsa did not have a gift for business and died in relative poverty. Motsa was a Christian convert and a monogamist.

MPAKA. A mining and transport center located in the **lowveld**, 12 miles (19 kilometers) east of **Siteki**, 1986 population 1,041. The Mpaka coal mine sits atop a gigantic lowveld reserve (estimated one billion tons) of low-sulphur, low-volatility, and high-energy coal. The mine is jointly owned by the **Tibiyo takaNgwane Fund** and Danish capital. What coal is exported goes exclusively to Kenya's cement industry. Mpaka is also a stopping point for the **Swaziland Railway**, connecting it to both Maputo, Mozambique, and Richards Bay, Natal.

MPANDE. *See* ZULU, MPANDE kaSENZANGAKHONA

MSIBI, DR. GEORGE (1931–). A medical doctor and politician who played an active role during the mid-1980s' *liqoqo*-instigated constitutional crisis following the death of *iNgwenyama* Sobhuza Dlamini II, before fleeing into exile in South Africa in 1986. Dr. Msibi received his medical education in India and Japan, but upon his return to Swaziland in 1961 he entered business (bottle stores) and politics instead of practicing medicine. In 1962, as the kingdom was debating the shape of the new pre-independence constitution, Msibi formed the National Convention as his political vehicle to power. Later that year he merged his movement with the Mbandzeni Party (**Clifford Nkosi**) to form the **Mbandzeni National Convention (MNC)**. In 1963 he was chosen by the British to represent the MNC at the London **constitutional conference**, where he affiliated the MNC with the **Joint Council of Swaziland Political Parties**. The MNC's eclectic platform doomed it to accomplish little beyond further fragmenting the opposition to Sobhuza's **Imbokodvo National Movement (INM)**, and it died before the 1964 **Legislative Council** (Legco) elections.

Meanwhile Msibi, ever the opportunist and sensing the potential of Imbokodvo, jumped ship in mid-1983 and joined Sobhuza, becoming the INM's secretary general prior to the 1964 elections. Those elections placed him in the Legco, and the following year he became the party's treasurer and a member of **Queen's Commissioner Sir Francis Loyd**'s independence constitutional commission. Then charges of corruption laid against him torpedoed his political career for several years, and he returned only in 1972 as one of Sobhuza's appointees to the Senate. In 1973, following the emergency declaration, Msibi was appointed by the *ingwenyama* to the royal constitutional commission.

Sobhuza's death breathed new life for a time into Dr. Msibi's political aspirations. As a member of the *liqoqo* during its short-lived "Supreme Council of State" period, he affiliated himself with the faction led by **Mnt. Mfanasibili Dlamini** that opposed the royalist faction (**Mnt. Gabheni Dlamini** and Queen Regent **Dzeliwe Shongwe**). Following Mfanasibili's arrest in 1986 Dr. Msibi fled into exile in South Africa and eventually became a businessman in Johannesburg.

MSIMANG FAMILY. The Msimang family, members of which figured prominently in the 19th-century mission and political history of Swaziland, was descended from Rev. Daniel M. Msimang (1831–1903). Msimang accompanied **Rev. James Allison** as a teamster when Allison established the Wesleyan mission at **Mahamba** in 1845. Msimang then retreated with Allison to **Edendale**, Natal, in 1846, where he became both an ordained clergyman and a prosperous farmer. In 1882 Msimang and his son, Rev. Joel Msimang (1854–1935), reestablished the Wesleyan mission near Mahamba, with the permission of *iNgwenyama* **Mbandzeni Dlamini**. That mission, which was found to be located in the **Transvaal**, was moved to its present location in Swaziland in 1897. Rev. Joel Msimang established an outstation with a chapel and a school at **Makhosini** in 1890, which in time became a thriving mission. In 1904, however, Joel Msimang broke with the Wesleyans and formed the Independent Methodist Church in Swaziland.

Joel Msimang's two sons, Richard and Selby Msimang, were raised at the Makhosini mission. Both later became founding members of what would become the **African National Congress (ANC)**. According to Christopher Lowe the Msimangs developed close ties with Edendale graduates **Josiah Vilakazi** and his brother Nehemiah, both of whom served as chiefs to the Christian community at Mahamba.[7] When Joel Msimang broke with the Wesleyans in 1904, Josiah Vilakazi cast his lot with him. That friendship put Richard Msimang in touch with the Swazi royal family, which Josiah Vilakazi served for a number of years as secretary. It was Richard Msimang, trained in the law, who introduced a fellow lawyer, **Pixley kaI. Seme**, to Queen Regent **Labotsibeni Mdluli**. Seme's fortunes would become intertwined with those of the Swazi royal house over the following three decades. Labotsibeni's son, **Mnt. Malunge Dlamini**, would also become acquainted with both Msimang and Seme, and through that association would play a prominent role in the ANC's college of chiefs until his death in 1915.

MTSETFWA, MANDANDA (1887–1982). The senior political officer (*indvunankhuluyesive*) of the nation during the reign of *iNgwenyama* **Sobhuza Dlamini II**, as well as *indvuna* of the royal **homestead** at **Zombodze**, the most prestigious of all such governorships. Mtsetfwa assumed the Zombodze governorship in 1916 during the regency of **Labotsibeni Mdluli**. He was also a member of the *liqoqo*, identified as its "vice-chairman" by the British administration in 1936. Their confidential report described him as "intelligent and courteous with sound judgement." By the time of Sobhuza's installation in 1921 Mtsetfwa had become one of the *ingwenyama*'s most trusted and respected councillors, and he remained so until Sobhuza died. Mtsetfwa was head of the Swazi deputation to the high commissioner in Pretoria during 1921 and was a member of the delegation to London led by Sobhuza in 1922–23. In 1947, when the **Standing Committee of the *libandla*** was established to represent its views directly to the colonial administration, Mtsetfwa was a founding member. As senior political officer of the nation Mtsetfwa exercised the privilege of performing the first ritual song of the annual *iNcwala* **ceremony** until, bent with age and nearly blind, he was freed from that responsibility. Mtsetfwa died just prior to Sobhuza's own death in 1982, both of them being dominant figures in the centralization of royal power during the 20th century.

MUSHROOM LAND SETTLEMENT SCHEME. A privately financed undertaking designed to assist the settlement of Swaziland by British yeoman farmers following the opening up of **crown lands** for sale in 1910. The **Partition Proclamation of 1907** had allocated 22 percent of Swaziland to be crown land, the bulk of which it secretly intended to parcel out to British settlers. (Poor Afrikaner *bywoners* ["tenant farmers"] were not automatically excluded as fallback purchasers as long as their numbers were kept to a bare minimum.) That was in keeping with **Lord Milner**'s vision of a South African countryside (in which Swaziland would be incorporated into the **Transvaal**) peopled by English-speaking farmers. Milner's vision was also that of his successor as **high commissioner, Lord Selborne**, and of local settlers led by **Allister Miller**. The vehicle to carry it out, the Mushroom scheme, was Miller's brainchild, and it was he who became its local director after 1910. The Mushroom syndicate purchased an initial 60,000 acres (24,300 hectares) of crown land in 1910. From then until 1925 hundreds of blocs of land ranging from 50 to 1,500 acres were sold to individual settlers under the aegis of the Mushroom scheme or the 1820 Settlers Association (another Miller enterprise), or, following World War I, through the British government–sponsored **Returned Soldiers' Settlement Scheme**. Most of the acreage thus settled was located north of the **Usutu River**; the less desirable land in the south was left to unsubsidized Afrikaner settlement.

All those schemes among themselves succeeded in placing Swaziland firmly within the realm of Milner's original vision of a wider South Africa as a mecca for white settlers. Following the visit of Colonial Secretary **Leopold S. Amery** to the territory in 1927 the government emphasis shifted from subsidizing the establishment of more British settlers to subsidizing those already there through developing the territory's infrastructure and agricultural marketing mechanisms. That change helped to bring about the end of all those settlement schemes by the time of World War II.

-N-

NAGANA. The South African/Swazi term for bovine trypanosomiasis, brought into Swaziland by a reappearance of the tsetse fly following World War II. The tsetse fly had first appeared in the **lowveld** at the turn of the century and had then been successfully eradicated. In 1946 the fly appeared again in the lowveld, in the south near Gollel (Lavumisa), and in the north along the Mozambican border. The colonial administration responded with a vigorous campaign of bush clearing (a two-mile [three-kilometer] swath through infected areas) and spraying of DDT by the South African air force. The campaign successfully eradicated the disease by 1948.

Its political effects, however, lasted considerably longer. First, the colonial administration elected to pay for its massive campaign with funds gleaned from two levies: one on European-owned cattle and the other in the form of a supplemental head tax on Swazi males, irrespective of cattle holdings. The government persuaded *iNgwenyama* **Sobhuza Dlamini II** to announce the tax levy and at the same time call for free labor to carry out the brush cutting. Because this was the same administration that had recently undercut his domestic authority with its implementation of the **Native Administration Proclamation** (1944), Sobhuza responded with (from the government's viewpoint) a decided lack of enthusiasm. Although the tax levy apparently was met, the labor requisition failed miserably. In 1947, during the height of the campaign, only 90 to 120 of the 300 men requested ever appeared. The government attributed this failure to a lack of chiefs' (and by implication the "**paramount chief**'s") control over their followers. It appeared clear to the government that the anti-nagana campaign was one aspect of Sobhuza's noncooperation with the 1944 proclamation. That proclamation was amended by the **Native Administration Proclamation** of 1950, which restored the *ingwenyama*'s authority over the chiefs.

NATIONAL TREASURY PROCLAMATION (1950). Proclamation 81/1950 was part of a package of three proclamations first proposed by the British administration in 1939 with the intention of formalizing **indirect rule** in Swaziland. Of the three the **Native Courts** and National Treasury Proclamations were to be the carrots, offering back to the Swazi authorities governance mechanisms that had been taken away from them early in the century. The third, the **Native Administration Proclamation,** was the stick, formalizing as it did the subordination of the *ingwenyama* and the chiefs to the **resident commissioner**. *iNgwenyama* **Sobhuza Dlamini II**, after a protracted and difficult struggle, ultimately was successful in reversing the objectionable provisions of the latter proclamation in 1950. The National Treasury Proclamation, implemented at the same time, provided for a Swazi national treasury to which a substantial portion of the native tax was to be allocated, and over which the *ingwenyama* would have considerable autonomy (with the resident commissioner's approval and subject to audit) in its expenditure.

For Sobhuza, who had found himself financially hobbled officially and personally throughout his entire reign, the treasury proclamation constituted a significant milestone in the restoration of his domestic sovereignty. Especially during the 1950s Sobhuza utilized much of the National Treasury resources to establish a school system independent of the Christian missions.

NATIVE ADMINISTRATION PROCLAMATIONS (1944, 1950). Beginning in 1939 the British **high commissioner** sought to formalize a style of administration known as **"indirect rule"** on Swaziland through the implementation of three proclamations: the Native Administration, **Native Courts**, and **National Treasury Proclamations**. Indirect rule (based on the Nigerian model) delegated certain administrative, police, court, and fiscal powers to native authorities that enabled them to maintain domestic law and order. Indirect rule consequently minimized the cost of the colonial administration and limited its focus to overseeing and policy-making. Native administration proclamations had previously been passed in most of British colonial Africa, including Bechuanaland (1934) and Basutoland (1938). In both of those territories the British proclamations had established that chiefs (and in the case of Basutoland the paramount chief) could be appointed and dismissed by the high commissioner. That was what was proposed to *iNgwenyama* **Sobhuza Dlamini II** and his *libandla* in 1939.

At the same time the colonial administration proposed to restore major elements of the Swazi monarchy's sovereignty by the implementation of the Native Courts (albeit with the **resident commissioner** as the final appellate authority) and National Treasury Proclamations. Sobhuza and his *libandla*, however, took the position that such an arrangement would violate previous British guarantees to preserve "native law and custom" written into the **third Swaziland Convention** (1894) and the British **Order-in-Council of 1903** establishing the high commissioner's sovereignty. Over the following decade Sobhuza fought a protracted and dogged campaign to prevent implementation of the administration proclamation, eager as he was to restore his criminal jurisdiction and fiscal autonomy.

Finally, the high commissioner, despairing of ever receiving Swazi assent, imposed the Native Administration Proclamation (44/1944) with the offending provision included, and without the courts and treasury proclamations to accompany it. Sobhuza's and his *libandla*'s responses of non-recognition and non-compliance kept the debate open, however, and eventually the administration backed away from the 1944 proclamation. The Native Administration (Consolidation) Proclamation (79/1950) expressly and specifically vested the powers to appoint and depose chiefs with the "**paramount chief**" (Sobhuza), although in the latter case the assent of the resident commissioner was required. It also (in conjunction with the Native Courts Proclamation) vested the "Paramount Chief in Libandhla" with the power to issue "Orders enforceable by the Native Courts" and to "make Rules for the peace, good order and welfare of the Natives of Swaziland."

Proclamation 79/1950 constituted a signal victory for Sobhuza and a vindication for his and the *libandla*'s tactics of argument, delay, and obstruction. (In 1941 Sobhuza had even threatened **Resident Commissioner Charles L. Bruton** with abdication over the issue.) Furthermore in that victory lay the groundwork for Sobhuza's protracted and ultimately successful campaign to regain total domestic sovereignty prior to independence in 1968.

NATIVE AREAS. Thirty-two parcels of land in Swaziland allocated to the Swazi under provisions of the **Partition Proclamation of 1907** and delineated by special commissioner **George Grey** in 1908. The native areas comprised 2,420 square miles (6,268 square kilometers) out of a total of 6,553 square miles (16,972 square kilometers), or about 37 percent of the total area. Underdevelopment theorists can find much in the delineation of Swaziland's native areas to suggest that land deprivation generates compliant, albeit undernourished, labor forces. Jonathan Crush has shown that colonial authorities deliberately allocated to the native areas lands too little and too poor for them to support an agricultural population for long without exporting much of their young male population to earn wages.[8] By the early 1930s many of the native areas were being officially reported as overpopulated and overstocked. By the 1940s a worried and embarrassed colonial government was adding to the native areas with **crown lands**, sold to the Swazi at heavily subsidized prices. Following independence the native areas came to be known in the aggregate as **Swazi Nation Land**. It is fair to argue that in the native areas allocated by the colonials can be seen the genesis of the Swazi population's chronic inability to feed itself in a territory that, if taken as a whole, is among the most fertile and well-watered in all of Africa.

NATIVE AUTHORITY. A term used by successive British colonial administrations in conjunction with their policy of "**indirect rule**" to designate and recognize the indigenous leadership structure to which the powers of internal government were to be delegated. The draft of the **Native Administration Proclamation** of 1944 was referred to during the protracted debate preceding its implementation as the "Native Authority Proclamation."

NATIVE COURTS PROCLAMATION (1950). Proclamation 80/1950 restored domestic criminal jurisdiction to the *ingwenyama*'s, *indlovukazi*'s, and chiefs' courts that had been withdrawn by **Swaziland Administration Proclamation 3/1904**. It was implemented as one of a package of three proclamations, the other two being the **National Treasury Proclamation** (81/1950) and the **Native Administration Proclamation** (79/1950). It differed from native courts proclamations in other British dependencies in that it vested the authority for establishing the Swazi court system and implementing rules and procedures (including record-keeping) in the *ingwenyama* and not the colonial officials. The reason for that important difference lay in the success of the argument over the Native Administration Proclamation put forward by *iNgwenyama* **Sobhuza Dlamini II** that previous British guarantees to preserve "native law and custom" had set Swaziland apart from other territories and were sacrosanct.

As first proposed in the late 1930s the Native Courts Proclamation had provided for the vesting of appellate jurisdiction from the *ingwenyama*'s court with the **resident commissioner**. Consequently Proclamation 80/1950 in conjunction with the other two laws constituted a significant victory for Sobhuza in his protracted struggle to regain British recognition of his internal sovereignty. In the event, and to the perpetual exasperation of the authorities, neither Sobhuza nor the chiefs ever maintained court records (or indeed ever codified Swazi laws), undoubtedly in part for fear that the British would begin to tamper with what was written down.

NATIVE LAND SETTLEMENT SCHEME. *See* SWAZILAND NATIVE LAND SETTLEMENT SCHEME

NATIVE RECRUITING CORPORATION (NRC). Founded in 1912, the monopsonistic labor recruiting arm of the **Transvaal** Chamber of Mines. The organization was formed out of necessity derived from the collapse of the Witwatersrand Native Labour Association's (WNLA's) infrastructure throughout southern Africa in 1906. After that time the NRC operated in British-administered territories and the WNLA operated in southern Mozambique. The NRC established itself in Swaziland in 1913 as one of several recruiting organizations operating there, notable among the others being Marwick & Norris, A.M. Mostert, and Taberer's Labour Organization. By 1916 the NRC was able to acquire exclusive **gold** mine recruiting rights in Swaziland, although it was 1920 before it was able to exploit that monopsony fully.

That was not to say that the NRC had no competition. Prior to World War I the Natal coal mines recruited heavily in Swaziland, but they quickly became notorious throughout the territory as excessively brutal and hazardous work environments. The NRC's most significant competition came locally, following the implementation of the **Partition Proclamation of 1907**, beginning in 1914. European-owned farms in Swaziland provided stiff competition for the services of their African tenants even though they paid wages averaging only one-third of gold mine levels. Still, the NRC was sending an average of 8,000 men annually, about 30 percent of the total working-age male population, to the Rand mines during the depression years down to World War II.

Following that war Swaziland became the theater of heavy capital investment in forestry, agribusiness, and manufacturing. As a consequence by the early 1960s the level of domestic employment reached 20,000. The Natal coal mines and sugar plantations again posted recruiters in Swaziland. All of that placed an unprecedented strain on the NRC's mine recruiting efforts, forcing it in 1949 to do what until then had been unthinkable: raise wages a full 9 percent. It also reduced its contract period to six months in order to compete with local employers who allowed workers to return home during planting and harvesting seasons. Still, the NRC continued to suffer from recruiting shortfalls throughout the 1950s, and it was only when local recruiting leveled off and the number of Swazi school-leavers began to outstrip employment levels that the NRC began once again to meet its recruitment quotas. Thereafter drops in mine quotas combined with Swazi demographics to ensure that never again did the organization want for recruits. During the late 1970s the NRC changed its name, but not its basic organization, to The Employment Bureau of Africa (TEBA) and moved its headquarters from **Siteki** to **Mbabane**.

NAZARENE CHURCH. One of the most significant Christian mission denominations in Swaziland in terms of numbers (1968: 6,000 members). The church sponsors educational and health institutions throughout the kingdom. It maintains Nazarene primary schools in **Manzini**, **Siteki,** and **Pigg's Peak**, and secondary schools in Manzini and Siteki. The church also operates the Nazarene Teacher Training College in Manzini, the Mbuluzi Leper Hospital near **Mbabane**, the Nazarene Bible College (Siteki) for training of missionaries, and the Raleigh Fitkin Memorial Hospital in Manzini. Raleigh Fitkin is a 250-bed facility, the largest in the country. Its doctors also staff the Mbuluzi Leper Settlement and 17 clinics throughout Swaziland north of the **Usutu River** on a visiting basis. The clinics are staffed with nurses trained at the hospital. The first Nazarene missionaries, Rev. and Mrs. H. F. Peak, arrived in 1910, while the most famous of them, **Dr.** and Mrs. **David Hynd** arrived in 1925.

iNCWALA **CEREMONY.** The central annual ritual in the Swazi cosmos, which at its core is the ritualization of the Swazi kingship in all of its dimensions. It is equally a religious and a political ceremony. Its dominant theme is in the nature of a first fruits ceremony, relating the rulers (primarily the *ingwenyama*) to the agricultural productive cycle as indicated by the orientations of the sun (*lilanga*) and moon (*inyanga*). On a deeper, political level the *iNcwala* ceremony is a powerful mechanism to engender and renew a unified sense of Swazi nationalism and loyalty to the monarchy. During the reign of *iNgwenyama* **Sobhuza Dlamini II** the main *iNcwala* ceremonies were held in the royal cattle enclosure (*sibaya*) of the ritual capital at **Lobamba**. Following the establishment of *iNgwenyama* **Mswati Dlamini III**'s reign the *iNcwala* was celebrated at **Ludzidzini**.

The *iNcwala* is a hallowed period lasting about three weeks toward the end of the calendar year, when regular daily routines are relegated to the second tier of the national consciousness. The period is divided into the Little *iNcwala*, which lasts two days beginning when the sun reaches its southern summer solstice and the moon is dark, and the Great *iNcwala*, which takes place for six days commencing with the night of the full moon. During the interim between the two, ritual songs and dances from the Little *iNcwala* are performed in important villages throughout the kingdom. The ritual itself is best described by Hilda Kuper and T. O. Beidelman.[9] Several weeks prior to the Little *iNcwala*, national "priests of the water" are dispatched to two distant locales (the Indian Ocean south of Maputo and certain rivers, notably the **Komati** and Mbuluzi) to fetch vessels of ritual water and other plant medicines in order to doctor the *ingwenyama*. On the eve of the Little *iNcwala* a black ox is slaughtered for strengthening medicine. On the moonless night of the Little *iNcwala* men dance from a crescent into a circle while a song expressing hatred and rejection of the *ingwenyama* and his isolation is sung, during which he is being doctored in his royal ritual enclosure (*inhlambelo*) for attainment of supernatural powers. Once doctored, the *ingwenyama* spits east and west from the enclosure, "stabbing" the new year. Thereupon the assemblage sings his praise for strengthening the earth and "biting" (confronting) the new year. The second day beginning at dawn the ceremony is repeated, following which the warriors go to weed the ***indlovukazi***'s gardens and afterwards are rewarded with a feast of meat.

The first day of the Great *iNcwala* finds the unmarried youths embarking on a quest for special tree branches with which to doctor the *inhlambelo*, which is done on the second dawn. The third day is dominated by the pummeling and slaughter of a black ox ("bull"), the symbol of potency. The bull is chosen by the *ingwenyama* using a doctored wand that drives it wild, and following its pummeling by the youths it is dragged into the *inhlambelo* where it is sacrificed and its parts are used for royal medicine or propitiating the ancestors. On the fourth day the *ingwenyama*, now properly doctored and fortified, walks naked (except for a penis cap) through the crowd from his *inhlambelo* to the hut where he had consummated the marriage to his first ritual queen. The crowd again sings songs of hatred and rejection. He is again doctored in the marital hut; then, spitting east and west, he again "stabs" and "bites" the new year. Others, youths and adults according to rank, cleanse themselves by "biting" various medicines for the new year.

Then ensues an elaborate dance by two groups: the royal clan (who drive the *ingwenyama* back to his *inhlambelo*) and the people (who try to entice him out). He finally emerges, clothed in a demonic costume of grass and animal skins, his body coated with black ointments, and dances in an agitated fashion pretending reluctance to join the people, appearing and disappearing, again and again. He finally disappears, which is the signal for royal kin and aliens to leave the *sibaya*. Then he again emerges, still anointed and doctored, but without his costume, holding a green calabash (the symbol of the Dlamini past and continuity), which he throws carefully on the horizontally held shield of a selected age-mate. So the old year has been left behind, the *ingwenyama* has demonstrated his strength anew, and the people are again united and prepared for the new year.

The *ingwenyama* spends that night with his first ritual queen, but all others are restricted in their behavior on that night and over the following day (the fifth, a day of seclusion for all). On the sixth and final day the remains of the slain ox-bull, all residual medicines, and all other ritual "dirt" are heaped together and set alight by the *ingwenyama*. A black cow is slaughtered, and the *ingwenyama*, after washing himself of medicines, walks naked around the *sibaya* sprinkling himself and the royal herd with cleansing medicines. As the fire burns rain is supposed to fall, quenching the flames and consecrating the final ritual. At long last, songs praising the *ingwenyama* and the nation are sung, followed by general feasting and dancing. Then, the *iNcwala* completed, the warriors retire over the next few days to work the royal fields.

Beidelman[10] offers the following interpretation of the Great *iNcwala*. The first half of the ritual enhances incrementally the formidable supernatural powers of the *ingwenyama* to the point where he can deal with all the metaphysical forces acting upon the world of the Swazi, for good and for bad. The loosing of his pent-up powers is symbolized by his demonic appearance, isolated from the common citizenry by the very potency of the chaotic supernatural forces now at their peak within him. The second half symbolizes the gradual depletion of those powerful forces within the *ingwenyama* and their distillation into good powers that may be kept and dangerous ones that must be discarded. The crucial point comes with his throwing of the green gourd symbolizing continuity, indicating his decision to end his isolation, rejoin the nation, place his now harmonized powers once again in the service of his subjects, and commit the discarded ones to the burning pyre.

It would be difficult to overemphasize the political significance of the *iNcwala* ceremony. This certainly became so following the reign of *iNgwenyama* **Mswati Dlamini II**, who gave it unprecedented emphasis as an annual ritual reaffirmation of the symbiosis between himself and the nation, as well as acknowledgment of his centrality to agricultural fertility. Because the *iNcwala* so explicitly equates the nation with the *ingwenyama*, for any person of political significance to purposely absent himself from the ritual would be regarded as a serious affront. That was the interpretation in 1960 when Sobhuza's nephew, the radical political activist **Mnt. Dumisa Dlamini**, conspicuously boycotted the *iNcwala* ceremony. Even worse, for a prince or chief to perform his own separate *iNcwala* ceremony has historically been regarded as rank treason and grounds for capture and execution. That was **Mnt. Somcuba Dlamini**'s fate at the hands of Mswati II when he danced the *iNcwala* during the early 1850s in the supposed safety of the **Lydenburg** Afrikaners. That makes the allowance by *iNgwenyama* **Sobhuza Dlamini I** of the Mamba clan (*see* **Mamba**, **Maloyi**) to perform its own *iNcwala* after 1819 seem all the more remarkable.

iNDLOVUKAZI. "Cow Elephant," Queen Mother. Constitutionally the political figure co-equal (or nearly so) to the *ingwenyama* in authority. According to Hilda Kuper, "The king and his mother . . . are the central figures in all national activities: they preside over the highest courts; they summon national gatherings, control the age classes, allocate land, disburse national wealth, take precedence in ritual, and help to organize important social events."[11] The *indlovukazi* is also *ex officio* a member of both the **liqoqo** and the **libandla**. The *indlovukazi* furthermore possesses various powers unique to her: certain ritual medicines of great power are in her exclusive possession, as are some important **rainmaking** medicines (she being equally responsible with the king for bringing rain).

Part of the *indlovukazi*'s importance derives heavily from the fact that upon the death of the *ingwenyama*, the heir is designated on the basis of the position and circumstances of his mother in relation to the deceased *ingwenyama* and his other wives. It was important, for instance, that the successful candidate have no other sons besides the heir, to prevent the sort of violent political crises that plagued the early reign of *iNgwenyama* **Mswati Dlamini II**. The requisite attributes are not fixed, however, and the character of the mother occasionally tips the balance in her favor, the most notable instance in recent memory being that of *iNdlovukazi* **Labotsibeni Mdluli**.

Constitutionally the *indlovukazi* acts as a balance to the *ingwenyama* in legal and economic matters as well as political. He presides over the highest court, she the second highest. He controls the army, but she commands certain **regiments** stationed at her capital. He allocates land, but she holds rainmaking powers to make it productive. Both enjoy ritual precedence at the *iNcwala* **ceremony** (he the greater, however). Both are addressed as "*iNkhosi*," the praise name of the royal **Dlamini** clan.

Historically the roles and powers of succeeding *tindlovukazi* over the years have varied widely. Some have exerted enormous influence on events both as *tindlovukazi* and as regents, notably **Tsandzile Ndwandwe** and Labotsibeni. Others have been notable for their lack of influence: that may be said of each of *iNgwenyama* **Sobhuza Dlamini II**'s first four *tindlovukazi*, **Lomawa**, **Nukwase**, **Zihlathi**, and **Seneleleni Ndwandwe**, beloved as each of them was. That was partly because Sobhuza, when he had the choice, did not normally select candidates noted for their strength of personality. It was also the case that they, like the current *indlovukazi*, **Ntombi Twala**, had the disadvantage of often being illiterate and unworldly in the new era of education and communications in which their *tingwenyama* moved with more ease.

Only in his final choice of an *indlovukazi* did Sobhuza select a woman known for her strength and intelligence, **Dzeliwe Shongwe**, probably because he knew that he was near death; and indeed it proved to be a provident decision. She proved that even in the modern era illiteracy can still be trumped by character. It was Dzeliwe who as *indlovukazi* during the mid-1980s, although she was herself illiterate, courageously stood up to the worldly but corrupt cabal that dominated the *Liqoqo* following Sobhuza's death, and she who helped as much as anyone to prevent its members from usurping power unconstitutionally.

NDWANDWE. A lineage of **Nguni**-speaking people occupying the northern reaches of Nguni territory, who were closely related to the royal **Dlamini** clan of the **Ngwane** lineage in Swaziland. Both lineages moved out of southern Mozambique during the time of **Dlamini III** (early 18th century), the Dlamini settling along the Pongola River where it cuts through the **Lebombo** range. During the reign of *iNgwenyama* **Ngwane** (late 18th century) the Dlamini moved west along the northern bank of the Pongola, while the Ndwandwe had long since migrated south into northern Natal, settling in the land giving rise to the Mkhuze and Black Mfolozi rivers. From then until well into the 19th century the Ndwandwe were destined to play a prominent role, both militarily and politically, in Swazi history. This was never more true than during the reign of Ndwandwe **King Zwide** (d. 1825), who became the military scourge of the nascent Dlamini polity in southern Swaziland. Zwide attacked repeatedly across the Pongola during the early reign of *iNgwenyama* **Sobhuza Dlamini I**, and it was probably only Zwide's defeat at the hands of Zulu **King Shaka** in 1819 that saved Sobhuza's fortunes. It was his perception of the gravity of the Ndwandwe threat that prompted Sobhuza to pull up stakes and move northward into central Swaziland at about that time.

The political impact that the Ndwandwe had on the Swazi during the post-Sobhuza era came principally from a marriage alliance. Sometime around 1816 Sobhuza, desperate to fend off Zwide's attacks, offered to take a daughter as his chief wife. Zwide dispatched a young girl, **Tsandzile Ndwandwe**, and several *tinhlanti* (subordinate co-wives), all of whom became mothers of prominent *bntfwanenkhosi* (princes). Tsandzile gave birth to Sobhuza's heir, *iNgwenyama* **Mswati Dlamini II**, in about 1825 and played a crucial role as *indlovukazi* in his becoming the "greatest of the Swazi fighting kings."[12] Of the *tinhlanti*, File was the mother of **Mnt. Ndwandwa Dlamini**, Lomawandhla was the mother of **Mnt. Maloyi Dlamini**, and la Vumisa was the mother of **Bnt. Malambule** and Tsekwane **Dlamini**. All of them were to figure prominently in 19th-century Swazi political history.

NDWANDWE, LaVUMISA (c. 1806–?). LaVumisa was one of the *tinhlanti* sent with **Ndwandwe** king **Zwide**'s daughter **Tsandzile**

Ndwandwe to marry *iNgwenyama* **Sobhuza Dlamini I** about 1813. Like Tsandzile she was a woman of forceful personality who wielded great influence with Sobhuza. LaVumisa was the mother of two headstrong sons, **Bnt. Malambule** and Tsekwane **Dlamini**. When Sobhuza was old and ill, laVumisa persuaded him to name Malambule to succeed him, only to see the dying king reverse his decision in the face of a storm of criticism. In 1846, following the installation of their half-brother *iNgwenyama* **Mswati Dlamini II**, the two princes launched an unsuccessful rebellion against him. When they fled to Zululand following their defeat at Mswati's hands, LaVumisa is thought to have accompanied them. When Tsekwane was allowed to return to Swaziland in 1893, he named the area in southwest Swaziland where he was allowed to settle kalaVumisa. Upon independence the border village formerly named Gollel was changed to Lavumisa. It is a major border crossing point and railhead (principally to Durban).

NDWANDWE, *iNDLOVUKAZI* LOMAWA (c. 1880–1938). Also Lomawa Nxumalo. The daughter of Ngolotjeni (Nxumalo) Ndwandwe, *indvuna* of the royal graves at Zikhotheni in southern Swaziland. She was sent to *iNgwenyama* **Bhunu Dlamini** in about 1898 as his third wife, together with two *tinhlanti* (subordinate co-wives), one of whom was **Nukwase Ndwandwe**. Ndwandwe was the mother of *iNgwenyama* **Sobhuza Dlamini II**. She spent her first two decades as queen mother under the strong personal influence of Queen Regent **Labotsibeni Mdluli**. Indeed Lomawa did not fully assume the duties of *indlovukazi* until Labotsibeni's death in 1925, when the rain and other important medicines that the dowager queen had retained unconstitutionally were finally relinquished to her.

Lomawa resided at **Lobamba**, the Swazi ritual capital. Unlike her predecessors as *indlovukazi* (notably **Tsandzile Ndwandwe**, **Sisile Khumalo**, and Labotsibeni), Lomawa largely distanced herself from domestic politics and the affairs of state, and instead placed a premium on maintaining harmonious relations with her son. A devout Christian, Lomawa was dissuaded from joining the Methodist Church as an official convert only after being strongly pressured by Labotsibeni and the *libandla* on the grounds that it would be incompatible with her duties as *indlovukazi*. Lomawa died in 1938, and her funeral was the occasion for the gathering of representatives from nearly every Christian and independent denomination in the kingdom. Lomawa was succeeded as *indlovukazi* by her sister and co-wife, Nukwase Ndwandwe.

NDWANDWE, MZILA (c. 1810–1884) and MAWEWE (d. 1872). Disputants over the succession to the throne of Gaza (Shangane) King Soshangane (d. 1858), into whose civil war *iNgwenyama* **Mswati Dlamini II** inserted himself to his lasting sorrow. Mawewe, the first-born son of Soshangane's chief wife, succeeded the king in accordance with **Nguni** custom at his death, but he was immediately attacked by his fraternal rivals. Four of them he killed, but the fifth, Mzila, fled for his life to the eastern **Transvaal**. Then Mawewe proceeded to rule in such a despotic and extortionate fashion that Mzila was able to gain popular backing for a return. Mzila, gathering followers and allying himself with the Portuguese at Lourenço Marques, routed Mawewe in battle at the end of 1861, forcing him to flee to the court of Mswati, who had married two of Mawewe's full sisters. A political alliance with Mawewe also opened to Mswati admittance to the elephant-hunting country of the Zoutpansberg region of the Transvaal, to which the Portuguese and the Shangane claimed access.

In response (early 1862) Mswati dispatched two *timphi* (military units), including the crack iNyatsi ("Buffalo") **regiment** under the command of **Sandlane Zwane**, to attack Mzila at his headquarters (Makotene), and they defeated him with heavy losses. The defeat, as it turned out, was not decisive, for Mzila regained the initiative following Mswati's withdrawal and routed Mawewe once again in mid-1862. Dabbling in the politics of the Gaza succession proved in the end to be enormously costly. Mawewe fled to his brother-in-law once more, and Mswati placed him on the Mzimpofu River in the wilds of northern Swaziland where he died, nursing to the end his resentment and plotting his return. Mswati spent the remainder of his life regretting his strategic blunders and contesting Mzila for control of the region dominated by the **Komati** and Crocodile rivers.

NDWANDWE, *iNDLOVUKAZI* NUKWASE (?–1957). Also Nukwase Nxumalo. Full sister and *inhlanti* (subordinate co-wife) to *iNdlovukazi* **Lomawa Ndwandwe**, and successor to her as *indlovukazi* following her death in 1938. Like her sister, Nukwase was a devout Christian, having been baptized in 1914. Nukwase was instrumental in persuading *iNgwenyama* **Sobhuza Dlamini II** to grant a piece of land in **Lobamba** for the building of the **Swazi National Church** during the mid-1950s. Also like her sister, Nukwase attended exclusively to her ceremonial duties as *indlovukazi*, leaving politics and diplomacy to Sobhuza. Upon her death Nukwase was succeeded as *indlovukazi* by **Zihlathi Ndwandwe**. Nukwase was the grandmother of **Mnt. Dumisa Dlamini**.

NDWANDWE, *iNDLOVUKAZI* SENELELENI (d. 1980). Also Seneleleni Nxumalo. Subordinate co-wife, sister, and successor to *iNdlovukazi* **Zihlathi Ndwandwe**. Unlike her two predecessors, who had ties to the Wesleyan church mission, Seneleleni belonged to an independent, fundamentalist church. Seneleleni was the last of *iNgwenyama* **Sobhuza Dlamini II**'s Ndwandwe queens. Upon her death she was succeeded as *indlovukazi* by **Dzeliwe Shongwe**.

NDWANDWE, *iNDLOVUKAZI* TSANDZILE (LaZIDZE; c. 1806–1874). Wife of *iNgwenyama* **Sobhuza Dlamini I** and mother of *iNgwenyama* **Mswati Dlamini II**. Tsandzile was a daughter of **Ndwandwe King Zwide**, the most formidable adversary of the Swazi south of the Pongolo River. She became the principal in a diplomatic marriage arranged between Zwide and Sobhuza. In about 1813, when she would have been age seven, Tsandzile was taken to Swaziland along with several *tinhlanti* (subordinate co-wives) to await her marriage to Sobhuza. Sobhuza married two of them, File and **laVumisa Ndwandwe**, before he married Tsandzile. Tsandzile bore Sobhuza three children; Mswati, Sobhuza's heir, was born about 1825. She proved to be a woman of extraordinary character, intelligence, and forcefulness who left a profound imprint on 19th-century Swazi history and who is regarded as one of the greatest of the *tindlovukazi*.

Upon Sobhuza's death in 1839 Tsandzile promptly demonstrated her mettle. Although she was not the officially designated *indlovukazi* she quickly emerged as the most prominent regent. She built a new **homestead** for herself and her son in the **Mdzimba** foothills, **Ludzidzini** ("Surrounded by Enemies"), and from there masterminded Mswati's accession to power and the smashing of his rivals—most of them the sons of her *tinhlanti*. The most significant of them, **Mnt. Malambule Dlamini**, son of *inhlanti* laVumisa Ndwandwe, was dispatched on the **Mahamba** slopes in 1846 by forces loyal to her and her son. Malambule fled to the Zulu, but their king, **Mpande**, upon hearing of his perfidy from Tsandzile, had him executed.

The installation of the youthful Mswati only added to Tsandzile's influence. She became the major force behind the sweeping administrative and political reforms that dominated his early reign. Philip Bonner argues that her model may have been her father's Ndwandwe state, which seems logical.[13] She established a system of *emabutfo* (age regiments) that cut across regional and clan lines to refocus national loyalties to the center. She established royal villages throughout the kingdom to symbolize central control and to keep watch on outlying regions. She breathed new life and innovation into the ages-old *iNcwala* **ceremony**, ritualizing her son's personification of the nation, his command of the new *emabutfo*, and his responsibility for agricultural productivity and national vitality. Tsandzile was a central element in Mswati's becoming Swaziland's greatest 19th-century king, rivaled only by his own father, *iNgwenyama* **Sobhuza Dlamini I**.

Mswati's death in 1865 did nothing to diminish Tsandzile's authority. She again became head regent, coordinating the efforts of an extraordinarily powerful political group (**Bnt. Malunge** and **Maloyi Dlamini**, and **Sandlane Zwane**) that deflected the ambitions of **Mnt. Mbilini Dlamini** to become successor in favor of **Mnt. Ludvonga Dlamini**. When *iNgwenyama* Ludvonga II died in 1874 Tsandzile was quick to implicate **Mnt. Ndwandwa Dlamini**, son of her *inhlanti* File Ndwandwe, and have him executed and his estate "eaten up." She then influenced the selection of **Mnt. Mbandzeni Dlamini** as Ludvonga's successor, just before she died. At her death Tsandzile was unrivaled by any political figure in the respect and prestige she enjoyed in the eyes of her people. She was buried at **Zombodze**.

NDWANDWE, *INDLOVUKAZI* ZIHLATHI (?–1975). Wife of *iNgwenyama* **Sobhuza Dlamini II** and successor to *iNdlovukazi* **Nukwase Ndwandwe**. Upon her death Zihlathi was succeeded as *indlovukazi* by her full sister and co-wife, **Seneleleni Ndwandwe**.

NDWANDWE, ZWIDE (c. 1770s–1825). **Nguni**-speaking builder and king of the **Ndwandwe** state during the era of political and military innovation in central and northern Natal of the late 18th and early 19th centuries. The forebears of the Ndwandwe state had migrated out of southern Mozambique along with the **Ngwane** in the early 18th century and settled along the Pongola River—they to the south and the Ngwane to the north. Eventually the Ndwandwe centered themselves near modern Nongoma, where Zwide succeeded his father Langa about 1805. Zwide's legendary fighting prowess resulted in his becoming the most formidable ruler in southeast Africa until the rise of **Shaka Zulu** after 1816. At about the same time the catastrophic effects of the early 19th-century **Madlathule famine** forced Zwide to escalate the aggressiveness of his tactics and to seek out watered lands in regions he had previously left alone. It was then that he became the scourge of *iNgwenyama* **Sobhuza Dlamini I**, headquartered at **Shiselweni** in the hills of the Pongola-iNgwavuma river watershed. Sobhuza's response was to pick up stakes and move north into central Swaziland, where he founded the modern Swazi state. Zwide then attacked the Ngwane of Matiwane, whom he drove across the Drakensberg mountains; then he turned south to attack the Mthethwa confederation of Dingiswayo. In 1816 he took on the Mthethwa army, captured Dingiswayo, and executed him.

That left the way open to the political aspirations of Shaka Zulu, who proceeded to consolidate his hold over the remains of the Mthethwa polity to a such a degree that Zwide determined to subdue him. That proved to be the undoing of Zwide, who sent an army south only to see it shattered by Shaka in two successive campaigns (1817 and 1819) that established the Zulu as the predominant power in the region. Zwide spent the rest of his life, along with his followers, in flight. His exact direction and timetable remain obscure. Generally he moved northward, skirting the western reaches of the Swazi kingdom and tarrying for a time in the central **Transvaal** southwest of the **Pedi** polity. Later, probably during the early 1820s, he moved eastwards to the valley of the upper **Komati River**, where he died.

NEW SCOTLAND. A 2,700 square mile (7,000 square kilometer) territory situated along the western border of Swaziland in the eastern **Transvaal**, the basis for which was a grant from the **South African Republic (SAR)** volksraad (legislature) in 1867. It was incorporated into the SAR (Transvaal) in 1893. *See also* McCorkindale, Alexander

NGONINI. A lumber-producing and irrigated citrus area in the extreme northern part of Swaziland, about five miles (eight kilometers) from the South African border. It is the site of an **irrigation** scheme drawing its water from the Mlumati River.

NGUNI. One of the principal linguistic clusters of Bantu-speaking peoples in southeastern Africa (the Drakensberg mountains to the Indian Ocean). They are generally regarded as having constituted the vanguard of the movement of the Bantu-speakers southward from central Africa. Their ancestors were Later Iron Age peoples who reached the Limpopo River in about the 4th century A.D. They all speak dialects of the common Nguni language, nearly all of them using three click consonants generally attributed to the Khoisan. Nguni-speakers are also characterized by strictures against exogamy, marriage among people tracing their descent from a common ancestor. Nguni-speakers are mixed farmers, growing grain crops and herding cattle. "Nguni," a European construct, is a linguistic and not a geographic term. The Swazi (Swaziland) are representative of Nguni-speakers inhabiting the northern reaches of the original settlement region; the Zulu (Natal) and Xhosa (Cape) are representative in the southern reaches. The **Pedi** (northern **Transvaal**), Ndebele (south-western Zimbabwe), and Ngoni (Malawi) are Nguni-speakers who migrated from the original area of settlement as the result of the formation of the Zulu empire during the early 19th century.

NGWANE. The traditional, organic name for the Swazi, believed to be after the 18th-century king **Ngwane Dlamini**. The term "Swazi" is thought to be a European construct, assigned to the Ngwane during the reign of *iNgwenyama* **Mswati Dlamini II**. Related **siSwati** terms are *emaNgwane* (Swazi people) and *kaNgwane* (in/to/from Swaziland).

kaNGWANE. "Place/Country of the Ngwane." **SiSwati** term for the national territory of the Swazi. Also the official name for the **South African** apartheid-era "homeland" for its siSwati-speaking African citizenry, abutting the western border of Swaziland. During the early 1980s the South African government concluded a secret agreement with *iNgwenyama* **Sobhuza Dlamini II** to transfer kaNgwane, in Sobhuza's mind historically Swazi territory, to Swaziland in return for certain political accommodations. The most consequential of them was Sobhuza's expulsion of the **African National Congress** from the kingdom, beginning in February 1982. That agreement, which created a firestorm of controversy throughout independent Africa when it became public, collapsed with the death of Sobhuza in August 1982. Sobhuza's successor, *iNgwenyama* **Mswati Dlamini III**, announced himself to be in favor of reviving negotiations with Pretoria leading toward the transfer of kaNgwane.

NGWANE III. *See* DLAMINI, *iNGWENYAMA* NGWANE

NGWANE IV. *See* DLAMINI, *iNGWENYAMA* SOBHUZA I

NGWANE V. *See* DLAMINI, *iNGWENYAMA* BHUNU

NGWANE NATIONAL LIBERATORY CONGRESS (NNLC). An opposition party formed in mid-1963 as political activities heightened in anticipation of pre-independence elections. The NNLC was formed as a consequence of the gradual fissioning of the **Swaziland Progressive Party (SPP)** during 1961–62. The final SPP split was partly ideological and partly a clash of personalities in the party leadership, those of **John J. Nquku** and **Dr. Ambrose Zwane**. Both Nquku's SPP and Zwane's NNLC stood for turning *iNgwenyama* **Sobhuza Dlamini II** and the *libandla* into a constitutional monarchy, and for establishing a political system based on a one man, one vote franchise and legalized opposition parties. Both the SPP and the NNLC, while espousing multiracialism, opposed giving the Europeans a privileged ("50–50") position in the proposed **Legislative Council**. Both advocated free and compulsory education and the fostering of **trade unions**. Zwane, who spent time in Ghana during the early and mid-1960s, went much further than Nquku was willing to go toward espousing Pan-Africanism and African socialism. He also accused Nquku (who was Zulu by birth) of personal cultism and corruption. Finally, Zwane was willing to go much further than Nquku toward fomenting labor activism as a means to achieving his political ends.

In 1963 Zwane became the NNLC's president, while **Mnt. Dumisa Dlamini** became its secretary general. During 1962 and 1963 Zwane, Dlamini, and **Macdonald Maseko** involved themselves deeply in labor activism, fomenting **strikes** in major industries and towns and occasionally inciting peaceful demonstrations to violence. As a consequence all three leaders were arrested and tried following the 1963 emergency declaration. That factor, plus the NNLC's superior organization, led it to do better in the 1964 Legislative Council elections than any party other than the royalist **Imbokodvo National Movement (INM)**. Still, the NNLC won no seats. Later, when Dlamini got into trouble with the law and jumped bail (early 1965), **Arthur Khoza** became acting general-secretary of the NNLC, although both he and Maseko resigned from the party in mid-1966. Still, the NNLC was the most popular opposition party running a full slate of candidates in the 1967 parliamentary elections, and it very nearly won the three seats of the Mphumalanga constituency. Once more, however, the INM won every seat in the new parliament, with 79 percent of the vote. Still, Zwane soldiered on.

In 1972 Zwane received his reward during the first post-independence election. The NNLC won a higher percentage of the vote than its 1967 showing, and in the same Mphumalanga constituency, a district heavy with industrial laborers and an independent peasantry, its slate (Zwane, Mageja Masilela, and **Bhekindlela Thomas Ngwenya**) handily defeated the INM candidates, one of whom, **Mnt. Mfanasibili Dlamini**, was a nephew of Sobhuza. Ironically, however, that small but signal electoral victory was to be the NNLC's last, for Sobhuza's government, already mistrustful of the British-engineered independence constitution, now proved itself to be unwilling to brook any voice of formal opposition in parliament. Ngwenya, one of the three winning NNLC candidates, was singled out, declared to be a prohibited immigrant on grounds of his South African birth, and summarily deported (May 1972).

The ensuing constitutional struggle between the NNLC and the *ingwenyama* played out over the following 11 months. Zwane, a strident but lonely opposition voice in **parliament**, stood up bravely for his party's principles in a starkly hostile atmosphere. Ngwenya appealed his expulsion to the courts while Sobhuza's parliamentarians attempted to outmaneuver him legislatively, until finally in March 1973 the Swaziland Court of Appeal found in Ngwenya's favor. Two weeks later Sobhuza declared an emergency, suspended the constitution, and prohibited all political parties. For a long time Sobhuza's move rang down the curtain on the NNLC, the only viable opposition party that could be said to have formally existed in Swaziland during the pre- and post-independence period.

The NNLC, however, rose again during the late 1990s. By 1997 several progressive groups and businessmen, impatient with the lack of cohesion and ineffectiveness of the opposition to the monarchist regime, revived the party as an opposition mechanism. Once again Mnt. Dumisa Dlamini, who had exiled himself to London, became its general secretary.

The death of its venerable founder, Dr. Zwane, in mid-1998 propelled the congress into yet another crisis of leadership. On the eve of the 1998 parliamentary elections the organization was split over the issue of whether or not to boycott them.

iNGWAVUMA. *See* INGWAVUMA

NGWENYA. "Crocodile." The second tallest mountain peak in Swaziland at 6,002 feet (1,829 meters) in altitude. Located near the border in northwest Swaziland, it is part of the Ngwenya range. Located in that area is what remains of Bomvu Ridge, which during the 1960s and 1970s was mined heavily for its iron ore. *See also* Swaziland Iron Ore Development Company

NGWENYA, BHEKINDLELA THOMAS. A member of the **Ngwane National Liberatory Congress (NNLC)**, Ngwenya became the subject of a political battle that led directly to Swaziland's constitutional crisis of 1972–73. Ngwenya, along with NNLC president **Dr. Ambrose Zwane** and Mageja Masilela, ran against and defeated the candidates of the royalist **Imbokodvo National Movement (INM)** in the Mphumalanga constituency in 1972. Because the INM had won every seat in each contest since the first pre-independence elections in 1964, the NNLC victory came as a profound shock to *iNgwenyama* **Sobhuza Dlamini II** and his political advisors. To Sobhuza, who had spent a lifetime reasserting the monarchy's sovereignty and who regarded the democratic **constitution** left in place by the British with profound hostility, the NNLC victory constituted a direct threat to his hard-won authority. That was the case in part because in Mphumalanga were two groups of voters whom Sobhuza feared were especially prone to anti-monarchist arguments: the Swazi peasantry on independent leasehold farms in the **Vuvulane** area and **sugar** workers on the **irrigated** estates in the **lowveld**. Sobhuza and his advisors, deciding that one taste of democracy was one too many, focused their attention on Ngwenya, who had been born in South Africa. In their private view Ngwenya had another strike against him: he was an independent smallholder farmer at Vuvulane, one of the sort who had turned the vote in Mphumalanga against the INM.

It was left to **Zonke Khumalo**, deputy prime minister and Sobhuza's son-in-law, to declare Ngwenya a prohibited immigrant and deport him to South Africa (May 1972). When Ngwenya subsequently returned he was arrested and jailed. The case against Ngwenya was hardly open-and-shut: he had lived in Swaziland all his life, had voted in previous elections without any question, and was the sort of upstanding, progressive farmer that Sobhuza claimed to admire. The NNLC appealed his expulsion to Swaziland's **High Court**, and in August it declared Ngwenya to be a Swazi citizen. The *ingwenyama*'s legislators responded by pushing through **parliament** the Immigration (Amendment) Act (1972), which made the prime minister, not the courts, the final arbiter of immigration cases. Ngwenya appealed on grounds that the new act was unconstitutional, and in March 1973 the Swaziland Court of Appeal ruled in his favor. Two weeks later Sobhuza revoked the constitution and embarked Swaziland on the era of rule by decree.

*i***NGWENYAMA.** "The Lion," the traditional title given to the Swazi king by his people. He is the sovereign, but he is much in addition to that. He is equated to, and the embodiment of, the nation, a concept that is reemphasized annually through the *i***Ncwala ceremony**. That ritual also symbolizes his centrality in the nation's agricultural productivity. Beyond that he is tantamount to the chief priest, in touch with both the occult (his ability to make rain) and the ancestors (symbolized during the *iNcwala* ceremony). As sovereign he shares power with the *indlovukazi*, to whom he owes the most in his own selection as *ingwenyama*. In theory he rules in a dyarchy, balanced in nearly every aspect by the *indlovukazi*, but in practice his ruling power is nearly always greater than hers. He presides over the highest court and wields capital jurisdiction, forms and controls age regiments, names and deposes chiefs, distributes land, holds enormous herds of cattle in trust for the nation, and is the central figure in the most significant national rituals. In the modern era the *ingwenyama* wields significant power from two new sources: dominance over public discourse through control or powerful influence over the media (radio, television, and newspapers) and control of enormous capital resources through two investment vehicles: the **Tibiyo takaNgwane Fund** and its real-estate counterpart, the Tisuka takaNgwane Fund. Never in history has the *ingwenyama* wielded more domestic power.

The procedure by which the new *ingwenyama* is selected is both fluid and shrouded in secrecy. There is no such thing as primogeniture involved—indeed, the sons of the first and second ritual wives are never considered. Instead the scrutiny of the *lusendvo* (council of kinsmen) falls primarily on the late *ingwenyama*'s wives as candidates. It is their pedigrees, their ages, their characters, and their numbers of sons that are weighed. Younger wives who have produced single sons are looked upon with favor because fraternal jealousy over the succession has often led to bloody complications and a weakened monarchy in the past. It is largely for reasons of kinship jealousy that the *inkhosana* (crown prince) is spirited away from his mother's homestead and hidden with trusted relatives or, in the case of *iNgwenyama* **Mswati Dlamini III**, sent to a school in England under guard. To a lesser degree the heir's character (if he is mature enough) is also judged, with intelligence and bravery valued, and tendencies to cruelty, violence, and obstinacy disdained. The choice of an heir is nearly always made following the *ingwenyama*'s death, the better to avoid palace coups and regicides.

Often these general principles are honored in the breach. *iNgwenyama* **Bhunu Dlamini**, for example, was the eldest of *iNdlovukazi* **Labotsibeni Mdluli**'s three sons and was known for his cruelty and impetuosity. Furthermore no Mdluli had ever become *indlovukazi*. In time of great national stress, however, her exceptional intelligence and strength of character were deemed to be so desirable that Bhunu, with all his impediments, was selected as the heir to *iNgwenyama* **Mbandzeni Dlamini** in 1889.

Until 1967 *iNgwenyama* **Sobhuza Dlamini II** had not been allowed by the British to use the title "king" but was referred to rather as "**paramount chief**." In the **1967 constitution**, however, his role as king and head of state was specifically provided for. In 1978, five years following his suspension of the **1968 (independence) constitution**, a new constitution was promulgated giving him authoritarian powers as king unchecked by any lawmaking or deliberative body.

NHLANGANO. "The Meeting Place." An agricultural (forestry) and tourist center in southwest Swaziland, 8 miles (13 kilometers) east of the **Mahamba** border post. Formerly named Goedgegun, it was the center of an Afrikaans-speaking farming population during the colonial era. Its 1986 population was 4,700. Nhlangano is the headquarters of the **Shiselweni** administrative region and of the Swaziland Tobacco Co-operative. A major industry is a sawmill processing local timber. It is also the location of the Evelyn Baring School and the Ngwane Teacher's Training College. Nhlangano's meaning, "The Meeting Place," refers to the meeting there between *iNgwenyama* **Sobhuza Dlamini II** and *libandla* and King George VI in 1947.

NKAMBULE, *iNDLOVUKAZI* TIBATI (c. 1840–1895). Also known as Madvolomafisha ("Short Thighs") because of her ample girth. Tibati was *inhlanti* (subordinate co-wife) of her sister Nandzi Nkambule, who was the mother of *iNgwenyama* **Mbandzeni Dlamini**. Nandzi was executed (c. 1860) by *iNgwenyama* **Mswati Dlamini II**, and the infant Mbandzeni was brought up by Tibati at the Gunundvwini royal **homestead** prior to assuming the throne in 1874. When Mbandzeni executed *iNdlovukazi* **Sisile Khumalo** (1881), Tibati succeeded her in that office, following which she occupied the royal homestead at **Nkanini**. During the **concessions** era Tibati had a falling out with Mbandzeni over the extent of his grants and over his firing of **Theophilus Shepstone, Jr.**, as his advisor and agent.

Following Mbandzeni's death in 1889 Tibati became queen regent. She spent the remainder of her life defending what was left of Swazi sovereignty as she viewed it. That meant that she restored Shepstone to his office, but she did not sign the **Organic Proclamations** of 1890 (establishing the triumviral **government committee**) and 1894 (allowing the **South African Republic [SAR]** to administer Swaziland). In 1894 she dismissed Shepstone and, to avert a SAR occupation, dispatched a **deputation** to London to request that **Britain** take over her kingdom as a protectorate, but it refused. By early 1895 Tibati was suffering from poor health and embarked on a running battle with her successor as *indlovukazi*, **Labotsibeni Mdluli**, for influence at court. In February 1895 she formally relinquished her office upon the installation of **Mnt. Bhunu Dlamini** as *ingwenyama*. She died later that year—perhaps, as was rumored at the time, by poisoning at the hand of Labotsibeni. Tibati was the mother of **Mnt. Logcogco Dlamini**, who served as her co-regent.

NKANINI. The ritual capital of Swaziland and royal **homestead** of the *tindlovukazi* (**Sisile Khumalo** and **Tibati Nkambule**) during the reign of *iNgwenyama* **Mbandzeni Dlamini**. The present ritual capital, **Lobamba**, stands near the site on which Nkanini was situated.

NKHOTFOTJENI. The name given to *iNgwenyama* **Sobhuza Dlamini II** when he was an infant, reputedly by his father, *iNgwenyama* **Bhunu Dlamini**. According to Hilda Kuper the name refers to a small, beautifully marked lizard.[14] Sobhuza's other boyhood name was Mona ("Jealousy"), referring to the jealousy and hatred that had killed his father.

tiNKHUNDLA. See TINKHUNDLA

NKOSI, ALPHEUS. A member of the **Edendale**-educated Wesleyan mission graduates at **Mahamba** who arrived at **Zombodze** just prior to the installation of *iNgwenyama* **Bhunu Dlamini** to become secretaries and advisors to the royal house. Nkosi, a former teacher at Mahamba, became a resident of Zombodze in 1894 and was appointed secretary to Bhunu after the latter's installation in 1895. Later he became secretary to the *indlovukazi* and (later) queen regent, **Labotsibeni Mdluli**. Like certain other of her Mahamba advisors (notably **Josiah Vilakazi** and **Cleopas Kunene**), Nkosi eventually came to be suspected of venality. In Nkosi's case the accusation was that he (and Kunene) took bribes from Pretoria in return for advising Labotsibeni to accept the paltry sum of £5,000 to settle the Swazi nation's claims against **Theophilus Shepstone, Jr.**, for financial irregularities while advising it. Nkosi was succeeded as secretary to the Swazi nation by Vilakazi, a fellow Mahamban, in 1901, but he served as a writing clerk for several years thereafter.

NKOSI, CLIFFORD. A former Johannesburg law clerk who returned to pre-independence Swaziland in early 1960s to enter politics. In 1962 Nkosi formed the Mbandzeni National Party. Its platform was, however, so eclectic that few understood whether Nkosi stood for democracy or monarchism. Later that year, going nowhere, Nkosi merged his party with that of another political pragmatist, **Dr. George Msibi**, to form the **Mbandzeni National Convention (MNC)**. Nkosi became its secretary general and then, following Msibi's resignation, its president. A year later, when Msibi resigned from the MNC (1963), Nkosi became its president. The MNC never amounted to anything and failed even to contest the 1964 **Legislative Council** elections.

iNKHOSANA. "Crown Prince." *See also* umntfwana

iNKHOSI DLAMINI. The lineage of the **Dlamini** clan name (*sibongo*) from which the ruling line of *tingwenyama* (kings) comes. Not all Dlamini lineages hold similar status with regard to the *ingwenyama*. Those more closely related to the royal line hold more status than those more distantly related. The iNkhosi Dlamini trace back to the legendary founder, Dlamini I, who migrated from **eMbo** in central Africa southward in about the 15th century.

NQUKU, JOHN J. (1899–1991). South African (Zulu)-born educator, journalist, and politician who played a dominant role in African intellectual and political life in Swaziland for nearly 60 years. Raised by Christian parents and educated in mission schools, Nquku served as a teacher and principal in South Africa (1920–29) before coming to Swaziland in 1930 as the first African inspector of schools (Supervisor of Native Education). He served in that capacity for 10 years, resigning in 1940 in protest over what he termed his racist treatment by the government. *iNgwenyama* **Sobhuza Dlamini II**, who took a keen interest in Swazi education throughout his lifetime and was impressed with Nquku's abilities, took him on in 1940 as advisor to the *libandla* and *liqoqo* on education and church matters. When Sobhuza established a **Standing Committee of the** *libandla* to liaise with the administration (1947), he named Nquku a member.

When Nquku arrived in Swaziland he took an immediate interest in the newly formed **Swaziland Progressive Association (SPA)** and served as its president from 1945 until it became the **Swaziland Progressive Party** in 1960. In 1934 he became founder and editor of *Izwi Lama Swazi* (1934–64), a vernacular newspaper. In 1955, following the takeover of *Izwi* by the Bantu Press, a South African company, Nquku founded and edited another newspaper, *The Swazilander*. In 1944 he became secretary-general of a merged religious group called the United Christian Church of Africa, and later for many years he was active with the Swaziland Council of Churches.

Nquku's relationship with Sobhuza, insofar as he was active in the SPA, which the king mistrusted, must have been ambiguous from the beginning. It became more so in 1957 when Nquku returned from an extended trip abroad full of enthusiasm for the new egalitarianism he saw being advocated in countries like Ghana. It came as no great shock to the *ingwenyama* when Nquku transformed the SPA into the Swaziland Progressive Party (SPP) in 1960 in order to position himself politically in anticipation of independence. Nquku continued to express strong support for Sobhuza, but as the SPP came increasingly under the influence of its radical secretary-general, **Dr. Ambrose Zwane**, Nquku's position with the *ingwenyama* became less and less tenable. Although Nquku had been a member of the 1963 London **constitutional conference**, beginning in 1964 following the **Legislative Council** elections (in which the SPP made a miserable showing) Nquku was effectively cut off from further serious official deliberations concerning Swaziland's constitutional future.

Nquku's SPP stumbled badly in the 1964 elections partly because the Zwane faction had split from it in 1963 over allegations of Nquku's dictatorial style and financial mismanagement. Zwane named his party the **Ngwane National Liberatory Congress (NNLC)**, and its radical platform along with his own style of labor activism attracted such a following as to leave the SPP far behind, never to regain its stature. The SPP was demolished in the 1967 elections (in which Nquku suffered the indignity of losing his own deposit) and again in the 1972 elections. Nquku spent the remainder of his life writing political commentaries to the local press.

iNSANGU. See INSANGU

NSIBANDZE, MBHABHA (?–1898). Senior political officer (*indvunankhuluyesive*) during most of *iNgwenyama* **Bhunu Dlamini**'s reign. Also chief *indvuna* of Queen Regent **Labotsibeni Mdluli**'s **homestead** at **Zombodze**. As the authoritarian character of the **South African Republic**'s (SAR's) administration of Swaziland became clear, especially as it touched on the imposition of taxes, Mbhabha's (and Labotsibeni's) relations with Bhunu became severely strained. Mbhabha's counsel to Labotsibeni was for peaceable responses to the SAR's initiatives, while Bhunu's volatile character inclined him toward confrontation. The anticipated explosion came in April 1898 when a troop loyal to Bhunu attacked Mbhabha's homestead at Zombodze and killed him. The murder unleashed a momentous political upheaval. The SAR confronted Bhunu over his responsibility for the execution, and it eventually tried and fined him. That incident was then used as the pretext for the SAR's termination, by a **protocol (1898)** to its 1894 convention with the British, of his criminal jurisdiction. Swazi criminal jurisdiction would not be restored until 1950.

iNSILA. See INSILA

NXUMALO, DR. ALLEN MALABHANE. Medical doctor trained at the University of the Witwatersrand (1957). The son of **Benjamin Nxumalo**, he was educated at the **Swazi National High School** at **Matsapha** and then Fort Hare University College in South Africa. A contemporary of Nelson Mandela at Ft. Hare, Nxumalo was active in the **African National Congress** Youth League during his years in Johannesburg. Upon his return to Swaziland he entered the government medical service and was also drawn into politics. Dr. Nxumalo was a delegate to the first constitutional conference (1960) representing the *libandla*. In 1963, however, he left the ranks of the royalists in protest over *iNgwenyama* **Sobhuza Dlamini II**'s endorsement of a "50–50" Swazi-European split in the membership of the proposed **Legislative Council**. Dr. Nxumalo joined the moderate, multiracial **Swaziland Democratic Party (SDP)** and became its president in late 1963. In 1964 Dr. Nxumalo and his party were crushed by Sobhuza's **Imbokodvo National Movement (INM)** in the Legislative Council elections, leading to its disintegration.

Dr. Nxumalo and others joined the INM in 1964–65, and he went on to win handily as an INM candidate in the 1967 elections. Sobhuza then selected him as minister of health in his first cabinet. Dr. Nxumalo did not contest the 1972 elections, but the *ingwenyama* nominated him to the House of Assembly, then made him minister for education and later minister for works, power, and communication. Following Sobhuza's repeal of the constitution in 1973, Dr. Nxumalo retired from politics and established a private medical practice.

NXUMALO, BENJAMIN (?–1941). Classificatory brother to *iNdlovukazi* **Lomawa Ndwandwe** and maternal uncle of *iNgwenyama* **Sobhuza Dlamini II**. Nxumalo championed Lomawa's candidacy to become *indlovukazi*, and he was throughout his lifetime a close and trusted advisor to Sobhuza. Nxumalo, educated at the Wesleyan mission at **Edendale**, Natal, became a lifelong member of the **African Methodist Episcopal Church** in Swaziland and advised Sobhuza on matters of both Western education and religion. During the **Anglo-Boer War** (1899–1902) Nxumalo campaigned in Swaziland on the side of the British. Following Sobhuza's installation in 1921, Nxumalo became royal secretary, replacing the dismissed **Josiah Vilakazi**. Nxumalo was secretary to both Sobhuza's deputations, to Pretoria (1921) and London (1922–23). His career suffered a reversal in 1924 when Sobhuza dismissed him for corruption, although he continued to draft many of the *ingwenyama*'s speeches thereafter. Nxumalo regained royal favor at least by 1930, when he was listed as a *liqoqo* member for the first time.

Nxumalo, as an educated Christian and a member of the royal circle, became with Sobhuza's support one of the earliest members of the emerging Swazi middle class. By 1936 he had amassed enough money (£175) as a trader and farmer to build a house and a stand (commercial shop) in Bremersdorp (**Manzini**), although he was refused permission to purchase the underlying land on account of his race. Politically, in 1929 he became a founding member of the **Swaziland Progressive Association (SPA)**, which he chaired until his death. That office undoubtedly complicated his relations with Sobhuza, who harbored suspicions of the SPA as a rival power base, but that did not stop Sobhuza from naming Nxumalo to represent him on the advisory board of the **Swazi National High School** at **Matsapha**, an institution he regarded as supremely important symbolically as well as educationally. Nxumalo was also head of the Swaziland branch of the **African National Congress**. Nxumalo was the father of **Dr. Allen Nxumalo**.

NXUMALO, *iNDLOVUKAZI* LOMAWA. *See* NDWANDWE, *iNDLOVUKAZI* LOMAWA

NXUMALO, MGCOBEYA. A longtime member of the *libandla* and trusted advisor of *iNgwenyama* **Sobhuza Dlamini II** who was one of the architects of Sobhuza's campaign against the British-proposed **Native Administration Proclamation** (1944), which began in 1939. The proclamation, which would have codified the authority of the **resident commissioner** over the *ingwenyama* and chiefs, was steadfastly opposed by Sobhuza and the *libandla*, ultimately successfully. Nxumalo was a member of the *libandla*'s **Standing Committee** established by Sobhuza in 1947 to liaise with the colonial administration. Nxumalo was the father of **Simon Sishayi Nxumalo**.

NXUMALO, *iNDLOVUKAZI* NUKWASE. *See* NDWANDWE, *iNDLOVUKAZI* NUKWASE

NXUMALO, *iNDLOVUKAZI* SENELELENI. *See* NDWANDWE, *iNDLOVUKAZI* SENELELENI

NXUMALO, SIMON SISHAYI (1936–2000). Educator and arguably the most astute and nimble politician Swaziland has ever produced. Son of chief **Mgcobeya Nxumalo**, he was raised and educated at Nkambeni in the **lowveld**, where he earned his junior (primary level) certificate and then taught primary school from 1954 to 1958. He then worked as a gold miner in Johannesburg before returning to Swaziland to enter business (1960). In 1961 he helped to found the Swaziland Sebenta Society (later **Sebenta National Institute**), an adult literacy and community development organization, which he helped to run for many years. Nxumalo's interest derived from his father's experience with a colonial literacy program when he was jailed by the British. When Mgcobeya was released he had married a literate woman who had taught all of his children how to read and write.

Nxumalo's mentor and backer in the Sebenta scheme was **Vincent Rozwadowski**, an expatriate from South Africa. In 1962, in response to the approach of independence, Nxumalo, Rozwadowski, and Jordan Ngubane (another exiled South African) founded the **Swaziland Democratic Party (SDP)**, the second of the significant opposition parties to be formed during the early 1960s. The other was the **Swaziland Progressive Party (SPP)**. The SDP's platform was the more moderate, favoring a constitutional monarchy based on an eventual (not immediate) universal franchise. Unlike the SPP, it explicitly eschewed Pan-Africanism. Nxumalo became president, while Rozwadowski became vice-president. When **Dr. Allen Nxumalo** briefly joined the SDP in 1963, he became president while Nxumalo became secretary-general. In the 1964 **Legislative Council** elections the SDP was soundly defeated by the royalist-settler political coalition of the **Imbokodvo National Movement (INM)** and the **United Swaziland Association (USA)**; it won not a single seat. Nxumalo was singularly humiliated by losing his own deposit in a constituency where his family was prominent and respected.

In responding, Nxumalo proceeded to demonstrate for the first time the political agility for which he later became famous. Fifteen weeks following the elections (October 1964) he bolted the SDP and joined *iNgwenyama* **Sobhuza Dlamini II**'s INM, the first of a flurry of such defections from across the spectrum of the opposition. Following Nxumalo's volte-face the SDP sank without a trace, but his own career took off. He ran as an INM candidate in the 1967 elections and won handily, following which Sobhuza named him assistant minister of finance in his new cabinet. Later he was named minister of commerce, industry, and mines. Following his reelection to **parliament** in 1972, he was appointed minister for industry, mines, and tourism. In those two positions Nxumalo was the power behind much of the dramatic buildup of the foreign-owned light manufacturing establishment in the **Matsapha** industrial site. Following Sobhuza's repeal of the constitution (1973), Nxumalo was named to the Royal Constitutional Commission that was to recommend the shape of the new constitution. At the time of Sobhuza's death in 1982 Nxumalo was managing director of the **Tibiyo takaNgwane Fund**, which he had helped to establish in 1968.

The *Liqoqo* period lasting from Sobhuza's death until the installation of **iNgwenyama Mswati Dlamini III** in 1986 was a politically volatile and dangerous time for Nxumalo, as it was for all the principals. Nxumalo, who was not a member of the *Liqoqo*, cast his lot with the traditionalists, notably **Mnt. Gabheni Dlamini** and the *indlovukazi*, **Dzeliwe Shongwe**. Nxumalo was named minister of finance in 1983, a promotion, but he then was dismissed as director of the **Tibiyo taka-Ngwane Fund**, a direct attack by the *Liqoqo* faction on his power base. Nxumalo responded by publicly accusing the *Liqoqo* leader, **Mnt. Mfanasibili Dlamini**, of corruption. In 1984 Nxumalo was dismissed from the cabinet by the *Liqoqo* faction and, along with other traditionalists, jailed. He was released in mid-1985 as the result of a palace countercoup that resulted in the Mfanasibili faction being arrested and placed on trial, as well as in the premature installation of Mswati as king in April 1986. Nxumalo had again landed on his feet.

Nxumalo quickly found a place in Mswati's inner circle of advisors after 1986. By the mid-1990s he was back in the cabinet as deputy prime minister. At the time of his death, Nxumalo was chairman of the Swaziland Investment Promotion Authority.

NXUMALO, ZIHLATHI. *See* NDWANDWE, ZIHLATHI

iNYANGA. See INYANGA

NYAWO, SAMBANE (?–1911). Chief of the independent Nyawo clan, occupying the **Lebombo** range bordered roughly by the Pongola River in the east, the western scarp of the Lebombo in the west, the iNgwavuma river gorge in the north, and the Pongola river gorge in the south. The area was excellent cattle country and was a trading crossroads, so that the Nyawo prospered. Sambane's father, Silevane Nyawo, maintained his independence by claiming allegiance to the Zulu, but when King **Dingane Zulu** was deposed and fled north to the Nyawo for safety in 1840, Silevane, Sambane, and others captured and executed him.

Sambane's diplomatic game changed dramatically during the 1880s, following the British defeat of the Zulu in 1879 and the intensification of the **South African Republic**'s (SAR's) campaign for an outlet to the sea. Because the north bank of the Pongola had been ceded to the **Lydenburg** Afrikaners by *iNgwenyama* **Mswati Dlamini II** in 1855, agents of the SAR began nosing around Sambane's territory in the late 1880s, signing a treaty with him acknowledging their special interests (1887). The British, however, argued that Sambane owed his allegiance to the Swazi, although there was no evidence to prove it, and *iNgwenyama* **Mbandzeni Dlamini** chose not to press his claim. That was as far as Swaziland ever came to access to the Indian Ocean through **Kosi Bay**. Squeezed between the two greater powers, Sambane proceeded to play an awkward diplomatic game, forging ties with the SAR and then claiming allegiance to the Zulu. Finally, in 1895 the British settled the issue by annexing the Nyawo as part of their wider claim to Tsongaland in order to deny the SAR its road to the sea.

NOTES

1. Bonner, *Kings, Commoners and Concessionaires*, pp. 23–24.
2. Crush, "The Culture of Failure," 187.
3. Bonner, *Kings, Commoners and Concessionaires*, p. 114.
4. Christopher Lowe, "Social Change and Ideological Struggle over Patriarchy in Colonial Swaziland," paper presented at the African Studies Association Conference, Baltimore, MD, November 1990, p. 36.
5. Bonner, *Kings, Commoners and Concessionaires*, p. 126.
6. Hilda Kuper, *Sobhuza II: Ngwenyama and King of Swaziland* (London: Duckworth, 1978), pp. 8–9.
7. Christopher Lowe, "The Tragedy of Malunge, or, The Fall of the House of Chiefs: *Abantu-Batho*, the Swazi Royalty, and Nationalist Politics in Southern Africa, 1894–1927," paper presented at the African Studies Association Conference, Boston, MA, December 1993, p. 18.
8. Jonathan Crush, "The Colonial Division of Space: The Significance of the Swaziland Land Partition," *International Journal of African Historical Studies*, XIII, 1 (1980), 81.
9. Hilda Kuper, *An African Aristocracy: Rank Among the Swazi* (London and New York: Oxford University Press for the International African Institute, 1969 edition [first published 1947]), pp. 197–225; T. O. Beidelman, "Swazi Royal Ritual," *Africa*, XXXVI, 4 (1966), 373–405, esp. 376–378.
10. Beidelman, "Swazi Royal Ritual," esp. 376–378.
11. Kuper, *African Aristocracy*, p. 54.
12. Ibid., p. 15.
13. Bonner, *Kings, Commoners and Concessionaires*, pp. 48–49.
14. Kuper, *Sobhuza II*, p. 32.

-O-

OHRIGSTAD. *See* LYDENBURG REPUBLIC

OLD LOBAMBA. *See* LOBAMBA

OLIFANTS RIVER. A major river flowing eastward in the eastern **Transvaal** about 110 miles (175 kilometers) north of Swaziland border. *iNgwenyama* **Mswati Dlamini II** once claimed the territory north of the modern border between the Crocodile and Olifants rivers (although the **Pedi** contested the claim), but he ceded it all to the **Lydenburg Republic** in 1846.

ORDER-IN-COUNCIL OF JUNE 25, 1903. A British order-in-council that constituted the formal basis for **Britain**'s claim to rule Swaziland from 1903 until it granted the kingdom's independence in 1968. That document was in turn based on powers specified under the Foreign Jurisdiction Act of 1890. The order did not declare Swaziland a British protectorate but rather specified Britain's right to administer Swaziland by virtue of its victory in the **Anglo-Boer War** over the kingdom's previous administrators, the **South African Republic (SAR)**. The document decreed that Swaziland fell under the governor of the **Transvaal** (then **Sir Alfred Milner**), who was authorized to rule by proclamation and to administer the territory through a **resident commissioner**. It stipulated that in administering the country the governor had to "respect" within certain limits "any Native laws" then existing that regulated Swazi society. That phrase, uttered repeatedly by *iNgwenyama* **Sobhuza Dlamini II** in defense of "native law and custom" on a variety of issues, would come back to haunt two generations of British administrators.

The order was used almost immediately as the basis for Britain's attack on the fundamental basis of the *ingwenyama*'s power, his criminal jurisdiction. That power had been curtailed once previously, by Britain's agreement with the SAR, in 1898, but it had been Queen Regent **Labotsibeni Mdluli**'s fervent hope that the war had abolished that protocol. The **Swaziland Administration Proclamation (3/1904)** however, dashed her hopes by extending the laws and the court system of the Transvaal to Swaziland, *mutatis mutandis*, in all criminal matters. Swazi courts were to exercise jurisdiction only in civil matters "in which aboriginal Natives only are concerned."

The British order-in-council of 1906, issued on the occasion of Britain's granting of internal self-government to the Transvaal, removed Swaziland from the administrative jurisdiction of the governor of the Transvaal and placed the kingdom under the British **high commissioner** for South Africa.

ORGANIC PROCLAMATION OF 1894. The British-**South African Republic (SAR)** Convention of 1890 guaranteed Swaziland's independence, but by 1893 Britain was becoming anxious to extricate itself from direct involvement with the kingdom. In the **second Swaziland Convention** (1893) Britain empowered the SAR to enter into negotiations with Swaziland in order to secure powers of administration and jurisdiction over it, but short of actual incorporation. The arrangement was to be included in an organic proclamation to be signed in 1894 by the queen regent and leading chiefs. The Swazi, led by Queen Regent **Tibati Nkambule**, flatly refused to sign that document, or even to negotiate toward such an agreement, citing the articles of the 1890 convention. Instead she dispatched a **deputation** to London in **1894** to persuade Britain to alter its position. London, however, rebuffed her and entered into the **third Swaziland Convention** (1894), which relieved the SAR of the obligation to obtain the organic proclamation from the Swazi. The successive conventions from 1890 to 1894 *in toto* documented the first instances of the utter cynicism with which the British repeatedly treated their obligations, stated and implied, toward the Swazi during the years immediately prior to and following their assumption of administration in 1903.

ORGANIZATION OF AFRICAN UNITY (OAU). Founded in 1963 to unite all the nations of Africa toward universal goals and the common good. The OAU's stated aims were to promote solidarity among member states, raise living standards among its member populations, defend sovereignty, and eliminate colonialism. By the late 1990s the OAU had 51 member nations, including **South Africa**, the only major non-member being Morocco. Swaziland's membership dates from 1968. Heads of state meet annually, and foreign ministers meet twice per year. During the early 1980s Swaziland was severely criticized by the OAU for expelling the **African National Congress** from its borders and for agreeing to accept **kaNgwane** and **Ingwavuma** from South Africa in compensation, in violation of that body's long-standing policy against adjustment of national borders.

OVERSEAS NATIVE LABOUR CONTINGENT (ONLC). A corps of African laborers recruited by Great Britain in 1916 to aid its war effort in Europe. The **resident commissioner, de Symons Honey**, put great pressure on Queen Regent **Labotsibeni Mdluli** to send Swaziland's 480-man quota forward. Labotsibeni chose instead to demonstrate the power of foot-dragging, in protest against the colonial government's expropriation of most of the royal house's finances and power. She also sought to undo the damage in public opinion caused to her reputation by her previous wholesale collaboration with South African mine labor recruiters. Only 57 men came forward, seriously embarrassing Honey, who referred to an assemblage of chiefs as "frightened women." Labotsibeni eventually sought to make amends by turning over to Honey the proceeds of her 1917 War Levy, £3,000. Later, *iNgwenyama* **Sobhuza Dlamini II** surely had history in mind when he vigorously supported recruiting for the **African Pioneer Corps** in 1941–42, for reasons of both loyalty and diplomatic leverage.

-P-

PALMER, WILLIAM W. *See* SELBORNE, LORD

PARAMOUNT CHIEF. As first outlined in the **third Swaziland Convention** (1894) and repeated in the **Protocol of 1898**, the term chosen by British colonial officials to indicate the highest chief in a given kinship, language, or regional group, known to them as a "tribe." The imperial theory was that in the British empire there was only one "king," and all colonial titles were necessarily subordinate to his. The matter of the *ingwenyama*'s English-language title never became an issue until the installation of *iNgwenyama* **Sobhuza Dlamini II** in 1921, because of the political circumstances prevailing since 1894. *iNgwenyama* **Bhunu Dlamini** had not objected to the title of "paramount chief," and the regency following his death in 1899 had obviated any raising of the issue until 1921. With Sobhuza's installation, however, the issue took on a new seriousness that bedeviled the administration until the British reversed themselves on the issue on the eve of independence in 1967.

Sobhuza, in his campaign to reverse things, chose several weapons, all of them subtle yet emphatic in the eyes of those who viewed titles and indicators of status to be important. He stamped his official correspondence with the imprint "Sobhuza II, Ngwenyama and King of Swaziland," which provoked occasional remonstrances from **Mbabane** but no change from him. His chiefs and followers refused on any occasion to accord visiting dignitaries, from **High Commissioner** Prince Arthur of Connaught (1922) to King George VI (1947), the royal salute "**Bayethe!**" ("Hail, Your Majesty!"), which they reserved for the king of Swaziland.

PARLIAMENT. Westminster-style legislative body established in Swaziland under British oversight in the **1967** (pre-independence) and

1968 (independence) constitutions. The Swaziland parliament lasted until *iNgwenyama* **Sobhuza Dlamini II** repealed the constitution in 1973. The new parliament established in 1978 under the *tinkhundla* (regional councils) electoral system was anything but a Westminster-style legislative body. The independence parliament consisted of two houses. The House of Assembly comprised 24 elected members, 6 more members nominated by the *ingwenyama*, and a speaker. Exclusive power to initiate legislation on taxation and financial matters belonged to the House of Assembly. The Senate consisted of a speaker, 6 members elected by the House of Assembly, and 6 appointed by the *ingwenyama*. The Senate had the power to initiate legislation on any matters other than finance, taxation, and Swazi law and custom. Election to the House was from eight three-member constituencies. Bills passed through both houses, assented to by the *ingwenyama*, and gazetted became law. The Swaziland parliament differed from Britain's in at least two important ways. First, parliament did not have the power to pass laws dealing with the *libandla*. Second, the *ingwenyama* retained the power to appoint the prime minister (from the membership of the House of Assembly) and the cabinet.

The 1978 parliament resembled the earlier one in that it was bicameral. The House of Assembly consisted of 40 elected members plus 10 appointed by the king. The Senate consisted of 10 elected members plus 10 appointed by the *ingwenyama*. Bills passed by both houses, signed by the king, and gazetted became law. The king retained his powers of appointment. Appearances notwithstanding, the new parliament was (aside from its important public debating function) simply a creature of the king. What made that so was the new electoral system based not on a secret democratic ballot but on 40 non-secret *tinkhundla* controlled by chiefs who owed their allegiance to Sobhuza. Voting was public in the form of acclamation by citizens who owed their access to land and patronage to the chiefs. Each *inkhundla* sent two representatives to an electoral college, where they chose 40 members of the House of Assembly. Activism for reform, which became a significant factor in Swazi politics by the late 1980s among movements such as the **People's United Democratic Movement (PUDEMO)**, was first aimed principally at democratizing the *tinkhundla*-based parliamentary electoral system.

PARSONSON, JOSEPH M. (1863–?). **South African** (Pietermaritzburg) stockbroker who by 1904 parlayed his business relationship with the **Mini** family of the **Edendale**, Natal, Wesleyan Mission into the position of influence as advisor to Queen Regent **Labotsibeni Mdluli**. By 1905

Parsonson had signed on as official advisor and agent of the Swazi nation, with power of attorney to handle financial matters. He never got to act on those powers because **High Commissioner Lord Selborne** was determined that the formidable Labotsibeni should not have access to competent European advice. Parsonson thereupon engaged an old Swazilander, **Albert Bremer**, to assist him in gaining entrance into Swaziland in order to carry out his new duties. Bremer instead undercut Parsonson in the queen regent's eyes with allegations of his corruption. In 1906 Labotsibeni dismissed Parsonson and engaged Bremer in his place, but the British refused the latter access to Swaziland as well.

PARTITION PROCLAMATION OF 1907. One of the most consequential decrees passed during the colonial era, the Proclamation legitimated the **concessions** earlier granted to European prospectors and speculators, and it awarded nearly two-thirds of the territory to European ownership or to itself as **crown lands**. In the greatest affront of all to the Swazi understanding on the original concessions (which were to be in usufruct only), the new European occupiers were granted **title deed** ownership of their new lands. The partition, carried out beginning in 1914 along the lines recommended by the **Swaziland Concessions Commission** and according to the delineations of the partition commissioner, **George Grey**, divided the country into European-owned farms, **crown land**, and Swazi "**native areas**." The proclamation also was meant to alleviate the insufficiency of Swazi labor, because the native areas were designed to support only a 50 percent increase in population and far less an increase in cattle. That meant that within half a generation after Swazi removal to them they would remain viable only as reservoirs of labor. As insurance against violence, Swazi removal to native areas or reclassification as tenants on European farms was to be delayed for five years, until 1914.

PEAK TIMBERS, LTD. The first significant post–World War II corporation involved in the development of Swaziland by foreign capital. **Robert P. Stephens**, a South African government forester, acted for a group of South African investors in concert with **High Commissioner Sir Evelyn Baring** to acquire and develop the northwestern Swaziland **highveld** for the cultivation of pine timber. Later the investor syndicate included Baring Brothers, Barclays Overseas Development Corporation, a Danish syndicate, and subsequently, the Anglo-American Corporation. The types of trees planted were principally *Pinus patula* (indigenous to the Mexican highlands) and the rapid-growing *Pinus elliotti* and *Pinus taeda* (indigenous to the southern United States). Later, eucalyptus trees were added, first as firebreaks, then to supply shoring timbers for South Africa's gold mines. A small amount of wattle (for tanning) is also grown. The combined forestry operations of Peak Timbers and Usutu Forests (**Usutu Pulp Company**) in the western Swaziland highveld comprise over 75 million trees, making it one of the largest commercial forests in the world. It is networked with 1,140 miles (1,840 kilometers) of tarred and secondary roads. Peak Timbers also possesses Swaziland's largest sawmilling complex.

Land for the Peak Timbers operation, eventually covering 197,680 acres (80,000 hectares), was acquired through the purchase of privately owned European acreage (at £5 an acre) and by the conversion of **Swazi Nation Land (SNL)** and lands previously committed to the **Swaziland Native Land Settlement Scheme (SNLSS)**. SNLSS lands were acquired by 1948, the peasantry being moved to the Impala ranch at **Pigg's Peak** and to a large farm in the southern highveld. The SNL transaction proved to be more difficult and infinitely more controversial. Without the SNL, lands that were held in trust for the nation by the *ingwenyama*, Peak Timbers's forest would have been pockmarked with unacceptable gaps.

Consequently in 1947 Baring, representing the capital interests, entered into negotiations with *iNgwenyama* **Sobhuza Dlamini II**, representing the Swazi nation. Sobhuza finally agreed to the exchange, enticed by Baring's offer to allocate 400 acres (162 hectares) of the proposed forest to the Swazi nation that might add as much as £180,000 to the Swazi treasury. SNL lands sufficient to accommodate 325 peasant families were bartered for **crown land** of comparable agricultural suitability elsewhere, mostly in the **middleveld**. For the families and the chiefs involved, the forced expulsion to alien and unfamiliar territory came as a cruel blow and was bitterly resented long afterwards. According to one Swazi historian, Sobhuza's barter was comparable to *iNgwenyama* **Mbandzeni Dlamini**'s concessions of three generations before.

For a number of years, as the young trees matured to sawmilling dimensions, the main product of the forest was chip board made from thinned-out trees, faced with veneer, and sold to furniture manufacturers mainly for the African market in South Africa. Once the trees matured fully (approximately 25 years), forest production was largely given over to sawn timber. Peak Timbers has for years been a subsidiary of the Anglo-American Corporation. A second commercial forest in the Pigg's Peak area, originally formed as Swaziland Plantations, is owned by the South African corporation Mondi.

PEDI. A Sotho-speaking nation occupying the northern and eastern **Transvaal**, rival claimants to the Swazi sphere of influence in the eastern Transvaal region throughout much of the 19th century. King Sekwati Maroteng (d. 1861) built the Pedi nation beginning in 1828 from the remains of the devastation wrought primarily by the **Ndwandwe** during the *difaqane* (Sotho: "time of crushing"). *iNgwenyama* **Mswati Dlamini II** (d. 1865), for whom the eastern Transvaal was a rich hunting ground for cattle and captives, kept the Pedi in constant fear of raids by his armies.

The reign of Sekwati's successor **King Sekhukhune Maroteng** (1861–79) was preoccupied from beginning to end by the Swazi threat. At first Sekhukhune restored Pedi military fortunes with a spectacular rout of the Swazi army at the battle of Ewulu in 1869, where according to tradition "[Swazi] princes fell like leaves in autumn." In 1875 the Pedi inflicted a second sharp defeat on the Swazi, this time on *iNgwenyama* **Mbandzeni**, at Mosega mountain, when a Swazi troop chasing a foiled pretender to the Swazi throne fleeing to Sekhukhune's protection ran into an ambush of defenders' rifles and was cut to pieces. Scarcely four years later it was the Swazi who triumphed, decisively and finally. By then the British had occupied the Transvaal, and Mbandzeni was persuaded by its administrator and commanding general, Sir Garnet Wolseley, to embark on a joint British-Swazi expedition against their common enemy, Sekhukhune.

In mid-November 1879 Mbandzeni, impressed by the British defeat of the Zulu and anxious to accommodate to British power, exceeded all expectations by dispatching nearly 8,500 troops (500 with rifles) under his ablest general, **Mbovane Fakudze**, to join the attack. In the savage battle against Sekhukhune's redoubt it was the Swazi who carried the day and who paid the price in casualties (up to 1,200) in the defeat and capture of Sekhukhune. In return the Swazi received two concessions from Wolseley: permission to ravage the villages for cattle and captives, and his word that Mbandzeni's assistance had earned a British guarantee of Swazi independence in perpetuity. The latter promise, although it was later inserted in the language of two separate conventions (1881 and 1884), was abrogated by the British in the **third Swaziland Convention** of 1894.

PEOPLE'S UNITED DEMOCRATIC MOVEMENT (PUDEMO). The principal popular opposition organization in Swaziland, which first surfaced during the mid-1980s in response to the *liqoqo*-instigated political crisis following the death of *iNgwenyama* **Sobhuza Dlamini II**. The movement, which is illegal, seeks to bring about true democratic rule in Swaziland, although it is not opposed to a constitutional monarchy. Its membership is young, centered among **trade union**, civil servant, and student and academic groups. Its activism during the late 1980s and early 1990s was aimed specifically at overturning the *tinkhundla*-based parliamentary electoral system. PUDEMO saw the *tinkhundla* system as being undemocratic and ultimately as the political basis of the monarchy's hegemonic control of the government and the economy. Secondarily PUDEMO sought to bring about political change through labor activism and was involved beginning in the late 1980s in instigating series of labor **strikes** among teachers, civil servants, and industrial and other workers. PUDEMO was widely understood to have had close ties with the **African National Congress** of **South Africa**, whose relations with Swaziland's monarchy soured following its 1982 expulsion by Sobhuza at Pretoria's behest.

By 1989 the government had begun to move against PUDEMO by turning the police loose on the campuses of the teacher training colleges and the **University of Swaziland** at Kwaluseni. In 1990 the government placed several alleged PUDEMO members on trial for sedition and treason, only to see them acquitted and released. Following that embarrassment the government moved to modify the *tinkhundla* system. By the late 1990s PUDEMO had moved to moderate its earlier radicalism and edged toward the political center, and as a consequence it attracted wider popular support. *See also* Swaziland Democratic Alliance (SDA); Swaziland Federation of Trade Unions (SFTU)

PIERCE, IVAN H. (1883–1971). One of the most successful and influential settler farmers in southern Swaziland. Born in Canada, Pierce taught at a commercial college in Durban and farmed in the Cape before arriving in Swaziland in 1915. He purchased a farm at Kubuta, where from the first he cultivated cash crops. He pioneered improved methods of tobacco farming and later specialized in banana cultivation, for which he again developed new methods, his research becoming internationally recognized. Pierce was one of the earliest farmers to turn to irrigated farming, surveying and excavating a 10-mile canal by himself. Pierce also operated a general store at Kubuta.

Pierce was also active in European politics. He was for many years a prominent member of both the **Swaziland Farmers Association** and the **European Advisory Council**.

PIGG, WILLIAM (1831–1902). Durban prospector who first arrived in Swaziland in 1880 to join **Thomas McLachlan** in prospecting the Phophonyane River region. In 1884 he discovered gold-bearing reefs on the hill in northern Swaziland bearing his name. The **Pigg's Peak** mine became the richest source of **gold** in all of Swaziland, eventually being mined to a depth of 800 feet (244 meters) and at one time employing 400 miners. Pigg, who moved his family to the Pigg's Peak area in 1886, was primarily a prospector and did not enter into the politics of concessioneering swirling around him at the time, although he did acquire stakes in a handful of mineral and land **concessions**. A couple of his later mineral concessions also produced payable gold. Pigg retired from Swaziland to Natal in 1895, leaving his stakes to be worked by his son. The Pigg's Peak mine closed following World War I but was reopened between 1941 and 1951.

PIGG'S PEAK. A commercial town in the **highveld** region of northwestern Swaziland, 26 miles (42 kilometers) southwest of the Matsamo border post. The population in 1986 was 3,223. Pigg's Peak, originally at the center of much of the **gold** prospecting and mining in Swaziland, has been since the late 1940s the administrative headquarters of the Pigg's Peak Plantation forestry complex as well as a population and shopping center for its workforce. With the region's spectacular scenery, its proximity to South Africa's Kruger National Park, and the building of the Protea Hotel in the 1980s, Pigg's Peak is also a hub of tourism.

PIM, SIR ALAN (1870–1958). Following the visit to Swaziland of Colonial and Dominions Secretary **Leopold S. Amery** in 1927, **Britain**'s policy of developmental neglect changed to one of making Swaziland a viable settler territory preparatory to its transfer to the **Union of South Africa**. For that to be done effectively an accounting of Swaziland's resources and economic potential was required. Accordingly Sir Alan Pim was dispatched to Swaziland in 1931 as head of a financial commission to take such an inventory. In keeping with Amery's purposes, Pim concerned himself primarily with the settler economy, which he saw (incorrectly) as being weighted down by the backwardness of the Swazi economy. He studied the Swazi side of the inventory only insofar as he perceived it giving light to the stagnation afflicting the territory's economy and administration as a whole.

The "Pim Report," *Financial and Economic Situation of Swaziland* (1932), did indeed paint a picture of stagnation. Mining development (**gold** and **tin**) had been disappointing. **Cattle** and cattle products exports were minimal. Agricultural production was meager, in part because of the antiquated farming methods being employed, so that Swaziland had become a net grain and foodstuffs importer. Scant attention had been paid to the **irrigation** potential of the major rivers. Transportation facilities, both within the territory and between Swaziland and the Witwatersrand, and for both people and agricultural commodities, were inadequate. Administratively the territory suffered from serious neglect of its native educational establishment and social services. As for the Swazi, the 32 **native areas** were already overstocked and becoming overpopulated, unrelieved by anything approaching modern husbandry methods. All of that added up to a territory woefully undeveloped in both the settler and the Swazi sectors, and consequently possessing a revenue base insufficient to build much of a development infrastructure without parliamentary assistance in the form of grants-in-aid.

The Pim Report served to focus official attention on Swaziland's economic plight, but it cannot be said, as Lord William Hailey does, that it marked a turning point in the territory's colonial history.[1] Parliamentary grants-in-aid, which had been implemented in 1928, were increased, but they scarcely affected the quality of administration or the welfare of the people. Little attempt, aside from the addition of a few more agricultural demonstrators, was made to improve Swazi agriculture or cattle husbandry. Education and social services remained primarily in the hands of the **missions**. Partly responsible for that was the growing awareness that Swaziland would not soon, if ever, be transferred to the Union. Swaziland's economic and financial fortunes awaited World War II and the passage of the **Colonial Development and Welfare Acts** of 1940 and 1945 to be rescued.

PREFERENTIAL TRADE AREA (PTA). *See* COMMON MARKET FOR EASTERN AND SOUTHERN AFRICA (COMESA)

PRETORIA CONVENTION (1881). Signed by the British and **Transvaal** governments in August 1881, the Pretoria Convention formally ended British claims to sovereignty over the Transvaal (which it had annexed in 1877). This retrocession was accompanied by two clauses of great importance to Swazi fortunes. Article 1 defined the boundary lines between the Transvaal and Swaziland, as delineated by the Alleyne Commission (**Transvaal-Swaziland Boundary Commission**). Article 24 confirmed Sir Garnet Wolseley's promise of future independence to the Swazi, as the result of the collaboration in war against the **Pedi**: "The independence of the Swazi within the boundary line of Swaziland . . . will be fully recognized." That paper guarantee was deemed insufficient by the British **high commissioner**, Sir Hercules Robinson, with the result that it was strengthened by the positioning of a border resident and police in the **London Convention** of 1884.

PREVENTIVE DETENTION LAW (1973). A law, similar in detail and purpose to South Africa's infamous apartheid-era General Law Amendment Acts (often referred to as the "90-day laws"), providing the Swaziland government with the power to detain any person without trial for a period of 60 days. Under the law the detention could be renewed following the 60 days as often as was deemed necessary in the public interest. The law was decreed in 1973 by *iNgwenyama* **Sobhuza Dlamini II** as a means of arming himself with the powers necessary to enforce his repeal of the **constitution**. The government retained that power until the mid-1990s and used it on several occasions to stifle dissent. The most notorious episode occurred during 1990–91 when the government detained 11 opponents under the preventive detention law and charged them with (among other things) violation of Sobhuza's 1972 decree banning all political activity. Following their 60-day jailing the government renewed the detention of five of them three additional times. The five were released only after an unprecedented attack on the detention law by the United States embassy as having a "chilling effect on the democratic process." Undoubtedly in response to that type of international attention, *iNgwenyama* **Mswati Dlamini III** repealed the 60-day detention law in 1993.

PRIVATE REVENUE CONCESSION (PRC, 1889). One of two concessions, the other being the **unallotted lands concession**, that were considered the most egregious, and the most consequential historically, of all those granted by *iNgwenyama* **Mbandzeni Dlamini** to foreigners. The two concessions are also the ones most often cited when the record of Mbandzeni's agent and advisor **Allister Miller** as the arch-betrayer of the *ingwenyama*'s trust is examined. The PRC, granted to **John R. Harington**, gave him the power to collect the private revenue of the *ingwenyama*, mainly from concessions, from which £12,000 was to be paid to the *ingwenyama* annually, the balance to be credited to Harington. The concession was good for as long as the commission was paid. The PRC document was witnessed by Miller at a time when Mbandzeni's capacities were diminished as he neared death. Harington later sold the concession to an agent of the **South African Republic (SAR)**, giving it one of the foundations on which it later based its claim to the right of governance over Swaziland.

The subsequent history of the *ingwenyama*'s income from the PRC was even less creditable to those officials involved. During the **Anglo-Boer War** (1899–1902) the funds were allowed by the SAR to accumulate in escrow, no commissions being paid to the Swazi queen regent, **Labotsibeni Mdluli**. Following Great **Britain**'s takeover in 1903, **Lord Milner**, governor of the **Transvaal**, expropriated those accrued commissions and further determined that the monarchy's revenue of £12,000 per annum was excessive. He cut it back to £1,000 annually, adding another £800 as a government allowance to the queen regent. The escrow amount owed to Labotsibeni, calculated to be as much as £85,000, was never seen by its legal beneficiaries again. Milner used some 30 percent of it to buy up certain concessions necessary for the running of the government. About £20,000 of it was placed by Milner in a Swazi Trust Fund (which supposedly replaced the cancelled private revenue concession trust), which was to be used primarily for Swazi education. The Swazi had no say in the matter. Even that trust fund proved to be a chimera: most of its resources were expended on government prophylactic measures against tick-borne cattle diseases, which were arguably intended to protect European-owned **cattle** as much as they were Swazi herds.

PROTECTED STATE AGREEMENT (1967). An agreement signed between Great **Britain** and Swaziland making the kingdom a protected state rather than an administered territory as it had been since 1903. It was on that occasion that *iNgwenyama* **Sobhuza Dlamini II** was allowed to assume the title of "king." The agreement was signed at **Lobamba**, the royal capital, in April following the implementation of the pre-independence **constitution** and the parliamentary elections. Finally, the agreement provided that Swaziland would become independent no later than December 31, 1969.

PROTOCOL OF 1898. A protocol significantly amending article II of the **third Swaziland Convention** (1894) between Great **Britain** and the **South African Republic (SAR)**, having the effect of depriving the Swazi monarchy and chiefs of their criminal jurisdiction. That constituted a major step toward the loss of Swaziland's independence. The pretext for the change, which the SAR had sought since its assumption of administrative responsibility over the kingdom in 1895, was a political execution at the hands of *iNgwenyama* **Bhunu Dlamini** in April 1898. The victim was the nation's prime minister (*indvunankhuluyesive*), **Mbhabha Nsibandze**, whose loyalties lay with *iNdlovukazi* **Labotsibeni Mdluli**, who was contesting Bhunu for power. Bhunu was charged, tried, fined for "permitting public violence" and then reinstated as **paramount chief**.

Then the SAR, under the terms of the 1898 protocol, placed the jurisdiction for all cases of serious crime under the landdrost's (magistrate's) court, with appeals to the high court of Swaziland. "Serious crimes" were defined as murder, manslaughter, rape, kidnapping, forgery, perjury, arson, and **witchcraft**. Only cases involving lesser crimes and civil matters were left to the paramount chief's and chiefs' courts. Britain, when it assumed the colonial administration of Swaziland in 1903, reimposed those provisions under its **Swaziland Administration Proclamation (3/ 1904)**. They were partly restored to the monarchy in 1950 (**Native Courts Proclamation**) and fully restored at independence.

Ironically, a provision of the 1898 protocol little noticed at the time had a profound impact on the restoration of *iNgwenyama* **Sobhuza Dlamini II**'s political fortunes some 30 years later. During the mid-1930s the administration sought to strengthen Sobhuza's domestic powers sufficient to make its new emphasis on "**indirect rule**" effective. It found itself unable to do so because of the *ingwenyama*'s lack of criminal jurisdiction, which meant that all too often his decrees went unheeded by the chiefs. In 1936 **Resident Commissioner Allan Marwick** dusted off a provision of the 1898 protocol criminalizing "resisting the authority of the paramount chief." He then saw to its use to prosecute and fine in colonial courts a number of chiefs who had ignored Sobhuza's decisions in a series of boundary disputes. Following those prosecutions (1937) Sobhuza's domestic hand was significantly strengthened.

PROVISIONAL GOVERNMENT COMMITTEE (1889–1890). A triumvirate committee that constituted the civil government of Swaziland (as distinct from the Swazi monarchy) beginning in 1889. The committee was composed of representatives from the Swazi nation (**Theophilus Shepstone, Jr.**), the **South African Republic** (SAR; **Daniel J. Esselen**), and Great **Britain** (**Col. Richard E. R. Martin**). It was formed on the recommendation of the **Anglo-Boer Joint Commission** of 1889 that the three **Swazieland Committees**, composed entirely of Europeans in order to administer the whites, had failed of their purpose. The Provisional Government Committee lasted from December 1889 until September 1890, when it was succeeded, in accordance with the terms of the **first Swaziland Convention** (1890), by the **Swaziland Government Committee** (1890–1895).

The Provisional Government Committee constituted a distinct improvement over the successive Swazieland Committees insofar as it institutionalized the overseeing by British and SAR officials of the generally self-serving dealings of Shepstone and the white concessionaires who had formed the membership of those committees.

-Q-

QUEEN'S COMMISSIONER. *See* HER MAJESTY'S COMMISSIONER

-R-

RAINMAKING. Part of the Swazi monarchy's claim to legitimacy since the 18th century and continuing to this day lies in its assertion of influence over certain important natural and supernatural phenomena. Not the least of those powers is rainmaking. Swazi rulers (male and female) claim exclusive possession of medicines that produce rain. For instance, during the final day of the *iNcwala* celebration it is supposed to rain, and it frequently does. It was not unknown for European farmers to have approached the *ingwenyama* in the past during prolonged droughts to request that he make rain. Part of the motivation for *iNgwenyama* **Sobhuza Dlamini I**'s conquering of certain clans (especially the Mnisi and the Magagula) on his early 1820s northern campaign was to capture certain potent rain medicines. It was said that Sobhuza ordered **Mnjoli Magagula**'s body slit open to retrieve missing rainmaking charms.

The most renowned of all Swazi royal rainmakers was Queen Regent **Labotsibeni Mdluli**, who was recognized throughout southern Africa for her special powers. Such was the power that she derived from her reputation that she refused (unconstitutionally) to give up certain rain medicines to *iNdlovukazi* **Lomawa Ndwandwe** until long after she was required to do so. Indeed some of them she kept until her death in 1925 as a sort of life insurance policy against her enemies. Lomawa by contrast was not renowned for her rainmaking powers.

The most effective rainmaking is performed by the *ingwenyama* and the *indlovukazi* secluded in concert, but they also work separately at times. Heavy rain and rainstorms are known as the *ingwenyama*'s rain (sometimes **Dlamini** rain), while light rain and mists are known as the *indlovukazi*'s (or sometimes Magagula) rain. The nature of the rain medicines is secret, but among them are a wand and a belt anointed with blood (wielded and worn by the *indlovukazi*, to be touched by no one else);

consecrated river water from the **Usutu**; a fetal calf with improperly formed bones, taken from the stomach of a slaughtered cow and wrapped in *inkondlwana* (a soft grass used to wrap ritual objects); and (most precious of all) a rain stone, which is kept secluded at the *indlovukazi*'s capital. The employment of these takes place in the *indlunkulu* (great hut), frequently but not always at night.

The ultimate power to bring and withhold rain lies with the *ingwenyama*, and he does not relinquish that power upon his death. **Hilda Kuper** (Papers, UCLA: S-XI, 6/12/35) notes that Sobhuza claimed his knowledge of rainmaking to have been received from the spirits of past *tingwenyama* and said that occasionally word from one of them (obtained through his intercession) was sufficient to produce rain without any other elaborate preparation. Conversely, **Mnt. Masumphe Dlamini** asserted in 1927 (RCS 662/27, SNA) that "no one can keep off [withhold] rain except the spirit of a deceased Paramount Chief [*ingwenyama*]. I am the son of a Paramount Chief but if I died I would have no power to keep off rain. It must be a Paramount Chief."

RALEIGH FITKIN MEMORIAL HOSPITAL. *See* HYND, DR. DAVID; NAZARENE CHURCH

RAND MONETARY AREA. *See* COMMON MONETARY AREA

RATHBONE, THOMAS B. (1842–?). Concessionaire who was deeply involved in royal politics during the eras of *tiNgwenyama* **Mbandzeni** and **Bhunu Dlamini**. Rathbone, fluent in **siSwati**, established a general store near the royal **homestead** at **Ludzidzini** and became close friends with the young Mbandzeni. He advised the *ingwenyama* in 1885 on the occasion of **Johannes Krogh**'s reputed attempt to have Swaziland declared a protectorate of the **South African Republic**. Rathbone, as the agent of the Durban-based Havelock Swaziland Prospecting Syndicate in 1886, obtained the concession that later formed the basis of the **Havelock Asbestos Mine** holdings. Rathbone became a friend and ally of **Theophilus Shepstone, Jr.**, and along with him obtained many **concessions** through his relationship of trust with the *ingwenyama*. Rathbone also weighed in on the side of Shepstone in his factional disputes with **John Thorburn**, at least until 1888 when Shepstone fell out of favor, at which point Rathbone switched sides. As a member of the **Swazieland Committee** Rathbone helped to oust Shepstone as Mbandzeni's advisor in 1889. Later Rathbone became a close friend and advisor to *iNgwenyama* Bhunu and took up residence at **Zombodze**. Unlike so many other concessionaires, Rathbone, in spite of his baneful influence on Swaziland's sovereignty, seems to have amassed little personal wealth from all of his dealings.

RAUCHER, JOSEPH (1851–1932). Hungarian photographer whose pictures of Swaziland (1887–1906) constitute a most important historical archive. Raucher first established himself in Steynsdorp (**Transvaal**) but by 1897 had established a shop and portrait studio in Bremersdorp (**Manzini**). Raucher's photographs of people at **Mbekelweni** beginning in 1887 are among his most valuable, along with the photographs he took in Bremersdorp at the time of *iNgwenyama* **Bhunu Dlamini**'s trial in 1898. Raucher was also a practicing paramedic, although he had no formal training, and was a member of the Bremersdorp hospital and health committees. Raucher fought on the Afrikaner side during the **Anglo-Boer War** (1899–1902), and as a consequence his wife was placed in a British concentration camp, where she died. Two small daughters, however, survived. There is a large collection of Raucher photographs housed in the Swaziland National Archives at **Lobamba**. They include two albums of photographs presented to the archives by one of his surviving daughters in 1971.

RECONSTITUTED EUROPEAN ADVISORY COUNCIL (REAC). An officially constituted European advisory and lobbying body that superseded the **European Advisory Council (EAC)**, which had existed since 1921. The EAC, comprising principally settler farmers, had grown increasingly disquieted since the early 1940s about the growing strength and influence of the *ingwenyama* and *libandla*. Consequently it had pressured the government to transform its status from an advisory to a legislative body, which the administration was continuously unwilling to do. Secondarily, with the advent of post–World War II capital investment in Swaziland, as the character of the settler population gradually transformed itself into a more cosmopolitan and entrepreneurial one, its impatience with the makeup and the agenda of the EAC grew. That tended to exacerbate the historical split in the EAC between representatives from north (British, urban, modern farming methods) and south (Afrikaner, rural, backward farming methods) of the **Usutu River**.

In response the government established the REAC by proclamation in 1949. The proclamation increased membership from 8 to 10, chosen by Europeans throughout Swaziland. In addition the government was represented by 7 non-voting officials. To the Europeans' consternation the REAC remained purely advisory and was limited in its activities to exclusively European interests. Like its predecessor the REAC had a standing committee to liaise with the government when it was not in session (meetings were held twice a year). In the event the REAC did not limit itself to purely European affairs but opined vigorously on a variety of subjects affecting Swazi affairs, including politics. On occasion it launched vehement attacks against the administration's policies when it considered them excessively pro-Swazi.

Like the EAC the REAC was very conservative and often reflected its membership's economic and ethnic ties with **South Africa**. It was chaired for many years by **Carl Todd**, a South African–born attorney, and it reflected his strong opposition to the one-man, one-vote principle put forward by the government for the pre-independence constitution. When in 1960 the REAC proposed the establishment of a multiracial **Legislative Council** its idea centered on a membership equally divided ("50–50") between Europeans, elected under its auspices, and Swazi nominated by the equally conservative *libandla*. That was rejected by the British government as preempting the formation of new political parties. With its ideas vetoed the REAC moved into politics, its membership forming the core of the **United Swaziland Association (USA)** in 1963. The USA contested the 1964 Legislative Council (**Legco**) elections in a coalition with the Swazi traditionalists' **Imbokodvo National Movement (INM)**. The REAC was superseded by the Legco in 1964.

REED DANCE. *See UMCWASHO*

REGIMENT. *See LIBUTFO*

REILLY, JAMES W. (1879–1954). Commonly referred to as "Mickey." Settler businessman and politician in colonial Swaziland. Reilly was for many years the operator of McReedy Tins Ltd., which worked the rich **tin** ore seams under the hills along the western edge of the **Ezulwini Valley**. Reilly oversaw the cheap removal of the earth overburden of the seams with high-pressure water hoses. The procedure was highly destructive of the ecology of the area; the scars persist to this day in the **Mlilwane Game Sanctuary**. Mining also polluted the **Lusushwana River** so seriously that Reilly was convicted in colonial court of river pollution in 1946 and paid a fine. Reilly also established the first electric generating company, which supplied electricity to the town of **Mbabane**. He served as a member of the **European Advisory Council** from 1935 until his death in 1954. Reilly was the father of **Terence Reilly**, the noted conservationist and member of the Swaziland Trust Commission.

REILLY, TERENCE E. Swazi conservationist and game warden. *See* Mkhaya Nature Reserve

"REINDEER REFERENDUM" (1964). A national referendum initiated by *iNgwenyama* **Sobhuza Dlamini II** and administered by the *libandla* in January 1964, which demonstrated overwhelming Swazi support for the *ingwenyama*'s point of view on the shape of the pre-independence constitution. In May 1963 the British government had imposed a "White Paper" constitution embodying a **Legislative Council** to be elected in mid-1964 on the basis of one-man, one-vote. Sobhuza, the *libandla*, and the (European) **United Swaziland Association** had argued to no avail for an equal "50–50" (European-Swazi) constituency. In November 1963 Sobhuza had unsuccessfully petitioned parliament to reverse the British government's position on the constitution.

It was then that **Resident Commissioner Sir Brian Marwick** questioned whether Sobhuza's petition spoke for the Swazi people or simply the *ingwenyama* and *libandla*. To answer Marwick's challenge Sobhuza called (over Marwick's opposition) for a referendum on the constitution. Sobhuza, in total control of the details and knowing that more than 75 percent of the population was illiterate, used symbolism to his own political advantage. To the question "Do you agree with the *iNgwenyama*'s petition?" voters chose one of two images. The lion indicated "yes"; the reindeer (totally alien to the Swazi experience) signified "no." When the returns were counted only 154 out of more than 122,000 Swazi votes went against Sobhuza's position. Symbolism was not the entire story, for only 8 out of 1,408 Europeans went against the *ingwenyama* as well. That in part reflected the strong support of Sobhuza's position by the **Reconstituted European Advisory Council** led by **Carl Todd**.

The referendum had important long-term consequences. The overwhelming nature of the results encouraged Sobhuza and the *libandla* to form a royalist political party (again in the face of strong opposition by Marwick and other officials) to contest the upcoming Legislative Council elections. The party they formed, the **Imbokodvo National Movement**, in concert with the Europeans' United Swaziland Association, went on to sweep those elections.

RESIDENT COMMISSIONER. The title of the principal British colonial administrative official in Swaziland. The title of resident commissioner superseded the office of special commissioner (1902–5) by virtue of the transfer of authority over Swaziland from the governor of the

Transvaal (once it returned to self-government) to the British **high commissioner** in Pretoria. Thereafter the resident commissioner reported to the high commissioner, and via him to the Colonial Office (1905–26), later the Dominions Office (1926–47), and still later the Commonwealth Relations Office (1947–68). The first resident commissioner was **Francis Enraght Moony** (1905), who had previously served as special commissioner (1902–5). The last resident commissioner was **Sir Brian Marwick** (1957–63; **Her Majesty's Commissioner for Swaziland**, 1963–64). The most consequential of all resident commissioners in terms of establishing policies setting the tone of relationships with the Swazi monarchy were **Robert Coryndon** (1907–16), **T. Ainsworth Dickson** (1928–35), **Allan G. Marwick** (1935–37), and **Sir Brian Marwick** (1957–64). The office of resident commissioner was superseded by terms of the pre-independence **constitution** (1964) with the title of Her Majesty's Commissioner for Swaziland. The Queen's Commissioner reported directly to the Commonwealth Relations Office, bypassing the high commissioner.

RETURNED SOLDIERS' SETTLEMENT SCHEME. A British government–sponsored scheme to subsidize the settlement of World War I veterans in the colonies as yeoman farmers, while at the same time helping to solve **Britain**'s postwar unemployment problem. In the case of Swaziland, soldiers were offered free passage and subsidized land (one-third of the market price), along with free agricultural training and low-interest loans to purchase and improve the land. Dozens of veterans settled in Swaziland, and some of them became successful farmers and cattlemen. Most prominent among them was **George Wallis**, who also served many years as a powerful member of the **European Advisory Council**. *See also* Mushroom Land Settlement Scheme

RITUAL MURDER. The practice of murdering victims for the purpose of obtaining medicines (*imitsi*) to strengthen and/or bring good fortune to the murderer. Ritual murders are sometimes (although very rarely) prescribed by *tinyanga* (*see* **inyanga**) in order to cure an illness or reverse bad fortune believed to have been caused by an evildoer (*umtsakatsi*). Ritual murder is a capital crime and is resorted to only on rare occasions. Instances proliferate, however, during periods of societal stress associated with ecological disasters (for the peasantry), political crisis (for chiefs or modern civil servants), or economic reverses (for entrepreneurs). Victims (referred to by their murderers as "bucks" [*tinyamatane*] as a means of assuaging self-guilt by depersonalizing them) are invariably from society's defenseless, the very young or very old. Medicines are strongest when excised from still-living victims. Eyes, internal organs, and genitals are said to make particularly powerful medicines.

During the 1930s and 1940s a number of those convicted were chiefs who perceived their influence with *iNgwenyama* **Sobhuza Dlamini II** on the wane as his own domestic authority revived. During the 1960s, 1970s, and 1980s those found guilty had often sought to increase the fertility of their fields, reverse fortunes in love, or ensure the success of new business undertakings. In 1974 Sobhuza felt the need to call a special meeting of the nation at **Lobamba** to denounce the epidemic of ritual murders.

ROAD MOTOR SERVICES. *See* SOUTH AFRICAN RAILWAYS AND HARBOURS ROAD MOTOR SERVICES

ROCK PAINTINGS. Paintings made by late Stone Age San (commonly but incorrectly known as Bushmen) on the sides or overhangs of caves, in at least 20 sites in Swaziland. Generally they depict animals, hunting and dancing scenes, and occasionally battles. They have been dated from between 20,000 to 10,000 years B.C. More than half the sites are within a 15 mile (24 kilometer) radius of **Mbabane**. There are archeological traces (including evidence of fires) of Middle Stone Age San occupying caves or overhangs in Swaziland 60,000 to 80,000 years B.C. Iron workings at **Ngwenya**, among the oldest known in the world, have been carbon-dated to 31,000 B.C. A few San still occupied Swaziland when the **Ngwane** moved across the **Lebombo** plateau to settle in Swaziland during the middle 18th century. The exact locations of the paintings are not published in an effort to preserve them. Generally speaking their locations are as follows. The best preserved are in the **Komati River** valley near the Nsangwini royal residence, but others are at Malutha, Ekuthandeni, Nkaba, and Ntungula; near Gege and near **Lobamba**; and along the banks of the Mpetsane River. One not necessarily of San origin is high on the **Lebombo** escarpment overlooking the **Hlane Royal National Park**.

ROMAN CATHOLIC CHURCH. One of the larger Christian denominations in Swaziland. There have been no demographic enumerations relating to religion since the 1956 census. A 1962 survey showed 7,630 Swazi and **EurAfrican** Roman Catholics, constituting 5.3 percent of the Christian population. A rough extrapolation suggests that there were as many as 19,000 communicants by the mid-1990s. Roman Catholic missionaries first arrived in 1914, an extension of the Natal Vicariate. The

Order of Servites of Mary purchased a plot in **Mbabane** on which they established the Mater Delarosa mission and school. Another mission, incorporating a school for deaf children, was established at St. Joseph's, 9 miles (15 kilometers) east of Bremersdorp (**Manzini**). Other missions, schools, and clinics were later established throughout Swaziland. In 1922 the mission was established as a separate prefecture under Fr. Pelligrino Bellezze. The Roman Catholic mission incurred the enmity of other Christian denominations because of its willingness to accommodate certain Swazi beliefs and traditional practices. They included *lilobolo*, the *iNcwala* **ceremony**, and the drinking of *tjwala* (traditional beer) in moderation. They did not include polygyny. The first Swazi Catholic bishop was Mandla Zwane (d. 1980). *iNdlovukazi* and Queen Regent **Dzeliwe Shongwe** was a Roman Catholic communicant.

ROYAL SWAZI NATIONAL AIRWAYS CORPORATION. The Swazi national airline, which began operations in 1978. It is primarily a passenger carrier. Until the mid-1990s the airline operated a single aircraft, a Fokker F-100 Fellowship turbojet, occasionally leasing other airliners when conditions warranted. In 1995 it purchased a second F-100, but then under both intense financial pressure and popular opposition it transferred it to Air Mozambique on a long-term lease basis. In 1999 *iNgwenyama* **Mswati Dlamini II** sought public funds (E195 million) for the retrieval from Air Mozambique of the second F-100 for his personal use.

Royal Swazi regularly flies to and from Johannesburg, and at varying times it has provided regular service to Gaborone, Maputo, Nairobi, Lusaka, and the Seychelles. Royal Swazi is wholly owned by the **Tibiyo takaNgwane Fund**. It has been from its inauguration a consistent and often massive money-loser, without question the largest single drain on Tibiyo's books and the beneficiary of periodic infusions of public funds. In 1998 efforts were being made by Tibiyo to merge Royal Swazi's operations with a consortium of South African commercial air carriers, led by South African Airways and including SA Express and Airlink.

ROYAL SWAZI POLICE FORCE. The first police force in Swaziland was established by the **Swaziland Government Committee** in 1890. It was composed of 12 European officers and 36 African constables, all from South Africa. The force was disbanded at the outbreak of the **Anglo-Boer War** in 1899. Following the war and the placement of Swaziland under the governor of the **Transvaal** a force of white officers and Zulu constables from the South African constabulary was deployed to Swaziland. They formed the basis of the colonial police for many years thereafter. Because the Zulu, historic enemies of the Swazi, were mistrusted and resented, and because the monarchy was forced to call on them as government constables to enforce its decisions, *iNgwenyama* **Sobhuza Dlamini II** developed a deeply ambivalent attitude toward them. That continued even after they came under his command in 1968 (renamed the Royal Swazi Police Force in 1969) and long after the last Zulu had been replaced by Swazi. That mistrust was a principal factor in the *ingwenyama*'s formation of the **Royal Umbutfo Defense Force** in 1973.

ROYAL UMBUTFO DEFENSE FORCE. Beginning in 1926 *iNgwenyama* **Sobhuza Dlamini II** based much of his claim to legitimacy on tradition. A principal element of that was his constant invocation of past glories bestowed on the Swazi through the military exploits of the royal *emabutfo*. When the Swazi contingent of the **African Pioneer Corps** fought in World War II, Sobhuza celebrated their departure and return with great ceremony reminiscent of former kings dispatching their *emabutfo* on glorious campaigns. He also formed a new *libutfo*, again with great ceremony, as each new generation came of age. The last one was formed in 1968 and named *Gcina* ("End [of an Era]"). Sobhuza's mistrust of the police had been heightened in 1963 when they had been unable to contain the countrywide labor unrest, necessitating Swaziland's occupation by British troops from abroad.

It was natural then that as he moved the nation toward the constitutional crisis of 1973, Sobhuza should look to the *emabutfo* as a source of loyal and reliable support. When he established the Royal Umbutfo Defense Force that year, its core came from the *Gcina libutfo*, and he exhorted it to emulate past glories in all of its actions. The defense force was equipped by the government of **South Africa**. Its main purpose was signified in its title: *umbutfo* was the term for the cohort of permanent warriors based in the royal villages throughout the kingdom to defend the monarchy and keep the peace. Since 1973 the defense force has been used exclusively in domestic shows of force and population control.

ROZWADOWSKI, VICEK (VINCENT) J. (d. 1970s). Emigrant from South Africa who made contributions to Swazi education and opposition politics during the 1960s. Rozwadowski, born in Poland, fought in the French underground during World War II before emigrating to **South Africa**, where he took up ranching. Rather than live under apartheid Rozwadowski moved his family to Swaziland during the 1950s and became a dairy farmer near **Mbabane**. In 1961 Rozwadowski, along with

Simon Sishayi Nxumalo founded the **Swaziland Sebenta Society** (SSS). Rozwadowski became its president. The SSS was a multiracial organization dedicated to the development of adult literacy and education, and (later) community development. In early 1962, as Swaziland moved toward establishment of a multiracial **Legislative Council**, Rozwadowski and Nxumalo became active in opposition politics. Joining with Jordan Ngubane, another South African exile (and former official of the **African National Congress**), they established the **Swaziland Democratic Party (SDP)**. Its platform was meant to be more moderate than that of the **Swaziland Progressive Party (SPP)** yet to the left of the European settler-Swazi traditionalist alliance's proposals. The SDP stood for a constitutional monarchy, a multiracial democracy based on a qualified (later universal) franchise, and an array of social welfare programs designed to improve overall living conditions. Nxumalo became president and served in that position until late 1963, when he was replaced by **Dr. Allen Nxumalo**, and Rozwadowski was named secretary general.

Rozwadowski's political career did not last much beyond the 1964 **Legislative Council** elections, when the SDP won no seats and he himself was badly beaten by **Robert P. Stephens** of the **United Swaziland Association**. Shortly afterwards the SDP disintegrated: Nxumalo beat a hasty retreat (October 1964) into the *ingwenyama*'s **Imbokodvo National Movement**, while Rozwadowski was drummed out of the party for having written an unauthorized letter to the commonwealth secretary in London. Rozwadowski retired from politics and established what became a very successful estate agency (VJR Agencies). Rozwadowski later claimed that his establishment of the SDP had been motivated by two things: his fear that under a traditionalist-settler alliance Swaziland would end up as another South African bantustan and his apprehension that the SPP would fall under the sway of the communists.

RURAL DEVELOPMENT AREA (RDA) PROGRAM. A Swaziland government program intended to improve the deteriorating condition of the Swazi peasantry on the 56 percent of the land designated as **Swazi Nation Land (SNL)**. (The remaining 44 percent is designated **title deed land**). The basis for SNL was the 32 **native areas**, then constituting 33 percent of the land, established under the **Partition Proclamation of 1907**. The native areas delineated by the British were made deliberately small and agriculturally marginal so that the Swazi occupants would be forced to labor for wages in order to provide for themselves. By the time of independence in 1968 much of the SNL had grown so eroded by overpopulation and overgrazing that its productivity was collapsing. Compounding the problem was that the rapid post–World War II capital development of Swaziland was luring the peasantry away from the rural areas to jobs in the industrial areas.

As a consequence the goals of the RDA program, launched in 1970, were to improve the agricultural and livestock productivity of SNL and concomitantly to retain the peasantry on the land by improving the quality of life there. Specifically it was hoped that maize production could be increased to the point of national self-sufficiency by 1983. It was envisioned that that would be accomplished while at the same time the protection of natural resources on SNL would be enhanced. Two methods were prescribed. One was to encourage scientific farming by destocking; the utilization of improved seeds, fertilizers, and insecticides; and the employment of tractors and related machinery. The other was to increase the number of Swazi **homesteads** on SNL engaged in commodity (principally **cotton** and tobacco) production. It was hoped to have 60 percent of SNL area devoted to RDA production by the mid-1980s. Creation of improved marketing, communications, and social services would follow. Initial funding was primarily from British, American, European Community, and World Bank resources.

The accomplishments of the RDA program were extremely modest. Maize production declined, falling at a rate of more than 5 percent a year, so that by the mid-1980s Swaziland was importing 35 percent of its grains consumed, rather than the 22 percent of the early 1970s. **Cattle** numbers, instead of declining, increased by 9 percent during the same period. Environmental deterioration continued in most areas. On the other hand cotton production by SNL smallholders increased dramatically, as did—modestly—vegetable production. The RDA program was terminated in 1986.

-S-

SAMKETI, KINGSWAY T. Swazi political opposition activist during the decade of the 1960s and early 1970s. Joining the **Swaziland Progressive Party (SPP)** in the early 1960s, Samketi was at first a supporter of its leader, **John J. Nquku.** Then in mid-1962 he joined a group of dissidents who first ousted Nquku but then failed to prevent the SPP from disintegrating. Samketi became president of one of the SPP factions for a number of months before resigning to join the **Ngwane National Liberatory Congress (NNLC)** under **Dr. Ambrose Zwane.** He became its vice-president and worked closely with Zwane for many years. In 1967 they gained publicity but no official acceptance when they staged a "lie-in" across the steps of Marlborough House in protest to their exclusion from the second constitutional conference in London. Samketi lost his bid for a seat in **parliament** in the 1967 elections, although coming closer than any other opposition candidate. In mid-1971, Samketi led the move to oust Zwane from the NNLC party leadership and, failing that, created his own faction, the NNLC (Samketi). It proved to be Samketi's political undoing: his candidates were overwhelmingly defeated in the 1972 parliamentary elections, while Zwane's NNLC won three seats in the Mphumalanga constituency. Following the 1972 elections Samketi retired to farming in **Vuvulane**.

SAN. *See* ROCK PAINTINGS

SANDYS, DUNCAN. British secretary of state for commonwealth relations and colonial affairs from 1960 to 1964, a period of primary importance in the constitutional history of Swaziland. When in early 1963 the second London **constitutional conference** stalemated between traditionalist and opposition politicians over the composition of the **Legislative Council**, Sandys stepped in to impose his own solution. That constitution ("White Paper," May 1963) satisfied no one, least of all *iNgwenyama* **Sobhuza Dlamini II**. To the disappointment of the traditionalists and the settlers, it vested some power in opposition parties. Conversely, to the disappointment of the opposition politicians, it guaranteed a preponderance of power to the traditionalists. Finally, to the disappointment of the *ingwenyama*, it vested executive power in the **Queen's Commissioner** and control of minerals in the Legislative Council. Against the entreaties of all to alter his constitution, Sandys never budged; the document was promulgated in January 1964 and was the basis on which the Legislative Council elections were contested in mid-1964.

SANGOMA (pl. *tangoma*). The most powerful (and most respected and often feared) ritual practitioner in Swaziland. *Tangoma*, who are more often women than men, divine the causes of illnesses or misfortunes by drawing on their unique ties with the occult world, especially their special communications with ancestral and other spirits. They also prescribe cures by supernatural means, expulsion or exorcism of evil spirits, rather than with physical medicines, as the *inyanga* does. *Tangoma* practice their craft utilizing a number of methods: throwing bones and noting their pattern, for instance, or a public séance to "smell out" evildoers (*batsakatsi*). The latter practice is outlawed under **witchcraft** ordinances because it has often led to murder. *Tangoma* claim legitimacy by virtue of family affinity to other *tangoma*, or by experiencing spirit possession.

During the colonial era the British administration outlawed all divining by *tangoma* (and most practices of *tinyanga* as well), under terms of the "witchcraft" proclamation of 1930. It did so for several reasons. First, *tangoma* were spiritual competitors with the missionary establishment, which by 1930 was enjoying increasing political influence. Second, *tangoma* were seen as an alternative locus of power by the administration, one that by claiming occult powers defied all temporal regulations. That proclamation (5/1930) did little to stop the practice of divining by *tangoma*.

inSANGU. *See INSANGU*

SCUTT, JOAN. Missionary, teacher, and author. Scutt arrived in Swaziland in 1937 as a missionary with the South Africa General Mission. She was attached first to the Bethany mission, then (1939–48) to the school at the Mbuluzi mission. She later taught and wrote at the Mseleni mission (1948–62), then at the school at the Ncabaneni mission. She was the author of 11 books, for both children and adults, most notably *The Story of Swaziland* (four editions, beginning 1966) and the autobiographical *Born a Rebel* (1987).

SEBENTA NATIONAL INSTITUTE (SNI). Formerly Swaziland Sebenta Society, founded by **Simon Nxumalo**, with the assistance of Nell Green and **Vincent Rozwadowski** in 1961. Nxumalo, who taught elementary school during the late 1950s, held the conviction that adult literacy contained a significant key to empowerment. His idea for the Sebenta scheme stemmed from the positive experience that his father, **Chief Mgcobeya Nxumalo**, had once had with a colonial literacy program while jailed by the British administration. Rozwadowski supplied the organizational experience and helped to secure funding. Nxumalo wrote and edited texts, and he kept his hand in running the society long after he had gone into politics and government service. The SNI now promotes both adult literacy and community development. It aims to enroll 100,000 adults continually over a five-year reading program. It is located and partially administered by the **Swaziland College of Technology** in **Mbabane**. Funding is from government, international, and private sources. The rate of illiteracy among Swazi adults remains above 60 percent.

SECOND SWAZILAND CONVENTION (NOVEMBER 1893). An agreement between **Britain** and the **South African Republic (SAR)** that provided for the SAR's sole takeover of the administration of Swaziland under certain conditions. Britain, which had ruled Swaziland jointly with the SAR and the Swazi monarchy since 1890 (**Swaziland Government Committee**), determined to withdraw from that arrangement as its strategic interests shifted northwards across the Limpopo River. The convention stipulated that the SAR obtain Swazi acquiescence to the new arrangement through direct negotiations and that its administration must stop short of incorporation. Swazi agreement was to be formalized in an "**organic proclamation**" signed by the queen regent, **Tibati Nkambule**, and her senior councillors. In the event Tibati adamantly refused to sign and instead in 1894 dispatched a **deputation** to persuade London to take her kingdom under its protection.

That, however, was not on Britain's agenda. It had already decided to use Swaziland, three successive prior guarantees to its independence notwithstanding, as a pawn in its negotiations with the SAR aimed at giving itself a free hand to the north beyond the Limpopo River. Furthermore the Colonial Office knew that Pretoria already possessed, through its purchase of the requisite **concessions**, the means to control Swaziland's political economy. Nevertheless, the second Swaziland Convention foundered over the Swazi refusal to sign the organic proclamation. As a consequence Great Britain signed the **third Swaziland Convention** in December 1894 dispensing with the queen regent's proclamation as a condition for the SAR's takeover. The **Transvaal** administration of Swaziland commenced in 1895 and lasted until the outbreak of the **Anglo-Boer War** in 1899. *See also* First Swaziland Convention

SEKHUKHUNE. *See* MAROTENG, SEKHUKHUNE I

SEKHUKHUNE'S STRONGHOLD, BATTLE OF (1879). On the request of Sir Evelyn Wood and Sir Garnet Wolseley, *iNgweyama* **Mbandzeni Dlamini** supplied an *imphi* of 8,000 men to fight the **Pedi** under **King Sekhukhune Maroteng** in November 1879. They attacked Sekhukhune's stronghold at dawn on the morning of November 28. A main column of several thousand Europeans and about the same number of Africans attacked from the front, while the Swazi plus less than a thousand Europeans attacked from the rear (actually, from high up the mountain). The Swazi *imphi* was under the command of **Mbovane Fakudze** and consisted of King Mbandzeni's *libutfo* plus several complementary regiments. Most of the battle was fought that day, with about

500 Swazi and 42 Europeans dead or wounded. Sekhukhune himself made his escape but was quickly hunted down and captured (December 2, 1879). As a reward for the aid of the Swazi, Sir Garnet Wolseley awarded Mbandzeni most of the captured **cattle** and promised that the independence of the Swazi would be assured forever.

SELBORNE, LORD (1859–1942). William Waldegrave Palmer, second earl of Selborne. Governor of the **Transvaal** and **high commissioner** for South Africa from 1905 to 1910, successor to **Lord Alfred Milner** (1897–1905). Selborne was ideologically suited to carry on with Milner's authoritarian policies *vis-à-vis* the Swazi monarchy and peasantry. His overarching plan for Swaziland was to complete its transformation into a productive settler territory preparatory to its incorporation into the future **Union of South Africa**. That meant paying particular attention to several details. First, the **concessions** granted during the reign of *iNgwenyama* **Mbandzeni Dlamini** must be legitimized and awarded to the settlers in such a manner as to place Swaziland in the hands of settler farmers without touching off a "native" rebellion. Second, the Swazi monarchy, which was resisting colonization far too spiritedly, had to be subdued.

By the time of Selborne's departure both those details had been more or less attended to. As for the concessions, Selborne drew up the **Partition Proclamation of 1907** in such a way that two-thirds of the most productive lands (far more than most Europeans had dared hope for) were transferred to the settlers and the crown while leaving the domains of the monarchy and the important chiefs relatively undisturbed. That delineation was deftly engineered by Selborne's agent, special commissioner **George Grey**, during 1908–9. Selborne also delayed implementation of the proclamation for five years (until 1914) in order to give the Swazi time to accommodate themselves to the idea of the expropriation before actually having to move. He also took measures to ensure that the practice of absentee farming ("kaffir farming," Selborne called it) would not impede the development of Swaziland's settler political economy as it had the Transvaal's.

On the question of the monarchy Selborne continued Milner's policy of hamstringing and humiliating the formidable queen regent, **Labotsibeni Mdluli**, and her councillors. His measures took many forms, a representative example of which was his handling of Labotsibeni's protest **deputation of 1907** to London. Labotsibeni hoped to obtain by that means the colonial secretary's reversals of the concessions proclamation, the high commissioner's expropriation of her private revenues, and his withdrawal of her criminal jurisdiction (**Swaziland Administration Proclamation 4/1907**). Selborne sought to orchestrate London's denial of her entreaties, which was a foregone conclusion, in such a way as to humiliate her in the eyes of her people. That would open the way for his deposition of her in favor of her young and more malleable grandson, the future *iNgwenyama* **Sobhuza Dlamini II**. In the event Selborne's plan backfired, for as a consequence of her pluck Labotsibeni's reputation with her people rose even though her petitions were denied, and she served in her office until 1921.

Selborne sought to carry out these authoritarian policies through an activist **resident commissioner** sympathetic to his views, **Robert Coryndon** (1907–16). Their policy of repression would not begin to be reversed until the commencement of **Resident Commissioner T. Ainsworth Dickson**'s term in 1928.

SELLSTROOM, AFFLECK (1909–c. 1985). A leading member of Swaziland's **EurAfrican** community. Son of a Swedish mariner and an **Nkhosi Dlamini** mother, he was educated at **Rev. Christopher Watts**'s St. Mark's School at Mpolonjeni. Sellstroom was active in the **EurAfrican Welfare Association (EWA)** and for many years served as its president. His letter to *The Times of Swaziland* (August 23, 1934) focused official attention on the plight of the EurAfrican and led to the building of St. Michael's School for EurAfricans in Bremersdorp (**Manzini**) in 1937. Sellstroom represented the EWA at the second **constitutional conference** in London (1963) and there associated the EWA with the **Constitutional Alliance of Swaziland Political Organizations**. Sellstroom was never able to make the EWA weigh significantly in any Swazi opposition party. Ultimately it collapsed as a political force, and Sellstroom became a member of the **Ngwane National Liberatory Congress**.

SEME, DR. PIXLEY kaI. (c. 1880–1951). A Zulu born at Inanda (American Zulu Mission) in Natal. Mission-educated, he obtained a bachelor's degree from Columbia University in New York City and studied law at Oxford. He practiced law in Johannesburg throughout his life. Seme was a co-founder of the **African National Congress (ANC)** and later served as its president (1930–36). He was awarded an honorary doctorate of laws degree from Columbia University in 1928.

Seme's ties with the Swazi royal house were deep and long-standing. One of his wives was a daughter of *iNgwenyama* **Mbandzeni Dlamini**. Seme also maintained a residence in **Mhlambanyatsi**. Beginning in about 1910 he began to serve as legal and political advisor to Queen

Regent **Labotsibeni Mdluli** and her son Prince Regent **Mnt. Malunge Dlamini**. Seme was introduced to them by Richard **Msimang** of the **Mahamba** Wesleyan mission, one of Labotsibeni's Mahamba-**Edendale** (Natal) advisors, a British-educated lawyer, and like Seme a co-founder of the ANC. Malunge and **Benjamin Nxumalo**, maternal uncle to *iNgwenyama* **Sobhuza Dlamini II**, both played influential roles in the early ANC, Malunge in the college of chiefs and Nxumalo as a co-drafter of the earliest ANC constitution (1919). When Seme founded the ANC newspaper *Abantu Batho* in 1912, he turned to Labotsibeni for financial support, and she became for a time a principal backer of the press. Sobhuza himself was a dues-paying member of the ANC until at least the late 1920s. Seme advised Labotsibeni on the need for the Swazi purchase of European-owned **concession** lands that came on the market and on ways to raise the necessary funds. Seme accompanied Sobhuza on his deputation to London in 1922 and later became the principal legal counsel in Sobhuza's lawsuit against **Allister Miller** (*Sobhuza II vs. Miller*), carrying it all the way to the Privy Council.

Seme's influence on the Swazi royal house, however, was distinctly mixed in its effects. It was he for instance who introduced both Labotsibeni and Sobhuza to the world of bank debit financing in order to purchase back the land and to initiate lawsuits. Labotsibeni eventually ran up liabilities totaling £48,000 to finance her real estate transactions. Sobhuza, who until 1926 imitated Seme in his "progressive" lifestyle, ran up countless debts with clothing, furniture, and other stores that he could not pay and ended up owing Seme £11,000 for the Miller case alone. Seme was charging Sobhuza an exorbitant £750 per annum retainer fee during those years, working on land issues and other matters for him into the early 1940s.

The problem was that both Sobhuza and Labotsibeni became politically hobbled by following Seme's financial schemes, and as a consequence each was forced to go hat in hand to the administration at the very times they were trying to defend the monarchy against it. Each also resorted to levying special taxes on the Swazi citizenry, in the process becoming visibly dependent on the administration's assistance for their collection, moves hardly calculated to enhance their popularity with their people at the very times when they desperately needed to enhance it.

SEPAMLA, FYNN F. (1888–1949). Arriving in Swaziland by bicycle in 1908, Sepamla became the first African clerk employed in the government secretariat (1909–49). Sepamla was also a founder (1929) and secretary of the **Swaziland Progressive Association** (1930–49). Sepamla had been born and educated in the Herschel district of South Africa. He was a prominent member of the emergent Swazi middle class and a frequent contributor of letters to the editor of *The Times of Swaziland* on the interests of the petit bourgeoisie.

SHABALALA, MNDENI. *iNdvuna ye tiNkhundla* (Officer of the *tiNkhundla*) from the 1970s to the early 1990s. Chief operating officer of the *tinkhundla* electoral system, Shabalala was charged with misappropriation of *tinkhundla* funds and with various other acts of corruption, especially with respect to the **Swaziland Railway**. In spite of his reputation for venality, Shabalala's political connections landed him a series of government positions during the decade of the 1990s, the last as a member of *iNgwenyama* **Mswati Dlamini III**'s **Constitutional Review Commission** (1996).

SHAKA. *See* ZULU, SHAKA kaSENZANGAKHONA

SHANGANE (GAZA) KINGDOM. Followers of Soshangane Ndwandwe (d. 1858), an ex-general under King **Zwide Ndwandwe** who broke off to the **Delagoa Bay** coast following Zwide's defeat by the Zulu (1819). Soshangane consolidated his chiefdom by defeating other coastal remnants of Zwide's former state. Soshangane called his kingdom Gazankulu (Gaza being his grandfather), but it and its inhabitants were more commonly referred to in the region as "Shangane." Soshangane's followers were mostly Tsonga, and all spoke the local dialect rather than his original **Nguni**. Soshangane's power was such that local Portuguese traders paid him tribute. Following his death the Shangane kingdom was beset by a succession struggle between two of his sons, **Mzila** and **Mawewe Ndwandwe**, in which *iNgwenyama* **Mswati Dlamini II** played a prominent role.

SHEPSTONE, THEOPHILUS, JR. (1843–1907). Known commonly as "Offy," the third son (of five) of Sir Theophilus Shepstone, secretary for native affairs in Natal. Shepstone was first a civil servant in Natal before becoming a lawyer and a member of the Natal legislative council. He served as a mounted officer during the Zulu war of 1879. Shepstone arrived in Swaziland in late 1886 and camped near the **Mbekelweni** headquarters of *iNgwenyama* **Mbandzeni Dlamini**, seeking **gold** prospecting **concessions** with an eye toward shoring up his shaky financial fortunes. In the process of obtaining his concessions Shepstone learned that Mbandzeni was seeking an advisor to assist him in dealing with the army of European prospectors arriving with hopes of striking gold.

Shepstone returned to Pietermaritzburg to wind up his affairs and then signed on as Mbandzeni's "resident adviser and agent" (February 1887). Shepstone immediately embarked on the dual tasks of consolidating his position against other scheming concessionaires and obtaining lucrative concessions for himself and his family. Unfortunately for Mbandzeni, his contract with Shepstone called for the latter to receive half of his revenues from concessions, giving Shepstone the incentive to grant as many as he could manage. Before he was through he managed a great many indeed, a number of them overlapping.

Shepstone the experienced politician determined that the way to consolidate his position and to turn away concessionaire criticism (he was by then hearing civil cases) was to form a governing committee to handle the affairs of the Europeans, which he could then control. The **Swazieland Committee**, which began sitting in August 1887, was easily managed by Shepstone through his manipulation of its pliable chairman, **James Forbes**. Meanwhile Shepstone's concessioning went on apace. By the end of 1887 he was charging concessionaires £20 each for beaconing their properties, and he had become involved with the government of the **South African Republic (SAR)**, which he knew to have designs on Swaziland as a potential railway route to the Indian Ocean. He first visited SAR President Paul Kruger in November 1887.

By that time **John Thorburn** had emerged as Shepstone's direct competitor for influence with Mbandzeni, the community of Europeans, and eventually the SAR. Thorburn owned the Embekelweni Hotel, which Mbandzeni took to frequenting, and it was probably from Thorburn that the *ingwenyama* learned the extent to which Shepstone was profiting from his position of trust. Mbandzeni's relations with Shepstone became increasingly strained, and by mid-1888 he had reduced the latter's status to secretary at a fixed annual salary of £600 per annum. By then the Europeans had divided into the Shepstone and Thorburn camps, and Shepstone's influence over a smaller, more focused and forcefully led (by **Allister Miller**) **Swazieland Committee** had been substantially reduced. By the end of 1888 Thorburn and his protégé Miller were in substantial control of the settler community through their domination of the Swazieland Committee. By early 1889 Mbandzeni had dismissed Shepstone as his secretary and replaced him with Miller, who thereupon commenced the pilfering of the *ingwenyama*'s remaining assets until his appointment expired at the end of July. None of that, however, prevented Shepstone from further intriguing both within Swaziland and beyond its borders.

Shepstone wrote letters to both the governor of Natal and President Kruger alleging such chaos at Mbekelweni and consequent danger to whites as to warrant their direct intervention. The result was the dispatching of ad hoc SAR and British commissioners to investigate affairs in Swaziland. In the meantime Mbandzeni had fallen deathly ill, and Shepstone had cultivated influence with the *indlovukazi*, **Tibati Nkambule**, to whom power was likely to accrue on his death. Indeed once Mbandzeni died (October 1889) Shepstone was quick to gain reappointment as advisor with all of his initial powers, and with great satisfaction he proceeded to assist Miller to the exits. Thus, when the **Anglo-Boer Joint Commission** arrived in November, Shepstone was in a position to reinforce his authority by getting himself appointed as the Swazi representative on the **Provisional Government Committee**, which was established on the commission's recommendation. He retained the same position on the permanent Government Committee, which was established in September 1890. This time he cashed in on his position, for he was able to obtain substantial commissions from the SAR for every concession granted or transferred to Pretoria that would enable it to govern Swaziland in the future. On the **private revenue concession** alone Shepstone received a £4,000 transfer fee plus £6,000 per year as an ongoing commissioner.

In that manner did Shepstone, who was in complete control of affairs from 1889 to early 1893, bargain away the future sovereignty of Swaziland in return for commissions and loans from the SAR. During that period the youthful *iNgwenyama* **Bhunu Dlamini** had not yet assumed his full authority; what real royal power there was lay with the *indlovukazi*, with whom Shepstone continued to enjoy considerable influence. By early 1893 Tibati had heard too many stories about his dealings with Pretoria not to believe some of them, and his influence dissipated. Shepstone stood to gain a handsome commission from the SAR for persuading her to sign the **organic proclamation** ratifying the **second Swaziland Convention** (1893) turning over the kingdom's administration to it, but he proved unable to do so. To the contrary, in August 1894 Shepstone was dismissed as secretary to the nation and replaced by a Natal lawyer, G. H. Hulett.

No European, not even Allister Miller, bore more responsibility for the selling out of the Swazi to both private and foreign interests in satisfaction of his own greed than did Shepstone. His unscrupulousness was breathtaking, matched only by his gall. In a final insult, when the Swazi laid claim against him in Pretoria (1896) for financial irregularities, he counterclaimed some £13,000 in unpaid fees and settled for £5,000.

SHISELWENI. Literally "The Place of Burning." The name of the region in southern Swaziland north of the Pongola River and west of the **Lebombo** range, into which the **Ngwane** took control and settled during the 1760s, during the reign of *iNgwenyama* **Ngwane Dlamini**. The Shiselweni region, superbly suited to the Ngwane mixed agricultural and pastoral way of life, was according to Philip Bonner a significant factor in the successful establishment of the early Swazi state.[2] It encompassed first the rich iNgwavuma River watershed for grain farming, and second both **lowveld** and **middleveld** environments, affording it year-round grazing potential. Finally, Shiselweni offered a relatively low danger of crippling drought; planting along the alluvial riverbanks offered insurance against famine. It was therefore indicative of the seriousness of *iNgwenyama* **Sobhuza Dlamini I**'s predicament that he decided to abandon the supportive environment of Shiselweni in order to escape the military danger posed by King **Zwide Ndwandwe**. Moving north with those relatively few followers still willing to cast their lot with him (the *Bemdzabuko*, "True Swazi"), Sobhuza finally settled in the **Ezulwini Valley**, where the environment and the fertile, well-watered alluvial soils were much like those of Shiselweni. It is Shiselweni, however, that has always been considered the birthplace of the Swazi nation.

SHONGWE, *iNDLOVUKAZI* **DZELIWE (c. 1925–).** Dzeliwe Shongwe was *iNgwenyama* **Sobhuza Dlamini II**'s last *indlovukazi* (1980–83) and the only one whose *sibongo* was other than **Ndwandwe**. She was the heroine of the anarchic interregnum following Sobhuza's sudden death in 1982. Largely untutored and unworldly, Dzeliwe summoned, in the face of the *Liqoqo*'s calculated assault on the monarchy, the character and fortitude to stand up to the conspirators at the crucial moment in 1983 when they attempted their *coup d'état*. Although she lost the standoff and was dismissed as *indlovukazi*, her exemplary courage emboldened others to confront the *Liqoqo* and ultimately prevail.

Dzeliwe was a devout Catholic who was preparing to be a nun when Sobhuza selected her as a queen. That background (all of Sobhuza's previous *tindlovukazi* had been Christians), along with the fact that she was childless, probably figured in her choice by Sobhuza to replace the late **Seneleleni Ndwandwe** as *indlovukazi*. Certainly the king, old and ill, also must have considered her strength of character and intelligence in the face of an uncertain future. Sobhuza's choice proved to be providential. In 1983 Dzeliwe, now widowed and as queen regent the senior royal official, strongly resisted the powerful and ambitious *Liqoqo* members in their attempt to rid themselves of the reformist prime minister, **Mnt. Mabandla Dlamini**, finally signing the dismissal order only when under threat of force. In August, however, when presented with a document placing her under the *Liqoqo*'s authority, she refused to sign it and instead dismissed them all. That order did not stand, for by then the *Liqoqo* had infiltrated too many of their allies into key positions. Dzeliwe was thereupon deposed, and in her place as both *indlovukazi* and regent was named **Ntombi Twala**, mother of the recently selected *iNkhosana* Makhosetive Dlamini (soon to be *iNgwenyama* **Mswati Dlamini III**).

Dzeliwe appealed these actions to the high court, but her argument (in the form of an affidavit presented by attorney **Douglas Lukhele**) that the *Liqoqo*'s actions were unconstitutional did not carry the day. Instead the high court bowed to the decree put forward by the "authorized person" and *Liqoqo* ally, Mnt. Sozisa Dlamini, that it had no jurisdiction over the dismissal of a queen regent, and it refused to proceed with the appeal. The *Liqoqo* thereupon removed Dzeliwe from the *indlovukazi*'s residence and ceremonial capital at **Lobamba**. Defiant to the end, Dzeliwe refused to return to her previous residence of **Masundwini** and instead chose the old capital of *iNdlovukazi* and Queen Regent **Labotsibeni Mdluli**. Also like Labotsibeni, Dzeliwe refused to relinquish certain powerful symbols of her office when she was taken from Lobamba. The symbolism was not lost on the Swazi citizenry. In their eyes Dzeliwe occupied a position of the highest esteem in the small pantheon of women instrumental in strengthening the monarchy in the past, notably Labotsibeni and *iNdlovukazi* **Tsandzile Ndwandwe**. *See also* Dlamini, *Mntfwanenkhosi* Mfanasibili

SIBACA. A colorful and graceful dance attributed to the Swazi but of no authentic ceremonial significance, commonly performed at non-traditional public occasions in Swaziland since the 1930s. Its origins trace to the South African gold mines where national groups of workers staged dance competitions on weekends. Such dances were encouraged by mining management as a tourist attraction and as a means to release ethnic and sexual tensions within the workforce, which was housed in single-sex hostels for long periods of time. Encouraged by *iNgwenyama* **Sobhuza Dlamini II**, who was once active in it himself, there is an annual competition between teams of distinctively dressed Sibaca dancers. The king himself is the judge.

SIBONGO. Clan (extended family) name. Plural: *tibongo*, clans; or praises, praise poetry. According to Thoko Ginindza the term derives from the verb *-bonga*: "to praise" or "to thank."[3] Every Swazi carries the *sibongo* of his or her father, and every woman is identified by her maiden *sibongo*. The *sibongo* is employed frequently in daily intercourse, used universally to show courtesy and respect. It is an element in every greeting and is frequently interjected into conversations by both speaker and listener. The *sibongo* is invoked at the commencement of a meal or beer drink, and a feast is the occasion for reciting and praising the *sibongo* of the host. When the *sibongo* of a stranger is not known, "*iNkhosi*" ("Sir/Madam") is used in its stead. Swazi who bear the same *sibongo* are regarded as related (i.e., descended from a common ancestor), and they do not intermarry.

In Swazi society *tibongo* are categorized in importance by three criteria: first, their historical order of incorporation into the state; second, their ethnic background (commonly **Nguni** or Sotho); and third, hierarchy on the basis of their practical or ritual roles in the monarchical system. As for order of incorporation and ethnic background, the ***Bemdzabuko*** ("True Swazi") include the **iNkhosi Dlamini** and related clans who made up the embryonic Swazi state in **Shiselweni**, among them the Fakudze, Hlope, Matsebula, Mhlanga, Tfwala, and Simelane (Nguni origins). The ***Emakhandza Mbili*** ("Those Found Ahead") included those clans that inhabited the regions north of Shiselweni into which *iNgwenyama* **Sobhuza Dlamini I** moved after 1819. Among them were the Bhembe, Gama, Gamedze, Gwebu, Magagula, Makhubu, Manana, and Motsa (Sotho in origin); and the Khumalo, Maseko, Mdlovu, Mncina, Shabalala, Shongwe, Tsabedze, and Zwane (Ntungwa-Nguni in origin). The ***Emafika Muva*** ("Latecomers") were mostly refugees from the wars accompanying the rise of **King Shaka Zulu**, incorporated during the reign of *iNgwenyama* **Mswati Dlamini II.** They included the **Ndwandwe** (and its subclans Mkhatjwa and Nxumalo) and the Mthethwa (Nguni in origin).

There is a recognized hierarchy of clans, although it has been blurred somewhat by time. At the pinnacle is the iNkhosi Dlamini, the lineage from which the *tingwenyama* (*sing.* **ingwenyama**) spring. Second in rank are the clans that have historically contributed the *tindlovukazi* (*sing.* *indlovukazi*; they are known as *ematala inkhosi*, "bearers of kings"): lineages of the Khumalo, Mdluli, Ndwandwe, Nkambule, and Simelane. Third in rank are those clans that for historical reasons have achieved a degree of independence: the Magagula, Mngometfulu, Mahlalela, and Mamba. Fourth in rank are those clans that were at one time exceedingly powerful and that have historically provided the *tindvuna* of royal villages: the Gwebu, Fakudze, Hlope, Nsibandze, and Zwane. Finally, there are clans that enjoy the status of having by tradition performed certain important practical and ritual functions for the monarchy. The Matsebula and the Motsa traditionally provide the *ingwenyama* with his initial queens. The Mdluli and the Motsa provide the senior *tinsila* to the *ingwenyama*, while the Matsebula and the Nkambule provide the junior *tinsila* (*sing. insila*). Lineages of the Gama, Mdluli, Nxumalo, and Simelane have traditionally guarded the royal gravesites. Aside from the iNkhosi Dlamini, the Magagula, Mngomentfulu, Mnisi, and Motsa have been historically renowned as rainmakers. Swaziland's most distinguished military generals have come from the Fakudze clan.

*in**SILA***. See *INSILA*

SIMELANE, *iNDLOVUKAZI* LOJIBA. Principal wife of *iNgwenyama* **Ndvungunye Dlamini**. Because Lojiba had no male issue, the son of her sister and *inhlanti* **Somnjalose Simelane**, **Mnt. Sobhuza Dlamini I**, was chosen to succeed Ndvungunye. After Sobhuza's installation Lojiba became *indlovukazi*, and following his relocation to central Swaziland he built the **Lobamba** royal village as her **homestead**. According to Huw Jones, because Somnjalose became queen regent upon Sobhuza's death in 1839, a title that constitutionally fell to the *indlovukazi*, Lojiba evidently preceded her husband in death.[4]

SIMELANE, *iNDLOVUKAZI* SOMNJALOSE (d. c. 1845). Younger sister and *inhlanti* to **Lojiba Simelane**, chief wife of *iNgwenyama* **Ndvungunye Dlamini**. Because Lojiba produced no son, Somnjalose bore the heir, *iNgwenyama* **Sobhuza Dlamini I**. It is likely that Somnjalose succeeded Lojiba as *indlovukazi*, undoubtedly because the latter died, perhaps fairly early in Sobhuza's reign. In any event Somnjalose was believed to have been the first *indlovukazi* to truly exercise the checks and balances powers of her office, reputedly in order to rein in the growing authoritarianism of Sobhuza. It was said that she had gained experience by using her influence in the *sigodlo* to restrain the excesses of **Ndvungunye**, who was reputed to be cruel. Once Sobhuza moved northward from **Shiselweni** (1819), Somnjalose occupied the **Ezulwini** royal **homestead**. When Sobhuza died in 1839 Somnjalose became queen regent, assisted by **Bnt. Malunge** and Mbukwane **Dlamini**, ruling during a turbulent interregnum riven by clan dissension until the investiture of *iNgwenyama* **Mswati Dlamini II** in 1840. At her death she bequeathed her newly powerful office to **Tsandzile Ndwandwe**, who proceeded to wield that authority with even greater effect.

SISWATI. *See* siSWATI

SITEKI. "The Place of Marriage." The administrative headquarters of the **Lubombo Administrative Region**, located at the western edge of the **Lebombo** escarpment overlooking the **lowveld** to the east, 40 miles (66 kilometers) west of **Manzini**, altitude approximately 2,050 feet (625 meters). Its 1986 population was 2,271 (estimated 1996 population 3,375). Siteki's colonial name was Stegi. The Good Shepherd Roman Catholic mission operates a hospital and schools (including a school for the handicapped) in Siteki.

SIVE SIYINGQABA. "The Nation Is a Fortress." The motto on the Swaziland national coat of arms. In 1996 *Sive Siyingqaba* became the title of a parapolitical "cultural group" (political parties being outlawed) espousing traditionalist political values. Its manifesto called for change, but not at the expense of the national heritage. To some observers the group recalled the royalist **Imbokodvo National Movement** of the pre-independence period. Others were reminded of the modern Zulu-based Inkatha Freedom Movement in **South Africa**, which by the 1980s had transformed itself into a militant and reactionary political party.

SMUTS, JOHANNES (1865–1937). British consular official who represented British interests in Swaziland during the period of the **South African Republic's** (SAR) administration (1895–1899). Smuts played a significant role in the summonsing and public trial of *iNgwenyama* **Bhunu Dlamini** following the murder of the prime minister and ally of *iNdlovukazi* **Labotsibeni Mdluli, Mbhabha Nsibandze**. Bhunu, who surmised (correctly) that the SAR sought to use his complicity as an excuse to dismiss him and reduce the power of his office, turned to Smuts and the British for assistance. Smuts used quiet diplomacy to work out a compromise that both kept Bhunu's office intact and satisfied the SAR authorities. Smuts departed from Swaziland on the eve of the **Anglo-Boer War** in October 1899, although he remained the principal British go-between with the queen regent, Labotsibeni Mdluli, for the duration of that conflict. Following the war Smuts was named president of the Concessions Commission (1904), whose task was to determine the value of existing **concessions** and recommend the amounts of land to be allocated to the settlers and the Swazi. Smuts also became registrar of deeds for Swaziland (1905) and served on the commission to delineate the boundary between eastern Swaziland and Portuguese Mozambique in 1907.

SOBHUZA II VS. MILLER (1924–1926). A landmark lawsuit undertaken by *iNgwenyama* **Sobhuza Dlamini II** for both legal and political purposes, the loss of which marked a major turning point in his career as king. Sobhuza had two things in mind in launching his suit. The first was to challenge the legitimacy of the **concessions** granted during the reign of his grandfather, *iNgwenyama* **Mbandzeni Dlamini**, in court, under British law, something that had never been done. The second was to revive the fortunes and popularity of his monarchy, under siege since Mbandzeni's time, by undertaking some dramatic and popular initiative. *Sobhuza II vs. Miller* fulfilled both purposes. The respondent, **Allister Miller**, was the owner of the farm Dalriach on the outskirts of **Mbabane**. Miller's acreage had originally been a portion of the **unallotted lands concession** owned by the **Swaziland Corporation**. The corporation, whose business was the exploitation of its previously acquired concessions, and in which Miller and **John Thorburn** were major shareholders, deeded a portion of Dalriach to him in 1921.

The Swazi, who had always contested the legitimacy of Mbandzeni's land concessions, and in particular the unallotted lands concession, which had been granted while Miller had been the king's advisor during his final days (July 1889), claimed that Dalriach was the domain of Chief Maloyi Kunene, son of **Chief Mbabane Kunene**. Consequently when Miller, who by 1924 was a hated man among the Swazi aristocracy, proceeded to expel many of Kunene's followers from Dalriach, often in an imperious manner, for refusal to perform farm labor, his actions were perceived by them as constituting a particularly egregious affront. Sobhuza's suit thus carried with it a powerful symbolism, but beyond that it was universally understood that the case constituted a challenge to the very basis of the settler-colonial state in Swaziland. It was primarily for that reason that the costs of Miller's defense were borne by the colonial administration.

Sobhuza's chief counsel was **Pixley kaI. Seme**, and the venue was the special court of Swaziland. Seme's main contention was that Mbandzeni had had no right under Swazi law to alienate any portion of his domains, but only their use, and that consequently all of his major concessions, including the one contested, had contained a proviso reserving the rights of his subjects. Miller's defense (presented by Albert Millin, a prominent Mbabane attorney) embraced two claims: that because Sobhuza was not a king but only a **paramount chief**, he enjoyed no sovereignty over the land; and that Miller had a perfect right under existing law to eject any tenant he wished for refusing to carry out his work obligation. The court's judgment, delivered in May 1924, found for Miller, mainly on the grounds that the **Partition Proclamation of 1907** was valid in law and had canceled any right Sobhuza might have had to the land in question.

Sobhuza thereupon appealed the verdict to the Privy Council and dispatched Seme to London to argue the case. The Privy Council rejected the appeal in April 1926. In May the **resident commissioner, de Symons Honey**, convened the *ingwenyama* and *libandla* at the courthouse in Mbabane to hear the judgment read in **siSwati** and to ask for comments. If Honey expected that the meeting would tidily end the chapter of the Miller case once and for all, he was mistaken. The comments of the assembled chiefs went on for three days, and the protest was capped by an extraordinary demonstration of young Sobhuza's leadership, acumen, and capacity for debate (RCS 90/23, SNA). Sobhuza engaged Honey in a dialogue worthy of Socrates. He defended Mbandzeni's concessions and laid the blame for Swaziland's predicament squarely on a succession of British perfidies stretching back to its guarantee of Swazi sovereignty in the aftermath of the joint campaign against the **Pedi** in 1879. In the process (the dialogue lasted an afternoon and the following morning in front of the assemblage) Sobhuza, apparently using no notes, repeatedly and devastatingly (but politely) demonstrated his superiority to Honey in both debating skills and command of the facts in his defense of Swazi tradition against Western machinations.

That day in May 1926 marked a major change in the direction of Sobhuza's life. Until then he had cast himself and shaped his royal career as an African "progressive," worldly in both style and substance. The Miller case had been an example of that: a lawsuit waged in the medium of Roman-Dutch law and in the colonial court system, argued by a lawyer educated in the United States and **Britain**. Its loss, which exacted a heavy psychological and financial toll on Sobhuza, also forced on him the realization of the need to abandon progressivism in favor of a return to his traditional roots as a mode of governance. His day-long Socratic humiliation of the resident commissioner was a dramatic indication of how decisive that change of directions was and an early indicator of how successful it was destined to be.

SOMHLOLO. "The Wonder." Popular name for *iNgwenyama* **Sobhuza Dlamini I**.

SOPHIATOWN. *See* SWAZI NATIONAL ROYAL CLUB

SOUTH AFRICA, GOVERNMENT OF (1994–). Swaziland's relationship with South Africa's Government of National Unity (1994–99) under President Nelson Mandela remained correct, but it was colored by the fact that Swaziland remained the only country in southern Africa in which political parties were banned. President Mandela became increasingly willing to use his own prestige and his country's membership in the **Southern African Development Community (SADC)** to pressure *iNgwenyama* **Mswati Dlamini III** to institute meaningful constitutional change. The general strike launched by the **Swaziland Federation of Trade Unions** in early 1997 on behalf of labor issues, and more broadly in favor of constitutional reform, was openly supported by the **African National Congress** and the Confederation of South African Trade Unions (Cosatu). Later that year Mandela, frustrated with the slow pace of change in the kingdom, advocated at a SADC meeting the imposition of sanctions against countries that refused to apply democratic values, a clear reference to Swaziland.

Meanwhile Swaziland's practical incorporation into South Africa's economic orbit continued apace, with both the Standard Chartered and Barclays Banks being taken over by major South African banks during 1995–97.

SOUTH AFRICA, REPUBLIC OF (RSA, 1962–1994). Swaziland's relationship with the Republic of South Africa during the heyday and decline of apartheid was dominated by several themes. The first was increasingly heavy South African capital investment in the kingdom. The second was the development of Swaziland as a theater of conflict between the South African security establishment and the revived forces of African nationalism after 1975. The third, stemming from the second, was the heightening of South African diplomatic domination of Swaziland's foreign policy centering on an offer of land (**kaNgwane** and **Ingwavuma**) to the kingdom in return for its repression of the **African National Congress (ANC)** within its borders. The fourth was the conservative reaction of Swaziland's monarchist government to the progressive democratization of South African society beginning in 1990.

As for capital investment, until about 1968 the preponderance of capital investment in Swaziland was British (principally through the Colonial [later **Commonwealth**] **Development Corporation**). Following Swaziland's independence, however, South Africa gradually became the main source of foreign capital, which now dominates the kingdom's economy, especially in the areas of banking, brewing, citrus, food processing, forestry, manufacturing, mercantile and grocery trade, mining, tourism, and transportation. Because the **Tibiyo takaNgwane Fund** became the principal joint investor in those sectors during that same period, thus forming a commonality of interests with South African capital, Swaziland placed itself in a position whereby the material prosperity of its aristocracy was dependent in large part on its alliance with foreign—especially South African—capital during the height of the apartheid era. That fact inevitably influenced Swaziland's diplomatic relations with Pretoria, which beginning in the early 1980s could be characterized as increasingly accommodationist.

To be fair, Swaziland's collaborationism during that period was attributable to a wide range of factors beyond Tibiyo's alliances. Its antecedents lay in the politics of the early 1960s leading to independence, when *iNgwenyama* **Sobhuza Dlamini II** had maintained publicly cordial and secretly close relations with the Nationalist regime, refraining from strong criticism of apartheid and seeking its political counsel when he decided to enter domestic politics in 1964. It was also the case that following independence in 1968 Swaziland remained tied to the **Southern African Customs Union** and the **Common** (Rand) **Monetary Area**, obtained 95 percent of its imports from the **South African Republic (SAR)**, and was heavily dependent on remittances from migrant labor employed there.

Still the fact remained that between 1975 and 1982 there were many signs that Swaziland recognized the realities and implications of the "winds of change" sweeping through the subcontinent. First was the fact that Swaziland determined to maintain cordial relations with the Marxist Front for the Liberation of Mozambique (FRELIMO) government following its takeover of Mozambique in 1975. One of the consequences flowing from that was Swaziland's becoming within months of the FRELIMO victory a major corridor for the flow of ANC arms and cadres from Mozambique into the **Transvaal**. The kingdom also became a haven for South African youths fleeing government retribution following the Soweto disturbances in 1976. There many of them were recruited by local ANC operatives and sent abroad for training.

As time went on other signs of a clash of loyalties within the kingdom became evident. By the late 1970s Swaziland was signaling its sympathy for many of the **Organization of African Unity**'s goals. It was a signatory to the anti-Pretoria Southern African Development Coordination Conference charter in 1979, and at the same time it declined South Africa's invitation to join its rival Constellation of Southern African

States. Then, during the prime ministership of **Mnt. Mabandla Dlamini**, the warming of Swaziland's attitude toward Mozambique was signaled by an invitation (1980) to its president, Samora Machel, to pay an official visit to the kingdom. Mabandla also signed a joint declaration with Mozambique, Lesotho, and Botswana condemning South Africa's regional destabilization campaign. Consequently by the early 1980s, with ANC agents and armaments flowing across the kingdom into the Transvaal, Pretoria had come to consider the state of its border with Swaziland to be one of its most pressing security concerns.

It was Sobhuza himself who reversed that situation before it progressed any further. That he did so could be attributed to Pretoria's astute diplomacy based on its understanding of what really motivated the old king. Since the 1930s Sobhuza had talked longingly of reincorporating the **siSwati**-speaking citizens of the eastern Transvaal region historically claimed by the kingdom into a greater Swaziland. That region had been since 1975 the South African bantustan, kaNgwane. Likewise Sobhuza had, like his predecessors, long decried the 1895 British incorporation into northern Natal of the Ingwavuma region, which had forever cut off Swaziland's hope of direct access to the Indian Ocean through **Kosi Bay**. Although it was true that Sobhuza had once belonged to the ANC and that he was the father-in-law of one of Nelson Mandela's daughters, it was equally true that the ANC's pro-democracy, anti-authoritarian ideals did not resonate well with him. Consequently, when Pretoria secretly approached him in 1981 with a deal involving his suppression of the ANC within Swaziland in return for its cession to him of both kaNgwane and Ingwavuma, it proved to be an offer he could not refuse. He signed a secret agreement to that effect in February 1982 and proceeded to carry out his end of the bargain with a vengeance. The Swaziland government embarked on a program of widespread arrests and deportations of ANC operatives and supporters. The official expulsion order was gazetted in 1984.

In the end, however, the land deal was never consummated, for several reasons. In Swaziland the death of Sobhuza in August 1982 opened the way for the voicing of opposition to the transfer, not the least of the opponents being the prime minister, Mnt. Mabandla. In South Africa, the virulent opposition to the arrangement by the kwaZulu government and the kaNgwane assembly prompted a change of heart in Pretoria, and the scheme was shelved indefinitely. In retrospect, part of Pretoria's diplomatic triumph lay in its persuading Sobhuza to sign the security agreement before the land was actually transferred.

Swaziland's reaction to the collapse of South African apartheid beginning in 1989 was muted. Its relationship with the ANC, which came to power in South Africa in 1994, was cool, stemming from its abrupt expulsion of the congress's Swaziland cadres beginning in 1982. Furthermore the ANC's platform espousing democratic rule and the redistribution of wealth was hardly one to be welcomed by Swaziland's monarchy. The government's official position therefore was that what was happening in South Africa bore no relevance to circumstances in Swaziland. That position did not sit well with the educated population and the nascent pro-democracy movements making their appearance at the same time. One of them, the **People's United Democratic Movement (PUDEMO)**, was widely believed to have close ties with the ANC and to be employing the ANC's advice in developing its own strategies. On a more visible level President Nelson Mandela, following his election in 1994, advised *iNgwenyama* **Mswati Dlamini III** on several occasions to move more quickly and decisively toward constitutional reform and multiparty elections. *See also* South Africa, government of

SOUTH AFRICA, UNION OF (1910–1962). When the constitution of the Union of South Africa was implemented in 1910 it specifically excluded from the Union the British **High Commission Territories** (HCTs), Basutoland (Lesotho), the Bechuanaland Protectorate (Botswana), and Swaziland. That development, according to Ronald Hyam, occurred primarily because of a sense of imperial *noblesse oblige* that prevailed in **Britain** during the Liberal government era (1905–15).[5] At the same time it was generally assumed that the HCTs would be incorporated at a future time—indeed, there was a schedule of incorporation attached to the constitution. That assumption envisioned that Swaziland would be the first to enter the Union, and relatively soon. One of the major themes in imperial policy toward Swaziland from 1910 to 1948 was the question of incorporation and the attitudes of the two domestic constituencies, the Swazi royal house and the European settler community, toward it.

The Swazi attitude was from the start against incorporation, especially following the Union's passage of the Natives Land Act of 1913, which made African ownership of land outside designated reserves illegal. Queen Regent **Labotsibeni Mdluli**, fearing that incorporation would only compound the Swazi loss of two-thirds of their lands (**Partition Proclamation of 1907**), proceeded to buy up as much of the lost lands as possible before the anticipated handover to the Union. She also helped to bankroll the **African National Congress** and its newspaper, *Abantu Batho*, whose early editorials lambasted South Africa's Natives Land Act

(1913), which similarly removed Africans to reserves. Following *iNgwenyama* **Sobhuza Dlamini II**'s installation in 1921 one of his first major initiatives was to lead a delegation to London to protest against the kingdom's projected incorporation to the Colonial Office. Thereafter, as the Union's oppressive policies toward its own African population became clearer, Sobhuza's position only hardened, although for diplomatic purposes he occasionally appeared to be open to discussion of his position.

The settlers were of two minds. In principle they opposed incorporation as threatening to their interests, but they could easily have been persuaded to reverse themselves in response to the Union's proffering of a railway from Johannesburg to Swaziland, which many settlers had come to believe spelled the difference between abundance and poverty for the settler economy. Pretoria kept them on the hook with periodic surveys of possible rail routes until 1922, when it took that carrot away and replaced it with the stick of a **cattle** embargo against Swaziland (1924) "for veterinary reasons." That heavy-handed measure, which remained in force until the outbreak of World War II, so alarmed and angered the Swaziland settlers as to begin to turn the preponderance of public opinion increasingly against incorporation.

That attitude was reinforced by Colonial and Dominions Secretary **Leopold S. Amery**, whose visit to Swaziland in 1927 served to reinforce his recently formed conviction that Swaziland should not be transferred as long as the Union continued along the reactionary course on native policy set for it by Prime Minister James B. Hertzog. This was in part because Amery observed at first hand Sobhuza's adamancy against transfer and in part because his discussions with the Europeans opened his eyes to the potential of an independent settler community acting as a counter against the example being set by the Union government. Following Amery's visit the question of Swaziland's transfer was in effect placed on indefinite hold. Several factors were to ensure that it was never lifted. One was the advent of World War II, during which the contemplation of major territorial changes took a back seat to pressing imperial considerations. Another was that the Dominions Office (under which the HCTs had fallen since 1926) became engaged during the 1930s in systematizing the powers of native authorities in all three territories (formalized in Swaziland's case in 1944), which until completed precluded any thought of incorporation. The last was the election of the Nationalists to power in South Africa in 1948, which decisively and finally trumped any further consideration of the question.

Swaziland maintained correct and cordial relations with the Union during its first decade and a half of apartheid rule. Economic ties remained close. The postwar period (1947–62) witnessed significant South African capital investment in Swaziland, particularly in forestry, citrus, iron and coal extraction, and light manufacturing. After 1948 Swaziland also became the haven for numbers of African refugees fleeing across the border from South African government repression and for resettling politically liberal South African whites who were no longer willing to live in such a racially oppressive society.

The Union of South Africa withdrew from the British Commonwealth in May 1962 and declared itself a republic. *See also* South Africa, Republic of

SOUTH AFRICAN RAILWAYS AND HARBOURS ROAD MOTOR SERVICE (SARHRMS). A bus service for both passengers and freight initiated by the state-owned transportation corporation of **South Africa** beginning in early 1928. The lack of transport and communications within Swaziland, and between the territory and the Johannesburg and Durban markets, had long been the subject of loud complaints by the European settler population, especially through the medium of the **European Advisory Council**. When the SARHRMS proposed establishing the service in 1927, the administration quickly agreed to its terms, which included **Mbabane's** substantial capitalization of internal road improvements. Three return routes were inaugurated, each three times per week: Breyten-Mbabane-Bremersdorp (**Manzini**); Bremersdorp-Gollel (Lavumisa; Pongola rail terminus); and Piet Retief-Dwaleni-Hlatikulu. The freight tariff between Breyten and Bremersdorp was two shillings three pence ($.55) per hundredweight. During the year 1928–29 (following on Colonial Secretary **Leopold S. Amery's** visit to the territory) the administration expended roughly £14,000 on the improvement of Swaziland's roads and bridges. By the end of 1928 the SARHRMS had eight six-wheeled busses plying the routes.

The effects of the SARHRMS vehicles on Swaziland's economy and society were profound. They lowered the cost of bulk transport, both of farm products to market and of imported fertilizers, materials, and equipment, by 50 percent. Mail service was regularized. According to the 1932 Pim Report (*see* **Pim, Sir Alan**) the SARHRMS, by improving the settlers' balance sheets and bolstering their confidence, became the making of commercial agriculture (initially **cotton, cattle** products, and tobacco) in Swaziland.[6] To the degree that the Swazi participated in the commodity economy (i.e., dealing in cattle products) they too benefited from the service, but during the early years it was the Europeans who were by far the main beneficiaries. That began to change with the establishment (1937) of the government creamery (butter factory) at Bremersdorp, which benefited both Swazi and settler cattlemen handsomely and that would not have been possible without the existence of the SARHRMS.

For the Swazi the social effects of the SARHRMS were less predictable. Women, whose social freedoms and opportunities hardly existed under Swaziland's tradition of rigid paternalism imposed on them at both the national and **homestead** levels, soon began to use the SARHRMS system to escape. The journey led first across the border to Breyten, **Transvaal** (a four-hour bus ride), and then by rail to the perceived freedoms and opportunities of Johannesburg. Some women migrated back and forth to Johannesburg, while others never returned to their homesteads. Because the viability of the Swazi social system was dependent in part on its commoditization of women, their ability to escape was quickly perceived as a grave threat by fathers and husbands, chiefs and the royal house, and, by extension, the colonial authorities. All parties quickly collaborated to put a stop to the practice. In 1931 the government issued a directive (with *iNgwenyama* **Sobhuza Dlamini II**'s assent) preventing Swazi women from riding the SARHRMS buses without a document attesting to male permission. Anecdotal evidence (in the absence of records) indicates that the restrictions did not seriously deter women from riding the busses. The directive was suspended during World War II, then revived in 1946, again with minimal effect.

Finally, World War II brought profound changes to the SARHRMS system, which had essentially been a monopoly until 1946. A few returning Swazi war veterans and others (notably **EurAfricans**) with wages accumulated during the conflict invested their savings in surplus South African army lorries, equipped them with benches, and began running them in competition over SARHRMS bus routes. Because most Swazi had long considered passenger service on the SARHRMS vehicles to be discriminatory and racist, the resulting loss of ridership quickly became a major problem for the company. This time there was no meeting of the minds between the Swazi authorities, who saw this as an opportunity for the lorry owners (many of them princes or clients of the monarchy) to break into the middle class, and the colonial administration, which was committed to maintaining the SARHRMS monopoly. The battle among the SARHRMS (which threatened to withdraw its busses from Swaziland), the administration (which was initially determined to pacify the SARHRMS), and Sobhuza's representatives (who stood firmly behind the lorry owners) went on for over two years, until the colonial authorities capitulated and allowed for the licensing of Swazi-owned bus lines. That episode constituted a significant milestone in the postwar formation of an affluent Swazi middle class.

SOUTH AFRICAN REPUBLIC (SAR, 1852–1902). Commonly referred to as the **Transvaal**; the state encompassing the Transvaal which was formed in 1852, and over which Martinus Pretorius succeeded his father Andries as president in 1855. The SAR incorporated the **Lydenburg Republic** in 1860, from which it inherited the diplomatic situation with Swaziland, then under the rule of *iNgwenyama* **Mswati Dlamini II**. Mswati had ceded lands to the Ohrigstaders in 1846 and subsequently more (in the eastern Transvaal) to their successors, the Lydenburgers, in 1855, and then had proceeded to settle the latter tract with royal villages. Only when the Zulu threatened him in 1860 did he reconfirm that cession. Mswati had further demonstrated his power by sending a troop into Lydenburg to kill the rebellious **Mnt. Somcuba Dlamini**, by supplying mercenary armies to the Afrikaners over the years, and by laying siege to Lourenço Marques and driving the Shangane out during 1863–64. The Afrikaners, on the other hand, were spread too thinly to be able to constitute any military power worthy of the name in the region, especially once their African neighbors began acquiring guns in numbers. Relations between Mswati and the SAR were further complicated by the ebbing and waning of their own diplomatic and military crises with the Zulu to the south and the **Pedi** to the north. The balance of power began to change decisively toward the SAR's favor only with Mswati's death (1865) and the Swazi regents' cession in that period of weakness of western lands in their border delineation with the Transvaal in 1866.

The SAR made further incursions on Swazi sovereignty during the reign of *iNgwenyama* **Ludvonga Dlamini II** (d. 1874), a period punctuated by Afrikaner incursions and by the disastrous defeats of Swazi invasions by the Pedi in 1869 (Ewulu) and 1875 (Mosega Kop). Most seriously in 1875, immediately following *iNgwenyama* **Mbandzeni Dlamini**'s installation, the Swazi in response to a war scare with the Zulu felt themselves obliged to sign, in return for its protection, a treaty with the SAR acknowledging its sovereignty, accepting (in principle) a SAR official, and allowing it the right to build a railway through their territory. Only the obvious inability of the Afrikaners, still divided among themselves, to enforce the treaty kept them at bay for another generation. Power swung back toward Mbandzeni's favor in 1879, however, when the king embarked on a joint campaign with the British occupiers of the SAR (1877–81) against Pedi **King Sekhukhune Maroteng**, in which the Swazi attackers carried the day, and on the strength of which the British proffered a guarantee of Swazi sovereignty forever.

The guarantee lasted only 15 years, principally because British strategic interests shifted north of the Limpopo River into central Africa after 1890, while the SAR (which regained its independence from the British in 1881) intensified its interest in Swaziland as its potential opening to the sea. To be sure, the underlying cause for the loss of Swaziland's independence could be said to have been Mbandzeni's **concessions**, for it was those monopolies, carrying with them the levers of governance in Swaziland, which were sold to the SAR by **Theophilus Shepstone, Jr.**, **Allister Miller**, **John Harington**, and others. That set in motion the chain of events beginning with the formation of the **Provisional Government Committee** of 1889, leading to the SAR's assumption of the kingdom's administration without Swazi assent under terms of the **third Swaziland Convention** (1894). Pretoria governed Swaziland from 1895 until the **Anglo-Boer War** broke out in October 1899. That war also brought an end to the SAR in 1902. *See also* first Swaziland Convention; Mdluli, *Indlovukazi* Labotsibeni; second Swaziland Convention; Swazieland Committee

SOUTH AFRICAN WAR. Also Second South African War. Alternative names for the **Anglo-Boer War**.

SOUTHERN AFRICAN CUSTOMS UNION (SACU). A customs union linking **South Africa** with Swaziland, Botswana, Lesotho, and Namibia. SACU, dating back to the early 1900s, is the oldest regional economic grouping existing in southern Africa. The union, which is administered by South Africa, collects customs duties on member states' imports from outside the SACU region along with excise duties on local production. It then distributes them back to member states on a *pro rata* basis. Some imports into SACU are subject to extremely high tariffs, the idea being to protect industries within the area. In practice that benefits South Africa primarily, partly because it discourages the smaller members from resorting to otherwise lower-cost alternative sources. Swaziland, like the other states, obtains the vast majority of its imports from South Africa; like the others, it depends heavily on SACU receipts for its income (42.1 percent of total government revenues 1989–93). The terms of the SACU agreement were being renegotiated in the late 1990s, with South Africa seeking a high percentage of gross revenues and the smaller countries holding out for higher compensation for SACU's distortion of their international trade patterns. In 1999 South Africa, upon entering into a free trade agreement with the European Union, declared that the revenue pool would shrink by about 31 percent, which would result in Swaziland's share diminishing by 14 percent.

SOUTHERN AFRICAN DEVELOPMENT COMMUNITY (SADC). A development union (by treaty, 1992) of Angola, Botswana, Congo (joined 1997), Lesotho, Malawi, Mauritius (joined 1995), Mozambique, Namibia, **South Africa** (joined 1994), Swaziland, Tanzania, Zambia, and Zimbabwe. The organization replaced the Southern African Development Coordination Conference (SADCC), which was formed in 1980 by the same states (excluding Congo, South Africa, and Namibia, the latter joining in 1990). The SADCC's purpose was to reduce member states' dependence on apartheid-era South Africa, but it failed of that intent. SADC's goals have shifted subtly from those earlier, apartheid-era SADCC goals to encourage southern Africa's (including South Africa's) general economic viability and independence. Within that broad framework the specific aims remain the same: to foster regional trade and economic integration and to act as a mechanism to attract and mobilize international support for regional and members' national projects. Toward those ends each SADC member nation was assigned a sector of responsibility, with Swaziland's being manpower development and training facilities, the same area of responsibility it had been assigned under SADCC.

Toward realization of the first aim of regional integration, the SADC's member states signed a protocol in 1996 aimed at creating a regional free trade area through the progressive reduction and eventual removal of all tariffs between member states. The SADC has also provided the framework for other undertakings: the establishment in 1994 of a rapid-deployment peacekeeping force within the region and the 1995 agreement to pool electric power derived mainly from South Africa's grid. Other SADC projects discussed during the late 1990s included a development bank, a common currency, and a regional parliament.

In 1998 the SADC came under great strain, stemming from the efforts of South African president Nelson Mandela's efforts to employ it as a diplomatic instrument to bring peace to the warring parties in the Congo, and later as a military instrument to quell the disturbances in Lesotho. Both countries were SADC member states, and both strongly resisted Mandela's efforts. In the case of the Congo, three other SADC members—Angola, Namibia, and Zimbabwe—inserted themselves into its civil war, which created serious new tensions within the conference.

SOUTHERN AFRICAN DEVELOPMENT COORDINATION CON-FERENCE. *See* SOUTHERN AFRICAN DEVELOPMENT COMMU-NITY

STANDING COMMITTEE OF THE *LIBANDLA* (SWAZI NATIONAL COUNCIL, SNC). The Standing Committee of the *libandla* was formed in 1947 and began regular meetings in 1950, following the implementation of the **Native Administration Proclamation** of 1950. Its origin lay in an address to the SNC in 1945 by **Resident Commissioner Eric K. Featherstone**, frustrated with the lack of cooperation by *iNgwenyama* **Sobhuza Dlamini II** and the *libandla* with the Native Administration Proclamation of 1944. Featherstone's stated concerns were with what he saw as the *libandla*'s unwieldiness (comprising every chief, headman, and councillor in the kingdom) and its non-productiveness (meeting only once annually over a week and producing little if any apparent substance). Out of the prolonged discussions that followed came the idea of a small, six-person standing committee of the *libandla* to liaise with the government on a regular basis, once every other week. The idea, which was analogous to the workings of the executive committee of the **European Advisory Council**, was proposed by the **high commissioner** but only reluctantly accepted by Sobhuza and the *libandla*, who were dragging their feet in protest to the 1944 proclamation.

When finally implemented the committee comprised a chairman, a secretariat, and one member from each of the six administrative districts, all nominated by the *ingwenyama* and *libandla*. The Standing Committee quickly came to be perceived by both the Swazi and the colonial administrations as an indispensable means of communication. For the British authorities it opened up a new avenue of access to the small circle of educated advisors on whom Sobhuza was increasingly relying for advice on policy formulation, and whom he placed on the standing committee. Over the years they included **Mfundza** and **Msindazwe Sukati**, **Polycarp Dlamini**, **Makhosini Dlamini**, Norman Nxumalo, **James S. M. Matsebula**, and **Abednigo Hlophe**. For Sobhuza it meant that the *libandla*, with which his relations had often been strained over the years, and which by the 1950s was in decline as an effectual political institution, could now be effectively bypassed as a primary sounding board with the authorities in favor of his close advisors. The Standing Committee ceased to function during the period of the **Legislative Council**, which began in 1964.

In 1996 *iNgwenyama* **Mswati Dlamini III** established another group termed the Standing Committee of the Swazi National Council. To that committee Mswati assigned the task of advising him on constitutional change. That Standing Committee was composed of many of the king's trusted advisors. By 1998, in the absence of a strong central authority directing it, the committee had assigned itself much wider powers than its original mandate had called for, including the settling of labor disputes.

STEGI. *See* SITEKI

STEINAECKER'S HORSE. *See* von STEINAECKER, BARON F. C. LUDWIG

STEPHENS, CORAL (c. 1910–). Wife of **Robert P. Stephens**, who arrived with him in 1947 and developed a small mohair weaving industry based on the grounds of the Stephens's residence, "Boshimela" ("The House of Many Chimneys") at **Pigg's Peak**. Ms. Stephens trained and employed Swazi women in the art of weaving and dyeing mohair drapes, upholstery, and rugs. She provided the women with sewing machines whose costs were to be amortized by her purchase of the products they produced on them. In establishing that enterprise Ms. Stephens created not only a world-renowned center of artistic production but also a place of reliable employment for dozens of Swazi women in a region of especially high unemployment for females and in a country not known for its support of economic independence for women. Ms. Stephens's fabrics have been exhibited in Paris and New York and are distributed through agents in the United States, the United Kingdom, Germany, and Australia.

STEPHENS, ROBERT P. (1905–). South African-born forester, industrialist, and politician who pioneered the period of post–World War II capital development of Swaziland. Stephens was a South African government forestry officer following his university education at Cape Town and Oxford (where he had been a Rhodes scholar). In 1947, following army service in World War II, Stephens and several South African colleagues (with financial backing from both the Barclays Overseas Development Corporation and Baring Brothers) established **Peak Timbers, Ltd.** in northern Swaziland. Stephens served as managing director of Peak Timbers until his retirement in 1968.

Stephens entered European politics in 1956 when he was first elected to the **Reconstituted European Advisory Council (REAC)**, serving until its demise in 1964. Stephens represented the REAC at the first (Swaziland, 1960) and second (London, 1963) **constitutional** conferences. He was also a founding member of the settler-dominated **United Swaziland Association (USA)**, which was committed to the preservation of the privileged position of Europeans in Swaziland. Stephens won election to the **Legislative Council** as a USA candidate in 1964, handily defeating the **Swaziland Democratic Party**'s **Vincent Rozwadowski**. When, following that election, *iNgwenyama* **Sobhuza Dlamini II** scotched his political coalition with the USA, Stephens maintained a close relationship with the king while stopping short of joining the traditionalist **Imbokodvo National Movement**.

Stephens served on the Constitutional Review Commission (1965) that drafted the pre-independence **constitution** of **1967**. Following the 1967 elections (in which Stephens did not stand), Sobhuza appointed him to the House of Assembly. In 1972 the king renewed Stephens's appointment and made him minister of finance. Following Sobhuza's repeal of the constitution (1973), an action that Stephens supported, Stephens was made a member of the Royal Constitutional Commission. Following his retirement from formal politics Stephens remained a close and loyal confidant of the king.

Stephens's father, Dr. Henry W. Stephens, was Swaziland government medical officer from 1892 until the turn of the century. Stephens's wife, **Coral Stephens**, manages a thriving mohair weaving industry adjoining their home in **Pigg's Peak**. Stephens's son, Dr. John W. Stephens, is a physician in **Mbabane**.

STEWART, BERTRAM B. (1868–1952). European police inspector, then trader, store owner, and hotelier in Nomahasha, then store owner in **Malkerns**. Stewart served as president of the Swaziland Chamber of Commerce and Industries for many years. During the **Anglo-Boer War**, a horse troop ("Steinaecker's Horse") commanded by **Ludwig von Steinaecker** raided Stewart's store and made off with £3,500 that the troopers found buried under the floor.

STEWART, VALLANCE M. (1869–1945). Trader and store owner in Bremersdorp (**Manzini**) who played an important role in European politics throughout his lifetime. Stewart was a member of the **European Advisory Council** (1924–32) and president of the **Swaziland Farmers Association**.

STRIKES, LABOR. Swaziland has a history of periodic labor unrest going back to the 1940s. Although the strikes have most frequently occurred over workplace issues there have always been underlying tensions, social or political, that have provided the context and determined the character of each work action. Especially in countries without working democratic political systems in place, labor activism has often constituted a means of expressing political opposition, and Swaziland has been no exception. The historically large percentage of Swazi males in **South Africa**'s politically volatile labor market since 1914 has undoubtedly contributed to that circumstance.

Modern labor walkouts began in Swaziland during 1944 with a strike at the **Havelock Asbestos Mine**. Worker resentment over mine management methods of controlling the brewing and consumption of beer and stronger drink touched off the strike. The walkout itself, although heavily destructive of certain mine property (notably the company beer hall) was brief and resulted in no loss of life. The underlying issue causing the strike was the company's disruption of the chain of command at the mine in its suppression of illegal brewing. Specifically it undercut *iNgwenyama* **Sobhuza Dlamini II**'s personal labor *indvuna* (officer), whose job had been to mediate between labor and management over worker grievances. Fundamentally, therefore, the strikers were reacting to being subjected to rigid modern industrial labor discipline. The shock of the strike resulted in the administration being more interventionist on the side of capital in the local labor market, in industry's reinforcement of the royal *indvuna* system of mediation, and in Sobhuza's movement into a closer alliance with industrial interests. In other words, in the fallout of the 1944 Havelock strike may be found the seeds of the wave of strikes that hit the Swazi economy in 1963.

The widespread labor unrest in 1963 had its roots in the massive post–World War II wave of capital investment in Swaziland beginning with commercial forestry in 1947. That development rapidly modernized the local labor market and gradually raised the level of worker consciousness. By the early 1960s economic and demographic forces had combined to transform a labor shortage into an oversupply, which industry addressed by freezing wages and withdrawing other incentives. The response of the labor force was to organize itself into increasingly militant unions. At the same time Swaziland's movement toward self-government, complete with the formation of sometimes radical opposition parties, touched off unprecedented public questioning of the domestic political status quo. One dimension of that was increasing worker dissatisfaction with Sobhuza's labor *indvunas* as perceived tools of management. In that atmosphere it proved irresistible to a handful of political activists, particularly those representing the radical **Ngwane National**

Liberatory Congress (NNLC), to attempt to turn widespread worker dissatisfaction to their own political advantage.

Six major labor disruptions swept over Swaziland in less than four months during 1963, involving 5,000 workers in many key industries. They were railway construction workers (February 28), **Ubombo Ranches** (March 18–28), **Peak Timbers** (March 29-April 6), **Havelock Asbestos Mine** (May 20-June 17), **Mbabane** workers and citizens (June 10–15), and again Ubombo Ranches (June 12–20). Union members threw out the *ingwenyama*'s labor *indvunas* and reacted with open derision to his public orders that they return to work and solve their grievances by traditional means. At that point, fearful of a further breakdown of royal authority and with his own police overextended, **Resident Commissioner Sir Brian Marwick** declared an emergency, summoned in the British army, arrested the leadership of the NNLC, and outlawed all strikes and union activity.

Since the *ingwenyama*'s repeal of the constitution in 1973 labor agitation and strikes have become a constant theme in the economic and political history of the kingdom. The strike that was second only to the 1963 disturbances in its destructiveness to property was waged by the Swaziland National Union of Teachers in 1977, again both over wages and the underlying system that denied them meaningful political representation. When the government responded to their demands with a paltry wage increase accompanied by the banning of their association, both teachers and students took to the streets until the police suppressed them. That strike set a new pattern, which was not infrequently followed thereafter, of vocal assaults on the king delivered with a tone of disrespect unimaginable until then.

By the mid-1990s real political opposition to the monarchy was being led by the union movement, notably the **Swaziland Federation of Trade Unions (SFTU)**, which had ties to the **People's United Democratic Movement (PUDEMO)** and the **Swaziland National Association of Teachers (SNAT)**. Beginning in April 1994 and lasting throughout the decade, SFTU-led mass strikes and stay-aways became a major ingredient in the political fare of the kingdom, each of them over wages, conditions, and unionization issues, but each also challenging the existing governmental structure. The underlying political theme of the strikes was opposition to the *tinkhundla* electoral system and the advocacy of a constitutional monarchy.

STUART, JAMES (1888–1942). Born in Natal, arrived in Swaziland in 1894 as interpreter to **Col. Richard Martin**, British representative on the **Government Committee**. Stuart became acting British consul in 1895, until relieved by **Johannes Smuts** later that year. He served as Smuts's replacement again in 1898–99. Later he became British magistrate at the **Ingwavuma** magistracy. Stuart, an accomplished linguist, was best known for his recording of the oral histories of the peoples of southeastern Africa. At his request *iNdlovukazi* **Labotsibeni Mdluli** and *iNgwenyama* **Bhunu Dlamini**, with both of whom he was on excellent terms, sent him several informants, including Mnt. Giba Dlamini and **John Gama**. Their interviews are among those included in the *James Stuart Archive* (4 vols. [of 7 projected], 1976–86).

SUGAR. Swaziland's most valuable single agricultural export. Swaziland produced 470,988 tons of sugarcane during 1996–97, of which 214,080 tons were exported, constituting by value 66 percent of all agricultural exports (including woodpulp) and about 17 percent of total exports. Principal markets were the European Union (EU), the United States, Canada, and Portugal. All sugarcane is grown in the **lowveld**, under **irrigation**. It was first cultivated on lands developed by the **Colonial Development Corporation** (CDC) under its **Swaziland Irrigation Scheme** during the early 1950s. The three main processing mills are at **Mhlume** and Simunye in the northern lowveld, and at **Ubombo** in the south. Mhlume and Simunye transport their sugar and molasses by road to the rail terminal at Mlawula, while Ubombo transports its product by road to the Phuzumoya rail station. Sugarcane is grown on **Swazi Nation Land** at Sihoya and Sivunga by the **Tibiyo takaNgwane Fund** and processed through the principal mills. In addition Tibiyo owns a half share of the CDC's Inyoni Yami Swaziland Irrigation Scheme in the northern lowveld. A number of smallholders around **Vuvulane** in the northern lowveld grow sugarcane for sale to the mills. Since 1964 all sugar has been marketed through the Swaziland Sugar Association.

In 1975 Swaziland became a signatory to the **Lomé Convention**, allowing it to sell 116,400 tons of sugar to the EU at an annually negotiated guaranteed price. Swaziland currently exports sugar under the terms of the Lomé IV Convention (signed 1989). Swaziland also markets sugar to the United States under a quota system. Those quotas at subsidized prices help to offset the much smaller revenues gained from the remainder of the exports at the world price. The 1999 crop was to be divided as follows: 174,000 tons to the EU, 20,000 tons to the United States, 17,000 tons to other **Southern African Customs Union** countries, and 35,000 tons to domestic consumption.

SUKATI, J. B. MFUNDZA (1915–). Swazi politician and royal advisor, son of **Lomadokola Sukati**. Sukati was selected by *iNgwenyama* **Sobhuza Dlamini II** in 1935 to be chief student officer of the experimental royal *libutfo* in the **Swazi National High School** at **Matsapha**. He then served as a clerk at the **Havelock Asbestos Mine** until he was commissioned by Sobhuza to be *indvuna* of the Swazi contingent of the **African Pioneer Corps** in 1941. Sukati, who achieved the rank of sergeant major, was mentioned in dispatches for bravery during the Anzio assault in 1944. In 1947 Sobhuza appointed him to the first **Standing committee of the** *libandla*. In 1964 Sukati was one of the *ingwenyama*'s nominees to the **Legislative Council**, and in 1965 he became a member of the Queen's Commissioner's Constitutional Review Commission. In 1967 Sukati stood successfully for **parliament** as an **Imbokodvo National Movement** candidate, following which he was named deputy prime minister (1967–71) by Sobhuza. In 1971 he became minister for power, works, and communication, but in 1972 he declined to stand for election to parliament and was dropped from the cabinet by Sobhuza. Sukati then served for several years as chairman of the Road Transportation Board.

SUKATI, LOMADOKOLA (?–1922). Prominent military officer, royal advisor, and *liqoqo* member. Sukati was a senior officer in *iNgwenyama* **Mbandzeni Dlamini**'s own iNdhlavela **regiment** and participated in the 1879 military campaign against **Pedi King Sekhukhune Maroteng**. Subsequently he became *indvuna* of *iNgwenyama* **Bhunu Dlamini**'s administrative headquarters at Zabeni. During the **Anglo-Boer War** (1899–1902) he served in the Swazi *imphi* that shadowed the Afrikaner forces in southern and eastern Swaziland. In 1915 Sukati was dispatched along with other notables to inspect the **Lovedale Missionary Institution** school for its suitability for *iNkhosana* Sobhuza Dlamini II's secondary education. Sukati was the father of **Mfundza** and **Msindazwe Sukati**, both of them important political figures during Sobhuza's reign.

SUKATI, DR. S. T. MSINDAZWE (1910–). Swazi civil servant, politician, diplomat, and trusted representative of and advisor to *iNgwenyama* **Sobhuza Dlamini II.** Sukati was educated at **Zombodze, Lovedale Missionary Institution**, Ft. Hare University College, and the University of South Africa, from which he obtained a B.A. by correspondence, the second Swazi to do so, in 1940. In 1944 Sobhuza appointed Sukati to a new and prestigious position of *lisolenkosi* (eye of the king), the senior liaison officer between the *ingwenyama* in *libandla* and the colonial administration. He served in that capacity for 15 years before handing the position over to **J. S. Mkhulunyelwa Matsebula** in 1959. Sukati served as *indvuna* of the royal party attending Queen Elizabeth's coronation in 1953. He was a member of the first constitutional commission convened by **Resident Commissioner Brian Marwick** in 1960 and the second **constitutional conference** in London (1963). He served as secretary to the first **Legislative Council** in 1964 and speaker of the House of Assembly in the pre-independence **parliament** in 1967. Beginning in 1968 Sukati embarked on a diplomatic career, becoming ambassador to both the United Nations and the United States. Beginning in 1975 Sukati served as ambassador to newly independent Mozambique. Sukati also served as chairman of the National Industrial Development Corporation of Swaziland (NIDCS). In 1968 Sukati was awarded an honorary doctorate of laws from the University of Botswana, Lesotho and Swaziland.

siSWATI. The language of the Swazi nation. Linguistically it is very closely affined to *isiZulu* and similar to other **Nguni** languages, themselves constituting a group of the Bantu language family. Until the era of World War II siSwati was a spoken language only; the Zulu language and dictionaries constituted the written medium. The official siSwati orthography was adopted by the Swazi government and incorporated into the first three years of the school curriculum in 1969. Hugh Macmillan sees that development to be in part an expression of cultural nationalism aimed at long-resented Zulu "immigrant intelligentsia."[7] The first comprehensive English-siSwati, siSwati-English dictionary, edited by David K. Rycroft, was published in 1981.

SWAZI COMMERCIAL AMADODA. A purchasing cooperative to benefit incipient Swazi traders and general dealers who lacked capital to purchase inventory, established in 1948 by *iNgwenyama* **Sobhuza Dlamini II**. Sobhuza understood at an early date the implications of the rise of economic activity and capital investment that made its appearance in Swaziland following World War II, and he was determined to ensure that a share of the wealth fell to the Swazi. He urged commoners to enter the wage labor market. For the aristocracy he attempted to ensure that a portion of new investment opportunities in small enterprise flowed to Swazi petty bourgeois interests (including, by extension, his own). Those enterprises included **cattle** dealing, the hides and skins trade, general merchandising, and commercial bus and bulk transport. In line with Sobhuza's intentions one of the organization's main objects was "to prevent the infiltration of foreign [i.e., Indian and European] capital into native trade" (File 1479, SNA). The board of the Commercial Amadoda was drawn from members of the emerging postwar elite closest to Sobhuza: chair, **Mfundza Sukati**; general secretary, Solomon Dlamini (a commercial transport entrepreneur); and treasurer, **Mnt. Dabede Dlamini**, a World War II veteran and business entrepreneur. The organization, which oversaw nine regional offices, was headquartered at Sobhuza's administrative homestead, **Lozithehlezi**.

The Commercial Amadoda never functioned successfully as a bulk-purchasing entity. Instead, by the early 1960s, with **Zonke A. Khumalo** as general secretary, the Commercial Amadoda had become a licensing agency for virtually every important class of Swazi business enterprise, from general dealerships and bottle stores to public busses. Under Kumalo the organization became the virtual arbiter of who gained access to the Swazi middle class and who did not. That immense power characterizes the Swazi Commercial Amadoda, the kingdom's premier trade association and lobbying organization, to this day.

SWAZI NATION LAND (SNL). Land in Swaziland held in trust (i.e., controlled in matters of tenure and distribution) by the *ingwenyama*. In the 1990s SNL comprised some 60 percent of the total land area of Swaziland, the remainder being **title deed land (TDL)**. SNL is allocated to the chiefs by the king and sub-allocated by them to individual **homesteads**. In return the homestead heads *khonta* (declare allegiance to), and traditionally pay either labor or cash tribute to, the chief and king. SNL is largely given over to subsistence agriculture (maize and **cattle**) and is mainly rain-fed. That being the case, SNL is highly susceptible to drought. The kingdom's maize crop is grown almost entirely on SNL, as is 80 percent of the **cotton** crop. More than 80 percent of the nation's cattle graze on SNL. Because Swazi cattle ownership is motivated primarily by social and financial liquidity considerations, low offtake has resulted in serious land degradation in areas, a condition that will only get worse unless the communal land tenure system is fundamentally altered. About three-quarters of all SNL farmers supplement their homestead agricultural income with wages.

SWAZI NATIONAL CHURCH. A Christian nondenominational church founded in 1939 with *iNgwenyama* **Sobhuza Dlamini II**'s assent by a number of his Christian relatives and followers. Leading proponents were **Mnt. Solomon Madevu Dlamini**, who had been excommunicated by the Wesleyans because he had advocated and practiced polygyny; **Benjamin Nxumalo** (Sobhuza's maternal uncle) of the **African Methodist Epis-**

copal Church; and *iNdlovukazi* **Nukwase Ndwandwe** of the Methodist Church. Sobhuza's motivations for establishing the national church were complex. On one hand, although he never came close to converting to Christianity, Sobhuza was a personal friend of several missionaries, notably **Dr. David Hynd** and Fr. Pelligrino Bellezze. Furthermore he appreciated fully the missions' contributions to the health and education of the Swazi.

On the other hand Sobhuza viewed the missions' acquisitiveness of land, their close ties with the administration, and certain of their teachings as serious threats to his own sovereignty and to Swazi tradition as he viewed it. Sobhuza even viewed the various **Zionist** sects, which opposed Christian teachings on—among other things—polygyny, **witchcraft**, and beer, with some apprehension as constituting powerful alternatives to royal, patriarchal authority, especially for women. Consequently Sobhuza saw the national church as a means to influence and perhaps even exert some control over independent churches. In 1944 Sobhuza granted a tract of land near **Lobamba** for establishment of the nondenominational church, which was renamed the United Church of Africa and whose secretary was **John J. Nquku**. A large, modern church was built on that site, begun in 1948 and completed in the late 1960s. *See also* Christianity

SWAZI NATIONAL COUNCIL. *See LIBANDLA*

SWAZI NATIONAL FUND. A fund started in 1911 by Queen Regent **Labotsibeni Mdluli** at the instigation of **Resident Commissioner Robert Coryndon**. The fund was intended by Coryndon as a kind of compensation for his having placed most of Labotsibeni's revenues from the **private revenue concession** out of her reach in the Swazi Trust Fund. Coryndon proposed the national fund to her as a way for her to foster the education of her people. The fund was based on a 2 shilling ($.50) per annum head tax on all Swazi males, to be collected at the tax camps along with the government levy. It soon became evident that Coryndon had no intention of using the fund for educational purposes, nor any idea of consulting her about its expenditure at all. That was a prime example of the cynicism that characterized much of Coryndon's administrative philosophy. From 1911 to 1916 the fund was expended in its entirety on eradication of East Coast Fever in **cattle**, which benefited Swazi and European cattle owners alike.

Only in 1916, following Coryndon's departure, did the administration agree to Labotsibeni's request that the fund be tapped to subsidize *iNkhosana* **Sobhuza Dlamini II**'s and his companions' education at the **Lovedale Missionary Institution** school in the Cape. Later, Sobhuza was forced to obtain the administration's permission to use Swazi National Fund monies to establish the **Swazi National High School** at **Matsapha** in 1931. Sobhuza complained continually into the post–World War II period over Swazi lack of control over the fund's expenditures. It was not until the 1950 implementation of the **National Treasury Proclamation** that the Swazi regained control of any of their national expenditures, including the Swazi National Fund. In 1957 the tax was raised to 5 shillings ($1.25) per annum by the Swazi.

SWAZI NATIONAL HIGH SCHOOL. *See* SWAZI NATIONAL SCHOOLS

SWAZI NATIONAL ROYAL CLUB. A social and political organization of Swazi and other middle-class intellectuals living in and around Johannesburg, founded by *iNgwenyama* **Sobhuza Dlamini II** in 1931. The club's headquarters was a house in Sophiatown that Sobhuza had purchased in 1921 (for about £400, or about $2,000) ostensibly as a place where Swazi—in theory even migrant mine laborers—could go to maintain and renew their Swazi ties. There was another purpose served by the Sophiatown house. That was the heyday of Sobhuza's "progressive" period, and the house had been purchased for him by **Dr. Pixley kaI. Seme**, his cosmopolitan lawyer and advisor, to afford him access to the metropolitan life. Sobhuza used the house to meet with expatriated Swazi and other African intellectuals in Seme's circle. He also was fond of visiting the annual Rand Agricultural Show, where the latest farm machinery, hybrid seeds, and prize animals were on display.

In 1926 (well before he founded the club) Sobhuza moved away from progressivism in favor of an emphasis on Swazi traditionalism as the ideological basis of his rule. Consequently the Sophiatown house became, somewhat incongruously, the headquarters of the National Royal Club and hence the locus for the fostering of traditional (i.e., monarchist) values. The stated purposes of the National Royal Club reflected that eclecticism: "to promote all aspects of Swazi welfare, encourage African cooperation, establish centers of discussion, help publish matters of African interest, obtain land for the purposes of the society, and raise funds for its support."[8] The club was renamed the Swazi National Royal Society in the late 1940s, and its Johannesburg representative (always close to the *ingwenyama*) was required to give periodic reports to him and the *liqoqo* on the state of Swazi expatriate values in South Africa. The club was said to have had a membership of 15,000 in the early 1960s, but it died out following independence.

SWAZI NATIONAL SCHOOLS. Two schools, one elementary and one secondary, were founded by the Swazi monarchy during the early 20th century to afford a Western education to *bntfwanenkhosi* (princes/princesses) and selected Swazi elite. The elementary school was founded by Queen Regent **Labotsibeni Mdluli** at her **homestead** at **Zombodze**. Labotsibeni, who had rejected the idea of a modern education for *iNgwenyama* **Bhunu Dlamini** and had seen the baneful consequences of that decision, reversed herself when the question of her grandson *iNkhosana* (Crown Prince) **Sobhuza Dlamini II**'s education arose; however, she was mistrustful of mission education. That was perhaps an outgrowth of the education that her two sons, **Bnt. Malunge** and **Lomvazi Dlamini**, had received at the Wesleyan mission schools at **Edendale** (Natal) and **Mahamba**, which she felt had carried unacceptable cultural baggage with it.

The Zombodze school was established in 1906, and although it was at first staffed by Edendale graduates (**Edgar Mini** and **Robert Grendon**), the fact that it was under her eye afforded her a certain confidence. Indeed, it was the government more than any missionaries with whom she habitually fought the hardest over the school's staffing and curriculum. Finally in 1908 **Resident Commissioner Robert Coryndon**, who was deeply suspicious of Grendon's politics, forced a teacher of his own choice on her, **Rev. Joseph Xaba**, whom she had bitterly resisted, in the new government-built school at Zombodze. When Sobhuza returned from the **Lovedale Missionary Institution** school in 1919 to be taught individually, the government again dictated the tutor, Lancelot Msomi.

In 1931 Sobhuza, himself appreciative of Western education but suspicious of what he perceived to be the deleterious effects of the mission agenda on traditional values, established the **Swazi National High School** at **Matsapha** to educate the elite. Perhaps recalling his grandmother's travails, Sobhuza used entirely non-governmental resources (the **Swazi National Fund**) to finance the school, and he kept a keen eye on its staffing and curriculum through the mechanism of an advisory board that he established and dominated. It was at the Swazi National High School that Sobhuza instituted the student *emabutfo* system (versus the missions' Pathfinder Scouts movement) in order to reinforce traditional (i.e., monarchist) values in the face of the inevitably Western-oriented standards of the curriculum. He did so over the spirited opposition of the

European mission establishment and against skepticism within certain elements of the government.

SWAZI NATIONAL TREASURY. Established by the **National Treasury Proclamation** of 1950, the Swazi national treasury was to receive its funds principally from court fines (by virtue of the **Native Courts Proclamation** of 1950) and a portion of the native tax. The treasury and courts proclamations had been withheld by the British authorities in 1944 as an incentive to force *iNgwenyama* **Sobhuza Dlamini II** and the *libandla* to comply with the terms of the **Native Administration Proclamation** (1944), which had empowered the **resident commissioner** at the expense of the **paramount chief**'s sovereignty. The 1950 Native Administration Proclamation excised the offending terms and was therefore accompanied by the implementation of the courts and treasury proclamations. By terms of the National Treasury Proclamation the *ingwenyama* in *libandla* was granted power to regulate the treasury's constitution and the expenditure of its funds for the purposes of the Swazi nation as distinct from those of the colonial administration. Also by its terms the **Swazi National Fund** was to be administered through the Treasury.

SWAZI OBSERVER, THE. A national daily newspaper founded in 1982 on the occasion of *iNgwenyama* **Sobhuza Dlamini II**'s diamond jubilee. A weekend edition was added during the mid-1980s. *The Swazi Observer* became the second such newspaper in Swaziland, alongside (and rivaling) the independent and foreign-owned *The Times of Swaziland*. The monarchy and the government had long been frustrated with what they considered the overly inquisitive and critical independent press (principally *The Times* in **Mbabane** and *The Star* in Johannesburg). *The Swazi Observer* expressed the point of view and interests of the monarchy and was entirely financed (aside from advertising revenue) by the king's **Tibiyo takaNgwane Fund**.

SWAZI PIONEER CORPS. *See* AFRICAN PIONEER CORPS

SWAZIELAND COMMITTEE (1887–1889). Also known as Swaziland Governing Committee, White Committee, and White Governing Committee. A committee (actually three successive committees) of European concessionaires established in 1887 to govern the European community as distinct from the Swazi monarchy. The first Swazieland Committee was established in 1887 by **Theophilus Shepstone, Jr.**, with the approval of *iNgwenyama* **Mbandzeni Dlamini**. Shepstone's private purpose was to consolidate his own position as Mbandzeni's advisor and agent in the face of mounting criticism from European residents and concessionaires that he was authoritarian and greedy. Shepstone convened a meeting of Europeans at **Mbekelweni** in May 1887, where it was decided that there was need for a government for whites and for a means to resolve their legal disputes separately, albeit ultimately subject to the *ingwenyama*'s sovereignty. The first Swazieland Committee of 25 elected members met in August, with **James Forbes** as chairman. Because Forbes was not an assertive man, Shepstone was able to dominate the committee's business, setting tariff rates and establishing various other regulations. As European resentment of Shepstone's slippery and arbitrary ways mounted over the following year, however, committee pressure was exerted on Mbandzeni for change. Forbes was replaced with a forceful chairman, **Capt. Andrew Ewing**. Then Ewing and others persuaded the *ingwenyama* to sign a proclamation in August 1888 (the "White Charter"), in effect gazetting the Swazieland Committee and lowering its membership to a more wieldy 15. Finally, **Allister Miller** was engaged for the new position of committee secretary at the same time as Mbandzeni finally signed a document reining in Shepstone's powers.

As a consequence the second Swazieland Committee (October 1888) acted far more independently, even demanding that Shepstone hand over the **concessions** register and related documents. Shepstone refused and then demonstrated that he retained enough power to force the committee to dissolve itself and stand again for election. Consequently by the time the third Swazieland Committee met (November 1888) it was no longer accepted as a viable means of European self-government. Politically by that time the Europeans had split into the **Thorburn** and **Shepstone** factions, which vied for the *ingwenyama*'s favor. As for the committee itself, as it became obvious by early 1889 that Mbandzeni was dying, its membership plunged headlong into the unseemly business of grabbing whatever concessions remained. The failure of the Swazieland Committee was one of several reasons behind the formation of the **Anglo-Boer Joint Commission** (October 1889) to determine the true dimensions of the difficulties in Swaziland. In December 1889, upon the commission's recommendation, the Swazieland Committee was replaced by the **Provisional Government Committee**.

SWAZIELAND CORPORATION. *See* SWAZILAND CORPORATION

SWAZILAND ADMINISTRATION PROCLAMATIONS (NUMBERS 3/1904 AND 4/1907). Swaziland Administration Proclamation 3/1904 and its amending Proclamation 4/1907 were the most important administrative decrees issued in newly colonized (1903) Swaziland by the British authorities. The 1904 proclamation specified that Swaziland was to be governed as a district of the **Transvaal**, whose laws were to be applied to the kingdom. It then established in the kingdom the same courts (in terms of powers and jurisdiction) as operated in the Transvaal, headed by an appellate court staffed by Transvaal judges. That meant in effect that the Swazi monarchy and chiefs once again lost their criminal jurisdiction, as they had prior to the **Anglo-Boer War** (1899–1902) by virtue of the **protocol of 1898.** They were not to regain that jurisdiction until it was partially restored by the **Native Courts Proclamation** of 1950 and fully restored at independence. The proclamation anticipated that Swaziland would soon be incorporated into the future **Union of South Africa**. Finally, the proclamation gave the title of **resident commissioner** to the senior British administrative official in Swaziland.

SWAZILAND AFRICAN NATIONAL UNION (SANU). *See* JOINT COUNCIL OF SWAZILAND POLITICAL PARTIES

SWAZILAND COLLEGE OF TECHNOLOGY (SCOT). Formerly the Swaziland Industrial Training Institute. Founded in **Mbabane** in 1946, SCOT provides training for middle-level craftsmen, technicians, and administrators. SCOT designs its courses to fit the needs of private and public sector employers, within the framework of the following departments and divisions: automotive, building, commercial, computer and electronic, electrical and telecommunications, hotel and catering, laboratory assistance, mathematics, mechanical engineering, plumbing, teacher training, technical drawing, and woodwork. Its examinations are set by British technical institutions. In 1996 SCOT enrolled 1,000 students.

SWAZILAND COMMITTEE. *See* SWAZIELAND COMMITTEE

SWAZILAND CONCESSIONS COMMISSION (1905–1908). A commission established by proclamation in 1904 by the British **high commissioner Lord Milner** in order to sort out conflicting claims among Europeans and Swazi over the legitimacy and scope of the **concessions** granted during the reign of *iNgwenyama* **Mbandzeni Dlamini**. Responding to intense settler pressure to grant the Swazi 15 percent of the land at best, balanced by Swazi hostility to the thought of any loss of territory at all, Milner established the commission to settle the matter and to determine the extent of the reserves (also provided for in the proclamation) intended for Swazi occupation.

The commission, chaired by **Johannes Smuts**, carried out the bulk of its work during 1905, following Milner's departure and replacement by **Lord Selborne**. The commission's principles were to accord the settlers the bulk of the land but also to leave the Swazi with enough territory so that they would not touch off a violent reaction against the Europeans, yet not so much as to allow them to "pass a life of idleness."[9] The commission further determined (also in the interests of peace and stability) that the physical disturbance to the Swazi population be kept to a minimum and that the royal house and prominent chiefs especially be allowed to retain as much of their domains as possible.

The commission's report was delivered to Selborne in early 1906 and became the basis for his **Partition Proclamation of 1907**. The proclamation awarded 37 percent of the land to the Swazi, with the majority of their **homesteads** to fall in the new "**native areas**" under chiefs, the remainder of them to remain on the new European estates under tenancy agreements. The final delimitation of the 32 native area boundaries was carried out by Partition Commissioner **George Grey** during 1908–9. Removal of those Swazi not entering into tenancy agreements was to begin in 1914.

SWAZILAND CONSTITUTIONAL COMMITTEE (1960–1962). A committee of Swazi traditionalists (i.e., *libandla* members) and opposition politicians, settlers (both **Reconstituted European Advisory Council** members and independents), and colonial government officials, convened by **Resident Commissioner Brian Marwick** in November 1960 to discuss issues concerning the drafting of a pre-independence **constitution**. The impetus for the committee's formation had come from two events: the "Winds of Change" speech delivered before the South African parliament by British Prime Minister Harold MacMillan in early 1960 and a meeting of many potential committee members convened by *iNgwenyama* **Sobhuza Dlamini II** in April 1960 to discuss the makeup of a possible internal **Legislative Council**. The membership of the committee read like a Who's Who of pre-independence politics. *Libandla* members included **Mnt. Makhosini Dlamini** (later Sobhuza's first prime minister), **Polycarp Dlamini** (secretary of the Swazi nation), **Msindazwe Sukati** (*lisolenkhosi*), **James S. M. Matsebula** (liaison officer), **Abednigo K. Hlophe, Dr. Malabhane Allen Nxumalo** (later president of the **Swaziland Democratic Party**), and **Douglas Lukhele**. Opposition party members included **John J. Nquku, Dr. Ambrose Zwane**, and **Obed Mabuza**, all from the only existing viable opposition party, the **Swaziland Progressive Party** (SPP; all three SPP members were also *libandla* councillors). Reconstituted European Advisory Council (REAC) members included **Ivan H. Pierce**, **Robert P. Stephens**, and **Carl F. Todd**. Other European members who would figure prominently in 1960s politics were **Dan Fitzpatrick**, **Willie Meyer**, and **Dr. David Hynd**. Several government officers were also members.

The committee met throughout 1961 in Swaziland, and then in December of that year a subcommittee met in London to present its proposed constitution to the colonial secretary, **Reginald Maudling**. During its 1961 discussions the committee broke into three factions. The Swazi traditionalists and their European allies each sought to codify the privileged status of their political organizations (the *libandla* and the REAC, respectively) in the structure of the new Legislative Council. Conversely, the opposition members sought a legislature based on the one-man, one-vote principle and without any reserved seats for Swazi or Europeans. The government members sought a constitution embodying Western-style, nonracial representative democratic principles. They meant to start with **trade unions** and local councils, and culminate in a sovereign **parliament**, with mention of the monarchy as nothing more than a ceremonial institution. The Swazi traditionalists and Europeans prevailed at first, for the proposals they carried off to London (the first constitutional conference, December 1961) specified a legislature that preserved half its seats for Europeans and placed two-thirds of the Swazi seats firmly in the *ingwenyama*'s hands. That was made possible only because the SPP members either had been expelled or had resigned from the committee in April 1961, and the government members had walked out of the meeting before the vote on the "50–50 constitution" proposal was taken.

The London conference was short and perfunctory, and the British government waited until February 1962 to make its response. It did so by releasing the previously secret committee document to the public, which with its guarantee of half the legislature's seats to Europeans so scandalized the full Swazi *libandla* that Sobhuza was forced to disavow the proposal, effectively killing it. With that the constitutional committee passed out of existence. When the British government called a second London **constitutional conference** in early 1963 it was a new constitutional committee with a wider roster of representatives that convened. It included members from the **Swaziland Democratic Party**, the **Mbandzeni National Convention**, and the **EurAfrican Welfare Association**. That committee quickly fractured along roughly the same fault lines as the original one, prompting Commonwealth Secretary **Duncan**

Sandys to dismiss the committee and impose his own constitution, published as a "White Paper" in May 1963.

SWAZILAND CONVENTION. *See* FIRST SWAZILAND CONVENTION; SECOND SWAZILAND CONVENTION; THIRD SWAZILAND CONVENTION

SWAZILAND CORPORATION. Prior to 1907 the Swazieland Corporation. Formerly the Umbandine Swazieland Concessions Syndicate Ltd., formed in 1891 by **Allister Miller** and **John Thorburn**, and capitalized at £50,000 ($250,000). The syndicate's assets comprised the mineral, **unallotted lands,** and monopoly **concessions** amassed by Miller and Thorburn from their dealings with *iNgwenyama* **Mbandzeni Dlamini** during the 1880s. In mid-1898 those assets were transferred to a new entity, the Swazieland Corporation, nominally capitalized at £300,000 ($1,500,000). Its directors were principally London-based, although the controlling interest in the corporation was held by the South African firm Lewis & Marks. Miller became the corporation's Swaziland manager. Aside from its extensive holdings in mining and industrial monopolies, the Swazieland Corporation aspired to sell its concessioned land to prospective British settlers and to establish itself in profitable agribusiness ventures such as **cotton,** timber, and **cattle.** The heart of the corporation's ambitions, however, remained in its land, which it claimed covered one-third of the territory and which Miller, ever the optimist, hoped to market at premium prices.

Miller's hopes were dashed with the arrival of **Lord Selborne** as the new British **high commissioner** (1905). Selborne took a dim view of the potential of large, influential land speculation companies to torpedo his vision of southern Africa as one vast, thriving white settler economy based on a compliant African proletariat. Selborne feared that such corporations would, in the event of an adequate settler market not materializing, sell their lands instead to wealthy Africans, which he likened derisively to "farming kaffirs." Selborne consequently undercut Miller's intended land-office business by offering **crown lands** for sale at prices much reduced from what the corporation intended to charge. One after another the corporation's major undertakings under Miller's direction—land, cotton, and ranching—failed to achieve his original expectations. Land after 1910 was marketed through the **Mushroom Land Settlement Scheme.** Cotton fell victim to the fluctuations in the world price following World War I. Swaziland Ranches, Miller's cattle venture in the

lowveld, sold out in the early 1920s, and shortly thereafter the Swaziland Corporation ceased operations.

SWAZILAND DEFENSE FORCE. *See* ROYAL UMBUTFO DEFENSE FORCE

SWAZILAND DEMOCRATIC ALLIANCE (SDA). An umbrella organization of **trade unions**, political groups, and churches, formed during the 1990s, whose aim was to bring about more representative government in Swaziland by non-violent means. Its most important members are the **Swaziland Federation of Trade Unions (SFTU)** and the **People's United Democratic Movement (PUDEMO).** Its power and influence were diminished in 1996 when the general **strike** and demonstrations that it was instrumental in organizing collapsed.

SWAZILAND DEMOCRATIC PARTY (SDP). Moderate opposition party formed in March 1962 by **Simon Nxumalo, Vincent Rozwadowski**, and Jordan Ngubane. It was intended to fill the gap between the European settler–Swazi traditionalist alliance on the right and the **Swaziland Progressive Party (SPP)** on the left. Like the Liberal Party in South Africa, its platform called for extensive social welfare legislation to improve the lot of the average Swazi citizen. Like the Liberal Party it advocated an eventual, but not immediate, universal franchise. The SDP acknowledged the historic role of the royal house but advocated making the *ingwenyama* into a constitutional monarch. In contrast to the **Ambrose Zwane** wing of the SPP (by mid-1963 the **Ngwane National Liberatory Congress [NNLC]**) the SDP eschewed Pan-Africanism on grounds of national sovereignty. Nxumalo became SDP president, while Rozwadowski became vice-president. When **Dr. Allen Nxumalo** joined the party briefly in 1963, he became its president, while Simon Nxumalo, the grassroots organizer, became its secretary-general.

During the 1963 labor unrest the SDP generally opposed the NNLC-inspired **strikes**. The SDP was destined for an early demise. In the 1964 **Legislative Council** elections it won not a single seat, with both Simon Nxumalo and Rozwadowski losing decisively to their opponents in the settler-traditionalist (i.e., **United Swaziland Association** and **Imbokodvo National Movement [INM]**) coalition. Following his defeat Simon Nxumalo bolted to the INM, and Rozwadowski was expelled for "taking independent action," both of which actions rang down the curtain on the SDP as a viable party.

SWAZILAND DEVELOPMENT AND SAVINGS BANK (SWAZI-BANK). A statutory body, wholly owned by the Swaziland government, whose designated purpose is to provide credit to and assist in the development of the rural cash economy. SwaziBank, which is managed by a publicly appointed board, encourages rural Swazi to develop a bank savings mentality and provides credit for agricultural development and construction of low-cost housing. During the 1990s SwaziBank was rocked by repeated revelations of scandal centering on multiple occurrences of mismanagement and misappropriation on the part of the board. The most prominent board member apparently involved was **Mnt. Masitsela Dlamini**, who was alleged to have walked away from a personal bank loan of about E3 million.

SWAZILAND ELECTRICITY BOARD (SEB). A statutory body that supplies electricity to a large portion of the country's domestic, commercial, industrial, agricultural, and **irrigation** infrastructures through the national grid. Many of the nation's major timber, **sugar**, mining, and irrigation industries generate portions of their own power requirements and purchase the balance from the SEB. In 1993 the SEB generated 52 percent of its power requirements (from diesel and three hydropower generating sites) and imported the balance from **South Africa** (Eskom). In 1998 the Swaziland government announced plans to privatize the SEB.

SWAZILAND FARMERS ASSOCIATION. The first of a number of European farmers' interest organizations that served educational, social, and political functions during much of the 20th century. Formed in 1909 and headed for many years by **Allister Miller**, the association became the most powerful and effective lobbying group with the Swaziland administration prior to the formation of the **European Advisory Council** in 1921. The association attempted (unsuccessfully) to monopolize the sale of maize to the government in 1911. The second most powerful interest group was the Hlatikulu Farmers Association, formed in 1911. By the 1920s the farmers' associations had become the primary vehicles by which government subsidized agricultural inputs and set up commodity marketing arrangements and educational schemes. Until the World War II–generated agricultural emergency changed things those subsidies were channeled almost exclusively to the European farming sector and away from Swazi agriculturalists.

SWAZILAND FEDERATION OF TRADE UNIONS (SFTU). The major **trade union** federation in Swaziland, led by Jan Sithole, which in the absence of legal opposition parties took on during the mid-1990s a political agenda. Its membership in the late 1990s stood at about 80,000. The other powerful unions operating in Swaziland during the late 1990s, also with political agendas, were the **Swaziland National Association of Teachers (SNAT)**, the National Association of Civil Servants (NCAS), and the Post and Telecommunications Union. Beginning in 1994 and lasting until the end of the decade the SFTU led a series of mass **strikes**, stay-aways, and demonstrations in quest of higher wages, better working conditions, and union recognition. As time passed it became clear that the SFTU had become less concerned with economic issues than with protest politics, for the clear context within which all its labor actions were waged was its increasingly strident criticism of the non-representative nature of the Swazi government, its excesses, and its corruption.

The SFTU's tactics clearly had some effect during the 1990s, for in response to its (and other unions') activism the government raised wages and bettered conditions, and the king reshuffled cabinets and reviewed the *tinkhundla* electoral system with an eye to making it more representative. In 1996 *iNgwenyama* **Mswati Dlamini III** attempted to mollify the SFTU and other opposition groups by establishing a **Constitutional Review Commission** with a mandate to draft a new constitution that would better satisfy the popular wish for a more representative government. By then the SFTU had ratcheted up political tensions by presenting the government with 27 largely political demands, most notably calling for the unbanning of opposition parties and the reining in of the king's powers. What was clear was that in the absence of lawful opposition parties the SFTU continued to regard itself as the leading agent of protest politics in Swaziland.

SWAZILAND GOVERNMENT COMMITTEE (1890–1895). A triumvirate governing committee representing the Swazi nation (**Theophilus Shepstone, Jr.**), the **South African Republic** (SAR; **Daniel J. Esselen**), and **Britain** (**Col. Richard E. R. Martin**). The committee superseded the **Provisional Government Committee** (1889–90), whose membership was identical, but which went out of existence with the implementation of the **first Swaziland Convention** in September 1890. The committee's purpose was to provide a civil government of the European community in Swaziland, as distinct from the Swazi monarchy. The committee was headquartered at **Albert Bremer**'s hotel in Bremersdorp (**Manzini**). It established the first civil (five officials) and judicial (five justices of the peace, eight officials) administrations in the kingdom. It also established a police force consisting of 12 Europeans and 36 African constables. Finally, it established a **Chief Court** in Bremersdorp to inquire into the disputed **concessions**.

From 1892 to 1893 Shepstone was replaced by **Godfrey Lagden**, government secretary in Basutoland. Otherwise Shepstone, when he acted as the Swaziland representative, attempted to dominate and manipulate the committee in ways similar to his actions on the **Swazieland Committee** prior to 1889. Shepstone habitually signed official papers as "Chairman of the Swazieland Government Committee" although he was never so designated officially. He got away with that behavior in part because of the running dispute going on between Esselen and Martin over a succession of issues. The committee was disbanded in February 1895 with the implementation of the **third Swaziland Convention** (1894) initiating the **Transvaal**'s administration of Swaziland.

SWAZILAND INDEPENDENCE FRONT (1964). A short-lived political association formed in April 1964 by politically moderate Europeans in order to contest the **Legislative Council** elections in June. The association's idea was to present the European voters with a relatively liberal alternative to the conservative **United Swaziland Association** for the four seats reserved for the European voters' roll. Its platform envisioned Swaziland as a nonracial country under majority (i.e., Swazi) rule. Losing all four contests, the front collapsed.

SWAZILAND IRON ORE DEVELOPMENT COMPANY. Formed in 1958 by the Anglo-American Corporation of South Africa in partnership (90%-10%) with the British steel-making corporation of Guest, Keen, and Nettlefolds. Anglo formed the company to prospect and develop the rich (62.5% iron) ore deposit at **Ngwenya** in the mountainous region of northwestern Swaziland. The deposit, amounting to some 30 million tons, had been discovered in the late 1940s as the result of an archeological investigation of an iron-age site. The company, capitalized at £3,500,000 ($16,500,000), signed an agreement in 1961 with two major Japanese steel producers (Yawata and Fuji) to supply an initial 12 million tons of ore over a 10-year period. At that time the Colonial (later **Commonwealth) Development Corporation (CDC)** took a 7 percent stake in the company, valued at £250,000 ($1,250,000). Such was the volume of ore to be transported that a railroad was built from Ngwenya to **Matsapha** and thence across Swaziland's eastern border to Lourenço Marques (Maputo). The **Swaziland Railway** was capitalized (£5,000,000, or $25,000,000) principally by Anglo American, the CDC, the Swaziland government, and the British high commission. The company constructed the railroad in two years, 1962–64. Three giant ore transports were constructed with foreign capital to carry the ore from Lourenço Marques to Japan. At no point during the years-long negotiations were the *ingwenyama*, **Sobhuza Dlamini II**, or the *libandla* officially consulted or invited to participate.

The company operated from 1961 to 1981, mining out all the high and medium grade ore, then shutting down once it was exhausted. The Swaziland administration's refusal to share any of the operation's returns with the Swazi (aside from laborers' wages) created such ill feeling on the part of Sobhuza and the *libandla* that it became a major determinant in his unequivocal demand that the mineral wealth of the kingdom fall to him at the time of independence.

SWAZILAND IRRIGATION SCHEME (SIS). A massive **irrigation** project near **Tshaneni** in the northeastern Swaziland **lowveld** developed by the **Colonial Commonwealth** Development Corporation (CDC) beginning in 1950. Its basis was a 105,000-acre tract of land purchased from Swaziland Ranches Ltd. (originally concessioned to **John Thorburn** in 1889), with water rights from both the **Komati** and Mbuluzi rivers. In 1957 work was completed on a 42-mile canal from the Komati, which provided the basis for the irrigated **sugarcane**, citrus, and (for the first 20 years) rice estates that were developed. By the mid-1970s rice growing, because of excessive salinity buildup, gave way to other cropping: pineapples, bananas, and **cotton**. The two initial developments were Tambankulu estates (citrus) and **Mhlume** (Swaziland) Sugar Company, which began milling in 1960. Mhlume, at first owned jointly by the CDC and Huletts, became wholly owned by the CDC in 1966. In 1964 a dam was constructed across the Sand River valley to act as a supplement to the canal and as insurance against drought.

A third 3,000-acre estate complex connected to the Komati canal, the **Vuvulane** Irrigated Farms, was established in 1963. This combined irrigated agriculture with a CDC attempt at social engineering whereby Swazi farmers were to have access to farms and smallholdings in freehold or with long-term leases. The farms were intended to grow cane for the Mhlume mill, while the smallholdings were to be devoted to cotton, maize, and vegetables. Agriculturally the venture was successful, with the Swazi proving themselves to be productive farmers, but politically Vuvulane was perceived by *iNgwenyama* **Sobhuza Dlamini II** and other traditionalists as a threat to the Swazi custom of communal land tenure that constituted the ultimate basis for the power of the monarchy and chiefs. Consequently following independence, when the long-term leaseholdings came up for renewal, they were canceled.

SWAZILAND NATIONAL ASSOCIATION OF TEACHERS (SNAT). Until 1990 the Swazi National Union of Teachers (SNUT). A historically strong and militant teachers' union whose actions since 1973 should be viewed in the context of the move of opposition politics from **parliament** to organized labor following *iNgwenyama* **Sobhuza Dlamini II**'s repeal of the constitution in that year. Sobhuza's suspension of parliament and banning of political parties gave new life to the **trade union** movement, which had been on the wane since the mid-1960s. The most militant of the unions was the Swaziland National Union of Teachers, registered with the government in the late 1960s. SNUT was the main force behind the joining of all major unions into the **Swaziland Federation of Trade Unions (SFTU)**, registered in 1973. It was SNUT that led the first nationwide **strike** in 1977, and both the strike's violent character and the dual nature of its protests (over both economic and political issues) became the models for subsequent labor activism over the following two decades. SNUT itself was banned following the 1977 strike but re-emerged as SNAT under the provisions of the Industrial Relations Act (4/1980). During the 1980s and early 1990s SNAT, under the leadership of Albert Shabangu, staged a succession of nationwide teachers' strikes demanding higher wages while at the same time making explicit its position that the root cause of the teachers' plight was political authoritarianism. By the mid-1990s leadership of the political aspects of the labor opposition campaign had been largely taken over by the SFTU.

SWAZILAND NATIVE LAND SETTLEMENT SCHEME (SNLSS). Following the awarding of two-thirds of the territory to European settlers and the crown by provision of the **Partition Proclamation of 1907**, the colonial government saw the Swazi over two ensuing generations become progressively starved of land. Landlessness was the result of population growth in the **native areas**, the expulsion of Swazi squatters from European farms, and the refusal of the administration to transfer **crown lands** to the Swazi nation under any terms. So critical had the situation become by 1938 that the **resident commissioner** recommended the sale of land, both crown and private, for Swazi occupation. His recommendation was rejected by the **high commissioner** on the grounds that such a policy would upset the European settlers and endanger the viability of the labor market both in Swaziland and on the Rand.

It was the World War II–generated need for the loyalty and productivity of the colonies that prompted **Britain**'s change of policy on land for the Swazi. Pressure for that change was applied by the shrewd initiative of *iNgwenyama* **Sobhuza Dlamini II**, who in 1941 dramatically petitioned the British parliament to alleviate Swazi landlessness and obtained the support of the Anti-Slavery and Aborigines Protection Society. In 1942 London authorized the expenditure of **Colonial Development and Welfare Act** (1940) funds to establish the Swaziland Native Land Settlement Scheme. It provided for an initial £150,000 ($750,000) with which to purchase sufficient acreage to alleviate the landlessness of 20,000 Swazi (4,000 families). By the end of the 1940s more than £200,000 ($1,000,000) had been expended to purchase 342,000 acres (138,510 hectares) for three principal settlements: **Pigg's Peak**, Herefords, and Nkwene. Each settler family was allotted about 75 acres (30 hectares), which provided for agricultural fields, a residential area, and grazing for 10 head of **cattle**.

What seemed like a total victory for Sobhuza was in his (and the *libandla*'s) eyes marred by a gigantic flaw that quickly turned the SNLSS into the subject of a highly contentious, running confrontation with the administration. Colonial officials, partly to maximize wartime productivity, mandated that the Swazi settlers be awarded the land in leasehold, and not in traditional, communal land tenure controlled by the *ingwenyama* through the chiefs. Quickly Sobhuza and the *libandla* came to view the SNLSS as a direct threat to the monarchy, whose ultimate control over the peasantry lay in its power to allocate and withhold land. The irony was that London had created the SNLSS in the first place partly to mollify Sobhuza's opposition to the **Native Administration Proclamation**, initially proposed in 1939, which had also embodied provisions threatening his sovereignty. Consequently Sobhuza withheld his support from the SNLSS as long as control of land and tenure remained with colonial authorities.

Partly for that reason the SNLSS failed in its primary objectives. By 1950 less than 3,000 of the planned 20,000 peasants had been relieved of their landlessness. Peasants were reluctant to become SNLSS settlers for a variety of other reasons as well, such as poor lands in the settlements and restrictions on cattle and goat holdings. Those who did settle on the land proved to be no more productive in terms of bags of maize per acre than the peasantry on **Swazi Nation Land** and no more progressive in instituting new methods of agriculture.

The SNLSS ended up falling short of Britain's original goals one by one, with the exception of restoring land to the Swazi. The final blow to British intentions came in 1946 when, the war over, the resident commissioner capitulated to Sobhuza's demands and declared all SNLSS lands subject to Swazi traditional tenure, under the control of the *ingwenyama*. That proved to be a signal victory in Sobhuza's campaign to regain his domestic sovereignty.

SWAZILAND POLICE. *See* ROYAL SWAZI POLICE FORCE

SWAZILAND PROGRESSIVE ASSOCIATION (SPA). An association of educated Swazi founded in 1929 for the purpose of furthering the interests of the nascent Swazi middle class. The first president was **Benjamin Nxumalo**, and the secretary was **Fynn Sepamla**. In 1945, following Nxumalo's death, **John J. Nquku** was elected president, and he edited its newsletter, *Ngwane*. Initiative for the formation of the SPA came from **Resident Commissioner T. Ainsworth Dickson** (1928–35), who sought an established means of communication with both the **EurAfrican** population and "native intellectuals" (or "exempted [from native tax, but paying poll tax] natives"). At his instigation the SPA, at first comprising both EurAfrican and Swazi members (except at Hlatikulu, where there were separate organizations), met with him twice yearly to discuss matters of concern. Subsequently the EurAfricans formed a separate interest group, the **Coloured** (later **EurAfrican**) **Welfare Association**. With Dickson the SPA raised a number of middle-class issues, and each of them got a fair and often sympathetic hearing from him. Early agenda items included discriminatory treatment at hospitals and on **South African Railways and Harbours Road Motor Transport** buses; a request that educated Africans have access to agricultural loan funds, and that they be allowed to purchase **crown lands** and urban business stands (especially eating houses and hotels); a query about increasing the number of African clerks employed by the government; and a petition that SPA members sit on educational advisory boards. Later concerns were education and tax policies, and labor conditions.

Somewhat to Dickson's surprise he found *iNgwenyama* **Sobhuza Dlamini II**, with his past reputation as a progressive, cool to the idea of a formal association of Swazi intellectuals. Sobhuza always harbored suspicions of associations not fully under his control, and in 1929 he was in the midst of his transformation from a progressive chief who admired Western ways to one who evoked "tradition" (i.e., conservative nationalism) as his political mantra. Sobhuza questioned the need for the SPA with Dickson, and when that did not work he insisted that it function only through the *libandla*, which to some degree it subsequently did. The SPA's efforts to accommodate itself to the monarchy were hampered by the king's continuing hostility toward it and the *libandla*'s consequent reluctance to associate with it. Part of Sobhuza's concern lay with the fact that so many SPA members were South African–born, which in his mind brought into question their loyalty to him in any future confrontation with the government. Dickson, who did not retreat from his support of the SPA, was however quick to pick up on Sobhuza's hostility to its separate line of communication and warned its members at their second meeting that their primary loyalty remained to the *ingwenyama* in *libandla*. For a few years Sobhuza attended all SPA meetings with the **resident commissioner**, and thereafter he kept tabs on the organization through its officers who were also *libandla* members and loyal to him: Nxumalo, then Nquku.

Nquku, once he became president in 1945, increasingly viewed the SPA as an appropriate vehicle for his own ambitions, which were considerable and which by the late 1950s had become transparently political. As a consequence his (and assuredly the SPA's) relations with Sobhuza became strained, the more so following Nquku's return from Ghana in 1957 full of enthusiasm for its brand of Pan-Africanism. It came as no surprise, then, that as Swaziland entered the pre-independence era Nquku transformed the SPA into Swaziland's first opposition party, the **Swaziland Progressive Party (SPP)**, which he hoped would place him in the political spotlight. That transformation (mid-1960) rang down the curtain on the SPA.

SWAZILAND PROGRESSIVE PARTY (SPP). The earliest, and for a while the most significant, of the opposition political parties founded in pre-independence Swaziland during the early 1960s. The SPP was established by **John J. Nquku** out of the shell of the **Swaziland Progressive Association (SPA)**, of which he was president. Nquku, a man of exceptional ability and ambition, considered the independence movements in West Africa to be replicable in Swaziland. On his return from Ghana in 1957 he set about politicizing the SPA in preparation for that day. It came in mid-1960, following Prime Minister MacMillan's "Winds of Change" speech and moves by both *iNgwenyama* **Sobhuza Dlamini II** and **Resident Commissioner Brian Marwick** to initiate a dialogue on the formation of an internal legislature.

Nquku's SPP, launched in July 1960, was largely the SPA made over into a political machine, with a membership drawn like the SPA from urbanized, educated Swazi and foreign-born Africans. Its platform, like the SPA's, was liberal, not radical, espousing a nonracial constitutional democracy based on universal suffrage (i.e., one person, one vote). Nquku became president, while **Dr. Ambrose Zwane** became secretary general. The SPP's early efforts at building a constituency beyond that base were hampered by the fact of Nquku's Zulu birth, which was unpopular with many Swazi. In addition the political conservatism of the average Swazi did not brook the fascination for Ghanaian-style Pan-Africanism and African socialism espoused by the SPP leadership, especially Zwane. Compounding that was the leadership's failure to establish effective local branches needed to turn the party into a grassroots organization.

Zwane, Nquku, and **Obed Mabuza**, another SPP official, were made members of the first constitutional committee convened by Marwick in November 1960. They proceeded to use its meetings as a forum for their radical political ideas, which served only to polarize the committee and drive the Swazi traditionalists and the conservative settler politicians closer together. Finally in early 1961 Nquku was expelled from the committee for his "disruptive" tactics, and Zwane and Mabuza resigned in protest. Still the SPP sought to establish a solid base for itself in the coming political fray. In early 1961 it engaged Professor **Dennis V. Cowen** of the University of Cape Town, a distinguished liberal constitutional authority, to draw up a draft constitution that would both recognize the then current political realities and point the way toward a future democratic order. The Cowen Report, published in September 1961, was never officially adopted, but it later became the basis for the **1967** pre-independence Swaziland **constitution**.

Meanwhile the SPP itself was giving way to internal factionalism. The main cause was Nquku's character and style of leadership, both authoritarian. Zwane and others accused him of rule by personality cult and of high living and misappropriation of funds during his frequent trips abroad to African capitals and to the United Nations. During one such absence (1961) Zwane attempted to take over the party but failed. The irretrievable split came in early 1962 when Zwane left the party with his followers (including **Mnt. Dumisa Dlamini**, head of the SPP youth wing) and established his own organization. He renamed his faction the **Ngwane National Liberatory Congress** in early 1963, with himself as president and Dlamini as secretary general. Later in 1962 Mabuza split with Nquku (again absent abroad) and formed yet another splinter group of the SPP.

Practically speaking that spelled the end of the SPP and of Nquku's dream of a political place in the sun. Over the next several months Nquku and his new secretary general, Albert Nxumalo, kept the semblance of a party organization maintained and themselves in the public eye by writing letters to *The Times of Swaziland* and other newspapers. Results of the 1964 **Legislative Council** elections, however, made a mockery of the party and its leadership. The SPP won no seats, and Nquku himself lost to his opponent by a vote of 13,500 to 56. In the 1967 parliamentary elections the SPP garnered only 0.1 percent of the popular vote, with Nquku receiving 34 votes and losing his deposit. Nquku retired officially as party leader in 1972. By the time Sobhuza outlawed political parties in 1973 the SPP was long gone.

SWAZILAND RAILWAY. A railway established by statute in 1962 in order to transport iron ore from the **Ngwenya** mines in western Swaziland to the ocean port at Lourenço Marques (Maputo), Mozambique, a distance of 137 miles (219 kilometers). The western terminus was at kaDake, while the eastern border crossing point was at Mlawula. The railway took a circuitous route to the border in order to service the industrial regions of Swaziland, notably **Matsapha** and **Mpaka**. Distances are eastern border to Matsapha, 88 miles (142 kilometers), and Matsapha to kaDake, 43 miles (69 kilometers). Following the closing of the Ngwenya mine, the Matsapha-kaDake segment became dormant.

Until the late 1990s the Swaziland Railway carried only freight, with the occasional exception of holiday passenger excursions and the repatriation of Mozambican refugees during the mid-1990s. In 1998 the railway established a regular passenger service between Mpaka and Durban, and it announced plans to initiate similar service to Johannesburg. During the 1980s new rail lines were added, mainly to service the coal and agribusiness industries. One is from Phuzmoya to Lavumisa (Golela, Natal), 56 miles (90 kilometers) in length, linking Swaziland with the South African ports of Durban and Richards Bay. The other is from Mpaka north via Mananga to the South African rail terminus at Komatipoort, **Transvaal**, 60 miles (97 kilometers) in length. South African rail traffic substantially cuts distances and eliminates steep gradients by transiting Swaziland from Komatipoort to Richards Bay and Durban. A dry port was completed at Matsapha in 1993, making it an international port of entry and exit for goods transported by rail. During 1992–93 Swaziland Railways transported 4.2 million tons of freight, of which 3.2 million tons (76 percent) was transit traffic. *See also* Swaziland Iron Ore Development Company

SWAZILAND SEBENTA SOCIETY. *See* SEBENTA NATIONAL INSTITUTE (SNI)

SWAZILAND UNITED FRONT. *See* JOINT COUNCIL OF SWAZILAND POLITICAL PARTIES

SWAZILAND YOUTH CONGRESS (SWAYOCO). A student protest organization formed in mid-1991 to campaign for representative democracy in Swaziland. In many ways a companion organization to the **People's United Democratic Movement (PUDEMO)**, SWAYOCO, led by Mphandlana Shongwe, staged a succession of peaceful marches and increasingly strident confrontations with the police and government authorities in protest of the *tinkhundla* electoral system, which it viewed as both root and symbol of much wider social and political ills. SWAYOCO sought to enhance its image as a peaceful and popular organization by couching its protests in terms of clean-up, squatters' and vendors' rights campaigns in towns and land rights movements in the countryside. SWAYOCO, according to Richard Levin, quickly emerged as a leading force for change and a means through which "the youth of Swaziland increasingly came to spearhead the campaign for democracy."[10] It did not, however, begin to rival PUDEMO's influence as the leading political protest group in Swaziland at the turn of the century.

NOTES

1. Lord Hailey, *Native Administration in the British African Territories. Part V. The High Commission Territories: Basutoland, The Bechuanaland Protectorate, and Swaziland* (London: HMSO, 1953), p. 383.

2. Bonner, *Kings, Commoners and Concessionaires*, pp. 14–17.

3. Thoko T. Ginindza, *Sibongo: Swazi Clan Names and Clan Praises* (Manzini: Swazi Heritage Series, 1992), p. 7.

4. Jones, *Biographical Register*, p. 543.

5. Ronald Hyam, *The Failure of South African Expansion, 1908–1948* (New York: Africana Publishing, 1972), p. 18.

6. Pim, *Financial and Economic Situation of Swaziland*, p. 13.

7. Macmillan, "Swaziland: Decolonisation," 664.

8. Kuper, *Sobhuza II*, p. 101.

9. Crush, *Struggle for Swazi Labour*, p. 147.

10. Richard Levin, *When the Sleeping Grass Awakens: Land and Power in Swaziland* (Johannesburg: Witwatersrand University Press, 1997), p. 219.

-T-

THE EMPLOYMENT BUREAU OF AFRICA (TEBA). *See* NATIVE RECRUITING CORPORATION (NRC)

THIRD SWAZILAND CONVENTION (1894). Signed by the British and **South African Republic (SAR)** governments, the convention wrenched from the Swazi the independence they had been guaranteed by the **Pretoria** (1881) and **London** (1884) **Conventions** and by the **first Swaziland Convention** (1890). It did so by awarding the SAR "all rights and powers of protection, legislation, jurisdiction and administration over Swaziland and the inhabitants thereof," although it fell short of physical incorporation. Finally, it dispensed with the stipulation that to validate the convention the queen regent and *libandla* must sign on to its provisions by means of an **organic proclamation**, which they refused to do. A variety of provisions left intact the trappings of internal sovereignty. The Swazi would be allowed a "**paramount chief**" (**Bhunu Dlamini**), along with such traditional laws and customs as did not clash with the convention, and along with their grazing and agricultural rights. The convention further stipulated that no railway would be constructed through Swaziland without British assent, and no taxes would be levied for three years. The SAR administered Swaziland through a special commissioner and other administrative and judicial officials from 1895 to the outbreak of the **Anglo-Boer War** in 1899.

THORBURN, JOHN (1836–1909). Early concessionaire and businessman in Swaziland, arriving via a circuitous route in 1886. Born in **Britain**, Thorburn had fought for the Union in the American Civil War, dug diamonds near Kimberley, and plied the waters of **Delagoa Bay** in a steamboat he had hauled overland from the Vaal River. Thorburn obtained a land **concession** in the shadow of the *ingwenyama*'s headquarters at **Mbekelweni**, where he established a hotel (the Embekelweni Hotel) and a store. The hotel's main attraction was a canteen dispensing spirits, which soon became the favored watering spot of the growing concessionaire community. *iNgwenyama* **Mbandzeni Dlamini** frequented the bar and formed a close relationship with Thorburn, which the latter proceeded to exploit, much to the anger of **Theophilus Shepstone, Jr.**, Mbandzeni's advisor.

In 1888 Thorburn obtained a concession granting him the banking monopoly, but Shepstone refused to register it until Thorburn interceded with the *ingwenyama* and forced the issue. So began a bitter enmity between the two powerful men that quickly divided the European community into two camps. Most concessionaires backed Thorburn, who enjoyed such influence with Mbandzeni as to be able to influence him decisively against Shepstone. In mid-1888 Thorburn helped to persuade Mbandzeni to dismiss Shepstone (the *ingwenyama* then rehired him at a fixed salary) and to sign the "**White Charter**" allowing the concessionaires to govern themselves. Thorburn was elected a member of the second and third **Swazieland Committees** in October–November 1888. By early 1889 Shepstone was out, replaced by **Allister Miller**, Thorburn's henchman, as secretary. The Thorburn forces thenceforth were in command.

Thorburn then proceeded to cash in on his influence. In 1888 he was granted a 50-year concession for lands north of the **Komati River** (211,070 acres; 85,419 hectares) in return for an annual rental of £2 ($10). He also received the unallotted minerals concession covering areas not already concessioned and lapsed concessions over all of Swaziland. Liquor importation and surveying monopolies followed. Thorburn's wife was granted two more monopolies, and Thorburn charged and received quarter shares of concessions granted to others through his influence with the king. In July 1889 Thorburn received the infamous 50-year **unallotted lands concession** covering all lands not previously allotted and lapsed concessions south of the Komati River, in return for an annual payment of £50 ($100).

Meanwhile Thorburn and Miller were shopping those and allied concessions to the government of the **South African Republic**, which later would enable it to govern Swaziland. They included the surveying, postal, and customs monopolies. In 1893 Thorburn and Miller incorporated themselves as the Umbandine Swazieland Concessions Syndicate Ltd., capitalized on Thorburn's (and his wife's) concessions, and sold shares. The syndicate later became the **Swazieland Corporation**, which in 1898 was listed on the London City (stock) Exchange with a capitalization of £300,000 ($1,500,000). Miller became the managing director in Swaziland, while Thorburn retired to Britain to live out most of the rest of his days. Thorburn, equally with Miller and Shepstone, bears the primary responsibility for betraying Mbandzeni's trust and friendship with such disastrous consequences to Swaziland. The best that can be said of Thorburn is that he never held an official position with which to compound his treachery, as did the other two.

umuTI. *See* HOMESTEAD

TIBIYO takaNGWANE FUND ("Tibiyo"). "The Wealth of the Swazi Nation." The royal investment trust established by *iNgwenyama* **Sobhuza Dlamini II** upon independence in 1968, when he was constitutionally vested with the mineral wealth of the nation. One of the hottest issues of contention between Sobhuza and the British government (along with the Swazi opposition parties) prior to independence was the ownership of Swaziland's natural (principally mineral) wealth. **Britain** wished to vest it in the new parliamentary government, but Sobhuza fought to have it vested in him "in trust for the Swazi nation." Sobhuza finally won, and he established Tibiyo to invest the revenues. His charter to Tibiyo dedicated it to advancing the "material welfare, standard of living and education" of the people, while at the same time preserving their "customs and traditional institutions." Tibiyo is overseen by a governing board appointed by the king.

Since 1968 Tibiyo claims to have continuously promoted the economic and cultural progress of the people through land repurchase, small business development, agricultural investments, educational scholarships, and the like. Substantial resources went into the purchase of freehold land from non-Swazis, much of which it developed into its own maize and dairy estates. It also set up a number of enterprises from butcheries to a national airline and a state television broadcasting service. The extent to which Tibiyo's resources are invested in the Swazi nation as a whole is unknown because its books are not open to the public. Basically Tibiyo is a closed-end corporation, largely secretive in nature, whose revenues are used in substantial portion to accumulate wealth on behalf of the monarchy and its interests. That is to say that Tibiyo's revenues do not accrue to the Ministry of Finance in **Mbabane**, but rather to Tibiyo's headquarters in **Lozithehlezi**. Although it is true that a portion of its wealth (there is really no telling how much, although its chairman valued its investments in 1999 at E552 million [$88 million]) is also used for the public good, the public arguably pays for much of it by virtue of the fact that Tibiyo is not subject to government taxation. Particularly in the case of Tibiyo, the phrase "in trust for the Swazi nation" resonates with an especially hollow ring.

By the 1990s Tibiyo had long ceased to be a mineral-based corporation. Much of its resources had been used since the 1960s to purchase large equity stakes (normally half interest) in most of the significant foreign investment ventures in the kingdom: **sugar**, timber, meat and food processing, **asbestos**, construction, insurance, and hotels and casinos. Many of its shares were acquired from the relevant foreign corporations with minimal capital expenditure, all in the name of "the national interest." Others were purchased at something closer to fair market value, as was the case of Usutu Forests (**Usutu Pulp Company**), which it owns outright. The architect for most of Tibiyo's domestic investment program was **Simon Sishayi Nxumalo**, a member of Tibiyo's founding committee in 1968, and subsequently either the general manager of the corporation or secretary of its governing committee from then until the time of Sobhuza's death.

By 1976 Tibiyo had accumulated sufficient capital for it to spin off many of its operations (principally in housing projects, office buildings, and commercial farms) to a second closely held royal investment trust, the Tisuka takaNgwane ("Foundation of the Nation") Fund. The most conspicuous of Tibiyo's publicly acknowledged commercial failures has been the **Royal Swazi National Airways Corporation**, which has hemorrhaged capital since its establishment in 1978 and which in 1998 was seeking an operating partner from among South Africa's group of private regional air carriers.

TIMES OF SWAZILAND (TOS), THE. Originally *The Times of Swazieland*. The principal English-language newspaper in Swaziland, founded in 1897. The *TOS* has been published from 1897 to 1899 (the outbreak of the **Anglo-Boer War**, when the *TOS*'s offices and printing facilities were destroyed), 1903 to 1909, and 1931 to the present. Its part owner, editor, and publisher was **Allister Miller**, whose previous newspaper experience had been with the *Cape Argus* (Cape Town) and the *Gold Fields News* (Barberton). Miller's early editorial mission was to lobby for the development of Swaziland as a European-dominated colony, settled by English-speakers, subsidized by roads and a railway built with metropolitan capital, and based on what he termed a "detribalized" (i.e., proletarianized) Swazi population. With the passage of the **Partition Proclamation** in 1907 the *TOS* had, in his words (*TOS* January 30, 1909) "done the work it was intended to perform," and it ceased publication for the following 22 years.

In late 1931, at a time when Miller and much of the rest of the settler community feared that Swaziland would be incorporated into the **Union of South Africa** before its settler economy had been "fully developed," publication of the *TOS* was resumed. Jonathan Crush associates the resumption of publication more directly to settler fears that the new, post-**Robert A. Coryndon/de Symons Honey** generation of colonial officials was exhibiting a disquieting sympathy toward Swazi culture and interests.[1] Editorially the newspaper was somewhat more circumspect. It promised its readers that the *TOS* "has again become a necessity as an instrument for public service," defining the public as "all Swaziland's inhabitants." Until the 1940s most of the *TOS*'s editorials were written by Allister Miller. Later they were written largely by **John Houlton**.

A Zulu-language edition of the *TOS* (**siSwati** not being a written language until the 1960s) was published on an irregular basis beginning in 1936. During and after World War II the *TOS* was published by the Swaziland Printing and Publishing Company, whose owner was Allister Miller, Jr. In 1950 the newspaper was sold to the High Commission Territories Printing and Publishing Company, owned by the Bantu Press of South Africa. During the late 1950s the *TOS* became a daily paper, and in the mid-1980s it began to publish the *Weekend Times*. Daily circulation in 1998 was 50,000. A competing newspaper, **The Swazi Observer**, owned by the **Tibiyo takaNgwane Fund** and reflecting the views of the royal house, began publication in 1982.

TIN. A major source of mineral wealth in Swaziland, mined from the turn of the century until 1948.[2] The heyday of tin mining in Swaziland was from 1905 to 1920. Cassiterite tin (i.e., tin dioxide) was discovered during the early 1890s. The seam ran from the vicinity of Oshoek (northwest Swaziland) in a southwesterly direction, 64 miles (104 kilometers) to the Mhlatuzane River near Maloma. Payable tin was found only along the 19-mile (31-kilometer) stretch from Oshoek to the southern end of the Lupholo and Mantenga hills, which formed the western rim of the **Ezulwini Valley**. Most of the tin mining (with the exception, briefly, of Forbes Reef) took place around **Mbabane** and the Lupholo/Mantenga hills, where the earth overburden was sufficiently thin and the water (for "sluicing" the overburden from the ore) plentiful enough to make mining profitable. Small mines were also operated along the iNgwenpisi River and near Sitobela.

Between 1905 and 1920 tin constituted more than 50 percent of Swaziland's exports by value. By 1920 with the decline of **gold** mining, tin constituted 95 percent of Swaziland's mineral exports by value. The strongest tin mining profits were earned during World War I, when tin prices reached more than £300 ($1,500) per dressed ton. After the mid-1920s profitability declined erratically until mining ceased in 1948. The earliest mining company of note was the Ryan Tin Syndicate Ltd. (Sidney T. Ryan, manager), which operated from 1890 to 1899. The primary producer afterwards was Swaziland Tin Ltd., formed from the Ryan syndicate's remains and owned by the Johannesburg mining firm of H. Eckstein & Co., which by the end of World War I was producing 90 percent of the tin exported. The second largest mining concern was Mc-Creedy Tins Ltd. (founded by George B. McCreedy), which worked the hills west of the Ezulwini Valley near present-day **Mlilwane**. Profitability was sapped by lack of rail transport to Johannesburg, but after 1911 costs of tin production were reduced dramatically by the introduction of high-pressure water hoses to break up the overburden. The resultant cost to Swaziland's ecology, however, was high. Great scars still mar the countryside around Mlilwane, and the resultant pollution of the **Lusushwana River** was the scourge of downstream European and Swazi farmer alike for many years. In 1946 **James ("Mickey") Reilly**, at that time head of McReedy Tins, was fined for polluting the Lusushwana. The cumulative value of tin exports from Swaziland totalled £2 million ($10 million).

TINKHUNDLA. Regional councils. *iNkhundla* refers to the space outside the **cattle** byre where men meet to discuss local affairs. *Tinkhundla* were first established by *iNgwenyama* **Sobhuza Dlamini II** in 1955 in an effort to bring the traditional administrative system up to date in the modern era when governance through chiefs had diminished in effectiveness, particularly in dealings with the colonial administration. Each *inkhundla* was a royal administrative center, dating back to their World War II origins as **African Pioneer Corps** recruiting facilities. To each *inkhundla*, chiefs in a designated area were attached, and each center was under a governor appointed by the *ingwenyama*. Although traditional criteria of heredity and loyalty to the king remained of primary importance, qualifications for appointment to the new governorships also included some formal education, a degree of administrative ability (including knowledge of the law), and clerical efficiency. By the time of independence 22 *tinkhundla* had been established.

By the early 1960s the *tinkhundla* system was considered by colonial administrators and Swazi authorities alike to be deeply in trouble. *Tinkhundla* meetings were infrequently held and scantily attended. *iNkhundla* governors were considered lazy and inept. Furthermore the entire system was viewed with deep suspicion by chiefs as a means by which they were being bypassed by Sobhuza and thus rendered less relevant. Finally, in the words of one district official, "the Swazi National Council [*libandla*] has jealously refused to delegate authority [to the *tinkhundla*] and its pathological reluctance to make decisions has brought . . . tribal administration to a state of affairs closely akin to anarchy" (P. Simkin, File 3118B [1962], SNA).

For his part Sobhuza vigorously denied those accusations, but that did not make them go away. The system continued largely in name only throughout the 1960s and into the early 1970s, when the king resuscitated it as a mechanism by which to restore his total control of the parliamentary electoral system. He did so in 1978, five years following his repeal of Swaziland's **constitution**.

In that year the king decreed the establishment of a new *tinkhundla*-based electoral system for a bicameral **parliament**. The number of *tinkhundla* was increased to 40, then subdivided into four regions, each under a regional administrator. At the top stood the governor (*indvuna yetinkhundla*), appointed by the king. All candidates for parliament not directly appointed by the *ingwenyama* were selected by an electoral college chosen by the *tinkhundla* through public acclamation. Practically speaking, the *tinkhundla* system ended Swaziland's five-year experiment in parliamentary democracy, for under it "individual rights," in Hilda Kuper's words, "were subordinated to the interests of an autocratic aristocracy."[3] The *tinkhundla* system has served that purpose ever since. Realizing the chiefs' worst fears, the system further eroded their already diminished power under Sobhuza's rule. Furthermore the *tinkhundla* bureaucracy gradually usurped the powers of the central governmental bureaucracy of district commissioners and subcommissioners left behind by the British, until the latter became little more than a shadow government.

Popular opposition to the *tinkhundla* grew palpable by the mid-1980s. It was during that decade that the political trauma of the post-Sobhuza *Liqoqo* era, followed by the achievement of democracy in **South Africa**, created a political opposition movement of unprecedented strength in Swaziland. Not a little of that force was derived from the fact that the **People's United Democratic Movement (PUDEMO)** and other groups soon recognized the deeply evocative power of their criticisms of the *tinkhundla* system as anti-democratic. Finally in 1991, in response to popular dissatisfaction, *iNgwenyama* **Mswati Dlamini III** ordered a review of the system. The result was a cosmetic reform of the procedures featuring a two-stage legislative election through 55 *tinkhundla*, which allowed for a secret ballot at the second stage. At the same time the widespread demand for a return to multiparty politics was rejected, so that the unpopularity of the *tinkhundla* system was scarcely abated. The 1993 elections under the new regulations served to confirm to the voters that the system remained rigged, and consequently 1994 saw the beginnings of mass labor activism and sporadic political violence.

In mid-1996 Mswati, in response to the escalation of domestic opposition and to pressure exerted by the South African and other governments in the region, announced the formation of a **Constitutional Review Commission (CRC)**, whose charge was to produce within two years a new constitution that would represent the people's wishes. That deadline was extended for another two years in mid-1998. Given the *ingwenyama*'s penchant for forming advisory commissions largely for the purpose of buying time, what the CRC would finally produce was anyone's guess.

TITLE DEED LAND (TDL). Land in Swaziland held in permanent, legal possession under title deed, as opposed to the communally held **Swazi Nation Land (SNL)**. The origin of TDL was the **concessions** granted to Europeans during the reign of *iNgwenyama* **Mbandzeni Dlamini**, confirmed by the **Swaziland Concessions Commission** in 1906, and codified by the **Partition Proclamation of 1907**. That proclamation allocated approximately two-thirds of Swaziland either to European concessionaires in title deed or to the colonial government in the form of **crown land**, much of which was later sold to settlers in title deed. Following World War II much of that land was sold to development corporations and partnerships that combined, developed, and irrigated it in order to produce crops and timber products for export. Almost all of Swaziland's commercial agricultural production comes from TDL. Much TDL is either wholly (in the case of Usutu Forests of the **Usutu Pulp Company**) or partially owned by the **Tibiyo takaNgwane Fund** in partnership with foreign capital. A small amount of TDL is owned by Swazi smallholders cultivating **sugarcane**. In the late 1990s TDL constituted about 40 percent of Swaziland's total area.

TODD, CARL F. (1903–). South African–born settler farmer and politician who played a major role in national politics during the 1960s leading to independence. Todd was a Johannesburg lawyer who purchased extensive acreage in the Swaziland **lowveld** near Stegi (**Siteki**) beginning in the late 1930s. By the early 1960s he had major holdings in **cattle** and **sugar**. All the while he pursued his life in Johannesburg as a lawyer and corporate director, living part of the year there and part in Stegi. He was first elected to the **European Advisory Council** in 1948 and by the early 1960s was head of the **Reconstituted European Advisory Council (REAC)**. As such Todd was at the center of the political maneuverings leading to the drafting of Swaziland's pre-independence **constitution** in **1964**. Todd represented the REAC on the first constitutional committee in 1960–61; he lobbied aggressively, and at first successfully, for a **Legislative Council** comprising equal representation by Swazi (mainly *libandla* councillors) and Europeans (principally REAC members). It was that "50–50" draft constitution vesting power among the most conservative Swazi and European elements that Todd and a handful of other committee members presented to the British government at the first London constitutional conference in late 1961. That recommendation was strongly opposed by **Resident Commissioner Brian Marwick**, whose strained relationship with Todd lasted until his own departure in 1964. (Many years later Marwick wrote that Todd "stood head and shoulders above his colleagues in the EAC intellectually and as a man of affairs.") When the British government responded by rejecting the 50–50 proposal and convoked a second **constitutional conference** in London in early **1963**, Todd again headed the REAC delegation. This time the new opposition delegates deadlocked the conference and opened the way for the British-imposed constitution (May 1963) allowing for a Legislative Council (Legco) open to all groups, including political parties.

Among the parties formed to contest the 1964 elections was the **United Swaziland Association (USA)**, which Todd was instrumental in forming and which was essentially the conservative wing of the REAC dressed up for the fray. Once *iNgwenyama* **Sobhuza Dlamini II** had formed the royalist **Imbokodvo National Movement (INM)** to contest the elections, Todd left the USA and, with Sobhuza's agreement but to the surprise of the INM itself, joined the king's party. More moderate-leaning Europeans formed the **Swaziland Independence Front**. Todd was elected to the Legco amid the sweep of the IMF-USA electoral coalition and was appointed to the Legco executive as member for natural resources by the **Queen's Commissioner**, **Francis Loyd**. Todd subsequently served on the second constitutional committee (1965). By 1967 Sobhuza had divorced the INM from its coalition with the USA and had driven Europeans from its ranks, and Todd was left out of that year's parliamentary elections. Sobhuza did, however, make him one of his European nominees to the Senate and reappointed him in 1972.

Sobhuza's repeal of the constitution in 1973 spelled the end of Todd's career in Swazi politics. His influence with Sobhuza during the early 1960s, when Sobhuza had supported a privileged place for Europeans in the government, had been substantial. In the process Todd had made bitter enemies in the administration and with the political heavyweights among the Europeans, and when Sobhuza later cut his political ties with the Europeans Todd was left stripped of a constituency.

TRADE UNIONS. Trade unions are a relatively recent phenomenon in Swaziland. Although in theory Swazi workers have had the right to organize since 1942 (the Swaziland Trade Union and Trade Disputes Proclamation, reaffirmed by Law 12 of 1966), in fact the hostility of the colonial administration and *iNgwenyama* **Sobhuza Dlamini II** toward unions prevented their formation until the early 1960s. Sobhuza, who regarded the existence of any organization with the potential of rivaling his power with grave suspicion, attempted to substitute a royal *indvuna* (officer) system to handle grievances at the workplace in place of unions. The system was at first accepted by Swazi laborers, as was demonstrated during the **strike** at the **Havelock Asbestos Mine** in 1944, which was in part a protest against management's attempts to undercut Sobhuza's labor *indvuna*.

As late as 1960 the Catchpole *Report on Labour Legislation in Swaziland* remarked on the absence of any trade unions at that time, yet by then the development of an industrial infrastructure following World War II had produced a modern workforce that was prone to unionization. With the reduction in employment levels beginning in the early 1960s, militant trade unions soon established themselves in important industries. When they struck in 1963 (*see* **strikes, labor**), the unions demonstrated in dramatic fashion their unwillingness to accept Sobhuza's system of labor *tindvuna*, who could be too easily co-opted by management, in place of their own negotiators. When Sobhuza ordered the workers to cease their strikes and negotiate their grievances through his chief labor representative, **Mnt. Masitsela Dlamini**, they blatantly ignored him in favor of their own leaders. That unprecedented example of Sobhuza's inability to control his followers led to the government's declaration of an emergency in June 1963.

Trade unions were outlawed by decree during the emergency (1963–68), and Sobhuza's 1973 repeal of the constitution effectively barred them again. Swazi workers, left with no other means of political expression, repeatedly chose labor activism to vent their grievances in spite of all restrictions. In 1975 **Swaziland Railway** workers struck and marched on the royal residence. In 1977 teachers boycotted and took to the streets. In 1978 **sugar** workers at Big Bend struck and set cane fields alight. In each case the immediate grievances were wages, working conditions, and inadequate grievance procedures, but every action quickly turned into an explicit expression of underlying political disaffection.

In recognition of the deteriorating situation the government in 1980 enacted the Industrial Relations Act (IRA), which scrapped the old management-dominated grievance system based on the *ndabazabantu* (king's labor representative). In its place the act established a mechanism involving workers, employers, and government representatives, capped by an industrial court. Although the new grievance arrangement proved to be scarcely more acceptable to labor than the one it replaced, the IRA did specifically acknowledge the right of every worker to freedom of association and to organize. Under its provisions the government recognized several unions during the 1980s. Notable among them were the **Swaziland National Association of Teachers (SNAT)**, which had been banned following the 1977 strike, and the **Swaziland Federation of Trade Unions (SFTU)**, which had first been registered in 1973 but which had quickly become incapacitated during the emergency declared that year by the king.

During the 1990s, in the absence of any perceived constitutional reform, the unions took on once again, as in the post-1973 period, the leadership role in political opposition to the status quo. Led by the SFTU and SNAT, they staged a number of labor actions, including general strikes, whose underlying aims were to pressure the monarchy into moving toward real democratization.

TRANSVAAL. *See* SOUTH AFRICAN REPUBLIC

TRANSVAAL-SWAZILAND BOUNDARY COMMISSION. A three-man Royal Commission appointed in December 1879 by Sir Garnet Wolseley to decide on the boundaries between Swazi territory and the **Transvaal**. Chaired by **Major James Alleyne**, it also included G. M. Rudolph, landdrost of Utrecht district, and Lieutenant R. P. Littledale, Royal Engineers, as members. It was accompanied throughout its travels by three Swazi *tindvuna* (officials) appointed by *iNgwenyama* **Mbandzeni Dlamini**. Its delineation of Swaziland's northern and southern borders (January–March 1880) was most heavily influenced by Swazi failure to press their territorial claims and their consequent loss of them, including access to the Pongola River in the south, and a substantial portion of the modern Transvaal from Komatipoort south to the present border in the north.

umTSAKATSI **(pl.** *baTSAKATSI*). *See* WITCHCRAFT

TSHANENI. "Where the Grass Is." An agricultural settlement of 3,682 persons (1986 census) in northeastern Swaziland, it is five miles (eight kilometers) northwest of **Mhlume** and five miles (eight kilometers) south-southwest of Bordergate. Tshaneni is the headquarters of the **Swaziland Irrigation Scheme**, with citrus being the main crop. Tshaneni draws its **irrigation** water from both the **Komati River** and the Sand River reservoir.

TWALA, *iNDLOVUKAZI* **NTOMBI (c. 1948–).** Mother of *iNgwenyama* **Mswati Dlamini II** whose selection (1982) as queen mother was controversial in part because her *sibongo*, Twala, was not one of those historically associated with the parenting of kings. There were several others of *iNgwenyama* **Sobhuza Dlamini II**'s wives whose pedigrees made them more logical candidates, but Twala had been a handmaiden, and a favorite, of Sobhuza's most influential and beloved wife, laMasuku (**Pauline Fikelephi Masuku**) whose judgment the king had always trusted. According to Hilda Kuper, it was laMasuku who persuaded Sobhuza to take the young woman as a wife.[4] Also in Twala's favor as a candidate was the fact that she bore only one child, a son (Mnt. Makhosetive, "King of Many Nations"), who was from the time of his birth a favorite of the *ingwenyama*.

There was also great controversy over the manner of Ntombi's accession to the office of *indlovukazi* in 1983. On the face of it the move was unconstitutional, because normally an *indlovukazi* succeeds to the office only with the crowning of a new *ingwenyama* or upon the death of the previous *indlovukazi*. In this case the legitimate officeholder who had been named by Sobhuza in 1980, *iNdlovukazi* **Dzeliwe Shongwe**, was dismissed by the *Liqoqo* in 1983 in its attempted *coup d'état*, an act exceedingly unpopular at the time and one that was cited in its subsequent dismissal. Ntombi at that point agreed to the council's nomination of her as both *indlovukazi* and queen regent. She also signed the statement, one that Dzeliwe had refused to endorse (leading to her dismissal), recognizing the authority of the *Liqoqo* over her as queen regent. Mswati was crowned in 1986, and the *Liqoqo* was dismissed, its more unsavory members either being jailed or fleeing the country. Once legitimately in office, *iNdlovukazi* Ntombi became popular with the commoners, although her reputation among the intelligentsia remained colored by her actions during the interregnum. *See also* Dlamini, *Mntfwanenkhosi* Mfanasibili

TWELVE APOSTLES. *See* COMMITTEE OF TWELVE

-U-

UBOMBO RANCHES, LTD. One of the largest **sugar**-producing companies in Swaziland, second only to Simunye sugar complex in tonnage produced. Ubombo is located in the southwestern **lowveld** at Big Bend, encompassing about 36,600 acres (about 14,800 hectares), of which about 15,000 acres (about 6,000 hectares) are under **irrigation**. Ubombo was started in 1949 with the objects of ranching **cattle** for beef production and growing crops under irrigation. Initially rice was Ubombo's principal crop, grown until a drop in the world price and the increased salinity of the soil produced by the rice culture made it uneconomic. The first sugarcane was grown in 1957. The harvest was crushed in a small mill that had been dismantled in Natal and transported to Swaziland. A large modern mill was built and began production in 1960. Starting with 26,000 tons of sugar milled in 1961, Ubombo was producing over 145,000 tons of raw and refined sugar and 40,000 tons of molasses annually by 1987. The Ubombo Ranches complex, along with the Mhlume-Simunye mill group, constituted an unparalleled socioeconomic stimulus to Swaziland during the 1950s and 1960s. They opened up theretofore undeveloped regions of Swaziland, and in the process they generated a larger number of jobs for Swazi than had the gold mines on the Johannesburg reef. Ubombo, which employs 4,000 workers, is 60 percent owned by the Swaziland Sugar Milling Company and 40 percent owned by the **Tibiyo takaNgwane Fund**.

In 1963 Ubombo Ranches was the site of major labor unrest that, along with other **strikes**, led to the government declaration of an emergency in June. A **trade union** had been organized among workers, frustrated by poor working conditions and low wages, by **Mnt. Dumisa Dlamini**, later of the **Ngwane National Liberatory Congress (NNLC)**. In March, led principally by Dlamini, **Macdonald Maseko**, and **Dr. Ambrose Zwane**, nearly the entire workforce of 2,500 struck. Management persuaded them to return to work with a promise to look into their grievances, but when it then failed to follow through a higher-intensity walkout was staged in June. Dlamini and Maseko once again incited the workers, who this time used violence against non-strikers, and the unrest spread to Big Bend. Consequently some of the British troops flown in from Kenya on June 13 were immediately deployed to break the strike at Ubombo Ranches and arrest the leaders.

UMCWASHO. Coming of age ceremony. Now called *umhlanga* (Reed Ceremony). An annual nationwide organization of nubile but unmarried girls formed for the purpose of indoctrinating them with correct morals and values. Its ancillary purposes are to honor the coming of age of a princess or daughter of a principal chief, and also to honor the *indlovukazi* through tribute labor and praises. The week-long ritual involves dancing and singing—both praises for the *indlovukazi* and ridicule for those girls who were unchaste—and feasting. It is held in late August or early September, and it begins and ends with communal labor (wood cutting and reed gathering for fencing) at the *indlovukazi*'s **homestead**. An *umcwasho* ceremony was first performed nationally in 1935; until then it had been held locally. *iNgwenyama* **Sobhuza Dlamini II** established it as one element of his campaign to re-regiment Swazi youth as a means to reinvigorate support for the monarchy. At that time the *umcwasho* was intended to roughly parallel his *emabutfo* system for schoolboys.

The laws of the *umcwasho* covered food, clothing, language, group discipline, and moral behavior. At its heart was the imposition of chastity for its duration (two years) followed by emphasis on the need for sexual restraint. Stiff fines and public mockery were the fate of lawbreakers, both girls and their lovers. The centerpiece of the celebration was a ceremonial dance (the "reed dance") by the maidens, scantily clad and at their loveliest, in slow motion in front of the *ingwenyama* and assembled aristocracy. It soon became the universal assumption that, whatever the *umcwasho* laws, the reed dance was the ideal venue for comely girls to be observed by those with marriage on their minds—including the king. The atmosphere at the reed dance can best be described, consequently, as galvanic.

Immediately subsequent to its celebration in 1935, *umcwasho* fell into disuse because of strong opposition by the Christian missions on the grounds that it was immoral and "heathen." Sobhuza stoutly defended it, as he did the *emabutfo*, but the ceremony was not performed again nationally until 1946 (the return of the **African Pioneer Corps** from World War II service), and then not again until 1968 (independence). By the time it came to be performed again regularly during the 1970s times had changed and so had its character, which emphasized less the *umcwasho* laws and more the *umhlanga* (reed dance). The ceremony is now known commonly as *Umhlanga*, and it centers on the ceremonial repair of the *indlovukazi*'s fences with reeds, and the reed dance itself. It remains a popular attraction for the foreign diplomatic community and for tourists.

UMHLANGA. See UMCWASHO

UMNTFWANA. Literally "Child" (of the Nation). Also *iNkhosana* (Crown Prince). The title given to the newly designated heir to the Swazi kingship following the death of an *ingwenyama*. After a mourning period he lives in his new capital with his mother, the *nabomntfwana*, and stays in communication with the queen regent until he comes of age. He may neither rule "with power" nor take the lead in national affairs until he is considered old enough to marry his first ritual wife. He then relinquishes the title *umntfwana* and becomes *ingwenyama*.

UMTSAKATSI (pl. *BATSAKATSI*). *See* WITCHCRAFT

UMUTI. *See* HOMESTEAD

UNALLOTTED LANDS CONCESSION (UAC, 1889). One of the two most egregious **concessions** granted by the ailing and mentally unsound *iNgwenyama* **Mbandzeni Dlamini** a few weeks prior to his death. The other was the **private revenue concession** (also 1889). The UAC, granted to **John Thorburn** and Frank Watkins, gave them the rights to all lands not previously conceded south of the **Komati River**, plus the right of first refusal on all lapsed and forfeited concessions, for an annual rental of £50 ($250). The amount of land involved constituted about 16 percent of the territory. The term of the UAC was 50 years, with the right of renewal for another 50 years. The man responsible for the grant was the *ingwenyama*'s agent and advisor, **Allister Miller**, a close friend and business partner of Thorburn, and soon to be his son-in-law. The UAC transaction, constituting as it did such a massive betrayal of the *ingwenyama*'s trust, sullied Miller's name in Swazi history as much as anything else he did. In 1891 the rights embodied in the UAC were ceded to the Umbandine Swazieland Concessions Syndicate Ltd. (later the **Swaziland Corporation**), in which Thorburn and Miller were major shareholders.

Finally, the concession figured heavily in the lawsuit that *iNgwenyama* **Sobhuza Dlamini II** filed against Miller in 1924 (*Sobhuza II vs. Miller*). Because Miller's farm Dalriach (near **Mbabane**) was carved from UAC land conveyed to Miller by the Swaziland Corporation, Sobhuza's suit was actually against the validity of the UAC, which in turn stood as representative of all the concessions granted by Mbandzeni.

UNION OF SOUTH AFRICA. *See* SOUTH AFRICA, UNION OF

UNITED CHURCH OF AFRICA. *See* SWAZI NATIONAL CHURCH

UNITED KINGDOM. *See* BRITAIN

UNITED SWAZILAND ASSOCIATION (USA). A political association formed mainly by the conservative members of the **Reconstituted European Advisory Council (REAC)** in late 1963 in order to contest the election for the European roll seats in the new **Legislative Council** (Legco) scheduled for mid-1964. Its platform espoused "partnership" with the *ingwenyama* (**Sobhuza Dlamini II**) and allied Swazi tradition-alists, which meant from the outset, according to Christian Potholm, a privileged position for the settler population ("white supremacy was never far from its ultimate goal").[5] The leading forces behind the USA's formation were **Carl Todd** and **Robert Stephens**, but its political base lay more among the Afrikaans-speaking farmers in southern Swaziland, and it elected as its chairman **Willie Meyer**, a southern Swaziland farmer who had never relinquished his South African citizenship. The alterna-tive European party, the **Swaziland Independent Front**, while it agreed with much of the USA's platform (including reserved seats for settlers in the Legco), balked at the racial beliefs of certain individuals among its membership.

Almost immediately upon the formation of the royalist **Imbokodvo National Movement (INM)** in April 1964, it quietly struck an agree-ment with the USA to form an unofficial coalition for purposes of con-testing the election. The idea of both was to perpetuate the existing *de facto* sharing of power between the REAC (which formed the basis of the USA's membership) and the *libandla* (which formed the core of the INM's membership). The USA contested all the European and a share of the national roll seats, while Todd, by agreement with Sobhuza, ran as an INM candidate. In the June 1964 elections the USA-INM coali-tion succeeded perfectly in its purpose. The USA swept all the European seats, and between them the USA and the INM won every national roll seat.

Scarcely were the returns in before Sobhuza turned the tables on the USA. First, he began to strengthen the base of the INM by persuading some of the leadership of the other opposition parties to abandon the struggle and join Imbokodvo. Then in 1965 the INM membership on the second constitutional committee reversed its previous position and op-posed the concept of reserved seats for Europeans in the pre-indepen-dence constitution. When the USA persisted in pressing for a "50–50" sharing of power in the new **parliament**, the INM dismissed it as har-boring a "Kenyan mentality." In the end the USA's inability to achieve any compromise with the INM over the shape of the **1967 constitution** led to its collapse as a political movement, leaving its membership the option either to accept Swazi majority rule or to leave Swaziland. Most chose the first alternative, and the USA failed even to contest the 1967 elections.

UNIVERSITY OF SWAZILAND (UNISWA). The origins of UNISWA are found in Pius XII University College, opened at Roma, Basutoland, by the Roman Catholic mission in 1945. In 1963 the British government purchased the campus and re-established it by royal charter as the University of Basutoland, The Bechuanaland Protectorate and Swaziland. Following the independence of Basutoland and Bechuanaland in 1966, the institution became the University of Botswana, Lesotho, and Swaziland (UBLS). During the era of white minority rule UBLS matriculated many of its students from South Africa and Rhodesia as well as the former British territories. Financial aid came from **Britain**, the United States, Canada, the Netherlands, and the European Community.

In 1973, in part because of the political turmoil prevailing in Lesotho, UBLS was dissolved and each country eventually established its own university. UNISWA was built beginning in 1973 at Kwaluseni on land donated by *iNgwenyama* **Sobhuza Dlamini II**, who became chancellor of the university. Subsequently a UNISWA agricultural campus was established at Luyengo. Resources were provided by the Swaziland government and by the foreign supporters named above.

Degree courses are offered in agriculture (Luyengo campus), arts, commerce (including accounting, business studies, economics, and statistics), education, humanities, law, social science, and science. Evening extension business classes are offered in **Manzini** and **Mbabane**. Student enrollment in 1998 stood at 2,500, and the university was staffed with a faculty of 150. As is common among African universities, UNISWA has been over the years the theater of student political activism against the prevailing political institutions. The most serious incident occurred in November 1990 when UNISWA students protested against the government arrest of several members of the **People's United Democratic Movement**, including a UNISWA student and a lecturer. The protest was brutally put down by the police, resulting in one student death and several injuries, followed by the temporary closure of the university. Student bitterness over the incident, and the ways in which the university dealt with the students involved, lingered for the better part of a decade.

USUTU FORESTS. *See* USUTU PULP COMPANY

USUTU PULP COMPANY. Established in 1959 to process the coniferous timber products of Usutu Forests (now the Usutu Forest). Usutu Forests had been established in 1949, two years after the start-up of **Peak Timbers**. The forest, commissioned by **High Commissioner Sir Evelyn**

Baring and laid out by **Ian Craib**, originally covered the western highveld between the **Usutu** and **Lusushwana rivers**, with **Mhlambanyatsi** as its headquarters. Land was originally purchased (much of it from **Transvaal** sheep graziers) for a flat rate of £5 ($25) per acre (.405 hectares). Subsequent **highveld** acreage was forested by Usutu south of Bhunya, south of Gege, and around modern **Nhlangano**. Usutu Forests was originally developed by the **Colonial** (later **Commonwealth**) **Development Corporation**. Planting of the original trees was carried out over a nine-year period. In 1950 the company undertook to assist the Swazi nation to plant coniferous trees on its lands adjacent to the company's acreage. Actual afforestation of the Swazi area (originally 3,700 acres [1,500 hectares]) was commenced in 1955 and completed in 1959. The Usutu forest today covers about 160,600 acres (about 6,500 hectares) and is planted with more than 55 million trees. Of those, 74 percent are coniferous, 23 percent are eucalyptus, and 3 percent are wattle. By the 1990s the Usutu forest was producing 12 percent of the world's wood pulp.

The Usutu Pulp Company mill, which was established jointly by the CDC and Courtaulds, Ltd. on the banks of the Usutu River near Bhunya, commenced production of unbleached kraft pulp in late 1961. The original mill produced 90,000 tons of kraft pulp annually. Subsequently Usutu Forests was incorporated into the pulp company as "Usutu Forest," whose acreage is owned entirely by the Swazi crown. Since 1990 the pulp operation has been owned jointly by the South Africa pulp and paper corporation Sappi, the Commonwealth Development Corporation, and local investor combinations. The mill's current capacity is 220,000 tons of pulp per year. Exports, administered by Sappi, are mainly to South Africa, Europe, Korea, Taiwan, and Japan.

USUTU RIVER. Properly Lusutfu or Great Lusutfu River. The Swazi river incorporating the greatest water volume. Rising near the headwaters of the Vaal River in the **Transvaal**, it enters Swaziland at latitude 26° 32' south, 16.5 miles (26.5 kilometers) west of Bhunya. It moves generally east-southeast across the center of the kingdom, in a straighter line than most rivers, until it dips south 4 miles (7 kilometers) east of Siphofaneni and commences a fishhook pattern ending at Big Bend, whence it flows east-southeast again to the Mozambique border. Leaving Swaziland at the town of Abercorn, it joins the Pongola River along the South African border with Mozambique. The two then become the Maputo River, which flows north-northeast to the Indian Ocean at **Delagoa Bay** near Bela Vista. The Usutu River is a vitally important natural resource for the economy, servicing a pulp mill at Bhunya and several **irrigation** schemes, most notably in the **Malkerns** and Big Bend regions. The river drains most of the heartland of Swaziland, its major tributaries being the Mbuluzi, **Lusushwana**, iNgwempisi, Mkhondvo, Sidvokodvo, Mhlamanti, Mzimphofu, Mhlathuzane, Mtsindzekwa, Mhlatuze, and Nyetane rivers. Additionally the Usutu plays an important part in Swazi ritual. In preparation for the *iNcwala* ceremony, *bemanti* ("people of the water"; priests) are sent with sacred vessels to obtain water from the Indian Ocean at the mouth of the Usutu River (the Mputo River in Mozambique), as well as from three other rivers: the Lusaba, the **Komati**, and the Mbuluzi.

-V-

VERMAAK, COENRAAD J. (1822–early 1890s). The first European to obtain a written **concession** of land in Swaziland. The grant, from *iNgwenyama* **Mswati Dlamini II** in 1860, was for a large tract of land south of the **Usutu River** bounded by the **Lebombo** ridge on the east and the hills giving rise to the iNgwavuma River in the west. Mswati's probable motive was strategic, for Vermaak observed Zulu movements in the region and periodically delivered reports on them to the king. In return, and for an annual rental of £5 ($25), Vermaak was made chief of the region and was allowed to hunt in and farm it, but Mswati specifically retained sovereignty. Vermaak lived there with his family in a wattle and daub house. Because he was a professional hunter, that was the main use to which he put it. In 1889 Vermaak attempted to persuade *iNgwenyama* **Mbandzeni Dlamini** to transform the tract into a land concession but was refused. Eventually, however, long after his death, the **Swaziland Concessions Commission** designated the area as a land concession (1906).

VILAKAZI, JOSIAH (occasionally VILAKATI; 1869–?). Secretary to Queen Regent **Labotsibeni Mdluli** from 1901 until 1921, when *iNgwenyama* **Sobhuza Dlamini II** was crowned. Vilakazi was the son of Levi Vilakazi (d. 1898), who had come to Swaziland from the **Edendale** (Natal) Wesleyan mission in 1880 as one of **John Gama**'s fellow concessionaires. Levi Vilakazi eventually became chief of the **Mahamba** Wesleyan mission, as did his son Josiah for a time. Josiah had been educated at Edendale and became the teacher of the primary school at **Mahamba** during the 1880s. He served as secretary to Labotsibeni from

1893 to 1896 before resigning to enter business. In 1901 he was again appointed her secretary, replacing **Alpheus Nkosi**. Vilakazi quickly became one of Labotsibeni's trusted advisors and an intimate of **Mnt. Malunge Dlamini**. There were few initiatives by Labotsibeni toward the British, few of her speeches or protest documents, and few of her most important domestic undertakings during those years that did not have Vilakazi's imprint on them. In fact the British administration during the early 1900s took to referring to the three as the "**Zombodze** party" and suspected them of plotting to replace *iNkhosana* (Crown Prince) **Sobhuza Dlamini II** with Malunge as the next *ingwenyama*. (Sobhuza was then living at his mother's [**Lomawa Ndwandwe's**] **homestead** at **Lobamba**. That may have been one reason why Sobhuza dismissed Vilakazi as royal secretary early in 1922.)

In 1907 Vilakazi and his brother and assistant secretary, Nehemiah Vilakazi, accompanied the Swazi **deputation** to London led unofficially by Malunge to protest the provisions of the **Partition Proclamation of 1907**. Christopher Lowe believes that Vilakazi met **Pixley kaI. Seme**, who was studying law at that time, in London.[6] In any event Vilakazi became a principal in the early meetings leading to the formation of what became the **African National Congress** in 1912. None of Vilakazi's activities as a royal advisor or political activist sat well with the British authorities, who launched an extended campaign of harassment against him that included intimidation, mail openings, and attempts to entrap him in illegal activities, all in order to neutralize him as an effective royal advisor and advocate.

In the end it was Vilakazi's own frailties that destroyed his influence with the monarchy. First, Vilakazi was accused of embezzlement, which in itself was hardly unheard of in the inner circle. Much more seriously, Vilakazi the "progressive" was done in by his defiance of tradition, being caught (1919) in a liaison with a daughter of **Mnt. Lomvazi Dlamini**, Labotsibeni's only surviving son. Defiling a member of the royal household entailed grave consequences, and the situation was made all the worse by the fact that Vilakazi had contracted a venereal disease in 1915. His behavior earned him the bitter enmity of the royal family until the end of his life. He tendered his resignation in 1919 but was kept on until Sobhuza replaced him as secretary with **Benjamin Nxumalo** and then evicted him from his house in 1922.

VOCATIONAL AND COMMERCIAL TRAINING INSTITUTE MAT-SAPHA. *See* GWAMILE VOCATIONAL AND COMMERCIAL TRAINING INSTITUTE MATSAPHA

von STEINAECKER, BARON F. C. LUDWIG (1854–1917). Prussian army veteran who arrived in **South Africa** in 1889, where he eventually joined the Colonial Scouts of Natal as an intelligence officer. His first action during the **Anglo-Boer War** (1899–1902) was to lead a column northward to blow up bridges in the **Transvaal** in order to hamper Afrikaner mobility. In 1900 he organized and led a corps of 300 mounted irregular men, known as Steinaecker's Horse, to patrol the border with Portuguese Mozambique. The corps (which eventually totaled 450 Europeans and 300 Africans) was headquartered at Komatipoort in the Transvaal. There it established its own workshops and transport system (including a rail line) and developed a proprietary intelligence arm.

In 1901 a 110-man detachment of Steinaecker's Horse occupied Bremersdorp (**Manzini**) and used it as a base for foraging and freebooting expeditions, as well as forays against Afrikaner scouting parties, in Swaziland. Steinaecker's troops were undisciplined, however, and he further made the mistake of treating the Swazi badly. Consequently Steinaecker's Horse never attained control of the countryside. In July 1901 a troop of Afrikaners from Ermelo (Transvaal) marched on Bremersdorp to rout the detachment. Steinaecker, upon hearing the news, decamped for **Barberton** and left no one in command. The remaining rabble, upon being probed, retreated from Bremersdorp to the east, and the Ermelo troop sacked and burned the town. Steinaecker's Horse fought the rest of its wartime skirmishes, none of them consequential, in the Transvaal. The corps was disbanded in early 1903, and Steinaecker (according to Huw Jones) lived out his days as a farmer and handyman in South Africa. He failed at both, and he committed suicide in 1917.[7]

VUVULANE. A progressive agricultural community established in 1962 by the **Swaziland Irrigation Scheme (SIS)** under the auspices of the **Colonial** (later **Commonwealth**) **Development Corporation (CDC)**. The CDC conceived of Vuvulane as both an agricultural and a social engineering experiment. One hundred small farms were laid out to be allocated in freehold to private Swazi cultivators. Because of the strident objections by *iNgwenyama* **Sobhuza Dlamini II** and the *libandla*, the allocations were altered to 20-year leaseholds. **Sugarcane** was to be the principal crop, to be sold to the **Mhlume** mill. Later, vegetables were also grown and marketed. Within a decade Vuvulane had developed into a thriving peasant community. From the CDC's point of view the experiment was both economically and socially successful.

Politically it was a different matter. Vuvulane's innovative land tenure arrangements, which removed its smallholders from their communal obligations to the king and chiefs, were viewed with deep apprehension by the traditional power structure. That apprehension turned to alarm when Vuvulane and other population centers in the Mphumalanga constituency voted against the king's **Imbokodvo National Movement (INM)** in favor of the opposition **Ngwane National Liberatory Congress (NNLC)** in the first post-independence election in 1972. That reversal, which confirmed all of Sobhuza's worst fears about Vuvulane, set in motion a chain of events ending with his repeal of the constitution in 1973 (*see* **Ngwenya, Bhekindlela Thomas**).

That left the problem of Vuvulane's land tenure arrangements. In 1983 the CDC was persuaded to transfer Vuvulane to the **Tibiyo takaNgwane Fund** gratis. The Tibiyo officer placed in charge of the scheme was **Mnt. Mfanasibili Dlamini**, one of the INM candidates whom the Vuvulane voters had thrown out of office in 1972. Under Tibiyo the Vuvulane smallholdings were converted into **Swazi Nation Land**, and the farmers' leases were not renewed. Subsequently, in response to the protests of 14 farmers over its treatment of them, Tibiyo destroyed their homes and threw them and their families off the land. Following extensive coverage of the affair in the independent press, the 14 were returned to their plots by *iNgwenyama* **Mswati Dlamini III**.

-W-

WALLIS, GEORGE (1887–1979). British-born farmer, **cattle** breeder, and politician. Wallis was trained as a lawyer, but a wound incurred during World War I left him deaf and consequently unable to practice law, so in 1919 he emigrated to Swaziland, subsidized under the **Returned Soldiers' Settlement Scheme**. Two other British war veterans accompanied him: Donald R. Keith and Percy J. Lewis. Together they lease-purchased a tract of about 6,700 acres (about 2,700 hectares) in the **middleveld** along the White Mbuluzi River near Mafutseni from the **Mushroom Land Settlement Scheme** in 1921. Lewis later resettled to **Matsapha** (now the prison and industrial site), where he became the largest maize farmer in Swaziland, while Keith purchased a farm, "Ravelston," at Stegi (**Siteki**), where he cultivated tung oil and edible nut trees. On the original farm, "Dinedor," Wallis cultivated **cotton**, maize, and cowpeas, but he soon became known mainly as an innovative and successful cattle breeder. Wallis started with 150 head of local (Nguni) cattle, cross-bred them with Herefords, and then combined them with Afrikanders, eventually building his herd to about 1,000 head. The result was a breed that for many years predominated among Swaziland's commercial cattle herds. During his heyday there was no more successful and influential settler farmer in the territory.

Once established on Dinedor, Wallis ventured into settler politics. During the 1930s and 1940s that meant two organizations: the **Swaziland Farmers Association** (SFA), a settler trade and lobbying group, and the **European Advisory Council (EAC)**, the principal interest group representing settler concerns to the administration. Wallis served as president of the SFA from 1936 to 1946 and as an EAC member from 1938 to 1961. During those 25 years Wallis forcefully articulated the EAC position that Swaziland's future depended on a prosperous and secure settler community favored by appropriate government land and water, veterinary, roads, education, labor, and tax policies. Wallis retired from active politics just as the kingdom was commencing its move toward internal self-government.

WATERFORD-KAMHLABA SCHOOL. Originally the Waterford School for boys, a private, multiracial school established in Swaziland in 1962 by a British-born educator, Michael Stern. As a center for liberal and progressive education, a rarity in southern Africa at the time, Waterford attracted students of all races, classes, and (later) sexes. Waterford especially attracted the children of middle-class Africans and liberal Europeans from **South Africa** during the apartheid era. On the occasion of its fifth anniversary celebration, *iNgwenyama* **Sobhuza Dlamini II** added the term *Kamhlaba*, "The World," to its original name.

WATTS, ARCHDEACON (later BISHOP) CHRISTOPHER C. (?– 1958). Anglican missionary to Swaziland, arriving in 1907 and serving as pastor of the All Saints Church. Watts was best known for his establishment of two private schools: St. Mark's School for European children in **Mbabane** and St. Mark's Coloured (**EurAfrican**) School at Mpolonjeni, 6 miles (10 kilometers) west of Mbabane. The Mbabane school he started with his own resources, the first students sitting on the floor and using chairs as their desks. Watts was the author of *Dawn in Swaziland* (1922).

WHITE CHARTER. *See* SWAZIELAND COMMITTEE

WHITE COMMITTEE. *See* SWAZIELAND COMMITTEE

WHITTLE, FREDERICK L. (?–1983). District superintendent (DS) of the **Native Recruiting Corporation (NRC)**, 1947–65. Whittle, South

African–born, was a career NRC official (1928–65) who worked in Johannesburg and in Basutoland before becoming DS in Swaziland in 1947. His assigned task was twofold. First, he was to increase the numbers of mine labor recruits from Swaziland, and from Mozambique being processed through Swaziland. Second, he was to change the system of compensation paid to NRC labor recruiters from capitation fees (then roughly £3 [$15] per recruit) to salaries. That was both a cost reduction measure and an NRC response to the colonial administration's demand that it end the arrangement known as "black-birding," a practice by which store-owners-cum-recruiters encouraged men to go so deeply into debt that they were then vulnerable to recruitment for the mines. The capitation system had been introduced into Swaziland in 1904 by the NRC's predecessor, the **Witwatersrand Native Labour Association (WNLA)**. Whittle successfully met both assignments, although the latter success was conditional. Numbers of recruits from Swaziland rose until the late 1950s, when a combination of factors leveled them off. They included a change in the mix of recruits from the corporation's various "catchment areas" and competition both from within industrializing Swaziland and from competing industries in **South Africa**.

Whittle was also the chief WNLA officer in Swaziland. That organization's legal catchment area was southern Mozambique, and Whittle processed both legal recruits from the Mozambique border area (principally its **Ingwavuma** office) and Mozambicans registering illegally as Swazi, through the NRC headquarters at Stegi (**Siteki**). Mozambicans choosing the latter alternative commonly bribed chiefs in southern Swaziland to obtain tax receipts that would enable them to be "repatriated" to Swaziland once their contracts in Johannesburg had been completed.

WILLIAMS, SIDNEY B. (1880–1980). Colonial official who was responsible for developing Bremersdorp (**Manzini**) into a modern town. Williams arrived in Swaziland in 1903 as a member of the 150-man troop of the South African constabulary accompanying special commissioner **Francis Enraght Moony**. Williams transferred to the civil administration in 1910 and was district commissioner at Bremersdorp from 1920 to 1939, then transferring to Hlatikulu until his retirement in 1941.

WITCHCRAFT. Practiced by evildoers (*batsakatsi*). *Batsakatsi* include both witches, whose destructiveness can be both physical and psychological, and sorcerers, who utilize poisons and other physically violent techniques to destroy people or property. *Batsakatsi* are most often females and are believed to network with other *batsakatsi* and to operate at night. They work either by casting spells from a distance or by direct personal contact, doctoring, for example, the victim's food. *Tangoma* (sing. *sangoma*) determine the nature of the evil and the evildoer's identity by various means of divining: throwing bones and observing their patterns (borrowed from the Sotho), or public séances or ordeals. Public "smelling out" of evildoers is, however, outlawed.

The gravest of all witchcraft offenses is **ritual** (*umutsi*, medicine) **murder**, which, although a capital offense, is still practiced. Its objects, all related to personal aggrandizement, are various: to ensure crop fertility or to reverse ill fortune in love, politics, or business. Flesh of the still-living victim (society's defenseless most often—the very young, the mentally deficient, or the elderly) is excised and mixed with other substances to concoct a powerful medicine that is used to doctor the aspirant, or perhaps his fields. The victim is killed in secret and referred to as the "buck" (*inyamatane*) in order to depersonalize him/her. The specialists in these cases are often (but not always) *batsakatsi*, and in the past their patrons have often been chiefs suffering some form of economic or political insecurity. In today's world the client might just as well be a businessperson who has suffered a reverse.

In 1930 the colonial government outlawed by proclamation all divining by *tangoma* along with many activities of *tinyanga* (sing. *inyanga*) involving diagnosis, labeling them all—inaccurately—as "witchcraft." Swazi, especially during the 1930s and 1940s, decried the law on the grounds that it protected *batsakatsi* and left the rest of the populace vulnerable to their evildoings.

WITWATERSRAND NATIVE LABOUR ASSOCIATION (WNLA). The main recruiting arm of the South African Chamber of Mines in Swaziland until its reorganization in 1906. Until that time the WNLA's "catchment area" had been subcontinent-wide: **South Africa**, the British colonies and territories (including Swaziland), Portuguese Mozambique, and "tropical Africa" south of 22° South latitude. After 1906 the WNLA's recruiting region was narrowed to southern Mozambique. Consequently the character of the WNLA's operations in Swaziland was transformed (although they were not eliminated) after 1906. The WNLA was replaced in Swaziland by the **Native Recruiting Corporation (NRC)**, which established an office there in 1913.

Prior to its withdrawal from Swaziland the WNLA's efforts were never more then modestly successful, for several reasons. Most important was that the Swazi were never prime candidates for labor recruiting as long as their economy was still self-sufficient. The British rendered it non-viable only by about 1914, following their imposition of heavy taxes (payable only in cash) and their expropriation of two-thirds of the land (**Partition Proclamation of 1907**, carried out in 1914). The other reason was that the WNLA's operation in Swaziland (which was also the recruiting ground for a number of individual labor agents) was never more than modest. Perhaps the most consequential aspect of the WNLA's efforts in Swaziland was its effort to forge a partnership with the Swazi royal house in its recruiting efforts. That agreement produced few recruits (mainly because it was illegal), but it did set a precedent that was followed by later—and more successful—agents, who enlisted first Queen Regent **Labotsibeni Mdluli** and her son **Mnt. Malunge Dlamini**, and later *iNgwenyama* **Sobhuza Dlamini II** in their recruiting efforts.

-X-

XABA, REVEREND JOSEPH J. The fourth teacher to be employed by Queen Regent **Labotsibeni Mdluli** at **Zombodze** to tutor the scions of the royal family at the turn of the century following her decision that they should be exposed to Western education. The first instructor had been **Cleopas Kunene**, the second had been **Robert Grendon**, and the third had been **Edgar Mini**.

Upon Mini's retirement the British administration, which had grown wary of the nascent social activism of the **Edendale** (Natal) Zulu community, imposed itself on the selection of his successor. Reverend Xaba, an elderly, conservative, Xhosa-speaking graduate of a mission school in the Cape, was chosen. He taught Sobhuza and other children of the elite until Sobhuza left for the **Lovedale Missionary Institution (South Africa)** school in 1916. Following Sobhuza's permanent return to Swaziland in 1918 the need for a tutor once more arose, and again the government, determined to influence what the *inkhosana* was taught, intervened. Labotsibeni insisted on re-employing Grendon, whom Sobhuza admired. **Resident Commissioner de Symons Honey** just as adamantly refused, because Grendon had a reputation for mixing politics into his curriculum and was also co-editor of the ANC newspaper *Abantu Batho* (although whether Honey was aware of that is unclear). Still, Honey appeared ready to relent when he received a letter from Xaba attacking Grendon's candidacy on the grounds that he was anti-British and a spy. Xaba's missive was enough to torpedo Grendon's candidacy, although the latter was allowed to remain and teach elsewhere in Swaziland. Sobhuza's tutoring was taken over by Lancelot Msomi, who previously had been a teacher at Zombodze.

-Z-

ZIONISM. The term "Zionist" is often used in southern Africa to denote any church professing adherence to a syncretic **Christianity** (or some aspect of it) that is controlled by Africans. Zionists are distinct from the two other main Christian institutions: mission churches (often European-controlled) and independent churches (doctrinally similar to mission churches but African-controlled). In Swaziland the term "Apostolic" can also be used as a generic term for an African-controlled quasi-Christian church. Both types are characterized more by their ethnic separatism from European-controlled mission churches than by important doctrinal differences. Zionist churches thus tend to be the modern descendants of the late-19th- and early-20th-century "Ethiopian" separatist movement that swept through the Christian missions (with the general exception of the **Roman Catholics**) in **South Africa**. In Swaziland the formation of Zionist churches occurred relatively late, gaining large followings beginning only in about 1940. Hilda Kuper's research during the 1930s revealed 21 separatist sects, 13 of which bore the name "Zion/Zionist" in their titles.[8] J. F. Holleman during the 1960s identified nine main separatist churches, five of which identified themselves as Zionist.[9] In 1962, of about 73,000 Swazi professing Christianity, approximately 29,000 (40 percent) were Zionists. There is reason to believe that by the 1990s that figure was closer to 50 percent. The attraction of Zionism lay in part in its tolerance of polygyny and the levirate, beer drinking, and the profession of both magic and **witchcraft**.

As compared with mission and independent church members, adherents to Zionism are more heavily rural and female, and they are much less well educated. Historically Swazi women have sought personal and spiritual fulfillment, denied them by the intensely patriarchal society, in Christian churches. In Zionism they found solace in the church garb, roles, and rituals, as well as in its emphasis on group support and spiritual healing. Although individual churches vary, central to all Zionist ritual is the role of the holy spirit and its force in healing. Jean Comaroff, writing of the Tswana, describes the ritual invocation of the Zionist holy spirit in four successive elements: invocation, testimony, strengthening, and healing.[10] It is in its ritual invocations that Zionism moves in closest sympathy with the practices of specialists in the occult. Zionism also commonly proscribes substances and practices regarded as defiling, such as tobacco, alcohol, and sexual promiscuity.

iNdlovukazi **Lomawa Ndwandwe**, a practicing Christian although she was forbidden to be baptized, was particularly drawn to a Zionist sect that both espoused Christianity and recognized the metaphysical claims of her son, *iNgwenyama* **Sobhuza Dlamini II**, to the kingship.

ZOMBODZE. The name of *iNgwenyama* **Ngwane Dlamini**'s national headquarters built during the mid-18th century in southern Swaziland near modern Dwaleni. It was at Zombodze that the *iNcwala* **ceremony** was first celebrated within the borders of modern Swaziland. More than a century later, during the reign of *iNgwenyama* **Bhunu Dlamini**, his mother, *iNdlovukazi* **Labotsibeni Mdluli**, built her **homestead** under the eastern shadow of the **Mdzimba** range about 5 miles (8 kilometers) east of modern **Lobamba** and named it Zombodze. As Bhunu grew progressively less stable and power accrued to Labotsibeni, more and more state business came to be carried on at Zombodze, Bhunu often residing there although his administrative homestead (*lilawu*) was located at Zabeni, 4 miles (7 kilometers) to the north-northeast. It was at Zombodze that the senior political officer and royal homestead *indvuna* **Mbhabha Nsibandze** was murdered by Bhunu's agents in 1898, touching off a series of events that seriously damaged the monarchy for the ensuing half-century. It was also at Zombodze where Bhunu died during the *iNcwala* ceremony in December 1899. During Labotsibeni's regency Zombodze served as the administrative and diplomatic headquarters of the nation. Zombodze was the site of the first **Swazi national school** established by Labotsibeni in 1906, in which *iNgwenyama* **Sobhuza Dlamini II** received his first formal education.

ZULU, CETSHWAYO kaSENZANGAKHONA (d. 1884). *See* ZULU, MPANDE kaSENZANGAKHONA

ZULU, DINGANE kaSENZANGAKHONA (c. 1795–1840). Half-brother, murderer, and successor of **Shaka Zulu** as Zulu king, reigning 1828–40. Owing his power to the army, Dingane dispatched it periodically to the north to squeeze the surplus out of his rich Swazi neighbors. An 1836 incursion against *iNgwenyama* **Sobhuza Dlamini I** netted Dingane 6,000 **cattle**, although Sobhuza escaped the trap Dingane had set for him. In 1839 Dingane's fortunes were reversed when a Swazi *imphi* led by **Mngayi Fakudze** repulsed the Zulu invading regiments with heavy casualties at the **Battle of Lubuya**, putting an end to the Zulu king's plans to colonize southern Swaziland. In fact Lubuya helped to seal Dingane's fate, for his requisitioning of troops for the battle so alarmed his half-brother **Mpande Zulu** that the latter fled with his army and formed an alliance with the Natal Afrikaners, and then jointly with them defeated Dingane at the Battle of the Maqongqo hills in early 1840. Mpande thereupon succeeded Dingane to the Zulu throne. Dingane fled to southern Swaziland, settling at Sankolweni, bordering the Hlatikulu forest on the southern Lubombo range just north of the Pongola River. There in March 1840 he was put to death on the lands of chief Silevane Nyawo.

ZULU, MPANDE kaSENZANGAKHONA (c. 1798–1872). Son of Chief Senzangakhona Zulu and half-brother to **Shaka Zulu** and **Dingane Zulu**. Mpande was the dynastic rival of Dingane, the murderer of and successor to King Shaka. In 1839 Mpande, foiled in his ambition to rule the Zulu and fearful of his own assassination by Dingane's men, crossed the Thukela River into Afrikaner territory and entered into a political alliance with Andries Pretorius, leader of the Afrikaner "trekboer" community in Natal. In early 1840 Mpande and an army of followers, in league with an Afrikaner military column, attacked and defeated Dingane's forces and forced him to flee, ultimately to his death in southern Swaziland. The Afrikaners then proclaimed Mpande king of the Zulu.

Throughout his life Mpande remained an enigma. Although he perpetuated the Zulu kingdom for more than 30 years he did so at enormous cost in land, **cattle**, and humiliating demonstrations of fealty toward his Afrikaner patrons. Indeed many Zulu followed him because of his perceived weaknesses rather than his strengths. Consequently Mpande sought compensation, as his predecessors had before him, in military adventurism against the Swazi to the north, who possessed enticing numbers of cattle and much land that was fertile and well watered. Mpande also discreetly sought out the goodwill of the British administration in Natal.

Mpande first attacked in 1846, taking advantage of the dynastic dispute disrupting *iNgwenyama* **Mswati Dlamini II**'s early reign. At that time Mswati's main adversary was **Mnt. Malambule Dlamini**, who reached an agreement with Mpande whereby the rebel would withdraw his troops toward the Pongola River headquarters whereupon Mpande would engage Mswati's pursuing army. That is essentially what happened: Mpande repulsed Mswati and made off with a large number of Swazi cattle. In early 1847 the Zulu king, invoking once again Mswati's "provocation" of the previous October, sent his columns crashing across the Pongola and through Swazi territory, chasing the Swazi and their cattle north to the Crocodile River. There Mswati's men holed themselves up in caves and then found further refuge with their **Lydenburg** Afrikaner allies. Mpande withdrew from Swaziland nearly six months later, and then only because he feared stirring up the emnity of the **Transvaal** Afrikaners.

Mpande renewed his attack once more at the end of 1848. Although the assault was much diminished in scale it was enough to frighten Mswati (whose relations with the Lydenburghers were at that moment in disarray) into making an accommodation with the Zulu king. According to Philip Bonner, Mswati ended up becoming Mpande's "tributary," but the arrangement lasted only until 1852, when Mpande returned to his old form and went on the attack against his old adversary.[11] Mpande's apparent aim was to turn Swaziland into his virtual colony, and he came within a whisker of achieving it. The Swazi were once more relieved of vast cattle herds and driven to their caves after sustaining heavy casualties.

Two events, however, saved them. The first was Mswati's by then celebrated diplomatic maneuvering, this time aimed at warming up with the British Natal administration (notably Sir Theophilus Shepstone, secretary for native affairs), with the aim of giving Mpande pause enough to call off his troops. Mswati even offered his sister in a marriage alliance to the Shepstone family, whom the secretary ceremonially accepted and then "gave" to one of his Zulu allies. In the end the king's array of diplomatic gestures succeeded of their basic intent. The second event was triggered by the very success of Mpande's invasion. One of the regiments fielded by Mpande was commanded by a son, Cetshwayo (d. 1884). That regiment's spectacular performance during the invasion elevated Cetshwayo's candidacy to succeed his father at the expense of a brother and rival, Mbuyazi, who was preferred by Mpande. Shortly a dynastic struggle was touched off within the Zulu kingdom that eventually escalated into a civil war. Both events combined to prompt Mpande to withdraw his army from Swaziland and to prevent further Zulu adventurism into Swazi territory for the remainder of his life.

ZULU, SHAKA kaSENZANGAKHONA (c. 1787–1828). Military general and state builder who forged the formidable Zulu nation from the remnants of the shattered Mthethwa confederacy in southern Natal (1819) and moved to defeat the **Ndwandwe** in northern Natal (1826), emerging as the pre-eminent leader of the most powerful northern **Nguni** state. The causes of the resulting *mfecane* (isiZulu for "crushing") period are the subject of an ongoing academic debate (*see* Bibliography, Section IV.2.a). Shaka constituted the greatest foreign military and political threat south of the Ndwandwe kingdom facing *iNgwenyama* **Sobhuza Dlamini I**. Sobhuza resorted to diplomacy to keep Shaka at bay: he made rain for him, he gave two of his daughters in marriage to him (both of whom Shaka later executed), and he even made a visit to Shaka's palace to demonstrate his fealty. In this instance diplomacy with Shaka turned out to count for little.

Much more important, and fortunately for Sobhuza, the Zulu king was destined to live a short life, during most of which his attention was turned in other directions, sorting out the territory south of the Thukela River and establishing trade relations with the Cape. When in 1827 Shaka turned his attention back north he had but a year longer to live. During 1827–28 the Swazi were on the receiving end of two separate Zulu attacks. Against the first Sobhuza chose discretion as the better part of valor and sought refuge in the impregnable **Mdzimba** caves. Against the second Sobhuza first checked the Zulu attack and then harried its retreat. Shaka's death did not remove the Zulu threat to Swazi; they would remain a constant source of concern to Sobhuza's successors for generations to come. *See also* Zulu, Dingane kaSenzangakhona

ZWANE, DR. AMBROSE P. (1922–1998). Medical doctor and politician whose labor and political activism during the 1960s changed the face of Swazi politics more than that of any other political figure with the exception of *iNgwenyama* **Sobhuza Dlamini II**. Zwane was the son of Amos Zwane, a renowned practitioner of Swazi traditional medicine and both personal doctor and trusted councillor of the *ingwenyama* (Zwane had accompanied Sobhuza to London in 1922–23). Ambrose Zwane was Swaziland's first qualified medical doctor, receiving his degree from the University of the Witwatersrand in 1951 and practicing as a Swaziland government medical doctor from 1953 until 1960. Zwane resigned his post that year to enter politics.

In mid-1960 Zwane joined the **Swaziland Progressive Party** as its secretary general. In that capacity he was appointed later that year to the first Constitutional Committee by **Resident Commissioner Brian Marwick**, along with SPP president **John J. Nquku** and SPP executive member **Obed Mabuza**. Their party position in favor of a one-man, one-vote provision in the proposed constitution led to Nquku's dismissal and

Zwane's and Mabuza's resignations from the committee. Even then a serious split over both personality and ideology had developed between Zwane and Nquku, with Zwane complaining more and more openly that Nquku was authoritarian, excessively moderate in his political philosophy, and too prone to luxurious foreign travel. The break came in early 1962 when Zwane left the SPP along with **Mnt. Dumisa Dlamini**, head of the SPP youth wing, and formed a faction called the SPP (Zwane), with Zwane as president and Dlamini as secretary general. In April 1963 the faction was renamed the **Ngwane National Liberatory Congress (NNLC)**. Its platform reflected Zwane's political views: immediate independence, with power vested in a democratically elected and multiracial Swaziland government, espousing African socialism (including the nationalization of basic industries), **trade unionism**, and compulsory education. Under such a system the *ingwenyama* would be no more than a figurehead. Events were to prove that Zwane's ideas were far ahead of their time, but they also proved that he was a man of his convictions.

Zwane visited Accra, Moscow, and Beijing. Alleging his radicalism, the British government barred Zwane from the second London **constitutional conference** in 1963. Zwane shifted his focus. In February 1963 the first of what turned out to be a wave of labor walkouts occurred in Swaziland. Zwane and Dlamini, sensing that political capital could be made from the underlying worker frustrations, embarked thereafter on a campaign of labor activism, fomenting **strikes** where there were none and agitating the ones that they found under way, hoping to touch off a political crisis. What they reaped instead was Marwick's declaration of an emergency, garrisoning of the country with a British army detachment, and rounding up of the NNLC leadership on grounds of inciting public violence. Zwane was jailed for two months, then tried and acquitted, although several others (including Dlamini) were convicted and imprisoned. The trials, however, proved to be a disaster for Zwane in another way, for the NNLC was immobilized for nearly a year in organizing its legal defense, and thus was ill-prepared to mount an effective campaign to contest the 1964 **Legislative Council (Legco)** elections. The party won not a single seat in the Legco, although it garnered more than 12 percent of the popular vote and emerged from the process as the most viable opposition party.

Following its 1964 showing and with evidence of the escalating strength of the royalist **Imbokodvo National Movement (INM)** party, the NNLC was hit with a wave of defections to Imbokodvo. Not the least of them was that of Dumisa Dlamini in 1966. Zwane's activities during those years were in the nature of a holding action. Still the NNLC was able to field a full slate of candidates for the 1967 parliamentary elections. Again it won no seats (Zwane lost badly in **Mbabane**), but it came within an eyelash of winning the Mphumalanga constituency. Encouraged, Zwane bided his time and seemingly basked in his role as the lone voice crying in the wilderness. (When Sobhuza addressed the new **parliament** in 1967 Zwane stood outside the entrance waving the NNLC flag; when Zwane was excluded from the third London constitutional talks in 1968 he lay down on the front steps of Marlborough House in protest until the London police carted him away). Again in the 1972 elections the NNLC contested every constituency, and this time the party won Mphumalanga.

For Zwane the Mphumalanga victory was a sweet vindication, but for Sobhuza it constituted an ominous sign. The ultimate basis of the king's power resided in his control over the distribution of land to the peasantry, yet Mphumalanga was heavily populated with two constituencies not under that control. The first comprised the smallholder farmers of **Vuvulane**, who held their land in long-term leaseholds administered not by Sobhuza but by the **Swaziland Irrigation Scheme**. The second comprised the sugar workers in and around Big Bend, who were dependent primarily on wages, not land, for their livelihood, and who had once (1963) staged a strike in defiance of the king's orders. Consequently Sobhuza moved quickly to invalidate the Mphumalanga election. One of the victors, **Bhekindlela Thomas Ngwenya**, was deported to **South Africa** as a prohibited immigrant. Ngwenya appealed to the **high court**, while Zwane used his new seat in parliament to heckle the government over its treatment of Ngwenya and a number of other controversial issues. Zwane finally proposed a motion of no confidence, giving Sobhuza a taste of what a real opposition would be like. Then twice over the following year the courts showed their independence by torpedoing Sobhuza's plan to unseat Ngwenya, once (August 1972) by declaring Ngwenya a Swazi citizen, and then (March 1973) by declaring unconstitutional an act of parliament making the prime minister and not the courts the final arbiter of immigration cases. Two weeks later Sobhuza repealed the constitution, disbanded parliament, and outlawed political parties.

For Zwane, whose 1972 Mphumalanga victory had touched off the events leading to Sobhuza's *coup d'état*, that event ended his political life, but not without a fight. Zwane served several periods of detention during the 1970s for holding illegal political meetings. He then retired from politics and returned to his private medical practice for the following 20 years. At the time of his death in 1998 Zwane was leading a revival of the NNLC in order to challenge once again the hegemony of the Swazi monarchy, this time by either contesting or boycotting—as future events would dictate—the parliamentary elections of that year.

ZWANE, SANDLANE (c. 1810–1888). A prominent military officer in the tiChele regiment under *tiNgwenyama* **Sobhuza Dlamini I** and **Mswati Dlamini II** who rose to become commander in chief of the army (*indvunankhuyemabutfo*) during the latter's reign. Zwane also attained the pinnacle of Swazi politics, first being appointed *indvuna* of *iNdlovukazi* **Tsandzile Ndwandwe**'s **homestead** at **Ludzidzini** and ultimately becoming recognized as prime minister of the nation (*indvunakhuluyesive*).

As a military commander Zwane led Mswati's army that intervened in the **Ndwandwe** (Gaza) civil war in southern Mozambique, which pitted **Mzila** against **Mawewe** following the death of their father Soshangane Ndwandwe. Zwane's troops in support of Mawewe inflicted a major defeat on Mzila's army at Makotene in 1862, although Mzila ultimately prevailed in the succession dispute. Politically Zwane remained the ally of Tsandzile throughout her lifetime, notably during the volatile period of her regency following Mswati's death in 1865, when she deflected the pretensions of **Mnt. Mblini Dlamini** in favor of **Mnt. Ludvonga Dlamini** as successor. Zwane subsequently played a prominent role in the selection of *iNgwenyama* **Mbandzeni Dlamini** as Ludvonga's heir. Tsandzile was also involved, along with **Bnt. Malunge** and **Maloyi Dlamini**, in that fateful choice, their primary motive appearing to have been that Mbandzeni's "exceptional lack of qualities" would allow them to continue to control the levers of power.[12] That proved to be a decision of breathtaking myopia, and Zwane compounded it by stepping into the resulting power vacuum and making choices that sealed Swaziland's unfortunate fate. He participated in the granting of most of Mbandzeni's significant **concessions** after 1883, and he sanctioned the appointment (1886) of **Theophilus Shepstone, Jr.**, as royal advisor and the establishment (1887) of the **Swazieland Committee**.

Zwane's wielding of power was accompanied by his repeated public displays of contempt for Mbandzeni, which infuriated the king and undoubtedly led to his own downfall. In late 1888 a plot to overthrow Mbandzeni in favor of a half-brother, **Mnt. Nkhopolo Dlamini**, was uncovered. The *ingwenyama*, whose innate suspicion of Zwane needed little to excite it, ordered him executed. Zwane, along with several other leading councillors, was clubbed to death.

NOTES

1. Crush, "The Culture of Failure," 186.

2. Jonathan Crush, "Tin, Time and Space in the Valley of Heaven," *Transactions of the Institute of British Geographers*, XIII (1988), 211–221.

3. Kuper, *The Swazi*, p. 138.

4. Kuper, *The Swazi*, pp. 163–164.

5. Christian Potholm, *Swaziland: The Dynamics of Political Modernization* (Berkeley: University of California Press, 1972), p. 104.

6. Lowe, "The Tragedy of Malunge," p. 18.

7. Jones, *Biographical Register*, p. 607.

8. Hilda Kuper, *The Uniform of Colour: A Study of White-Black Relationships in Swaziland* (Johannesburg: Witwatersrand University Press, 1947), p. 122.

9. J. F. Holleman (ed.), *Experiment in Swaziland: Report of the Swaziland Sample Survey, 1960* (Cape Town: Oxford University Press, 1964), pp. 154–155.

10. Jean Comaroff, *Body of Power, Spirit of Resistance: The Culture and History of a South African People* (Chicago and London: University of Chicago Press, 1985), p. 207.

11. Bonner, *Kings, Commoners and Concessionaires*, p. 61.

12. Ibid., p. 160.

Bibliography

CONTENTS

INTRODUCTION

Swaziland until the 1980s was one of the most underresearched countries on the African continent. Apart from official government publications, there existed few substantial scholarly monographs focused solely on Swaziland. The exceptions were the scholarship of a geographer, two anthropologists, a historian, and a political scientist. Dorothy Doveton's *The Human Geography of Swaziland* (1937) was the first full-length geographical study of the territory, which from a modern viewpoint was marred by its explicitly

Eurocentric bias. By contrast, Hilda Kuper's thoroughly researched studies *An African Aristocracy* (1947; reprinted 1980) and *The Uniform of Colour* (1947) served for more than a generation as the main scholarly resources on the Swazi for virtually all the social sciences and humanities. Those seminal works were preceded and supplemented by Brian Marwick's *The Swazi* (1940; reprinted 1966). Kuper's useful, modernized abridgment of her earlier works appeared as *The Swazi* in 1952 (revised and expanded in 1963 and again in 1986). Beginning in 1972 the pioneering Swazi historian James S. Mkhulunyelwa Matsebula's *A History of Swaziland* (revised editions 1976, 1988) became the standard comprehensive history of the kingdom. Its strength lay in its emphatically Africanist perspective at a time when scholarship on southern Africa was only beginning to change from its predominantly Eurocentric, albeit liberal, point of view. Christian Potholm's balanced *Swaziland: The Dynamics of Political Modernization* (1972) became the essential work on the period of constitutional development and political maneuverings leading to Swaziland's independence in 1968. In 1978 Kuper's biography *Sobhuza II* provided a detailed view of the political history of his times from the 1890s to the mid-1970s.

Both Kuper and Matsebula viewed Swaziland from an essentially royalist perspective. Beginning in 1983 a new body of scholarship balanced these earlier works with solidly researched studies emphasizing materialism and class analysis, and viewing the political development of the kingdom with a decidedly more critical eye. Most notable among them were Philip Bonner's *Kings, Commoners and Concessionaires* (1983), Jonathan Crush's *The Struggle for Swazi Labour, 1890–1920* (1987), Laurel Rose's *The Politics of Harmony* (1992), and Richard Levin's *When the Sleeping Grass Awakens* (1997). Those works have been supplemented by a growing body of articles, pamphlets, and papers on Swazi history, politics, sociology, economics, agriculture, and education over the past generation by (among others) Alan Booth, Margaret Zoller Booth, John Daniel, Fion de Vletter, Martin Fransman, Donald Funnell, Thoko Ginindza, Carolyn Hamilton, Huw Jones, Allan Low, Christopher Lowe, Hugh Macmillan, Patricia McFadden, Michael Neocosmos, Randall Packard, Margo Russell, and Hamilton Sipho Simelane.

The main comprehensive bibliographical source (which was very helpful in this compilation) is Balam Nyeko's *Swaziland* (revised 1994). The most useful guide to Swaziland historical documents and official publications is *Swaziland Official Publications, 1880–1972* (1975), which serves as the guide to an extensive compilation of those documents available on microfiche from the State Library, Pretoria.

Contemporary coverage of Swaziland has become fairly extensive. The main local newspaper (daily) is *The Times of Swaziland* (*TOS*), whose editorial independence was substantially curbed by the Swaziland government by means of periodic expulsion threats against its expatriate ownership and editorial staff beginning in the early 1990s. *TOS* is available on microfilm from the State Library, Pretoria. A second daily newspaper, *The Swazi Observer*, is owned by the Tibiyo takaNgwane Fund and strongly reflects the views and interests of the Swazi monarchy in both its news columns and its editorials. More objective and critical reporting is to be found in two South African newspapers: *The Weekly Mail and Guardian* and especially *The Star* (Johannesburg). Political analysis can be found in *Africa Confidential* (occasional) and *The Economist Intelligence Unit: Country Report* (quarterly) and *Country Profile* (annual). Important events are also covered regularly by the British Broadcasting Corporation (BBC) in its daily "Profile on Africa" radio segments. Finally, on the Internet there exist a Swaziland web page (http://www.realnet.co.sz) and "Swazi-Net" addresses on e-mail (realim@realnet.co.sz and swazi-net@list.pitt.edu).

I. GENERAL

A. Bibliographies and Dictionaries

Andor, Lydia E. *The Small and the New in Southern Africa: The Foreign Relations of Botswana, Lesotho, Namibia, and Swaziland Since Their Independence: A Select and Annotated Bibliography.* Johannesburg: South African Institute of International Affairs, 1993.

Arnheim, Johanna. *Swaziland: A Bibliography.* Cape Town: School of Librarianship, 1963. (Reprint of 1950 edition)

Balima, Mildred (comp.). *Botswana, Lesotho, and Swaziland: A Guide to Official Publications 1868–1968.* Washington: Library of Congress (U.S. Government Printing Office), 1971.

Grotpeter, John J. *Historical Dictionary of Swaziland.* Metuchen, NJ: Scarecrow Press (African Historical Dictionaries No. 3), 1975.

Nkabinde, Thokozile (comp.). *Library and Information Science: An Annotated Bibliography of Theses and Dissertations on Botswana, Lesotho and Swaziland.* Roma, Lesotho: University of Lesotho, Institute of Southern African Studies, 1989.

Nyeko, Balam (comp.). *Swaziland.* Rev. ed. Oxford: Clio Press, Santa Barbara, CA: ABC-CLIO (World Bibliographical Series No. 24), 1994.

Parsons, Neil (comp.). *The High Commission Territories, 1909–1964: A Bibliography.* Kwaluseni, Swaziland: University of Botswana, Lesotho and Swaziland (Swaziland Libraries Publication No. 3), 1976.

Steinhauer, D. R. (comp.). *A Guide and Index to the Swaziland Government Gazette, 1963–1977.* Kwaluseni, Swaziland: University College of Swaziland (University of Botswana and Swaziland), 1978.

Steinhauer, D. R. (comp. and ed.). *Swaziland National Bibliography, 1972–1976, with Current Information.* Kwaluseni, Swaziland: University College of Swaziland (University of Botswana and Swaziland), 1977.

Steinhauer, D. R. (comp.). *Swaziland National Bibliography, 1977, with Current Information.* Kwaluseni, Swaziland: University College of Swaziland (University of Botswana and Swaziland), 1978.

Swaziland, Government of. *Socio-Economic Development Bibliography.* Mbabane: Economic Planning Office, 1994.

Swaziland Official Publications, 1880–1972: A Bibliography of the Original Microfiche Edition. Pretoria: State Library (Bibliographies No. 18), 1975.

Thorn, Lynne (comp.). *Swaziland National Bibliography, 1978–1982, with Current Information.* Kwaluseni, Swaziland: University of Swaziland, 1984.

University of Swaziland Library. *Swaziland National Bibliography, 1983–1985, with Current Information.* Kwaluseni, Swaziland: University of Swaziland, 1986.

Wallace, Charles Stewart (comp.). *Swaziland: A Bibliography.* University of the Witwatersrand, Department of Bibliography, Librarianship and Typography, 1967.

Webster, John B. and Paulus Mohome. *Bibliography of Swaziland.* Syracuse, N.Y.: Maxwell School of Citizenship and Public Affairs, Program of Eastern African Studies, Bibliographic Section (Occasional Bibliography No. 10), 1968.

Willet, Shelagh M. *A Checklist of Reference Books on Lesotho, Botswana and Swaziland.* Grahamstown, South Africa: Rhodes University, Department of Librarianship (Bibliographical Series No. 1), 1971.

Woodson, Dorothy C. "The J.S.M. Matsebula Collection at the University of Swaziland," *History in Africa,* XVIII (1991), 381–397.

B. General Information

Ashton, Hugh. "The High Commission Territories," in *Race Relations Handbook* (London: Oxford University Press, 1949).

Barker, Dudley. *Swaziland.* London: HMSO, 1965.

Becker, Peter. *Trails and Tribes in Southern Africa.* London: Hart-Davis, MacGibbon, 1975.

Booth, Alan R. "Priorities and Opportunities for Research in Swaziland," *History in Africa,* IX (1982), 325–335.

———. *Swaziland: Tradition and Change in a Southern African Kingdom.* Boulder, CO: Westview Press (Africa Profile Series), 1983.

Coryndon, R. T. "Swaziland," *Journal of the African Society,* XIV (1915), 250–265.

Hailey, Lord (William M.). *An African Survey.* Rev. ed. London: Oxford University Press, 1957.

Hancock, W. Keith. *A Survey of British Commonwealth Affairs.* London: Oxford University Press, 1963.

Hendy, H. R. *Swaziland, South Africa.* Mbabane: Swaziland Chamber of Commerce and Industries, 1953.

Houlton, John. "The High Commission Territories in South Africa," *Geographical Magazine,* XXVI (August, 1953), 175–181.

Miller, Allister M. "Swaziland," *Transactions of the Royal Colonial Institute,* XXXI (1899–1900), 274–304.

———. *Swaziland.* London: Weightman and Company, 1934.

Nxumalo, Simon S. *Our Way of Life.* Mbabane: Mabiya Publications, 1976.

Pott, Douglas. "The Story of the Swaziland Protectorate," *Race Relations Journal,* XVIII (1951), 125–165.

———. *Swaziland: A General Survey.* Rev. ed. Johannesburg: South African Institute of Race Relations, 1955.

Scutt, Joan. *The Story of Swaziland.* 4th ed., rev. Mbabane: Websters, 1983.

Swaziland Government. *A Handbook to the Kingdom of Swaziland.* Mbabane: Government Information Services, 1968.

C. Guides, Yearbooks, and Reports

Andrew, Bruce. *The Guide to Swaziland.* Johannesburg and Mbabane: Winchester Press, 1970.

British Information Service. *The High Commission Territories.* London: Central Office of Information, 1963.

Great Britain, Government of. *Swaziland.* Colonial Annual Reports. London: HMSO, 1906–1939; 1946–1968.

Great Britain, Government of. Colonial Office. *Swaziland.* London: Central Office Information, 1963.

Schwager, Dirk. *Swaziland.* Stellenbosch: Dirk and Colleen Schwager, 1980. (Reprint 1998)

Swaziland, Government of. *Census of Swaziland, 1956.* Mbabane: Government Printer, 1958.

———. *Development Plan 1988/89–1993/94.* Mbabane: Ministry of Economic Planning and Development, 1988.

———. *Development Plan 1994/95–1996–97.* Mbabane: Ministry of Economic Planning and Development, 1994.

———. *Development Plan 1997/98–1999/00.* Mbabane: Ministry of Economic Planning and Development, 1997.

———. *4th National Development Plan 1983/84–1987/88.* Mbabane: Swaziland Printing and Publishing Company Ltd., 1983.

———. *Handbook to the Kingdom of Swaziland.* Mbabane: Swaziland Government Information Services, 1968.

———. *Post Independence Development Plan.* Mbabane: Swaziland Printing and Publishing Company Ltd., 1969.

————. *Report on the 1966 Swaziland Population Census* (H. M. Jones, Census Commissioner). Mbabane: Swaziland Printing and Publishing Company Ltd., 1968.

————. *Report on the 1976 Swaziland Population Census.* 3 vols. Mbabane: Swaziland Printing and Publishing Company Ltd., 1979.

————. *Report on the 1986 Swaziland Population Census.* 4 vols. Mbabane: Central Statistical Office, 1986.

————. *Report on the Swaziland Population Projections (1986–2016).* 5 vols. Mbabane: Central Statistical Office, n.d.

————. *Second National Development Plan 1973–1977.* Mbabane:Swaziland Printing and Publishing Company Ltd., 1973.

————. *Third National Development Plan 1978/79–1982/83.* Mbabane: Swaziland Printing and Publishing Company Ltd., 1978.

D. Statistical Abstracts

Great Britain, Swaziland Government Information Services. *Annual Statistical Bulletin.* Mbabane: Swaziland Government Information Services, 1966–1968 (annual).

Swaziland, Government of. *Annual Statistical Bulletin.* Mbabane: Ministry of Economic Planning and Statistics, 1969–1996 (annual).

E. Travel and Description

Bulpin, Thomas V. *Lost Trails of the Low Veld.* Cape Town: H. B. Timmins; London: Hodder and Stoughton, 1950.

————. *Scenic Wonders of Southern Africa.* Muizenberg, South Africa: Books of Africa, 1985.

Campbell, Alec, David Ambrose, and Dave Johnson. *The Guide to Botswana, Lesotho and Swaziland: A Comprehensive Companion for Visitors and Investors.* Saxon, South Africa: Winchester Press, 1983.

Crewe-Brown, Mike. *A Traveller's Companion to South Africa Including the Kingdom of Swaziland.* Johannesburg: CBM, 1994.

Crush, Jonathan and Paul Wellings. "The Southern African Pleasure Periphery, 1966–83," *Journal of Modern African Studies,* XXI, 4 (1983), 673–698. Reprinted in S. Britton and W. Clarke (eds.), *Ambiguous Alternative: Tourism in Small Developing Countries* (Suva, Fiji: University of the South Pacific, 1987).

Davis, A. *Umbandine: A Romance of Swaziland.* London: 1898.

Filmer, Harry J. and Patricia Jameson. *Usutu! A Story About the Early Days of Swaziland.* Johannesburg: Central News Agency, 1960.

Forbes, David. *My Life in South Africa.* London: Witherby, 1938.

Griffithes, T. P. *From Bedford Row to Swazieland.* London: Bradley, 1898.

Harrison, David. "Tradition, Modernity and Tourism in Swaziland," in *Tourism and the Less Developed Countries* (New York: Halsted Press, 1992), pp. 148–162.

Hawthorn, Vic. *South Africa, Lesotho & Swaziland*. Berkeley, CA: Lonely Planet, 1993.

Hendy, H. R. *Swaziland: The Tourist's Paradise*. Durban, South Africa: John Ramsey, 1953.

Hussey, Hazel A. *Swaziland Jumbo Tourist Guide: A Travel Guide for Tourists and Visitors to the Kingdom of Swaziland*. Mbabane: R. O. Hussey & Co., 1994.

Leigh, Nila K. *Learning to Swim in Swaziland: A Child's-Eye View of a Southern African Country*. New York: Scholastic, 1993.

Miller, Allister M. *Swaziland*. (n.p.): Mendelson, 1900.

———. *Swaziland: The California of South Africa*. Mbabane: Swaziland Mining, Commercial and Industrial Chamber, 1907.

———. *Swaziland: The Land of Green Pastures and Running Streams*. Johannesburg: The Mushroom Land Settlement Company, 1936.

O'Neil, Owen Rowe. *Adventures in Swaziland*. New York: Century, 1921.

Scutt, Joan F. *This Is Our Life in Swaziland*. London: Edinburgh House Press, 1962.

Settlers Emigration Society. *Land and Farming Prospects in the Transvaal and Swaziland*. London: R. Clay and Sons, 1910.

Spurdens, Constance. *Sunshine in Swaziland: Reminiscences of Africa*. Saltburn, England: J. Parks, 1930.

Turco, Marco. *Visitors' Guide to Swaziland: How to Get There, What to See, Where to Stay*. Johannesburg: Southern Book Publishers, 1994.

Watts, Christopher J. "Swaziland," *Travel in Africa*, 1 (March 1952), 25–26.

Wentzel, Volkmar. "Swaziland Tries Independence," *National Geographic*, CXXXVI, 2 (August 1969), 266–293.

II. CULTURAL

A. Archeology and Prehistory

Barham, Lawrence S. "A Preliminary Report on the Later Stone Age Artifacts from Siphiso Shelter in Swaziland," *South African Archaeological Bulletin*, XLIV, 149 (June 1989), 33–43.

Beaumont, Peter B. and J. C. Vogel. "On a New Radiocarbon Chronology for Africa South of the Equator," *African Studies*, XXXI, 2 & 3 (1972), 65–89, 155–182.

Boshier, Adrian K. "Archaeology: Swaziland, Birthplace of Modern Man," *Science Digest*, LXXIII, 3 (March 1973), 42–47.

Boshier, Adrian K. and P. B. Beaumont. "Mining in Southern Africa and the Emergence of Man," *Optima*, XXII, 1 (March 1972), 2–12.

Dart, Raymond A. and P. B. Beaumont. "Evidence of Iron Ore Mining in Southern

Africa in the Middle Stone Age," *Current Anthropology*, X, 1 (February 1969), 127–128.

———. "Ratification and Retrocession of Earlier Swaziland Iron Ore Mining Radiocarbon Datings," *South African Journal of Science*, LXIV, 6 (June 1968), 241–246.

Hamilton, C.N.G. "Ancient Workings in Swaziland," *South African Archeological Bulletin*, XVI, 64 (December 1961), 128–133.

Jones, T. Rupert. "Exhibition of Stone Implements from Swaziland," *Journal of the Royal Anthropological Institute*, XXVIII (Old Series, 1899), 48–54.

Masson, John. R. "Rock-Paintings in Swaziland," *South African Archeological Bulletin*, XVI, 64 (December 1961), 128–133.

Price-Williams, David. "Archaeology in Swaziland," *South African Archaeological Bulletin*, XXXV, 131 (June 1980), 13–18.

———. "A Preliminary Report on Recent Excavations of Middle and Late Stone Age Levels at Sibebe Shelter, N.W. Swaziland," *South African Archaeological Bulletin*, XXXVI, 133 (June 1981), 22–28.

Price-Williams, David and A. Watson. "New Observations on the Prehistory and Paleoclimate of the Late Pleistocene of Southern Africa," *World Archaeology*, XIII (1982), 372–381.

Price-Williams, David, A. Watson, and A. S. Goudie. "Quaternary Colluvial Stratigraphy, Archaeological Sequences and Paleoenvironment in Swaziland," *Geographical Journal*, XLVIII, 1 (March 1982), 50–67.

Stephen, Michael F. "The Great Diamond Rush? Or What Archaeology Tells of Swaziland Before the Swazi," in J. Daniel and M. Stephen (eds.), *Historical Perspectives on the Political Economy of Swaziland* (Kwaluseni: University of Swaziland, Social Science Research Unit, 1986), pp. 7–16.

B. Fine Arts

Ginindza, Theresa Thoko. "The Aesthetic Component of Swazi Artifacts," *Ufahamu*, II, 1 (Spring 1971), 27–30.

———. "SiSwati Traditional Dress and Costume," *Swaziland National Centre Yearbook* (1974), 16–31.

Harding, J. R. "A Note on the Conus Shell Disc Ornament in Swaziland," *Man*, LXIV, 222 (1964), 185–186.

Huskisson, Yvonne. *A Survey of Musical Practices of a Swazi Tribe*. Pretoria: National Council for Social Research, 1960.

Rohrmann, G. F. "House Decoration in Southern Africa," *African Arts*, VII, 3 (Spring 1974), 18–21.

Rycroft, David K. "The National Anthem of Swaziland," in M. Shaw (ed.), *National Anthems of the World* (London: Blandford Press, 1969), pp. 368–370.

———. "Stylistic Evidence of Nguni Song," in K. Wachsmann (ed.), *Essays on*

Music and History in Africa (Evanston, IL: Northwestern University Press, 1971), pp. 213–241.

———. *Swazi Vocal Music*. Tervuren, Belgium: Musée Royal de l'Afrique Centrale & Belgische Radio en Televisie, 1968. (Monograph [40 pp.] and LP disc)

———. *Zulu, Swazi and Xhosa Instrumental and Vocal Music*. Tervuren, Belgium: Musée Royal de l'Afrique Centrale & Belgische Radio en Televisie, 1970. (Monograph [55 pp.] and LP disc)

C. Linguistics and Languages

Davey, A.S. "A Swati Comparative List," *South African Journal of African Languages*, X, 4 (1990).

Lanham, L. W. "The Proliferation and Extension of Bantu Phonemic Systems Influenced by Bushmen and Hottentot," *Proceedings, Ninth Annual Congress of Linguistics* (Cambridge, MA, 1962), pp. 382–391.

Rycroft, David K. *Concise SiSwati Dictionary*. Pretoria: J. L. van Schaik, 1981. (Reprinted 1998)

———. *Essential SiSwati: A Phrase Book*. Pretoria: J. L. van Schaik, 1981.

———. *Say It in SiSwati*. 2d ed. London: School of Oriental and African Studies, University of London; Mbabane: Websters, 1979. (Manual, with language laboratory cassette tapes)

Sibiya, A. K. *An Elementary Course in SiSwati*. 2d ed. Mhlambanyati, Swaziland: Usutu Pulp Company Training Centre, 1975.

Ziervogel, D. *Swazi Texts with an English Translation, Notes, and a Glossary of Swazi Terms*. Pretoria: J. L. van Schaik, 1957.

Ziervogel, D. and E. Mabuza. *A Grammar of the Swati Language (SiSwati)*. Pretoria: J. L. van Schaik, 1976.

D. Literature

Dube, Oswald B. *The Arrow of King Sobhuza II*. Mbabane: Websters, 1986.

Kuper, Hilda. *Bite of Hunger*. New York: Harcourt, Brace, and World, 1965.

———. *A Witch in My Heart*. London: Oxford University Press, 1970.

Lynne, Suzanna. *Red Feather Love*. Toronto and Winnipeg: Harlequin, 1975.

Matsebula, J.S.M. *The King's Eye*. Cape Town: Maskew Miller Longman, 1983.

———. *A Tribute to the Late His Majesty King Sobhuza II*. Mbabane: Websters, 1983.

Miller, Allister M. *Mamisa: The Swazi Warrior*. Pietermaritzburg: Shuter and Shooter, 1933. (Reprinted 1955; Siswati edition, 1960)

Mzizi, Joshua B. *Man of Conscience: The Life History of Albert Hashane Shabangu and Selected Speeches*. Mbabane: Websters, 1990.

Savory, Phyllis. *Swazi Fireside Folktales*. Cape Town: Howard Timmins, 1973.

Scutt, Joan. *Born a Rebel*. Mbabane: Websters, 1987.

———. *Sipho, the Swazi: A Children's Story*. Roodeport: Mission Press, 1976.

III. ECONOMIC

A. General

Barclays Bank of Swaziland. *Barclays Business Guide to Swaziland*. Mbabane: Barclays Bank of Swaziland Ltd., 1989.

———. *Swaziland: A Businessman's Profile*. Mbabane: Barclays Bank of Swaziland Ltd., 1986.

———. *Swaziland: An Economic Survey and Businessman's Guide*. Mbabane: Barclays Bank of Swaziland Ltd., 1981.

de Vletter, Fion (ed.). *The Swazi Rural Homestead*. Kwaluseni: University of Swaziland, Social Science Research Unit, 1983.

Economist Intelligence Unit. *Country Profile: Namibia [and] Swaziland*. London: Economist Intelligence Unit, 1967–present (annual). (Former title: *Quarterly Economic Review of Namibia, Botswana, Lesotho, Swaziland: Annual Supplement*)

———. *Country Report: Namibia [and] Swaziland*. London: Economist Intelligence Unit, 1967–present (quarterly). (Former title: *Quarterly Economic Review of Southern Africa: Republic of South Africa, South West Africa, Botswana, Lesotho and Swaziland*)

Great Britain, Government of. Commonwealth Relations Office. *Basutoland, Bechuanaland Protectorate, and Swaziland: Report of an Economic Survey Mission*. London: HMSO, 1960.

Howick, Lord. "The Emergence of Swaziland (Personal Reminiscences of the Economic Advance of the Territory)," *Optima*, XII, 2 (June 1962), 104–109.

Pim, Sir Alan. *Financial and Economic Situation of Swaziland: Report of the Commission Appointed by the Secretary of State for Dominion Affairs*. London: HMSO, 1932. (Cmd. 4114)

Southern African Economist. Harare: Southern African Development Coordination Conference (now Southern African Development Community) Press Trust, 1988– .

Stephen, Michael F. " 'Small Is Beautiful'—An Overview of the Swazi Economy," in J. Daniel and M. Stephen (eds.), *Historical Perspectives on the Political Economy of Swaziland* (Kwaluseni: University of Swaziland, Social Science Research Unit, 1986), pp. 193–219.

Wekwete, K. H. (ed.). *Planning Urban Economies in Southern and Eastern Africa*. Brookfield, VT and Aldershot, England: Avebury, 1994.

B. Agriculture and Pastoralism

Baton, E. *Swaziland Agricultural Survey*. Cape Town: University of Cape Town, School of Social Studies, 1953.

Best, A.C.G. "Development of Commercial Agriculture in Swaziland, 1946–1963," *Papers of the Michigan Academy of Science, Arts and Letters*, LII (1967), 269–287.

Carr, M.K.V. "Irrigation Issues in Swaziland: Large-Scale Projects," *Outlook on Agriculture*, XVI, 2 (1987), 54–58.

"Cotton Growing in Swaziland," *Bulletin of the Imperial Institute*, 24 (1923), 468–474.

Daniel, John B. McI. *The Geography of the Rural Economy of Swaziland*. Durban, South Africa: Institute for Social Research, University of Natal, 1962.

———. "The Influence of Processing Industries on Swazi Agriculture," in G. Stewart (ed.), *Processing and Financing African Primary Products* (Edinburgh: Edinburgh University, Centre for African Studies, 1967), pp. 97–127.

———. "Some Government Measures to Improve African Agriculture in Swaziland," *Geographical Journal*, CXXXII, 4 (December 1966), 506–515.

———. "Swaziland: Some Problems of an African Rural Economy in a Development Country," *South African Geographical Journal*, XLVIII (December 1966), 90–100.

Derman, P. J. "Cash Crops in Swaziland: An Anthropological Perspective," *South African Journal of African Affairs*, II (1977), 115–119.

———. "Stock and Aristocracy: The Political Implications of Swazi Marriage," *African Studies*, XXXVI, 2 (1977), 119–129.

Dlamini, P. M. and S. Adams. "Pricing Policies in Relation to Agricultural Productivity and the Environment," *UNISWA Research Journal*, III (June 1990), 1–10.

Doran, M. H., A. Low, and R. Kemp. "Cattle as a Store of Wealth in Swaziland: Implications for Livestock Development and Overgrazing in Eastern and Southern Africa," *American Journal of Agricultural Economics*, LXI, 1 (1979), 41–47.

Funnell, Donald C. "Changes in Farm Incomes and the Rural Development Program in Swaziland," *The Journal of Developing Areas*, XVI (1982), 271–290.

———. "The Quiet Innovators: Small-Scale Irrigation on Swazi Nation Land," in H. Tielmann (ed.), *Scenes of Change: Visions on Developments in Swaziland* (Leiden: African Studies Centre, 1988), pp. 121–136.

———. *Under the Shadow of Apartheid: Agrarian Transformation in Swaziland*. Aldershot, England: Avebury, 1991.

Hackel, Jeffrey D. "Rural Change and Nature Conservation in Africa: A Case Study from Swaziland," *Human Ecology*, XXI, 3 (1993), 295–312.

Low, Allan R. C. *Agricultural Development in Southern Africa: Farm-Household Economics and the Food Crisis*. London: James Currey; Portsmouth, NH: Heinemann; Cape Town: David Phillip, 1986.

Low, A.R.C., R. Kemp, and M. Doran. "Cattle as a Store of Wealth in Swaziland: Reply," *American Journal of Agricultural Economics*, LXII (1980), 614–617.

———. "Cattle, Wealth and Cash Needs in Swaziland: Price Response and Rural Development Implications," *Journal of Agricultural Economics*, XXXI, 2 (1980), 225–236.

Murdoch, G. "Soil Survey and Soil Classification in Swaziland," *African Soils*, IX, 1 (January–April 1964), 117–123.

Rauniyar, Ganesh P. "Managing Green Revolution Technology: An Analysis of a Differential Practice Combination in Swaziland," *Economic Development & Cultural Change*, XLIV, 2 (1996), 413–437.

———. "Technology Adoption on Small Farms," *World Development*, II, 2 (1992), 275–282.

Russell, Margo, N. Mbatha, and V. Sithole. "Sample Survey of Maize Growing in Swaziland." University of Swaziland, Social Science Research Unit, Research Paper No. 1, c. 1983.

Sikhondze, Bonginkhosi B. "The Development of Swazi Cotton Cultivation: Some Theoretical Problems, 1904–1985," *Mohlomi: Journal of Southern African Historical Studies*, VI (1990), 117–138.

———. "Monopoly Commodity Production in Swaziland: The Case of Cotton," *Eastern Africa Social Science Review*, VI, 2 (June 1990) and VII, 1 (January 1991), 171–181.

———. "The Role of the Money Economy in Changing the Nature of Swazi Agriculture with Special Reference to the Development of Cotton Cultivation, 1900–1968: A Case Study of the Middle and Low-Veld of Swaziland." Institute of Commonwealth Studies, University of London, 1980. (Mimeo)

———. "Swazi Responses and Obstacles to Cotton Cultivation, 1918–1945," *Transafrican Journal of History*, XIII (1984), 177–187.

Simelane, Hamilton Sipho. "The Colonial State, Peasants and Agricultural Production in Swaziland, 1940–1950," *South African Historical Journal*, XXVI (1992), 93–115.

Testerink, J. "Agricultural Commercialization in Swaziland: Farmers Compared." University of Swaziland, Social Science Research Unit, Research Paper No. 11, 1984.

UNISWA Journal of Agriculture: A Publication of the Faculty of Agriculture. Luyengo: University of Swaziland, Faculty of Agriculture, 1992– .

University of Swaziland. *Agricultural Policy for the 1990s.* Kwaluseni: University of Swaziland, Social Science Research Unit, 1991.

Wood, R. C. "Cotton in Swaziland," *Empire Cotton Growing Review*, IV (1927), 13–19.

———. "A Report on Experimental Working on Cotton in Swaziland Season, 1925–1926," *Empire Cotton Growing Review*, IV (1927), 64–78.

C. Land Tenure

Armstrong, Alice K. *Legal Aspects of Land Tenure in Swaziland.* Mbabane: United States Agency for International Development, 1985.

Bowen, Paul N. *A Longing for Land: Tradition and Change in a Swazi Agricultural Community*. Brookfield, VT: Ashgate; Aldershot, England: Avebury, 1993.

Hughes, A.J.B. "Reflections on Traditional and Individual Land Tenure in Swaziland," *Journal of Local Administration Overseas*, III, 1 (January 1964), 3–13.

———. "Some Swazi Views on Land Tenure," *Africa*, XXXII, 3 (July 1962), 253–278. Reprinted in C. Turnbull (ed.), *Africa and Change* (New York: Alfred A. Knopf, 1973).

———. *Swazi Land Tenure*. Durban, South Africa: University of Natal, Institute for Social Research, 1964.

Levin, Richard. "Contract Farming in Swaziland: Peasant Differentiation and the Constraints of Land Tenure," *African Studies*, XLVII, 2 (1988), 101–120. Reprinted in M. Neocosmos (ed.), *Social Relations in Swaziland: Critical Analyses* (Kwaluseni: University of Swaziland, Social Science Research Unit, 1987), pp. 171–189.

———. "Traditional Land Tenure in Swaziland: Technical Efficiency, Problems of Democratic Organization and the Value of Legalistic Classifications," *Journal of Contemporary African Studies*, VII, 1/2 (1988), 57–79. Reprinted in M. Neocosmos (ed.), *Social Relations in Swaziland: Critical Analyses* (Kwaluseni: University of Swaziland, Social Science Research Unit, 1987), pp. 151–170.

Magagula, Glenn T. "Land Tenure and Agricultural Production in Swaziland," in J. W. Arntzen, L. Ngcongco, and S. Turner (eds.), *Land Policy and Agriculture in Eastern and Southern Africa* (Tokyo: United Nations University, 1986), pp. 133–140.

Matthews, Kgomotso. "'Squatters' on Private Tenure Farms in Swaziland: A Preliminary Investigation," in M. Neocosmos (ed.), *Social Relations in Rural Swaziland: Critical Analyses* (Kwaluseni: University of Swaziland, Social Science Research Unit, 1987), pp. 191–219.

Mugyenyi, Joshua. "Land Tenure Systems and Its Implications for Rural Development in Swaziland," in I. C. Lamba and B. Kandoole (eds.), *Mobilization of Resources for Rural Development in Swaziland* (Zomba, Malawi: Southern African Universities Social Science Conference, 1988), pp. 239–264.

Rose, Laurel L. *The Politics of Harmony: Land Dispute Strategies in Swaziland*. Cambridge: Cambridge University Press (African Studies Series No. 69), 1992.

———. "'A Woman Is Like a Field': Women's Strategies for Land Access in Swaziland," in Jean Davison (ed.), *Agriculture, Women and Land: The African Experience* (Boulder, CO: Westview Press, 1988), pp. 177–201.

Russell, Margo. *African Freeholders: A Study of Individual Tenure Farms in Swazi Ownership*. Madison: University of Wisconsin, Land Tenure Center, 1990.

———. "Why Communal Land Tenure Survives in Swaziland," *Ceres*, XIX, 5 (1986), 30–34.

Scott, Peter. "Land Policy and the Native Population of Swaziland," *Geographical Journal*, CXVII, 4 (December 1951), 435–447.

Silitshena, Robson. "The Impact of Colonialism on Land Use in Central and Southern Africa," in Paul A. Olsen (ed.), *The Struggle for the Land* (Lincoln: University of Nebraska Press, 1990), pp. 146–170.

D. Finance, Credit, and Banking

Central Bank of Swaziland. *Quarterly Review.* Mbabane: Central Bank of Swaziland, 1979–present (quarterly).

Collings, Francis d'A., G. Doneley, A. Petersen, C. Puckahtikom, and P. Wickam. "The Rand and the Monetary Systems of Botswana, Lesotho and Swaziland," *Journal of Modern African Studies,* XVI, 1 (1978), 97–121.

International Monetary Fund. *Surveys of African Economies, Volume 5: Botswana, Lesotho, Swaziland, Burundi, Equatorial Guinea and Rwanda.* Washington, DC: International Monetary Fund, 1973.

Matsebula, Michael S. *Public Spending in Swaziland Since Independence.* Kwaluseni: University of Botswana and Swaziland, Economics Department (Occasional Paper No. 2), 1976.

———. "Tax Incentives in Botswana, Lesotho and Swaziland: A Case for Policy Harmonizing and Re-Gearing," *Journal of Southern African Affairs,* IV, 1 (January 1979), 45–54.

———. "Tax Incentives in Swaziland: Some Efficiency Considerations," *Journal of Southern African Affairs,* II, 4 (1977), 489–497.

Mercey, Charles. "The Swaziland Development and Savings Bank and Credit to Small Farmers in Swaziland: Three Measures of Success," in F. de Vletter (ed.), *The Swazi Rural Homestead* (Kwaluseni: University of Swaziland, Social Science Research Unit, 1983), pp. 209–276.

"South Africa, Lesotho and Swaziland," *Southern Africa Record,* XLIII (1986), 15–25.

Swaziland, Government of. *Statistical News.* Mbabane: Central Statistical Office, 1983–present (quarterly).

E. Commerce and Industry

Best, Alan C. G. *Swaziland Railway: A Study in Politico-Economic Geography.* East Lansing: Michigan State University, African Studies Center, 1966.

Booth, Alan R. "South African Sanctions-Breaking in Southern Africa: The Case of Swaziland," in Robert Edgar (ed.), *Sanctioning Apartheid* (Trenton, NJ: Africa World Press, 1990), pp. 323–338.

Cobbe, James H. "The South African Trade Control System and Neighboring States," *South African Journal of Economics,* XLII, 4 (December 1974), 438–442.

Dinwiddy, Bruce. *Promoting African Enterprise.* London: Croom Helm (Overseas Development Institute), 1974.

Evans, Julian and D. Wright. "The Usutu Pulp Company—the Development of an Integrated Forestry Project," in M. Carr (ed.), *Sustainable Industrial Development* (New York: Intermediate Development Group of North America, 1988), pp. 151–171.

International Labour Organisation. *The Small Enterprises Development Company Limited (SEDCO): An Approach to Developing the Local Construction Industry.* Geneva: International Labour Organisation, 1981.

Kamalkhani, Sylvie K. "The Constraints on Small Business in Swaziland," *Africa Insight*, XIX, 4 (1989), 219–224.

———. "Promoting Local Capital: The Role of the Small Enterprise Development Corporation (SEDCO) in Swaziland," *Journal of Southern African Studies*, XVII, 2 (1991), 191–196.

Maasdorp, Gavin. "Industrialization in a Small Country: The Experience of Swaziland," in John Barratt, D. Collier, K. Glaser, and H. Mönnig (eds.), *Strategy for Development* (London: Macmillan, 1976), pp. 179–192.

Matsebula, Michael S. "Entrepreneurial Success in Swaziland's Urban Informal Sector: A Profit-Function Framework," *Eastern Africa Economic Review*, IV, 1 (1988), 36–41.

———. "Swaziland's Urban Informal Sector: Its Characteristics, Constraints and Production from an Aggregate Viewpoint," in H. Tieleman (ed.), *Scenes of Change: Visions on Developments in Swaziland* (Leiden: African Studies Centre, 1988), pp. 137–149.

———. *The Urban Informal Sector: A Historical and Structural Analysis with Special Reference to Swaziland.* Harare: SAPES Books, 1996.

McPherson, Michael A. "Determinants of Small and Micro Enterprise Registration: Results from Surveys in Niger and Swaziland," *World Development*, XXIV, 3 (1996), 481–487.

Nxumalo, Sishayi S. "International Trade and Investment: The Case of Swaziland," in J. Barratt, S. Brand, D. Collier, and K. Glaser (eds.), *Accelerated Development in Southern Africa* (New York: St. Martin's Press, 1974), pp. 525–533.

Robson, Peter. "Economic Integration in Southern Africa," *Journal of Modern African Studies*, V, 4 (December 1967), 469–490.

Sandee, Henry, and H. Weijland. "Dual Production and Marketing of Vegetables in Swaziland: A Case of Marginalization of Female Traders," in H. Tieleman (ed.), *Scenes of Change: Visions on Developments in Swaziland* (Leiden: African Studies Centre, 1988), pp. 150–162.

Selwyn, Percy. *Industries in the Southern African Periphery: A Study of Industrial Development in Botswana, Lesotho and Swaziland.* Boulder, CO: Westview Press; London: Croom Helm, 1975.

Smit, P. and E. J. van der Merwe. "Economic Co-Operation in Southern Africa," *Journal of Geography*, III, 3 (September 1968), 279–294.

Sonko, Karamo N. M. "A Tale of Two Enterprises: Swaziland's Lessons for Privatization," *World Development*, XXII, 7 (1994), 1083–1096.

Swazi Review of Commerce & Industry. *Swaziland: A Review of Commerce & Industry.* Matsapha: Swazi Review of Commerce & Industry (Pty.) Ltd., 1998.
Turner, Biff. "A Fresh Start for the Southern African Customs Union," *African Affairs*, LXX (1971), 269–276.

F. Development

Fair, T.J.D. and L. Green. "Preparing for Swaziland's Future Growth," *Optima*, X, 4, (December 1960), 194–206.
Fair, T.J.D., G. Murdoch, and H. Jones. *Development in Swaziland: A Regional Analysis.* Johannesburg: Witwatersrand University Press, 1969.
Great Britain, Government of. *The Development of the Swaziland Economy.* London: HMSO, 1965.
International Labour Office. *Reducing Dependence: A Strategy for Productive Employment and Development in Swaziland.* Addis Ababa: International Labour Office, Jobs and Skills for Africa, 1977.
Kendrick, A. R. "The Role of the Commonwealth Development Corporation in Project Formulation and Implementation with Particular Reference to Agriculture in Swaziland," in John Barratt, D. Collier, K. Glaser, and H. Mönnig (eds.), *Strategy for Development* (London: Macmillan, 1976), pp. 111–148.
Lea, John P. "Underlying Determinants of Housing Location: A Case Study from Swaziland," *Journal of Modern African Studies*, XI, 2 (1973), 211–225.
Leistner, G.M.E. and P. Smit. *Swaziland: Resources and Development.* Pretoria: African Institute of South Africa (Communication of the Africa Institute No. 8), 1969.
Low, Allen. "Rural Development and Farm Homestead Economic Behaviour," in F. de Vletter (ed.), *The Swazi Rural Homestead* (Kwaluseni: University of Swaziland, Social Science Research Unit, 1983), pp. 163–208.
See also Section I.C above for the development plans listed under "Swaziland, Government of."

G. Labor

Booth, Alan R. "Capitalism and the Competition for Swazi Labour, 1945–1960," *Journal of Southern African Studies*, XIII, 1 (1986), 1–26.
———. "The Development of the Swazi Labour Market, 1900–1968," *South African Labour Bulletin*, VII, 6 (1982), 34–57.
———. "Homestead, State and Migrant Labor in Colonial Swaziland," *African Economic History*, XIV (1985), 107–145. Reprinted in J. Daniel and M. Stephen (eds.), *Historical Perspectives on the Political Economy of Swaziland* (Kwaluseni: University of Swaziland, Social Science Research Unit, 1986), pp. 17–50.

Catchpole, F. C. *Report on Labour Legislation in Swaziland*. Mbabane: Government Printer (High Commission Publication No. J499), 1960. (Mimeo)

Cobbe, James H. "Wage Policy Problems in the Small Peripheral Countries of Southern Africa, 1967–1976," *Journal of Southern African Affairs*, II, 4 (1977), 441–468.

Crush, Jonathan. "Landlords, Tenants and Colonial Social Engineers: The Farm Labour Question in Early Colonial Swaziland," *Journal of Southern African Studies*, XI (1985), 235–257.

———. "Swazi Migrant Workers and the Witwatersrand Gold Mines, 1886–1920," *Journal of Historical Geography*, XII (1986), 27–40.

———. "Uneven Labour Migration in Southern Africa: Conceptions and Misconceptions," *South African Geographical Journal*, LXVII (1984), 115–132.

Crush, Jonathan, A. Jeeves, and D. Yudelman. *South Africa's Labour Empire: A History of Black Migrancy to the Gold Mines*. Boulder, CO: Westview Press; Cape Town: David Philip, 1991.

De Vletter, Fion. "Labour Migration in Swaziland," in W. R. Bohning (ed.), *Black Migration in South Africa* (Geneva: International Labour Organisation, 1981), pp. 45–89.

———. "Labour Migration in Swaziland: Recent Trends and Implications," *South African Labour Bulletin*, VII, 6 (1982), 114–139.

De Vletter, Fion, M. Doran, A. Low, and P. Amoah, "Labour Migration to South Africa: The Swaziland Case Study," in *Migratory Labour in Southern Africa* (Addis Ababa: United Nations Economic Commission for Africa, 1985), pp. 431–461.

Elkan, Walter. "Labour Migration from Botswana, Lesotho and Swaziland," *African Perspectives*, I (1978), 145–156. Reprinted in *Economic Development and Cultural Change*, XXVIII, 3 (1980), 583–596.

Fransman, Martin. "Labour, Capital and the State in Swaziland," *South African Labour Bulletin*, VII, 6 (1982), 58–89.

Kowet, Donald K. *Land, Labour Migration and Politics in Southern Africa: Botswana, Lesotho and Swaziland*. Uppsala: Scandinavian Institute of African Studies, 1978.

Lipton, Merle. "Men of Two Worlds: Migrant Labour in South Africa," *Optima*, XXIX, 2/3 (November 1980), 72–201.

Low, A.R.C. *Migration and Agricultural Development in Swaziland: A Micro-Economic Analysis*. Geneva: International Labour Office (ILO Migration for Employment Project, Working Papers No. 13), 1977.

McFadden, Patricia. "Women and Revolution: Women Workers in Southern Africa," in J. Daniel and M. Stephen (eds.), *Historical Perspectives on the Political Economy of Swaziland* (Kwaluseni: University of Swaziland, Social Science Research Unit, 1986), pp. 153–160.

———. "Women in Wage-Labour in Swaziland: A Focus on Agriculture," *South African Labour Bulletin*, VII, 6 (1982), 140–166.

Milazi, Dominic. *The Politics and Economics of Labour Migration in Southern Africa*. Maseru, Lesotho: Lesotho Printing & Publishing Co., 1985.

Prinz, F. and B. Rosen-Prinz. *Migrant Labour and Rural Homesteads: An Investigation into the Sociological Dimensions of the Migrant Labour System in Swaziland.* Geneva: International Labour Organisation, 1978.

Russell, Margo. "High Status, Low Pay: Anomalies in the Position of Women in Employment in Swaziland," *Journal of Southern African Studies,* XII, 2 (1985), 293–307.

Simelane, Hamilton Sipho. "Labour Migration and Rural Transformation in Post-Colonial Swaziland," *Journal of Contemporary African Studies,* XIII, 2 (1995), 207–226.

Simelane, Nomthetho G. "The State and the Working Class: The Case of Swaziland," in *Southern African Studies: Retrospect and Prospect* (Edinburgh: Centre of African Studies, 1983), pp. 99–118. Reprinted in J. Daniel and M. Stephen (eds.), *Historical Perspectives on the Political Economy of Swaziland* (Kwaluseni: University of Swaziland, Social Science Research Unit, 1986), pp. 142–152.

Swaziland, Government of. *Big Bend Strike: Report of the Commission Appointed to Inquire into the Causes and Circumstances of the Strike Which Took Place in the Big Bend Area During March, 1963.* Mbabane: Government Printer (High Commission Publication No. AG847), 1963. (Mimeo)

See also Section IV.C below ("History: Colonial").

H. Investment and Foreign Aid

"Business Outlook Abroad: Swaziland," *Business America,* CXII, 18 (September 9, 1991), 26–27.

Cobbe, James. "Possible Side Effects of Aid to South Africa's Neighbors," *African Affairs,* LXXXIX, 354 (1990), 85–96.

De Vletter, Fion. "Footloose Foreign Investment in Swaziland," in Alan W. Whiteside (ed.), *Industrialization and Investment Incentives in Southern Africa* (Pietermaritzburg: University of Natal Press; London: James Currey, 1989), pp. 142–166.

Jones, David. *Aid and Development in Southern Africa: British Aid to Botswana, Lesotho and Swaziland.* London: Croom Helm; New York: Holmes & Meier, 1977.

I. Regional Economic Linkages, Unions, and Conferences

Askin, Steve. "The Sanctions-Busting Boom: A World-Wide Network Supports South Africa's Fastest Growing Export Industry," *Southern African Political & Economic Monthly,* IX (June 1988), 10–14.

Baffoe, Frank. "Some Aspects of the Political Economy of Economic Co-operation and Integration in Southern Africa: The Case of South Africa and the Countries of Botswana, Lesotho and Swaziland (BLS)," *Journal of Southern African Affairs,* III, 3 (1978), 327–342.

——. "Southern Africa," in Adebayo Adedeji (ed.), *Indigenization of African Economies* (London: Hutchinson, 1981), pp. 278–308.

Fair, T.J.D. *Towards Balanced Spatial Development in Southern Africa.* Pretoria: Africa Institute of South Africa, 1981. Reprinted (abridged) in *Journal of Contemporary African Studies,* I, 2 (1982), 253–267.

Gargano, Michael. "Withdrawal from the Rand Monetary Area: Swaziland's Prospects," *Africa Insight,* XVI, 2 (1986), 79–82.

Harris, Betty J. *The Political Economy of the Southern African Periphery: Cottage Industries, Factories, and Female Wage Labour in Swaziland Compared.* New York: St. Martin's Press, 1993.

Lemon, Anthony. "Swaziland," in Colin Clarke and A. Payne (eds.), *Politics, Security and Development in Small States* (London: Allen & Unwin, 1987), pp. 156–169.

Leys, Colin. "Scandinavian Development Assistance to Botswana, Lesotho and Swaziland," in D. Anglin, T. Shaw, and C. Widstrand (eds.), *Canada, Scandinavia and Southern Africa* (Uppsala: Scandinavian Institute for African Studies, 1978), pp. 47–64.

Maasdorp, Gavin. "Economic Co-operation in Southern Africa: Prospects for Regional Integration," *Conflict Studies,* CCLIII (1992), 1–30.

——. "A Strategy for Rail and Road Transportation in Southern Africa," *Africa Insight,* XXI, 1 (1991), 7–13.

Maasdorp, Gavin and A. Whiteside (eds.). *Towards a Post-Apartheid Future: Political and Economic Relations in Southern Africa.* London: Macmillan, 1992.

Sembajwe, Israel. "Population and Development in Southern Africa: The 1990s and Beyond," in *Southern Africa in the 1980s and Beyond: Institute of Southern African Studies 1980–1990* (Roma: National University of Lesotho, Institute of Southern African Studies, 1993), pp. 136–155.

Takirambudde, Peter N. "Rethinking Regional Integration Structures in Eastern and Southern Africa," *Africa Insight,* XXIII, 3 (1993), 149–158.

Van der Merwe, Derek. "Economic Cooperation in Southern Africa: Structures, Policies, Problems," *Comparative and International Law Journal of Southern Africa,* XXIV, 3 (1991), 386–404.

Weeks, John. "Regional Cooperation and Southern African Development," *Journal of Southern African Studies,* XXII, 1 (1996), 99–117.

Wood, Robert and Kathryn Morton. "Has British Aid Helped Poor Countries," *ODI Review,* I (1977), 40–67.

1. Southern African Customs Union

Ayee, Joseph R. A. "Swaziland and the Southern African Customs Union," *Journal of African Studies,* XV, 3/4 (1988/89), 61–70.

Cattaneo, Nicolette. "Piece of Paper or Paper of Peace: The Southern African Customs Union Agreement," *International Affairs Bulletin,* XIV, 1 (1990), 44–58.

Gibb, Richard. "Regional Integration in Post-Apartheid Southern Africa: The Case of Renegotiating the Southern African Customs Union," in *Journal of Southern African Studies*, XXIII, 1 (1997), 67–86.

Hall, P. H. "The Revenue Distribution Formula of the Southern African Customs Union," *South African Journal of Economics*, XLVIII, 3 (1980), 268–275.

Hoohlo, Setsomi G. "The Southern African Customs Union (SACU) and the Post-Apartheid South Africa: Prospects for Closer Integration in the Region," in Sehoai Santho and M. Sejanamane (eds.), *Southern Africa After Apartheid: Prospects for the Inner Periphery in the 1990s* (Harare: Southern Africa Political Economy Series Trust, 1990), pp. 92–108.

Kumar, Umesh. "Southern African Customs Union and BLS Countries (Botswana, Lesotho and Swaziland)," *Journal of World Trade*, XXIV, 3 (1990), 31–53.

Landell-Mills, P. M. "The 1969 Southern African Customs Union Agreement," *Journal of Modern African Studies*, IX, 2 (1971), 263–281.

Maasdorp, Gavin. "The Southern African Customs Union—an Assessment," *Journal of Contemporary African Studies*, II, 1 (1982), 81–112.

Mosley, Paul. "The Southern African Customs Union: A Reappraisal," *World Development*, VI, 1 (January 1978), 31–43.

Robson, Paul. "The Southern African Customs Union: A Comment," *World Development*, VI, 4 (April 1978), 461–466.

Tsie, Balefi. "States and Markets in the Southern African Development Community (SADC): Beyond the Neo-Liberal Paradigm," *Journal of Southern African Studies*, XXII, 1 (1996), 75–98.

Turner, Biff. "A Fresh Start for the Southern African Customs Union," *African Affairs*, LXX, 280 (1971), 269–276.

IV. HISTORY

A. General

Ginindza, T. Thoko. *Sibongo: Swazi Clan Names and Clan Praises*. Manzini: Swazi Heritage Series, 1992.

Matsebula, J.S.M. *A History of Swaziland*. 3d ed. Cape Town: Longman Southern Africa, 1988.

Parsons, Neil. *A New History of Southern Africa*. London: Macmillan, 1982.

Shillington, Kevin. *History of Southern Africa*. Harlow: Longman, 1987.

B. Pre-Colonial

Agar-Hamilton, J.A.I. *The Native Policy of the Voortrekkers: An Essay in the History of the Interior of South Africa 1836–1858*. Cape Town: Maskew Miller, 1928.

Bonner, Philip L. "Classes, the Mode of Production and the State in Pre-Colonial Swaziland," in Shula Marks and A. Atmore (eds.), *Economy and Society in Pre-Industrial South Africa* (London: Longman, 1980), pp. 80–101.

———. "Factions and Fissions: Transvaal/Swazi Politics in the Mid-Nineteenth Century," *Journal of African History*, XIX, 2 (1978), 219–238.

———. *Kings, Commoners and Concessionaires: The Evolution and Dissolution of the Nineteenth-Century Swazi State*. Cambridge: Cambridge University Press (African Studies Series No. 31); Johannesburg: Ravan Press, 1983.

———. "Mswati II, c. 1826–65," in Christopher Saunders (ed.), *Black Leaders in Southern African History* (London: Heinemann, 1979), pp. 61–74.

Bryant, A. T. *A History of the Zulu and Neighboring Tribes*. Cape Town: C. Struik, 1964.

———. *Olden Times in Zululand and Natal*. London: Longmans, Green & Co., 1929.

Cook, P.A.W. "History and Izibongo of the Swazi Chiefs," *Bantu Studies*, V, 2, (1931): 181–210.

Garson, Noel G. "The Swaziland Question and a Road to the Sea," *Archives Yearbook for South African History*, II (1957), 263–434.

Gillis, D. Hugh. *The Kingdom of Swaziland*. Westport, CT and London: Greenwood Press, 1999.

Jones, Huw M. *A Biographical Register of Swaziland to 1902*. Pietermaritzburg: University of Natal Press, 1993.

———. "Mbandzeni kaMswati (c.1857–1889)," *Africana Notes and News*, XXVIII, 8 (1989), 319–327.

———. "The Pre-colonial Distribution of the Swazi Population," *African Historical Demography*, II (1981), 331–369.

Malan, B. D. "The Middle Stone Age in the Eastern Transvaal and Swaziland," *South African Journal of Science*, XLVII, 5 (1950), 146–150.

Miller, Allister M. *Swazieland and the Swazieland Corporation*. London: The Swazieland Corporation, 1900.

Nyeko, Balam. "Pre-nationalist Resistance to Colonial Rule: Swaziland on the Eve of Imposition of British Administration, 1890–1902," *Transafrican Journal of History*, V, 2 (1976), 66–83.

———. "The Rule of the Dlamini in Nineteenth-Century Swaziland," *Tarikh*, IV, 2 (1973), 42–48.

Omer-Cooper, J. D. *The Zulu Aftermath: A Nineteenth Century Revolution in Bantu Africa*. London: Longman, 1966.

Peires, J. B. (ed.). *Before and After Shaka: Papers in Nguni History*. Grahamstown, South Africa: Rhodes University, Institute of Social and Economic Research, 1981.

Raddatz, H. *The Transvaal and the Swaziland Gold Fields*. Cape Town: Saul Solomon, 1886.

Sikhondze, Bonginkhosi B. "State Within a State: The History of the Evolution of the Mamba Clan of Swaziland," *Transafrican Journal of History*, XV (1986), 144–163.

Simelane, Hamilton Sipho. "Swazi Resistance to Boer Penetration and Domination, 1881–1898," *Transafrican Journal of History*, XVIII (1989), 117–146.

Umlandvo, Kulandza. *In Pursuit of Swaziland's Precolonial Past* (Swaziland Oral History Project, Carolyn Hamilton, ed.). Manzini: Macmillan Boleswa, 1990.

Webb, C. de B. and J. B. Wright (eds.). *The James Stuart Archive of Recorded Oral Evidence Relating to the History of the Zulu and Neighboring Tribes*. 4 vols. Pietermaritzburg: University of Natal Press; Durban, South Africa: Killie Campbell Africana Library, 1976–1986. (See especially vols. 1 [1976] and 3 [1982])

Westcott, Michael and Carolyn Hamilton. *In the Tracks of the Swazi Past: A Historical Tour of the Ngwane and Ndwandwe Kingdoms* (Swaziland Oral History Project, Carolyn Hamilton, ed.). Manzini: Macmillan Boleswa, 1992.

Wright, John. "Politics, Ideology, and the Invention of the 'Nguni,'" in Tom Lodge (ed.), *Resistance and Ideology in Settler Societies* (Johannesburg: Ravan Press and the University of the Witwatersrand, African Studies Institute, 1987), pp. 96–118.

1. The Mfecane *Reconsidered*

The contemporary scholarly controversy being waged over the origins and character of the *Mfecane* (the period of demographic chaos in southeast Africa following the death of Shaka Zulu in 1828), while geographically somewhat peripheral to the Swazi kingdom, is still of direct relevance to Swaziland's pre-colonial historiography. Representative elements of that important dialogue follow.

Cobbing, Julian. "The *Mfecane* as Alibi: Thoughts on Dithakong and Mbolompo," *Journal of African History*, XXIX, 3 (1988), 487–519.

Eldredge, Elizabeth A. "Sources of Conflict in Southern Africa ca.1800–30: The '*Mfecane*' Reconsidered," *Journal of African History*, XXXIII, 1 (1992), 1–35.

Hamilton, Carolyn A. " 'The Character and Object of Chaka': Reconsideration of the Making of Shaka as '*Mfecane*' Motor," *Journal of African History*, XXXIII, 2 (1992), 37–63.

———. *Terrific Majesty: The Powers of Shaka Zulu and the Limits of Historical Invention*. Cambridge, MA and London: Harvard University Press, 1998.

Omer-Cooper, John D. "Has the *Mfecane* a Future? A Response to the Cobbing Critique," *Journal of Southern African Studies*, XIX, 2 (1993), 273–294.

Peires, J. B. "Paradigm Deleted: The Materialist Interpretation of the *Mfecane*," *Journal of Southern African Studies*, XIX, 2 (1993), 295–313.

Saunders, Christopher. "Conference Report: *Mfecane* Afterthoughts," *Social Dynamics*, XVII, 2 (1991), 171–177.

Wright, John. "A.T. Bryant and 'The Wars of Shaka,'" *History in Africa*, XVIII (1991), 409–425.

C. Colonial

Arden-Clarke, Sir Charles. "The Problem of High Commission Territories," *Optima*, VIII, 4 (1958), 163–170.

Baring, Sir Evelyn. "The Emergence of Swaziland," *Optima*, XII, 2 (1962), 104–109.

———. "Problems of the High Commission Territories," *International Affairs*, XXVIII (April 1952), 184–189.

Booth, Alan R. "Capitalism and the Competition for Swazi Labour, 1945–1960," *Journal of Southern African Studies*, XIII, 1 (1986), 125–150.

———. " 'European Courts Protect Women and Witches': Colonial Law Courts as Redistributors of Power in Swaziland, 1930–1950," *Journal of Southern African Studies*, XVIII, 2 (1992), 253–275.

———. "Lord Selbourne and the British Protectorates 1908–1910," *Journal of African History*, X (1969), 133–148.

Cell, John W. *Hailey: A Study in British Imperialism, 1872–1969.* Cambridge: Cambridge University Press, 1992.

Cockram, Ben. "The Protectorates: An International Problem," *Optima*, XIII, 4 (1963), 177–183.

Coryndon, R. T. *Some Account of George Grey and His Work in Africa.* London: Chiswick Press, 1914.

Crush, Jonathan S. "Colonial Coercion and the Swazi Tax Revolt of 1903–07," *Political Geography Quarterly*, IV (1985), 179–190.

———. "The Colonial Division of Space: The Significance of the Swaziland Land Partition," *International Journal of African Historical Studies*, XIII, 1 (1980), 71–86.

———. "The Colour of Civilization: White Farming in Colonial Swaziland, 1910–1940," in Alan Jeeves and J. Crush (eds.), *White Farms, Black Labor: The State and Agrarian Change in Southern Africa, 1910–1950* (New York: Heinemann; London: James Currey; Pietermaritzburg: University of Natal Press, 1997), pp. 214–227.

———. "The Construction of Compound Authority: Drinking at Havelock, 1938–1944," in Jonathan Crush and A. Ambler (eds.), *Liquor and Labor in Southern Africa* (Athens: Ohio University Press; Pietermaritzburg: University of Natal Press, 1992), pp. 367–394.

———. "The Culture of Failure: Racism, Violence and White Farming in Colonial Swaziland," *Journal of Historical Geography*, XXII, 2 (1996), 177–197.

———. "The Genesis of Colonial Land Policy in Swaziland," *South African Geographical Journal*, LXII, 1 (1980), 73–88.

———. "Settler-Estate Production, Monopoly Control and the Imperial Response," *African Economic History*, VIII (1979), 183–197.

———. *The Struggle for Swazi Labour, 1890–1920.* Kingston and Montreal: McGill-Queens University Press, 1987.

―――. "Tin, Time and Space in the Valley of Heaven," *Transactions of the Institute of British Geographers*, XIII (1988), 211–221.

Doxey, G. V. *The High Commission Territories and the Republic of South Africa*. London: Oxford University Press, for the Royal Institute for African Affairs, 1963.

Dundas, Sir Charles and H. Ashton. *Problem Territories of Southern Africa: Basutoland, Bechuanaland Protectorate, and Swaziland*. Johannesburg: South African Institute of International Affairs, 1952.

Fairlie, Michael. *No Time Like the Past*. Edinburgh, Cambridge, and Durham: The Pentland Press, 1992.

Filmer, Harry J. and P. Jameson. *Usutu! A Story About the Early Days of Swaziland*. Johannesburg: Central News Agency, 1960.

Fransman, Martin. "The Colonial State and the Land Question in Swaziland, 1903–1907," in *The Societies of Southern Africa in the 19th and 20th Centuries, Volume 9* (London: University of London, Institute of Commonwealth Studies, Collected Seminar Papers No. 24, 1979), pp. 27–38.

Great Britain, Government of. *Basutoland, the Bechuanaland Protectorate, and Swaziland: History of Discussions with the Union of South Africa, 1919–1939*. London: HMSO, 1952.

Hailey, Lord. *Native Administration in the British African Territories. Part V. The High Commission Territories: Basutoland, the Bechuanaland Protectorate, and Swaziland*. London: HMSO, 1953.

―――. *The Republic of South Africa and the High Commission Territories*. London: Oxford University Press, 1963.

Halpern, Jack. *South Africa's Hostages: Basutoland, Bechuanaland, and Swaziland*. Baltimore: Penguin Books, 1965.

Headlam, Cecil (ed.). *The Milner Papers*. 2 vols. London: Cassell & Company, 1931, 1933.

Hyam, Ronald. "African Interests and the South Africa Act, 1908–1910," *Historical Journal*, XIII (1970), 85–105.

―――. *The Failure of South African Expansion, 1908–1948*. New York: Africana Publishing, 1972.

Konczacki, Z. A., J. Parpart, and T. Shaw (eds.). *Studies in the Economic History of Southern Africa: Vol. 2. South Africa, Lesotho and Swaziland*. London: Frank Cass, 1991.

Kuklick, Henrika. *The Savage Within: The Social History of British Anthropology, 1885–1945*. Cambridge: Cambridge University Press, 1991.

Kuper, Hilda. "The Colonial Situation in Southern Africa," *Journal of Modern African Studies*, II (1964), 149–164.

―――. *Sobhuza II: Ngwenyama and King of Swaziland*. London: Duckworth, 1978.

―――. *The Uniform of Colour: A Study of White-Black Relationships in Swaziland*. Johannesburg: Witwatersrand University Press, 1947.

Macmillan, Hugh. "Administrators, Anthropologists and 'Traditionalists' in Colonial Swaziland: The Case of the 'Amabhaca' Fines," *Africa*, LXV, 4 (1995), 545–564.

———. "A Nation Divided? The Swazi in Swaziland and the Transvaal, 1865–1986," in Leroy Vail (ed.), *The Creation of Tribalism in Southern Africa* (London: James Currey; Berkeley and Los Angeles: University of California Press, 1989), pp. 289–323.

———. "Swaziland: Decolonisation and the Triumph of 'Tradition,'" *Journal of Modern African Studies*, XXIII, 4 (1985), 643–666. Reprinted in John Daniel and M. Stephen (eds.), *Historical Perspectives on the Political Economy of Swaziland* (Kwaluseni: University of Swaziland, Social Science Research Unit, 1986), pp. 104–125.

Marwick, A. G. "The Attitude of the Swazi Towards Government and Its Causes." Manuscript (1955) copy in the Swaziland National Archives, Lobamba: RCS 591/30.

Mashasha, Francis J. "The Swazi Land Partition, 1902–1910," in *The Societies of Southern Africa in the 19th and 20th Centuries, Vol. 4* (London: University of London, Institute of Commonwealth Studies, Collected Seminar Papers No. 17, 1974), pp. 87–107.

Maud, Sir John. "The Challenge of the High Commission Territories," *African Affairs*, LXIII (1964), 94–103.

McGregor, JoAnn. "People Without Fathers: Mozambicans in Swaziland, 1888–1993," *Journal of Southern African Studies*, XX, 4 (1994), 545–567.

Miller, Allister M. *The South East Coast of Africa and Its Development*. St. Albans, England: Cambridge Press, 1923.

———. *Swaziland: The Land of Green Pastures and Running Streams*. Mbabane: The Mushroom Land Settlement Company, 1936.

Nyeko, Balam. "The African Voice in Colonial Swaziland: The Question of Transfer, 1910–1939," *Mohlomi: Journal of Southern African Historical Studies*, III/IV/V (1981), 20–34.

———. "The Extension of British Colonial Administration into Swaziland," *Makerere Historical Journal*, II, 2 (1979), 133–144.

Packard, Randall M. "Maize, Cattle and Mosquitoes: The Political Economy of Malaria Epidemics in Colonial Swaziland," *Journal of African History*, XXV, 2 (1984), 189–212.

Perham, Margery and L. Curtis. *The Protectorates of South Africa: The Question of Their Transfer to the Union*. London: Oxford University Press, 1935.

Pim, Sir Alan. "British Protectorates and Territories: An Address Delivered at a Meeting of the Royal Empire Society," *United Empire*, XXV, 5 (1934), 266–279.

———. "Questions of the South African Protectorates," *International Affairs*, XIII, 3 (1934), 668–688.

Rich, Paul B. *White Power and the Liberal Conscience*. Johannesburg: Ravan Press, 1984.

Scutt, J. F. *The Story of Swaziland*. 3d ed. Mbabane: Swaziland Printing and Publishing Co., 1986.

Simelane, Hamilton Sipho. "The Colonial State, Peasants and Agricultural Production in Swaziland, 1940–1950," *South African Historical Journal*, XVI (1992), 93–115.

———. "Labor Mobilization for the War Effort in Swaziland, 1940–1942," *International Journal of African Historical Studies*, XXVI, 3 (1993), 541–574.

———. "Land, Labour and the Establishment of Commercial Forests in Swaziland, 1947–1962," *Journal of Eastern African Research and Development*, XVII (1987), 124–146.

———. "Landlessness and the Imperial Response in Swaziland 1938–1950," *Journal of Southern African Studies*, XVII, 4 (1991), 717–741.

———. "Landlords, the State and Child Labor in Colonial Swaziland, 1914–1947," *International Journal of African Historical Studies*, XXXI, 2 (1998).

Spence, J. E. "British Policy Towards the High Commission Territories," *Journal of Modern African Studies*, II, 2 (1964), 221–246.

Stevens, Richard P. "The History of the Anglo-South African Conflict over the Proposed Incorporation of the High Commission Territories," in Christian P. Potholm and R. Dale (eds.), *Southern Africa in Perspective: Essays in Regional Politics* (New York: Free Press, 1972), pp. 97–109.

———. *Lesotho, Botswana, and Swaziland: The Former High Commission Territories in Southern Africa*. New York: Frederick A. Praeger, 1968.

Torrance, David E. *The Strange Death of the Liberal Empire: Lord Selborne in South Africa*. Montreal and Kingston: McGill-Queen's University Press, 1996.

Vail, Leroy. "Swazi Royal Praises: The Invention of Tradition," in Leroy Vail and L. White (eds.), *Southern African Voices in History* (Charlottesville: University Press of Virginia; London: James Currey, 1991), pp. 155–197.

Youé, Christopher P. "Imperial Land Policy and the African Response," *Journal of Imperial and Commonwealth History*, VII, 1 (1978), 56–70.

———. *Robert Thorne Coryndon: Proconsular Imperialism in Southern and Eastern Africa, 1897–1925*. Waterloo, Ontario: Wilfred Laurier Press, 1986.

D. Post-Colonial

Daniel, John. "Swaziland in the Context of South African Destabilization," in John Daniel and M. Stephen (eds.), *Historical Perspectives on the Political Economy of Swaziland* (Kwaluseni: University of Swaziland, Social Science Research Unit, 1986), pp. 181–192.

Daniel, John and M. F. Stephen (eds.). *Historical Perspectives on the Political Economy of Swaziland: Selected Articles*. Kwaluseni: University of Swaziland, Social Science Research Unit, 1986.

Daniel, John and J. Vilane. "Swaziland: Political Crisis, Regional Dilemma," *Review of African Political Economy*, XXXV (1986), 54–67. Reprinted in H.

Tieleman (ed.), *Scenes of Change: Visions on Developments in Swaziland* (Leiden: African Studies Centre, 1988), pp. 38–51.

Davies, Robert H., D. O'Meara, and S. Dlamini. *The Kingdom of Swaziland: A Profile.* London: Zed Books, 1985.

Esterhuysen, Pieter. "The Legacy of Sobhuza II," *Africa Insight*, XIV, 1 (1984), 5–13.

Fox, Edward. *Obscure Kingdoms.* London: Hamilton, 1993. (See especially the chapter "Swaziland—Kings and Rulers.")

Gininzda, Z. R. *King Mswati III.* Mbabane: Macmillan Swaziland National Publishing Co., 1988.

Levin, Richard. "Swaziland's 'Tinkhundla' and the Myth of Swazi Tradition," *Journal of Contemporary African Studies*, X, 2 (1991), 1–23.

———. *When the Sleeping Grass Awakens: Land and Power in Swaziland.* Johannesburg: Witwatersrand University Press, 1997.

Lister, L. D. and B. George. "The Role of Tradition in the Recent Political and Economic Development of Swaziland," *Manchester Papers on Development*, I, 3 (1985), 30–44.

Selected Speeches of His Majesty, King Sobhuza II. Mbabane: Websters, n.d. (Selected addresses from 1967 to 1978)

Simelane, Hamilton Sipho. "The Post-colonial State, Class and the Land Question in Swaziland," *Journal of Contemporary African Studies*, XI, 1 (1992), 22–50.

Tieleman, Henk J. (ed.). *Scenes of Change: Visions on Developments in Swaziland. Papers Presented at the Seminar "Social Sciences in Swaziland," Free University Amsterdam, February 1986.* Leiden: African Studies Centre, 1988.

Winter, Isobel. "The Post-colonial State and the Forces and Relations of Production: Swaziland," *Review of African Political Economy*, IX (1978), 27–43.

V. LAW

A. General

Adinkrah, K.O. "'We Shall Take Our Case to the King': Legitimacy and Tradition in the Administration of Law in Swaziland," *Comparative and International Law Journal of Southern Africa*, XXIV, 2 (1991), 226–239.

Bennett, T. W. and N. Peat. *A Sourcebook of African Customary Law for Southern Africa.* Cape Town: Juta, 1991.

Juta, H. C. *Revised Edition of the Laws of Swaziland in Force on the First Day of April, 1949.* 3 vols. London: C. F. Roworth, 1951.

Ndwandwe, R. M. and S.M.B. Dlamini. *Teach Yourself Employment Law in Simple English.* Part 1. Mbabane: Ministry of Education, Primary Curriculum Unit, c. 1998.

Nhlapo, R. T. "Legal Duality and Multiple Judicial Organisation in Swaziland: An Analysis and a Proposal," in P. N. Takirambudde (ed.), *The Individual Under African Law* (Kwaluseni: University of Swaziland, 1982), pp. 66–76.

Nhlapo, Thandabantu. *Marriage and Divorce in Swazi Law and Custom.* Mbabane: Websters, 1992.

Okoth-Obbo, George. "Remedying Wrongful Termination of Employment in Lesotho and Swaziland Through Reinstatement: A Comparative Analysis," *Lesotho Law Journal*, V, 1 (1989), 31–76.

Pain, J. H. "The Reception of English and Roman-Dutch Law in Africa with Reference to Botswana, Lesotho and Swaziland," *Comparative and International Law Journal of Southern Africa*, XI, 2 (1978), 137–167.

Rubin, Neville N. "The Swazi Law of Succession: A Restatement," *Journal of African Law*, IX, 2 (1965), 90–113.

———. "Swaziland," in A. N. Allot (ed.), *Judicial and Legal Systems in Africa*, 2d ed. (London: Butterworth, 1970), pp. 230–247.

———. "Swaziland Legislation: The Marriage Proclamation, 1964," *Journal of African Law*, IX, 1 (1965), 60–64.

Rweyemamu, Novatus. *The Swazi Chief and the Written Law.* Mbabane: Websters, 1990.

Sanders, A.J.G.M. "The Internal Conflict of Laws in Swaziland," *Comparative and International Law Journal of Southern Africa*, XIX, 1 (1986), 112–120.

———. "Legal Dualism in Lesotho, Botswana and Swaziland—a General Survey," *Lesotho Law Journal*, I, 1 (1985), 47–67.

Takirambudde, Peter N. "External Law and Social Structure in an African Context: An Essay About Normative Imposition and Survival in Swaziland," *Comparative and International Law Journal of Southern Africa*, XVI, 2 (1983), 209–228.

———. "State Regulation and Control of the Insurance Business: The Case of Swaziland," *Zimbabwe Law Journal*, XXI, 2 (1981), 100–112.

———. "Stealing from a Bank Account," *Comparative and International Law Journal of Southern Africa*, XV, 2 (1982), 215–223.

———. "The Swaziland Contractual Regulation of Land Transactions: Trading Efficiency for Social Justice," *Comparative and International Law Journal of Southern Africa*, XIV, 2 (1981), 179–195.

Thompson, A. C. *The Laws of Swaziland.* 4 vols. Mbabane: n.p., 1960.

Wanda, B. P. "Swaziland," in Andrew Harding and J. Hatchard (eds.), *Preventive Detention and Security Law: A Comparative Survey* (Dordrecht and Boston: M. Nijhoff, c. 1993), pp. 241–246.

B. Women and the Law

Adinkrah, K. O. "Folk Law Is the Culprit: Women's 'Non-Rights' in Swaziland," *Journal of Legal Pluralism and Unofficial Law*, 30/31 (1990/91), 9–31.

Armstrong, Alice. "Access to Health Care and Family Planning in Swaziland: Law and Practice," *Studies in Family Planning*, XVIII, 6 (1987), 371–382.

―――. "Consent in Rape Cases in Swaziland: A Woman's Right to Decide," *Zimbabwe Law Review*, IV, 1/2 (1986), 112–124.

―――. "Evidence in Rape Cases in Four Southern African Countries," *Journal of African Law*, XXXIII, 2 (1989), 172–184.

―――. "Maintenance Statutes in Six Countries of Southern Africa," *Journal of African Law*, XXXIV, 2 (1990), 132–144.

―――. "A Note on Several Aspects of Rape in Swaziland," *Comparative and International Law Journal of Southern Africa*, XIX, 3 (1986), 474–482.

―――. "Traditionalism and Access to Health Care: Law Relevant to Women's Health in Swaziland," in A. Armstrong (ed.), *Women and Law in Southern Africa* (Harare: Zimbabwe Publishing House, 1987), pp. 221–236.

―――. (ed.). *Women and Law in Southern Africa*. Harare: Zimbabwe Publishing House, 1987.

―――. "Women as Victims: A Study of Rape in Swaziland," in A. Armstrong (ed.), *Women and Law in Southern Africa* (Harare: Zimbabwe Publishing House, 1987), pp. 255–275.

Armstrong, Alice K. and R. Thandabantu Nhlapo. *Law and the Other Sex: The Legal Position of Women in Swaziland*. Mbabane: Websters, 1986.

Nhlapo, R. Thandabantu. "Law Versus Culture: Ownership of Freehold Land in Swaziland," in A. Armstrong (ed.), *Women and Law in Southern Africa* (Harare: Zimbabwe Publishing House, 1987), pp. 35–55.

―――. "The Legal Status of Women in Swaziland and Some Thoughts on Research," in Julie Stewart and A. Armstrong (eds.), *The Legal Situation of Women in Southern Africa* (Harare: University of Zimbabwe, 1990), pp. 97–138.

―――. "No Cause for Optimism: Bigamy and Dual Marriage in Swaziland," in A. Armstrong (ed.), *Women and Law in Southern Africa* (Harare: Zimbabwe Publishing House, 1987), pp. 125–134.

C. The Constitution and Human Rights

Baloro, John. "The Development of Swaziland's Constitution: Monarchical Responses to Modern Challenges," *Journal of African Law*, XXXVIII (1994), 19–34.

Bischoff, Paul. *Peace, Nationalism and the State of Human Rights in Swaziland*. Roma: National University of Lesotho, Institute of Southern African Studies, 1989.

Cowen, D. V. *Report on Constitutional Reform*. Cape Town: Lincey and Watson, 1961.

Maope, K. A. *Human Rights in Botswana, Lesotho and Swaziland: A Survey of the BOLESWA Countries*. Roma: National University of Lesotho, Institute of African Studies, 1986.

Neff, Steven. *Human Rights in Botswana, Lesotho and Swaziland: Implications of Adherence to International Human Rights Treaties.* Roma: National University of Lesotho, Institute of African Studies, 1986.

Rautenbach, I. M. "Reflections on the Swaziland 'Bill of Rights,'" *Speculum Juris,* IV (1968), 44–49.

Wanda, B. P. "The Shaping of the Modern Constitution of Swaziland: A Review of Some Social and Historical Factors," *Lesotho Law Journal,* VI, 1 (1991), 137–178.

Weisfelder, Richard F. "Human Rights in Botswana, Lesotho, Swaziland and Malawi," *Pula: Botswana Journal of African Studies,* II, 1 (1980), 5–32.

D. Law Reports

Amoah, P.K.A. "Current Legal Developments—Swaziland," *Comparative and International Law Journal of Southern Africa.* (This law report appears in each number of the journal, beginning with Vol. XIII [1980], with occasional exceptions. The journal appears three times each year. Beginning in 1992, the reports are written by Muhawa I. Maziya.)

Sanders, A.J.G.M. "Law Reporting in Swaziland," *Journal of African Law,* XXIX, 1 (1985), 94–101.

VI. POLITICS

A. General

Abena, Joyce. "Swaziland: The Beginning of the End of Monarchist Domination?," *Southern African Political & Economic Monthly,* IV, 5 (1991), 30–33.

Baloro, John. "The Human Right to Free Association and Assembly and Multi-Party Democracy: A Study of the Law and Practice in Swaziland," *Africa Insight,* XXII, 3 (1992), 206–211.

Daniel, John. "The Political Economy of Colonial and Post-colonial Swaziland," *South African Labour Bulletin,* VII, 6 (1982), 90–113.

Levin, Richard. "Is This the Swazi Way? State, Democracy and the Land Question," *Transformation,* XIII (1990), 46–66.

Lister, Laurel D. and B. George. "The Role of Tradition in the Recent Political and Economic Development of Swaziland," *Manchester Papers on Development,* I, 3 (1985), 30–44.

Mugyenyi, Joshua. "Popular Alliances and the State in Swaziland," in P. Anyang' Nyongo (ed.), *Popular Struggles for Democracy* (London: Zed Books; Tokyo: United Nations University, 1987), pp. 265–285.

Nxumalo, Simon. *Profiles of Parliamentarians in the Kingdom of Swaziland.* Mbabane: Swaziland Printing and Publishing Co., 1968.

"The Post-Sobhuza Power Struggle," *Africa Report,* XXIX, 1 (1984), 51–54.

Potholm, Christian P. "Changing Political Configurations in Swaziland," *Journal of Modern African Studies*, IV (1966), 313–322.

――――. "The Ngwenyama of Swaziland: The Dynamics of Adaptation," in R. Lemarchand (ed.), *African Kingships in Perspective: Political Change and Modernization in Monarchical Settings* (London: Frank Cass, 1977), pp. 126–159.

――――. "Remembrance of Things Past? The Process of Institutional Change in Swaziland," *Africa Quarterly*, XIII, 1 (1973), 1–22.

――――. "Swaziland," in Christian Potholm and R. Dale (eds.), *Southern Africa in Perspective* (New York: The Free Press, 1972), pp. 141–153.

――――. "Swaziland in Transition to Independence," *Africa Report*, XII, 6 (1967), 49–54.

――――. *Swaziland: The Dynamics of Political Modernization*. Berkeley: University of California Press, 1972.

Schoeman, Stan. "The Monarchy in Swaziland," *Africa Insight*, XVI, 3 (1986), 163–175.

――――. "Swaziland: The Monarchy at Work," *Africa Institute Bulletin*, XXVII, 3 (1987), 37–40.

Stevens, Richard P. "Swaziland Political Development," *Journal of Modern African Studies*, I, 3 (1963), 327–350.

Van Wyck, Adam J. *Swaziland: A Political Study*. Pretoria: Africa Institute of South Africa, 1969.

Vieceli, Jacqueline. "Swaziland After Sobhuza: Stability or Crisis?" *Issue*, XII, 3/4 (1984), 56–63.

B. Government and Administration

Butler, I. E. "Swaziland," in Willam B. Vosloo, D. Kotzé, and W. Jeppe (eds.), *Local Government in Southern Africa* (Pretoria: Academica, 1974), pp. 164–182.

Dlamini, M. P. "Development Planning and Administration of Development in Swaziland: The Gap Between Theory and Reality," *African Review*, XVII, 1/2 (1990), 108–127.

Lea, John P. "Swaziland: Urban Local Government Subjugation in the Post-Colonial State," *Review of African Political Economy*, XV/XVI (1979), 146–147.

Macartney, W.J.A. "The Parliaments of Botswana, Lesotho and Swaziland," *Parliamentarian*, L, 2 (1969), 92–101.

Onadipe, Abiodun. "Overhauling the Feudal Regime in Swaziland," *Contemporary Review*, CCLXIX, 1571 (1996), 296–301.

Picard, Louis A. "Traditionalism, the Bureaucracy, and Local Administration: Continuity and Change in Swaziland," *Journal of African Studies*, XIII, 4 (1986/87), 116–125.

Proctor, J. H. "Traditionalism and Parliamentary Government in Swaziland," *African Affairs*, LXXII, 288 (1973), 273–287.

C. Foreign Affairs

Ajulu, Rok and Diana Cammack. "Lesotho, Botswana, Swaziland," in Phyllis Johnson and D. Martin (eds.), *Destructive Engagement: Southern Africa at War* (Harare: Zimbabwe Publishing House, 1986), pp. 138–169.

Belfiglio, Valentine J. "South Africa's Relations with Botswana, Lesotho and Swaziland," *Journal of Asian and African Studies*, XV, 3/4 (1980), 217–228.

Bischoff, Paul-Henri. "Swaziland: A Small State in International Relations," *Afrika-Spectrum*, XXI, 2 (1986), 175–188.

———. *Swaziland's International Relations and Foreign Policy: A Study of a Small African State in International Relations.* Bern, Frankfurt, New York, and Paris: Peter Lang, 1990.

———. "Why Swaziland Is Different: An Explanation of the Kingdom's Political Position in Southern Africa," *Journal of Modern African Studies*, XXVI, 3 (1988), 457–471.

Black, David R., J. Mugyenyi, and L. Swatuk. *Foreign Policy in Small States: Botswana, Lesotho, Swaziland in Southern Africa.* Halifax: Dalhousie University, Centre for Foreign Policy Studies, 1988.

Booth, Alan R. "South Africa's Hinterland: Swaziland's Role in Strategies for Sanctions-Breaking," *Africa Today*, XXXVI, 1 (1989), 41–50.

Crush, Jonathan S. "The Parameters of Dependence in Southern Africa: A Case Study of Swaziland," *Journal of Southern African Affairs*, IV, 1 (1979), 55–66.

Daniel, John. "A Comparative Analysis of Lesotho's and Swaziland's Relations with South Africa," in South African Research Services, *South African Review, II* (Johannesburg: Ravan Press, 1984), pp. 228–238.

Esterhuysen, Pieter. "Greater Swaziland?" *Africa Insight*, XII, 3 (1982), 181–188.

Griffiths, Ieuan and D. Funnell. "The Abortive Swazi Land Deal," *African Affairs*, XC, 358 (1991), 51–64.

Grundy, Kenneth. *Confrontation and Accommodation in Southern Africa: The Limits of Independence.* Berkeley: University of California Press, 1973.

Hanlon, Joseph. "Post-Apartheid South Africa and Its Neighbors," *Third World Quarterly*, IX, 2 (1987), 437–449.

Harries, Patrick. "History, Ethnicity and the Ingwavuma Land Deal: The Zulu Northern Frontier in the Nineteenth Century," *Journal of Natal and Zulu History*, VI (1983), 1–27.

Johnson, Phyllis and D. Martin (eds.). *Frontline Southern Africa: Destructive Engagement.* New York: Four Walls and Eight Windows, 1988.

Keller, Edmund J. and L. Picard (eds.). *South Africa in Southern Africa: Domestic Change and International Conflict.* Boulder, CO: Lynne Rienner, 1989.

Mugyenyi, Joshua B. "Swaziland: The Vagaries of Geopolitics, Subordination and Collaboration," in Stephen H. Arnold and A. Nitechi (eds.), *Culture and Development in Africa* (Trenton, NJ: Africa World Press, 1990), pp. 267–285.

"KaNgwane, South Africa," *The Review of the International Commission of Jurists*, XXXII (1984), 21–25.

Potholm, Christian. P. "The Protectorates, the O.A U. and South Africa," *International Journal*, XXII, 1 (1966–67), 68–72.

Robbins, David. "Swaziland: The South African Land Deal," *Africa Report*, XXVII, 6 (1982), 18–22.

Sejanamane, Mafa. "Dependency and the Foreign Policy Options of Small Southern African States," in Sehoai Santho and M. Sejanamane (eds.), *Southern Africa After Apartheid: Prospects for the Inner Periphery in the 1990s* (Harare: SAPES Trust, 1990), pp. 15–25.

D. Swaziland in the Southern African Development Community

The Southern African Development Community was formerly the Southern African Development Coordination Conference (SADCC).

Anglin, Douglas. "SADCC After Nkomati," *African Affairs*, LXXXIV, 335 (1985), 163–181.

Gwaradzimba, Fadzai. "SADCC and the Future of Southern African Regionalism," *Issue: A Journal of Opinion*, XXI, 1/2 (1993), 51–59.

Hill, Christopher. "Regional Cooperation in Southern Africa," *African Affairs*, LXXXII, 327 (1983), 215–239.

Leys, Roger and A. Tostensen. "Regional Cooperation in Southern Africa: The Southern African Development Coordination Conference," *Review of African Political Economy*, XXIII (1982), 52–71.

Mhone, Kandako. "Law as a Factor for Regional Cooperation: SADCC—Problems and Prospects," *Comparative and International Law Journal of Southern Africa*, XXIV, 3 (1991), 379–385.

Nsekela, Amon J. (ed.). *Southern Africa: Towards Economic Liberation*. London: Rex Collings, 1981.

Saasa, Oliver S. "Regional Cooperation and Integration in Southern Africa: The Case of the SADCC Industrial Sector," in *Southern Africa in the 1980s and Beyond: Institute of Southern African Studies 1980–1990* (Roma: National University of Lesotho, Institute of Southern African Studies, 1993), pp. 101–126.

Simelane, Nomthetho. "Swaziland Within SADCC," in Timothy M. Shaw and Y. Tandon (eds.), *Regional Development at the International Level: African and Canadian Perspectives,* Volume 2 (Lanham, MD: University Press of America, 1985), pp. 265–275.

Tostensen, Arne. *Dependence and Collective Self-Reliance in Southern Africa: The Case of the Southern African Development Coordination Conference (SADCC).* Uppsala: The Scandinavian Institute for African Studies, 1982.

VII. NATURAL SCIENCE

A. Botany

Anderson, John M. and H. Anderson. *Palaeoflora of Southern Africa: Prodromus of South African Megafloras Deronian to Lower Cretaceous.* Rotterdam: A. A. Balkema, 1985.

Craib, Ian. "Exotic Softwood Forestry in Southern Africa," *Optima*, IX, 2 (1959), 73–78.
Palgrave, Keith C. and R. Drummond. *Trees of Southern Africa* (E. J. Mall, ed.). Cape Town: C. Struik, 1977.

B. Geography

Crush, Jonathan. "The Southern African Regional Formation: A Geographical Perspective," *Journal of Economic and Social Geography*, LXXIII, 4 (1982), 200–212.
Daniel, John B. McI. *The Geography of the Rural Economy of Swaziland*. Durban, South Africa: University of Natal, Institute for Social Research, 1962.
De Blij, Harm. J. *A Geography of Southern Africa*. Chicago: Rand McNally, 1964.
———. "A Note on the Relationship Between the Swaziland Low Veld and Adjoining Areas," *Transactions and Proceedings of the Geological Society of South Africa*, LXIII (1960), 175–187.
Doveton, Dorothy M. "The Economic Geography of Swaziland," *The Geography of Swaziland*, LXXXVIII (1936), 322–331.
———. *The Human Geography of Swaziland*. London: George Philip & Son, 1937.
Funnell, Donald C. "Selective Spatial Closure and the Development of Small-Scale Irrigation in Swaziland," *Journal of Economic and Social Geography*, LXXVII, 2 (1986), 113–122.
———. "Water Resources and the Political Geography of Development in Southern Africa: The Case of Swaziland," *Geoforum*, XIX, 4 (1988), 497–505.
Gibbons, C.L.M.H. "Tors in Swaziland," *Geographical Journal*, CXLVII, 1 (1981), 72–78.
Keast, Allen. "Environmental Sciences: Biotic Diversity in Southern Africa: Concepts and Conservation" (J. B. Huntley, ed.), *Quarterly Review of Biology*, LXVI, 3 (1991), 359–360.
Lea, John P. "The Differentiation of the Rural Periphery in Swaziland: A Multi-Variate Analysis," *South African Geographical Journal*, LIV (1972), 105–123.
Masson, John. "The First Map of Swaziland, and Matters Incidental Thereto," *Geographical Journal*, CLV, 3 (1989), 335–341.
Murdoch, G. and J. Andriesse. *A Soil Irrigability Survey of the Lower Usutu Basin (South) in the Swaziland Lowveld*. London: HMSO, 1964.
Nquku, J. J. *Geography of Swaziland*. Bremersdorp: Servite Fathers, 1936.
Reilly, Terence E. *The Mlilwane Story: A History of Nature Conservation in the Kingdom of Swaziland and Fund Raising Appeal*. Mbabane: Mlilwane Trust, 1985.
Wellington, J. H. "Notes on the Physiography of Swaziland," *South African Geographical Journal*, XXXVIII (1956), 30–36.
Whittington, G. W. "Towards Urban Development in Swaziland," *Erkunde*, XXIV, 1 (1970), 26–39.

C. Geology

Dart, R. A. and P. Beaumont. "Ratification and Retrocession of Earlier Swaziland Iron Ore Mining Radio Carbon Datings," *South African Journal of Science*, LXIV, 6 (1968), 241–246.

Davies, D.N.A. and J. Urie. *The Bomvu Ridge Hematite Deposits*. Mbabane: Government Printer, 1956.

Dingle, R. V., W. Slesser, and A. Newton. *Mesozoic and Tertiary Geology of Southern Africa*. Rotterdam: A. A. Balkema, 1983.

Hawkins, L.A.W. "Rich Iron Ore Deposits Give Swaziland Its Long-Awaited Railroad," *Optima*, XIV, 2 (June 1964), pp. 84–87.

Hunter, D. R. "Geology, Petrology and Classification of the Swaziland Granites and Gneisses," *Transactions of the Geological Society of South Africa*, XL (1957), 85–125.

———. *The Mineral Resources of Swaziland*. Mbabane: High Commission Printing and Publishing Co., 1962.

Lowe, Donald R. "Accretionary History of the Archean Barberton Greenstone Belt (3.55–3.22 Ga), Southern Africa," *Geology*, XXII, 12 (1994), 1099–1102.

Mushala, Hezekiel M. "Application of Remote Sensing Techniques in the Study of the Geology of the Great Usutu River Basin in Swaziland," *Swaziland Journal of Science and Technology*, XI, 1/2 (1990), 29–37.

Saggerson, E. P. and L. Turner. *A Review of the Metamorphism in the Republic of South Africa and the Kingdoms of Lesotho and Swaziland*. Pretoria: Council for Geoscience, Geological Survey of South Africa, 1995.

Spargo, P. E. "The Thermal Springs of the Pigg's Peak District, Swaziland," *South African Journal of Science*, LXI, 4 (1965), 179–182.

Turner, B. R. and W.E.L. Minter. "Diamond-Bearing Upper Karoo Flurial Sediments in N.E. Swaziland," *Journal of the Geological Society*, CXLII, 5 (1985), 765–766.

Watson, Andrew. "The Origin and Geomorphological Significance of Closed Depressions in the Lebombo Mountains of Swaziland," *Geographical Journal*, CLII, 1 (1986), 65–74.

Way, H.R.J. *Mineral Ownership as Affecting Mineral Development of Swaziland*. Mbabane: Government Printer, 1955.

Wellington, J. H. "Notes on the Physiography of Swaziland and Adjoining Areas," *South African Geographical Journal*, XXXVIII (1956), 30–36.

D. Zoology

Abbott, Clare and Stephen Hanning. *Southern African Butterflies*. Johannesburg: Macmillan South Africa, 1984.

Branch, Bill. *Field Guide to the Snakes and Other Reptiles of Southern Africa*. Cape Town: C. Struik, 1988.

Broadley, Donald G. *FitzSimmon's Snakes of Southern Africa*. Johannesburg: Delta Books, 1983.

Bruton, M. N., P. Jackson, and P. Skelton. *Pocket Guide to the Freshwater Fishes of Southern Africa*. Cape Town: Centaur Publishers, 1982.

Cillie, Burger. *Mammals of Southern Africa: A Field Guide*. Sandton: Frandsen Publishers, 1987.

De Moor, Irene J. and M. Bruton. *Atlas of Alien and Translocated Indigenous Aquatic Animals in Southern Africa*. Pretoria: Council for Scientific and Industrial Research Foundation for Research Development, 1988.

Kessler, Cristina. *All the King's Animals: The Return of Endangered Wildlife to Swaziland*. Honesdale, PA: Boyds Mills Press, 1995.

Roberts, Austin. *The Birds of South Africa*. London: H. F. & G. Witherby; Johannesburg: Central News Agency, 1953.

Rowan, Steyn. *Birds of Prey of Southern Africa: Their Identification and Life Histories*. Cape Town: David Philip, 1985.

VIII. SOCIAL SCIENCE

A. General

Southern African Political & Economic Quarterly. Harare: Southern African Political Economy Series Trust, 1987– .

UNISWA Research Journal. Kwaluseni: University of Swaziland, 1988– .

B. Anthropology and Ethnology

Beemer [Kuper], Hilda. "The Swazi Rain Ceremony," *Bantu Studies*, IX (1935), 275–280.

Comaroff, Jean. *Body of Power, Spirit of Resistance: The Culture and History of a South African People*. Chicago and London: University of Chicago Press, 1985.

Derman, P. J. "Stock and Aristocracy: The Political Implications of Swazi Marriage," *African Studies*, XXXVI, 2 (1977), 119–129.

Dumbrell, H.J.P. "Pyre Burning in Swaziland," *African Studies*, XI (1952), 190–191.

Engelbrecht, J. A. *Swazi Texts with Notes*. Cape Town: Nasionale Pers, 1930.

Evans, Jeremy. " 'Where Can We Get a Beast Without Hair?' Medicine Murder in Swaziland from 1970 to 1988," *African Studies*, LII, 1 (1993), 23–42.

Green, Edward C. "Mystical Black Power: The Calling to Divine-Mediumship in Southern Africa," in C. S. McClain (ed.), *Women as Healers: Cross Cultural Practises* (Rutgers, NJ: Rutgers University Press, 1989), pp. 186–200.

Kuper, Adam. "The Anthropologist's Vocation in South Africa," *African Studies*, XLV, 1 (1986), 1–15.

———. "Rank and Preferential Marriage in Southern Africa: The Swazi," *Man*, XIII, 4 (1978), 567–579.

Kuper, Hilda. *An African Aristocracy: Rank Among the Swazi*. London and New York: Oxford University Press for the International African Institute, 1947. (Reprinted 1980)

———. "Colour, Categories and Colonialism," in Victor Turner (ed.), *Colonialism in Africa 1870–1960: Vol. 3. Profiles of Change: African Society and Colonial Rule* (Cambridge: Cambridge University Press, 1971), pp. 286–309.

———. "Costume and Cosmology: The Animal Symbolism of the *Ncwala*," *Man*, VIII, 4 (1973), 613–630.

———. "Costume and Identity," *Comparative Studies in Society and History*, XV, 3 (1973), 348–367.

———. "The Development of a Primitive Nation," *Bantu Studies*, VI, 4 (1941), 339–368.

———. "Kinship Among the Swazi," in A. R. Radcliffe-Brown and D. Ford (eds.), *African Systems of Kinship and Marriage* (London, New York, and Toronto: Oxford University Press, for the International African Institute, 1950), pp. 86–110.

———. "The Language of Sites in the Politics of Space," *American Anthropologist*, LXXIV, 3 (1972), 411–425.

———. *The Swazi*. London: International African Institute, 1952.

———. *The Swazi: A South African Kingdom*. New York: Holt, Rinehart and Winston, 1963. (2d edition, 1986)

———. "The Swazi Reaction to Missions," *African Studies*, V, 3 (1946), 177–189.

———. "The Swazis of Swaziland," in J. L. Gibbs (ed.), *Peoples of Africa* (New York: Holt, Rinehart and Winston, 1965), pp. 479–511.

———. "The Uniform of Colour in Swaziland," *African Studies*, II, 2 (1943), 97–107.

Lystad, Mary H. "Adolescent Social Attitudes in South Africa and Swaziland," *American Anthropologist*, LXXII, 6 (1970), 1389–1397.

Marwick, Brian. *The Swazi: An Ethnographic Account of the Natives of the Swaziland Protectorate*. Cambridge: Cambridge University Press, 1940. (Reprinted 1966, London: Frank Cass)

Myburgh, A. C. *The Tribes of Barberton District*. Pretoria: Department of Native Affairs (Ethnological Publications No. 25), 1949.

Ngubane, Harriet. "The Predicament of the Sinister Healer," in M. Last and G. Chavunduka (eds.), *The Professionalisation of African Medicine* (Manchester: Manchester University Press, 1988).

Schapera, I. (ed.). *The Bantu-Speaking Tribes of South Africa*. London: Routledge, 1937.

Schoeman, P. J. "The Swazi Rain Ceremony," *Bantu Studies*, IX (1935), 168–175.

Twala, R. G. "Beads as Regulating the Social Life of the Zulu and Swazi," *African Studies*, X (1951), 113–123.

1. Monarchy and Royal Ceremony

Apter, Andrew. "In Dispraise of the King: Rituals 'Against' Rebellion in South-East Africa," *Man*, XVIII, 3 (1983), 521–534.

Astuti, Rita. "Ritual, History and the Swazi *Ncwala*: Sacred Kingship and the Origin of the State," *Africa*, XLIII, 4 (1988), 603–620.

Beidelman, T. O. "Swazi Royal Ritual," *Africa*, XXXVI, 4 (1966), 373–405. Reprinted in Colin M. Turnbull (ed.), *Africa and Change* (New York: Alfred A. Knopf, 1973).

Cook, P.A.W. "The First-Fruits Ceremony," *Bantu Studies*, IV, 3 (1930), 205–210.

Gluckman, Max. *Rituals of Rebellion in South-East Africa*. Manchester: Manchester University Press, 1954.

————. "Social Aspects of the First Fruits Ceremonies Among the South-Eastern Bantu," *Africa*, XI (1938), 25–41.

Kuper, Hilda. "Celebration of Growth and Kingship: Inqwala in Swaziland," *African Arts*, I, 3 (1968), 56–59; 90.

————. "A Ritual of Kingship Among the Swazi," *Africa*, XIV, 5 (1944), 230–257.

————. "A Royal Ritual in a Changing Political Context: The *Ncwala* of the Swazi," *Cahier d'Études Africaines*, XII, 48 (1972), 593–615.

Lincoln, Bruce. "Ritual, Rebellion, Resistance: Once More the Swazi *Ncwala*," *Man*, XXII, 1 (1987), 132–156.

2. Military Organization and Regimentation

Beemer [Kuper], Hilda. "The Development of the Military Organization in Swaziland," *Africa*, X, 1 (1937), 55–74; X, 2 (1937), 176–205.

Kuper, Hilda. "The Monarchy and the Military in Swaziland," in John Argyle and E. Preston-Whyte (eds.), *Social System and Tradition in Southern Africa: Essays in Honour of Eileen Krige* (Cape Town: Oxford University Press, 1978), pp. 222–239.

3. Marriage

Engelbrecht, J. A. "Swazi Customs Relating to Marriage," *Annals of the University of Stellenbosch*, VIII, 3 (1930), 1–27.

Kuper, Hilda. "The Marriage of a Swazi Princess," *Africa*, XV, 3 (1945), 145–155.

Matsebula, J.S.M. "A Traditional Swazi Wedding," *Swaziland Teachers' Journal*, LV (1967), 42–44.

Ngubane, Harriet. "The Consequences for Women of Marriage Payments in a Society with Patrilineal Descent," in David Parkin and D. Nyamweya (eds.), *Transformations of African Marriage* (Manchester: Manchester University Press, for the International Africa Institute, 1987).

C. Demography

Fair, Denis. "Sub-Saharan Africa and the Population Issue: The Cases of Kenya and Swaziland," *Africa Insight*, XV, 4 (1985), 252–255; 261.

Kuczynski, R. R. *Demographic Survey of the British Colonial Empire* (Vol. II). London: Oxford University Press, 1949.

Van Warmelo, Nicolaas J. *Preliminary Survey of the Bantu Tribes of South Africa* (Union of South Africa, Department of Native Affairs, Ethnological Publications, Vol. V). Pretoria: Government Printer, 1935.

D. Medicine, Health, and Diet

Beemer [Kuper], Hilda. "Notes on the Diet of the Swazi in the Protectorate," *Bantu Studies*, XIII, 3, (1939), 199–236.

Cappetta, Marlene. "Population, Food and Nutrition: Swaziland, 1940–1982," in Fion de Vletter (ed.), *The Swazi Rural Homestead* (Kwaluseni: University of Swaziland, Social Science Research Unit, 1983), pp. 163–208.

Gort, Enid. "Health Care Selection in Swaziland," *Journal of African Studies*, XV, 3/4 (1988/89), 71–75.

Green, Edward C. "The Integration of Modern and Traditional Health Sectors in Swaziland," in R. M. Wulff and S. Fiske (eds.), *Anthropological Praxis* (Boulder, CO: Westview Press, 1987), pp. 87–97.

———. "The Planning of Health Education Strategies in Swaziland," in R. M. Wulff and S. Fiske (eds.), *Anthropological Praxis* (Boulder, CO: Westview Press, 1987), pp. 15–25.

———. "Sexually Transmitted Disease, Ethnomedicine and Health Policy in Africa," *Social Science and Medicine*, XXXV, 2 (1992), 121–130.

———. "Traditional Healers, Mothers and Childhood Diarrheal Disease in Swaziland: The Interface of Anthropology and Health Education," *Social Science and Medicine*, XX, 3 (1985), 277–285.

Green, Edward C. and L. Makhubu. "Traditional Healers in Swaziland: Toward Improved Co-operation Between the Traditional and Modern Health Sectors," *Social Science and Medicine*, XVIII, 12 (1984), 1071–1079.

Hoff, Wilbur, and D. Maseko. "Nurses and Traditional Healers Join Hands," *World Health Forum*, VII, 4 (1986), 412–416.

Huppert, Eric L. "Rural Health," in Fion de Vletter (ed.), *The Swazi Rural Homestead* (Kwaluseni: University of Swaziland, Social Science Research Unit, 1983), pp. 305–315.

Jones, Sonya M. *A Study of Swazi Nutrition: Report of the Swaziland Nutrition Survey 1961–62 for the Swaziland Administration*. Durban, South Africa: University of Natal, Institute for Social Research, 1963.

Makhubu, Lydia P. *The Traditional Healer*. Kwaluseni: University of Swaziland, 1978.

Matbaum, O. "The Past and Present Position of Malaria in Swaziland," *Journal of Tropical Medicine and Hygiene*, L, 5 (1960), 119–127.

Robertson, L. "Breast Feeding Practices in Maternity Wards in Swaziland," *Journal of Nutritional Education*, XXIII, 6 (1991), 284–287.

Serdula, M. K., J. Aphane, and P. Kunene. "Acute and Chronic Undernutrition in Swaziland," *Journal of Tropical Pediatrics*, XXXIII, 1 (1987), 35–42.

E. Urbanization and Migration

Davies, Robert and J. Head. "The Future of Mine Migrancy in the Context of Broader Trends in Migration in Southern Africa," *Journal of Southern African Studies*, XXI, 3 (1995), 439–450.

Lea, John P. "Housing Priorities and Policies in Swaziland: A Spatial Approach," *South African Journal of African Affairs*, IV, 1 (1974), 50–61.

———. "Population Mobility in Rural Swaziland: A Research Note," *Journal of Modern African Studies*, XII, 4 (1974), 673–679.

———. "Squatting as an Epiphenomenon: The Evolution of Unplanned Settlement in Swaziland," in R. A. Obudho and C. Mhlanga (eds.), *Slum and Squatter Settlements in Sub-Saharan Africa* (New York: Praeger, 1988), pp. 281–294.

———. "Underlying Determinants of Housing Location: A Case Study from Swaziland," *Journal of Modern African Studies*, XI, 2 (1973), 211–225.

Poulsen, Kirsten. "Community Development in Swaziland," in Fion de Vletter (ed.), *The Swazi Rural Homestead* (Kwaluseni: University of Swaziland, Social Science Research Unit, 1983), pp. 277–304.

Wilsenach, André. "The Provision of Urban Housing in Botswana, Lesotho and Swaziland: Policy and Strategy Since Independence," *Insight*, XIX, 2 (1989), 82–87.

———. *Urban Housing in Botswana, Lesotho and Swaziland: Symptoms and Strategies*. Pretoria: Africa Institute of South Africa, 1985.

F. Religion and the Occult

Butler, P. "Ritual Murder," *Outspan*, LI (1952), 38–41.

Chapman, Louise R. *Africa, O Africa*. Kansas City: Nazarene Publishing House, 1989.

Dlamini, Timothy L. L. "The Nkonyane Church Revisited: Recent Developments Centred Around a Financial Dispute in the Christian Catholic Apostolic Holy Spirit Church in Zion," *Transafrican Journal of History*, XIII (1984), 40–47.

Du Plessis, J. *A History of Christian Missions in South Africa*. Longman, Green, & Co. Ltd., 1911.

Etherington, Norman. *Preachers Peasants and Politics in Southeast Africa, 1835–*

1880: African Christian Communities in Natal, Pondoland and Zululand. London: Royal Historical Society, 1978.

Froise, Marjorie (ed.). *Southern Africa: A Factual Portrait of the Christian Church in South Africa, Botswana, Lesotho, Namibia and Swaziland.* Monrovia, CA: MARC, 1989.

———. *Swaziland Christian Handbook 1994.* Johannesburg: Christian Info, 1994.

Gardner, Juanita. *The Promise.* Kansas City: Nazarene Publishing House, 1992.

Hall, James. *Sangoma: An Odyssey into the Spirit World of Africa.* New York: Putnam, 1994.

Hutchinson, Vivian. *Following Jesus in Africa.* Mogadore, OH: Chandler Books, 1994.

Kasenene, Peter. *Religion in Swaziland.* Johannesburg: Skotaville, 1993.

———. *The Swazi Catholic Church Comes of Age.* Mbabane: Websters, c. 1993.

———. *Swazi Traditional Religion and Society.* Mbabane: Websters, 1993.

Kuper, Hilda. "The Swazi Reaction to Missions," *African Studies*, V, 3 (1946), 177–188.

Mears, Gordon. *Methodism in Swaziland.* Rondebosch: Methodist Missionary Department, 1955.

Meintjes, Sheila. "Family and Gender in the Christian Community at Edendale, Natal, in Colonial Times," in Cherryl Walker (ed.), *Women and Gender in Southern Africa to 1945* (Cape Town: David Phillip; London: James Currey, 1990), pp. 125–145.

Nilsen, Marie and Paul H. Sheetz. *Malla Moe.* Chicago: Moody Press, 1956.

Ramsey, Evelyn M. *Show Me, Lord.* Kansas City: Beacon Hill Press, 1982.

Robertson, T. C. "Swaziland Magic," *Libertas*, IV, 12 (1944), 18–37.

Schmelzenbach, Elmer. *Sons of Africa: Stories from the Life of Elmer Schmelzenbach* (Leslie Parrott, collaborator). Kansas City: Beacon Hill Press, 1979.

Schmelzenbach, Harmon F. *Schmelzenbach of Africa: The Story of Harmon F. Schmelzenbach, Missionary Pioneer in Swaziland, South Africa.* Kansas City: Nazarene Publishing House, 1971.

Scutt, Joan Frances. *The Drums Are Beating.* London: H. E. Walter, 1951.

Sundkler, Bengt G. M. "Chief and Prophet in Zululand and Swaziland," in Meyer Fortes and G. Dieterlen (eds.), *African Systems of Thought* (London: Oxford University Press, 1965), pp. 276–290.

———. "The Concept of Christianity in African Independent Churches," *African Studies*, XX, 4 (1961), 203–213.

———. *Zulu Zion and Some Swazi Zionists.* London and New York: Oxford University Press, 1976.

Watts, Christopher C. *Dawn in Swaziland.* London: Society for the Propagation of the Gospel in Foreign Parts, 1922.

Ziervogel, D. "A Swazi Translation of 1846," *African Studies*, IX, 4, (December 1950), 167–184. (A Wesleyan Methodist catechism)

G. Social Conditions

Astuti, Rita. "'Cattle Beget Children'—But Women Must Bear Them: Fertility, Sterility and Belonging Among Women in Swaziland," in Henk J. Tielman (ed.), *Scenes of Change: Visions on Developments in Swaziland* (Leiden: African Studies Centre, 1988), pp. 191–201.

Barendregt, Jaap and M. Brouwer. "Family Cycle or Social Stratum: An Analysis of Spending Behaviour of Swazi Urban Workers," in Henk J. Tielman (ed.), *Scenes of Change: Visions on Developments in Swaziland* (Leiden: African Studies Centre, 1988), pp. 104–120.

Dlamini, Thinie N. "Teenage Pregnancies in Swaziland." Kwaluseni: University of Swaziland, Social Science Research Unit, Research Paper No. 31, c. 1991.

Guma, Xolile. "Cash Income and Expenditure," in Fion de Vletter (ed.), *The Swazi Rural Homestead* (Kwaluseni: University of Swaziland, Social Science Research Unit, 1983), pp. 123–149.

Holleman, J. F. (ed.). *Experiment in Swaziland: Report of the Swaziland Sample Survey, 1960*. Cape Town: Oxford University Press, 1964.

Kabagambe, John C. "Labour Utilisation in the Swazi Homestead," in I. C. Lamba and B. Kandoole (eds.), *Mobilization of Resources for National and Regional Development in Southern Africa* (Zomba, Malawi: Southern African Universities Social Science Conference, 1988), pp. 357–370.

Kuper, Adam. "Symbolic Dimensions of the Southern Bantu Homestead," *Africa*, L, 1 (1980), 8–23.

Kuper, Hilda. *The Uniform of Colour: A Study of White-Black Relationships in Swaziland*. Johannesburg: Witwatersrand University Press, 1947.

Leliveld, André. "The Effects of Restrictive South African Migrant Labor Policy on the Survival of Rural Households in Southern Africa: A Case Study from Rural Swaziland," *World Development*, XXV, 11 (1997), 1839–1849.

———. *Social Security in Developing Countries: Operation and Dynamics of Social Security Mechanisms in Rural Swaziland*. Amsterdam: Thesis Publishers, 1994.

Malepe, Thandile B. "Alcohol-Related Problems in Swaziland," *Contemporary Drug Problems*, XVI, 1 (1989), 43–58.

McFadden, Patricia. "The Condition of Women in Southern Africa: Challenges for the 1990s," *Southern African Political and Economic Monthly*, III, 10 (1990), 3–9.

Ngubane, Harriet. "The Swazi Homestead," in Fion de Vletter (ed.), *The Swazi Rural Homestead* (Kwaluseni: University of Swaziland, Social Science Research Unit, 1983), pp. 95–121.

Russell, Margo. "Beyond Remittances: The Redistribution of Cash in Swazi Society," *Journal of Modern African Studies*, XXII, 4 (1984), 595–615.

———. "A Landed Proletariat? Coming to Terms with a Contradiction in Terms," in Henk J. Tielman (ed.), *Scenes of Change: Visions on Developments in Swaziland* (Leiden: African Studies Centre, 1988), pp. 215–229.

————. "Why Swaziland Does Not Have an Old Age Problem," *Pula: Botswana Journal of African Studies*, IV, 2 (1984), 50–55.

Simelane, Nomthetho G. *Social Transformation: The Swaziland Case*. Dakar: Codesria, 1995.

Warren, Charles W., J. T. Johnson, G. Gule, E. Hlope, and D. Kraushaar. "The Determinants of Fertility in Swaziland," *Population Studies*, XLVI, 1 (1992), 5–17.

Women and Law in Southern Africa Research Trust. *Family in Transition: The Experience of Swaziland*. Mbabane: Ruswanda Publishing Bureau, 1998.

H. Gender and Women

Armstrong, Alice. *A Sample Survey of Women in Wage Employment in Swaziland*. Kwaluseni: University of Swaziland, Social Science Research Unit (Research Paper No. 15), 1985.

————. *Struggling over Scarce Resources: Women and Maintenance in Southern Africa*. Harare: University of Zimbabwe Publications, 1992.

Armstrong, Sue. "Choice Would Be a Good Thing," *New Scientist*, CXLVIII (1995), 44–45.

Blumberg, Rae L. "Gender, Microenterprise, Performance , and Power: Case Studies from the Dominican Republic, Ecuador, Guatemala, and Swaziland," in Christine E. Bose and E. Acosta-Belén (eds.), *Women in the Latin American Development Process* (Philadelphia: Temple University Press, 1995), pp. 194–226.

Kappers, Sophieke. "Sitanani: Let's Help Each Other: Women and Informal Savings, Credit, and Funeral Organizations in Swaziland," in Henk J. Tielman (ed.), *Scenes of Change: Visions on Developments in Swaziland* (Leiden: African Studies Centre, 1988), pp. 163–190.

Miles, Miranda C. "Housing for Domestic Workers in Swaziland," in Ann Schlyter (ed.), *A Place to Live: Gender Research on Housing in Africa* (Uppsala: Nordiska Afrikainstitutet, 1996), pp. 94–111.

Stading, Hilary. "Gender Relations and Social Transformation in Swaziland: Some Comments on Future Research Possibilities," in Michael Neocosmos (ed.), *Social Relations in Rural Swaziland: Critical Analyses* (Kwaluseni: University of Swaziland, Social Science Research Unit, 1987), pp. 127–149.

See also works on women in other sections, especially Sections III.C, III.G, V.B, VIII.C, VIII.D, VIII.G, IX, and X.

IX. EDUCATION

Armstrong, Sue. "The Obstacle Course," *New Scientist*, CLXVIII (1995), 58–59.

BOLESWA Educational Research Journal. Gaborone: University of Botswana,

Faculty of Education; Roma: National University of Lesotho, Faculty of Education; Kwaluseni: University of Swaziland, Faculty of Education, 1982– .

Booth, Margaret Zoller. "Children of Migrant Fathers: The Effects of Father Absence on Swazi Children's Preparedness for School," *Comparative Education Review*, XXXIX, 2 (1995), 195–210.

———. "Parental Availability and Academic Achievement Among Swazi Rural Primary School Children," *Comparative Education Review*, XL, 3 (1996), 250–263.

———. "Western Schooling and Traditional Society in Swaziland," *Comparative Education*, XXXIII, 3 (1997), 433–451.

Daniel, John. "Swaziland," in *Academic Freedom 2: A Human Rights Report* (London and Atlantic Highlands, NJ: Zed Press, 1993), pp. 136–152.

Datta, Ansu. "Education and Development in Southern Africa," in *Southern Africa in the 1980s and Beyond* (Roma: National University of Lesotho, Institute of Southern African Studies, 1993), pp. 70–84.

Dlamini, Barnabas M., M. Simelane, and D. Khumalo. "Training for Agriculture Self-Sufficiency in Swaziland," in Richard Mkandawire and K. Matlosa (eds.), *Food Policy and Agriculture in Southern Africa* (Harare: SAPES Books, 1993), pp. 220–244.

Geary, Kevin. "Indicators of Educational Progress—a Markov Chain Approach Applied to Swaziland," *Journal of Modern African Studies*, XVI, 1 (1978), 141–151.

Gilbert, Dan. "Local Hero," *Vocational Education Journal*, LXVII, 7 (1992), 35.

Green, Edward C. "Evaluating the Response of Swazi Traditional Leaders to Development Workshops," *Human Organization*, LI, 4 (1992), 379–388.

Kingsley, Phillip. "Home-Based Training of Pre-School Children in Rural Swaziland," *SIER Bulletin*, VIII (1987), 11–29. (Published by the University of Swaziland, The Swaziland Institute for Education Research)

Knox, Donald M. "A Needs Assessment for Educational Research in Swaziland," *SIER Bulletin*, VII (1986), 16–25.

Magagula, Cisco. *Implementing Education Policies in Swaziland*. Washington, DC: World Bank, 1990.

Matsebula, J.S.M. *Education Administration in Swaziland and United Kingdom*. London: University of London, 1965.

Micklos, John, Jr. "Women's Education: A Key to Development," *Reading Today*, XIV, 2 (1996), 14–16.

Molewa, Julia. *Modern and Traditional Recipes for Junior Secondary Home Economics*. Harlow: Longman, 1994.

Myeni, Annie D. "Practical Experience in Preventive Alcohol Education in Swaziland," *Contemporary Drug Problems*, XVI, 1 (1989), 81–93.

Nxumalo, S. "Developing Women's Income-Generating Skills in Swaziland," *Adult Education and Development*, XXIII, 6 (1991), 62–82.

Ping, Charles J., J. Turner, and W. Mamba. *University of Swaziland, Commission on Planning, 1986*. Kwaluseni: University of Swaziland, 1986.

Raum, O. F. "The Imbalance of Educational Development in Southern Africa," *South African Journal of African Affairs*, I (1971), 8–30.

Rose, Brian W. "Education in the Former High Commission Territories of Bechuanaland (Botswana), Basutoland (Lesotho) and Swaziland," in Brian W. Rose (ed.), *Education in Southern Africa* (Johannesburg and London: Collier-Macmillan, 1970), pp. 195–221.

———. "Educational Policy and Problems in the Former High Commission Territories of Africa," *Comparative Education*, I, 2 (1965), 113–118.

Rwomire, Apollo. "Education and Development in Swaziland: Aims, Strategies and Challenges," in Rukhsana A. Siddiqui (ed.), *Sub-Saharan Africa: A Sub-Continent in Transition* (Aldershot, England and Brookfield, VT: Avebury, 1993), pp. 149–166.

Sargent, R. A. "Projections and Policies in Swaziland's Education System," *SIER Bulletin*, VII (1986), 1–15.

Stevens, Richard P. "Southern Africa's Multiracial University," *Africa Report*, IX, 3 (1964), 16–18.

Swaziland, University of. *SIER Bulletin*. Kwaluseni: University of Swaziland, The Swaziland Institute for Educational Research, 1979–c. 1989. (Annual)

White, A. "Swazi National Schools," *Overseas Education*, XXX, 2 (1958), 62–63.

X. PAPERS, THESES, AND DISSERTATIONS ON SWAZILAND

A more comprehensive listing of M.A. theses and Ph.D. dissertations relating to Swaziland can be found in Balam Nyeko's 1994 bibliography (see above, Section I.A). This is a selected list and also includes titles not included in the above-named work.

Allen, Carole J. "Dimensions of Swazi Households in Rural and Urban Areas," Ph.D. dissertation, University of Massachusetts, 1974.

Armitage, Fiona L. "Abakamuya: People of the Spirit. A Study of the Zionist Movement in Swaziland with Special Reference to the Swazi Christian Church in Zion of South Africa and the Nazarethe Branch," M.A. thesis, University of Aberdeen, 1976.

Atkinson, Craig J. "Regional Industrial Change in Southern Africa: A Case Study of Swaziland in the 1980s," M.A. thesis, Queen's University, 1993.

Beemer [Kuper], Hilda. "Rank Among the Swazis of the Protectorate," Ph.D. dissertation, University of London, London School of Economics and Political Science, 1943.

Best, Alan C. G. "The Swaziland Railway: A Study in Politico-economic Geography," Ph.D. dissertation, Michigan State University, 1965.

Bischoff, Paul-Henri. "Swaziland in International Relations: Swaziland's International Relations and Foreign Policy up to 1982," Ph.D. dissertation, Manchester University, 1985.

Bonner, Phillip L. "The Rise, Consolidation and Disintegration of Dlamini Power in Swaziland Between 1820 and 1889: A Study in the Relationship of Foreign External Affairs to Internal Political Development," Ph.D. dissertation, University of London, 1977.

Booth, Margaret Zoller. "Children of Migrant Fathers: A Study of the Effects of Father-Absence on Swazi Children's Preparedness for School," Ph.D. dissertation, Ohio University, 1991.

Cazziol, Roger. "The Origins and Development of the Zionist Movement in Swaziland," M.A. thesis, University of Natal, 1986.

Crush, Jonathan S. "The Spatial Impress of Capital and the Colonial State in Swaziland, 1903–14," M.A. thesis, Wilfrid Laurier University, 1978.

———. "The Struggle for Swazi Labour, 1890–1920," Ph.D. dissertation, Queen's University, 1982.

Daniel, John B. McI. "The Geography of the Rural Economy of Swaziland," Ph.D. dissertation, University of Natal, 1963.

De Blij, Jan Harm. "The Physiographic Provinces and Cyclic Erosion Surfaces of Swaziland," Ph.D. dissertation, Northwestern University, 1959.

Dlamini, Barnabas M. "Evaluation of the Agriculture Program in the Secondary Schools of Swaziland as Perceived by Agriculture Teachers and Headmasters," M.S. thesis, University of West Virginia, 1982.

———. "Perceptions of Professionals in Agricultural Education Regarding the Agricultural Teacher Education Program in Swaziland (Evaluation Adequacy)," Ph.D. dissertation, Ohio State University, 1986.

Dlamini, Nesta. "Attitudes of In-Service Teachers Toward Reading Instructional Practices in Swaziland Primary Schools," Ph.D. dissertation, Ohio University, 1993.

Dlamini, Patrick S. "The Dynamics of Government Intervention and Implications for Policy Reform: The Case of the Swaziland Agricultural Marketing Board (NAMB) and the National Maize Corporation (NMC)," M.A. research paper, Williams College (Massachusetts), Center for Development Economics, 1995.

Dlamini, Timothy L. L. "The Christian Catholic Apostolic Holy Spirit Church in Zion: As It Exists in Swaziland—Its Development, Life and Worship," M.A. thesis, University of Botswana and Swaziland, 1976.

———. "Rural-to-Urban Migration of Swazi Youth and Educational Implications for Swaziland," Ph.D. dissertation, University of Pittsburgh, 1981.

Doveton, Dorothy M. "The Human Geography of Swaziland," B. Litt. thesis, Oxford University, 1937.

Dube, Musa M. A. "Perceptions of Field Officers, Extension Officers and Farmers Regarding Agricultural Extension Education in Swaziland," Ph.D. dissertation, Iowa State University, 1993.

Evans, Jeremy P. "Medicine Murder in Swaziland Between 1970 and 1988: An Assessment of an Increase in Killings for Medicine," B.A. honours dissertation, University of the Witwatersrand, 1990.

Fauniyar, Ganesh P. "An Econometric Model of Rate of Adoption of Agricultural

Technology for Developing Countries [Swaziland]," Ph.D. dissertation, Pennsylvania State University, 1990.

Fransman, Martin J. "The State and Development in Swaziland, 1960–1977," D.Phil. dissertation, Sussex University, 1978.

Gailey, C. R. "Change in the Social Stratification of the Swazi, 1936–1967," D.Phil. dissertation, University of South Africa, 1968.

Garson, Noel G. "The Swaziland Question and a Road to the Sea, 1887–1895," M.A. thesis, University of the Witwatersrand, 1955.

Genge, Manelisi. "Law and the Imposition of Colonial Rule in Swaziland, 1890–1898," M.A. thesis, Ohio University, 1992.

———. "Power and Gender in Southern African History: Power Relations in the Era of Queen Labotsibeni Gwamile Mdluli of Swaziland, ca. 1875–1921," Ph.D. dissertation, Michigan State University, 1999.

Ginindza, T. Thoko. "SiSwati Oral Poetry," Ph.D. dissertation, International College (Los Angeles), 1985.

Grotpeter, John J. "Political Leadership and Political Development in the High Commission Territories," Ph.D. dissertation, Washington University, 1965.

Gule, Gugulethu Z. "Childhood Mortality in Swaziland: Levels, Trends and Determinants," Ph.D. dissertation, University of Pennsylvania, 1990.

Gule, Jeremiah M. "Creating Excellence: A Study of the Administration, Content and Process of Management Training in the Public Sector in Swaziland," Ed.D. dissertation, Harvard University, 1991.

Heilbronn, Selwyn G. "Water Law Development and Irrigation in Swaziland, 1910–80," Ph.D. dissertation, Cambridge University, 1982.

Hughes, A.J.B. "Land Tenure, Land Rights and Land Communities on Swazi Nation Land: A Discussion of Some Inter-Relationships Between the Traditional Tenure System and Problems of Agrarian Development," Ph.D. dissertation, University of Natal, 1970.

Hunter, Raymond H. "The Precambrian Terrain in Swaziland with Particular Reference to the Granite Rocks," Ph.D. dissertation, University of the Witwatersrand, 1968.

Kasenene, Peter. "Ecumenical Progress in Swaziland 1880–1982," Ph.D. dissertation, University of Cape Town, 1988.

Kuby, David J. "Elitism and Holiness in Swazi Conversion," Ph.D. dissertation, University of California, Los Angeles, 1979.

Kunene, Euphrasia C. L. "The Acquisition of SiSwati As a First Language: A Morphological Study with Special Reference to Noun Prefixes, Noun Classes, and Some Agreement Makers," Ph.D. dissertation, University of California, Los Angeles, 1979.

Kunene, Gerald S. "British Colonial Policy in Swaziland, 1920–1960," Ph.D. dissertation, University of York, 1992.

Lea, John P. L. "The Geographic Determinants of Housing Policy in Swaziland," Ph.D. dissertation, University of the Witwatersrand, 1974.

Levin, Richard M;. "Hegemony and Crisis: Swazi Royal Power in Transition," Ph.D. dissertation, Liverpool University, 1985.

Lowe, Christopher. "Elite Reactions to Colonialism in Swaziland: The Case of Prince Mavela Dlamini," paper presented at the African Studies Association Conference, Seattle, WA, November 1992.

———. "Land and Chiefship in Swaziland 1910–1940: Some Preliminary Reflections," paper presented at the University of Swaziland, Social Science Research Unit seminar, November 1989.

———. "Social Change and Ideological Struggle over Patriarchy in Colonial Swaziland," paper presented at the African Studies Association Conference, Baltimore, MD, November 1990.

———. "Swaziland's Colonial Politics: The Decline of Progressivist South African Nationalism and the Emergence of Swazi Political Traditionalism, 1910–1939," Ph.D. dissertation, Yale University, 1998.

———. "The Tragedy of Malunge, or, The Fall of the House of Chiefs: *Abantu-Batho*, the Swazi Royalty, and Nationalist Politics in Southern Africa, 1894–1927," paper presented at the African Studies Association Conference, Boston, December 1993.

Lukele, Andrew. "Economic Growth and Underdevelopment in Swaziland," Ph.D. dissertation, Harvard University, Harvard Law School, 1973.

Maasdorp, Gavin G. "Transportation and Development in Small Peripheral Countries: A Case Study of Swaziland," Ph.D. dissertation, University of Natal, 1975.

Maepa, Linda N. "Television in Swaziland: An Ethnographic Study of Seven Swazi Families," Ph.D. dissertation, University of Iowa, 1994.

Magagula, Cynthia McD. "The Multi-national University in Africa: An Analysis of the Development and Demise of the University of Botswana, Lesotho and Swaziland," Ph.D. dissertation, University of Maryland, 1978.

Magagula, Glenn T. "A Socio-economic Analysis and Evaluation of Rural Development Areas in Swaziland," Ph.D. dissertation, University of Maryland, 1978.

Mamba, Rotter Sicheme. "A History of the Mamba Kingdom: The Unknown Aspect of Swazi History," B.A. thesis, University of Swaziland, 1985.

Marwick, Brian A. "*Abantu ba Kwa N'gwane*: An Ethnological Account of the Natives of the Swaziland Protectorate," M.A. thesis, University of Cape Town, 1939.

Mashasha, Francis J. "The Road to Colonialism: Concessions and the Collapse of Swazi Independence, 1875–1926," Ph.D. dissertation, Oxford University, 1977.

McCullough, Douglas. "Agricultural Development, Wage Labor and Social Change: The Political Contingencies of 'Good Employer' Policies in the Swaziland Sugar Industry, 1945–1965," M.A. thesis, Ohio University, 1989.

McFadden, Patricia. "Proletarianisation in Swaziland: The Case of the Sugar Industry," Ph.D. dissertation, Warwick University, 1987.

Miles, Miranda C. "Missing Women: A Study of Swazi Female Migration to the Witwatersrand, 1920–1970," M.A. thesis, Queen's University, 1991.

Mkatshwa, Thab'sile D. "Differences in Student Performance Between Schools: A Comparative Analysis of Two Swazi High Schools," Ph.D. Dissertation, University of Pennsylvania, 1991.

Mlahagwa, Josiah R. "Capital, Class and State in Colonial Swaziland, c. 1850–1948," Ph.D. dissertation, University of Dar es Salaam, 1987.

Mlangeni, T. "The Reception of Roman-Dutch Law in Swaziland," MLS thesis, University of Adelaide, 1985.

Mndebele, Comfort B. S. "Professional Vocational Technical Education Competencies for Swaziland Teachers of Agricultural, Commercial, Home Economics, and Technical Studies," Ph.D. dissertation, Virginia Polytechnic Institute and State University, 1994.

Murdoch, George. "Soil and Land Capability in Swaziland," Ph.D. dissertation, University of Edinburgh, 1968.

Ndlovu, Hebron L. "The Royal Easter Ritual and Political Actions in Swaziland," Ph.D. dissertation, McMaster University, 1994.

Ngcobo, Zipho G. "Health Information Seeking Behaviour of Women in Rural Swaziland," Ph.D. dissertation, University of Pittsburgh, 1994.

Nkambule, N. M. "A Diagnosis of Adverse Effects of Customary Land Tenure on Land Use in the Kingdom of Swaziland: Is a Land Privatisation Policy the Answer?" M.A. thesis, University of Wisconsin, 1983.

Nkosi, Abner G. "Education and Culture Among the Swazi of the Protectorate," M.S. thesis, Yale University, 1950.

Nyeko, Balam H. L. "The Swazi Leadership's Response to Colonial Rule, 1902–1930," Ph.D. dissertation, Makerere University, 1977.

Perkins, Floyd J. "A History of Christian Missions in Swaziland to 1910," Ph.D. dissertation, University of the Witwatersrand, 1974.

Potholm, Christian P. "Political Development in Swaziland," Ph.D. dissertation, Tufts University, Fletcher School of Law and Diplomacy, 1966.

Riba, Matofobhi. "Privatisation of a Natural Monopoly: The SEB Case," M.A. research paper, Williams College (Massachusetts), Center for Development Economics, 1995.

Rosen-Prinz, Beth. "Urbanization and Political Change: A Study of Urban Local Government in Swaziland," Ph.D. dissertation, University of California, Los Angeles, 1976.

Russell, Margo. "Texture and Structure in Race Relations: A Comparison of Interpersonal Relations in Two Southern African Communities Under Conditions of Apartheid and Non-Racialism," Ph.D. dissertation, University of East Anglia, 1977.

Schmidt, Charles F. "South Africa and Former High Commission Territories: Political Independence in an Interacting Space Economy," M.A. thesis, Southern Illinois University, 1969.

Scott, Peter. "The Agricultural Geography of Swaziland," M.Sc. thesis, University of London, 1948.

Shongwe, Adam B. "Making and Implementing Educational Decisions Under a

Diffused Authority Structure in Swaziland," Ed.D. dissertation, Columbia University, Teachers' College, 1990.

Shongwe, Musa M. "Genesis, Morphology, and Classification of Soils in Two Ecological Zones in Swaziland," Ph.D. dissertation, Ohio State University, 1992.

Sikhondze, Bonginkhosi B. "The Development of Swazi Cotton Cultivation, 1904–1985," Ph.D. dissertation, University of London, School of Oriental and African Studies, 1989.

Simelane, Hamilton Sipho. "Capital Penetration and Commercial Afforestation in Swaziland, 1947–1962," M.A. thesis, Ohio University, 1985.

———. "War, Economy and Society in Colonial Swaziland, 1939–1945," Ph.D. dissertation, University of Toronto, 1991.

Simpson, Angela G. "Aptitude, School Grades, Cambridge Examination Results, and University Performance: The Swaziland Case," Ph.D. dissertation, Ball State University (Indiana), 1990.

Sukati, Nonhlanhla A. "Primary Health Care in Swaziland: An Exploration of Women's Opinions," Ph.D. dissertation, University of California, San Francisco, 1996.

Tabibian, Nasrin. "Women and Rural Development in Africa: A Case-Study of Women's Income-Generating Activities in Swaziland (Non-Formal Education)," Ed.D. dissertation, University of Massachusetts, 1985.

Upvall, Michel J. "The Articulation of Nurses and Indigenous Healers in Swaziland: A Nursing Perspective," Ph.D. dissertation, University of Utah, 1990.

Urie, John G. "The Geology of the Bovu Ridge Iron Deposits, Swaziland," M.Sc. thesis, University of the Witwatersrand, 1958.

Van Biljon, Willem J. "The Nature and Origin of Chrysolite Asbestos in Swaziland and the Eastern Transvaal," Ph.D. dissertation, University of the Witwatersrand, 1959.

Vieceli, Jacqueline. "Formal Education and Manpower Development in Swaziland: A Policy Analysis," Ph.D. dissertation, Indiana University, 1987.

Wallender, Helena E. "Demographic and Environmental Factors Affecting Fertility Decisions in Swaziland," Ph.D. dissertation, Michigan State University, 1977.

Youé, Christopher P. "The African Career of R. T. Coryndon," Ph.D. dissertation, Dalhousie University, 1978.

Appendix A
Kings of Swaziland

The early genealogy of Swazi *tingwenyama* is disputed as to both its nomenclature and its length. This list starts with the mid-18th century Dlamini migration from the eastern slopes to the Lebombo range to the banks of the Pongola River in southern Swaziland.

Those wishing to trace the Swazi royal genealogy in greater detail should consult Kuper's *An African Aristocracy* (p. 232) and Matsebula's *A History of Swaziland* (3rd ed., p. 8 and "Genealogical Table" facing p. 18).

Ngwane II (c. 1735–c. 1775). *Lilawu*: Lobamba.

Ndvungunye (Zikhodze; c. 1755–c. 1805). *Lilawu*: Zombodze.

Sobhuza I (Ngwane IV; Somhlolo; c. 1780–1839). *Lilawu*: Ezulwini.

Mswati II (Mavuso II; c. 1825–1865). *Lilawu*: Hhohho.

Ludvonga II (Macaleni; c. 1855–1874)

Mbandzeni (Dlamini IV; c. 1857–1889). *Lilawu*: Mbekekweni.

Bhunu (Ngwane V; c. 1877–1899). *Lilawu*: Ezabeni.

Sobhuza II (1899–1982). *Lilawu*: Lozitehlezi.

Mswati III (1968–). *Lilawu*: Lozita.

Appendix B
Queen Mothers of Swaziland

iNgwenyama Ngwane II: laYaka Ndwandwe.

iNgwenyama Ndvungunye: Lomvulo Mndzebele.

iNgwenyama Sobhuza I: Lojiba Simelane; Somnjalose Simelane (d. c. 1844)

iNgwenyama Mswati II: Tsandzile Ndwandwe (d. 1875).

iNgwenyama Ludvonga II: Sisile Khumalo (d. 1881).

iNgwenyama Mbandzeni: Sisile Khumalo (d. 1881); Tibati Nkambule (d. 1895).

iNgwenyama Bhunu: Labotsibeni Mdluli (d. 1925).

iNgwenyama Sobhuza II: Lomawa Ndwandwe (d. 1938; Nukwase Ndwandwe (d. 1957); Zihlathi Ndwandwe (d. 1975); Seneleleni Ndwandwe (d. 1980); Dzeliwe Shongwe.

iNgwenyama Mswati III: Ntombi Twala.

About the Author

Alan R. Booth received his Ph.D. in African History in 1964. He is Professor of History and J. Richard Hamilton/Baker & Hostetler Professor of Humanities at Ohio University. He has been the recipient of three Fulbright grants, the first to Basutoland (lecturer at the University of Basutoland, the Bechuanaland Protectorate and Swaziland) in 1964, and the others to Swaziland in 1980 (lecturer at the University of Swaziland) and 1989 (research). He is the author of several articles and books on Swaziland. Articles include "The Development of the Swazi Labour Market 1900–1968" (*South African Labour Bulletin*, 1982); "Homestead, State, and Migrant Labor in Colonial Swaziland" (*African Economic History*, 1985); "Capitalism and the Competition for Swazi Labour, 1945–1960" and " 'European Courts Protect Women and Witches': Colonial Law Courts as Redistributors of Power in Swaziland, 1920–1950" (*Journal of Southern African Studies*, 1986, 1992); and "South African Sanctions-Breaking in Southern Africa: The Case of Swaziland (*Sanctioning Apartheid* [Africa World Press], 1990). His books include *Swaziland: Tradition and Change in a Southern African Kingdom* (Westview Press, 1983).